Regulation and Economic Opportunity: Blueprints for Reform

Edited by Adam Hoffer and Todd Nesbit

The Center for
Growth and **Opportunity**
at Utah State University

Cover design and typesetting by Brooke Jacques

The Center for Growth and Opportunity at Utah State University
3525 Old Main Hill
Logan, UT 84322
www. thecgo.org

This book is dedicated to Jerry Ellig. A thoughtful colleague, friend, and mentor. He made invaluable contributions to the field of regulatory studies and inspired countless scholars. He will be missed.

William F. Shughart II

> Errors are not what men live by or on. If an economic policy
> has been adopted by many communities, or if it is persistent-
> ly pursued by a society over a long span of time, it is fruit-
> ful to assume that the real effects were known and desired.
> Indeed, an explanation of a policy in terms of error or con-
> fusion is no explanation at all—anything and everything is
> compatible with that "explanation."[1]

On the same page as the passage just quoted, the late Nobel laurate
George Stigler instructs students of regulation "to look, as precisely and
carefully as we can, at who gains and who loses, and how much," when
a regulation is contemplated or already has been imposed. In seeking
to explain why a particular regulatory policy is adopted and persists,
especially in the face of evidence that its actual effects are "unrelated
or perversely related"[2] to its announced goals, Stigler's seminal theory
of economic regulation teaches that *"the truly intended effects should be
deduced from the actual effects."*[3]

Good intentions—the road to hell is paved with them—are not
enough to justify government interventions into the private sector's
affairs. A decision to intervene requires careful analysis of the problem

(the ostensible "market failure") to be corrected. Before any regulation is adopted, the analysis likewise must conclude that the public sector's intervention actually will improve somehow on the outcomes observed in a status quo, unregulated market, avoiding what Harold Demsetz calls the "nirvana fallacy": comparing actual market processes (the "naturally occurring world") with some ideal, unobtainable alternative.[4] What is most important, however, is to be a "good economist" in the sense of Frédéric Bastiat,[5] who grasps not only the obvious, visible effects of regulation ("what is seen"), but also the second- and third-order effects that emerge only after a regulation has been promulgated ("what is unseen") and therefore must be *anticipated*.

Far too often the effects of a regulatory intervention that conflict with, or undermine, its announced goals are excused as "unintended consequences" of the public sector's benevolent attempts to change the behaviors of individual producers and consumers in directions that generate benefits for society as a whole. Consequently, the politicians responsible for regulatory statutes and the employees of the regulatory agencies that enforce them are much like Adam Smith's "man of system," who

> is apt to be very wise in his own conceit; and is often enamoured with the supposed beauty of his own plan of government, that he cannot suffer the smallest deviation from any part of it. . . . He seems to imagine that he can arrange the different members of a great society with as much ease as the hand arranges the different pieces upon a chess-board. He does not consider that the pieces upon the chess-board have no other principle of motion besides that which the hand impresses upon them.[6]

In reality, however,

> in the great 'chess-board' of human society, every single piece has a principle of motion of its own, altogether different from that which the legislature might chuse to impress

upon it. If those two principles coincide and act in the same direction, the game of human society will go on easily and harmoniously, and is very likely to be happy and successful. If they are opposite or different, the game will go on miserably, and the society must be at all times in the highest degree of disorder.[7]

Social and economic interactions in the real world are multifaceted, and so it should be no surprise that regulatory interventions often produce consequences that are "unintended." But if those consequences become known—that is, obvious even to the most casual observer—and are not corrected, then, as Stigler concludes, the actual effects of regulation, no matter how perverse or counterproductive, must be intentional. They cannot be explained as unforeseen "mistakes."

The book now in your hands, *Regulation and Economic Opportunity*, supplies a catalog of regulatory failures across the spectrum of industries and economic activities subject to myriad federal, state, and local regulatory rules. The spontaneous orders emerging from the interactions of autonomous adult human beings in voluntary and mutually beneficial market exchanges are displaced by the edicts of politicians and their bureaucratic agents, who lack access to knowledge about the special circumstances of time and place[8] necessary for operation of the "invisible hand" that guides buyers and sellers pursuing their own parochial interests toward collective prosperity.

What is much more important is that the volume's contributors explain *why* government failure often is more problematic than the market failures to which intervention supposedly serves as a salutary corrective. Chief among the explanations is one of the principles of public choice: the same model of rational individual behavior applies to both the private and the public spheres of action. Politicians and policymakers are not selfless pursuers of the "public's interest," the "general welfare," or any other such fuzzy goal. Like anyone else, they want to advance their careers by being reelected to office or promoted, by getting paid more, or by gaining positions that allow them to manage more people and control more-generous organizational budgets.

Second, to return to Stigler's seminal contribution to the economic theory of regulation,

> the state—the machinery and power of the state—is a potential resource or threat to every industry in the society. With its power to prohibit or compel, to take or give money, the state can and does selectively help or hurt a vast number of industries.[9]

The state's massive legislative power and its administrative machinery have expanded exponentially since the New Deal. They have grown and been reinforced by the public sector's responses to the crises of the 20th century's two global wars,[10] to the financial meltdown of 2007–2008, and, more recently, to the pandemic-justified lockdowns caused by SARS-CoV-2. An enlarged and much more potent government means that many individuals and groups will mobilize to gain access to the benefits or to avoid the costs – the helps and hurts – delivered by selective regulatory interventions. The logic of collective action[11] teaches that small, well-organized special interest groups will tend to dominate the political process that creates and enforces regulations constraining economic and social interactions, thereby successfully capturing rents.[12] Those factions' gains predictably come at the expense of less-well-organized groups, such as the consumers of the regulated industry's products and the general taxpaying public, who must finance the regulatory agencies' operations.

The rents created by regulatory interventions are transitory, leading to a hopeless and socially costly trap.[13] Restrictions on entry into a market (and sometimes on exit from it), ceilings or floors on the prices regulated firms can charge, controls on the qualities of the goods and services offered, limits on allowable days and hours of business operation, health and safety rules for employers and their employees, and even directives designating some businesses as "essential" (and others not)—all can generate economic benefits for the owners of the affected firms, at least in the short run. But in the long run, regulatory rents are capitalized into asset prices (as when a regulated firm is sold by its original owner) or competed away by nonprice or service quality rivalry among the regulated entities. The consequence is that the new owners of regulated firms no longer earn extraordinary returns on their investments. Meanwhile, consumers continue to pay regulatorily elevated prices and perhaps suffer deteriorations in product quality because of regulated producers' weakened incentives to innovate.

The transitional gains trap leads to the worst of all possible worlds: high prices for customers and low (or no) profits for suppliers. Rent-seeking does not create wealth; it merely redistributes the wealth existing when regulation is adopted. The trap also helps explain why deregulation is such a rare event.[14] Rent-seeking costs incurred in the past to capture regulation's transitory gains are sunk. To the extent that they are not, dismantling a regulatory regime triggers rent-defending efforts because of the threat of capital losses faced by the owners of regulated firms. Society is permanently poorer. Since rent-seeking activities are ubiquitous, the only sure way of evading the trap is to avoid promiscuous regulation in the first place and to follow the lessons taught in *Regulation and Economic Opportunity*.

A third feature of most regulatory regimes is that the same rules apply to all affected parties: "one size fits all." Uniformity can be justified as a way of reducing the costs of administering regulations by requiring compliance by everyone subject to them. Although exceptions are possible if one or more of the affected parties can bring sufficient political influence to bear on the legislature that enacts a regulatory statute or the agency that enforces it, such exceptions complicate the regulatory process and force regulators to accept responsibly for apparently unequal treatment of the individuals, organizations, or companies they supervise. So regulatory rules tend to be inflexible, requiring compliance by all firms, by all consumers, and by all employees. Such inflexibility, along with the frequently high costs of regulatory compliance, which place heavier burdens on small firms than on large ones able to spread fixed compliance costs over larger volumes of output, means that regulation often has regressive effects. It drives smaller firms out of business (or into the arms of their larger rivals through mergers) and prices low-income households out of regulated markets. The rigidities of

regulatory regimes contrast sharply with more decentralized com-
mon-law processes, which allow for "contracting around" the decisions
of courts when their rulings interfere with economically efficient, mutually beneficial exchanges.[15]

One reason that the administrative state has expanded by leaps and
bounds over the past century, displacing more decentralized, democratic market processes, can be found in the deference increasingly
conceded by courts to the supposed expertise of specialized regulatory agencies. A showing of due process—that a regulation has been
reviewed by some legislative or administrative body and deemed to
be in the "public's interest" and to fall broadly within the state's police
powers—is all that normally is required nowadays for the judiciary to
allow a regulation to stand. Long gone is *substantive due process*, in which
courts require more than just the following of proper procedures.[16]
Under that older doctrine, regulations were reviewed on the basis of
their consistency with certain rights and liberties of a free and prosper-
ous society, such as those of employers and employees to contract on
mutually beneficial terms. Minimum-wage laws, for example, would be
rejected on substantive due process grounds. The sanctity of contracts
between buyers and sellers likewise would doom regulatory label-
ing of some businesses as "nonessential" during public health panics.

Regulation and Economic Opportunity is an indispensable guide to both
older and more contemporary theories of economic and social regulation, in realms running the gamut from entrepreneurship to the markets
for labor, land, energy, tobacco, vaping, and alcohol, and from the internet to K–12 schooling. The volume's contributors take seriously Stigler's
instruction to deduce the intended effects of regulation from its actual
effects, and in doing so they take advantage of the fine-grained information that recently has become available for measuring regulation's
scale and scope. The actual effects of many regulatory interventions
discussed in the volume impede entrepreneurship, burden small enterprises with heavy compliance costs, slow innovation, and deny many
people opportunities to raise their standards of living.

At present, public discourse on government intervention often echoes
a mantra to "follow the science." But science never is settled. Even if it

were, though, the proponents of regulation and the scholars who study it must acknowledge that applying provisional scientific findings in practice requires navigating political processes wherein special interests exercise decisive influences on policy outcomes. Recognizing that politics frequently trumps science, including economic science, is the most important lesson the readers of *Regulation and Economic Opportunity* ought to take away.

Contents

FOREWORD
William F. Shughart II

INTRODUCTION
An Introduction to Regulation   **xvii**
Adam Hoffer and Todd Nesbit

Section 1
Regulation, Entrepreneurship, and Opportunity   **1**

CHAPTER 1
Regulation and Entrepreneurship: Theory, Impacts, and Implications   **3**
Russell S. Sobel

CHAPTER 2
Regulation and the Perpetuation of Poverty in the US and Senegal   **19**
Steven Horwitz and Magatte Wade

CHAPTER 3
Social Trust and Regulation: A Time-Series Analysis of the United States   **45**
Peter T. Calcagno and Jeremy Jackson

CHAPTER 4
Regulation and the Shadow Economy   **85**
Travis Wiseman

Section 2
Regulation and Labor Market Outcomes   **103**

CHAPTER 5
An Introduction to the Effect of Regulation on Employment and Wages   **105**
James Bailey

CHAPTER 6
Occupational Licensing: A Barrier to Opportunity and Prosperity   **121**
Alicia Plemmons and Edward Timmons

CHAPTER 7
Gender, Race, and Earnings: The Divergent Effect of Occupational Licensing on the Distribution of Earnings and on Access to the Economy   **155**
Kathleen M. Sheehan and Diana W. Thomas

CHAPTER 8
How Can Certificate-of-Need Laws Be Reformed to Improve Access to Healthcare?   **173**
Alexander Ollerton and Christopher Koopman

Section 3
Land Use and Energy Standards   **193**

CHAPTER 9
Land Use Regulation and Housing Affordability   **195**
Emily Hamilton

CHAPTER 10
Building Energy Codes: A Case Study in Regulation and Cost-Benefit Analysis   213
Matthew J. Holian

CHAPTER 11
The Tradeoffs between Energy Efficiency, Consumer Preferences, and Economic Growth   231
James Broughel

Section 4
Energy Markets and Environmental Regulations   257

CHAPTER 12
Cooperation or Conflict: Two Approaches to Conservation   259
Jordan K. Lofthouse and Megan E. Jenkins

CHAPTER 13
Retail Electric Competition and Natural Monopoly: The Shocking Truth   289
Jerry Ellig

CHAPTER 14
Governance for Networks: Regulation by Networks in Electric Power Markets in Texas   315
Michael Giberson and L. Lynne Kiesling

Section 5
Divisive Cases of Regulating Products and Services   351

CHAPTER 15
Net Neutrality: Internet Regulation and the Plans to Bring It Back   353
Ted Bolema

CHAPTER 16
Unintended Consequences of Regulating Private School Choice Programs: A Review of the Evidence   377
Corey A. DeAngelis and Lindsey M. Burke

CHAPTER 17
"Blue Laws" and Other Cases of Bootlegger/Baptist Influence in Beer Regulation   403
Stephan F. Gohmann and Adam C. Smith

CHAPTER 18
Smoke or Vapor? Regulation of Tobacco and Vaping   423
James E. Prieger

CONCLUSION
Moving Forward: A Guide for Regulatory Policy   459
Adam Hoffer and Todd Nesbit

Endnotes   475

An Introduction to Regulation

Adam Hoffer and Todd Nesbit

Regulatory expansion has been stunning. The *Code of Federal Regulations* (CFR)—the accumulation of rules imposed by the departments and agencies of the federal government—now exceeds 180,000 pages.[1] At a reading speed of two minutes per page, the average American would need more than 250 days of consecutive, around-the-clock reading to wade through the comprehensive list of regulations promulgated by federal government agencies.

The CFR has gotten so long that no individual can possibly comprehend the full set of federal regulations. The CFR does not even include the additional regulations imposed by executive orders, state governments, and local municipalities.

Regulation matters. Functional, evidenced-based regulation can provide significant public benefits, such as protecting uninformed consumers, limiting the effects of monopoly power, improving public health and safety, safeguarding civil rights, and protecting the environment.

Poor regulation can be devastating. Interest groups can convince the government to use its coercive powers to their own benefit and profit at the expense of everyone else. The financial and time costs of complying with regulations can drastically outweigh the benefits. Even regulations created with the best of intentions can have such perverse effects in the form of eroding the fundamental market processes that underpin the remarkable level of economic development those in the West enjoy, leaving in its wake poverty and civil unrest.

The goal of this volume is to study regulation. We ask fundamental questions that lead us to study not only the actual effects of regulation, but also how regulations are created.

Regulations are not born in a vacuum. Rather, regulation is the result of exchanges taking place in the political marketplace. The participants in this marketplace—namely, politicians, bureaucrats and parties interested in regulatory outcomes—are not benevolent social planners. Volumes of research point to the conclusion that politicians and bureaucrats respond to incentives just as other human beings do. Sometimes these incentives lead the politicians and bureaucrats to promote regulation in the broad public interest. At other times, these incentives lead the same individuals to pursue personal objectives, such as reelection, job security, larger budgets, and more influence. The entire regulatory process is plagued by imperfect information and unchecked self-interest.

Proponents of regulation often point to a distrust of free enterprise and provide anecdotes of "market failures" as justification for a larger regulatory, administrative, or managerial state. Free markets are astonishingly effective at allocating scarce resources in the most efficient manner. Sometimes members of society are not satisfied with that final distribution of resources. Some market characteristics, such as externalities, public goods, market power, and asymmetric information, may indeed lead markets to produce less than efficient results.

The question we must ask is whether we can trust government regulators to create rules that improve on market outcomes. All data point to one answer: no! Americans do not trust "the government" or "elected officials." Opinion surveys showing a deep lack of trust in the United States government are rich and robust (for an example, see table 1).

According to a Pew Research Center poll, trust in the US government is at an all-time low. Only 17 percent of respondents in 2019 reported that they "trust the government in Washington always or most of the time," down from 73 percent for a similar poll in 1958.[2]

Table 1. Trust in US Public Figures

Profession	% of US adults who have a great deal of or a fair amount of confidence that _____ will act in the best interest of the public
The military	85
Scientists	84
Principals (K–12)	84
Police officers	83
Professors	71
Religious leaders	65
Journalists	58
Business leaders	46
Elected officials	39

Source: Lee Rainie, Scott Keeter, and Andrew Perrin, "Trust and Distrust in America," Pew Research Center, July 22, 2019.

Approval of Congress ("Do you approve or disapprove of the way Congress is handling its job?") was 22 percent in March 2020.[3] The congressional approval rating has not exceeded 30 percent in the 11 years preceding the publication of this book.

When government institutions are put head to head with specific product brands and companies, Americans clearly trust private companies more than they do the US government.[4] When people were asked whether they trusted the following (e.g., company, brand, person, institution) "a lot to do the right thing," tech companies like Amazon, Google, PayPal, and the Weather Channel scored among the highest of all surveyed companies, with 35 percent of respondents placing a lot of trust in the company about which they were asked. The United States government earned a lot of trust only from 7 percent of respondents. Seven percent! Roughly 14 out every 15 people do *not* place much trust in the government.

The bottom line of these findings is stunning. Americans have little faith in elected officials or the government. Yet the same government officials that Americans distrust control the ever-growing regulatory landscape designed to "solve" our problems. Regulatory policymaking proceeds with little oversight, and most policymakers and citizens have little idea about what is written into a regulation.

We need a clear understanding of regulation and its effects to draw conclusions about its contributions to economic well-being and to create beneficial public policy. Unfortunately, regulation's scope is notoriously difficult to quantify. Broad empirical studies of federal regulations have been impractical until only recently.

Technological advances in machine learning facilitated the creation of RegData,[5] a revolutionary and evolving dataset that quantifies regulatory restrictions and identifies the specific industries affected by them. For the first time, researchers are able to employ this new dataset to build on the existing literature consisting of individual event and case studies. The empirical findings can now provide to the public and policymakers more reliable estimates of the direct and indirect effects of regulatory policy.

The present volume collects scholars to answer essential empirical questions related to how regulations are created and the effects of a growing regulatory state. The goal of the book is to increase awareness of the consequences of regulatory policies and encourage a more informed debate about such policies. It is important to evaluate public policy outcomes as they are rather than as proponents might wish them to be.

Outline of the Book

We organize *Regulation and Economic Opportunity* in five sections:

Section I: Regulation, Entrepreneurship, and Opportunity

We begin our examination of the effects of regulation with a look at entrepreneurship, given the critical role that it plays as a driver of innovation, economic prosperity, and overall economic growth. In **chapter 1**, Russell Sobel examines not only how regulations affect the market economy, but also how the political process influences the nature of the regulations promulgated. Sobel, using the public choice model of regulation, goes on to show that the incentives inherent in the political process generally lead to inefficient regulations that tend both to stay on the books and to encourage unproductive rent-seeking. Given the substantial costs involved in rent-seeking, the political environment tends to favor large, established firms at the expense of new start-ups that otherwise might have brought about more innovation, competition, and cost reductions. Sobel's key takeaway is that the current regulatory environment is costly—much more so than it superficially appears.

In **chapter 2**, Steven Horwitz and Magatte Wade expound on one of those costs, which is often overlooked by many others: that regulation blocks at least some entrepreneurial upward mobility and thus perpetuates poverty. The authors explore the role that regulatory restrictions play in causing two outcomes: (1) many households, particularly nonwhite households, in the West persistently fall below the Western poverty line, while others enjoy greater income mobility, and (2) that many households and even entire countries in the Global South, particularly in Africa, have been unable to achieve anything close to Western levels of material comfort.

Regulation, particularly for those who are poor and marginalized in the political process, has stood in the way of the market innovation and creative destruction that was instrumental in the Great Enrichment. The effect of regulation in the United States has been highly regressive and tends to trap many people in poverty. In Senegal, regulatory burdens, in terms of both time and financial resources, are so heavy that it is nearly impossible to start a small business. Consequently, many entrepreneurs choose to remain in the extralegal sector with no legal rights or protections. Furthermore, large multinational firms in Senegal are able to use their financial advantages and influence not only to better navigate the regulatory environment but also to gain special exemptions unavailable to small entrepreneurs. The result is an underdeveloped legal small business sector and an economic climate rife with distrust and corruption.

Chapter 3 extends and generalizes the discussion of regulation and distrust of market exchange. As mentioned earlier in this chapter, a major motivation for government interventions is the absence of trust in other market participants. For example, if consumers do not trust sellers not to defraud them, they may appeal to government to impose regulations to prevent such fraud. However, chapter authors Peter Calcagno and Jeremy Jackson suggest that regulation also can, in theory, degrade social trust by magnifying economic and political inefficiencies. They test the causal relationship between social trust and regulation empirically. While they present some evidence that less social trust causes regulation, the evidence that regulation reduces social trust is more convincing. That finding is important because other research has indicated that countries with more social trust tend to experience faster economic growth. Calcagno and Jackson's results likewise offer additional support for the finding that regulation hinders entrepreneurial activity, discussed in chapter 1.

Horwitz and Wade mention in chapter 2 that regulatory burdens have, in part, encouraged many Senegalese entrepreneurs to operate outside the legal sector. That observation is far from unique to Senegal. In **chapter 4,** Travis Wiseman explores how overregulation leads to perverse incentives encouraging individuals to engage in socially unproductive activities and in the shadow economy. Wiseman, expanding on William Baumol's distinction between productive and unproductive entrepreneurship,[6] argues that in the face of an increasingly overregulated economic environment, otherwise productive entrepreneurs respond by engaging in rent-seeking to influence future regulations and by moving some of their activities underground or offshore in order to engage in productive, unproductive, and sometimes destructive activity.

Many labor-market regulations discussed in section II, such as occupational licensing, scope-of-practice restrictions, and minimum wages, commonly lead to participation in the shadow economy. Although the size of the shadow economy is sometimes difficult to gauge accurately, it can be a reliable indicator of the onerousness of public policy as it relates to earning income or making a business profit.

On the one hand, the existence of the shadow economy serves as an escape valve or a substitute for legal markets, permitting trade in many items that would be too costly or offer too low of a profit in the legal sector. On the other hand, operating in the shadow economy increases the risk of being defrauded, undermining social trust.

Moreover, investments in both human and physical capital are abridged in shadow economies, leading to slower growth as well.

Section II: Regulation and Labor Market Outcomes

We begin our analysis of labor market regulations in **chapter 5.** James Bailey provides a broad analysis of how regulation affects labor markets by answering two questions: Does regulation kill or create jobs, and does regulation raise or lower wages? Consistent answers to those questions are not easy to find in the literature. To find answers, we must first acknowledge that many types of regulations affect labor market outcomes and that their effects vary substantially. Bailey categorizes regulations into seven types: (1) cost-increasing regulations, (2) bans, (3) entry barriers, (4) occupational licensing, (5) minimum wages, (6) mandated employment benefits, and (7) make-work regulations. After walking through the consensus about regulation's effects on jobs and wages for each type of regulation, Bailey acknowledges that we still have a lot to learn regarding the overall consequences of regulatory growth on employers and employees.

In **chapter 6,** Alicia Plemmons and Edward Timmons provide a more detailed introduction to occupational licensing, expounding on the research addressing the expansion of such regulations since the early 20th century. Support for occupational licensing has its roots in protecting and promoting individual liberty; licensing therefore should not necessarily be viewed as bad policy. Plemmons and Timmons's analysis is consistent with arguments made by Christopher Tiedeman, the 19th-century classical liberal author and student of constitutional law: the legitimate purpose of licensing is to limit the frequency of injurious trade by restricting from the market incompetent traders who seek to defraud consumers.

Plemmons and Timmons show that the number of occupations requiring licenses and the stringency of the requirements for obtaining these licenses has expanded dramatically in recent years. The authors explore the effects of occupational licensing on numerous economic measures: occupational choice, job mobility, wages, consumer access, and product or service quality, to name a handful. While some of the research findings highlighted by Plemmons and Timmons support that occupational licensing is associated with improved service quality select industries, the consensus in the relevant literature suggests that the growth in licensing almost certainly extends beyond the legitimate purpose described by Tiedeman.

The coverage of occupational licensing laws continues in **chapter 7**, in which Kathleen Sheehan and Diana Thomas examine the laws' effects on the so-called gender and race wage gaps. Occupational licensing is a barrier to entry that reduces the supply of labor in the licensed industry. Basic economics indicate that wages will rise for workers who are able to gain entry into the industry. However, wage gains will not necessarily be equally distributed among all workers. Furthermore, less entry into the field can lead to more unemployment—and that effect, again, may not be the same across all races and genders.

Chapter 8 discusses regulation employed widely in the healthcare industry: certificate-of-need (CON) laws. Alexander Ollerton and Christopher Koopman examine how CON laws can be reformed to improve access to care. These laws regulate the building, expansion, and modernization of healthcare facilities and of the medical equipment available to these facilities. The original intent of CON laws was to improve access to healthcare facilities, particularly in rural areas, while also driving down healthcare costs. Ollerton and Koopman argue that CON laws instead have, in many cases, reduced access and raised costs. The authors suggest that states with these laws should follow the lead of the 14 states that have repealed their CON laws. If this proves unachievable, states should consider phasing the requirements out over time or removing them for specific types of providers, to improve access to needed care.

Section III: Land Use and Energy Standards

Section III is a three-chapter unit that covers land use, building codes, and energy standards. Emily Hamilton begins her treatment of land use regulation in **chapter 9** with an analysis of how such regulations affect housing affordability. Hamilton discusses how zoning and other land use regulations, such as minimum unit size or lot size requirements, have contributed to the elimination of many of the market innovations that can provide affordable housing options in cities with otherwise high land prices. Ultimately, the land use restrictions, largely supported by homeowners seeking to increase the value of their principal asset, have limited new housing construction and driven up housing prices and rents. Rent controls, introduced to combat some of the housing price effects of other regulations, have contributed to less housing and job mobility; rent-controlled properties often are repurposed (as condominiums or other owner-occupied dwellings) and sold at higher prices than rental housing not covered by such controls. However, as Hamilton discusses, some local and state efforts to liberalize land use regulations have shown promise.

The contributions of **chapter 10** are twofold: First, Matthew Holian analyzes the effects of building codes designed to reduce household energy consumption. Second, in the process of presenting that analysis, Holian walks readers through the main steps in a sound cost-benefit calculation, which is a method used widely in regulatory analyses. Building and energy codes can be defended, in part, on efficiency grounds. Specifically, home buyers are at an informational disadvantage relative to builders because buyers cannot easily observe how much insulation or what type of wire or ductwork was used in the construction. Furthermore, homebuyers may underestimate the long-run benefits of improved energy efficiency, focusing on the up-front costs only, leading to less demand for energy-efficient building materials or heating and cooling systems. However, Holian also notes that energy efficiency regulations can be counterproductive because consumers change their behaviors in predictable ways that offset the benefits of regulatory standards. Determining which effects dominate thus becomes an empirical question. Holian demonstrates a cost-benefit analysis of building energy codes in Florida.

James Broughel continues the discussion of energy-efficiency standards in **chapter 11**. Rather than examining building efficiency standards as Holian does in chapter 10, Broughel focuses on standards for appliances. The Department of Energy asserts that consumers and businesses exhibit irrational behavior in energy markets. However, those claims of irrationality depend on myriad assumptions, including assumptions about a product's use over its lifetime, quality differences between more- and less-efficient devices, and the consumer's or business's discount rate.

Broughel concludes **chapter 11** with a longer-run, intertemporal analysis, rather than adopting the typical static analysis. He provides an intriguing approach that deserves more attention, because such an intertemporal analysis leads to the possibility that stringent energy efficiency regulations can produce faster economic growth and therefore improve future well-being at the expense of decision makers today. One must then question how much present sacrifice is appropriate in the pursuit of these benefits and, what is more important, who is in position to make such a determination: private individuals or government regulators?

Section IV: Energy Markets and the Environmental Regulations

In **chapter 12**, Jordan Lofthouse and Megan Jenkins discuss how the typical approach to public policy, particularly environmental policy, often pits individuals and groups against one another. That need not be the case, however. Regulatory policy can be developed in ways that lead to cooperation and joint achievement of collective goals rather than cutthroat political competition. Markets work well when private property rights can be well defined and protected; however, many cases, especially concerning environmental issues, can be identified wherein such rights cannot be well defined. Thus, public policy often is the next best option, but its effectiveness frequently is tarnished by the political process. Lofthouse and Jenkins's solution is to employ "market-like regulations" that merge the best aspects of markets and public policy while limiting the worst aspects of politics. They adopt the American Prairie Reserve as a case study. The authors finish the chapter with a discussion of how existing laws and regulations can be reformed in similar manners and lead to more-cooperative outcomes.

The electricity distribution and retail power industry has long been argued to be a natural monopoly, and its prices and conditions of service have generally been regulated by public utility commissions across the United States since the 1930s. In only 13 states can most consumers choose their electricity supplier, but even in those states electric power distribution is a publicly regulated monopoly. In **chapter 13**, Jerry Ellig advances the discussion of competition in electricity markets. In both models he examines—one in which suppliers compete for retail customers on a regulated wire network monopoly and another with duopolistic competition between electric utilities with overlapping wire networks—additional competition is associated with cost reductions, lower prices, improved innovation, and more product differentiation.

Michael Giberson and Lynne Kiesling continue the discussion of electricity market regulation in **chapter 14**. Like Ellig in the previous chapter, the authors challenge the traditional natural monopoly governance framework for electricity markets, arguing instead that competition can improve efficiency. They specifically examine the electricity market in Texas, which they identify as the only US state with a fully competitive market design at both the wholesale and retail levels. They argue that Texas's policy has encouraged network governance that has expanded investment in transmission infrastructure and new energy generation technologies (such as wind and solar projects). While Texas's institutional framework is not perfect, it serves as an example of the "market-like regulation" that Lofthouse and Jenkins describe in chapter 13 and can serve as a model for other states.

Section V: Divisive Cases of Regulating Products and Services

The fifth and final section of the book is reserved for four areas of regulation that have generated heated debate in recent years. Ted Bolema in **chapter 15** discusses an internet regulation known as "net neutrality," promulgated in 2015 and repealed in 2017. Both net neutrality's promulgation and its repeal were contested hotly and generated lively debates among policy wonks. However, much of the discussion likely left audiences confused, given the technical nature of the controversy. Bolema begins the chapter by defining *net neutrality* before dissecting the economic analysis presented in the Federal Communications Commission's 2015 Open Internet order, which established the policy.

Bolema argues that internet consumers have benefited from the 2017 repeal of net neutrality, but the battle is far from over.

Corey DeAngelis and Lindsey Burke discuss in **chapter 16** the unintended consequences of regulating private school choice programs. The competition introduced by school choice programs generally has been found to improve student achievement. Regulations restricting school choice programs threaten to limit these benefits. Such regulations include open-admission mandates, state testing or a nationally normed testing requirement, random-admissions mandates, and rules that participating schools must accept vouchers as tuition payments in full.

DeAngelis and Burke review the empirical evidence on the effects of school choice program regulations and find that the preponderance of the evidence suggests that such regulations are associated with reductions in the quantities, qualities, and specialties of private schools participating in choice programs. The two most intrusive program regulations are found to be random-admissions mandates and state testing mandates.

Chapters 17 and 18 address the regulation of vice. In **chapter 17**, Steve Gohmann and Adam Smith examine state alcohol regulations before James Prieger explores the regulation of tobacco and vaping in **chapter 18**. The passage of the 21st Amendment left the control of alcohol in state hands and created numerous peculiar variations in public policies across the states. The three-tier system (wholesale, distribution, and retail), however, has been a mainstay across the majority of states. Gohmann and Smith apply the "Bootleggers and Baptists" model to analyze the regulatory constraints on alcohol. In that model, an odd alignment of political interests occurs between an economic interest group—the Bootleggers—who seek to reduce competition and a moral interest group—the Baptists—who seek to achieve some social ideal. The authors detail some recent events in Kentucky (restrictions on brewery ownership by distributors) and Indiana (restrictions on cold beer sales and Sunday alcohol sales) to demonstrate the applicability of the Bootleggers-and-Baptists model.

Arguments for regulating e-cigarettes and vaping often are made on paternalistic grounds, buttressed by claims that users do not properly understand the long-term consequences of their behavior. But, as Prieger discusses, the consequences of regulating e-cigarettes are not so simple. To understand the consequences one must establish whether and to what extent e-cigarettes are complements to or substitutes for tobacco cigarettes and determine the health effects of vaping relative to smoking, the dangers of exposure to second-hand vapor or smoke, and the potential unintended consequences of regulation, such as exacerbation of illicit trade. Given Prieger's answers to these questions, the costs of regulating e-cigarettes and vaping very likely exceed the benefits. Prieger concludes by presenting seven steps to informed regulation of e-cigarettes and vaping. It is important to note here that, as in many of the other cases examined in the book, Prieger's alternatives are not limited to the status quo (current regulation) or no regulation at all. Rather, his goal is improved regulation: his prescriptions permit some nonzero level of regulation.

The conclusion summarizes the major themes and policy prescriptions offered throughout the book, as identified by the editors and this introduction's authors, Adam Hoffer and Todd Nesbit. One consensus revealed throughout is that the costs associated with overregulation or unjustified regulation are substantial. Consequently, many existing regulations should be scaled back or eliminated altogether—though this might prove difficult given vested special interests and the existence of the transitional gains trap. That is not to say that all regulation should be eliminated; far from it. Many good regulations exist and many more would exist if rules were rewritten to take advantage of market-like forces to minimize the costs associated with political divisiveness.

Conclusion

We hope to provide readers of this book with analyses related to regulation in a wide array of industries and applications. Regulation has been difficult to study empirically owing to a lack of data and computational abilities. Consequently, we believe that individuals have been quick to accept regulations as easy, politically palatable solutions to societal problems. However, the benefits of regulation often are overpromised, and its costs often hidden from public view.

The primary purpose of this book is to present a more complete analysis of the benefits and costs of public regulation—both the seen and the unseen—such that the actors engaged in the political process can form better conclusions concerning the appropriateness of regulatory policy. Our expectation is that this book will provide the analysis of the regulatory environment and regulatory policy necessary to motivate improved policymaking.

Regulation, Entrepreneurship, and Opportunity

CHAPTER 1

Regulation and Entrepreneurship: Theory, Impacts, and Implications

Russell S. Sobel

This chapter examines the impact of regulation on entrepreneurship. Doing so requires a basic understanding of both the role of regulation in a competitive market economy and how the democratic political process (that ultimately sets regulatory policy) affects which types of regulation are enacted. Specific applications to the size, quantity, and quality of new establishments and innovations are discussed in this chapter.

Entrepreneurship is a key source of economic growth due to the ongoing process of innovation it embodies. Approximately one-half of the differences in national economic growth rates among countries is explained by differing levels of entrepreneurial activity.[1] The actions of entrepreneurs create not only jobs, income, and wealth, but also new goods and services that improve consumer well-being. Over the past century, for example, medical innovations have improved life expectancy by approximately 30 years in the United States—and those years have been rendered more comfortable thanks to entrepreneurs such as Willis Carrier and Candido Jacuzzi, who invented modern air conditioning and soothing hydrotherapy pumps for bathtubs, respectively.

Explaining the critical role entrepreneurs play in economic development has been an important part of the work of scholars such as Joseph Schumpeter, who describes how entrepreneurs search for new combinations of resources. Guided by the profit and loss system entre-preneurs unleash a process of "creative destruction" in which new goods and services replace old ones.[2] Other authors, such as Israel Kirzner, explicitly focus on the entrepreneurial discovery process as integral to the market process.[3]

The fact that good economic policies are essential for economic growth has been recognized since the time of Adam Smith, the father of modern economics. One of the key reasons for this relationship is that good policies help to promote entrepreneurship.[4] Regulation of business has the potential to significantly affect the entrepreneurial process. Because of this, regulation can have serious consequences for the economic health and prosperity of a nation, and understanding this relationship can lead to better economic policy.

The Role of Regulation in Free Market Capitalism

What, then, is the proper role of government regulation? Adam Smith put it best: "Little else is requisite to carry a state to the highest degree of opulence from the lowest barbarism, but peace, easy taxes, and a tolerable administration of justice; all the rest being brought about by the natural course of things."[5] What Smith meant was that for a market economy to function properly, property rights must be well-defined and enforced and individuals must be held accountable for any dam-ages they cause to the person or property of others without consent.

One major point of common confusion involves the difference between "regulation" and the role of the legal and judicial system. Criminal laws concern issues such as theft and murder, and civil laws normally protect the private rights of citizens and offer legal remedies in disputes related to contracts, torts, property law, family law, and so forth. If, for example, a firm sells a defective product that injures a con-sumer, the issue is usually handled under the legal and judicial system and does not involve what economists normally consider or measure as "regulatory policy," which is enacted as part of the system of statu-tory law created through the democratic political process.

By *regulatory policy* or *regulation*, then, scholars usually mean the *addi-tional* rules that are adopted through the democratic political process

to govern private decision-making, going beyond what would normally be considered the basic protections of life, liberty, and property,
and compensation for unwanted third-party harm. To differentiate
between regulation and these normal civil and legal protections that
are necessary for the functioning of a market economy and should be
in place, for the remainder of this discussion I will call normal civil and
legal protections "the rule of law." Thus, *the rule of law* hereafter refers
to the basic protections of legal rights against harm caused by others.

What, then, are some examples of what economists mean by *regulation*? Some countries, for example, have regulations that stipulate the
maximum number of hours per week employees may work. In France,
for example, the legal length of the working week is 35 hours, and
employees may not work for more than 4.5 hours without a break. Many
countries (and even subnational governments) have legal minimum
wages and mandated worker benefits. Certain types of businesses often
operate under rules related to accessibility for people with disabilities
and to hours of operation. Other government rules may require the preferential use of local companies in sourcing. Ridesharing services such
as Uber and Lyft and travel-lodging services such as Airbnb are now
subject to widespread bans, limitations, and specific rules. Some alcoholic beverages cannot be sold on certain days of the week, at certain
times of day, in certain types of stores, or with certain levels of potency.
The adult recreational purchase and use of drugs such as marijuana
are restricted in some locations but not in others, as are gambling and
prostitution. Regulations also include bans on cigarette smoking, plastic bags, straws, and plastic-foam containers.

While the normal legal protections I've termed *the rule of law* involve
preventing violations and compensating victims in cases where one
party harms another against the second party's will, in contrast, regulatory policy generally interferes with voluntary contracting in cases
were no third-party harm or violation of rights has taken place. Regulation bans, prohibits, or restricts the extent or conditions under which
voluntary agreements (or trades) take place.

Another important point is that in free markets, individuals in their
private dealings may impose restrictions—*private regulation*. Even

before local government bans on cigarette smoking, for example, many restaurants did not allow smoking. Some neighborhoods have home-owners' associations that ban short-term property rentals for profit. These types of restrictions that occur in the private sector are part of a normal competitive market economy, one in which some restaurants may not allow smoking while others may choose to allow it, and con-sumers' dollars represent votes that determine which businesses will be profitable and survive given the rules they have chosen to adopt.

But what I mean by regulation in this chapter is government regu-latory policy, in which restrictions on voluntary choice are chosen and imposed by the political process, applied uniformly across a geograph-ic-political jurisdiction in addition to any existing privately adopted rules and the rule of law.

The Public Interest versus Public Choice Views of Regulation

Now that I have defined *regulation* for the purposes of this chapter, I will turn to a careful consideration of the environment in which rules replacing or restricting private choice are decided upon and enacted— the democratic political process.

In which cases should the voluntary choices of individuals be replaced by government mandates? The traditional arguments for such interventions answer that regulation is justified in cases when the choices individuals might make are in some regard immoral, societally or culturally wrong, unfair or costly to certain groups of individuals, or harmful to the person making the choice or to others that may be affected. Examples of such choices include drinking too much alcohol or drinking it on the day that should be devoted to religious worship, committing suicide, selling one's body for money, recreationally alter-ing one's mental state with substances that reduce personal productivity, or having rules that (even inadvertently) disadvantage one group of possible consumers over another.

Yet another avenue of argument maintains that while the rule-of-law protections may work in terms of providing after-the-fact compensation for harms done, more can be done to prevent the harm from occurring in the first place. For example, under a rule-of-law system a drug manufacturer that sells a dangerous drug can be held accountable for any actual harm caused, and this risk of punishment may deter future incidents, but this doesn't change the fact that someone has been harmed.

According to these views, the government can and should interfere in private decisions to improve the overall functioning of society. Some argue that these types of restrictions in certain cases are good for the individuals whose behaviors are restricted. Parents, for example, often place rules on their children "for their own good," because children may make decisions that, with hindsight, they will later regret. The view that the government may perform a similar role for otherwise rational adults is often termed *paternalism*.

The view that the government should use regulatory policy to restrict private choice when doing so "helps" society and the individuals in it—that is, when the benefits of the intervention outweigh or justify the potential costs—is known as the *public interest* view of regulation.[6] Those who adopt this view show a willingness to, for example, slow the rate of entrepreneurship or economic growth if this would achieve some desirable social goal in the process.

The problem with this view in practice, however, is that these regulatory restrictions are decided upon within a democratic political process—one in which individual voters, special interest groups, lobbyists, bureaucrats and government employees, and elected legislators or representatives each have their own private interests and incentives that influence which rules are proposed and adopted. Often, for instance, restrictions on Airbnb rentals are favored and pushed through by heavily funded lobbyists representing the hotel industry, while restrictions on Uber and Lyft are similarly imposed not in the interest of consumers, but in the interest of seeking votes and campaign contributions from the local taxi industry. Employees of the Drug Enforcement Administration or local police whose jobs and funding may depend on the war on drugs may have a vested interest that influences decisions about marijuana policy.

This view—that outcomes of the democratic political process may not always be the policies that are in the overall public interest, but rather the ones designed to benefit narrow special interest groups—is known as the *public choice* view of regulation. The field of public choice, pioneered by Nobel laureate James Buchanan, attempts to apply the basic principles of economics to understand the decisions made within the political process.[7] By using the same tools economists use to understand how consumers or business owners may make decisions in their own interests, scholars have recognized ways in which these tools also apply to individuals in their public-sphere activities. Someone who steps into a voting booth or a job in government does not magically transform into a fundamentally different person—people operating in the public sphere still desire to make decisions that further their own self-interest.

Thus, certain activities may be banned or regulated not because these restrictions help society, but because the restrictions benefit certain individuals or organized special interest groups—often at the expense of others. In this public choice view, widespread use of government regulations become less desirable. Regulatory-making bodies and agencies may be captured by special interests who then use them against the public good to limit competition and transfer income or other private benefits to themselves at the expense of others.[8] Firms are often able to manipulate and use regulations to limit competition and attack competitors.

In contrast to the rule of law, which prevents individuals from taking from one another, overzealous and overreaching regulations may become an instrument of plunder in which rules are imposed to transfer income and benefits to those who have the most political connections, clout, or votes.[9]

The best way to conclude this section is by discussing the "bootleggers and Baptists" theory, made famous by noted economist Bruce Yandle.[10] Yandle noted that in many cases individuals' and groups' private justifications for government regulations are hidden or masked in public interest motives. In other cases, two very different groups have private interests that simply align to pose a powerful political force. From the name of the theory you may have assumed—correctly—that Yandle was referring to bootleggers' and Baptists' shared interests in policies regarding alcohol prohibition. During Prohibition, bootleggers benefitted from the regulations restricting the production and sale of alcohol. Moonshiners who distilled hard liquor, and the mobsters and bootleggers who transported and distributed it, were benefitting from the restrictive policies and were just as much in favor of keeping them in place as those who supported prohibition on moral grounds (the "Baptists," in Yandle's terms).

Thus, while a current regulatory policy may at first seem to be imposed for public-interest or moral reasons, the real underlying reasons are likely private economic benefits. For example, a lobbyist representing the taxi industry, in an effort to ban Uber, may find it effective to publicize rare cases in which Uber drivers have committed crimes rather than simply arguing that Uber's business model lowers the profitably of the taxi industry.

This reality should lead a careful thinker to consider that many regulations imposed for seemingly social reasons may, rather, be in place because of the private interests they serve at the public expense. Looking at the larger picture, however, one needs to carefully consider the true public benefits and costs of regulations when deciding which regulations may or may not be warranted.

The Cost of Regulation

The last general consideration that must be clarified before a discussion can begin about the specific impact of regulations on entrepreneurial activity regards the potential measurement of the costs of regulations. The noted 19th-century economic philosopher Frédéric Bastiat was well known for his forceful arguments that the true costs of government actions often far exceed what is obvious and visible.[11] The "unseen" or "secondary" effects, often referred to as "unintended consequences," play an important role in computing the true costs of regulations—the costs that must be weighed against any potential benefit.

In many cases, these unintended consequences of regulation simply result in the actual costs of a regulation being greater than what was anticipated. For example, local bans on alcohol sales (i.e., in "dry counties") are usually associated with obvious costs such as lost tax revenue and fewer eating and drinking establishments. However, an often-overlooked cost is that these regulations result in more individuals driving to neighboring counties to purchase and consume alcohol, leading to increased drinking-and-driving fatalities. In some cases, a regulation may be passed that in hindsight creates costs so much higher than anticipated that its passage would not have been justified to begin with if the true costs had been known.

One might think that such inefficient regulations would simply be overturned once their costs are known (as was done when the federal alcohol prohibition was repealed). But there is a well-documented bias in political action against such changes. Regulations, once imposed, are often hard to remove or change, even if they are later outdated, unnecessary, or inefficient. For example, they may create vested-interest groups that benefit from the inefficient rules and fight for them to remain in place. Noted economist Gordon Tullock called this the "transitional gains trap," and illustrates it at work in the political support to keep in place inefficient agricultural subsidies and taxi medallions.[12] In other cases, bad or outdated regulations remain on the books simply because they are not on the political radar; they go unnoticed amid the many new high-profile items on the political agenda. This is why it is strongly desirable to have normal procedures in place to review existing regulations, or mandatory sunset provisions that cause newly adopted regulations to expire at some time in the future.[13]

Frequently, these unintended consequences result not just in higher costs of regulation, but also in much lower (or nonexistent) benefits. In some cases, regulations may hurt the very groups or causes they were intended to help. For example, the employment provisions of the Americans with Disabilities Act were passed with the intention of lowering barriers to employment for people who are disabled. The legislation prohibits discrimination based on disability status and further requires employers to make reasonable accommodations for employees with disabilities. However, there is evidence that the Americans with Disabilities Act has harmed the employment opportunities for disabled Americans by increasing the cost of hiring disabled workers and making it harder to fire them, resulting in a decrease in the employment of disabled individuals.[14] Similarly, the Endangered Species Act created regulations allowing large areas around the nesting grounds of the red-cockaded woodpecker to be declared "protected habitats," a designation that imposes stringent restrictions on the surrounding property owners. This unleashed a frenzy of destruction as landowners rushed to cut down trees in which woodpeckers might potentially nest, leading to a large decrease in the potential habitat for the birds.[15] More recently, researchers have found that bans on plastic grocery bags have resulted in at least a 25 percent increase in emergency room visits and deaths related to harmful *E. coli* and other bacteria from unwashed reusable bags.[16] Once you consider the harmful secondary effects, these regulations are significantly less beneficial than they might at first appear.

Regulation, Rent-Seeking, and "Unproductive" Entrepreneurship

Widespread regulation also works to lessen private-sector entrepreneurship indirectly by distorting the private returns (profit rates) to private-sector activity versus political activities. When regulation causes large changes in the wealth or income of individuals, these individuals are willing to spend resources to affect the political process and alter the course of action on the regulation in question. That is, a regulation that would make the XYZ company a monopolist in an industry by restricting competition would be very valuable to the company, enough so that the company might be willing to devote substantial resources to making sure the regulation gets enacted. Its efforts might take the form of political contributions, lobbying, or other means. There is now a large literature documenting the enormous amounts spent by individuals attempting to sway the political process in their favor, a process known as *rent-seeking* in the academic literature.[17] According to the Center for Responsive Politics, for example, in 2018 alone $3.46 billion was spent lobbying the federal government to influence legislation, and more than 11,000 registered lobbyists were doing the lobbying. This is in addition to the $3 billion in campaign contributions individuals and interest groups gave to support federal political candidates.[18] And this is just at the federal level; similar amounts were spent to influence state and local political actions.

There is yet another important cost policymakers should consider before they enact regulations—one that also has the potential to render regulations more costly than they appear at first glance. This is the fact that regulation directly results in a reallocation of entrepreneurial talent away from the private sector and toward activities that are innovative in the political arena.[19] Some members of society who could have become accomplished private-sector entrepreneurs instead become accomplished lobbyists or lawyers and spend their talents attempting to sway public policy in the direction they or their clients favor.

Simply put, the more government gets involved in the economy, and the more influence it has over the allocation of resources and flows of income, the greater is the incentive for talented individuals to devote their time and careers to the political sector (and consequently not to the private sector). Compounding this effect is the fact that high levels of government regulation and taxation generally lower the profitability of private-sector business activities and thereby further reduce the incentive to engage in private-sector entrepreneurship. Thus, more government influence and control over private actions through regulation reduces the relative return to becoming a private-sector entrepreneur and increases the return to becoming a public-sector entrepreneur (a talented and innovative lobbyist, for example).

Economists have constructed several overall indexes that measure the extent to which governments do (and do not) intervene in private markets across both states and nations. The most famous of which is the Economic Freedom of the World index, but there are also ones for states and other political jurisdictions. While the index includes more policy measures than just regulation, regulation is a major component of the index. As regulation grows, economic freedom declines.

In a 2008 study, I showed that states with higher economic freedom scores have both more productive private-sector entrepreneurship and less unproductive entrepreneurship.[20] I constructed an index of "net entrepreneurial productivity" that grows with the proportion of entrepreneurial talent allocated to the private sector and falls with increasing political activity or lawsuit abuse. There was a clear and strong relationship between the economic freedom scores of US states and their levels of net entrepreneurial productivity. Higher levels of economic freedom therefore not only promote the good types of entrepreneurship but also decrease the destructive types of entrepreneurship.

While measures of unproductive entrepreneurship aren't widely available at the international level, there is clear evidence of a similar relationship between more government regulation (as reflected in lower economic freedom scores) and lower rates of productive entrepreneurship. In a 2015 study I ranked countries by their level of economic freedom and computed average levels of entrepreneurship for each of three groups—countries with economic freedom scores in the top third of scores, countries with scores in the middle third, and countries with scores in the bottom third.

The third of countries with the lowest economic freedom scores in 2014 (indicating the most government regulation of business) had just slightly more than one new private entrepreneurial venture per 1,000 people, while the third of countries with the highest economic freedom scores achieved a rate of new venture formation of more than six per 1,000 people. So, for every 1,000 people in a country, there were roughly five more business start-ups in the least-regulated economies than in the most-regulated economies.

Regulation, Start-Up Activity, and Firm Size

When regulations make it more costly or difficult to open or run a business, we should generally expect they will result in fewer businesses.[21] Until recently, studies attempting to examine the impact of regulation on entrepreneurship did so either theoretically, on a case-study basis, or by using proxies for the level of regulation, such as enforcement agency budgets, page counts of regulatory codes, survey measures, procedure counts, or cost estimates.

One study, for example, finds that the Clean Air Act, in its first 15 years, caused a loss of almost 600,000 jobs and $75 billion in economic and business activity.[22] There is also evidence that when countries take steps to enact regulatory reform to lessen business regulation these efforts have substantial positive impacts.[23]

More recently, a new measure of regulation has appeared that may allow more extensive research on this issue in the future. The publication and availability of RegData now offers a comprehensive metric of US federal regulation by agency and by industry (classified using the North American Industry Classification System) going back to 1970, on the basis of a statistical computer analysis of words and phrases embedded in agency regulatory restrictions.[24] Using these new data, economists James Bailey and Diana Thomas have examined how levels of industry regulation impact firm births, firm deaths, and new hires, and have done so separately for small and large firms. Using the data for all firms, they find that a 10 percent increase in regulation leads to a 0.47 percent decline in firm births and 0.63 percent reduction in new-firm hiring, and they find that this relationship is even stronger and larger for smaller firms—which means that regulation hurts small business activity disproportionately.[25]

Regulation and Firm Size

While it is perhaps unsurprising that states or countries with more regulation have fewer new entrepreneurial ventures, what may not be so obvious is that higher levels of regulation also affect the sizes of firms—or, more precisely, the viability of businesses of differing sizes.

Most regulations function as "fixed costs," meaning that the cost of compliance is similar for both large and small firms. For example, the cost of installing one entrance ramp for people with disabilities is the same for a small diner with 10 seats as it is for a larger diner with 500 seats. Similarly, the time cost of permitting and paperwork involved in opening a business might be nearly the same for a small firm as for a large firm. The implication is that these fixed costs of regulations disproportionately affect small firms. As a proportion of their costs, dealing with regulations is less costly for larger firms than for smaller ones.

Using measures of US state-level regulatory enforcement costs, researchers have found that more state-level regulation is associated with a significantly lower proportion of establishments with only the owner working (no employees) or with one to four employees—in other words, small businesses.[26] These results suggest that one additional cost of the regulatory system, often overlooked, is its impact on the efficiency of firm structure. By inefficiently influencing firm size, regulatory systems create additional costs within the economic system.

While regulations generally increase costs for all businesses, higher regulatory hurdles generally give a relative cost advantage to larger establishments, which can maintain internal tax and legal departments, as opposed to smaller firms that usually need to build external networks. Individual entrepreneurs simply have a difficult time dealing with the costs associated with these regulatory barriers by themselves. This effect of regulation has substantial implications for economic growth because it implies greater regulatory burdens lead to fewer small entrepreneurial start-ups. If there is less entrepreneurial experimentation in the economy, fewer business successes will be present in the marketplace, leading to slower economic progress and innovation.

This is particularly harmful because small businesses are disproportionately responsible for new innovations and growth. Several authors, including famous economists such as Joseph Schumpeter and William Baumol and noted Harvard Business Professor Clayton Christensen, have all stressed that while large firms are generally better at improving existing products (what they term "incremental improvements"), it is small firms that have pioneered most of the major new innovative goods and services in the economy (the "disruptive innovations").[27] By disadvantaging the small-business, first-time entrepreneur types, regulation can disproportionately influence innovation in an economy.

In the end, the best form of regulation is competitive markets with low entry barriers, an argument famously made by Nobel laureate Milton Friedman. When one firm is behaving poorly, new firms can come in and earn its customers if there is freedom of entry into industries (i.e., "contestable markets").[28] According to this logic, the worst thing regulation can do is make it more difficult or costly for competitors to enter industries and threaten incumbent firms that aren't doing a good job satisfying consumers at the lowest cost.

The Regulation of Entrepreneurial Inputs

An additional facet of regulation's impact on entrepreneurship is worth discussing—this is how it distorts choices regarding the mix of inputs in the productive process. Normally, a business would select the combination of labor, capital, and land that minimizes the cost of production for its desired level of output. It would also choose the location, advertising strategies, and quality best suited to winning and satisfying its customers. Often, however, regulations either distort the relative prices of various options or restrict which choices can be made. For example, labor regulations regarding hours, benefits, and minimum wages distort the choices of entrepreneurs who must decide among labor and machinery and equipment.

One example case is the regulations that restrict businesses attempting to operate in the historic districts of cities. For example, the New York City Landmarks Preservation Commission placed an ordinary gas station within the bounds of its SoHo historic district when the district was drawn up, preventing or at least significantly complicating the owner's plans to redevelop the property into a mid-rise condo development.[29] The owner even needed city approval to install new doors on a shed on his property. Even though the gas station was no longer profitable, the historic designation prevented the resource from being properly and efficiently reallocated.

Regulation and Corruption

A final issue related to the regulation of entrepreneurial start-ups and of business more generally is that it creates opportunities for the corruption of public officials.[30] When a country (or state) imposes particularly onerous or burdensome procedures on those seeking to open a new business, entrepreneurs may find they can bribe their way through the process much more easily. In the literature this is often referred to as "greasing the wheels" of the regulatory process.[31]

Perhaps nowhere is the anecdotal and empirical evidence for this effect stronger than in post-socialist economies, which have some of the highest corruption rates in the world.[32] The recent headline-making admission of casino owner Sheldon Adelson that he likely violated US law by bribing Chinese officials provides a case in point, though admittedly an anecdotal one. The *New York Times* reports, "As with many lucrative business spheres in China, the gambling industry on

Macau is laced with corruption. Companies must rely on the good will of Chinese officials to secure licenses and contracts. Officials control even the flow of visitors, many of whom come on government-run junkets from the mainland."[33]

The general idea is that when the barriers to opening a business are high, being able to bribe political agents can ease the business start-up process. When government agents control the flow of licenses, contracts, or customers, the entrepreneurs who provide favors to these government agents are better equipped to successfully navigate the process of opening a successful business. In a nutshell, for many entrepreneurs around the globe, paying bribes can be viewed simply as a cost of entering an industry—equivalent to, say, having to purchase a business license. The problem, of course, is that government corruption is generally harmful and destructive to achieving economic growth and prosperity, and to the growth-generating process of entrepreneurship.[34]

Policy Reform

As this chapter has argued, government regulations often create significant costs and unintended consequences. The potential benefits of any regulation, proposed or existing, should be weighed against these costs. Careful consideration and requirements that cost-benefit analysis be performed on existing and proposed regulations are a step in the right direction, but those who prepare cost estimates must try to include the harder-to-see costs in areas such as lobbying, rent-seeking, and corruption. Enacting and enforcing sunset provisions is another step toward a more efficient regulatory code. It is also important for policymakers to ensure that regulations do not lessen competition, restrict entry, or create burdens so high they interfere with the ability of new small businesses to open.

Conclusion

The academic literature on regulation's impact on entrepreneurship suggests, unsurprisingly, that excessive regulation is harmful to the level of entrepreneurship, the productivity of entrepreneurship, and the level of innovation, and consequently to economic growth. The problematic issue, however, is understanding the level beyond which regulation becomes "excessive" or "inefficient." Some may argue that achieving certain social, moral, or fairness goals is worth the cost of reduced entrepreneurship. While the values placed on these trade-offs are subjective, often regulations imposed with noble goals do not deliver the level of benefits expected because of unintended consequences or the inherent "public choice" shortcomings of the political process that give undue influence to concentrated special interest groups.

In the end, regulations are costly—more costly than they at first appear. The true benefit of each potential regulation needs to be weighed against the considerable cost regulations impose, and all regulations should be forced to prove their worth before they are adopted (or continued) as policy. Competition among firms, enabled by contestable markets, is the best form of dynamic regulation in an economy, and in order to function properly an economy requires a strong rule of law within which the life, liberty, property, and individuals' contracts are upheld and people are held accountable for damages to others. Regulations beyond this scope generally cause individuals and firms to devote resources toward attempting to influence government policy and often lead to the corruption of government officials.

CHAPTER 2

Regulation and the Perpetuation of Poverty in the US and Senegal

Steven Horwitz and Magatte Wade

Our attempt to explore the issue of poverty starts with the recognition that poverty has been the typical state for most human beings throughout human history. It is only in the past 200 years or so that more than a tiny fraction of human beings have been able to live long lives of material and physical comfort. In some sense, the intellectual puzzle of human economic history is not explaining the causes of poverty, but the causes of the much more exceptional wealth of the modern era. Put differently, how did humans ever escape a world where nature-given resources cannot possibly enable more than a small number of people to survive at a subsistence level? What are the causes of what economic historian Deirdre McCloskey calls "the Great Enrichment?"[1]

Even as the Great Enrichment has raised living standards in the Western world and lifted billions out of severe poverty across the globe in the past few decades, poverty still exists in multiple forms worldwide. In the West, there are still too many people who have not been able to share fully in the cornucopia of the Great Enrichment. Nonwhite households are more likely to be persistently below the Western poverty line, even as others move up and down the income ladder. In the rest of the world, especially in Africa, too many households, and whole countries, have not been able to escape to anything close to Western levels of material comfort, even where they aspire to that goal and are willing to work for it. In the West, we see household-level poverty in the midst of societies that have great riches, while elsewhere we see both household- and country-level poverty in the midst of increasing worldwide plenty.

The task of this chapter is to offer some insight about these two outcomes. If the Great Enrichment has done so much for the West and is starting to do the same elsewhere, why has it not spread to all in the West, and why have so many elsewhere in the world not shared in its benefits? The answer we will propose is that the freedom to trade in the marketplace and the ethical approval of such activity, both of which were crucial to the Great Enrichment, have been restricted through government regulations in ways that perpetuate poverty. In the Western world, these regulations affect entry-level labor markets and the entrepreneurship associated with new small businesses, thereby making it more difficult for lower-skilled workers to rise out of poverty. In many other parts of the world, the regulatory state is more encompassing, making it very difficult for most citizens, and not just the poor within those countries, to start new businesses and to operate in an environment of generalized freedom to trade. In both parts of the world, these regulations restrict what has been termed the "permissionless innovation" necessary to reap the benefits of the discovery process of competitive markets. The more often that people need permission from government regulators to try out new ideas or to tweak earlier innovations, the more difficult it is to create the wealth that raises living standards and pushes back against poverty.

The next section explores in greater detail the question of how the West grew rich and why that Great Enrichment has not fully spread elsewhere. Understanding who benefits from regulation is crucial to providing that answer. The two following sections provide examples from the US and Senegal of the way restricting trade and requiring permission to innovate has perpetuated the pockets of poverty in the West and the more widespread poverty in other parts of the world.[2] The potential for bringing the benefits of the Great Enrichment to all the world is real, if only we can identify the regulations that prevent economic growth and upward mobility and then remove them and allow markets and competition to spread the Great Enrichment globally.

Trade and the Great Enrichment

The facts of the Great Enrichment are well known and largely uncontroversial. In the 19th century, a significant and growing portion of humanity began to escape the grinding poverty that had characterized human history up to that point. Although in earlier times a small portion of the privileged, such as royalty, had lived comparably well, even the quality of their lives paled in comparison to what the Great Enrichment would bring. One of the great accomplishments of the past 200 years has been the rise in the living standards of more and more ordinary people. It may well be true that the rich today live incredibly well, but the average westerner lives far better than the kings and queens of old—even the average African outdoes them. One need only consider that approximately 80 percent of adult sub-Saharan Africans own either a basic cell phone or a smartphone.[3]

More generally, we can follow McCloskey's calculation that the average human now consumes 8.5 times more than the average human 200 years ago and lives twice as long (after making it to age 16), and that the earth is able to support 7 billion people as opposed to 1 billion.[4] If we do the multiplication (8.5 × 2 × 7), the result is that humanity is 119 times better off, in terms of total consumption by the total number of human life-years, than 200 years ago. There are now more people living longer lives with more ability to consume, and by a factor of 119.[5]

We have seen the effects of this enrichment in the United States and globally. Of course a comparison between 2019 and 100 or 200 years prior would clearly show those gains in wealth, but one number is worth considering: the percentage of income spent on food, clothing, and shelter has fallen over the past 100 years, from about 75 percent to 35 percent.[6] The value of labor has climbed and market competition has kept prices affordable, with the result that members of the average US household today have a great deal more discretionary income than their grandparents and great-grandparents did. Even if we look at the past 50 years, we can see that the percentage of US households that possess basic appliances such as washing machines, dishwashers, and dryers, as well as goods such as TVs, air conditioning, and microwaves, has increased, in some cases substantially (see table 1). In addition, average (and poor) US households have goods that didn't even exist 50 years ago, such as smartphones, personal computers, and other electronics, not to mention access to new lifesaving drugs and other medical treatments. Economist Michael Cox and economic journalist Richard Alm provide a useful nice list of items available at the end of the 20th century that did not exist a generation earlier.[7] This standard of living should be, but is not always, available to all Americans, and finding ways enable more people to enjoy that standard is the problem that needs to be addressed.

Table 1. Percentage of Households
with Various Consumer Items, 1971–2005

	% of poor households				% of all households	
Item	1984	1994	2003	2005	1971	2005
Washing machine	58.2	71.7	67.0	68.7	71.3	84.0
Clothes dryer	35.6	50.2	58.5	61.2	44.5	81.2
Dishwasher	13.6	19.6	33.9	36.7	18.8	64.0
Refrigerator	95.8	97.9	98.2	98.5	83.3	99.3
Freezer	29.2	28.6	25.4	25.1	32.2	36.6
Stove	95.2	97.7	97.1	97.0	87.0	98.8
Microwave	12.5	60.0	88.7	91.2	1.0	96.4
Color TV	70.3	92.5	96.8	97.4	43.3	98.9
VCR	3.4	59.7	75.4	83.6	0.0	92.2
Personal computer	2.9	7.4	36.0	42.4	0.0	67.1
Telephone	71.0	76.7	87.3	79.8	93.0	90.6
Air conditioner	42.5	49.6	77.7	78.8	31.8	85.7
Cellular telephone	—	—	34.7	48.3	0.0	71.3
At least one car	64.1	71.8	72.8*	—	79.5	—

* This number is for 2001.

Source: US Census Bureau, "Extended Measures of Well-being: Living Conditions in the United States, 2005," 2005, https://www.census.gov/data/tables/2005/demo/well-being/2005-tables.html.

Figure 1. Changes in Global Poverty, 1990–2013

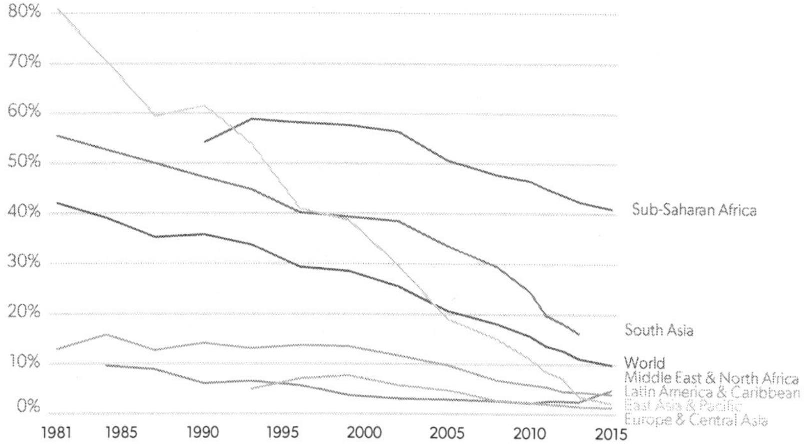

Source: http://ourworldindata.org/extreme-poverty, using data from World Bank, "PovcalNet: An Online Analysis Tool for Global Poverty Monitoring," http://iresearch. worldbank.org/PovcalNet/. Accessed September 17, 2020.

Globally, one of the unheralded stories of the past few decades has been the enormous decline in extreme poverty. We have seen the rise of global consumption as more and more people across the world have begun to approach Western standards of living. Less obvious has been the decline of extreme poverty. The World Bank reports that the percentage of people living in extreme poverty, defined as less than $1.90 per day, fell to 10 percent in 2015, which is a historic low. The total number of people living on less than $1.90 day fell to 736 million. This represents an enormous decline over the past few decades, as more than 1 billion people moved out of extreme poverty between 1980 and 2015.. The World Bank estimated that the number for 2018 would be 8.6 percent of the world's population below the extreme poverty line. [8]

Despite these accomplishments, it remains the case that parts of the world have not had as much success as others. Sub-Saharan Africa, for example, is expected to have more than 10 percent of their population below the extreme poverty line for at least another decade.

To understand these data on the Great Enrichment, and why poverty persists in the midst of plenty, we need to understand the causes of the explosion in wealth of the past 200 years. [9] The key factors were the freedom to trade in markets and an ethical system that accepted, if not approved of, the innovation that markets produced and the profits that they generated.

More specifically, we might break the "freedom to trade in markets" into two pieces: the first is "permissionless innovation" and the second is "trade-tested betterment." What happened in the early 19th century is that it became possible for more people to try out new ideas without having to obtain a license or other permission from governments. Rather than being seen as a threat to the established traditions, innovations became tolerated and encouraged as the risks of failure lessened thanks to more stability in agricultural output. The problem then became determining which innovations were truly beneficial and which were not. What McCloskey calls "trade-tested betterment" is the process by which the profit and loss generated through market exchange provides the test for whether particular innovations are sources of social improvement. Profits tell us that value has been created and that we are better off, while losses tell us that value has been destroyed and that we need to try something different.[10]

Trade-tested betterment through the guide of profit and loss requires a number of other institutions. Having new ideas and inventions is not enough. The right institutions are necessary to turn inventions into innovations that improve people's standard of living. First and foremost, there must be private property rights, and those rights must be clearly defined and effectively and fairly enforced. The wealth-creating processes of innovation and testing by profit and loss require that people know that their property is theirs and will remain theirs into the indefinite future. This means that it is protected from the predation of both other private actors and governments. State actions ranging from the uncompensated use of eminent domain to full nationalization (or the threat thereof) will discourage property owners from being willing to take the risks associated with innovation. So will regulations that impose excessive and unnecessary costs on potential producers.

Along with private property, these processes require the rule of law. The law must be clear and public and those who write and enforce the law must be subject to it as well. The rule of law also enables actors to form reliable expectations about the future and know that they will be treated fairly.

The last institutional requirement is sound money. All of the market transactions that drive economic progress take place in terms of money, and if money's value is constantly fluctuating because of inflation or deflation, market exchange and the calculation of profit and loss are much more difficult. In such situations we will get less innovation and weaker market tests, leading to less wealth creation. The parts of the world that respect private property, adopt the rule of law, and have sound money have historically experienced the most widespread enrichment.

Alongside these institutional requirements, the Great Enrichment also requires that people have an ethical system that encourages the openness, innovation, and profit-seeking that is associated with market exchange. In McCloskey's terms, our "habits of the lip" are at least as important as the institutional structures in which we operate. A society that has these institutions but also expresses strong disapproval of innovation or profit-making would have a hard time generating enrichment. In her work, McCloskey argues that changes in how entrepreneurial activity was perceived, along with an increasing tolerance for people striking out on their own and seeking their fortune rather than staying with family and community, were crucial to the Great Enrichment.[11] How people talked about trade, markets, and profits shifted in important ways, and the behavior associated with those institutions was increasingly seen as virtuous. That shift provided a necessary complement to the institutional requirements noted above. Together they produced the Great Enrichment.

To the degree that these institutional and ethical requirements are in place today in various countries around the world, those countries have continued to prosper. There is nothing in the story of the Great Enrichment that suggests that any group of people, be it an ethnic group or an entire nation, cannot share in its bounty. Adopting the right institutions and ethical perspective is what is needed, and this path is available to all humanity.

If we know what reduces poverty, why does it persist in pockets in the West and more broadly elsewhere in the world? Why haven't the right institutions been adopted more consistently worldwide? There are a variety of answers to that question, but the overarching explanation is that the benefits of good institutions are widely dispersed across the population and are often subtle and slow to develop. This makes it hard for people to appreciate them, especially when regulation and intervention into markets has benefits for well-organized groups that can be part of creating them. The benefits from intervention and regulation are concentrated in the hands of a small number of people who therefore have an incentive to argue for regulation, while the costs in terms of lost overall growth are spread thinly across the whole population, and are often hidden and long-run, giving the larger population little incentive to oppose the regulation.

For example, when a group of producers argues for a regulation that will prevent others from entering their line of work, they stand to benefit significantly from it, while the costs in terms of higher prices, lower quality, and less innovation are spread across a much larger number of people and the per capita cost is quite small. Those with political power, or with the resources to access political power, will frequently have exactly this sort of incentive to favor regulation and the weakening of wealth-creating institutions, unless there are political safeguards in place to prevent them from doing so.[12]

In some cases this dynamic takes the form of what is known as the "bootleggers and Baptists" problem.[13] Those who gain materially from regulation or from weak institutions often find themselves getting support from others who have a strong ideological or moral belief that a regulation is needed. For example, suppose a big-box store wants to open across the street from a shopping mall. The owners of the mall, and the owners of the stores that occupy it, might have many financial reasons to oppose the new big-box store. They stand to benefit from a regulation that would prevent such a store from opening. They are the "bootleggers" who benefit from preventing market exchange. They might find common cause with environmentalists who, while they have no financial interest in stopping the big-box store, have a strong commitment to making sure the new store does no environmental harm. They are the "Baptists" whose moral or ideological beliefs are satisfied by stopping the new store.

A good number of regulations give rise to this kind of alliance of strange bedfellows, making it more likely that they will pass, even if they are harmful in terms of overall economic well-being. The challenge for those seeking to generate consistent enrichment is finding ways to develop and preserve the wealth-enhancing institutions in the face of the incentives that well-organized interest groups have to lobby for regulatory interventions that benefit themselves at the expense of others or weaken wealth-enhancing institutions. Poverty exists where that challenge has not been overcome.

The Regressive Effects of Regulation in the United States

Most people assume that the purpose of regulating economic activity is to protect the most vulnerable people against the predation of those with economic power who often take advantage of what economists call "market failures." We imagine that the primary effects of regulation are to restrain the activities of those who prevent consumers and smaller producers from surviving the competitive process. In that imagining, we forget that it's not possible to regulate just one side of an exchange. All regulation, of necessity, limits the choices of both buyers and sellers. For example, if we pass a law that says employers cannot pay their workers less than $15 per hour, we are also passing a law that says workers cannot accept a job for less than $15 per hour, even if they might very much wish to do so. The same is true of regulations on producers, such as zoning laws. They do indeed limit the choices about where sellers can locate, but they also limit the options available to buyers in the areas sellers are prohibited from operating. Combining this point with the discussion in the previous section about the way some sellers can use regulation to raise the costs of their rivals and profit without improving the price or quality of their product, we cannot assume that regulation will always benefit the little guy.

Economist Diana Thomas describes a different pathway for the regressive effects of regulation.[14] If we view regulation as an attempt to manage perceived risks, we see that regulations often focus on low-probability risks that the relatively wealthy are unable, or simply do not wish, to manage themselves. If we imagine households both spending their own funds and lobbying for public expenditures to reduce risks, the costs of regulations that focus on low-probability risk will fall disproportionately on lower-income households. Thomas argues that these costs displace private household spending that might have served to mitigate higher-probability risks than those being regulated.

Thomas uses the example of mandating rear-view cameras in cars. Such regulations raise the cost of cars, including used ones, and they save very few lives. To the extent that these sorts of regulations reduce the disposable income of poorer households, they crowd out the expenditures such households would make to mitigate much higher-probability risks (e.g., spending on medical care). Wealthier households supporting such regulations are far less likely to be subject to that crowding-out effect. Thomas concludes, "Regulation has a regressive effect: It redistributes wealth from lower-income households to higher-income households by forcing lower-income households to subsidize the risk mitigation preferences of the wealthy and pay for risk reductions they would not otherwise choose."[15] Whether through the effects of limiting choice for consumers and rivals by lobbying for regulations, or through exploiting differences in the cost of risk mitigation, regulation benefits those with more resources more often than it does those with fewer.

Regulations designed to end poverty, for example, often end up promoting more poverty than they relieve. One example of this phenomenon is minimum-wage laws. From the employer's perspective, minimum-wage laws are minimum-productivity laws. If I have to pay you $15 per hour, I'm only going to hire you if you produce at least $15 per hour of value for my firm. If your skills are such that you cannot produce that much, you will not be hired. Minimum-wage laws thereby cut off the bottom rungs of the economic ladder by making it impossible for lower-skilled workers to enter the labor market. As a result, not only do those lower-skilled workers not have the opportunity to earn an income to relieve their current poverty, they cannot obtain basic job skills, as well as good references, that would increase their productivity and enable them to climb the ladder out of poverty. Moving out of poverty in a sustainable way requires employment, and the empirical evidence, while not unanimous, generally shows that minimum-wage laws cause some degree of unemployment among those who need jobs the most.

Unsurprisingly, when negative effects on employment and income are found, they tend to be concentrated among younger workers and those with weaker educations and less human capital in general.[16] Historically, minimum-wage laws have often been supported by higher-productivity workers playing the role of bootleggers (partnered with the "Baptists" arguing for the supposed injustice of market wages) who correctly see such laws as shutting out lower-wage competition from the market. If it is illegal to hire someone willing to work for $10 per hour, I will be that much more likely to hire higher-productivity workers who can justify the $15 per hour I must pay them. The history of minimum-wage laws shows the ways in which wealthier, higher-wage workers supported such laws as a way to foreclose lower-wage competition, especially competition being offered by immigrants and people of color.[17] Minimum-wage laws thereby perpetuate poverty among the lower-skilled, lower-wage groups.

Other regulations can affect wages in ways that disproportionately harm the least well-off. Economists James Bailey, Diana Thomas, and Joseph Anderson argue that regulation redistributes wealth from the poor to the rich by creating more high-paying job opportunities at the expense of lower-paying ones.[18] Specifically, they investigate whether an increased regulatory burden causes firms to have to bear more compliance costs by hiring more employees who are better compensated, such as lawyers and accountants. If it does, the effect may involve firms reallocating labor resources from lower-paying production jobs to higher-paying compliance-related jobs, thereby harming lower-wage workers relative to higher-wage ones. Bailey, Thomas, and Anderson find "some evidence that the costs associated with regulation lead to slower wage growth and that the burden is borne disproportionately by lower-wage workers."[19] Even if lower-wage workers are not made *absolutely* worse off by increased regulation, their relative position is worsened, making the effects regressive.

Though inflation is not a regulation, strictly speaking, maintaining sound money is one of the keys to fostering widespread increases in wealth that improve the well-being of the least well-off. Inflation also has regressive effects. Inflation imposes "coping costs" (which are economically identical to the "compliance costs" of regulation) that necessitate new expenditures by firms in high-inflation environments.[20] The costs of coping with inflation include a relative shift away from workers involved in direct production to those hired to cope with the effects of inflation. As with the compliance costs of regulation, this will mean hiring more accountants, financial experts, and lawyers relative to production workers. Because those jobs are higher-paying, we would expect to see the same regressive effects on real wages during inflation as we see from an increase in the regulatory burden on firms.

In addition their effects on wages directly, regulations can affect the quantity of labor, and in so doing create more poverty by limiting job opportunities. Occupational licensure laws provide one good example of such poverty-inducing regulations.[21] Occupational licensure laws are found at the state and municipal level and set the conditions required to obtain licenses to perform a variety of different jobs. Getting a license frequently involves costly and time-consuming preparation for exams. These costs serve as barriers to entry that limit competition in the industry being licensed, resulting in higher profits for incumbents and lost job opportunities for potential competitors. Occupational licensure laws provide another excellent example of the bootleggers-and-Baptists phenomenon mentioned earlier, given the coincidence of the economic interests of the incumbents and the moral concern of those who believe such regulation is needed to protect the safety of consumers. The "public safety" argument for licensure is less than persuasive when licenses are required for jobs such as interior design, which pose no safety threat to the public.

Licensing clearly increases the wages of incumbents, or those fortunate enough to obtain a license in the face of these barriers.[22] However, these gains have to be set against the costs borne by those trying to get a license and the costs of less employment or pay for those who choose lower-paying alternatives after being discouraged by the costs of the licensing process. Even those who get licenses and higher pay may see some or all of their gains absorbed by dues or fees to the licensing

boards required to maintain their protected status. But most important for our argument is the fact that incumbents and those most likely
to obtain licenses are likely to have higher incomes than those they
are attempting to exclude. If the potential workers excluded by licensing are poorer than those who benefit from it, occupational licensing
is regressive and helps to perpetuate existing poverty.

The Institute for Justice looked at 102 low- and moderate-income occupations that require licenses. The researchers found that all 50 US states
and the District of Columbia require licenses for at least some of these
occupations. The number of occupations licensed in each jurisdiction
ranges from 24 to 71 of the 102 studied.[23] The licensed worker categories included florists, interior designers, auctioneers, manicurists, and
preschool teachers. Some occupations are licensed in certain states but
not in others.[24] The licensed incumbents also tend to control the licensing boards, and there is evidence they can adjust fee amounts and the
difficulty of tests to raise or lower the barrier to lower-income applicants. On average, the licensing process required "$209 in fees, one exam
and about nine months of education and training," but that average is
highly variable across states.[25] For those with lower incomes, particularly
new entrants to the labor market, these requirements are burdensome.[26]

Part of the burden concerns the fact that about half of the licensed
occupations pertain to businesses that can be run easily and cheaply
from one's home or a low-rent storefront. Licensing blocks the path
to business creation, ownership, and expansion, which is often a path
out of poverty. Finally, those who practice in these licensed lower-income occupations are more likely to be nonwhite and less-educated
than the general population, and they have an annual average income
37 percent lower than the average for the US population as a whole.[27]
Occupational licensing has a clear tendency to harm the relatively poor
more than the relatively well-off, and thereby make it more difficult
to escape poverty.

Another effect of both minimum-wage laws and occupational licensure is that they increase the prices of various goods and services. In
general, lower-income households are less able to absorb such price
increases than higher-income households, because the added costs are

larger as a percentage of their household budgets. The result is that poor households find their budgets stretched, making it more difficult for them to save or to become licensed themselves, which further traps them in poverty. For example, consider cities in which regulators have banned ride-sharing services such as Uber or Lyft. Besides restricting employment opportunities for the poor, this policy raises the price of transportation services by reducing competition from lower-priced providers.[28] By decreasing the amount of transportation that consumers can afford and requiring them to pay more for what they use, this policy contributes to the perpetuation of poverty in the midst of plenty in the US.

Occupational licensing laws frequently affect professions that can easily be the source of small business start-ups. For example, incredibly strict cosmetology licensing laws make it very difficult for people, especially women of modest means, to go into business for themselves providing those services. Licensing day-care providers both increases the costs of day care, which particularly burdens lower-income households, and makes it harder for prospective providers, who are themselves often relatively poor, to start a day-care business.[29]

In addition to licensing laws, a variety of business regulations raise the cost of starting small businesses, which makes upward mobility more difficult in the US and other advanced economies. These regulations include zoning and other restrictions on home-based businesses, as well as limits on mobile businesses such as food carts and street vendors. Although the effects in advanced economies are real, they pale in comparison to the problems created by similar but more draconian laws in poorer countries.

Despite what might be the good intentions behind them, zoning laws, like occupational licensure laws, suffer from a bootleggers-and-Baptists problem, because they are often a tool used by the politically influential to block market access by lower-cost competition. In Chicago, for example, starting a new business requires a $250 license that must be renewed every two years, and violating this law will cost at least that amount per day. Renovating a home to accommodate a business requires completing a variety of forms, as well as an application process controlled by the Department of Planning and Development.[30] Even something as small as changing a sign can require dozens of hours and forms. Chicago regulations limit home-based businesses to no more than one employee who does not live in the home, and such businesses cannot manufacture or assemble products unless they sell them directly to retail customers who come to the home.[31] It is not clear what the Baptist argument is here, but the bootleggers are obvious.

Street vending and operating food trucks offer an excellent way for lower-income people to start the climb out of poverty, because they require relatively little start-up capital and make use of preexisting skills. Unfortunately, municipal regulations frequently make working in this way harder than necessary. Chicago requires a "peddler's license" and puts severe limitations on the places street vendors can operate. Food trucks cannot prepare food "on the street" without a specific, additional license and are subject to a large number of restrictions, including a requirement that they operate at least 200 feet away from a physical restaurant.[32] That regulation is a classic bootleggers-and-Baptists story: the owners of the brick-and-mortar restaurants play the role of bootleggers by lobbying for the restriction (among other restrictions), while Chicago aldermen play the Baptists by claiming that such rules are necessary to promote "entrepreneurship" in the restaurant industry. Unlike other provisions of Chicago regulations, which might plausibly be related to food safety or traffic issues, this rule is clearly designed to protect industry incumbents from the real entrepreneurial threat of food trucks.[33]

Many Chicago food trucks end up operating "in the shadow of the law," and more than a third of them have reported harassment from law enforcement while almost half have complained that legal uncertainty is one of the biggest impediments to their business.[34] The vast majority of food truck operators in Chicago are nonwhite and many of them report that that they got started with a food truck because of poor employment options in the city, or because of their age or health.[35] Food trucks offer a way out of poverty, and regulations and police harassment that raise the costs of entering or continuing in that business perpetuate poverty.

Street vendors in Philadelphia and other cities face similar restrictions.[36] New York City has a citywide limit on the number of food vending permits it issues, and it can take months and multiple forms to get a permit. Some of these forms are only available in English, raising the costs of getting started as a vendor for low-income immigrants.[37] The result of these regulations is a black market for the various permits, with prices ranging from $10,000 to $20,000 for a permit lasting two years. Such costs will be prohibitive for many low-income households, which in turn will extend their time in poverty.[38]

Finally, the general business permit approval process can be highly burdensome, and it varies significantly across cities. A recent US Chamber of Commerce study found that Chicago not only averaged 32 days to approve a permit for a professional services business, it charged $900 for doing so.[39] The state of Illinois then charged an additional $500, plus an annual fee of $250, to let a business organize as a limited liability company. The Chicago examples are above the national average, but almost every major city imposes some sort of significant permit-related burden on new businesses. Because all the regulations discussed in this section have regressive effects, it is not surprising that economists Dustin Chambers, Patrick McLaughlin, and Laura Stanley found that, at the state level, a 10 percent increase in the "effective federal regulatory burden . . . is associated with an approximate 2.5% increase in the poverty rate."[40]

If we are serious about addressing poverty in the US, one way to start is to remove all the barriers discussed in this section and allow people of modest means to seek out the jobs they want at wages they are satisfied with, allow them to enter various occupations without the regulatory barriers associated with licensing, and make it easier for them to start small businesses, whether out of their home, a food truck, or a street vendor's cart. For example, certification provides an effective and much-lower-cost alternative to licensing. The municipal regulatory process has too often been captured by wealthy, politically influential incumbents who see lower-income households wanting to work or start new businesses as competition to be eliminated rather than as people whose aspirations for upward mobility should be encouraged.

Reducing the burdens placed on those who want to work would help address the poverty amid plenty that characterizes parts of the US and other places in the Western world.

Regulation and Poverty in Senegal

Drawing on one of the authors' experience as an entrepreneur in both the US and Senegal, we can explore the effects of regulation in Africa with a case study of the challenges facing entrepreneurs in Senegal. Senegal is a former French colony that gained independence from France in 1960. The newly independent nation largely inherited French colonial law. Senegal's first two presidents, who governed the country from 1960 to 2000, were socialists. Thus the Senegalese legal system is inherited from a state-centric civil law nation in Europe, modified by 40 years of socialism and its associated cronyism and rent-seeking. It is very far from an optimal legal system for business and generating economic growth.

In fact, most African nations place near the bottom of the World Bank's Ease of Doing Business rankings as well as the Fraser Institute's Economic Freedom of the World rankings.[41] Senegal ranks 124th out of 162 countries on the Economic Freedom of the World Index (on the basis of 2017 data), placing it in the least economically free quartile. On regulation, Senegal ranks 147th out of 162, putting it among the most regulated economies in the world, with only about 10 percent of countries scoring worse. It ranks 114th on the measure for Legal System and Property Rights, which puts it in the lower end of the third quartile.[42] Senegal is also among the world's poorer countries. In regard to GDP per capita, Senegal ranks 149th out of 185 countries on the basis of 2018 data from the World Bank.[43] Given Senegal's lack of economic freedom, particularly its high regulatory burden, weak property rights, and ineffective legal system, as well as an ethical legacy from colonialism and socialism that is not friendly to markets and trade, Senegal's poverty is not a surprise.

Table 2 compares the US and Senegal on the Economic Freedom of the World rankings by specific category. Although the two countries are not that far apart in terms of the *size* of government, where they

diverge is on the issues central to our argument: legal systems and property rights, as well as regulation. The combination of a high regulatory
burden and a lack of rule of law and lack of protection for property
and contracts is particularly problematic for economic growth in general and poverty relief specifically.

Table 2. Economic Freedom of the World Rankings—US and Senegal, 2017

	Overall rank	Overall score	Size of Government score	Legal System and Property Rights score	Sound Money score	Freedom to Trade Internationally score	Regulation score
US	5	8.19	7.16	7.44	9.80	7.67	8.86
Senegal	124	6.17	7.02	4.28	7.22	6.70	5.63

Note: Rank is out of 162 countries. All scores are out of 10.

Source: Data on US and Senegal at the Fraser Institute's Economic Freedom database, https://
www.fraserinstitute.org/economic-freedom/map?geozone=world&page=map&-
year=2017&countries=SEN#country-info (accessed August 27, 2020), which uses data
from James Gwartney et al., *Economic Freedom of the World: 2019 Annual Report* (Vancouver, BC: Fraser Institute, 2019).

A closer look at the regulatory burden on entrepreneurs helps to
explain the link between Senegal's economic freedom ranks and its
poor economic performance In the US, entrepreneurs can set up a limited liability company in minutes online, and also quickly open a bank
account. Prospective entrepreneurs have hundreds of choices in banking with diverse service packages all competing for their business. In
the US, entrepreneurs can easily have ingredients, packaging, manufacturing equipment, shipping materials, and so forth shipped to them
quickly, in many cases overnight. Orders can be made online and paid
for with a credit card, and firms have thousands of choices of vendors
all competing to serve them. US entrepreneurs can more or less hire and
fire as they please, and—while taxes normally require an accountant—
compliance with tax law is not overly burdensome for a small business.

In Senegal, by contrast, it can take a year to open a new business if
one follows the official, formal procedures. Opening a business requires
entrepreneurs to work with several bureaucratic offices. As part of the

process, a notary public must be paid a fee of $200, which is about a one-fifth of a year's income for the average Senegalese.[44] Often bureaucrats do not show up to meetings, or show up late. Once they arrive, they often are not sure whether they are using the right procedure. They might lose paperwork, or they might stall in an attempt to get a small bribe to move forward. All these impediments are significant regulatory barriers and transaction costs that prevent entrepreneurs with good ideas from putting those ideas into practice in ways that could benefit the Senegalese public.

If they can get their business approved, entrepreneurs have very limited banking options because banking in Senegal is a state-managed oligopoly. The few players provide customers with few options and high fees. There are substantial minimum deposits needed to open a business account—again, often in excess of a year's salary for the average Senegalese person.[45] Once the funds are in the bank, transfers are expensive and time consuming. In contrast to the US, in Senegal bank personnel are more like government bureaucrats than service providers competing for customers.

After the long process of getting the needed approvals and bank accounts, when entrepreneurs want to begin operations, they find that almost nothing is available in Senegal. Take a simple cardboard box. In the US, one finds an endless array of cardboard box options and multiple firms that provide them. In Senegal, there are exactly two vendors and they offer only custom sizes, with a minimum quantity of 1,000 boxes per size, which is often much more than is needed. (As of January 2021, the larger vendor forced the smaller vendor out of business. There is now just one.) The result is wasted capital investment in supplies that will not be needed for far into the future. Because the costs of opening a new small business are so high, even a for-profit entity supplying something like boxes in a competitive market is typically accustomed to working with a relatively small number of large corporate customers rather than with small entrepreneurs.

These obstacles to creating legal businesses have created a massive "missing middle" problem in Senegal and across Africa. The "missing middle" refers to the fact that there are plenty of "microentrepreneurs" (i.e., poor people struggling to buy and sell out of necessity but with little or no real business structure because they remain in the black or gray market), and there are larger multinational corporations that have the resources to jump through the hoops of African bureaucracies. What is missing are entrepreneurial small businesses that have the protection of the law because they operate in a legal market.

The microentrepreneurs either cannot afford to create a legal business or prefer not to because they do not want the tax and regulatory hassles associated with doing so. As a consequence, they largely remain invisible, as black-market businesses must be. They have no legal rights to anything, they cannot obtain a bank account, they have no insurance, and they cannot guarantee their products through public certifications of quality—thus they do not typically develop into substantial businesses. This is one reason why cardboard boxes are not readily available in Senegal: there is not an adequate small business market to support them.[46] Because there are so few entrepreneurs, there is no ecosystem of professional small business service providers to support fast, efficient business operations.

The Dutch Good Growth Fund, an impact fund seeking to address the missing middle issue in West Africa, commissioned several studies in 2018. The researchers confirmed that most informal entrepreneurs perceive the process of going formal as too costly (in time and money) and too complex to make it worthwhile. In part, this is because one of the ways in which small business can get access to the formal credit system does not exist in West Africa. In the words of one researcher, "There are barely any players that can offer external funding (that is not collateralized debt) in the range of 10,000–1 million Euros."[47] Without the ability to get loans of that size, it does not pay to try to make use of the formal credit system.

At the other end, the multinational corporations have dedicated teams of lawyers and accountants to help them navigate the formal credit processes. This parallels the US situation, because multinational firms in Africa face substantial compliance costs. There is no reason to think that a displacement of lower-wage jobs does not take place in Africa as in the US, with the same regressive consequences. The multinational firms also have enough influence that politicians will grant them special exemptions unavailable to small entrepreneurs in order to attract their business. Because the multinational companies can rely on their own internal support services, they never have to deal with the absence of firms and institutions that Western businesses take for granted. Small businesses, by contrast, must find a way to deal with the fact that there are no networks of FedEx locations, no Office Depots, and no overnight delivery of millions of products.

In Senegal, all these things are personal rather than routinized through formal institutions. When economic activity is based on who one knows, the transaction costs of getting things done rise substantially. The ability of multinational firms to avoid those costs by doing things internally gives them a huge advantage over small businesses. The way in which regulations prevent new small businesses from opening, combined with the lack of a structure to support small businesses, contributes to the impoverishment of the Senegalese through both higher prices and fewer opportunities to earn an income.

Labor market regulations also impose large costs on entrepreneurs. When one hires an employee in Senegal, one is essentially married to the employee for life. By law, the government requires that entrepreneurs obtain approval before they lay off an employee. This situation encourages businesses not to hire people in the first place and to become more capital-intensive, reducing employment opportunities for those who need jobs the most. These employment rules make it hard for small businesses to adjust to inevitable fluctuations in demand by varying their labor force.[48] In practice, most Senegalese companies hire people as independent contractors to avoid the costs associated with these rules. However, doing so means that entrepreneurs cannot provide a real benefits package to their employees. Not only do these labor regulations mean fewer jobs, they also mean fewer benefits for those who do get work.

Paying business taxes in Senegal is an impossible, Kafkaesque task. The complexities of Senegalese value-added tax law are such that even government officials do not understand how rules of the tax apply, which might explain why Senegal is ranked near last on the Ease of Doing Business index on taxation. The ambiguity of the law opens up the possibility of selective enforcement and the use of regulation as a political weapon, further raising the costs of starting and maintaining small businesses. Similar ambiguities and selective enforcement affect everything from property rights to building permits, creating an environment of uncertainty that discourages entrepreneurship and the wealth and jobs it brings. The environment of uncertainty also encourages those with resources and access to political power to seek out regulations that benefit them or harm their (potential) competition, diverting resources from the positive-sum game of trade to the negative-sum game of transfers. Table 3 summarizes Senegal's ranks on all the elements of the World Bank's overall Ease of Doing Business index.

Those businesses that do manage to get started in Senegal and deal with all these problems will also face tariffs as high as 35 percent on a large variety of imports, as well as a value-added tax of an additional 18 percent, making the full tax burden potentially over 50 percent.[49] Some entrepreneurs may be able to get specific exemptions by spending enough time jumping through the right bureaucratic hoops, but doing so is only worthwhile for a small number of businesses selling relatively high-end consumer goods for the US market. Most small businesses either smuggle goods into the country or use inferior local substitutes—or they never come into existence at all.

Note the devastating impact of the regulations, tariffs, taxes, uncertain property rights, and permit systems described in this section: collectively they have almost completely killed off the ecosystem of legal, entrepreneurial small and medium-sized businesses that are essential to employment and broad-based growth and prosperity. This is why almost all business in Senegal is either informal or captured by large corporations, and why Senegal suffers from the missing middle. It is also why youth unemployment is such that "more than 70% of the youth in the Republic of the Congo, the Democratic Republic of the Congo, Ethiopia, Ghana, Malawi, Mali, Rwanda, Senegal and Uganda are either self-employed or contributing to family work."[50] It is also why so many young Senegalese leave for Europe in small fishing boats, accepting a very real risk of dying at sea. The costs of regulation are not just about material well-being.

Table 3. Rank for Senegal in World Bank Ease of Doing Business Index, 2019

Category	Rank out of 188 countries
Starting a business	60
Dealing with construction permits	131
Getting electricity	119
Registering property	116
Getting credit	67
Protecting minority investors	114
Ease of paying taxes	166
Trading across borders	142
Enforcing contracts	132
Resolving insolvency	96
Overall rank	123

Note: Rank is out of 188 countries.

Source: World Bank, "Ease of Doing Business Rankings," *Doing Business 2019*, accessed September 17, 2020, https://www.doingbusiness.org/en/rankings.

An Agenda for Reform

As policymakers and researchers think through how to reform the regulatory state to reduce its regressive effects, there are important differences between the challenges facing the US and those facing Senegal and other places where the Great Enrichment has yet to spread. But one common reform that could help in both places is requiring that all new regulatory proposals include an analysis of their effects on lower-wage workers and the poor more generally. The stated rationale for many regulations is such that those who analyze their effects have little reason to ask questions about their effects across income levels. Analyses should cover the effects on employment and new business creation as well as prices of outputs, because all of those can affect poverty. Requiring that analysts ask the question about distributional effects is no guarantee that analyses will be performed well or that their results will influence political decision makers, but it would at least recognize that regulations can often prevent upward mobility (in the US) or the development of a middle class in general (in Senegal and elsewhere).

A second general proposal for reform starts by recognizing that many regulations are intended to protect larger incumbent firms against competition from smaller firms, or those considering entering the industry. Our discussion of the bootleggers-and-Baptists phenomenon indicates that we need to watch for the "bootleggers" who are proposing regulations that use the arguments of the "Baptists" as cover for their own financial self-interest. Requiring statements of financial interest by those proposing or supporting new regulations (much as is expected of researchers who take positions on policy issues) would be helpful, as would soliciting the views of smaller competitors in the regulated industry or of small entrepreneurs in other industries who have faced similar regulatory barriers. These are difficult problems to overcome because of the concentrated benefits and dispersed costs of regulation, but calling attention to them would be a start.

A third general reform that all could benefit from, particularly those in the poorer parts of the world, is to ensure that the regulation that does exist remains clear and predictable and is enforced consistently. As we saw in the case of Senegal, a lack of clarity and weak enforcement of the rule of law exacerbate the ways in which regulation contributes to poverty. Barriers to the creation and continued operation of businesses are problematic enough on their own, but they are worse when entrepreneurs are unsure about the nature of the rules and their enforcement.

In Senegal, the necessary changes will be more difficult given the more deeply entrenched institutional problems. One strategy for reform should be to find ways to enable the existing informal economy to become part of the formal economy. There is clearly no lack of entrepreneurial spirit in Senegal's informal economy. Rather, those entrepreneurs are prevented from having the maximum positive effect on economic growth and upward mobility by the regulatory barriers that raise the costs of entering the formal economy, and thereby favor the larger multinational companies that can pay those costs.[51] The foundation for a reduction in poverty is there, both through more employment opportunities and greater output leading to lower prices, but it is being suffocated by the regulatory state and the lack of clear, consistent, and equitably enforced rules.

The problems in the US are much more specific, because particular regulations, rather than the deep institutional structure, are the relatively larger problem. Poverty reduction through regulatory reform will require a close look at regulations such as occupational licensure, zoning, business licenses, and others that raise the cost of starting a business, or staying in business, without a clear, corresponding social benefit. The benefits to incumbents of raising rivals' costs are private gains reflecting a negative-sum and regressive transfer. Absent a clear social benefit to such regulations, they need to be repealed so that the least well-off can reap the full benefits of competition. The evidence is clear that a vigorous and competitive market economy, framed by well-defined and enforced property rights, the rule of law, and sound money, has enabled much of humanity to emerge from poverty. The reforms listed above would enhance that vigor and competitiveness in any place that adopts them.

Conclusion

A close look at the effects of economic regulation in the US and Senegal indicates the ways in which it perpetuates poverty among both least well-off in the West and the global poor. If we want to encourage upward mobility in the West and significantly reduce poverty in places like Senegal, we need to free the skills and energy of entrepreneurs from the burden of excessive regulation. For places like the United States, this means taking seriously the regressive effects of a whole variety of regulations that inevitably serve the interests of incumbent firms with access to political power rather than actually protecting consumers, workers, or entrepreneurs. Much of the regulatory structure is, in practice, a redistribution from the poor and powerless to the wealthier and more powerful.

In places like Senegal, the scale of change will have to be greater, and it will require a serious commitment to the more fundamental liberal institutions: the rule of law, contracts, and property rights. It will also require a recognition that markets, exchange, and liberal institutions more broadly have their own African roots and are the path to prosperity, not a harmful legacy of Western colonialism and imperialism. The West grew rich by giving people the freedom and moral approval to author their own life projects, in which entrepreneurial ventures and choices of employment are often central, by ending arbitrary political interference and regressive regulations. That recipe still works today as a way to extend the wealth currently enjoyed by so many in the West to the poor in the West and across the globe.

CHAPTER 3

Social Trust and Regulation: A Time-Series Analysis of the United States

Peter T. Calcagno and Jeremy Jackson

Whom do you trust? The typical measure of the social trust concept is through responses to survey questions such as this one: "Do you think most people can be trusted?" Unfortunately, data from many sources are documenting a decline in social trust in the US, as measured by such questions. 2019 Pew Research survey data show that 79 percent of US adults believe that "Americans have 'far too little' or 'too little' confidence in each other," while 70 percent believe that "Americans' low trust in each other makes it harder to solve the country's problems."[1] The role of social trust and social capital in developing economic and political institutions is becoming a prevalent topic among social science researchers. Social trust and social capital are similar concepts that attempt to measure the health and connectivity of a society's social fabric. Social trust is closely related to cultural heritage, and has been found to be associated with the development of constitutions, with economic growth, with happiness, and with economic freedom. Because social trust is associated with so many beneficial outcomes, it is important to find the cause of the erosion of social trust among the US population. It is not just social trust, which is a trust for one another, that is eroding.

Table 1. Trust and the US Government

Survey date	Source	Individual polls (%)	Moving average (%)
25 Mar 2019	Pew	17	17
21 Mar 2010	Pew	22	24
14 Feb 2000	Pew	40	34
1 Dec 1990	ANES	28	33
15 Oct 1980	ANES	25	30
1 Dec 1970	ANES	54	54
15 Oct 1964	ANES	77	77
1 Dec 1958	ANES	73	73

Note: The poll results provided here are the percentages of people who reported that they trust the government in Washington "always" or "most of the time."

Sources: Pew = Pew Research Center; ANES = American National Election Studies

According to a recent Pew Research Center poll, only 17 percent of Americans "trust the government in Washington to do what is right 'just about always' or 'most of the time.'" This is a historic low: in 1958 this number was at at 73 percent.[2] Table 1 shows the change in trust in the federal government over the past seven decades. In addition, Americans think that other Americans' trust in Washington, DC, has declined—75 percent of poll respondents believe that trust in the federal government has been shrinking, and 41 percent believe that Americans lack of trust in the federal government is a major problem.[3]

Similarly, Gallup polls have surveyed individuals regarding trust in the three branches of the US government, and all three are accorded historically low levels of trust. In 2019 the percentages of people who have a "great deal" of trust in the current executive, judicial, and legislative branches are 24, 16, and 4 percent, respectively.[4] In addition, Gallup finds that trust in the American people to make good judgments under the democratic system is also down.[5] In 1974, 83 percent of people thought that the American people had either a great deal or a fair amount of confidence in making democratic decisions; however, in 2018 only 58 percent thought they had a great deal or fair amount of confidence. If trust in the federal government and its citizens is at a low and people do not think others trust the government, then what effect does this have on our economic system and, more importantly, on the regulatory environment that is supposed to protect individuals from a variety of potential harms?

Meanwhile, numerous studies examine the various effects of regulation on an economic system. Regulation consists of rules, mandatory prescriptions that must be followed, and prohibitions stipulating what must not be done. Regulation acts as a constraint on the behavior of the regulated. The academic literature argues theoretically and empirically that regulation can introduce inefficiencies and drag to an economic system,[6] affecting economic growth,[7] entrepreneurship,[8] workers,[9] and firms.[10] While government regulations can be necessary to promote the safety or well-being of its citizens, overwhelming regulatory burdens can be costly to firms that must comply and to customers that pay higher prices.[11] Excessive regulation can raise the possibility of regulatory capture, whereby industries gain control of the agencies tasked with regulating them,[12] or rent-seeking behavior, whereby firms seek preferential treatment in exchange for political favors.[13] Each of these pitfalls reflects a tendency for regulation to protect firms from their competition instead of protecting citizens.

One might argue that an economic system with high trust and simple but effective rules might not require as much regulation. After all, if you trust fellow citizens to do the right thing, then you don't need regulation to constrain their behavior. Indeed, researchers have found that those with low social trust demand more regulation while those with high social trust prefer less.[14] However, those with low social trust are also likely not to trust the state regulating agencies, whereas those with high social trust are likely to trust the regulating agencies.

Attitudes toward regulation and intervention are found to be conditional on institutional trust: an individual with high social trust is more likely to support regulation when confidence in regulating agencies is high and confidence in companies (the entities needing regulation) is low. This creates a possibility that social trust and regulation could display a positive correlation. Social trust itself is not developed in a vacuum, but is rather derived from the cumulating of social development through experiences. This development requires a feedback mechanism whereby praiseworthy behavior is rewarded and blameworthy behavior is punished.[15] Regulation circumvents the feedback mechanism in which individuals develop their sociality , leaving one with lower social trust as a result.[16]

With trust at historic lows and regulation at historic highs, we want to examine the relationship that may exist between them. This chapter's objective is to pull together the literature on regulation and social trust, along with data from the US, to examine what role social trust plays in the determination and development of regulation.

There is little literature that examines the relationship between social trust and regulation. The literature that does exist only examines cross-country data. For instance, economists Philippe Aghion, Yann Algan, Pierre Cahuc, and Andrei Shleifer argue that there is a negative relationship between trust and regulation. They argue that the causation should go both ways, with increased distrust causing increased regulation and increased regulation further degrading trust.[17] However, they are unable to implement an empirical test of bidirectional causation and rely purely on correlation across countries in one time period. Paolo Pinotti, a researcher with the Bank of Italy, uses individual data across multiple countries from a single year.[18] He looks at the relationship between social trust and individual preferences about regulation and finds evidence that low social trust is correlated with an increased preference for regulation. He puts forward a theoretical framework that suggests trust may causally influence preferences for regulation and the level of regulation itself, yet this causal link cannot be established by his study.

We intend to add to this research by focusing on one country—the United States—and using time-series data as opposed to a cross section of countries. Using social trust data from the General Social Survey and regulation data from RegData, we examine the relationship between social trust and regulation from 1972 to 2017. This long period of data allows us to see whether the same results that are present in the cross-country analysis are present over time, and in a single developed country. While our data do not allow for a full-scale determination of causation as opposed to correlation, we are able to take advantage of the long time horizon of our data to test for what is known as "Granger causality." Granger causality has been likened to predictive causality. It requires that the *cause* (increased regulation) occur before the *effect* (decreased social trust). Essentially, past movements in a *cause* variable can be tested for subsequent movements in an *effect* variable. One of the useful aspects of this concept and statistical technique is that it allows for and tests for bidirectional causality.

The rest of the chapter develops as follows: The next section explores the literature on regulation, social trust, and the overlap between them. The third section presents the data and model used to examine social trust and regulation. The fourth section presents the results of our empirical analysis. The fifth section summarizes the results in the context of recommendations for policy reform, and the final section offers a conclusion.

Literature and Background

Regulation

To begin examining the impact of social trust on regulation, we bring together two broad areas of research in the economics literature. The first area examines the impact of regulation on economic activity. The literature on regulation presents empirical evidence that higher levels of regulation are negatively correlated with business activity, entrepreneurship, and economic growth.[19] Several studies suggest that the agencies that set and impose regulations seek to gain job security, power, and prestige by providing greater amounts of regulations.[20] These agencies pass new regulations to benefit the special interest groups that dominate the political landscape. Firms might hire lobbyists to represent them within an industry to rent-seek for regulations that will lessen competition, or interest groups might promote "public interest" concerns about issues such as the environment or land use policy. In some cases, both forces might be in play, as in situations that follow economist Bruce Yandle's "bootleggers and Baptists" theory of special-interest-group activity.[21] Researchers have found that countries with high costs of entry into the market due to a high regulatory burden also have a weaker perception of marketplace competition and lower-quality private and public goods.[22]

Research suggests that higher levels of government intervention reduce entrepreneurial activity at the cross-country level.[23] Specifically, regulatory scholars Andrew Hale, David Borys, and Mark Adams contend that regulation has become so burdensome and complex, owing to its overly vague and difficult-to-interpret language and the large investments in time and resources required to discover and interpret it, that it actually reduces safety—contrary to the good intentions of the regulators.[24] Using economist William Baumol's theory of productive and unproductive entrepreneurship, several researchers argue that regulation will not lessen entrepreneurship, but will rather redirect it into unproductive channels.[25] One study uses data from the US to explore the possibility that trends of increasing regulation, measured by RegData, can lead to a trend of declining entrepreneurial activity. The authors find little evidence to suggest that regulation affects entrepreneurial activity in the US economy.[26]

At the state level, research shows that states with higher levels of economic freedom and with less regulation tend to spur on more entrepreneurial ventures.[27] Regulations can also affect the size and scope of firms. One study suggests that regulation can operate as a fixed cost to firms and deter the growth of small firms.[28] Firms will also purposely remain small in an attempt to avoid or be exempt from regulation.[29] Specifically, regulations like Sarbanes-Oxley seem to encourage firms to remain just small enough to maintain exemption from regulation as small businesses.[30] Economists Daron Acemoglu and Joshua Angrist argue that the Americans with Disabilities Act actually reduced the employment of people who are disabled.[31] The act requires employer accommodations for disabled workers and makes workplace discrimination based on disability illegal. Its advocates intended to make the workplace more open and inclusive to those with disabilities by providing legal protections, yet the evidence paints a different picture of the workplace that now exists. The required accommodations make hiring someone with a disability very costly—in some cases, more costly than the expected cost of litigation owing to noncompliance.

The Nobel Prize winning economist, Joseph Stiglitz argues that market failures such as externalities are one motivation for regulation. He notes that environmental regulations have given us cleaner air and water and that we could not fathom a world without food safety regulations.[32] Financial regulation is an area of debate over the net costs or benefits of regulation. Stiglitz argues that the problem with financial markets is not that they are regulated, but that financial regulation tends to be very specific.[33] The high level of specificity makes it possible for financial entrepreneurs to leverage the specificity and circumvent regulatory restriction. The highly dynamic nature of financial markets presents a unique set of challenges for regulators. Lynn Stout, Professor of Law, argues that financial speculation creates real welfare losses and that there are regulatory solutions that could reduce these welfare losses.[34]

The issue, according to Stiglitz, is that markets do not operate as our models of perfect competition predict they should and that issues such as asymmetric information create a real need for regulation in the market. The question is not whether we need regulation: "The debate is only whether we have gone too far, and whether we could have gotten the desired results at lower costs."[35] In addition, there is the issue of market irrationality, which—behavioral economics argues that individuals will make less-than-optimal decision and that behavioral economics might provide insights into creating regulation that can improve an individual's well-being. Economist Cass Sunstein argues that paying attention to choice architecture in designing regulation could change how regulation is imposed and improve the regulatory environment.[36] Richard Thaler and Sunstein similarly argue, in their book *Nudge*, that designing regulations so as to make the most beneficial option the easiest choice—that is, giving people a *nudge*—is a way to create regulatory benefits to improve on market irrationality. Thus, by employing lessons learned from behavioral economics, nudges could allow for better and more efficient types of regulation.[37]

According to Economists Patrick McLaughlin, Nita Ghei, and Michael Wilt, overall regulatory restrictions in the US have increased by almost 20 percent since 1997. It is estimated that if regulations had remained at the same level they were in 1980, the US GDP would have grown by an additional $4 trillion as of 2012. Thus the inefficiencies and burdens associated with regulations can slow economic growth, increase the prices of goods to consumers, distort labor markets, and increase inequality.[38]

Social Trust

Political Scientist Robert Putnam defines *social capital* as "features of social organization, such as trust, norms, and networks, that can improve the efficiency of society by facilitating coordinated actions."[39] *Social trust*, which is considered to be a component of social capital, has been found to be a determining factor in the development of several political and economic institutions. Similarly to regulation, social trust has been found to affect economic growth. One study found that countries with high social trust grow faster than countries with low social trust.[40] Another researcher argues that social trust can influence growth through other factors such as governance and education.[41] Using an econometric technique known as three-stage least squares regression, which controls for many confounding factors, Christian Bjørnskov, economist, finds that social trust causes economic growth through the intermediary channels of increased education and improved governance.[42] Social trust causes increased schooling and increases an index for the "rule of law" (improved governance). Each of these has an effect on economic growth. However, political scientist Peter Nannestad argues that high social trust in Scandinavian countries has also led to the development of a large welfare state, which is likely to reduce growth.[43]

A study by economists Ryan Murphy, Meg Tuszynski, and Jeremy Jackson (one of the authors of this chapter) brings together these disparate literatures on trust (social capital), economic freedom, growth, entrepreneurship, and well-being. Using data on the US, its authors find weak evidence of a positive effect of trust on economic freedom in the US. Conversely, they also find weak evidence of a negative effect of economic freedom on trust.[44] Neither effect was large, which tends to agree with the results of previous studies that also explore the effect of economic freedom on social capital in the US.[45]

These studies stand in contrast to a 2006 study that finds a positive causal relationship between economic freedom and trust using international data from the Economic Freedom of the World report and the World Values Survey.[46] While social capital and social trust remain separate concepts, social trust is a key element of social capital and is often touted as the component of social capital that is most economically relevant.[47] This chapter is not focused on the concept of economic freedom, yet economic freedom and regulation are certainly linked concepts. A society with high levels of economic freedom will tend to have lower levels of regulation.

Social capital and social trust can be described as binding, when tightly knit communities are bound together in solidarity, and bridging which refers to the connectedness of disparate communities and groups to one another. Social trust provides a community with what it needs to overcome problems of collective action and may reduce the need for regulations to restrict the behavior of those who don't comply with the community standards of conduct and behavior. Likewise, a highly regulated community may be one in which social trust isn't needed. You don't need to trust others if you can instead trust the state to enforce compliance with community standards of conduct and behavior. At a more extreme level, high levels of regulation may even destroy social trust by eliminating the feedback loop required for the development of sociality. Or perhaps trust develops because regulation creates compliance that then allows individuals to trust one another. The direction of the effect between social trust and regulation can go either way—it could be positive or negative. Before we review the literature on trust and regulation, we discuss relationship between government and trust more broadly.

Trust and Government Level, Size, and Scope

Beyond cross-country studies, there are studies that examine political trust at the local and state levels in the United States. One 2005 study attempts to determine political trust at the local level. The authors find that the more diverse cities are with regard to ideology, income inequality, and education level, the lower political trust is.[48] Other researchers, looking at the state level, argue that political trust in state and local government is consistently high in the United States—and much higher than trust in the federal government. They argue that economic conditions such as unemployment and fiscal condition explain why there is more trust at the state level.[49]

Large government is often associated with slow growth and economic inefficiency, but these issues are separate from the economic consequences of regulation. Many of the Scandinavian countries are associated with a large welfare system, but they are also known for their high levels of social trust.[50] However, these countries are not necessarily heavily regulated. Table 2 shows that, among the countries of Norway, Sweden, Denmark, Finland, and the Netherlands, social trust has been increasing across the waves of the World Values Survey, beginning in the 1980s. At the same time, social trust in the US has been decreasing. Table 3 indicates the size of government (as measured by the Economic Freedom of the World index) for these same countries. The Economic Freedom of the World index measures economic freedom on a scale of 0–10, with higher values indicating greater economic freedom. Evaluating economic freedom over the same period as the World Value Survey, in these countries has improved slightly, but on average they score between 4 and 5. The US has an average size-of-government score of approximately 7 over this period. Thus, the US has a smaller government than all of these countries, but less social trust.

However, these are not overly regulated countries. Table 4 demonstrates that the Economic Freedom of the World index for all of these countries has been improving with regard to regulation, increasing their index scores by between 1 and 2 points. For instance, Norway went from 5.35 in 1980 to 7.32 in 2009. The US has experienced only slight decreases in economic freedom. Thus, Norway, Sweden, Denmark, Finland, and the Netherlands score relatively well on this measure of regulation, and this evidence suggests that regulation in these countries has been decreasing while their social trust has been increasing. Several researchers have argued that social trust must precede the large welfare state to keep the other parts of the government, such as regulation, in check.[51] The high social trust is what allows the large welfare state to function effectively. Similarly, others suggest that the quality of governance is what is necessary to maintain a stable welfare state.[52]

The US has not seen much change in the economic freedom measure of regulation—there is a slight decrease over this time period, while trust levels have declined. This suggests that regulation and trust are inversely related, but the level of trust is a separate issue from the overall size of government. We now review the literature on the relationship between regulation and trust more explicitly.

Table 2. Social Trust Scores

Country	Early 1980s	Early 1990s	Mid-1990s	2000	2005–2007	2008–2009	Average score
Norway	61.2	65.1	65.3	—	—	75.1	66.7
Sweden	57.1	66.1	59.7	66.3	68.0	70.7	64.7
Denmark	56.0	57.7	—	66.5	—	76.0	64.0
Finland	57.2	62.8	47.6	58.0	58.8	64.7	58.2
Netherlands	46.2	55.8	—	59.8	—	61.7	55.9
US	46.8	50.0	35.6	35.8	39.6	—	41.6

Source: Average scores from the World Values Survey, http://www.worldvaluessurvey.org/wvs.jsp.

Table 3. Government Size Scores

Country	1980	1990	1995	2000	2005	2009	Average score
Norway	3.63	3.69	3.88	3.90	5.85	5.09	4.34
Sweden	2.70	3.49	3.74	4.60	4.60	4.26	3.90
Denmark	3.80	3.89	3.81	4.74	4.40	4.09	4.12
Finland	5.17	4.76	3.59	5.04	5.01	5.00	4.76
Netherlands	5.01	5.53	5.35	4.69	5.04	4.27	4.98
US	5.89	7.32	7.25	7.38	7.71	7.15	7.12

Source: Economic Freedom of the World report Fraser Institute, https://www.fraserinstitute.org/economic-freedom/dataset.

Table 4. Regulation Scores

Country	1980	1990	1995	2000	2005	2009	Average score
Norway	5.35	6.08	7.05	7.33	7.42	7.32	*6.76*
Sweden	5.85	6.17	6.33	7.54	7.69	7.50	*6.85*
Denmark	6.44	7.00	7.57	8.02	8.60	8.46	*7.68*
Finland	6.38	6.52	6.90	7.51	7.83	7.59	*7.12*
Netherlands	6.21	6.05	6.96	8.06	7.89	7.63	*7.13*
US	8.63	8.66	8.33	8.55	8.61	8.09	*8.48*

Source: Economic Freedom of the World report Fraser Institute, https://www.fraserinstitute.org/economic-freedom/dataset.

Regulation and Trust

Some researchers claim that trust is an important aspect of having a society flourish and that when trust and ethical behavior are low, citizens will demand regulation.[53] Regulation can bring with it economic and political inefficiencies and costs as well as further damaging social trust, as noted above. Therefore, low trust and demands for regulation can form a vicious cycle in which social trust spirals downward. For instance, there seems to be evidence that social trust affects contracts. Two 1997 studies found that contracts will be longer and more verbose where there are low levels of social trust.[54] The authors of one article claim that in places that lack formal institutions to enforce contracts and secure property rights social capital can aid in facilitating economic activity.[55] Therefore, where institutions that formally enforce contracts and secure property rights are not present and where trust is low the return on investment for regulations is high. A later study applies this argument to national constitutions and finds that countries with high social trust have shorter constitutions.[56] Another study finds similar relationship between social trust and constitutions for US states.[57]

There are a few studies that bring together the areas of regulation and social trust. Aghion, Algan, Cahuc, and Shleifer, using a cross-country study, argue that there is a negative relationship between trust and reg-ulation. They argue that individuals in low-trust countries will demand more regulation from their government even when citizens perceive that the government is corrupt. Developing a model of civic-minded-ness, the authors claim that communities that are civic-minded will have low regulation and corruption.[58] They argue that distrust is a source of disorder, and this relationship leads individuals to demand more reg-ulation. Using the World Values Survey, they examine both countries in the Organization for Economic Co-operation and Development and former Soviet countries to demonstrate that regulation and corruption flow from distrust.[59]

Similarly, Pinotti—also using cross-country data—shows that low levels of trust increase the levels of regulation. In particular, Pinotti claims that studies of regulation and corruption have omitted the important variable of trust.[60] Furthermore, he argues that accounting for trust reduces the effects of regulation on entry into markets. He suggests that it is the low levels of trust that are at the source of the problem, as opposed to the regulations themselves.[61]

Economists Hans Pitlik and Ludek Kouba claim that the influence of social trust on attitudes about government intervention is conditional on the perception of the reliability, honesty, and incorruptibility of state actors and major companies.[62] Pitlik and Kouba's results support the idea that the impact of social trust on attitudes about government inter-vention is conditional on individual confidence in state actors relative to private companies.

There is a well-established literature that examines trust in labora-tory experiments based on game theory. In *Humanomics*, economists Vernon Smith and Bart Wilson review that literature and extend it to include insights from Adam Smith's *The Theory of Moral Sentiments*.[63] They modify the traditional trust game by giving players the option to punish those who display blameworthy behavior (want of beneficence) and subsequently the option to reward behavior that is praiseworthy (beneficent action). Laboratory experiments of these modified trust games support Adam Smith's description of how morality, sociality, and trust are developed through the feedback loops of social interaction that reward that which is praiseworthy and punish that which is blame-worthy. When this feedback loop is bypassed by state regulation, the opportunity for society to develop the social norms required for gener-ating social trust is missing. This is the mechanism by which "regulation can erode social trust.

Using trust experiments, economists Thomas Rietz, Eric Schniter, Roman Sheremeta, and Timothy Shields find that if a system based on trust is functioning well, it is best not to interfere with it by impos-ing minimum standards of behavior. However, if a trust-based system is not performing well in the absence of rules, it might be improved with the addition of rules, but only when the rules are very restrictive. In the researchers' experimental environment, trust and reciprocity are damaged by the imposition of rules (which we interpret as regula-tions), further damaging the welfare aspects of the game.[64] Regulation damages the individuals' ability to learn about and influence norms of trust and reciprocity.

We are building on the work that brings together the literature on regulation and trust by looking at social trust in the US over time. The General Social Survey provides us with data for the US from 1972 to 2017. We add to the literature by examining the relationship between regulation and social trust in a single country over time. Previous stud-ies have used data from many countries at one point in time. Such studies are subject to error because many cultural factors, which vary from country to country, are hard to control for. A lack of multiple time periods also eliminates the ability to observe a cause and effect over time. By focusing on one country over time, we overcome these diffi-culties to the extent that cultural factors are constant over time.

As noted above, we know that regulation has been increasing in the US, which lets us ask two questions: Do increases in regulation have a degrading effect on social trust? Does lower social trust lead to an increase in regulation as a response? Our time-series data allow us to further test the direction of causality between regulation and trust. We are also able to test whether a negative relationship between regula-tion and trust exists over time.

Data and Methodology

Data

Our data come from two major sources. The General Social Survey (GSS) provides trust data at the US level for the years 1972–2018. The survey asks individuals questions on a variety of topics that range from social media, workplace conflict, and religion all the way to national security issues. A variety of questions address an individual's confidence or trust in government, business, the press, the judiciary, and individuals. The survey also includes a question regarding general social trust. The GSS has long been one of the main sources for social trust data in the US and has been used in numerous frequently cited research studies.[65]

The general trust question in the GSS asks, "Generally speaking, would you say that most people can be trusted or that you can't be too careful in dealing with people?" Our variable *Trust* is the proportion of respondents in a given year who choose the response "most people can be trusted."

The GSS data contain annual data for 1972–1993, although with some gaps, and biennial data beginning in 1994. To measure overall confidence and trust levels in a given year, we compute the simple average of all responses that year. In years where there are no GSS data available, we impute the value as the average of the years before and after. Where two consecutive data points are missing, we impute the data points with a simple linear projection. This gives us an annual time series of trust data from 1972 to 2017.[66]

Because Pitlik and Kouba find that the effect of social trust on the demand for regulation is mitigated by institutional confidence,[67] we also consider a GSS question regarding confidence in institutions. Here is the question: "I am going to name some institutions in this country. As far as the people running these institutions are concerned, would you say you have a great deal of confidence, only some confidence, or hardly any confidence at all in them?" The responses are coded on a scale of 1 to 3, with higher values indicating greater confidence. We construct variables using responses about confidence in the following institutions: Congress (*ConLegislature*), press (*ConPress*), medicine

(*ConMedicine*), finance (*ConFinance*), and business (*ConBusiness*). Our variables for institutional confidence are the proportion of respondents that report having "a great deal of confidence." (The confidence variables were added to the GSS in 1973.)

The data on regulation come from RegData, a database published by the Mercatus Center at George Mason University. RegData includes two primary metrics: restrictions and industry relevance. We focus on restrictions, which is a proxy for the number of regulatory restrictions contained in the regulatory text (*Restrictions*). Restrictions are measured by counting select words and phrases, such as *shall* or *must*, that are typically used in legal language to create binding obligations or prohibitions. RegData also offers a secondary measure of restrictions—the total word count of the regulatory text—as an alternative measure of the volume of regulation over time (*Words*). We use both of these measures to account for regulation in the US over time. RegData provides us with annual data on restrictions and words from 1970 to 2017, which match well with our GSS data. Thus, combining the two data sets, we have a time series that goes from 1973 to 2017.

The relationship between social trust (or social capital) and economic growth is well established in the literature.[68] Income inequality as measured by the Gini coefficient has also been shown to be causally related to social trust.[69] Unemployment is also related to general macroeconomic conditions, to economic growth, and to regulation.[70] While our main focus is the relationship between social trust and regulation, it is important to include control variables in our analysis to mitigate the potential that omitted variable bias could lead to false conclusions about Granger causality. For this reason, in addition to the variables of interest—social trust and regulation—we include three control variables: the US GDP growth rate (*Growth*), income inequality measured by the Gini coefficient (*Gini*), and the US unemployment rate (*Unemployment*). While it is possible to conceive of other potentially relevant control variables, the relatively short length of the data set (44 years of observations) and the lag structure of the model make adding a large number controls problematic.[71]

Summary statistics for all data are given in table 5, where the data have first been transformed by the natural logarithm.

Table 5. Summary Statistics

Variable	Observa- tions	Mean	Standard deviation	Minimum	Maximum
Restrictions	48	13.540	0.264	12.91	13.900
Restrictions_Health	48	9.675	0.476	8.425	10.520
Restrictions_Finance	48	11.260	0.210	10.90	11.760
Restrictions_Mining	48	9.348	0.495	7.930	9.843
Trust	47	−0.999	0.120	−1.176	−0.736
ConLegislature	46	−2.213	0.375	−2.934	−1.421
ConPress	46	−2.021	0.382	−2.500	−1.239
ConMedicine	46	−0.824	0.142	−1.033	−0.489
ConFinance	44	−1.513	0.367	−2.248	−0.851
ConBusiness	46	−1.515	0.237	−2.041	−1.123
Growth	49	6.373	2.998	−1.800	13.000
Gini	49	−0.821	0.070	−0.931	−0.722
Unemployment	49	1.805	0.240	1.361	2.273

Methodology

Since our data are a time series and we want to determine whether trust affects regulation and regulation affects trust, our main empirical method is a regression technique known as vector autoregressive (VAR). All variables enter into the VAR model after we have first taken the log and then the first difference (which is calculated by subtracting the value at time t from the value at time $t - 1$).[72] This method treats each of the key variables, *Trust* and *Restrictions*, as endogenous variables that depend on lagged values of itself and each of the other variables. This model allows us to conduct what are known as tests of Granger causality. Granger causality refers to the ability of past values of one variable to predict the current values of another. This method corresponds to an empirical test of cause (a change in a current value of one variable) producing an effect (a change in the future value of another variable). We will conduct Granger causality tests to answer two questions: Does regulation "Granger cause" trust and, conversely, does trust "Granger cause" regulation?[73] The VAR methodology also allows one to track the dynamic effects of a one-time change in one variable on another variable with what is known as an impulse response function. We compute impulse response functions that allow us to examine the dynamic effects of a change in trust on regulation and the dynamic effects of a change in regulation on trust.

A more detailed description of the methodology can be found in this chapter's appendix.

Results

To begin our examination of the relationship between regulation and trust, we examine the raw data. We plot the annual mean of *Trust* and the annual number of *Restrictions* (figure 1). Figure 1 shows *Trust* (the proportion of people who responded "most people can be trusted") at just over 45% in 1972 and declining over the period of observation to just over 30% in 2018. *Restrictions* in 1970 was at 40,000 and by 2017 was at just over 1 million. Thus, the annual trends of the raw data suggest a strong negative relationship between the two variables. In figure 2 we plot *Trust* and *Words*: the same strong negative relationship is also present using the volume measure of regulation.

To examine this relationship further, we can similarly plot out social trust and confidence in our various institutions. Figure 3 shows the trends in *Trust, ConPress, ConMedicine, ConLegislature, ConBusiness,* and *ConFinance.* A few observations can be made as we compare the respondents' confidence in these various institutions. Confidence in all of these institutions, like social trust, is declining over the period in question. Respondents have the most confidence in medicine and the least confidence in Congress. Confidence in financial institutions shows the most volatility, with declines in confidence corresponding with economic downturns.

Figure 1. Social Trust and Regulatory Restrictions

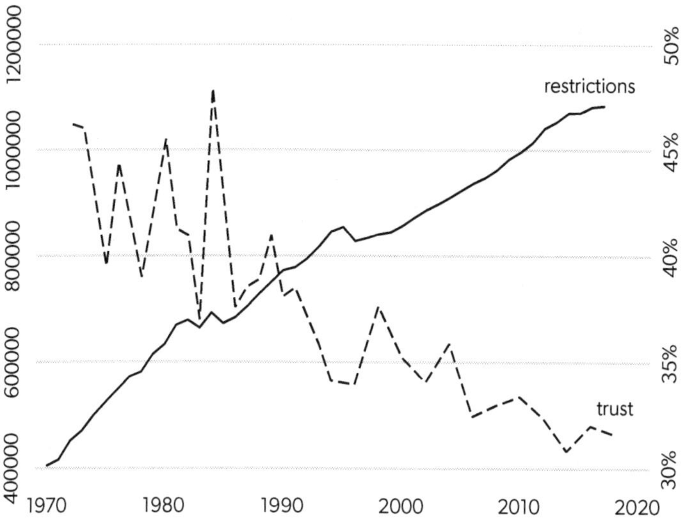

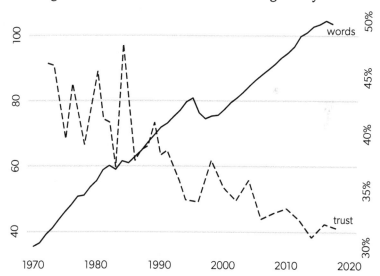

Sources: General Social Survey (data set), NORC at the University of Chicago, 2018 data (release 2), March 2019; Patrick A. McLaughlin and Oliver Sherouse, RegData US 3.1 Annual (data set), QuantGov, Mercatus Center at George Mason University, Arlington, VA, 2018.

Figure 2. Social Trust and Volume of Regulatory Text

Sources: General Social Survey (data set), NORC at the University of Chicago, 2018 data (release 2), March 2019; Patrick A. McLaughlin and Oliver Sherouse, RegData US 3.1 Annual (data set), QuantGov, Mercatus Center at George Mason University, Arlington, VA, 2018.

Figure 3. Social Trust and Confidence in Various Institutions

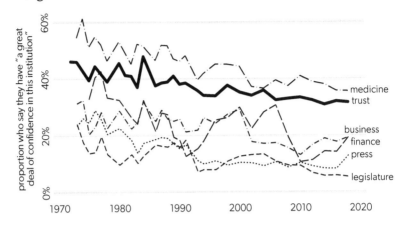

Source: General Social Survey (data set), NORC at the University of Chicago, 2018 data (release 2), March 2019.

Figures 1 and 2 suggest that *Restrictions* and *Words* appear to be increasing at a steady and smooth rate, but if we examine various industries, we see that there is variation in regulation. We identify three industries to examine closer: healthcare, finance, and mining. RegData provides data broken down by the codes used in the North American Industry Classification System, so we focus on the two-digit codes for our three chosen industries. In the figures that follow, we plot *Trust* against *Restrictions* and *Words* limited to these specific industries.

We identify these industries as ones that are heavily regulated. Finance and healthcare/medicine are industries that have confidence measures in the GSS, noted in figure 3, but both are service industries. Mining is an industry that is heavily regulated because of the potentially dangerous conditions associated with working in mining, but there is no corresponding GSS data available for confidence in mining and it is not an industry that most individuals would pay close attention to. For this reason, we include it to determine whether the relationship between general social trust and regulation in mining is different from the relationships between general social trust and regulation in the other two industries.

Figures 4 and 5 show *Trust* plotted alongside *Restrictions_Health* and *Words_Health*, respectively. Figure 4 shows that *Restrictions_Health* was increasing during the early 1970s, then appears to plateau from the late

1970s through the early 1990s before beginning to increase again. The negative relationship between social trust and regulatory restrictions is still obvious. Figure 5 shows a similar pattern, with some spikes and dips in *Words_Health* over the time frame.

We repeat this exercise with the finance industry (figures 6 and 7) and the mining industry (figures 8 and 9). We will limit our discussion here to *Restrictions_Finance* and *Restrictions_Mining*. Figure 6 depicts *Restrictions_Finance* increasing during the 1970s, declining during the early to mid 1980s, increasing again aside from a couple of dips just before 2000, and then increasing steadily after 2000—with a sharp increase following the Great Recession. However, *Restrictions_Mining* is perhaps the most interesting variable relative to *Trust*, and shows the greatest amount of change. The restrictions on mining increased dramatically in the mid to late 1970s, and then declined somewhat during the mid 1980s. Restrictions on mining increased again around 1990 before falling around 2000. Since then, they have steadily increased. Again, the negative relationship between social trust and regulatory restrictions is present in these industries, although it is less pronounced in mining.

Figure 4. Social Trust and Regulatory Restrictions Related to the Healthcare Industry

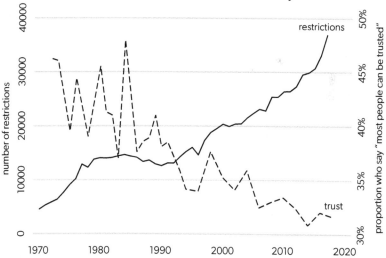

Sources: General Social Survey (data set), NORC at the University of Chicago, 2018 data (release 2), March 2019; Patrick A. McLaughlin and Oliver Sherouse, RegData US 3.1 Annual (data set), QuantGov, Mercatus Center at George Mason University, Arlington, VA, 2018.

Figure 5. Social Trust and Volume of Regulatory Text Related to the Healthcare Industry

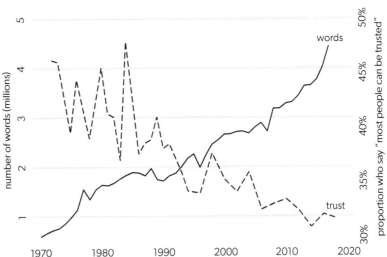

Sources: General Social Survey (data set), NORC at the University of Chicago, 2018 data (release 2), March 2019; Patrick A. McLaughlin and Oliver Sherouse, RegData US 3.1 Annual (data set), QuantGov, Mercatus Center at George Mason University, Arlington, VA, 2018.

Figure 6. Social Trust and Regulatory Restrictions Related to the Finance Industry

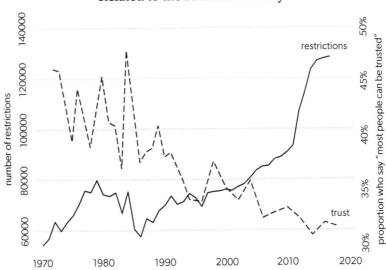

Sources: General Social Survey (data set), NORC at the University of Chicago, 2018 data (release 2), March 2019; Patrick A. McLaughlin and Oliver Sherouse, RegData US 3.1 Annual (data set), QuantGov, Mercatus Center at George Mason University, Arlington, VA, 2018.

Figure 7. Social Trust and Volume of Regulatory Text Related to the Finance Industry

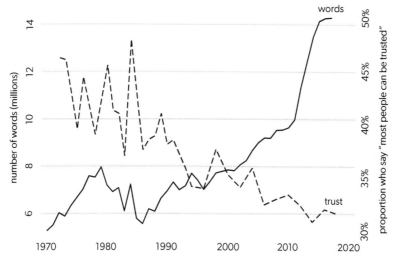

Sources: General Social Survey (data set), NORC at the University of Chicago, 2018 data (release 2), March 2019; Patrick A. McLaughlin and Oliver Sherouse, RegData US 3.1 Annual (data set), QuantGov, Mercatus Center at George Mason University, Arlington, VA, 2018.

Figure 8. Social Trust and Regulatory Restrictions Related to the Mining Industry

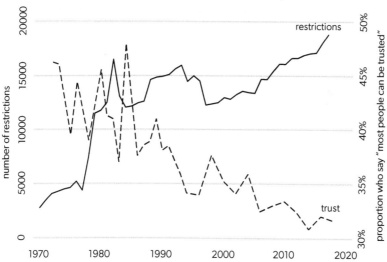

Sources: General Social Survey (data set), NORC at the University of Chicago, 2018 data (release 2), March 2019; Patrick A. McLaughlin and Oliver Sherouse, RegData US 3.1 Annual (data set), QuantGov, Mercatus Center at George Mason University, Arlington, VA, 2018.

Figure 9. Social Trust and Volume of Regulatory Text Related to the Mining Industry

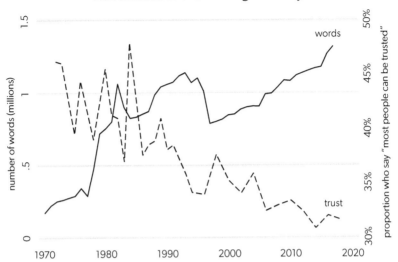

Sources: General Social Survey (data set), NORC at the University of Chicago, 2018 data (release 2), March 2019; Patrick A. McLaughlin and Oliver Sherouse, RegData US 3.1 Annual (data set), QuantGov, Mercatus Center at George Mason University, Arlington, VA, 2018.

Aghion, Algan, Cahuc, and Shleifer argue that causality runs from higher levels distrust leading to demanding regulation.[74] However, their analysis is a cross-country study. Given our time series of data, we can examine a Granger causality between *Trust* and regulation (as measured by *Restrictions*) to determine whether *Trust* Granger causes *Restrictions*, whether *Restrictions* Granger causes *Trust*, or whether Granger causality runs in both directions.

A Wald test is used to determine Granger causality from the VAR output. (See the appendix for details concerning the VAR model, output, and Wald tests.) Our results indicate that changes in *Trust* do not Granger cause later changes in *Restrictions*.[75] That is, changes in *Trust* do not have the ability to predict future changes in *Restrictions*. However, the converse is confirmed. Changes in *Restrictions* do Granger cause changes in *Trust*. Current changes in regulation as measured by *Restrictions* can be used to forecast future changes in *Trust*. This relationship of *Restrictions* Granger causing *Trust* holds across the three industries we examine as well. Additionally, *Trust* Granger causes *Restrictions_Finance* and *Restrictions_Mining*—thus, when it comes to the finance and mining industries, Granger causality runs in both directions.

Finally, to further assess the relationship between trust and regulation, we employ an impulse response function (IRF). An IRF estimates the dynamic effect of a one-time change (shock) in one variable as it interacts with other variables, leading them to all change over time. The IRFs that we compute and graph presumes that a one-time shock to a variable happens at time zero and then maps the dynamic impact on another variable over the following 10 time periods. Again, we test this relationship in both directions. Figure 10 illustrates the effect of a one standard deviation increase (shock) in *Trust* on the number of regulatory restrictions. The estimated effect is the solid line, while the shaded area around the line represents the 90 percent confidence interval around the estimated effect.

In the period following the shock to trust, there is a small negative effect on restrictions. However, the confidence interval contains zero, which demonstrates that the size of the effect is statistically insignificant. The initial small negative effect quickly goes to zero after the first period. Similarly, the dynamic effect on *Trust* of a one standard deviation increase (shock) in *Restrictions* is computed in an IRF and displayed in figure 11. *Trust* has no immediate response to the initial shock in *Restrictions*. However, in time period 2, there is a significant decrease in *Trust* by just over 1 percent, which is about half a standard deviation in *Trust*. In the third period and following after the shock in *Restrictions*, there are no further changes to *Trust*. This demonstrates that a one standard deviation increase in *Restrictions* will tend to correlate with a half a standard deviation decrease in *Trust* two periods later. These results provide further evidence for the negative relationship between social trust and regulation.

The dynamics of the relationship between changes in social trust and changes in regulation differ by industry. To examine this more fully, we also compute IRFs for *Trust* and regulation in each of the industries previously examined: healthcare, finance, and mining. These IRFs are presented in figures 12 through 17. The IRF showing the dynamics between a one standard deviation increase in healthcare restrictions and its impact on social trust is found in figure 12. This graph shows the familiar pattern we saw for overall restrictions in figure 11: Initially, there is no impact on social trust, but two periods after an increase in healthcare regulations, there is a significant decrease in social trust. Figure 13 demonstrates that a one standard deviation increase in social trust has no dynamic impact on healthcare restrictions. Figures 14 and 15 graph the corresponding IRFs for the finance industry. A one standard deviation increase in finance regulations leads to an immediate (although statistically insignificant) decrease in social trust, followed by another (this time statistically significant) decrease in social trust two years later.

Interestingly, a one standard deviation increase in social trust also leads to a decline in finance regulation one year later. Thus, there is evidence of a vicious cycle in the finance industry, as increased regulation leads to decreased social trust and decreased social trust leads to increased regulation. The mining industry presents an entirely different set of relationships. Figures 16 and 17 graph the corresponding IRFs for the mining industry. As shown in figure 16, a one standard deviation increase in mining restrictions actually leads to subsequent increases in social trust in years 2 and 3 following the increase. This is the opposite of the effect we saw for regulation overall and in the healthcare and finance industries.

Figure 17 demonstrates that a one standard deviation increase in social trust leads to a decrease in mining restrictions the following year—a decrease that disappears in subsequent years.

Figure 10. Impulse Response Function: *Trust* to *Restrictions*

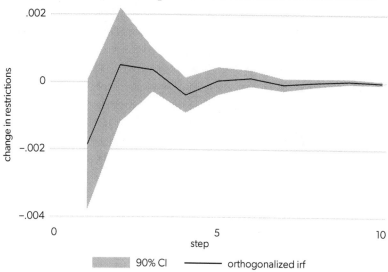

Figure 11. Impulse Response Function: *Restrictions* to *Trust*

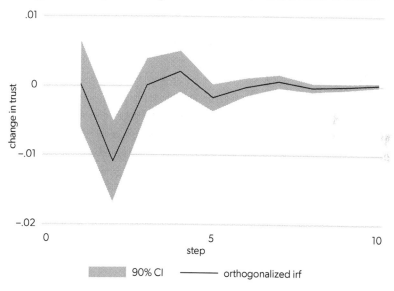

Figure 12. Impulse Response Function: *Restrictions_Health* **to** *Trust*

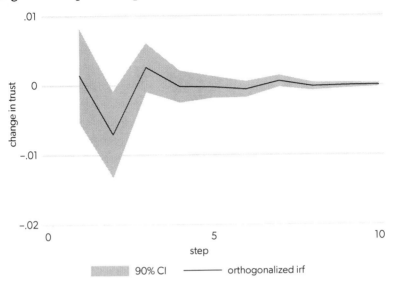

Figure 13. Impulse Response Function: *Trust* **to** *Restrictions_Health*

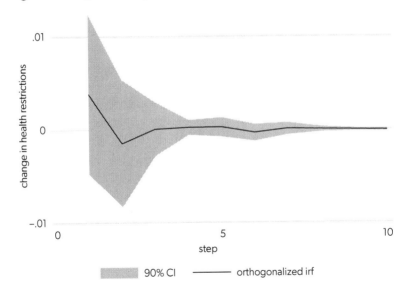

Figure 14. Impulse Response Function:
Restrictions_Finance to *Trust*

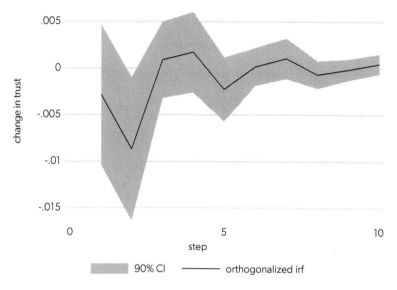

Figure 15. Impulse Response Function:
Trust to *Restrictions_Finance*

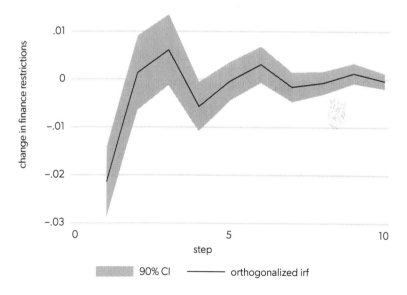

Figure 16. Impulse Response Function:
Restrictions_Mining to *Trust*

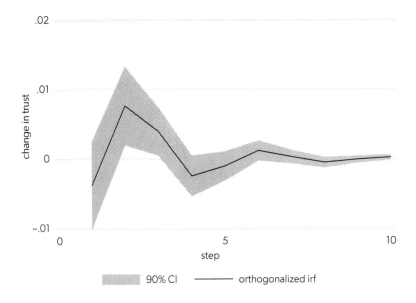

Figure 17. Impulse Response Function:
Trust to *Restrictions_Mining*

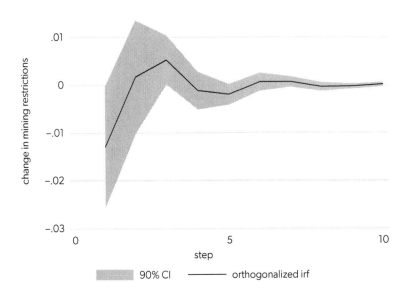

Policy Reform

Social trust has been found to be correlated with economic growth[76] and subjective well-being,[77] making its promotion an ideal objective for policy. While there are often specific benefits that accrue from specific and targeted pieces of regulation, there are also benefits to be had from general and broad deregulation efforts and reforms that reduce the complexity and burden of regulation. Regulation can get in the way of the necessary social feedback loops that create social trust as social interactions reward that which is praiseworthy and punish that which is blameworthy. Our findings demonstrate that, in addition to traditional benefits, general deregulation may also bring an increase in social trust.

While we do not find evidence that increases in social trust would lead to decreases in overall regulation, thus revealing a virtuous cycle of deregulation, we do reveal such a virtuous cycle of deregulation in the finance industry. A general reduction of the regulatory burden in the finance industry can lead to increases in social trust. These increases in social trust then lead to further general reductions of regulation in the finance industry—thus perpetuating a cycle that will see further increases in social trust.

These results bring to the fore two main policy recommendations. First, policymakers should look for ways to reduce the overall regulatory burden on the economy. Doing so would promote economic efficiency, economic growth, and social trust. Second, policymakers should look for ways to reduce the regulatory burden on the finance industry specifically. Such reductions may bring additional benefits owing to the virtuous cycle. A reduced regulatory burden in the finance industry will lead to increased social trust, which will further propagate itself from further reductions in the financial regulatory burden.

Conclusion

We set out to empirically examine the question of causality between regulation and social trust. Our analysis adds to the existing literature by providing a new time-series data set of regulation and trust in the US. Other studies have all been cross-sectional and cross-country. Our findings are consistent with those of previous researchers, who have found that there is a negative relationship between social trust and regulation.[78] However, Granger causality tests provide strong evidence that regulation Granger causes trust. There is less compelling evidence that trust Granger causes regulation.

This relationship is tested with a data set encompassing all the regulations in the US as well as a select set of industry regulations, and the results continue to hold. These results suggest that a vicious cycle does not exist between the degradation of social trust and growth in regulation that have been observed in the US since the 1970s. Because social trust doesn't Granger cause regulation, it is possible to implement policies that can support social trust without the negative consequences generated from regulation. Furthermore, policies that reduce the regulatory burden have the added benefit of leading to increased social trust along with increased efficiency and economic growth. This is especially beneficial because social trust is known to be associated with so many other desirable outcomes.

Appendix: Methodology in Detail

To conduct our tests of Granger causality, we first determine whether the variables contain a unit root and, if so, whether stationarity can be achieved by first-differencing the data. We confirm that the first differences of all data are stationary, so all VAR regressions are performed using first differences of the data. This allows us to use a simple VAR econometric specification on which we can conduct Wald tests for Granger causality. In all VAR regressions, the data are first logged and then first-differenced. The summary statistics of the data in log first differences appear in table A1.

Each VAR model we estimate is a system of two linear regression equations, as expressed in equations A1 and A2, where subscript t indexes time, *Trust* is the first difference of the log level of trust, *Restrictions* is the first difference of the log level of the number of restrictions (from RegData), and X is a vector of log first differences of control variables.[79] Letting i index each equation, the error term is $e_{i,t}$ and the parameters to be estimated are (1) the constants for each equation, C_i; (2)

the coefficients for lagged differences of endogenous variables, $\rho_{i,t}$; and (3) the vector of coefficients for lagged differences of exogenous variables, $\gamma_{i,t}$.

$$Trust_t = C_1 + \rho_{1,1} Restrictions_{t-1} + \rho_{1,2} Restrictions_{t-2} + \gamma_{1,1} X_{t-1} + \gamma_{1,2} X_{t-2} + e_{1,t}. \quad (A1)$$

$$Restrictions_t = C_2 + \rho_{2,1} Trust_{t-1} + \rho_{2,2} Trust_{t-2} + \gamma_{2,1} X_{t-1} + \gamma_{2,2} X_{t-2} + e_{2,t}. \quad (A2)$$

VAR model 1 is a simple two-way VAR specification between the log first differences of *Restrictions* and *Trust*. Diagnostic tests indicate that a VAR model of lag order 2 is most appropriate. The VAR model includes the confidence measures of our institutions and our controls for economic conditions. This model generates an R^2 of .62 on *Restrictions* and .86 on *Trust*, indicating that the model is better able to predict *Trust* than *Restrictions*. The VAR coefficients for model 1 can be seen in table A2. We continue in this same vein with our restrictions in the specific industries of healthcare, finance, and mining in VAR models 2, 3, and 4, respectively. These results can be found in tables A3, A4, and A5, respectively. Table A6 displays the Wald test statistics for all Granger causality tests.

Table A1. Summary Statistics in Log Differences

Variable	Observations	Mean	Standard deviation	Minimum	Maximum
Restrictions	47	0.0209	0.0212	−0.0317	0.0820
Restrictions_Health	47	0.0445	0.0673	−0.0897	0.2360
Restrictions_Finance	47	0.0183	0.0614	−0.2200	0.1340
Restrictions_Mining	47	0.0407	0.1270	−0.2320	0.5310
Trust	46	−0.0082	0.0650	−0.1290	0.2580
ConLegislature	45	−0.0336	0.1740	−0.5840	0.3340
ConPress	45	−0.0133	0.1160	−0.2850	0.2490
ConMedicine	45	−0.0095	0.0652	−0.1790	0.1450
ConFinance	43	−0.0125	0.1690	−0.3700	0.3000
ConBusiness	45	−0.0109	0.1350	−0.4660	0.2490
Growth	48	−0.0020	2.3560	−7.9000	5.6000
Gini	48	0.0043	0.0095	−0.0150	0.0474
Unemployment	48	−0.0049	0.1510	−0.2450	0.4730

Table A2. Vector Autoregression Model 1: Regulatory Restrictions and Social Trust

Variable	Equation A1 (restrictions) Coefficient	Equation A2 (trust) Coefficient
$Restrictions_{t-1}$	0.2881** (0.1527)	0.0523 (0.3303)
$Restrictions_{t-2}$	0.0082 (0.1388)	−0.9699*** (0.3003)
$Trust_{t-1}$	−0.0784* (0.0488)	−0.2742*** (0.1056)
$Trust_{t-2}$	0.0222 (0.0450)	−0.2708*** (0.0974)
$ConLegislature_{t-1}$	−0.0187 (0.0195)	0.0187 (0.0422)
$ConLegislature_{t-2}$	0.0443*** (0.0150)	−0.0172 (0.0324)
$ConPress_{t-1}$	−0.0130* (0.0406)	−0.1872** (0.0879)
$ConPress_{t-2}$	−0.0039 (0.0289)	0.3511*** (0.0626)
$ConMedicine_{t-1}$	−0.0476 (0.0930)	0.1350 (0.2012)
$ConMedicine_{t-2}$	−0.0364 (0.0675)	−0.4872*** (0.1461)
$ConFinance_{t-1}$	−0.0486** (0.0229)	−0.0223 (0.0495)
$ConFinance_{t-2}$	0.0566*** (0.0230)	−0.1059** (0.0497)
$ConBusiness_{t-1}$	0.0435 (0.0515)	0.0570 (0.1114)
$ConBusiness_{t-2}$	−0.0247 (0.0354)	0.2173*** (0.0766)
$Growth_{t-1}$	0.0061* (0.0036)	0.0071 (0.0077)
$Growth_{t-2}$	−0.0015 (0.0016)	−0.0051 (0.0034)
$Gini_{t-1}$	0.3339 (0.3882)	−2.3076*** (0.8397)
$Gini_{t-2}$	−0.2039 (0.2393)	1.0465** (0.5176)
$Unemployment_{t-1}$	0.0063 (0.0344)	0.1038 (0.0745)
$Unemployment_{t-2}$	0.0605* (0.0340)	−0.0437 (0.0735)
Constant	0.0087 (0.0043)	0.0147 (0.0093)
N	41	41
R^2	0.62	0.86

Note: Standard errors are in parentheses.
* $p < .1$; ** $p < .05$; *** $p < .01$.

Table A3. Vector Autoregression Model 2: Healthcare Industry Regulatory Restrictions and Social Trust

Variable	Equation A1 (healthcare restrictions) Coefficient	Equation A2 (trust) Coefficient
$Restrictions\_Health_{t-1}$	−0.0940 (0.1555)	0.0241 (0.0887)
$Restrictions\_Health_{t-2}$	0.2920*** (0.1231)	−0.1564** (0.0702)
$Trust_{t-1}$	0.1502 (0.2030)	−0.3010*** (0.1157)
$Trust_{t-2}$	0.0026 (0.1658)	−0.3971*** (0.0945)
$ConLegislature_{t-1}$	−0.0065 (0.0794)	0.0335 (0.0453)
$ConLegislature_{t-2}$	0.0056 (0.0642)	−0.0333 (0.0366)
$ConPress_{t-1}$	−0.0282 (0.1493)	−0.0344 (0.0851)
$ConPress_{t-2}$	0.0880 (0.1145)	0.3060*** (0.0653)
$ConMedicine_{t-1}$	−0.3870 (0.3753)	−0.0946 (0.2140)
$ConMedicine_{t-2}$	0.0503 (0.2625)	−0.3185** (0.1496)
$ConFinance_{t-1}$	0.1457 (0.0962)	−0.0273 (0.0548)
$ConFinance_{t-2}$	−0.2323*** (0.0965)	−0.1058** (0.0550)
$ConBusiness_{t-1}$	0.3176 (0.2219)	0.1221 (0.1265)
$ConBusiness_{t-2}$	0.1238 (0.1356)	0.1648** (0.0773)
$Growth_{t-1}$	−0.0124 (0.0152)	0.0080 (0.0087)
$Growth_{t-2}$	0.0029 (0.0061)	−0.0066** (0.0035)
$Gini_{t-1}$	−1.5642 (1.5776)	−2.1198*** (0.8995)
$Gini_{t-2}$	0.2731 (0.9825)	0.9432* (0.5602)
$Unemployment_{t-1}$	0.1696 (0.1403)	0.1062 (0.0800)
$Unemployment_{t-2}$	−0.2178 (0.1367)	−0.0762 (0.0779)
$Constant$	0.0328 (0.0154)	0.0025 (0.0088)
N	41	41
R^2	0.44	0.84

Note: Standard errors are in parentheses.
* $p < .1$; ** $p < .05$; *** $p < .01$.

Table A4. Vector Autoregression Model 3:
Finance Industry Regulatory Restrictions and Social Trust

	Equation A1 (finance restrictions)	Equation A2 (trust)
Variable	Coefficient	Coefficient
$Restrictions\_Finance_{t-1}$	0.2436 (0.1762)	−0.0817 (0.1378)
$Restrictions\_Finance_{t-2}$	−0.1207 (0.1783)	−0.2592* (0.1394)
$Trust_{t-1}$	−0.8420*** (0.1467)	−0.2208** (0.1147)
$Trust_{t-2}$	0.0725 (0.1665)	−0.2877** (0.1302)
$ConLegislature_{t-1}$	0.0298 (0.0688)	−0.0320 (0.0538)
$ConLegislature_{t-2}$	0.0656 (0.0489)	−0.0154 (0.0382)
$ConPress_{t-1}$	0.1460 (0.1098)	−0.0898 (0.0859)
$ConPress_{t-2}$	−0.0679 (0.0898)	0.3610*** (0.0702)
$ConMedicine_{t-1}$	−0.9179*** (0.2660)	−0.0719 (0.2080)
$ConMedicine_{t-2}$	0.4137** (0.2078)	−0.4405*** (0.1625)
$ConFinance_{t-1}$	−0.0362 (0.0681)	−0.0150 (0.0533)
$ConFinance_{t-2}$	−0.0615 (0.0731)	−0.1537*** (0.0571)
$ConBusiness_{t-1}$	0.5232*** (0.1510)	0.1005 (0.1181)
$ConBusiness_{t-2}$	−0.0783 (0.1135)	0.2369*** (0.0887)
$Growth_{t-1}$	0.0250** (0.0111)	0.0042 (0.0086)
$Growth_{t-2}$	−0.0083 (0.0053)	−0.0044 (0.0042)
$Gini_{t-1}$	−2.4821* (1.3701)	−3.1778*** (1.0713)
$Gini_{t-2}$	1.5484 (0.8404)	1.4110** (0.6571)
$Unemployment_{t-1}$	0.2049** (0.1027)	0.0852 (0.0803)
$Unemployment_{t-2}$	0.0268 (0.0988)	−0.0742 (0.0773)
$Constant$	0.0251 (0.0107)	0.0063 (0.0084)
N	41	41
R^2	0.72	0.84

Note: Standard errors are in parentheses.
* $p < .1$; ** $p < .05$; *** $p < .01$.

Table A5. Vector Autoregression Model 4:
Mining Industry Regulatory Restrictions and Social Trust

Variable	Equation A1 (mining restrictions) Coefficient	Equation A2 (trust) Coefficient
$Restrictions\_Mining_{t-1}$	0.5309*** (0.1488)	−0.0374 (0.0510)
$Restrictions\_Mining_{t-2}$	−0.0776 (0.1317)	0.1394*** (0.0451)
$Trust_{t-1}$	−0.5371* (0.3158)	−0.2752*** (0.1083)
$Trust_{t-2}$	0.2100 (0.2591)	−0.4662*** (0.0888)
$ConLegislature_{t-1}$	0.0343 (0.1393)	0.0529 (0.0478)
$ConLegislature_{t-2}$	−0.1030 (0.0995)	−0.0643* (0.0341)
$ConPress_{t-1}$	−0.1309 (0.2444)	0.0000 (0.0838)
$ConPress_{t-2}$	0.0905 (0.1850)	0.3102*** (0.0634)
$ConMedicine_{t-1}$	−0.4356 (0.5770)	−0.1036 (0.1978)
$ConMedicine_{t-2}$	0.5519 (0.4197)	−0.2645* (0.1439)
$ConFinance_{t-1}$	−0.2912** (0.1487)	−0.0313 (0.0510)
$ConFinance_{t-2}$	0.4542*** (0.1556)	−0.1375*** (0.0533)
$ConBusiness_{t-1}$	−0.2494 (0.3214)	0.0281 (0.1102)
$ConBusiness_{t-2}$	−0.6501*** (0.2219)	0.2616*** (0.0761)
$Growth_{t-1}$	0.0652*** (0.0226)	0.0046 (0.0077)
$Growth_{t-2}$	−0.0359*** (0.0094)	−0.0060* (0.0032)
$Gini_{t-1}$	−1.3635 (2.4885)	−1.6225** (0.8532)
$Gini_{t-2}$	0.8076 (1.5357)	0.7921 (0.5265)
$Unemployment_{t-1}$	−0.1380 (0.2157)	0.0346 (0.0740)
$Unemployment_{t-2}$	0.3461 (0.2223)	−0.0565 (0.0762)
Constant	0.0151 (0.0201)	−0.0088 (0.0069)
N	41	41
R^2	0.70	0.85

Note: Standard errors are in parentheses.
* $p < .1$; ** $p < .05$; *** $p < .01$.

Table A6. Granger Causality Wald Tests

Effect variable	Cause variable	X^2
Model 1		
Restrictions	*Trust*	3.40
Trust	*Restrictions*	12.27***
Model 2		
Restrictions_Health	*Trust*	0.57
Trust	*Restrictions_Health*	5.13*
Model 3		
Restrictions_Finance	*Trust*	35.43***
Trust	*Restrictions_Finance*	5.33*
Model 4		
Restrictions_Mining	*Trust*	4.73*
Trust	*Restrictions_Mining*	9.68***

Note: * $p < .1$; ** $p < .05$; *** $p < .01$.

CHAPTER 4

Regulation and the Shadow Economy

Travis Wiseman

Regulation creates many perverse incentives. This chapter explores the pressures that overregulation puts on individuals to hide their economic activity from tax authorities and other public officials—that is, to engage in the shadow economy. It is well documented in the academic literature that overregulation relates positively to the size of the shadow economy. This chapter explores shadow economies and investigates some of the leading regulatory burdens that cause them to grow. I also discuss several sensible and low-cost regulatory reforms that discourage informal activity by promoting productive, wealth-generating participation in the formal sector.

Institutions, Entrepreneurship, and Shadow Economies

Institutions are the rules that govern individual action, and social *interaction*. Economists call them "rules of the game," and there are formal and informal variants.[1] The rules we find listed among states' and national constitutions, for example, are *formal* rules. Those that are not codified, but often adhered to, socially, are informal. Social norms such as handshakes, and holding the door for persons behind you are examples of informal institutions. In this chapter, I will focus primarily on formal rules and how they relate to individuals' decisions to participate in shadow economies.

In his paper "Entrepreneurship: Productive, Unproductive, and Destructive," economist William Baumol suggests that entrepreneurs are guided by institutions into various forms of activity.[2] Productive outcomes, he asserts, are encouraged by institutions that reward wealth creation, and unproductive outcomes by institutions that reward zero- or negative-sum activities—for instance, rent-seeking and frivolous lawsuits.[3] Baumol's insights into the potential for various forms of entrepreneurship are important. He challenges the common perception of entrepreneurship. Most people, I think, reasonably identify entrepreneurs as those who innovate and accumulate wealth from the popularity of their innovations. We often identify brands such as Apple and Microsoft as outcomes of entrepreneurship—indeed, what Baumol identifies as *productive* entrepreneurship. However, Baumol alerts his audience to the ubiquity of entrepreneurs—to the fact that the innovative minds around us aren't limited to those who present us with the goods and services we value most. There are, for example, entrepreneurial minds hard at work innovating new ways to capture wealth through redistribution and the political process! According to Baumol, there is potential to refocus the efforts of such entrepreneurs on wealth creation, simply by adjusting the rules to make productive activity worthwhile and unproductive activity costly.

I mention Baumol here because, while I think his hypotheses are valid, I want to alert the reader to markets people exploit under unfavorable institutions. One question that arises concerning Baumol's productive and unproductive entrepreneurship hypothesis is this: How do people presently engaged in productive entrepreneurship respond to rule changes that decrease the relative rewards of productive activities? Individuals operating in the legal sector of the economy who are faced with an unfavorable institutional change may, of course, choose to bear the full cost of that adjustment. For example, if a tax policy targeting their industry reduces their disposable income, they may simply carry on their productive activity, only with lower income. However, there are other possible responses. Individuals may migrate to more favorable institutional conditions—such as other states with fewer regulatory burdens—or they may refocus their efforts on legal but unproductive activity. For instance, an electrician burdened by new, onerous code enforcement might choose to become a lobbyist (not likely, but hear me out). Or individuals may simply choose to give up entrepreneurship entirely. Alternatively, they may move their entrepreneurial efforts *underground*! (This is perhaps the most likely outcome in the case of the overburdened electrician.) By refocusing their efforts this way, these entrepreneurs join the count of shadow economy participants. It is this possibility that I'll explore in this chapter.

In the sections that follow, I will define the shadow economy and discuss how shadow economies theoretically come to fruition, and how scholars measure shadow economic activity. (After all, we're talking about activity purposefully undertaken in a way to avoid detection.) I will provide examples of shadow economies in action and discuss associated costs and consequences of shadow economic activity. I will conclude with some suggestions about what can be done to reduce the size of the shadow economy moving forward.

The Shadow Economy

The phrase *shadow economy* often summons thoughts of prostitution rings and illicit drug sales, of dark alleyways and dimly lit corridors that serve as venues for shady dealings. But shadow transactions, while they may certainly unfold in the sketchiest of places and involve these risky businesses, include much more. The *shadow* designation generally implies a realm of economic activity in which participants simply prefer to remain out of sight.[4]

There is some debate over the formal definition of *shadow economy*.[5] Most empirical methodology used to estimate shadow economies focuses narrowly on market activity that is otherwise legal.[6] Here, I contend that shadow economic activity consists of *all* market activity deliberately undertaken in a way to avoid detection by public officials. That is, I consider a shadow economy to include both activity that is at all times illegal—for example, dealing in illegal narcotics—and activity that would be legal if it were not purposefully hidden—for example, under-the-table moonlighting. An unlicensed hairdresser who styles hair for cash and doesn't report it on her taxes is one example of a shadow economy participant. A contractor working without permits is another. They are working in the shadows along with prostitutes and drug dealers. While some of the services offered by such "entrepreneurs" are questionable, in the Baumolian sense they are all engaged in productive activity—only off the books.

Shadow economies around the world have garnered quite a bit of attention in recent years. In a study of 162 countries (including developing countries, high-income members of the Organisation for Economic Co-operation and Development, eastern European countries, and central Asian countries), economists Andreas Buehn and Friedrich Schneider find that, on average, shadow economy size is roughly equivalent to 34 percent of GDP.[7] Countries such as Zimbabwe, Panama, and Bolivia have relatively large shadow economies – with measured sizes of 61.8, 63.5, and 66.1 percent of GDP, respectively.[8] For economies like these, formal economic activity, in terms of value, is less important than underground activity.

The shadow economy of the United States is certainly smaller than the world average, but underground markets in the US still play an important role. Famed journalist Robert Neuwirth, for example, writes of the nation's black markets during World War II:

> In order to channel the nation's resources for World War II, the United States instituted stringent price controls. Yet, all across the land, people and producers smuggled products across state lines and price-gouged with impunity. As much as 80 percent of the nation's meat was sold above the price the government mandated, along with 60 to 90 percent of the country's lumber and one-third of all clothing. Gas was strictly rationed, but 2.5 million gallons a day disappeared, to be sold on the black market. And this doesn't count counterfeited ration coupons.[9]

Economist Hans Sennholz focuses on more recent events:

During the 1960s and 1970s, the U.S. Government, in cooperation with the state governments, destroyed millions of jobs.
It forcibly raised the cost of labor through sizeable boosts
in Social Security levies, unemployment taxes, Workman's
Compensation expenses, Occupational Safety and Health
Act expenses, and many other production costs. The mandated raises inevitably reduced the demand for labor and
added millions of workers to the unemployment rolls. The
boosts also reduced the take-home pay of the remaining
workers as market adjustments shifted the new costs to the
workers themselves. Both effects, the rising unemployment
and the falling net wages, provided powerful stimuli to off-
the-books employment.[10]

And Buehn and Schneider's average estimate of the US shadow economy from 1999 to 2007 is 8.6 percent of GDP.[11] This is small only in a
relative (to other countries) sense; it is by no means an economically
negligible fraction of total economic activity. When government-man-
dated prices result in shortages, underground markets step in to fill the
void. Shadow economies provide a platform for consumers to acquire
the goods and services they desire, but are difficult to acquire in the
formal sector. Often, shadow economies come to fruition as a response
to new policies – and can sometimes counter the intentions of political actors. Therefore, shadow economic activity can have important
policy implications. For example, where a larger portion of the population is engaged in underground activity, there will likely be less
income from that activity reported to the government. This can result
in smaller tax bases from which governments may collect revenue to
fund their liabilities. This, in turn, may result in higher budget deficits
or tax rates.[12] Hence, political actors across the world search for ways
to reduce shadow economic activity.[13]

In general, a growing shadow economy can be described as a response
of individuals who feel overburdened by the state. Participants either
choose the "exit option" if burdens in the formal sector grow sufficiently

large, or, alternatively, they never choose the "entry option" as they approach the productive periods of their lifetimes.[14]

But what burdens promote shadow market participation? And how do we measure that participation? Researchers have developed theories along with a number of creative ways to measure shadow economic activity.

Measuring the Shadow Economy

Common among the determinants of shadow economic activity are tax and social welfare burdens; licensing, educational requirements, fees and other regulatory barriers to doing business; and labor market burdens. Measuring the effects of these burdens on shadow economy size is not easy, largely because shadow market participants go out of their way to remain undetected. Thus, measuring shadow economy size requires innovative statistical methods, to say the least. The following paragraphs outline a few common methods.

There are both direct and indirect ways to estimate shadow economic activity. Direct methods rely almost exclusively on surveys—which require participants to discuss with a researcher the work they're doing in the underground. As with any survey data, results are often questionable. (Would you be entirely honest with someone questioning your whereabouts and means of earning illegal income?)

More often, studies of the shadow economy make use of indirect estimation techniques. The use of available indirect techniques varies by the level of the study (e.g., state-level, regional, national) and by data availability. Two widely used indirect methods are the electricity consumption approach and the MIMIC model approach.

The electricity consumption approach dominates the literature surveying shadow economies of central and eastern European countries in the mid to late 1990s and the first few years after 2000,[15] and relies on differences between electricity consumption and GDP. This method of underground estimation is based on the assumption that production requires electricity in both the formal sector and the informal sector. While GDP reports only formal-sector economic activity, electricity— or, more precisely, growth in the consumption of electricity—will give a researcher a better idea of total (formal and informal) production. Researchers track the differences between growth in GDP and electricity consumption, and contest that where there is large divergence (e.g., electricity use growth rates outpace GDP growth rates), there must be unrecorded, unofficial production occurring.

MIMIC is short for multiple-indicators-multiple-causes, and the MIMIC model makes use of a system of equations that relates both potential causes of shadow economic activity and potential indicators that shadow economic activity is occurring to a measure of shadow economy size. While the *shadow economy* variable is unobservable, the basic idea of this model is to evaluate how several observable causal variables and several observable indicator variables interact with each other. I will spare the reader further technical detail,[16] but note that this is the most popular method used in present-day shadow economy studies.

Some Determinants of Shadow Economic Activity

Institutions that discourage productive entrepreneurship simultaneously *encourage* participation in underground economies. For example, labor market regulations such as occupational licensing effectively restrict the supply of goods and services in the market.

Since their licenses represent protection from potential competitors, license-holders can raise prices on the goods and services they provide. This works to discourage both consumers and future producers from entering the market—that is, the *legal* market. Entrepreneurs and consumers excluded from the legal sector will often undertake transaction illegally—which can sometimes be dangerous. Economists Sidney Carroll and Robert Gaston demonstrate that in the 1960s as states began implementing licensing requirements for electricians, two things unfolded: (1) the supply of electricians fell (in the *formal* sector, at least) and (2) incidents of electrocution increased.[17] High barriers to entry in the formal sector for electricians raise prices for their services. For some prospective customers, those prices are prohibitively high—though they still want the job done. As a result, inexperienced do-it-yourselfers take high risks that sometimes result in bad outcomes.

Corporate incentive programs produce similar results. When firms win special privilege through the political process—often in the form of tax breaks, credits, and exemptions, for example—they effectively secure a leg up over their competition in the market. And, consumers and non-favored firms suffer for it. Firms that lack the same political privilege may turn to the shadow economy to gain more customers, or they may be forced to downsize their legal operations or, worse, leave the market entirely. Downsizing in any degree results in unemployed workers, who themselves may turn to shadow economies to survive.

Minimum wages drive up the price of low-skilled labor—essentially raising production costs for producers who employ this labor—and force employers to focus their hiring decisions on higher-skilled employees. Minimum-wage rules have the effect of (1) preserving employees who are at least worth (to their employers) the current minimum wage and (2) forcing workers who employers perceive as less valuable employees into the shadow economy. Some of these workers will be forced out of work entirely. It is true that, in a minimum-wage-free world, many of these workers would likely earn very low wages, but pushing them into the shadow economy (or out of work entirely) decreases their opportunity to engage in the official economy, which can hurt them in many other ways—such as missing out on resume development and skill building.

Taxes are often used to regulate consumer and producer behavior. High taxes tend to increase underground activity. Taxes increase the cost of producing goods and services, raise prices that consumers pay for final products, and reduce disposable income. This heightens the incentive for buyers and sellers to bargain off the books. Have you ever been offered a discount on your purchase for paying in cash?

Welfare programs also generate perverse incentives that encourage shadow economic activity. Many programs are designed to reduce the dollar amount of benefits as recipients earn more income from formal employment—economists sometimes refer to this as an *implicit marginal tax*. As a result, many people get trapped inside the welfare program. For example, if a welfare recipient finds formal-sector work and her income from said work rises by $6,000 but her welfare benefits are reduced by $4,000, she gains only $2,000 in disposable income. This amounts to a substantial marginal tax rate of approximately 67 percent.

Suppose that, in addition to welfare transfers, this person is also earn-ing an off-the-books income of $3,000 that she would have to give up when she accepts the legal-sector position. This amounts to $7,000 in combined welfare benefits ($4,000) and underground income ($3,000) that she would forgo, while earning $6,000 at her new job.

In this case, the welfare beneficiary experiences negative returns (an implicit tax rate of 116 percent), which makes her *worse off* financially for choosing to pursue legal employment in the face of the welfare pro-gram option. She may choose, rationally, to remain in both the welfare program and the shadow economy. The important point here is that income earned in the shadow economy is not reported and therefore does not affect the benefits received from government programs—in contrast to income earned from legal employment. Therefore, high implicit marginal tax rates make participation in the shadow econ-omy more attractive.

Any policy or regulation that raises the cost of doing business in a legal setting, or discourages searching for formal employment, will invariably lower the cost of doing business in the shadow economy. Underground exchanges make up a not-insignificant portion of total US economic activity. Studies suggest that the value of total US shadow economy transactions, in recent years, rests between $1 trillion and $2 trillion annually.[18] This is a clear indication that shadow economies have important policy implications. Shadow economic activity amounts to potentially billions of dollars in lost tax revenue.

If you've ever paid cash to a neighbor for mowing your lawn or babysitting your children,[19] chances are that you've taken part in an underground exchange. A recent study of US shadow economies doc-uments shadow economy size for each of the states, over more than a decade. As an example, on average, Mississippi's shadow economy is the largest among the 50 states.[20] Estimates place Mississippi's shadow economy size at 9.54 percent of the state's economy, on average. What this means is that for every $10 of income generated in the state's legal sector, nearly one additional dollar is earned in the shadow economy and not reported. In terms of value, on the basis of a 2016 estimate of the state's real GDP as \$95.3 billion, the state's shadow economic activity amounted to approximately \$9.1 billion in 2016. That translates to approximately \$3,044 per person.[21]

Consequences of the Shadow Economy

Shadow economies are largest where states rely less on free markets and more on government. Figure 1 illustrates the relationship between economic freedom, from the Economic Freedom of North America index,[22] and shadow economy size in the US states. Large shadow economies are an indication of just how difficult it is to create wealth in the formal, legal economy. And this difficulty produces a number of downsides. For policymakers, one downside is the lost tax revenue from unreported transactions. However, the downsides to the actual buyers and sellers of underground goods and services may be even worse. Transactions undertaken off the books expose parties of the exchange to risk of being swindled in a number of ways. The purchaser of an underground good or service might end up with a faulty product—we've all heard stories of the unlicensed handyman who destroyed more than he fixed or left the job unfinished, then fled the scene. Or the seller of services may be left with a bad check, or with no payment at all. The risks are high because in the underground world there is little legal recourse for bad outcomes.

The situation is more ominous in the market for goods that are at all times illegal—that is, prohibited goods. Prohibitions encourage a lot of bad behavior. Drug markets provide great examples. Since drug suppliers lack legal recourse to, say, prevent the theft of their product, they often take the law into their own hands or purchase protection services from others willing to risk their lives in the underground. History reveals that large underground protection agencies tend to develop around prohibited products for which there remains a very high demand. We know these protection and supply agencies as gangs, mafias, and cartels. When exchanges in these markets go wrong, these problems simply cannot be reported to the legal authorities for restitution. Imagine a drug buyer calling the police to report that the drugs he purchased were tainted, or to report a theft that occurred during the transaction.

Figure 1. Shadow Economy Size and Economic Freedom

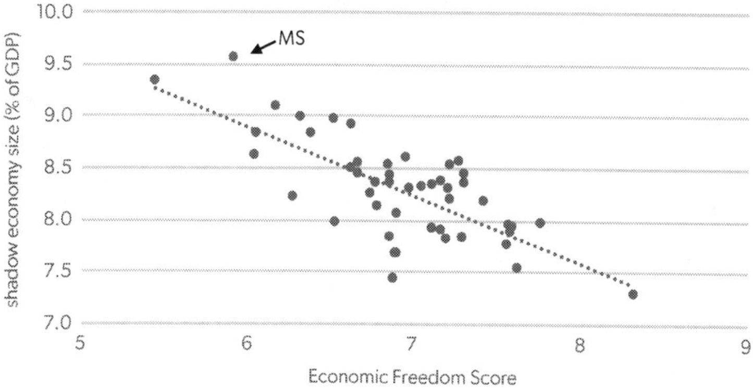

Source: Average shadow economy size versus average EFNA score, 1997–2008, constructed by the author, using data from Dean Stansel, José Torra, and Fred McMahon, *Economic Freedom of North America 2016* (Vancouver, BC: Fraser Institute, 2016), and shadow economy estimates from Travis Wiseman, "US Shadow Economies: A State-level Study," *Constitutional Political Economy* 24, no. 4 (2013): 310-35.

In a recent study published by the Institute for Justice, *License to Work,* the authors explore 102 low- and middle-income occupations, and document, by state, the number of these that require occupational licensing. It may come as no surprise that states that erect higher barriers to entry in these occupations also tend to exhibit relatively large shadow economies. For example, the states of Mississippi and West Virginia require licenses for approximately 65 percent and 69 percent of these 102 occupations, respectively. These two states also host two of the largest shadow economies, as a percentage of GDP, in the nation (9.54% and 9.32%, respectively). By contrast, two of the smallest shadow economies belong to Colorado and Delaware (7.52% and 7.28%). These states require licenses only for approximately 33 percent and 43 percent, respectively, of the 102 studied occupations.[23]

"Low- and middle-income" equates to low- and middle-range skill sets—that is, individuals who are *limited in their education and training.* In other words, licensing in these 102 occupations is aimed disproportionately at those who might benefit most from a job, but simultaneously have the most difficulty overcoming barriers to market entry because they lack competitive skill sets, knowledge, and the income to better develop themselves.

Table 1. Shadow Economy, Income, Entrepreneurship, and Education

	Shadow economy size (% of GDP)	Real GDP per capita	Productive entrepreneurship score	% population with bachelor's degree or more
Large shadow economies				
Mississippi	9.54	$31,881	16.33	20.80
West Virginia	9.32	$36,315	7.85	19.60
Average of the two	9.43	$34,098	12.09	20.20
Small shadow economies				
Colorado	7.52	$52,795	41.06	39.20
Delaware	7.28	$63,664	37.09	30.90
Average of the two	7.40	$58,230	39.08	35.05

Sources: For shadow economy size, Travis Wiseman, "US Shadow Economies: A State-Level Study," *Constitutional Political Economy* 24, no. 4 (2013): 310–35. For real GDP, Bureau of Economic Analysis (https://www.bea.gov/data/gdp/gross-domestic-product). For productive entrepreneurship score, Travis Wiseman and Andrew Young, "Religion: Productive or Unproductive," *Journal of Institutional Economics* 10, no. 1 (2014): 421-33. For population with bachelor's degree or more, Census Bureau, Educational Attainment in the United States, 2016.

Though licensing doesn't explain the full size of shadow economies, barriers like licensing requirements keep the poorest of the population locked in precarious situations—unable to get their footing on the first rung of the economic ladder to prosperity.

Additionally, for comparison, table 1 shows the record of wealth and well-being in Mississippi, West Virginia, Colorado, and Delaware, relative to shadow economy size. Averages of all estimates are provided to demonstrate the remarkable differences in important indicators, such as the states' real GDP per capita (of legally reported activities), productive entrepreneurship scores,[24] and educational attainment at the bachelor degree level or higher. The states with smaller shadow economies have, on average, a more highly educated population (35.05% with bachelor's degrees versus 20.20%), experience more formal-sector productive entrepreneurship (an average score of 39.08 versus 12.09), and realize a higher real per capita GDP ($58,230 versus $34,098).

Reducing the size of the underground economy in any of these states would vastly improve the human condition—but would be especially beneficial in the states that consistently demonstrate the largest shadow economies. But how should a state approach its shadow economy? Research suggests that decreases in tax and social welfare burdens, as well as in labor market regulations, are associated with large decreases in shadow economic activity.[25] For example, a recent study of US underground economies suggests that a 1 percentage point decrease in burdens from taxes and charges (e.g., licensing fees) is associated with an approximately 0.30 percentage point decrease in shadow economy size, on average.[26] This may not sound like much, but consider the value of 0.30 percent of Mississippi's 2016 real state-level GDP. With GDP at a little over $95 billion, a 0.30 percentage point reduction in shadow market activity amounts to approximately $286 million annually. Much of this might be captured in the formal sector once barriers to market entry have been lowered. Most shadow market participants would prefer to do business on the up and up, and they will as long as operating in the legal economy is not prohibitively costly.

Alternatively, the same study suggests that direct attempts to identify and regulate the shadow economy—for instance, increasing police forces to combat underground activity—are associated with much smaller decreases in shadow economic activity. Increasing state expenditures (as a percentage of GDP) for shadow market task forces by 1 percentage point amounts to about a 0.05 percentage point reduction in shadow economy size, on average. Compare this to the aforementioned effect of reducing burdens from taxes and charges (0.30 > 0.05). Moreover, task force measures put additional pressure on taxpayers to fund such initiatives. It is plausible that the increased tax burdens might simply crowd out the efforts of task forces—that is, as task forces reduce shadow economic activity, the taxes required to fund those forces might incentivize more participation in the underground—creating a vicious cycle. Furthermore, entrepreneurs and firms already operating in the shadow economy have an increased incentive under pressure from task force initiatives to innovate new methods to avoid detection.[27] Pushing shadow market participants deeper underground only increases the costs of maintaining an effective task force.

In fact, prohibitions are possibly the most troublesome regulations imposed in any one place, because they push market activity very deep into the shadows. In addition to incentivizing off-the-books transactions, prohibitions often have consequences that are much more dire—indeed, *deadly*! Prohibitions—for instance, bans of alcohol or drugs—are often based on the common misperception that if the good or service is prohibited outright, social ills and anxieties associated with consumption of the good or service will simply go away. However, history tells a different story.

In his autobiography, published one year before his death, famed Spanish filmmaker Luis Buñuel declared, "I never drank so much in my life as the time I spent five months in the United States during Prohibition."[28] Buñuel's assertion illustrates a grand miscalculation among regulators—Prohibition did not destroy demand.

Ratification of the Eighteenth Amendment to the US Constitution, on January 16, 1919, ushered in a nationwide alcohol prohibition. Alcohol consumption *did* decline at the onset of Prohibition—due mostly to an immediate and sharp increase in supply costs and search costs (which include the cost and added risk of evading detection by Prohibition agents, etc.), but within a few short years, consumption bounced back to 60–70 percent of its pre-Prohibition levels.[29]

Underground consumption demands underground supply—and in a world where suppliers lack legal recourse to remedy infringements on their property (such as theft of their booze), they turn to underground protection. Gangsterism is most closely associated with William Baumol's "destructive" entrepreneur. Gangsters generate wealth in their underground enterprises, but they also loot and murder their competitors.[30] Economist Mark Thornton documents a 67 percent increase in homicides during Prohibition (from 6 persons per 100,000 pre-Prohibition to nearly 10 persons per 100,000 by 1933).[31] The number of homicides dropped substantially following Prohibition's 1933 repeal.

States Should Provide Shadow Market Participants with an Incentive to Join the Official Economy

The following list is a summary of suggested reforms:

- *Reduce taxes.* Reducing taxes – be it sales, corporate, or personal income taxes — will lower the cost of engaging in the formal economy. Simplifying the tax code is another step states could take to constrain wealth redistribution. Doing this would have the added benefit of reducing the power of lobby groups to profit from the demands they place on bureaucrats, since bureaucrats would be equipped with less to supply. Delaware is one of the nation's most inviting tax environments for business—the state offers low, fixed corporate income taxes, accompanied by no sales tax. Delaware also has the smallest shadow economy in the US, on average.

- *Reduce or eliminate occupational licensing requirements and other labor market regulatory burdens.* Hotels, cabs, beauty salons, and mail delivery services are just a few of the business types that are influenced by occupational licensing in many states. In the formal sector, these industries all profit in a big way from exclusive trade licensing. Unfortunately, such licensing is also responsible for the wasting of many states' limited resources, as states often focus their task force efforts on squashing the many relatively harmless underground jobs that come to fruition under strict, onerous licensing rules.

- *Reduce or eliminate price controls.* Minimum-wage hikes primarily serve those who are at present employed in minimum-wage positions; they do little to incentivize employers to hire new labor from the low-skilled labor pool. With the bottom rung of the economic ladder removed, many people entering the labor force for the first time with little experience will turn to the underground economy—and, incidentally, never show up in official unemployment statistics. Rent controls are another form of price control that create perverse incentives for owners of rental properties. Under strict rental pricing regimes, landlords will search for ways to bust through the price cap. Some convert their apartments into

makeshift hotel suites – think Airbnb. In this way, landlords earn
profits by offering accommodations at prices lower than those
charged by legal, *licensed* hotels, but at higher fixed rents.

- *Reconsider prohibitions.* Undoubtedly, there is substantial shadow
  economic activity associated with goods that are outright illegal
  to produce and consume under any circumstances. The choice
  to outlaw a good necessarily forces its remaining production
  and consumption underground. For example, since the legalization of marijuana for recreational use in Colorado, Washington,
  and other states, consumption and production has become more
  visible. The good is taxed, and producers and consumers have
  recourse to the legal system and experience workplace and quality standards that go along with the above-ground economy.[32]

Conclusion

This chapter introduces the reader to the shadow economy—what it
is, what causes it, what can be done to reduce its size—and highlights
tax and regulatory environments as determinants of entrepreneurial
decisions to do business off the books. Onerous occupational licensing,
burdensome tax policies and incentive programs, and outdated prohibitions all work against entrepreneurs by obstructing their path to
prosperity. Productive entrepreneurs thrive in places where barriers to
market entry are low—where they participate less in the shadow economy and more in the legal sector. This means also that they commit
fewer crimes, dedicate less effort toward unproductive rent-seeking
activity, and instead focus their efforts on wealth creation. It must be
recognized that governments will not pave the path to prosperity with
wasteful tax and spending initiatives and burdensome regulation. To
expand economic opportunities, we must work to eliminate the government's role in picking who gets to participate in the market and who
doesn't. Instead, let the free-enterprise system determine that.

Regulation and Labor Market Outcomes

CHAPTER 5

An Introduction to the Effect of Regulation on Employment and Wages

James Bailey

Does regulation kill jobs or create them? Push wages up or push them down? In fact it can have any of these effects, depending on how it is written and where it is applied. In this chapter, I first use economic theory to distinguish among certain common types of regulation and explain their varying effects on wages and employment. I then summarize the empirical literature from economics and adjacent fields that attempts to determine whether the effects predicted by simple economic theory hold true in the real world, measure how large these effects are in practice, and quantify the net effect of all US regulations on wages and employment.

In short, the literature finds that the directional predictions of simple economic theory generally hold true, but that the estimated size of these effects varies widely. Several attempts to quantify the "cumulative" cost of US regulation have produced estimates in the neighborhood of $2 trillion per year, but in fact these studies only estimate the cost of about a quarter of all federal regulations.

What Is Regulation?

A typical regulation states a set of actions that certain types of individuals or firms must or must not take. Take, for example, chapter 2, section

1420.3, from Title 16 of the *Code of Federal Regulations*—"requirements for four-wheel ATVs"—which begins,

> Each ATV shall comply with all applicable provisions of the American National Standard for Four-Wheel All-Terrain Vehicles (ANSI/SVIA 1–2017), ANSI-approved on June 8, 2017. The Director of the Federal Register approves this incorporation by reference in accordance with 5 U.S.C. 552(a) and 1 CFR part 51. You may obtain a copy from Specialty Vehicle Institute of America. . . .

In short, the regulation is adding design requirements to a manufacturing process, presumably with the goal of enhancing consumer safety.

In some cases regulations do not constitute binding constraints that actually affect producers, either because they are not enforced or because producers would have done things that way without being told to. But in the typical case regulations do matter, and do change the decisions made by economic actors.

Different types of regulations have different effects, and the scope, scale, and variety of regulation can be bewildering even to experienced researchers and to those in regulated industries. To keep things simple, rather than attempting to discuss every possible type of regulation, in this chapter I focus on a few major types of regulation that have clear ties to labor markets. These include common general regulations (cost-increasing regulations, bans, and entry barriers) that can have spillover effects on labor markets, as well as labor-specific regulations that target labor markets directly (minimum wages, mandated benefits, and employment regulations).

What Does Basic Economic Theory Predict about How Different Types of Regulation Affect Wages and Employment?

Cost-Increasing Regulations
A typical cost-increasing regulation, such as the ATV rule described

above, directs producers to change their products in costly ways, often for the purpose of benefiting a third party such as consumers or the environment. In basic economic terms, an increase in the cost of production is a leftward shift in the supply curve, which leads to higher prices, reduced production, and lower revenue for producers. In the case of consumer-safety regulation, these effects may be partly offset by an increase in demand, to the extent that consumers see the regulated product as higher quality. But apart from unusual cases in which producers were making a systematic error and producing goods below the profit-maximizing quality, the effect of cost-increasing regulation on a market remains the same: higher prices, reduced production, lower revenue.

What does this mean for wages and employment? In general, as revenue falls, the marginal revenue product of workers falls, and therefore so do wages and employment. However, certain workers in occupations related to regulatory compliance may become more valuable and see their wages and employment rise, as long as the regulation is not so onerous that it shuts down the industry entirely.

Bans

Sometimes regulations do simply shut down an industry, either intentionally or as an unintended consequence of cost increases.[1] In such cases the effect on wages and employment is clearly negative:[2] all workers in the industry lose their jobs, though most will become reemployed as they move to other, next-best jobs.

Entry Barriers

To the extent that regulatory compliance is a fixed cost, larger firms will be better able to bear it. Larger firms may even lobby for cost-increasing regulations in the hopes of raising rivals' costs more than their own and thereby gaining a relative competitive advantage.[3] But while a typical regulation applies to all firms, at least on paper, entry barriers are an important exception. Regulatory entry barriers explicitly apply only to new firms—incumbents may be exempted through grandfathering or may have already paid the fixed cost of entry. Examples of entry barriers include the need to obtain a business license and the need to gain the approval of a state board before starting a business.

The obvious effect of such entry barriers is to reduce entry—that is, to reduce the number of new firms in the affected industry or region. What is less obvious is how this affects wages and employment. Do entry barriers work like the typical regulation—shifting supply leftward, reducing the marginal revenue product of most workers, and so reducing employment and wages? Perhaps. But while entry barriers raise costs for new firms, they do not raise costs for existing firms, which instead become more profitable because the reduced competition allows them to charge higher prices. Incumbent firms gain more "monopsony" market power over workers, which they can use to push down wages and employment, but they also gain more "monopoly" market power over consumers. A textbook monopoly raises prices and cuts back production. Reduced production generally leads to lower employment, and this monopoly employment effect is in the same direction as the monopsony employment effect, so we can be confident that entry barriers lead to lower employment.

But entry barriers' effect on wages is ambiguous. The monopsony effect pushes wages down, but the monopoly effect can push them up, though the monopoly effect is itself ambiguous. Monopolies may lead to lower wages because the lower production drops the demand for labor, or to higher wages because of "rent sharing," in which the more-profitable monopoly leads to workers with a higher marginal revenue product and employers better able to pay high wages (think of 1960s-era Detroit automakers).

This latter effect is especially pronounced in the case of occupational licensing, where the entry barrier targets workers directly rather than targeting the products they make or the firms that employ them (see chapter six in this volume for a more in-depth discussion of occupational licensing). If a certain type of workers, say cosmetologists, must go through a costly licensing process before they are able to legally work in their field, this situation functions as a reduction in the supply of cosmetologists, reducing their numbers but increasing their wages.

Occupational licensing is not merely an entry barrier but also a form of regulation that targets workers specifically. Given our subject (employment and wages), occupational licensing and other types of labor-specific regulations deserve a closer look.

Labor-Specific Regulations

While most regulations affect workers only unintentionally, a large minority of regulations do target labor. Among the 41 titles of the *Code of Federal Regulations* are Title 20, "Employees' Benefits," and Title 29, "Labor"; many other titles also include regulations targeting labor. According to 2019 data from Quantgov,[4] the Department of Labor was the sixth-largest regulatory agency out of 130 federal regulatory agencies.[5]

Labor-specific regulations generally affect wages and employment through one of three mechanisms: they target wages directly, they target employee benefits or working conditions, or they target employment or the demand for workers directly. Each of these mechanisms affects wages and employment differently and so merits separate analysis. But economic logic ties wages, benefits, and employment together. Employers aim to offer a compensation package (including cash wages and nonwage benefits) that is generous enough to attract the employees they want but not so generous that it exceeds the revenue the employees add through their work. When regulations attempt to improve workers' wages, benefits, or job security, they can sometimes improve workers' bargaining power and make workers better off at the expense of employer profits and consumer prices. But profit-maximizing employers are always looking for ways around these regulations, leading to trade-offs across wages, benefits, and employment.

Minimum wages.

Minimum wages increase wages for some workers but lead employers to reduce job benefits in an attempt to bring total compensation back down to the desired, profit-maximizing level. Curtailed benefits could include benefits directly funded by employers, such as health insurance and retirement matching, but also other perquisites of the job, such as flexible hours. Minimum-wage jobs may not have many such benefits to cut, however. Therefore, minimum wages will be partly paid for through lower profits—but if the profitability of a worker falls below zero, the job may simply be cut.

Mandated benefits.
A similar logic applies to regulations that mandate employee benefits such as health insurance or workers' compensation. Employers attempt to reduce the total compensation package to its profit-maximizing level by cutting wages or other benefits. To the extent that they are unable to do so, or to the extent that employees value the mandated benefit below its cost of provision, employment will fall.[6]

Employment regulation.
Employment-targeting regulations take two common forms. One tries to make the jobs of existing employees more secure through protections against arbitrary firing.[7] This functions as an employee benefit—employers can offer slightly lower wages or other benefits and still attract employees—with the twist that it makes employers more cautious about hiring in the first place. The other type of employment regulation aims to increase the total number of employees rather than to make individual employees more secure in their jobs. These regulations may be motivated by a desire to "create jobs" (think of the mandatory full-service gas stations in Oregon and New Jersey), or by the belief that the additional workers will improve product quality or consumer safety (think of the requirement that a copilot be present on flights). In general, this type of regulation increases the demand for workers and so increases both employment and wages, unless the costs imposed by the regulation are so great as to shut down production.

Summary of Predictions
Table 1 summarizes the predictions made above. For the sake of simplicity, I only include the effect on employment and wages in the typical case, ignoring the other effects of regulation (on employee benefits, prices, profits, etc.) and ignoring the contrary effects on small subgroups (such as compliance workers benefiting while most workers

Table 1. Effect of Various Regulations on Employment and Wages (Basic Theory)

Type of regulation	Employment	Wages
"Typical" cost-increasing regulations	↓	↓
Bans	↓	↓
Typical entry barriers	↓	
Occupational licensing	↓	↑
Minimum wages	↓	↑
Mandated benefits	↓	↓
Make-work regulations	↑	↑

are harmed) or unusual cases (such as make-work regulations being so costly they shut down the industry).[8]

In short, regulations almost always harm employment on net, while their effects on wages are more mixed. But in order to fully evaluate the costs and benefits of a regulation, we need to know more than just how it affects employment and wages.

Remember: Bad Jobs Exist

We have now examined the simple economics explaining how various regulations affect employment and wages. A noneconomist may assume I intend to argue that the regulations that kill jobs and cut wages are bad, while the regulations that create jobs and raise wages are good. But neither of these inferences is necessarily true. To draw conclusions about the overall costs and benefits of regulation, we need to look a bit deeper.

Bad jobs exist. When regulation kills a bad job, most people are made better off. When regulation creates a bad job, most people are made worse off. By "bad jobs," I don't simply mean menial or low-paying jobs, but rather jobs that destroy more value than they create. Most jobs involving manual labor or low pay are not bad in this sense; for instance, sanitation and food preparation generally create great value.

Instead, one archetypal bad job might be manager in a lead paint factory. The job may have paid well and carried some status, and lead paint was a product that many people were willing to pay for. But it also contributed to a mass poisoning that made the world a dumber and more violent place,[9] and these costs almost certainly outweigh the benefits of lead-paint-factory jobs and longer-lasting paint. The regulation banning lead paint certainly reduced employment in the short run, and this should be counted as a cost of regulation, but a job-killing regulation may nevertheless be worthwhile if it brings sufficient benefits to others.

Conversely, a job-creating regulation is not necessarily a good one. Besides the manager of a lead paint factory, another archetypal "bad job" may be that of the bureaucrat who must approve beneficial activities. Suppose an activity is generally beneficial and carries no special risk to consumers or the environment, yet a regulation requires it to receive bureaucratic approval before proceeding.[10] The regulation may create bureaucratic jobs, and the recipients of those jobs will appreciate the salary, but the regulation that created their jobs can only delay or deny benefits to others. Everyone would be better off if the regulation were repealed, even if the bureaucrat received the same salary for doing nothing.[11]

While the labor-market effects of regulations are important, they are far from the only cost or benefit of regulations, and do not themselves constitute sufficient grounds for accepting or rejecting a regulation. There's a reason why this study of labor-market effects is only one chapter in a larger work on regulation.

What Has Empirical Research Found Regarding Regulation, Wages, and Employment?

Now we've seen what basic economic theory has to say about which types of regulations push employment and wages up or down. In this section, we turn to the empirical literature on specific regulations to see whether this theory holds in the real world, and to measure just how big the effects of regulation are.

Entry Barriers

The most generic and universal form of entry barrier is the process that every new business must go through to legally form. The World Bank's Ease of Doing Business index has measured the intensity of this barrier in almost every country since 2003.[12] According to the 2019 report, in New Zealand starting a new business requires only a single step that takes less than a day, while in other countries such as Haiti and Venezuela, starting a new business requires at least a dozen steps that may take several months to complete, and costs several times the average annual income.[13] The scholars who created the initial version of this index confirmed that higher entry barriers lead to less product market competition and a higher share of employment in the unofficial economy.[14] This reduction in (legal) employment matches what economic theory predicts (as discussed above), as well as the findings of other empirical work—specifically, that new firms create a disproportionate share of new jobs.[15] But the large literature using the Ease of Doing Business index has generally not studied the effect of business entry restrictions on wages.

The literature on occupational licensing has reached a near-consensus that occupational licensing reduces employment while increasing wages for workers in the licensed profession. From economists Milton Friedman and Simon Kuznets in their classic study of professional licensing to the authors of more recent work, researchers consistently find slower employment growth and higher wages in licensed professions.[16]

Labor-Specific Regulations

Minimum wages.

There are at least as many articles on the minimum wage as there are labor economists; a search on EconLit reveals 3,140 written since 1945. To sum up an immense and varied literature too quickly: economic theory works, but the employment effects are smaller and slower than you might think after looking at a typical textbook supply and demand graph. A substantial minority of papers find that a minimum wage is not associated with any significant dis-employment. Specifically, a

minimum wage increase is more likely to slow the hiring of new workers than it is to cause layoffs of existing workers.[17]

Mandated benefits.
Benefit regulations include mandates that employers cover health insurance[18] and mandates that employer health insurance cover specific
treatments.[19] Studies consistently find that many benefit regulations
reduce wages. As economic theory predicts, though, the effect of benefit
mandates on employment is more mixed.[20] In some cases benefit mandates seem not to harm employment at all.[21] This could be due to firms
finding regulatory loopholes,[22] or to the logic of the model by Lawrence
Summers (former Harvard president and US Secretary of the Treasury),
where the cost of the benefit is fully passed back to employees in the
form of lower wages (so employers have no incentive to reduce hiring)
while employees fully value the benefit (so all continue working, since
they perceive their total compensation to be the same).

In other cases, though, benefit mandates do seem to have affected
employment. Some regulations attempt to benefit a specific group (such
as maternity benefits, which target younger women), and these can lead
to lower employment for that group without necessarily lowering overall employment. In a 2014 study I found this to be true for older men
in the case of prostate cancer screening,[23] but the most extreme example is likely the Americans with Disabilities Act. The act intended to
protect and promote employment by adding antidiscrimination protections for disabled workers and requiring employers to offer "reasonable
accommodations" for disabilities. But despite the explicit antidiscrimination parts of the law, employers reacted strongly; economists Thomas
DeLeire, Daron Acemoglu, and Joshua Angrist estimate that the act
reduced the employment of disabled workers by at least 10 percent.[24]

Summarizing empirical work on specific regulations.
Table 2 summarizes the empirical estimates for certain types of regulations. These generally accord with the theoretical predictions
summarized in table 1 about how different types of regulation affect
employment, and the empirical research gives us an idea of how strong

these effects are. Before we start celebrating the excellent predictive track record of economic theory, however, I must advise some caution about the state of the empirical evidence. It is challenging to find empirical work estimating the effect of some types of regulation on wages or employment, which is why these types of regulation are not included in the table, and why there is only a question mark for the effect of entry barriers on wages (the paper cited does not attempt to measure the effect on wages, only on employment). Other types of regulation have the opposite problem: there are many estimates available but they don't all agree, either because of disagreements over the proper estimation methodology (as for the minimum wage) or because even within a category of regulation there can be a variety of effects (as for various mandated benefits). Still, economic theory is looking good overall: Where empirical work exists it generally confirms the direction predictions of economic theory, and at worst it finds no effect rather than an effect in the opposite direction of the prediction.

Table 2. Estimated Effect of Certain Regulations on Employment and Wages

Type of regulation	Employment	Wages	Source
Typical entry barrier[a]	↓ 14%	?	Djankov et al.
Occupational licensing	↓ 20%	↑ 18%	Kleiner and Krueger
Minimum wage[b]	↓ 1%	↑ 10%	Wolfson and Belman
Mandated benefit[c]	↓ 2%	↓ 2.8%	Bailey

[a] To be precise, Djankov et al. find that employment shifts to the unofficial economy, but do not test whether it falls overall.

[b] The minimum wage estimate is from a meta-analysis that summarizes 37 other studies, many of which estimated dis-employment effects larger or smaller than the pooled 1% estimate.

[c] The effect size is particularly likely to vary with the specific benefit; Lahey finds that employment falls with no effect on wages, while Gruber finds that wages fall with no effect on employment.

Sources: Simeon Djankov et al., "The Regulation of Entry," *Quarterly Journal of Economics* 117, no. 1 (2002): 1–37; Morris Kleiner and Alan Krueger, "Analyzing the Extent and Influence of Occupational Licensing on the Labor Market," *Journal of Labor Economics* 31, no. 2 (2013): S173–S202; Paul Wolfson and Dale Belman, "15 Years of Research on US Employment and the Minimum Wage," *Labour* 33 (2019): 488–506, https://doi.org/10.1111/labr.12162; James Bailey, "Who Pays the High Health Costs of Older Workers? Evidence from Prostate Cancer Screening Mandates," *Applied Economics* 46, no. 32 (2014): 3931–41.

Aggregate effect of labor-specific regulations.

The research on how specific labor regulations affect wages and employment is generally excellent—researchers have used the latest empirical methods to carefully identify the effect of the regulations they study. This excellent research is made possible by the nature of the regulations being studied, which tend to target only some groups or to be enacted in only some states, leaving other groups or states to serve as controls. But not every specific regulation can be studied this way, and it is particularly difficult to determine the effect of aggregate regulation with as much certainty. Do mandated benefits and other labor-market regulations merely change who gets hired, or do they really reduce overall employment?

Here the evidence is more suggestive than definitive, but there is a lot of it. Europe generally has more labor-market regulation than the United States, together with higher unemployment.[25] Moreover, the labor force participation rate of prime-age men in the US has fallen from a peak of 94.7 percent in 1967 to 86.4 percent in 2019.[26] In other words, the proportion of men aged 25–54 who have no job and are not trying to get one has more than doubled. The causes of this change remain poorly understood and much debated,[27] but it has occurred alongside a huge expansion of federal regulation (as measured by number of words and restrictions in the *Code of Federal Regulations*);[28] of occupational licensing;[29] and of health insurance benefit mandates (which increased more than fortyfold since the 1960s[30]).

If all this regulation has increased the cost of hiring faster than the value employers see in new employees, we would expect employment to fall. The growth in US nonemployment has been concentrated at lower skill levels,[31] which may be because employer demand has grown more at higher skill levels (the "job polarization" discussed by economist Didem Tuzemen and many others noting a growing wage and employment gap by skill and education level). Alternatively, it could be because regulatory costs bind more at lower levels—an employer can simply cut wages for high-wage workers if regulation makes them more costly to employ, but for a worker who is already at the minimum wage and with minimal benefits, the employer's only choice is between cutting employment or accepting the loss in profits. This is one reason why regulation often has "regressive effects"—that is, it hits lower-income workers harder.[32]

The Overall Effect of Regulation

We've now considered the evidence on many specific types of regulation. But what does all this add up to? If a country or state engaged in a wholesale, across-the-board program of regulation or deregulation, how would this program affect labor markets? Perhaps surprisingly, only a handful of researchers have attempted to answer this question; as economists Mark Crain and Nicole Crain put it, "For the most part, the volume of regulations and their complexity have discouraged attempts by government agencies and private researchers to generate a comprehensive estimate of regulatory costs."[33]

The basic approach of most studies has been to compare the state of the labor market across more- and less-regulated countries, states, or industries. Some analyses are cross-sectional, making these comparisons at a single point in time; the challenge here is that states and countries differ in many ways besides their level of regulation, and controlling for all of these differences is difficult. Other time-series or panel analyses focus on changes in regulation over time, so that a state or country can be compared to itself before the regulatory change as well as to other polities.

An article in the *Journal of Economic Growth* measures total regulation in the US over time by counting the number of pages in the *Code of Federal Regulations*.[34] While its primary focus is on total output and total factor productivity, the results also imply that increased regulation in the postwar era led to slower wage and employment growth.

The advent of RegData has for the first time allowed researchers to easily quantify how the level of federal regulation varies by industry in the US.[35] In a 2017 study with Diana Thomas, I find that doubling the level of regulation in an industry leads to a 6.3 percent decline in new hires,[36] and a 2018 article finds a similar result using a similar approach.[37] Entrepreneurship scholars David Lucas and Christopher Boudreaux also find reduced net job creation in more-regulated industries, but find that this effect is moderated by state economic free-dom.[38] Also using RegData to compare industries, economists Bentley Coffey, Patrick McLaughlin, and Pietro Peretto estimate that in 2012, the economy was 25 percent smaller than it would have been in the absence of regulatory growth since 1980,[39] which translates to $13,000 less in per capita income. (The authors do not provide estimates for how much of this is due to declines in labor income as opposed to other income sources.)

While RegData's original goal was to quantify federal regulation in the United States,[40] its creators are in the process of expanding it to cover other countries and the regulatory codes of US states. Using a preliminary measure of US state regulatory codes, policy analyst Mark Febrizio finds very large dis-employment effects: "a 10 percentage point increase in [regulatory] restrictions is associated with a 11 to 13 per-centage point decrease in employment growth."[41]

Crain and Crain use a cross-country measure of regulation from the World Economic Forum's Global Competitiveness Report 2006–2013 to create an Economic Regulation Index. They find that GDP per capita falls by 8.1 percent for each one-point increase in the Economic Regu-lation Index; because the US has 26 percent more regulation than the "benchmark" lowest-regulation countries of the Organisation for Eco-nomic Co-operation and Development, they translate this to mean that US GDP would increase by $1.4 trillion (about 8 percent) if US regu-lation were cut to benchmark levels. After adding the costs of some other types of regulation not captured by the first index, they conclude that the annual cost of regulation in the US is about $2 trillion, which translates to about $10,000 per worker. Like the authors of several of the studies using RegData, they find that this cost is disproportionately borne by small firms.[42]

Wayne Crews states, "regulatory costs are unknowable in an elemen-tal sense, and estimates of them are not observable or calculable—much as the economic calculations necessary to enable central economic planning are impossible."[43] Still, Crews does his best to calculate the incalculable, and estimates that regulation causes a $1.9 trillion hit to US GDP, though he cautions that this is more of a lower bound: "This figure is based on a nonscientific, disclaimer-laden, fusion amalgam of GDP losses, and compliance costs derived from available official data and other sources. Even so, this assessment is more representative and inclusive than official estimates and more 'conservative' in that burdens conceivably are considerably more."[44] As with other GDP-based estimates, it is not clear how much of this reduction to income occurs because of lower wages or employment and how much because of other factors.

The Council of Economic Advisers (CEA) attempts to quantify the aggregate economic effects of the net deregulatory stance of the Trump administration. The CEA's main estimation strategy is to sum up the impact estimates of previous government reports on major recent (de)regulatory actions. The council concludes that if this regulatory approach is continued, it will raise US GDP by up to 2.2 percent over a decade, raising real income by $3,100 per household. Much of this effect occurs through the channel of lower consumer prices rather than higher nominal wages or employment. Unlike some researchers, the CEA has also attempted to quantify the nonpecuniary benefits of repealed regulation, and concludes that they amounted to $600 per year, so that the total net benefit of deregulation is $2,500 per household.[45]

In sum, research on the overall effect of regulation has produced a variety of estimates. This is partly because it has employed a variety of estimation strategies and data sets and partly because it has estimated the effect of regulation on different outcomes (GDP, productivity, new hires, etc.). Perhaps most importantly, different researchers considered different counterfactuals. Despite titles and abstracts that sometimes imply otherwise, none of these researchers has actually attempted to sum up the overall cost of all regulation—and they have been wise not to, as we have no real examples to study of a country cutting all or even most regulation.[46] Instead, their estimates are based on counterfactuals such as cutting regulation to the level the US had in 1980, or to the level of the current lowest-regulation countries in the Organisation for Economic Co-operation and Development (each roughly a 25 percent cut); or they measure the effects of smaller actual deregulations such as the net reduction in federal regulation since 2017.

While it would be nice to know the net effect of all US regulation on GDP, employment, and wages, from a practical standpoint it is more important to know the likely effect of changes to regulation *at the margin*, because a greater-than-25-percent cut to regulation seems unlikely.[47] This marginal effect will depend above all on which regulations are actually passed or repealed: this chapter has shown that different types of regulations have very different effects, this mix of regulations will vary with the political times, and for any given administration the best strategy is likely to involve measuring the effects of the specific regulations it has passed and repealed, as the CEA has done.[48]

CHAPTER 6

Occupational Licensing: A Barrier to Opportunity and Prosperity

Alicia Plemmons and Edward Timmons

Occupational licensing laws establish mandatory minimum entry requirements that must be met for aspiring professionals to begin working. These requirements include completing minimum levels of education and training, paying various fees, passing examinations, and satisfying "good moral character" standards. In the early 1950s, approximately 5 percent of workers in the United States were required to obtain a license to work.[1] As of 2019, the percentage of workers has grown to almost 22 percent.[2] This is nearly 10 times the fraction of workers (2.3%) receiving the federal minimum wage[3] and more than double the percentage of workers (10.3%) that are union members.[4] Occupational licensing primarily occurs at the state level, but there are some examples of federal licensing, as well as variation at the county and municipal levels.

Some occupations, such as those of physicians, dentists, and registered nurses, are licensed in every state with little variation in licensing requirements. Other occupations, such as barbering and cosmetology, are universally licensed but with significant state-to-state variation. Barbers, for example, must complete 2,100 hours of education in Iowa—more than double the number of hours mandated in New Hampshire (800).[5] Some occupations (such as those of massage therapists and radiologic technicians) are licensed in most states; others (e.g., lactation consulting and interior design) are licensed in only a few states. There are even examples of occupations that are licensed in only one state—such as florists in Louisiana.

To better understand the costs associated with occupational licensing requirements, we will use barbers as an illustrative example. As of September 2020, barbers require a license in all 50 states and the District of Columbia.[6] Using data provided through the Knee Center for the Study of Occupational Regulation at Saint Francis University, we find that there is a large discrepancy in the fees required to obtain a barber's license across states—from $10 in Pennsylvania to $450 in Alaska. Fees are far from the only requirement prospective barbers must meet to obtain a license. Other costs take the form of time spent on experience and training, different forms of examination, and good moral character requirements.

In the case of barbers, degree requirements range from none at all in some states to proof of graduation from a licensed barbering college in others. These educational programs can vary drastically in cost. In the 2019-2020 academic year, the average cost of tuition, books, and supplies was more than $15,000 per year.[7] This is a comparatively high cost considering that the 2019 median pay for barbers and other hairstylists was approximately $26,270 a year, or just under $13 per hour.[8] In most states, after completing the education or experience requirements (thousands of hours of hands-on experience in some cases), prospective barbers must complete examinations. States vary in their examination requirements, but exams may be written, practical, or theoretical—or a combination of all three. After paying for education expenses and examinations, prospective barbers are also required in most states to demonstrate good moral character by disclosing any criminal history. In many cases, good moral character requirements might bar individuals with non-dangerous records from employment.

Barbers have mixed feelings about the licensing requirements and prospects for future reform. For example, in Arkansas, where there was a senate bill to abolish the State Board of Barber Examiners, barbers protested and noted that the proposal "definitely takes the professionalism, and it definitely takes the craft out of what we do and it just puts us in layman's terms."[9] Others also struggle with the prospect of what's known as a *transitional gains trap*.[10] If licensing laws are repealed, then the time and money thousands have spent to obtain a license may become obsolete and, in the words of one director of an Arkansas barber college, the repeal "makes the license that they receive pointless."[11]

While these feelings do persist, there is also the long-term situation to consider. When a similar Texas bill that would abolish the requirement that barbers be licensed, Texas state representative Matt Shaheen explains that "the legislation was created to expand employment opportunities. . . . Texans that are willing to join the workforce and compete—especially low-income Texans looking to improve their lives—should face the fewest obstacles possible."[12] Both the Arkansas and Texas bills did not become law.

Why are occupations licensed and why are there such vast differences from state to state? Economists have developed two theories.[13] The first theory focuses on the supply side of the labor market. By making it more difficult for aspiring workers to enter the licensed profession, licensing ensures that fewer individuals have the ability to enter the occupation. This reduction in supply results in the licensed practitioners having the ability to earn higher wages and charge higher prices for their services. Therefore, this theory suggests that welfare declines as a result of occupational licensing. Occupational licensing comes about and is able to persist as a result of concentrated benefits being received by the licensed professionals and individuals that develop a financial stake in the persistence of the regulation (e.g., schools and examining bodies). The costs associated with licensing, on the other hand, are dispersed among a larger number of people, and thus individuals are less passionate about limiting new or eliminating existing occupational licensing legislation. Nobel prize winning economist Milton Friedman advanced this theory specifically in the case of occupational licensing, and the theory was more formally outlined and generalized by economist Mancur Olson.[14] Practitioners will actively attempt to implement licensing as a means of increasing their own benefit.[15] Practitioners' differing abilities to organize into interest groups and influence state legislators will result in significant differences in licensing legislation from state to state

An alternative theory of occupational licensing instead focuses on the demand side of the labor market. Consumers have less information about the qualifications, reputation, and ability of a professional than the professional has about him- or herself. By establishing minimum quality standards, occupational licensing alleviates this gap in information (known as the *asymmetric information problem*). As a result, occupational licensing may potentially increase welfare. This theory was originally developed by Nobel prize winning economist George Akerlof and later applied specifically to occupational licensing by economist Hayne Leland.[16] Berkeley economist Carl Shapiro also noted that occupational licensing may increase the human capital of licensed professionals by raising training levels, which may help to increase the quality of services that consumers receive.[17]

Shapiro's analysis showed that licensing may enhance welfare if professional qualifications and training are not observable, but will reduce welfare if training is observable. Professionals may use excessive investment into human capital as a signaling device—one that tends to benefit consumers who value high quality, but at the expense of consumers who do not value high quality. In addition, certification may potentially be inferior with respect to welfare than both licensing and market competition if professionals overinvest in training to serve as a signaling device.

Other scholars have further expanded on this public choice theory of licensure by estimating market equilibriums in which licensure restricted the workers' ability to supply their labor but also affected the demand for workers on the basis of quality and selection criteria. They find that licensing raised wages and hours but reduced employment and reduced average welfare.[18] Still other researchers studying the relationship between occupational licensing and public choice argue that practitioners favor licensing to reduce competition and keep inflated wages (which accords with the theory of public choice), but that public choice theory has limitations in capturing all of the potential harms of licensure.[19] The researchers also suggest that public choice theory fails to theoretically address potential threats to public health and safety and places a disproportionate emphasis on studying professions in which the justification for licensure is the weakest.

Some scholars have argued that advances in technology have significantly reduced the effects of asymmetric information.[20] Consumers can use websites such as Yelp, Angie's List, Google, and Facebook to gather information about the reputation and ability of professionals before completing a transaction. Research suggests that consumers may value and use consumer ratings in place of licensing status.[21] It is also not clear why requirements for occupational licensing would substantially vary from state to state if regulators were primarily motivated by improving welfare. Further, there is little documented evidence of consumers being the primary lobbyists for new occupational licensing—instead, professional associations (and individuals with financial ties to the regulation) are generally the fiercest defenders and supporters of occupational licensing.[22]

The fact that many licensed professionals fear that licenses will be "worthless" if barriers to entry are removed (the transitional gains trap) also seems to be more consistent with the supply-side theory than the demand-side theory. If licensing were primarily operating as a signaling device, the license should still serve an important purpose of signaling quality despite competition from unlicensed professionals.

Certification represents one regulatory alternative to occupational licensing. The state of California, for example, issues certificates to massage therapists. Individuals without a certificate are free to practice massage therapy, but may not use the protected title "certified massage therapist." Unfortunately, public perception often equates "regulation" with "licensing." In reality, occupational licensing represents the strictest form of occupational regulation—an outright ban on practice unless individuals meet entry requirements. In *Capitalism and Freedom*, Milton Friedman defines less stringent forms of regulation that he refers to as *certification* and *registration*. Certification protects a title but does not prohibit practice. Registration refers to the state collecting contact information from applicants and maintaining a list of practitioners. Each of these less-stringent types of occupational regulation is much less prevalent than licensing. Only 2.3 percent of workers are certified, and registration is likely even less prevalent.[23] Adding to public confusion, states often use all three terms interchangeably in statutes and administrative code—most often states use the terms *certification* and *registration* in place of *licensing*.[24]

The Institute for Justice has identified additional alternatives to occupational licensing besides certification and registration.[25] Figure 1 shows the "inverted pyramid" depicting alternative forms of regulation—beginning with the least-restrictive option at the top (market competition) and the most-restrictive option at the bottom (occupational licensing). The shape of the inverted pyramid represents the restrictiveness of a form of occupational regulation—a larger area within the pyramid corresponds with more freedom for the market to function without restriction.

Market competition is at the top of the pyramid and represents the least intrusive means of regulating the market. At the other extreme, licensure represents the most restrictive government-intervention approach to regulating an industry, in that it does not allow an individual to provide a good or service without the express consent and permission of a government organization. The menu of options shown in figure 1 provides regulators with nine less-costly and less-intrusive means of addressing possible market failures. As noted previously, advances in technology have likely reduced the potential for market failure, and the case that can be made for occupational licensing has weakened over time.

In the sections that follow, we trace the history of licensing and the origins of occupational licensing, before turning to a summary of the existing empirical literature on its effects. We then provide some important visualizations of the scope and effects of licensing before offering a framework for reform.

History of Occupational Licensing

Occupational licensing has a rich and expansive history. Rules governing occupations can be traced back to the Babylonian Code of Hammurabi, circa 1700 BC. These early rules outlined expectations

Figure 1. Alternatives to Occupational Licensing

Source: John K. Ross, "The Inverted Pyramid: 10 Less Restrictive Alternatives to Occupational Licensing" (report, Institute for Justice, November 2017).

about prices for medical services and punishments for negligent practitioners. There is evidence that occupational regulation also existed quite early in China: competency examinations were used as a determinant of job proficiency in small, wealthy circles as early as the Han dynasty, and were expanded in the late seventh century AD by Wu Zetian of the Tang dynasty. These occupational regulations were known as the Imperial Examination. Members of any socioeconomic class in the country could pay an application fee and take a civil service examination; those who passed met the requirements to become a candidate for the state bureaucracy.[26] Later, during the Song dynasty, the program was regularized into a three-tiered system that included local, provincial, and court exams. Over the following few hundred years, the Chinese government expanded rudimentary licensing systems for dentists, physicians, and acupuncturists.[27]

Eventually, the idea of restricting entry into occupations to maintain a standard of performance, ensure quality and safety, and limit competition began to appear in Europe in the 13th and 14th centuries with the popularization and expansion of medieval guilds.[28] Guilds were found within Germany, Naples, Sicily, and Spain. These were often made up of artisans or merchants who oversaw the entry into and practice of their craft or trade within a particular geographic region. These guilds often enforced their authority as a rudimentary professional association through grants of letter patents from monarchs. Gaining entry into these exclusive organizations often involved paying fees and dues and meeting competency requirements.

The foundations of occupational regulation in the United States were laid in the early colonies. Some later developments can be traced to the ideas of Scottish author Adam Smith, commonly regarded the father of modern economics. Smith discussed early forms of occupational regulation in his most well-known work, *An Inquiry into the Nature and Causes of the Wealth of Nations*, such as regulations that limited the number of apprentices a skilled craftsman could undertake and regulations that limited the length of apprenticeship programs.[29] Many of these ideas were incorporated into US state-level regulation concerning apprentices and property rights for many categories of workers such as bakers, leather merchants, lawyers, and innkeepers. During the 19th century some states and localities chose to progress from industry regulation to early forms of licensure that granted the right to practice to approved individuals only; examples can be found applying to barbers, embalmers, farriers, pawnbrokers, and a selection of other professionals.[30] These examples of occupational licensing were rare and hotly debated until a Supreme Court ruling in 1889 upheld the constitutionality of state efforts to regulate the medical profession for the purpose of promoting and maintaining health and safety.[31]

Within the United States, occupational licensing was sparse until early in the Progressive Era (1890–1920)[32] and was often undertaken by national professional organizations—most notably the American Medical Association (AMA) for physicians, which was established in 1847. The publicly stated mission of the AMA was to advance scientific research, improve public health, and create a consistent set of standards for medical education. The AMA also serves as a form of trade union by restricting the number of people who can enter a medical occupation, and therefore indirectly affects wages and limits potential competition by restricting the practice of medicine to exclude other professionals such as chiropractors and barbers.[33] In 1908, the Council on Medical

Education within the AMA contracted the Carnegie Foundation for the Advancement of Teaching to survey the American medical education system with regard to public health and safety. Abraham Flexner was chosen to survey the 155 medical schools that existed at the time within North America, and found substantial differences in curriculum, assessment, and requirements for graduation.[34]

In 1910, Flexner published his findings in a report, titled *Medical Education in the United States and Canada,* that outlined specific recommendations for creating a single model of medical education. Direct consequences of this report included the closure or consolidation of many inefficient or understaffed medical schools, a series of rules stating that a new medical school cannot be created without the permission of the state government, and a set standard of education for those intending to be considered medical practitioners. Flexner's report laid the groundwork for modern licensing, in that it established that all physicians receive at least six years of postsecondary formal instruction in order to practice medicine—instruction that adheres closely to the scientific method and maintains the protocols of scientific research.

The medical doctor field, though the most notable example, was not the only field that adopted a form of occupational regulation and licensure during the Progressive Era. Many states introduced licensing requirements for professionals including accountants, architects, chiropractors, engineers, nurses, optometrists, and plumbers.[35] By the mid-20th century, there were nearly 1,200 state licensing statutes and approximately 5 percent of jobs in the United States required an occupational license.[36]

The Progressive Era marked the beginning of modern occupational licensing systems in the United States. Occupational licensing underwent rapid expansion between 1950 and the late 2010s. There are many views about why this expansion occurred, two of which are referenced in the previous section. In summary, technological advances and increased professional specialization had made it increasingly difficult for consumers to judge differences between service providers.

Proponents of occupational licensing have often argued that they decrease consumer uncertainty and increase demand for licensed services while also providing a wage premium to incentivize individuals to invest in education and experience.[37] Opponents have often argued in response that these laws create unnecessary barriers to entry, limit competition by reducing the equilibrium labor supply, drive firms to locate inefficiently, reduce economic mobility, and raise prices—all while having negligible effects on the quality of products.[38]

The expansion of occupational licensing laws since the mid-20th century can be partially attributed to the structure of the economy. In 1950, when 5 percent of jobs required an occupational license, the US economy primarily consisted of manufacturing.[39] At the time, a large portion of manufacturing did not require specialized college-level education, and many employees were hired directly out of high school and gained training and experience on the job. These manufacturing jobs relied on unions to enact collective bargaining to maintain employee standards, employer-employee relations, and wages. In recent decades, there has been a shift as the US economy has become service-oriented. As service-oriented jobs have expanded in scope, so have the number of jobs with occupational licensing requirements.

During the expansionary period of occupational regulation, the percentage of jobs that require a license has grown substantially—nearly 22 percent of workers require an occupational license as of 2019.[40] In the early 20th century, most licensing requirements were set by state legislatures or by professional organizations. As service-based occupations have become more specialized and diverse, many states have elected to appoint a board of individuals familiar with the industry to review and set the requirements for entry. Almost all the time, individuals on these boards currently work within the industry and have an incentive to limit competition. In addition, the board members may work within institutions that train and educate applicants, giving them a financial incentive to increase education and training requirements. Also, many states do not have sunsetting procedures whereby potentially inefficient or outdated occupational licensing requirements can be reviewed to determine whether they are still necessary for the promotion of public health and safety.[41]

Literature

The appendix provides a list of studies divided by subject category. The first category focuses on how occupational licensing affects quality or the demand for goods and services. In general, these studies have been limited owing to data unavailability and the difficulty associated with measuring quality. The most common profession examined from the mid-1970s to shortly after the turn of the century was the dental industry. One study finds that the likelihood of adverse outcomes is reduced when licensing is present.[42] Two others, however, find little to no evidence of an effect on outcomes in dental hygiene.[43]

Quality studies have also been conducted in some other industries. A study that analyzed seven widely varying licensed occupations finds that licensing has either a negative impact or no impact on the quality of the services provided to consumers.[44] Carl Shapiro provides a comprehensive theoretical model of the quality impacts stemming from occupational licensing and concludes that wealthier consumers who value high-quality goods and services greatly benefit from licensing, but lower-income individuals lose from tougher licensing standards through reductions in access.[45]

Occupational licensing is also likely to have an effect on the wages of professionals. One study finds evidence that licensure generally increases rents for massage therapists rather than affecting the quality of the service provided to consumers.[46] These rents are most commonly depicted through wage increases, for which estimates vary drastically across industries. Significant evidence of wage premiums has been documented for barbers, radiologic technologists, construction workers, dental hygienists, childcare professionals, opticians, and veterinary technicians.[47] Survey data on government-issued occupational licensing are associated with an 11 percent differential in wages after controlling for other differences among of the applicants.[48] These wage premiums and barriers to entry reduce the equilibrium labor supply by an average of 17–27 percent.[49]

Since occupational licensing inspires diametrically opposed reactions among citizens, such regulations often become the topic of political campaigns. A researcher who used data on political spending in state-level elections finds that greater political spending by healthcare interest groups, mainly physicians and nurses, increased the probability that a state would maintain licensing laws that restrict practice.[50] This is interesting because it raises the question of why an organized group of individuals already inside a profession would actively seek regulatory barriers to the entry of new professionals. A part of the rationale for this behavior may be related to a paternalistic argument, according to which those already in the profession and government seek to keep out, in the best interest of the public, those attempting to enter the profession—though what constitutes the public's best interest is hotly debated.[51]

Occupational regulation also commonly has spillover effects on other areas of interest such as student loans. Though these connections remain understudied, they imply a larger problem that needs to be addressed. Recently, the *New York Times* investigated and found that 19 states have begun suspending people's professional licenses for unpaid student loans[52]—loans that students are taking out to meet ever-increasing licensing education and experience requirements.

Licensing can be viewed not only as assurance that services meet quality and safety standards, but also as a signal that the licensed workers themselves offer a threshold level of quality and competence. This signal affects workers' employment opportunities and employers' willingness to hire a diverse set of workers. One 2018 study finds that the information and human capital content supplied by licenses enable firms to rely less on race and gender as predictors of worker productivity.[53] The researchers find that licensing reduces the racial wage gap between white men and black men by 43 percent and the gender wage gap between white men and white women by 36–40 percent. Examining licensing regimes that include good moral character criteria, they find that a license tends to be a positive indicator of nonfelony status, particularly for black men.

It should be noted that additional work by the same authors agrees with previous literature about the costs associated with occupational licensing.[54] It is important to always weigh the potential benefits of occupational licensing against its associated costs, which are well documented and understood. From a policy standpoint, there are likely less costly ways for black men to signal nonfelony status.

Visualization and Discussion

In light of the growing presence of occupational licensing within the US labor force, it is important to be able to visualize how licensing requirements have changed during recent decades. Since many occupational licensing conditions are set at the state level, the fees, education requirements, and examinations can vary drastically among states. Some occupations are subject to multiple levels of regulation. In addition to state-level requirements, there are also a variety of federal requirements, and individual municipalities may maintain their own standards and requirements that apply to workers who practice or operate in their territory. For example, the Federal Aviation Administration maintains federal-level licensing requirements for aviation maintenance technicians, which apply on a national scale.[55] On the other end of the scale, tour guides are required to obtain a license in New York City, but there is no statewide requirement.[56]

This section considers only occupations that are subject to licensing, meaning that workers require government authorization to provide their services legally, in all or a subset of states. As an illustrative example, consider emergency medical technicians (a universally licensed occupation) and bartender. In every state, emergency medical technicians must have government permission to practice emergency medical response and to transport patients by ambulance to medical facilities, and it would be illegal for someone to perform these actions without authorization. On the other hand, in 38 states bartenders may obtain a voluntary certification to serve alcohol, but this certification is not required in any state and individuals can operate in this capacity without the certification.

Visualizing changes in occupational licensing requirements over time is difficult because, until recently, there was no consistent collection of state-level data that asked whether a person was subject to an occupational license or that surveyed known occupations for their entry requirements. Therefore, the discussion of data will be divided into three subsections. The first subsection identifies the growth in occupational licensing for low- and moderate-income professions between 1993 and 2012.[57] The second subsection examines the growth in the frequency and cost of occupational licensing for low- and middle-income professions between 2012 and 2017. Finally, the third subsection discusses current and future data sources and how changes in the Current Population Survey will affect how researchers and policymakers are able to address and analyze the effects of occupational licensing moving forward.

It is important to note that in this discussion of occupational licensing there is often a focus on low- and medium-income occupations. This focus reflects a limitation of the current literature due to data availability constraints. It is often argued, though, that these occupations are the ones that are most important to focus on, since licensing costs constitute a larger percentage of household income for lower- and middle-income households, and losing time to fulfill training and experience requirements can potentially disadvantage or harm households that rely on lower-paying occupations.

1993–2012

The study of occupational licensing drastically changed with the introduction of a publication from the Institute for Justice, titled *License to Work* (*LTW*). *LTW* presents the state-level occupational licensing requirements for 102 professions across all states and the District of Columbia.[58] It provided a benchmark for researchers to use as they sought to compare occupational licensing requirements at the state level. Before *LTW* was published in 2012, very little data about licensing at the national level was readily available.

In 2018, one of us (Edward Timmons) coauthored a study that used *LTW* to study economic mobility.[59] We used 1993 data from the *Professional and Occupational Licensing Directory*[60] and compared these data to the data for occupations that were listed in the 2012 *LTW*. Our study became one of the first analyses of growth in low-income occupational licensing. Though it does not provide an exhaustive list of all licensed professions, our study's comparison serves as an important basis point, offering a perspective from which to track the growth of licensing regulations over time.

Figure 2 reproduces the original map of growth in licensed occupations from that 2018 study. Growth in the 1990s and shortly after the turn of the century was not limited to a single geographic region, and states differed drastically in the number of new occupational licenses they enacted—from a low of 15 in Kentucky to 59 in Louisiana. We also found that within the 1993–2012 period occupational licensing is associated with substantial negative effects on economic mobility within states.

Figure 2. Newly Licensed Occupations Between 1993 and 2012

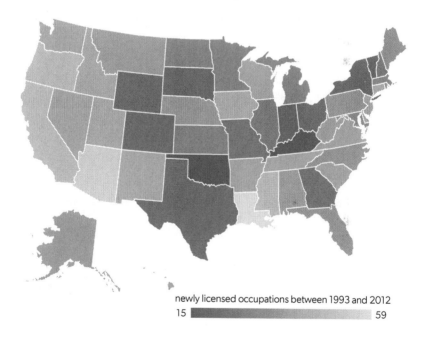

newly licensed occupations between 1993 and 2012

15 ▬▬▬▬▬▬▬▬▬▬ 59

Sources: Created using data from table 1 in Edward Timmons et al., "Assessing Growth in Occupational Licensing of Low-Income Occupations: 1993–2012," *Journal of Entrepreneurship and Public Policy* 7, no. 2 (2018): 180. Data from 2012 are from Dick M. Carpenter II et al., *License to Work: A National Study of Burdens from Occupational Licensing*, 1st ed. (Arlington, VA: Institute for Justice, May 2012); 1993 data were collected from David P. Bianco, ed., *Professional and Occupational Licensing Directory: A Descriptive Guide to State and Federal Licensing, Registration, and Certification Requirements* (Detroit: Gale Research, 1993).

2012–2017

License to Work was updated and rereleased in 2017.[61] Since the data collection and definition methodologies changed slightly between the 2012 and 2017 editions, there are limitations to the comparability of the aggregate state measures within these reports over time. Therefore, this subsection will discuss an overview of occupational licensing in 2017, as well as some observations about occupations for which data were collected consistently over this five-year period.

Table 1 presents summary statistics for occupational licensing costs across states for the 102 occupations included in the 2017 *LTW* update. One of the most notable and well-known costs of occupational licenses are fees. Comparing average fees is not the perfect way to capturing state variation, but it does provide a rough sketch of the regulatory environment. Figure 3 depicts the average fees to acquire a license in each state, and these vary drastically. Nevada is the most expensive state—on average, an occupational license costs $704. In Nebraska, the least expensive state, the average fee is $76. The average cost of a license across all states is $268.14; approximately two-thirds of states have averages within $113.77 above or below this average.

Table 1. Summary Statistics of 2017 Occupational Licensing Requirements

Requirement	Mean	Standard deviation	Minimum	Maximum
Number of 102 occupations licensed	54.12	15.21	26	77
Average fees	$268.14	$113.77	$76.00	$704.00
Average days to complete education and experience	373.69	199.54	117.20	987.70
Average number of exams	1.84	1.01	0	4

Source: Dick M. Carpenter II et al., *License to Work: A National Study of Burdens from Occupational Licensing*, 2nd ed. (Arlington, VA: Institute for Justice, November 2017).

Figure 3. Average Fee to Obtain an Occupational License, 2017

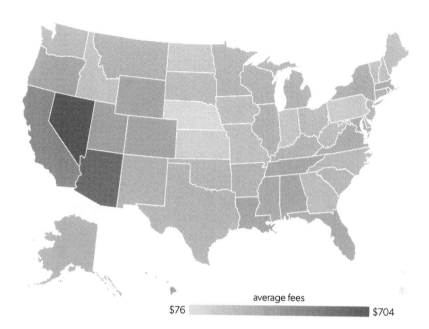

Source: Dick M. Carpenter II et al., *License to Work: A National Study of Burdens from Occupational Licensing,* 2nd ed. (Arlington, VA: Institute for Justice, November 2017).

Table 1 also contains information on the number of the 102 occupations that are licensed within each state, the number of exams required to obtain a license, and the days required to complete mandated training and experience.

Figure 4 is a map depicting the length of time mandated to fulfill licensing requirements. One of the first interesting things to note is the similarities between average fees (figure 3) and education requirements (figure 4), since these measures tend to be correlated and if a state has a high cost in one, it often has a high cost in both. The amount of time needed to complete the education and experience requirements for a license in the United States, in 2017, averaged 373.69 days, or slightly over a year. The length of time necessary to fulfill these requirements can vary widely, from 117.20 days on average in Pennsylvania to 987.70 days in Hawaii (almost three years).

Figure 4. Average Number of Days to Complete Education and Experience Requirements for an Occupational License, 2017

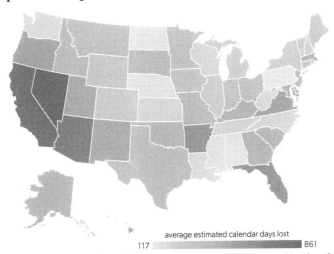

average estimated calendar days lost

117   861

Source: Dick M. Carpenter II et al., *License to Work: A National Study of Burdens from Occupational Licensing*, 2nd ed. (Arlington, VA: Institute for Justice, November 2017).

Professions that require licensing vary from state to state. For example, table 2 lists some of the many professions that require an occupational license. Some occupations are licensed in every state, such as those of bus drivers and emergency medical technicians. But many other licenses exist in only a selection of states. A few licensing regimes are entirely unique, in that only one state has enacted legislation to subject that profession to an occupational license. Some interesting examples include florists in Louisiana and home entertainment installers in Connecticut.

Since the 2012 edition of *LTW* differs in collection methodology from the 2017 edition, we can't make direct comparisons of the state averages in fees or education requirements. It can be observed, however, that many professions saw an increase in the number of states that required occupational licensing between 2012 and 2017. For example, childcare workers now require a license in an additional 11 states, crane operators now require a license in an additional 14 states, and earth drillers are now required to obtain a license in every state—a license that involves costs ranging from $50 to $1,000 and up to six years of education requirements.

Table 2. Examples of Licensing Prevalence

Licensed in all states	Licensed in 26–49 states	Licensed in 2–25 states	Licensed in only one state
barber	animal breeder	animal control officer	conveyor operator
bus driver	athletic trainer	animal trainer	florist
cosmetologist	auctioneer	bartender	forest worker
earth driller	worker who runs bill collection agency	carpenter, commercial	home entertainment installer
emergency medical technician	carpenter, residential	cement finishing contractor, commercial	psychiatric aide
pest control applicator	cement finishing contractor, residential	crane operator	social and human service assistant
school bus driver	childcare home operator	dental assistant	
truck driver	high school head coach	dietetic technician	
vegetation pesticide applicator	door repair contractor, residential	door repair contractor, commercial	
	drywall installation contractor, residential	drywall installation contractor, commercial	
	fire alarm installer	electrical helper	
	fisher, commercial	farm labor contractor	
	floor sander contractor, residential	floor sander contractor, commercial	
	gaming cage worker	funeral attendant	
	gaming dealer	insulation contractor, commercial	
	gaming supervisor	interior designer	
	glazier contractor	interpreter, sign language	
	HVAC contractor	locksmith	
	insulation contractor, residential	log scaler	
	iron/steel contractor	nursery worker	
	landscape contractor	optician	
	makeup artist	packer	
	manicurist	painting contractor, commercial	
	mason contractor	paving contractor, commercial	
	massage therapist	psychiatric technician	
	midwife	still machine setter	
	milk sampler	taxi driver	
	mobile home installer	teacher assistant	
	painting contractor, residential	terrazzo contractor	
	paving contractor, residential	title examiner	
	pharmacy technician	worker who runs travel agency	
	pipeline contractor	tree trimmer	
	preschool teacher	upholsterer	
	security alarm installer	weigher	
	security guard	wildlife control operator	
	shampooer		
	sheet metal contractor		
	skin care specialist		
	slot supervisor		
	taxidermist		
	travel guide		
	veterinary technician		

Source: Dick M. Carpenter II et al., *License to Work: A National Study of Burdens from Occupational Licensing*, 2nd ed. (Arlington, VA: Institute for Justice, November 2017).

Looking Forward

As of September 2020 there are a few great resources available that supply further information on occupational licensing. The Knee Center for the Study of Occupational Regulation at Saint Francis University, founded in 2016, provides insight and data about the occupational licensing requirements for a variety of occupations across socioeconomic classes. Likewise, as noted previously, the Institute for Justice has published the *License to Work* study, which provides summary statistics about the licensing costs of 102 occupations across all states. Additionally, since 2015 the Current Population Survey has incorporated questions meant to identify individuals with professional certifications or occupational licenses. For instance, the survey asks respondents whether they currently have an active professional certification or a state or industry license, whether the certification or license was issued by a government agency (and at which level of government), and whether the certification or license is required for their job.

There are also a range of new federal data sources beyond the Current Population Survey available to students and policymakers.[62] These include the Survey of Income and Program Participation, which in 2008 asked questions regarding professional certification and the Baccalaureate and Beyond which conducts four-year follow-up surveys on these 2008 degree recipients. The National Center for Education Statistics (within the US Department of Education) also provides the Beginning Postsecondary Students Longitudinal Study for 2012 and 2014. And the 2012 Education Longitudinal Study provides eight-year follow-ups on high school graduates from 2004.[63] These growing sources of data will assist legislatures to develop efficient policies and improve economic welfare.

Pathways for Reform

Momentum for reform of occupational licensing began to build up following the publication of Benjamin Shimberg, Barbara Esser, and Daniel Kruger's *Occupational Licensing* in 1972.[64] The book reports the findings of a five-year study examining occupational licensing and notes a litany of problems with the status quo. Interest continued into 1980, when a conference organized by the American Enterprise Institute led to the publication of an edited volume on licensure.[65] Interest from the academic community and the public policy community mostly languished for the next 20 years. Owing to a number of published works by economist Morris Kleiner (including three books), interest resumed in 2000. On the public policy front, the publication of the Obama White House report on licensing was also key.[66]

From 1973 to 2013, only eight occupations were successfully delicensed.[67] From 2011 to 2016, twelve states attempted to delicense groups of occupations.[68] Perhaps the occupation for which deregulation efforts have been most successful is hair braiding. In 2005, twenty-nine states required hair braiders to obtain a full cosmetology license. As of September 2020, only seven states still maintain this requirement.[69]

Instead of devoting efforts to delicensing individual occupations or groups of occupations, several states have successfully implemented comprehensive reforms. These reforms can be separated into three broad categories: (1) the Right to Earn a Living Act, (2) executive oversight, and (3) mandatory sunset review.

The Right to Earn a Living Act (passed in Tennessee in 2016 and in Arizona in 2017)[70] recognizes that citizens have a fundamental right to work that takes precedence over existing occupational licensing law. It gives citizens the opportunity to sue the state if they believe that licensing laws are infringing on this fundamental right. In March 2017, the law resulted in a change in licensing requirements for behavioral health specialists in Arizona.[71] As of September 2020, there have been no successful lawsuits in either state that have led to the complete removal of licensing laws.[72]

Executive oversight initiates a review process by a state's executive branch. Mississippi passed this type of reform in 2017.[73] An executive oversight law grants review power for all licensing rules to the state's governor, attorney general, and secretary of state. If two of these three individuals object to a new licensing rule, the rule can be blocked or vetoed. As of September 2020, we are not aware of any instances in which Mississippi's executive branch exercised this new authority to block licensing legislation.[74]

A number of states have instituted, by either legislation or executive order, a mandatory sunset review model. Under this type of reform, a mandatory review process is established that subjects existing occupational licensing to reviews. The frequency of these reviews varies depending on the state. Louisiana, Nebraska, and Oklahoma implemented this type of reform in 2018. Both Idaho and Ohio implemented it in 2019.[75]

There is a fourth type of reform that, as of early 2020, has not been implemented in any state. In October 2018, Governor Susana Martinez of New Mexico issued an executive order permitting consumers to seek service from unlicensed professionals.[76] Essentially, the order would transform existing occupational licenses into voluntary certification. Courts made the determination that legislation would be needed to make the change, and no such legislation has yet been proposed in New Mexico.[77] Legislation has been put forward in West Virginia,[78] but (as of September 2020) has not been approved.

It is too early to surmise what type of reform is most effective. Up until the past five years, the general trend nationwide has been an increase in the scale and scope of occupational licensing. A number of states are currently engaged in reform efforts and soon there will be data available to evaluate the effectiveness of these different types of reform to inform policymakers and provide a template for implementing future reform.

Appendix: Table of Occupational Licensing Studies

Quality Studies

Study	Outcome	Study Group	Results
Morris Kleiner and Robert Kudrle, "Does Regulation Affect Economic Outcomes? The Case of Dentistry," *Journal of Law and Economics* 43, no. 2 (2000): 547–82.	quality, prices, wages	dentists	There is no improvement in outcomes associated with licensing, prices are raised for consumers, and wages are raised for practitioners.
Hayne Leland, "Quacks, Lemons, and Licensing: A Theory of Minimum Quality Standards," *Journal of Political Economy* 87, no. 6 (1979): 1328–46.	quality	multiple	Licensing requirements are not the best way to increase quality, but do result in some improvement. When industry sets licensing standards, they are too high.
Daniel Hogan, "The Effectiveness of Licensing," *Law and Human Behavior* 7, no. 2–3 (1983): 117–38.	quality	multiple	Licensing does not increase quality. Boards fail to discipline practitioners with action against unlicensed members. Possible negative side effects result from limited supply.
Dick M. Carpenter II, "Testing the Utility of Licensing Evidence from a Field Experiment on Occupational Regulation," *Journal of Applied Business and Economics* 13, no. 2 (2012): 28–41.	quality	florists	Regulation does not result in a significant difference in quality.
Edward Timmons and Anna Mills, "Bringing the Effects of Occupational Licensing into Focus: Optician Licensing in the United States," *Eastern Economic Journal* 44, no. 1 (2018): 69–83.	quality, wages	opticians	Licensing results in as much as 16.9% in increased wages. No increase in quality based on observed malpractice insurance premiums.
John Barrios, "Occupational Licensing and Accountant Quality: Evidence from the 150-Hour Rule" (Research Brief No. 136, Cato Institute, 2018).	quality, wages, labor supply	accountants	An increase in education requirements does not result in higher quality, does lower supply of accountants, and increases wages.
Sidney Carroll and Robert Gaston, "Occupational Licensing and the Quality of Service: An Overview," Law and Human Behavior 7, no. 2–3 (1983): 139–46.	quality	several	There is a strong negative association between occupational licensing and quality of service received.

Study	Outcome	Study Group	Results
James Shilling and C. Sirmam, "The Effects of Occupational Licensing on Complaints against Real Estate Agents," Journal of Real Estate Research 3, no. 2 (1988): 1–9.	quality, competition	real estate agents	Restrictions on entry improve the quality of services but have significant anticompetitive effects.
Joshua Angrist and Jonathan Guryan, "Does Teacher Testing Raise Teacher Quality? Evidence from State Certification Requirements," Economics of Education Review 27, no. 5 (2008): 483–503.	quality, wages, demographics	teachers	State-mandated teacher testing is associated with higher wages; there is no evidence of quality improvement. Hispanics have lower test scores, resulting in a lower ratio of Hispanic teachers.
A. Frank Adams, "Occupational Licensing of Cosmetologists and Midwives: Two Empirical Studies on the Effects of Regulation" (PhD diss., Auburn University, 1996).	prices, quantities consumed, consumer welfare	midwifes and cosmetologists	Regulation increases prices and decreases quantity consumed; this results in detrimental consumer welfare effects.
Roger Feldman and James Begun, "The Welfare Cost of Quality Changes Due to Professional Regulation," Journal of Industrial Economics 34, no. 1 (1985): 17–32.	profits, quality, consumer welfare	optometrists	Increased regulation increases profits and quality.
Robert Jackson, "Post-graduate Educational Requirements and Entry into the CPA Profession," Journal of Labor Research 27, no. 1 (2006): 101–14.	quality, labor supply	accountants	Increasing education requirements for a license results in higher entrance exam scores but fewer exam takers.
Adriana Kugler and Robert Sauer, "Doctors without Borders? Relicensing Requirements and Negative Selection in the Market for Physicians," Journal of Labor Economics 23, no. 3 (2005): 437–65.	quality, wages	physicians	Relicensing requirements increase wages but decrease quality of service.
Carl Shapiro, "Investment, Moral Hazard, and Occupational Licensing," Review of Economic Studies 53, no. 5 (1986): 843–62.	quality, moral hazard, investment	multiple	Licensing benefits consumers who value quality highly, not those who do not. Licensing may raise total surplus if sellers' investments are not observable, but is Pareto-worsening if training levels are observable.

Study	Outcome	Study Group	Results
Marcus Dunn and Thomas Hall, "An Empirical Analysis of the Relationship between CPA Examination Candidate Attributes and Candidate Performance," Accounting Review 59, no. 4 (1984): 674–89.	licensing exams, quality	accountants	Scholastic aptitude test scores, accounting GPA, accounting hours completed, school attended, hours of self-study, and completion of CPA review course are significantly associated with CPA exam performance.
Chi-Wen Lee, Chiawen Liu, and Taychang Wang, "The 150-Hour Rule," Journal of Accounting and Economics 27, no. 2 (1999): 203–28.	quality, wages, consumer welfare	auditors	An increase of licensing requirements results in higher wages; quality may decrease; more grandfathered CPAs elect to enter audit market.
Deborah Haas-Wilson, "The Effect of Commercial Practice Restrictions: The Case of Optometry," Journal of Law and Economics 29, no. 1 (1986): 165–86.	quality, consumer welfare, prices	optometrists	Increased commercial practice restrictions increased prices for eye exams and eyeglasses by 5%–13%, with no change in quality.
Ronald Bond et al., "Staff Report on Effects of Restrictions on Advertising and Commercial Practice in the Profession: The Case of Optometry," Federal Trade Commission, Bureau of Economics, 1980.	quality	optometrists	Looser restrictions do not decrease quality.
Morris Kleiner, Licensing Occupations: Ensuring Quality or Restricting Competition? (Kalamazoo, MI: W.E. Upjohn Institute for Employment Research, 2006).	quality	multiple	Overview of quality related occupational licensing studies and the theoretical foundations of licensure
Darwyyn Deyo, "Licensing and Service Quality: Evidence Using Yelp Consumer Reviews" (working paper presented at San Jose State University, 2017).	quality	barbers, cosmetologists, manicurists, massage therapists	In states with licensing exams there is less competition, diminishing returns from licensure, and lower overall quality.

Wage Studies

Study	Outcome	Study Group	Results
Edward Timmons and Robert Thornton, "The Effects of Licensing on the Wages of Radiologic Technologists," *Journal of Labor Research* 29, no. 4 (2008): 333–46.	wages	radiologic technologists	Licensed radiologic technologists earn 3.3% more than those where licensing is not needed. The gap increases to 6.9% when controlling for endogeneity.
Morris Kleiner and Alan Krueger, "Analyzing the Extent and Influence of Occupational Licensing on the Labor Market," *Journal of Labor Economics* 31, no. 2 (2013): S173–S202.	wages	entire labor force	Licensees earn 18% higher wages, but government certification has a smaller effect.
Mario Pagliero, "The Impact of Potential Labor Supply on Licensing Exam Difficulty," *Labour Economics* 25 (2013): 141–52.	exam difficulty, wages	lawyers	A 1.0% increase in exam difficulty implies a 1.7% increase in median entry-level salaries.
Morris Kleiner and Alan Krueger, "The Prevalence and Effects of Occupational Licensing," *British Journal of Industrial Relations* 48, no. 4 (2010): 1–12.	wages, unions	all	Licensing increases wages by 15%; licensing and union membership increase wages by 24%; licensing does not reduce wage dispersion.
Robert Thornton and Edward Timmons, "Licensing One of the World's Oldest Professions: Massage," *Journal of Law and Economics* 56, no. 2 (2013): 371–88.	wages, labor supply	massage therapists	Licensing increases wages by 16.2% and reduces market size; there is less evidence that certification has such effects.
Edward Timmons and Robert Thornton, "The Licensing of Barbers in the USA," *British Journal of Industrial Relations* 48, no. 4 (2010): 740–57.	wages	barbers	Licensing provisions may increase wages for barbers by between 11% and 22%.
Peter Blair and Bobby Chung, "Job Market Signaling through Occupational Licensing" (NBER Working Paper No. 24791, National Bureau of Economic Research, Cambridge, MA, 2018).	wages, discrimination	multiple	When a profession is licensed, characteristics such as race and gender have less influence on wages and result in smaller wage gaps than in unlicensed areas.
Beth Redbird, "The New Closed Shop? The Economic and Structural Effects of Occupational Licensure," *American Sociological Review* 82, no. 3 (2017): 600–24.	competition, wages	multiple	Licensing does not limit competition, does not increase wages, creates institutional mechanisms that increase entry into occupation, and causes quality to stagnate.

Study	Outcome	Study Group	Results
Morris Kleiner and Evgeny Vorotnikov, "Analyzing Occupational Licensing among the States," *Journal of Regulatory Economics* 52, no. 2 (2017): 132–58.	wages, wage inequality, regional analysis	all	There are no regional patterns in the distribution of occupational licensing, and there is considerable variation across states in licensing's influence on earnings. There is a nationwide increase in wages of 11% when an occupation is licensed.
Maury Gittleman, Mark Klee, and Morris Kleiner, "Analyzing the Labor Market Outcomes of Occupational Licensing," *Industrial Relations: A Journal of Economy and Society* 57, no. 1 (2017): 57–100.	wages, employment levels, health	multiple	Licensing results in higher pay, a greater likelihood of being employed, and a higher probability of receiving employer-sponsored health insurance.
Edward Timmons, Jason Hockenberry, and Christine Durrance, "More Battles among Licensed Occupations: Estimating the Effects of Scope of Practice and Direct Access on the Chiropractic, Physical Therapist, and Physician Labor Market" (Mercatus Research, Mercatus Center at George Mason University, Arlington, VA, 2016).	wages, hours worked	chiropractors	An expansion of chiropractic scope caused in increase in chiropractors' wages and a slight reduction in their hours worked.
Morris Kleiner and Kyoung Park, "Battles among Licensed Occupations: Analyzing Government Regulations on Labor Market Outcomes for Dentists and Hygienists" (NBER Working Paper No. 16560, National Bureau of Economic Research, Cambridge, MA, 2010).	wages, employment growth	dentists and dental hygienists	In states that allow hygienists to be self-employed, they have 10% higher earnings and dentists have lower earnings and employment growth.
William Moore, Douglas Pearce, and R. Mark Wilson, "The Regulation of Occupations and the Earnings of Women," *Journal of Human Resources* 16, no. 3 (1981): 366–83.	wages	women	Licensing increases women's earnings by 20% per hour. Certification is not associated with a premium for women.
Maury Gittleman and Morris Kleiner, "Wage Effects of Unionization and Occupational Licensing Coverage in the United States," *ILR Review* 69, no. 1 (2015): 142–72.	unions, wages	multiple	Unions provide greater wage increases than licensing.

Study	Outcome	Study Group	Results
William White, "The Impact of Occupational Licensure of Clinical Laboratory Personnel," *Journal of Human Resources* 13, no. 1 (1978): 91–102.	wages, labor supply	laboratory personnel	Recent licensure laws have no effect on wages or employment, but older laws increase both.
Dean Lueck, Reed Olsen, and Michael Ransom, "Market and Regulatory Forces in the Pricing of Legal Services," *Journal of Regulatory Economics* 7, no. 1 (1995): 63–83.	wages, consumer welfare	attorneys	Licensing restrictions for attorneys do not increase the price of services or incomes for attorneys; market forces are more significant.
James Schaefer and Michael Zimmer, "Occupational Licensure in the Accounting Profession Effects of Public Regulation on Accountants Earning," *Journal of Applied Business Research* 11, no. 2 (1995): 9–16.	wages	accountants	Additional licensing requirements raise wages; decreased requirements lower wages.
U.S. Department of the Treasury Office of Economic Policy, Council of Economic Advisers, and the Department of Labor. "Occupational Licensing: A Framework for Policymakers". The White House (2015)	number of licensed professions, wages, prices	all	There has been a fivefold increase in the rate of US workers requiring a license since the 1950s. Licensing results in higher wages and higher prices. There are great variation in licensed professions among states; fewer than 60 occupations are covered by all states.
Maya Federman, David Harrington, and Kathy Krynski, "The Impact of State Licensing Regulations on Low-Skilled Immigrants: The Case of Vietnamese Manicurists," *American Economic Review* 96, no. 2 (2006): 237–47.	immigration, wages	Vietnamese immigrant manicurists	Greater language proficiency requirements increase the difficulty of assimilation, lower wages for the unlicensed, and raise wages for the licensed.
Morris Kleiner, "Occupational Licensing," *Journal of Economic Perspectives* 14, no. 4 (2000): 189–202.	policy, wages	multiple	Licensing may increase income inequality.
Mark Gius, "The Effects of Occupational Licensing on Wages: A State-Level Analysis," *International Journal of Applied Economics* 12, no. 20 (2016): 30–45.	wages	multiple	Licensing increases state-level wages for childcare workers, opticians, and veterinary technicians; no other studied occupations show statistically significant increases.

Study	Outcome	Study Group	Results
Edward Timmons and Robert Thornton, "There and Back Again: The De-licensing and Re-licensing of Barbers in Alabama," *British Journal of Industrial Relations* 57, no. 4 (2019): 764-790.	deregulation, wages, labor supply	barbers and cosmetologists	After deregulation, barbers' and cosmetologists' wages and labor force numbers shrank. Deregulation results in a small increase in barbershops and a decrease in cosmetology shops.
Alex Maurizi, "Occupational Licensing and the Public Interest," *Journal of Political Economy* 82, no. 2 (1974): 399–413.	wages, pass rates, excess demand	multiple	Increases in excess demand generates a decrease in the pass rate set by licensing boards, prolonging high incomes.
Jeffrey Perloff, "The Impact of Licensing Laws on Wage Changes in the Construction Industry," *Journal of Law and Economics* 23, no. 2 (1980): 409–28.	wages	workers in manufacturing and construction	There is evidence of inequalities resulting from regulation between manufacturing and construction wages.

Labor Supply Studies

Study	Outcome	Study Group	Results
Morris Kleiner and Evan Soltas, "A Welfare Analysis of Occupational Licensing in U.S. States" (NBER Working Paper No. 26383, National Bureau of Economic Research, Cambridge, MA, 2019).	labor supply	483 occupations	Licensing raises wages but reduces employment on the margin. There is an average welfare loss of 12% of occupational surplus.
Robert Thornton and Andrew Weintraub, "Licensing in the Barbering Profession," *ILR Review* 32, no. 2 (1979): 242–49.	labor supply	barbers	Minimum education requirements, barber school hours required, and months of apprenticeship required have had little or no significant effect on the number of entrants.
Joshua Hall and Shree Pokharel, "Barber Licensure and the Supply of Barber Shops: Evidence from U.S. States," *Cato Journal* 36, no. 3 (2016): 647–57.	labor supply	barbers	The number of exams required for a license is negatively related to the number of barbershops; no other state-level regulations are associated with fewer barbershops.
Edward Timmons and Catherine Konieczny, "Untangling Hair Braider Deregulation in Virginia," *Cato Journal* 38, no. 3 (2018): 679–99.	labor supply	hair braiders	Deregulation increased labor supply growth by 7%.

Study	Outcome	Study Group	Results
Marek Zapletal, "The Effects of Occupational Licensing: Evidence from Business-Level Data," *British Journal of Industrial Relations*, forthcoming.	labor supply, prices, mobility, training facilities and instructors	cosmetology	Licensing regulation does not reduce the number of practitioners or consumer prices, but lowers individual rates of entry and exit. States with more stringent licensing requirements regarding the number of instructors and the size of training facilities increase barriers to entry for training schools, but no with effect on instructor pay.
Dick M. Carpenter II and E. Frank Stephenson, "The 150-Hour Rule as a Barrier to Entering Public Accountancy," *Journal of Labor Research* 27, no. 1 (2006): 115–26.	labor supply	accountants	Increased licensing requirements result in a 60% decrease in candidates seated.
Jeff Boone and Teddy Coe, "The 150-Hour Requirement and Changes in the Supply of Accounting Undergraduates: Evidence from a Quasi-experiment," *Issues in Accounting Education* 17, no. 3 (2002): 253–68.	labor supply	accountants	38% of the decrease in accounting graduates can be attributed to the increase of education requirements to 150 course hours.
A. Frank Adams, John Jackson, and Robert Ekelund, "Occupational Licensing in a 'Competitive' Labor Market: The Case of Cosmetology," *Journal of Labor Research* 23, no. 2 (2002): 261–78.	labor supply, consumer welfare, wages	cosmetologists	An increase in licensing regulation results in a smaller workforce, greater wages, and additional deadweight losses.
Alicia Plemmons, "Occupational Licensing Effects on Firm Entry and Employment" (Working Paper no. 2019.008, Center for Growth and Opportunity at Utah State University, 2019).	labor supply, employment	low- and moderate-income occupations	States with greater occupational licensing requirements have decreased employment and firm presence.

Migration and Mobility Studies

Study	Outcome	Study Group	Results
Janna Johnson and Morris Kleiner, "Is Occupational Licensing a Barrier to Interstate Migration?" *American Economics Journal: Economic Policy* 12, no. 3 (2020): 347-373	interstate migration	multiple	Individuals are less likely to migrate across states when they face high relicensure costs. Costs.

Study	Outcome	Study Group	Results
Peter Pashigian, "Occupational Licensing and the Interstate Mobility of Professionals," *Journal of Law and Economics* 22, no. 1 (1979): 1–25.	mobility	lawyers	Lower mobility of lawyers is likely due to licensing, not investment in state-specific law.
Arlene Holen, "Effects of Professional Licensing Arrangements on Interstate Labor Mobility and Resource Allocation," *Journal of Political Economy* 73 (1965): 492–92.	labor supply, mobility	multiple	Licensing results in less interstate mobility and lowers the supply of workers in field.
Brian Meehan, "The Impact of Licensing Requirements on Industrial Organization and Labor: Evidence from the U.S. Private Security Market," *International Review of Law and Economics* 42 (2015): 113–21.	mobility	security guards	Increases in licensing requirements for individual private security guards and for security firms reduced the number of firms and increased the size of existing licensed firms.

Entrepreneurship Studies

Study	Outcome	Study Group	Results
Susanne Prantl and Alexandra Spitz-Oener, "How Does Entry Regulation Influence Entry into Self-Employment and Occupational Mobility?," *Economics of Transition and Institutional Change* 17, no. 4 (2009): 769–802.	self-employment levels, occupational mobility	German workers	Entry regulation reduces self-employment and occupational mobility.
Stephen Slivinski, "Weighing Down the Bootstraps: The Heavy Burden of Occupational Licensing on Immigrant Entrepreneurs" (Policy Report No. 2017-01, Center for the Study of Economic Liberty at Arizona State University, 2017).	immigrants, entrepreneurship	immigrant vs. native-born entrepreneurs	States with lighter licensing burdens had 14% higher immigrant entrepreneurship rates, while states with greater burdens had 11% lower rates.
Andrew van Stel, David Storey, and Roy Thurik, "The Effect of Business Regulations on Nascent and Young Business Entrepreneurship," *Small Business Economics* 28, no. 2–3 (2007): 171–86.	entrepreneurship, regulations	39 countries	Labor market regulations and minimum capital requirements lower entrepreneurship rates, while other administrative factors do not.

Summary Literature

Study	Type of Research	Occupations Studied	Contribution
Alex Bryson and Morris Kleiner, "Re-examining Advances in Occupational Licensing Research: Issues and Policy Implications," *British Journal of Industrial Relations* 57, no. 4 (2019): 721–31.	history	all	Available data set post-2010 and surveys eight papers.
Ryan Nunn and Gabriel Scheffler, "Occupational Licensing and the Limits of Public Choice Theory," *Administrative Law Review Accord* 4, no. 2 (2019): 25–41.	theory	all	Comparative analysis of public choice arguments of licensure.
Robert Thornton and Edward Timmons, "The De-licensing of Occupations in the United States," *Monthly Labor Review*, May 2015.	examining delicensing movements	various	Comparative overview of delicensing movements.
George Stigler, "The Theory of Economic Regulation," *Bell Journal of Economics and Management Science* 2, no. 1 (1971): 3–21.	theory	all	Theoretical background.
Edward Timmons et al., "Assessing Growth in Occupational Licensing of Low-Income Occupations: 1993–2012," *Journal of Entrepreneurship and Public Policy* 7, no. 2 (2018): 178–218.	number of occupations licensed	low- and moderate-income occupations	States licensed an average of 32 additional low- or moderate-income occupations in 2012 than in 1993. The high was 59, the low was 15.
Morris Kleiner, "Reforming Occupational Licensing Policies" *Discussion Paper 2015-01,* The Hamilton Project, (2015).	licensing reforms	multiple	Theoretical background.
Morris Kleiner, "Life, Limbs, and Licensing: Occupational Regulation, Wages, and Workplace Safety of Electricians, 1992–2007," *Monthly Labor Review* (United States Bureau of Labor Statistics), January 2014.	labor safety	electricians	Regulation's impact on deaths and injury is statistically significant.
Jeffrey Pfeffer, "Administrative Regulation and Licensing: Social Problem or Solution?," *Social Problems* 21, no. 4 (2014): 468–79.	review of studies: price, labor supply, wages	multiple	Licensing increases prices, restricts entry, and increases wages.

Study	Type of Research	Occu- pations Studied	Contribution
Marc Law and Sukkoo Kim, "Specialization and Regulation: The Rise of Professionals and the Emergence of Occupational Licensing Regulation," *Journal of Economic History* 65, no. 3 (2005): 723–56.	history	multiple	Empirical clarification of recent literature.
Morris Kleiner, "The Influence of Occupational Licensing and Regulation" *IZA World of Labor* (Institute of Labor Economics), October 2017.	literature review	all	Licensing may increase wages and benefits but also reduces access to work without providing clear benefits for consumers.
Paul Larkin Jr., "Public Choice Theory and Occupational Licensing," *Harvard Journal of Law and Public Policy* 39, no. 1 (2016): 209–331.	policy and law	all	Legal justifications for occupational licenses and criticisms.
Elizabeth Graddy and Michael Nichol, "Structural Reforms and Licensing Board Performance," *American Politics Quarterly* 18, no. 3 (1990): 376–400.	policy review	4 health occupations	Review of relevant literature.
Robin Roberts and James Kurtenbach, "State Regulation and Professional Accounting Education Reforms: An Empirical Test of Regulatory Capture Theory," *Journal of Accounting and Public Policy* 17, no. 3 (1998): 209–26.	policy	accountants	The adoption of a 150-hour accounting education requirement is related to individual states' CPA lobby strengths.
Simon Rottenberg, "The Economics of Occupational Licensing," *Aspects of Labor Economics* 1962, 3–22.	theory	multiple	Theoretical foundation.
Milton Friedman, *Capitalism and Freedom* (Chicago: University of Chicago Press, 1962).	policy, theory	multiple	Theoretical foundation.
Jason Jensen, "An Examination of the Burdens Faced by Entrepreneurs at Start-Up and Five Years Later," *Journal of Entrepreneurship and Public Policy* 4, no. 2 (2015): 152–70.	business success rates	multiple	Regulatory factors and taxes matter little early on, but taxes become a larger burden later. Capital and labor supply matter a lot early on; permitting and licensing matter later on.

Gender, Race, and Earnings: The Divergent Effect of Occupational Licensing on the Distribution of Earnings and on Access to the Economy

Kathleen M. Sheehan and Diana W. Thomas

Regulation, while usually well intended, can have detrimental effects on overall economic activity because it creates barriers to entry for firms and workers and because it hinders economic activity more generally. Economies that are more heavily regulated tend to have lower rates of new firm starts, lower levels of overall employment, and lower economic growth overall.[1] In addition, regulation has been shown to have disproportionately negative effects on low-income households and workers.[2] Price increases resulting from regulation are borne disproportionately by low-income consumers,[3] lower-wage professions tend to suffer decreasing wages as a result of regulation,[4] and states with higher levels of regulation tend to have higher levels of poverty.[5] Given the differential effects of regulation on different socioeconomic classes, an obvious question is whether regulation has differential and potentially negative effects on different genders and races as well. In this chapter, we explore this question in more detail by reviewing the literature on occupational licensing—a type of labor-market regulation—and its effect on gender and race wage gaps.

Occupational Licensing, Gender, and Race

More than a quarter of all workers employed in the United States in

2017 held a certificate or an occupational license.[6] This number has increased dramatically since the 1950s, when roughly 5 percent of the employed were licensed or certified.[7] As a result of this trend, occupational licensing has become an important institution in the analysis of labor markets.

Occupational licensing is a government credential that an individual is required to acquire to legally work for pay in an occupation. It can be required by a local, state, or federal government, but state requirements are the most common in the US. Licensure may entail receiving specific training, passing exams, completing continuing education requirements, and paying certification fees, and licensing requirements often contain some morality clause. The main rationale for a license is to protect the health and safety of customers and to ensure a high quality of service. However, the number of worker types covered by licensing regulation has increased dramatically since the 1950s, and states now require licenses not only for workers in traditional health and safety fields, such as doctors and electricians, but for more and more categories of workers, such as interior designers and travel agents.[8]

Traditionally, economic theory suggests that occupational licensing increases barriers to entry and results in increased, positive economic profit for incumbents in the labor market whose supply is now restricted.[9] Additionally, the literature on rent-seeking suggests that intra-industry rent-seeking can result in a skewed distribution of regulatory rents, where some suppliers benefit at the expense of others.[10] The implication of these theoretical contributions for the analysis of the effect of occupational licensing on wages is that, depending on the licensing institutions, distributional consequences may differ.

On the whole, Maury Gittleman, Mark Klee, and Moriss Kleiner find that credentialed (licensed or certified) workers earn on average 5.7 percent more than noncredentialled workers, are more likely to be employed, and are more likely to receive employer-provided health insurance.[11] In addition, Gittleman, Klee, and Kleiner find that licensing does not seem to have an effect on wage inequality. However, other researchers have found that countries with more stringent entry regulations for businesses do have increased income inequality (Chambers,

McLaughlin, and Stanley 2019). Occupational licensure is one example of an entry regulation, though one that these researchers did not examine specifically.[12] The expanding number of occupations requiring licensing has the potential to be regressive in nature, however, by providing greater benefits to those who are already wealthier. While a credential increases wages for those employed, it also has the potential to change worker selection into a field because of the higher barrier to entry and, as a result, it reduces overall employment in that field.[13]

Occupational Licensing and Gender

Gender differences in compensation are measured in terms of the widely discussed gender wage gap. In 2014, full-time female workers earned on average 81.1 percent of male weekly earnings on an annual basis.[14] This highly cited statistic continues to cause outrage among politicians and the public, and has been used as a justification for legislation requiring firms to release earnings data and prohibiting employers from retaliating against employees who disclose their own wages or inquire about their employer's wage practices.

In historical comparison, the earnings gap has decreased significantly since 1979, the first year for which comparable earnings data area available. Women earned on average 60 cents on the male dollar between 1950 and 1980, but the earnings ratio began to increase in the late 1970s and convergence has been significant since then. Women's weekly earnings ratio increased from 61.0 percent to 76.5 percent of male workers' between 1978 and 1999,[15] but progress has been slower and more differentiated since.

Economists have studied the wage gap and potential explanations for it extensively over the past several decades, and the most recent comprehensive study by Blau and Kahn (2017) suggests that up to 62 percent of the gap can now be explained.[16] In this study, economists Francis Blau and Lawrence Kahn examine traditional measures of human capital, such as education and experience, as well as additional controls for industry, occupation, and union coverage. The results for their full specification suggests that females earned 91.6% of male earnings in 2010, which leaves a gap of 8.4 cents between male and female earnings.[17] This remaining gap could be the result of either unobserved differences between male and female workers (statistical discrimination) or the discriminatory tastes of coworkers, customers, and employers.[18]

Claudia Goldin argues persuasively that the remaining female-to-male earnings gap comes from within-occupation differences in earnings rather than from between-occupation differences.[19] Put differently, it is not the systematic choice of lower-paying occupations on the part of women that drives the gender wage gap, but instead earnings differences within occupations. Across different occupations, women in the same occupation systematically earn less than their male counterparts, even when researchers control for education and experience.

Taking a closer look at the pharmacy profession, which has a comparatively low wage gap, Goldin and her coauthor, Lawrence Katz, suggest that growth of pharmacy employment in retail chains and hospitals and the decline of independent pharmacies over the past half century has created an environment of greater substitutability among pharmacists and subsequently greater linearity in pay (that is, a reduced penalty for part-time work) in which women, who are more likely to work part time, get paid the same as men, who have more traditional work schedules.[20]

In their discussion of this relatively egalitarian profession, Goldin and Katz highlight two particular factors that have resulted in greater substitutability of individual pharmacists: First, greater use of information technology and more pervasive prescription drug insurance have enhanced the ability of pharmacists to hand off clients. Second, the standardization of pharmacy products and the reduction of the prevalence of compounding by individual pharmacies have reduced the importance of the idiosyncratic expertise and talent of particular pharmacists. As a result, consumer preferences for particular pharmacists have decreased and pharmacists have become more substitutable. At the same time, the shift toward larger-scale retailing of drugstores facilitated a shift toward linearity in pay. This greater substitutability and pay linearity have helped close the within-occupation wage gap.

Pharmacists are paid an almost equal hourly wage—there is no wage premium for working traditional office hours and there is not a large wage penalty for part-time work. This helps to decrease the wage gap between men, who are more likely to be full-time workers, and women, who are more likely to work part time.[21]

Given these insights regarding the remaining disparities in earnings between men and women, as well as the insights regarding what features of an occupation may drive more equal pay, it appears that occupational licensing could have the potential to contribute to alleviating gender pay differences if it increases substitutability between workers and produces linearity in pay similar to what is seen in the pharmacy profession. In other words, occupational licensing may reduce the wage gap if licenses and related credentials make individual workers more substitutable. Licensing laws do likely make some workers more substitutable, since they establish a minimal requirement for work experience and education and offer some level of quality control. If the resulting greater substitutability increases temporal flexibility and linearity in pay, occupational licensing may accordingly reduce the wage gap.

Additionally, occupational licensing laws could increase pay transparency if trade organizations report average pay for workers. To the extent that this information is accurate and readily available, it could also potentially narrow the wage gap. Recent literature suggests that increased pay transparency narrows the gender wage gap by slowing down the growth of male wages[22] and increasing wages for women with higher education levels.[23]

Occupational licensing could increase the wage gap, on the other hand, by imposing geographic constraints on mobility, limiting job switching, increasing the costs of labor force absences, and encouraging nonentry into the licensed field.

If occupational licensure acts as a geographic constraint and limits worker mobility, the gender wage gap could increase. Research has shown that individuals who work in occupations that require state-specific licensing exams are much less likely to move across state lines than individuals in nonlicensed professions.[24] The license makes it more costly to move. Since women often increase their wages by changing employers, this limits their possibilities.

Geographic constraints are particularly important for employees trailing their spouses. Women are historically more likely to be trailing spouses, and the existing literature seems to suggest that they continue to be more likely than men to be the spouse who moves for a partner's job.[25] While good empirical evidence on the absolute number of trailing spouses by gender is nonexistent, William Bielby and Denise Bielby report that women are more likely than men to report reluctance to relocate for a better job (for themselves).[26] If a couple moves as a result of the trailed spouse's employment prospects and the move requires the trailing spouse to obtain a license or other credential in order to continue working in the same occupation, the credential can become a barrier to entry that results in the trailing spouse taking a lower-paying position or staying out of the labor force altogether.

Though it does not specifically examine the impact of licensure laws, research examining the effects of job relocation on spousal careers suggests that family relocation negatively affects women's earnings both in absolute terms and relative to their husbands' earnings, which increase.[27] Jeremy Burke and Amalia Miller look at evidence from military families and find that spousal earnings decline by 14 percent after a move, that a move increases the likelihood of no earnings for the spouse, and that these career costs persist for two years after the move.[28] The authors specifically note both that spouses may avoid entering fields that require a license because of the barrier to entry licenses create and that wages may be negatively affected for spouses in licensed fields. The military has noted the impacts of licensure on spousal careers by offering the Spouse Education and Career Opportunities Call Center for career and education counseling around licensure, and the Defense-State Liaison Office has recently worked to change state laws to better accommodate state reciprocity in licensure for military spouses. These actions suggest that female earnings are negatively impacted by some state licensing.

The continuing education requirements for many state-licensed occupations also have the potential to adversely impact women at higher rates than men. Women are more likely to take a break from their careers owing to concerns about childcare or elderly parents and to choose to work part time.[29] These decisions can make required continuing education credits prohibitively expensive for women to acquire, in terms of both time and money. Often larger employers will help employees meet continuing education requirements by hosting classes or by helping to offset the monetary outlay required for attending classes. Workers who take a break from their profession can find it difficult to gather information about continuing education requirements. Additionally, the opportunity cost of continuing education likely changes during a career break: Someone who is not currently employed in the licensed profession can't use work hours to meet continuing education requirements, but must instead take time that was allocated to childcare or elderly care, to other careers or schooling, or to dealing with health concerns. Finally, the relative costs of any testing and classes, in monetary terms and in terms of time spent, are significantly higher for a part-time worker (and earner) than for an individual currently working and earning a full-time salary in a licensed profession spending a similar amount of money and time.

For example, when Massachusetts adopted a continuing education requirement for licensed real estate agents in 1999, the number of licensed active agents decreased by between 39 and 58 percent.[30] The National Association of Realtors notes that the majority of realtors are women—meaning this regulatory change likely adversely affected women at higher rates than men.

An occupational license is now required in a large number and variety of fields. It is possible that a license decreases the wage gap in some fields, exacerbates it in others, and has dual effects (working in both directions) in still others. Occupational licensure likely also changes who enters the licensed field, further complicating attempts to understand licensure's impact on gender wage gaps. While empirical research can help bring better understanding of licensure's impacts, the complexity of the ways that licensing could impact wages complicates these studies.

Occupational Licensing and Race

As in the case of the gender wage gap, occupational licensing has the potential to decrease the racial wage gap if licensure increases substitutability for all workers along the lines suggested by Goldin and Katz and if it reduces the information asymmetry between employees and employers relating to employees' qualifications. Asymmetric information regarding employee qualification is particularly problematic for minority workers. Employee quality is difficult to observe ex ante—consequently, in the absence of sufficient information, employers may rely on observable characteristics such as race and gender to infer worker ability and productivity. As a result, individual applicants may be judged not solely on the basis of observable individual characteristics but also on the basis of the average characteristics of a group they are observed to belong to. If employers are legally prohibited from asking questions about criminal background, they may infer information about an individual's criminal background from the individual's race or gender. Women are less likely to have a criminal record than men, and white individuals are less likely to have a criminal record than black or Latino individuals, on average.[31] This kind of statistical discrimination is difficult for individual workers to overcome.

Amanda Agan and Sonja Starr provide some evidence for the presence of this kind of statistical discrimination. They show that black applicants were significantly less likely to receive resume callbacks and were less likely to be employed in "ban the box" states in which employers are prohibited from including questions relating to criminal background on job applications.[32] In an environment in which other job-market signals are unavailable, licenses can potentially help minorities overcome such asymmetric information problems with respect to worker productivity and qualification. While employers may not be able to ask questions about criminal background directly, they can require a license or certification—which often includes a criminal background check as a prerequisite. Having to show a license can therefore allow minority workers to signal qualifications beyond the average of the minority group they belong to and avoid statistical discrimination. In other words, if licenses provide consistent signals about worker qualities that are otherwise difficult to communicate, especially for minorities, they may reduce wage inequality.

Occupational licensing could, however, also aggravate the wage gap between workers of different races if the positive effect of increased substitutability is outweighed by negative effects of increasing and differentiating barriers to entry for different races. For example, occupational licensure laws are widely accepted to reduce the labor supply in the market—the credentialing aspect of the license means there are fewer suppliers of labor in that market. If this decrease in supply is felt more heavily by minority groups, the wage gap could increase.

The presence of licensing requirements might alter worker selection into a field. Individuals who are deterred from entering a profession because of licensing requirements would not show up in a wage gap study since they would not be considered to be in the field. It is possible that a license requirement would deter larger numbers of minority workers from entering a labor market than white workers. For example, occupational licensure laws often impose significant educational requirements workers must fulfill in order to obtain and maintain the license. If minorities graduate from trade schools and colleges at lower rates than their white counterparts, they will be ineligible for many licensed jobs at higher rates than white individuals.[33] Licensure rules that prohibit individuals with recorded felonies from entering the licensed professions could impact minorities at higher rates than white individuals.[34] Similarly, a lack of access to credit[35] to pay for exam and application fees could prevent minorities from entering a field at higher rates than white workers. In all these cases, the licensing requirement does not benefit minority workers unless they can meet the requirements of licensure. Statistics relating to within-occupation earnings for minority workers are therefore potentially skewed if minority workers are less likely to enter a profession in the first place.

Empirical Results

The empirical evidence on how occupational licensing affects female or minority labor-market outcomes is mixed. Recent contributions suggest that occupational licensing reduces both the gender wage gap and the racial wage gap, and that it does not effectively function as a barrier to entry with divergent effects on minorities and white workers. As noted earlier, however, there is concern that worker selection skews these results. Older research suggests that occupational licensing and regulation more generally benefited white men at the expense of women and minorities. For example, a 2010 paper finds that stricter regulations for funeral directors reduce the proportion of women in that profession by 24 percent.[36] This chapter's appendix summarizes the main results of a number of empirical contributions to this literature.

However, some recent empirical evidence suggests that occupational licensing increases wages within a profession, may reduce the gender and racial wage gap, and may increase the employment of women and minorities. Peter Blair and Brian Chung find that occupational licensing narrows the gender wage gap by 36–40 percent (36% for white women and 40% for black women, as compared to white men). More specifically, using data from the Survey of Income and Program Participation, they report that the license premium for white and black women was 13.7 percent and 15.9 percent, as compared to 7.5percent for white men. They also find that occupational licensing narrows the gender wage gap by 36-40% and the wage gap between black and white men by 43 percent.[37] Beth Redbird finds that occupational licensing does not increase wages, but that it improves access to licensed occupations for historically disadvantaged groups, including black and female workers.[38] Redbird hypothesizes that the increased share of minorities among licensed professionals is the result of formal procedures, such as licenses, replacing informal barriers to entry. She suggests that formal barriers to entry are more likely to be color-blind and measurable and can be publicized, while informal barriers to entry into a profession may encourage discrimination and homogeneity.

Blair and Chung find that black men in particular benefit from licenses that signal nonfelony status: in their sample, black men in a licensed profession on average earned a premium of 12.5 percent, as compared to a 7.5 percent premium for licensed white men. Blair and Chung argue that licenses serve as a job-market signal that allows minority workers to overcome asymmetric information between firms and workers, who are subject to statistical discrimination relating to employee productivity and to quality more generally.[39] More specifically, licenses help to overcome barriers to entry for African American men for whom employers overestimate the likelihood of a criminal past.[40]

One major concern regarding occupational licensing is that it will reduce the supply of labor in licensed professions[41] and will change the characteristics of those entering those professions. For example, a higher education requirement might encourage some women to not enter an occupation, or a nonfelony status requirement might exclude some minority workers who would otherwise have pursued a certain career. Evidence reported by Ryan Nunn supports the idea that licensing might skew access.[42] Nunn reports that 27 percent of non-Hispanic whites hold occupational licenses while only 22 percent of blacks and 15 percent of Hispanics hold licenses. The exclusion of these workers will not show up readily in an empirical analysis, but it certainly impacts the wages that people will or will not earn.

Blair and Chung may temper Nunn's results, however. They suggest that occupational licensing reduces labor supply by an average of 17–27 percent. But their results also suggest that the negative effects of licensing are stronger for white workers and weaker for black workers.[43] This reduction in the wage and employment gap cannot be a desirable result if it comes at the expense of absolute minority employment, however. The fact that a profession has relatively more minority employment or a smaller wage gap between white and black workers is only a desirable outcome if these changes are the result of minority workers being absolutely better off.

Shedding light on this concern, Morris Kleiner shows that licensed occupations grow at a rate that is 20 percent less than that of unlicensed occupations,[44] which suggests that, rather than improving opportunities for minorities, licensing may just reduce opportunities for employment overall. This evidence suggests that when the wage gap within a field decreases, this may not mean workers are doing better overall. In fact, some of the relative improvements among minorities may be the result of reductions in the wages and employment of white men rather than the result of increases in the wages or employment of black men. These mixed empirical results suggest that more research needs to be done to better understand the effects of licensure on market outcomes. It's possible that licensure laws help female and minority labor market outcomes in some circumstances and hurt them in others. Research needs to more closely examine the impact of licensure on worker selection, socioeconomic status, part-time work, style of work, and education in order to more clearly differentiate these effects.

Other Types of Regulation, Gender, and Race

A handful of studies consider the effect of specific regulatory reforms on minorities. A 1994 study finds that deregulation of trucking resulted in a dramatic increase in the proportion of black drivers, who had previously been prohibited from entering the industry by the predominantly white trucking business owners who were the beneficiaries of trucking regulation.[45] Sandra Black and Philip Strahan consider the differential effect of banking deregulation on male and female workers in the industry. They find that, while deregulation reduced earnings for all workers in banking, women were relative beneficiaries of the reforms, which reduced the gender wage gap in the banking industry. In addition, women's share of employment in managerial positions increased following deregulation.[46] A 2019 study finds that the cost of regulation in terms of wage effects is mostly borne by lower-wage workers and that workers in higher-earning managerial and compliance-relevant professions, such as accountants and lawyers, earn higher wages when an industry becomes more regulated.[47] These studies help highlight how the barrier-to-entry aspect of regulation may be more costly to women and minority workers than to white male workers.

While some of the effects discussed above may be small and may be considered negligible or justifiable costs by advocates of greater levels of regulation, an important downside of regulation, especially when it is ineffective in terms of achieving its desired goal, is that it creates a group with a vested interest in its persistence. Regulation that redistributes resources from one group to another but is otherwise ineffective will have advocates in those who benefit from the law, and thus will be more persistent than its relative policy success might suggest. Gordon

Tullock coined the term "transitional gains trap" to describe this phenomenon of regulatory persistence in the face of policy failure.[48]

Policy Reform

Even when it is well-intentioned, labor-market regulation such as occupational licensing laws can have unforeseen yet detrimental effects that are particularly burdensome for minorities and women. As we have shown above, the empirical record about occupational licensing laws is by no means easy to assess or clear cut. While such laws seem to increase wages for those in the licensed profession, they do so at the expense of reductions in employment both in the short term and dynamically in the long term. Several of the studies we reviewed earlier suggest that such employment effects are most severe for women and minorities, although there is recent evidence that suggests that the share of women and minorities in certain professions increases with licensure.

Overall, occupational licensing laws are similar to regulation more generally in that they redistribute earnings and employment among groups. While the specific redistributive effects of occupational licensing laws are difficult to trace, existing evidence suggests that incumbent workers in an industry benefit at the expense of newcomers, including women and minorities. Occupational licensing also changes who is able and willing to enter a field. Evidence also suggests that occupations with licensing laws are less dynamic—that is, less likely to grow. This is troubling if one policy goal is wage growth for women and minority groups. Wages grow the most in dynamic industries. This evidence is in line with an emerging literature on the regressive effects of regulation, which identifies detrimental effects for low-income households as an important cost of regulatory accumulation.[49]

In light of this evidence on occupational licensing and on regulation more generally, additional licensing laws should be considered with great caution. Empirical research on occupational licensure is mixed, researchers regularly question the data used in studies, and the necessity of many licensure laws for health and safety has also begun to be questioned.[50] With more than 25 percent of the workforce already required to hold a license to perform their jobs, policymakers should be cautious about expanding this practice to include even more professions and workers.

Given high existing levels of occupational licensing in the states, a move toward greater labor market freedom and general deregulation may be more effective for generating economic growth. Economic growth will, in turn, increase wage growth for women and minorities.

Most occupational licensure happens through state legislation. This makes blanket policy recommendations difficult to deliver. We caution all policymakers against enacting additional licensure laws without careful study of their impacts. We also suggest that existing licensure laws be carefully examined to see whether they are necessary for the health and safety of consumers. Such studies should also consider secondary effects of regulation.

In the process of considering new regulation or examining existing laws, policymakers should consider whether a voluntary certification program could provide similar benefits to consumers. Voluntary certification has the potential to provide many of the possible benefits of licensure discussed earlier (especially the benefits related to overcoming asymmetric information problems and avoiding statistical discrimination) without excluding from the labor market large segments of workers who cannot meet the educational, monetary, or time burden involved in obtaining a certificate. On net, voluntary certification would be more dynamic than licensure and would provide customers with more choice.

Conclusion

As described in this chapter, the evidence is largely inconclusive regarding the differential effect of regulation on women and minorities and, more specifically, the differential effect of occupational licensing laws on those groups. While some recent research seems to find that licensing laws have a positive effect on gender and minority wage gaps, the difficulty with the existing evidence is that it cannot control for potential effects of such laws on differential access to labor markets. If occupational licensing laws disproportionately disincentivize labor market participation by women and minorities, the narrowing of gender and minority earnings gaps comes at the high cost of dis-employment for such groups.

On the whole, licensure is likely an expensive way to help minorities and women, because it hurts consumers and potential entrants to licensed professions and increases unemployment, while not necessarily (or only imperfectly) creating the circumstances that promote wage equality.

Appendix: Table of Empirical Studies on Occupational Licensing and Gender or Race

Study	Data	Effect of occupational licensing on female workers	Effect of occupational licensing on minority workers
Beth Redbird, "The New Closed Shop? The Economic and Structural Effects of Occupational Licensure," *American Sociological Review* 82, no. 3 (2017): 600–624.	1983–2012 Current Population Survey	Licensing increases female employment.	Licensing increases black employment.
Peter Q. Blair and Brian W. Chung, "Job Market Signaling through Occupational Licensing" (NBER Working Paper No. 24791, National Bureau of Economic Research, Cambridge, MA, 2019).	Waves 13–16 of Survey of Income and Program Participation, 2008 panel	There are license premiums of 13.7% and 15.9% for white and black women, respectively (compared to a 7.5% license premium for white men), which translates to a reduction in the wage gap of between 36% and 40%.	There is a license premium of 12.5% for black men (compared to a 7.5% license premium for white men), which translates to a reduction in the wage gap of 43%.
Peter Q. Blair and Brian W. Chung, "How Much of a Barrier to Entry Is Occupational Licensing?," *British Journal of Industrial Relations* 57, no. 4 (2019): 919–43.	Wave 13 of Survey of Income and Program Participation, 2008 panel; 2015 Current Population Survey	There is no statistically detectable differential effect on labor supply.	Licensing reduces the relative labor supply of white men by 15.2% and of black men by 18.9%.
Marc T. Law and Mindy S. Marks, "Effects of Occupational Licensing Laws on Minorities: Evidence from the Progressive Era," *Journal of Law and Economics* 52, no. 2 (2009: 351–66.	1870–1960 United States Census of Population	Licensing increased female employment in engineering, pharmacy, plumbing, and registered nursing. Licensing reduced female employment among teachers. Licensing did not have a significant effect on female employment in other occupations.	Licensing reduced the employment of black workers in barbering and increased black employment in practical nursing. Licensing had a positive effect on black employment in the medical profession as well as teaching. Licensing did not have a significant effect on black employment in other occupations.

Study	Data	Effect of occupational licensing on female workers	Effect of occupational licensing on minority workers
Stuart Dorsey, "The Occupational Licensing Queue," *Journal of Human Resources* 15, no. 3 (1980): 424–34.	Applications for cosmetology licenses in Missouri (January–April 1975) and Illinois (June 1976)		Blacks, apprentices, less-educated individuals, and nonnatives are more likely to fail written licensing exams.
Stuart Dorsey, "Occupational Licensing and Minorities," *Law and Human Behavior* 7, no. 2/3 (1983): 171–81.	Candidates for cosmetology licenses in Illinois and Missouri (1976)		Licensing disproportionately excludes less-educated and minority workers.
Maya N. Federman, David E. Harrington, and Kathy J. Krynski, "The Impact of State Licensing Regulations on Low-Skilled Immigrants: The Case of Vietnamese Manicurists," *American Economic Review* 96, no. 2 (2006): 237–41.	Individual-level licensing records from occupational licensing agencies of 35 states; U.S. Census Bureau data for 2000		English proficiency requirements for manicurists harm nonnative workers (specifically, Vietnamese workers).
David E. Harrington, and Jaret Treber, *Designed to Exclude: How Interior Design Insiders Use Government Power to Exclude Minorities & Burden Consumers* (Washington, DC: Institute for Justice, 2009).	National sample of Interior designers based on U.S. Census Bureau data for 1990 and 2000		There are fewer black and Hispanic interior designers in states with regulation limiting practicing professionals to those with college degrees.
Joshua D. Angrist and Jonathan Guryan, "Teacher Testing, Teacher Education, and Teacher Characteristics," *American Economic Association Papers and Proceedings* 94, no. 2 (2004): 241–46.	Educational Testing Service Praxis II test results and teacher SAT scores		Teacher testing requirements do not improve teacher quality, but decrease the number of Hispanic teachers.

CHAPTER 8

How Can Certificate-of-Need Laws Be Reformed to Improve Access to Healthcare?

Alexander Ollerton and Christopher Koopman

When the Metcalf-McCloskey Act of New York passed in 1964, the United States was seeing its first certificate-of-need (CON) law. This law allowed the state of New York to regulate "the exact [healthcare] needs of the community prior to hospital construction."[1] The New York legislators meant to control healthcare costs by limiting the construction of healthcare facilities and encouraging their spread across the state—maximizing access for those seeking medical treatment. In order to expand an existing facility or build a new facility, interested parties (e.g., physicians/entrepreneurs) had to file an application with the state.[2] Through these regulations, New York hoped to increase access to healthcare (especially in rural areas), increase the quality of care, and decrease healthcare spending.[3]

In 1974, the National Health Planning and Resources Development Act (NHPRDA) brought the idea of certificate-of-need to the federal government. Like New York's law, this act implemented state agencies designated for the regulation of the building, expansion, and modernization of healthcare facilities and medical equipment.[4] In an effort to encourage the development of healthcare facilities in rural and low-income areas, The NHPRDA allocated $1 billion (about $4.2 billion in 2020 money) over three years to aid in the expansion of healthcare through resource development and health planning.[5] To be eligible for these funds, a community would need to implement its own CON law. Over the decade that followed, every state except Louisiana enacted some form of a CON law.[6]

Motivated by the lack of evidence that CON laws restrained costs and by the Reagan administration's deregulatory efforts, Congress, in 1986, repealed the federal requirement for CON laws in state healthcare systems.[7] Still, today the majority of states, 35, maintain CON laws.[8]

In this chapter we discuss the effects on CON laws, which have been studied extensively ever since the first law was passed in New York. Researchers have documented effects on access to care, affordability of care, quality of care, and—in a few cases—health outcomes. In short, previous studies show that CON laws are ineffective at improving access, affordability, or quality of care. On the basis of these findings, we lay out several potential policy alternatives. In most cases, patients will be best served by the repeal of state-level CON laws in favor of experimentation by entrepreneurs. Where that is not possible, policymakers should consider modifications to current CON laws or other options, such as administrative relief, to allow for increased access to healthcare.

Access to high-quality health services and care is vital for the well-being of individuals in communities across the US. Despite the intentions of CON laws' proponents, the evidence shows that the laws are more a barrier to achieving this goal than a pathway toward it.

What Are the Effects of Certificate-of-Need Laws?

Certificate-of-need laws were intended to support the expansion of healthcare by means of regulations that enhanced healthcare facilities and increased the use of medical devices. Many of the people who developed CON laws thought the laws could regulate costs to make healthcare more affordable and could facilitate the expansion of healthcare, allowing for accessible care in rural areas and optimizing the use of medical devices. [9] However, evidence suggests that the laws have instead reduced the quality, accessibility, and affordability of healthcare.

Quality of Care

A central goal of CON laws is to improve the quality of the care provided within the healthcare system. [10] Yet surgical research results suggest that CON laws may contribute to higher mortality rates and reduce the quality of care. Reforming CON laws in states that still have them likely improves the quality of health, based on evidence collected before and after the removal of CON laws in several states.

Every year, approximately 790,000 knee replacement surgeries and 450,000 hip replacement surgeries are performed in the United States.[11] (Since these are commonly performed surgeries, it may be more practical to observe how these are affected by CON laws.) One study of Pennsylvania's CON law repeal in 1996 examined the surgical outcomes of knee and hip replacements. Researchers discovered that the rate of death related to knee and hip replacement surgeries declined after the CON law's repeal.[12] It seems that if CON laws are removed elsewhere, their removal might correlate with an increase in longevity of life.

Cardiac care is another area that can be looked at to see the effects of CON laws. The researchers who conducted a different study focused on coronary artery bypass graft surgeries and found an increase in mortality rates prior to Pennsylvania's CON law repeal.[13] A similar study followed patients undergoing artery bypass surgery after the repeal of CON laws in multiple states. This study discovered that the removal of CON laws resulted in lower mortality rates. Additionally, there was no evidence suggesting that CON laws were associated with higher-quality care.[14] Overall, both of these surgical studies conclude that CON laws reduce the quality of care through their regulations and contribute to higher mortality rates.

An economic study of Vermont predicts that the quality of care would rise with the removal of CON laws: the researchers found a 4.5 percentage point increase in patient satisfaction rates. Perhaps more importantly, the study also suggests that eliminating CON laws would lower mortality rates.[15] A similar study for the state of Virginia found that if CON laws were repealed, the total number of post-surgery complications would decrease by 5.2 percent and patient satisfaction would increase by 4.7 percent.[16]

In a recent study, economists Thomas Stratmann and David Wille found that the CON law review process resulted in limited entry of fewer healthcare facilities and lower hospital quality.[17] The study showed that nearly all the measures normally used to gauge hospital quality are worse in CON states. Importantly, this paper avoids concerns about reverse causality. In the case of CON laws, the reverse causality argument holds that it is poor health conditions or a lack of healthcare options that encourage the passage of CON laws. However, Stratmann and Wille's study shows that it is CON laws that drive poor healthcare outcomes, and not the other way around. The study mitigates concerns about reverse causality by examining communities that span CON and non-CON states.[18]

Supporters of CON laws believe restricting medical services, especially limiting the number of providers, will ensure that each provider has a higher number of patients –resulting in better quality of care.[19] But this prediction relies on the assumption that the providers operating under CON laws will be more proficient and specialized since a specialization allows a physician to perform the same procedure often. However, this is not always the case. In fact, research has shown that the quality of care has no difference with physicians practicing in CON vs non-CON states.[20]

Ultimately, research has revealed that CON laws have negative impacts on mortality rates and quality of care. Removing or modifying CON laws may achieve an improvement in quality of care. This will lead to an increased opportunity for longevity and could result in greater economic growth. As long as CON laws remain, they will hinder efforts to achieve these goals—but this will not be their only effect. Accessibility to care is also affected in states with CON laws.

Accessibility of Care

CON laws were designed with the intent to increase access to healthcare. However, research has shown that CON laws, by limiting the ability of entrepreneurs to start medical businesses, have reduced access to care or at the most made no improvement.

Under CON laws it becomes more difficult for medical providers to obtain medical devices. This suggests that patients will experience both reduced quality and reduced accessibility of care. The evidence bears out this prediction: For example, one study found that states with CON laws experience decreased utilization of medical equipment (i.e., fewer MRI scans, CT scans, and PET scans) from nonhospital providers by 34 to 65 percent.[21] The rare use of these medical devices within CON states is likely due to the regulations for expanding current medical facilities.

Because of these restrictions imposed by CON laws, it is difficult for entrepreneurs to expand medical facilities. A lack of medical facilities can encourage consumers to travel long distances, even out of state, to receive medical care where it is more accessible.[22] This generates a decline in medical equipment usage in states with CON regulations because consumers would rather travel outside of their state to receive efficient medical care, perpetuating the cycle. Also, the potential smaller selection of medical devices in CON-regulated states consequently forces patients to travel out of state for their medical care.

According to Thomas Stratmann and Matthew Baker (a PhD student at George Mason University), there are "3.93 percent more MRI scans, 3.52 percent more CT scans, and 8.13 percent more PET scans" occurring outside CON-regulated states.[23] Removing CON laws would decrease barriers to entry for medical providers and provide increased access to medical devices, improving healthcare overall for patients who need access to medical devices. Because CON laws limit access to medical equipment and services, they limit patients' options. Patients facing a restricted supply are forced to travel further or wait longer for medical care.

The economic study of Vermont mentioned earlier estimates how the removal of CON laws would also provide more access to healthcare services. If CON laws were removed, there would be approximately six more hospitals available in Vermont (most in rural areas), 36.4 percent more MRI scans available, and 70 percent more CT scans available.[24] This study demonstrates an increase in accessibility with the removal of CON laws, but—like before—the increase can be more easily analyzed by looking at common surgical procedures.

A study by researchers at the University of Virginia revealed that fewer total hip replacement surgeries were performed in states that had

CON laws, compared to their counterparts without CON laws.[25] This suggests that CON laws likely play a role in inhibiting access to care.

We have examined how CON laws hinder access to medical devices and to healthcare in general. Now we will see how the CON application process also creates barriers to providing healthcare services.

In Tennessee, entrepreneurs must jump through several hoops and wait on the decisions of state regulation agencies before they can build new facilities, expand existing facilities, or buy new medical devices. As shown in figure 1, the process begins when an applicant files a letter of intent with the state. (This letter must also be published in the newspaper.) The applicant must then pay a filing fee before the request goes under review by the Tennessee Health Services and Development Agency. The review process often results in additional questions for the applicant. The applicant's responses are taken into consideration as the application enters a second cycle of review. Tennessee's review cycle begins on the first of each month and can take approximately 60 days for applicants to receive an approval or denial of their application. If the application is denied, the applicant may appeal within 15 days from their initial notification. If the application is approved, it can take an additional four weeks for the applicant to receive their certification. Once the certificate has arrived the changes requested in the application can be made.[26]

This lengthy process delays projects that would increase access to care and means entrepreneurs have weaker incentives to expand existing facilities. The entire CON application process in the state of Tennessee can take anywhere from 65 to 110 days.[27] Figure 1 illustrates how the complexity of the application process might be one reason why many potential entrepreneurs are hesitant to begin the process.

In order to help improve the accessibility of care, states should consider removing the long review process. Without the applications, fees, waiting times, and associated frustrations, facilities would be able to enter the construction phase sooner and would therefore be available to provide more care to their communities. Thanks to this increase in care and accessibility, there would be more opportunity for competition. This increased competition would incentivize entrepreneurs to

Figure 1. Tennessee Certificate-of-Need Application Process

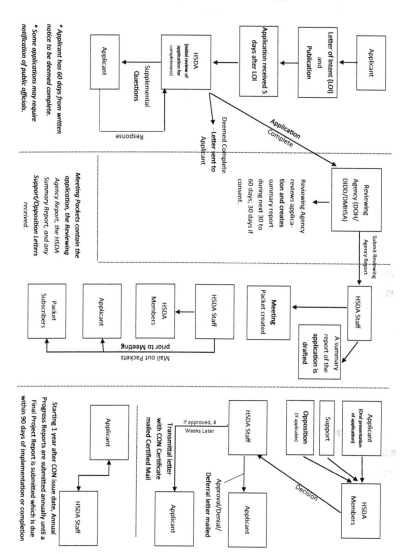

Note: DOH = Tennessee Department of Health, DIDD = Tennessee Department of Intellectual and Developmental Disabilities, DMHSA = Tennessee Department of Mental Health and Substance Abuse Services Agency, HSDA = Tennessee Health Services and Development Agency.

Source: Flowchart published by the Tennessee Health Services and Development Agency, accessed October 2, 2020, https://www.tn.gov/content/dam/tn/hsda/documents/con_process_flow_chart2014.pdf.

expand medical facilities and equipment within each formerly regulated state and encourage those seeking medical attention to stay inside state lines—bolstering the state's economy.

Affordability of Care

Despite CON law proponents' intentions, research suggests that the laws have failed to make healthcare affordable. In terms of geographic proximity and in terms of financial costs, CON laws have made care less accessible and less affordable. An early indication of the limitations of CON laws can be found in a thorough 1988 report conducted by the Federal Trade Commission (FTC). In its review, the FTC found that healthcare costs were not lower after CON laws were enacted.[28] In fact, contrary to what the law's proponents had anticipated, many of the states that had incorporated CON laws appeared to have higher healthcare spending than states that did not enforce CON laws.[29]

Ophthalmology, the branch of medicine that deals with eyes, illustrates why CON law modifications or removal can increase affordability of care. Ophthalmology is still regulated under CON laws, however, this focus of medicine seems to have a higher probability of building and using existing ambulatory surgical centers (ASCs). ASCs were first developed due to physician frustrations with local hospitals. [30] Physicians had a difficult time finding the resources needed to perform their surgeries at hospitals so they developed ASCs. [31] The use of ASCs is increasing in ophthalmology. Between 2001 and 2014, the use of ASCs (particularly for cataract surgery) has grown by 2.34 percent each year.[32] This shift from hospitals to ASCs increases accessibility for eye surgeries and drives down their costs for patients (and insurers) because of gains in convenience.[33] If CON laws were removed this could increase the number of ASCs, provide more resources to physicians (decreasing frustrations), and increase affordability for patients.

Cataract surgeries provide a good example of how costs can be brought down while a procedure remains easily accessible. Cataract surgery is a procedure that removes the natural crystalline lens in the eye and replaces it with an artificial lens.[34] Historically, cataract surgery has been performed mostly in hospitals. Over the past few decades, however, this has changed. Most cataract surgeries are now performed in ASCs. This shift from hospitals to ASCs has instigated a decline in costs for the procedure. For example, in 2014 the average co-pay for a cataract removal in an ASC was $190, compared to $350 in a hospital.[35]

Cataract surgeries are not the only eye procedures that highlight CON laws' failings—cosmetic eye surgeries also provide a great example. Laser-assisted in situ keratomileusis, better known as LASIK, has become a popular cosmetic surgery for many citizens in the United States. In 2010 approximately 800,000 LASIK surgeries and similar procedures were performed.[36] As technology improves and the market becomes more saturated with LASIK providers, the cost of LASIK declines. LASIK's decrease in price is also influenced by the transparency of the market.[37] For example, many businesses showcase the price of their LASIK procedures, encouraging competitive pricing. Some businesses even offer specials as cheap as $250 per eye in order to attract patients. This allows consumers to find the best option available to them.

One reason this procedure fosters a competitive market is the nature of the surgery. LASIK is an elective procedure, meaning the patient has the choice to undergo the surgery or not. Many insurers do not cover the cost of LASIK; others cover only a minimal amount. Therefore, individuals contemplating LASIK surgery have an incentive to consider the cost as well as the safety of the facility they choose to perform the procedure. CON laws do not allow such competition to arise around other healthcare procedures (many of which are urgent or non-elective), so patients and providers do not have similar incentives to decrease the costs. Theoretically, the removal of CON laws could allow more competition within the healthcare market and provide an incentive to decrease costs for other areas of healthcare.

Unfortunately, there are rare circumstances in which strict CON laws do not allow for ASCs. In 2017, a doctor in Cedar Rapids, Iowa, was unable to use an already-constructed ASC because the facility was denied certification. The doctor applied for certification four times, each time explaining the need for the ASC and demonstrating how the facility would provide for the community. However, the state denied each application. Iowa's Hospital Association pointed out that the facility would take paying patients away from hospitals.[38] Some studies demonstrate that preexisting facilities don't lose patients when new facilities are opened, however[39]—and even if they did, their loss might indicate that patients are receiving better care and services.

Many studies have found results suggesting that CON laws have failed to lower healthcare costs. These results, reported in the appendix, confirm the FTC's earlier findings that CON laws increase healthcare costs.[40] (The tables in the appendix summarize how CON laws affect spending and efficiency.) Overall, 13 of the studies included in the appendix show that CON laws increase healthcare costs or decrease efficiency. The other 9 show no effect on healthcare costs, or show that CON laws improve efficiency. Both the FTC's 1988 report and this more recent review of the research suggest that CON laws are at least questionable as a means of reducing healthcare costs.

Other studies continue to find similar results. For example, studies of Vermont and Virginia suggest that CON laws raise the prices of healthcare services in both states. According to estimates for Vermont, the removal of CON laws may reduce healthcare costs $228 per capita, and would decrease healthcare spending per physician per year by $68.[41] In the case of Virginia, the removal of CON laws would reduce spending by $79 per physician per year, and also would lower total healthcare spending by $205 per capita.[42] The authors of these two studies points out that this decline in healthcare costs happens because there are fewer restrictions to providing more healthcare services.

CON laws are not the only factor raising healthcare costs, however. Economists James Bailey and Tom Hamami have found that, on a national level (during 1996–2019), 10.5 percent of the increase in per capita healthcare spending was associated with CON laws.[43] To put this into perspective, for every dollar spent, approximately 10 cents could be saved by the removal of CON laws. This shows that the removal of CON laws has a significant effect on healthcare costs overall and could help improve access to care.

If CON laws were modified to encourage competition within the healthcare market, entrepreneurs would have an incentive to increase price transparency and provide lower-cost services. Recall how competition works: If store A sells a soda for one dollar, its competitor, store B, will want to sell the same product for 99 cents. This will encourage store A to lower its price to 98 cents. The back-and-forth will eventually level out and each store will charge the same price for a soda. This model could apply to the healthcare industry as well, if government policies encourage healthy competition to lower the cost of healthcare services and provide more affordable healthcare.

A Blueprint for Better Access and Higher-Quality Healthcare Services

Research suggests a number of alternatives to CON laws that will be more effective at providing access to high-quality healthcare services. They range from a full repeal of CON laws to changing how CON laws currently work.

The most straightforward policy response to the failures of CON laws is repeal. As of January 2020, 35 states maintain some kind of CON program. The positive experiences of the states that have repealed their own CON laws suggest that repeal improves access to healthcare and results in better-quality care at a lower cost.[44] Research shows that states that have removed CON laws do not experience a surge of healthcare spending and tend to see improved access to healthcare facilities.[45]

A second-best response is to modify existing CON laws. Such modifications have included near-repeal (see, e.g., Florida[46]) and a process of phasing out the laws over time (see, e.g., Georgia[47]), among other approaches. States should revise their regulations to prevent the denial of modifications to existing medical facilities because of economic costs. If a state is unable to repeal its CON laws entirely, then it should clarify that the only acceptable reason for denying applications to build new facilities, expand current medical facilities, or purchase additional medical technologies and tools are that existing facilities are lacking optimal capacity and use. In other words, the current medical facilities are not seeing a high volume of patients so the need for a new facility or expansion of a current facility may not be justifiable.

In 2020, nine states have introduced legislation to modify their current CON laws.[48] These bills have taken a number of forms. Florida's, for example, removed the CON application requirement for several types of providers. The legislation exempted general hospitals, complex medical rehabilitation beds, and tertiary hospital services from the application and state-level approval process.[49] Georgia's legislation increased the expenditure threshold for facilities from $2.5 million to $10 million, and for medical equipment from $1 million to $3 million. This means that some healthcare expansions that would formerly have been contingent on CON approval can now avoid the CON application process.[50] While there is no evidence yet about how this change will affect the application process, the hope is that there will be fewer CON applications and an increase in healthcare innovation. For example, a brand-new MRI machine can cost up to $3 million.[51] Under the new legislation, a facility that wants to add a machine will no longer have to go through a CON application process and be approved.

Maryland is following in Florida and Georgia's footsteps. The Maryland Health Care Commission did extensive research on CON laws and how they affected the healthcare system in the state.[52] One suggestion the commission came up with was to remove the expenditure threshold altogether. This would allow physicians to expand their current facilities without the hassle of trying to optimize their resources to fit under a specific monetary parameter.[53] Maryland's decision to modify its CON laws is a step in the right direction and will hopefully allow more access in areas where healthcare seems scarce.

Another minor, but perhaps meaningful, reform proposal is to wrap a CON process within existing community health needs assessment requirements.[54] When the Affordable Care Act was passed, Congress required hospitals to fill out a community health needs assessment (a form provided through the IRS). This document assesses the community impact a hospital provides and if the hospital can justify their community impact they can maintain a tax-exempt status. This document helps identify opportunities to improve the healthcare services within a community by requiring hospitals to implement strategies to meet the health needs of that community; in this way they are similar to CON laws. Combining the two would eliminate the need to enforce

CON laws because the health needs assessment identifies areas of need within the healthcare system, making CON laws redundant.[55]

Repealing CON laws through interstate agreements is another option that may appeal to those who defend CON laws.[56] Colorado and Arkansas have already decided to repeal their CON laws if other states are willing to also repeal their CON laws.[57] This type of agreement is not uncommon among states. For example, Utah has a similar interstate agreement in regards to Daylight Saving Time.[58] According to the bill, the state house and senate must approve the bill in addition to "four other western states" in order for Utah to have year-round standard time.[59] Using this type of alternative approach to address CON laws may be beneficial because it could influence neighboring states to follow suit.

A fifth option that could save time and money for those involved in the CON application process is administrative relief.[60] Examples of administrative relief include fee reduction and a simplified application process.[61] As mentioned earlier, the current Tennessee CON application process is quite complex. It can take months for an application to be approved and thousands of dollars to apply. This CON application process is similar in other CON regulated states as well. If the fees were significantly reduced and the application process were made much simpler, there might be an increase in applications—and eventually an increase in the healthcare system's accessibility.

One final recommendation that may assist with CON reform is early temporary suspension of CON laws during an emergency (i.e., a pandemic). On March 11, 2020, the United Nations and the World Health Organization declared a pandemic of SARS-CoV-2, the virus that causes COVID-19.[62] Because of the limitations imposed by CON laws, many states were unprepared for the increased need of healthcare during the pandemic.

While many states (e.g., New York, Tennessee, Virginia, Georgia) temporarily suspended their CON laws in spring 2020, their response was not quick enough to handle the COVID-19 outbreak.[63] New York, for example, suspended its CON laws in mid-March, but this gave healthcare providers only one week to prepare for the exponential growth in demand that they were about to experience.[64] According to a 2018 study, there are approximately 2.8 hospital beds per 1,000 people in the United States.[65] Compared to other countries this number is terribly low: for example, China has 4.3 beds per 1,000 and France has 6.5 beds per 1,000.[66] If states decide to retain their CON laws after the COVID-19 pandemic, it would be worthwhile for them to investigate the pre and post effects the temporary suspension had on healthcare accessibility and cost.

Conclusion

When certificates of need were first introduced, they were intended to increase equity in healthcare. Although they were well intentioned, these policies have contributed to increased healthcare costs and limited access to healthcare.

Research suggests that CON laws do not support the expansion of healthcare services that communities and patients desperately need. Overall, the best policy for improving access to care and attaining higher-quality care is to remove CON laws. For states where a full repeal is unachievable, an alternative strategy is to modify CON laws by allowing for more capital expenditure for existing facilities. Georgia's and Maryland's experiences with this strategy appear promising.

Access to high-quality healthcare services is vital for the well-being of individuals in communities across the US. Despite the intentions of their proponents, CON laws are more of a barrier to these goals than a pathway toward better health outcomes. Policymakers should pursue reforms that either remove CON laws or bring them into line with their intended outcomes of increased accessibility and lowered healthcare costs.

Appendix: Empirical Studies of Certificate-of-Need Regulation and Health Spending

Effect of CON Regulation on Per Unit Costs, Prices, or Charges

Study	Effect of CON regulation	Quotation
Monica Noether, "Competition among Hospitals," *Journal of Health Economics* 7, no. 3 (September 1988): 259–84.	CON regulation increases the average price for specific disease categories such as congestive heart failure and pneumonia.	"CON's strongest effect is that it creates cost-raising inefficiencies which are passed on in higher prices."
David C. Grabowski, Robert L. Ohsfeldt, and Michael A. Morrisey, "The Effects of CON Repeal on Medicaid Nursing Home and Long-Term Care Expenditures," *Inquiry: A Journal of Medical Care Organization, Provision, and Financing* 40, no. 2 (Summer 2003): 146–57.	CON repeal has no statistically significant effect on per diem Medicaid nursing home charges or per diem Medicaid long-term care charges.	"The results . . . show that regulatory change did not have a statistically significant effect on either Medicaid payment rates or overall days."
Vivian Ho and Meei-Hsiang Ku-Goto, "State Deregulation and Medicare Costs for Acute Cardiac Care," *Medical Care Research and Review* 70, no. 2 (April 2013): 185–205.	Removing CON regulation decreases the cost of some procedures.	"We found that states that dropped CON experienced lower costs per patient for coronary artery bypass grafts (CABG) but not for percutaneous coronary intervention (PCI)."
James B. Bailey, "Can Health Spending Be Reined In through Supply Constraints? An Evaluation of Certificate-of-Need Laws" (Mercatus Working Paper, Mercatus Center at George Mason University, Arlington, VA, July 2016).	Removing CON reduces hospital charges by 5.5% five years after repeal.	"CON repeal . . . is associated with . . . a statistically significant 1.1% reduction in average hospital charges per year (a 5.5% reduction for a mature CON repeal)."

Effect of CON Regulation on Expenditures

Study	Effect of CON regulation	Quotes
Frank A. Sloan and Bruce Steinwald, "Effects of Regulation on Hospital Costs and Input Use," *Journal of Law and Economics* 23, no. 1 (April 1980): 81–109.	Comprehensive CON programs have no effect on hospital expenditures per patient day; noncomprehensive programs increase hospital expenditures per patient day.	"The short-run effect of a mature, noncomprehensive program is to raise total expense per adjusted patient day by nearly 5 percent; the long-run effect is over twice this."
Frank A. Sloan, "Regulation and the Rising Cost of Hospital Care," *Review of Economics and Statistics* 63, no. 4 (November 1981): 479–87.	CON regulation has no effect on hospital expenditures per admission, per patient day, or per adjusted patient day.	"The certificate-of-need coefficients imply CON has had no impact on costs."
Joyce A. Lanning, Michael A. Morrisey, and Robert L. Ohsfeldt, "Endogenous Hospital Regulation and Its Effects on Hospital and Non-hospital Expenditures," *Journal of Regulatory Economics* 3 (June 1991): 137–54.	CON regulation increases per capita hospital, nonhospital, and total health expenditures.	"The coefficient of CON is positive and statistically significant in all three expenditure equations. The most pronounced effect is on hospital expenditures, where CON appears to add 20.6 percent to per capita hospital expenditures in the long run. This is consistent with the view that CON programs act to protect inefficient hospitals from competition."
John J. Antel, Robert L. Ohsfeldt, and Edmund R. Becker, "State Regulation and Hospital Costs," *Review of Economics and Statistics* 77, no. 3 (August 1995): 416–22.	CON regulation increases per-day and per-admission hospital expenditures but has no relationship to per capita hospital expenditures.	"CON investment controls imply higher per day and per admission costs, but have no statistically significant effect on per capita cost."
Christopher J. Conover and Frank A. Sloan, "Does Removing Certificate-of-Need Regulations Lead to a Surge in Health Care Spending?," *Journal of Health Politics, Policy and Law* 23, no. 3 (1998): 455–81.	CON regulation has no effect on total per capita health expenditures; there is no evidence of a surge in spending after repeal.	"Mature CON programs are associated with a modest (5 percent) long-term reduction in acute care spending per capita, but not with a significant reduction in total per capita spending. There is no evidence of a surge in acquisition of facilities or in costs following removal of CON regulations."

Study	Effect of CON regulation	Quotes
Nancy A. Miller, Charlene Harrington, and Elizabeth Goldstein, "Access to Community-Based Long-Term Care: Medicaid's Role," *Journal of Aging and Health* 14, no. 1 (February 2002): 138–59.	CON regulation increases per capita Medicaid community-based care expenditures.	"Use of a nursing home CON or combined CON/moratorium was associated with increased community-based care expenditures."
David C. Grabowski, Robert L. Ohsfeldt, and Michael A. Morrisey, "The Effects of CON Repeal on Medicaid Nursing Home and Long-Term Care Expenditures," *Inquiry: A Journal of Medical Care Organization, Provision, and Financing* 40, no. 2 (Summer 2003): 146–57.	CON repeal has no statistically significant effect on either aggregate Medicaid nursing home expenditures or aggregate Medicaid long-term care expenditures.	"Using aggregate state-level data from 1981 through 1998, this study found that states that repealed their CON and moratorium laws had no significant growth in either nursing home or long-term care Medicaid expenditures"
Patrick A. Rivers, Myron D. Fottler, and Zeedan Younis, "Does Certificate of Need Really Contain Hospital Costs in the United States?," *Health Education Journal* 66, no. 3 (2007): 229–44.	CON laws increase hospital expenditures per adjusted admission.	"The results indicate that CON laws had a positive, statistically significant relationship to hospital costs per adjusted admission. . . .These findings suggest not only that CON do not really contain hospital costs, but may actually increase them by reducing competition."
Fred J. Hellinger, "The Effect of Certificate-of-Need Laws on Hospital Beds and Healthcare Expenditures: An Empirical Analysis," *American Journal of Managed Care* 15, no. 10 (October 2009): 737–44.	CON regulation is associated with fewer hospital beds, which in turn are associated with slower growth in aggregate health expenditures per capita. But there is no direct relationship between CON regulation and health expenditures per capita.	"Certificate-of-need programs did not have a direct effect on healthcare expenditures. . . . Certificate-of-need programs have limited the growth in the supply of hospital beds, and this has led to a slight reduction in the growth of healthcare expenditures."

Study	Effect of CON regulation	Quotes
Patrick A. Rivers, Myron D. Fottler, and Jemima Frimpong, "The Effects of Certificate of Need Regulation on Hospital Costs," *Journal of Health Care Finance* 36, no. 4 (July 2010): 1–16.	Stringent CON programs increase hospital expenditures per admission.	"Implications from these results include the inability of CNR [CON regulations] to contain HC [hospital costs] as assumed or expected, and the possibility that CNR [CON regulations] may actually increase HC [hospital costs], while reducing competition."
Momotazur Rahman et al., "The Impact of Certificate-of-Need Laws on Nursing Home and Home Health Care Expenditures," *Medical Care Research and Review* 73, no. 1 (February 2016): 85–105.	CON regulation increases the growth in Medicare and Medicaid expenditures on nursing home care but decreases the growth in home healthcare expenditures.	"Compared with states without CON laws, Medicare and Medicaid spending in states with CON laws grew faster for nursing home care and more slowly for home health care."
James B. Bailey, "Can Health Spending Be Reined In through Supply Constraints? An Evaluation of Certificate-of-Need Laws" (Mercatus Working Paper, Mercatus Center at George Mason University, Arlington, VA, July 2016).	CON regulation is associated with higher overall per capita healthcare expenditures and with higher per capita Medicare expenditures.	"CON increases total health spending [per capita] by a statistically significant 3.1%. Increases are especially high for spending on physician care—a statistically significant 5.0%. . . . CON is estimated to increase overall Medicare spending [per capita] by a statistically significant 6.9%."

Effect of CON Regulation on Hospital Efficiency

Study	Effect of CON regulation	Quotation
B. Kelly Eakin, "Allocative Inefficiency in the Production of Hospital Services," *Southern Economic Journal* 58, no. 1 (July 1991): 240–48.	CON hospitals are less efficient than non-CON hospitals.	"Hospitals subject to CON regulations have a greater measure of allocative inefficiency by .88 to 1.03 percentage points."
Laurie J. Bates, Kankana Mukherjee, Rexford E. Santerre, "Market Structure and Technical Efficiency in the Hospital Services Industry: A DEA Approach," *Medical Care Research and Review* 63, no. 4 (2006): 499–524.	CON hospitals are not any less efficient than non-CON hospitals.	"Evidence . . . implies that the presence of a state certificate-of-need law was not associated with a greater degree of inefficiency in the typical metropolitan hospital services industry."

Study	Effect of CON regulation	Quotation
Gary D. Ferrier, Hervé Leleu, and Vivian G. Valdmanis, "The Impact of CON Regulation on Hospital Efficiency," *Health Care Management Science* 13, no. 1 (March 2010): 84–100.	CON hospitals are more efficient than non-CON hospitals.	"In general, we found that the hospital sector in states with active CON regulations performed better in terms of aggregate technical and mix efficiency, irrespective of the stringency or laxness of this oversight."
Michael D. Rosko and Ryan L. Mutter, "The Association of Hospital Cost-Inefficiency with Certificate-of-Need Regulation," *Medical Care Research and Review* 71, no. 3 (June 2014): 280–98.	CON hospitals are more efficient than non-CON hospitals.	"Average estimated cost-inefficiency was less in CON states (8.10%) than in non-CON states (12.46%)."

Effect of CON Regulation on Investment

Study	Effect of CON regulation	Quotation
David S. Salkever and Thomas W. Bice, "The Impact of Certificate of Need Controls on Hospital Investment," *Milbank Memorial Fund Quarterly: Health and Society* 54, no. 2 (Spring 1976): 185–214.	CON regulation does not decrease investment, but does change its composition.	"CON did not reduce the total dollar volume of investment but altered its composition, retarding expansion in bed supplies but increasing investment in new services and equipment."
Fred J. Hellinger, "The Effect of Certificate-of-Need Legislation on Hospital Investment," *Inquiry: A Journal of Medical Care Organization, Provision, and Financing* 13, no. 2 (June 1976): 187–93.	CON legislation induced hospitals to increase investments.	"The empirical results support the hypotheses that [CON] legislation has not significantly lowered hospital investment and that hospitals anticipated the effect of [CON] legislation by increasing investment in the period preceding the enactment of the legislation."

Source: Matthew D. Mitchell, "Do Certificate-of-Need Laws Limit Spending?" (Mercatus Working Paper, Mercatus Center at George Mason University, Arlington, VA, September 2016).

Land Use and Energy Standards

CHAPTER 9

Land Use Regulation and Housing Affordability

Emily Hamilton

Every city in the United States has implemented land use regulations that limit the amount of housing that can be built within city borders and raise the cost of new housing construction. These rules are framed as tools for reducing the negative externalities of development, such as noise that carries across property lines or shadows that buildings cast on their neighbors. However, these regulations also stand in the way of people's opportunity to live in the locality of their choice at a price affordable to their household. This chapter covers the history of land use regulations; the potential that a lightly regulated market could deliver housing at a wide range of price points; the effect of land use regulations on housing affordability; and, finally, potential solutions that could allow more people to live in the locations of their choice.

Localities implemented the early U.S. zoning codes during the Progressive Era. The first U.S. zoning code adopted in New York City in 1916 took steps toward limiting the mass of buildings as well as separating buildings by use. It was implemented at the behest of department store owners, who wanted to keep garment factories from encroaching on the blocks that they wanted to maintain as exclusive shopping destinations. Today, however, land use regulations primarily serve to separate single-family neighborhoods from land available for any other use and to prevent the redevelopment of a single-family home for any other use.

In addition to business interests, early supporters of zoning included progressive reformers. The reformers argued that tall buildings, made feasible by elevators and new construction techniques, contributed to disease by allowing high population density. With the advent of streetcar technology that made it possible for people to commute farther to their downtown jobs, these reformers supported clearing away densely populated, low-income neighborhoods and encouraging the residents to move to low-density, single-family homes with yards. Slum clearance was paired with the construction of public housing, but often there was a net loss of housing units and the public housing units were available to families with higher incomes than those who had been living in the bulldozed homes.[1]

When New York implemented its zoning code, other US cities were already working on their own land use ordinances that shared similar objectives of separating uses and limiting density.[2] Today, development in every US city is constrained by land use regulations. Houston is often cited as an example of an unzoned city. While it doesn't have a use-zoning code like all other major American cities, it does have land use regulations, including parking requirements and minimum lot size standards that serve some of the same purposes as zoning.[3]

Early zoning ordinances were not without their critics, primarily in the real estate industry. Some argued that land use regulations that reduced land values constitute an unconstitutional taking of private property and that localities lacked a rational basis for determining zoning designations. This theory was eventually put to the test in Euclid, Ohio. The Ambler Realty Company sued for the right to build an industrial project on land that was zoned for various other uses. In 1926, the case reached the US Supreme Court, and the court held that localities may legally separate land zoned for commercial and residential uses and multifamily from single-family zoned land.[4]

From the beginning, land use regulation in the US has been a tool of exclusion. The New York shopkeepers who supported zoning to keep factories out of shopping districts were often more concerned about keeping the factories' immigrant workers away from their stores than about the factories themselves.[5] Until *Buchanan v. Warley* in 1916, some municipalities implemented pre-zoning land use regulations that explicitly barred African Americans from purchasing homes in parts of localities.[6] Following the ruling that explicitly race-based zoning violated Fourteenth Amendment protections for freedom of contract, localities turned to zoning rules that drove up housing costs, including single-family zoning and minimum lot size requirements.[7] While these rules segregate neighborhoods by income rather than race, they have outsize effects on racial groups, including African Americans (who have lower incomes on average than the average for the country as a whole).

As legal scholar Bernard Siegan explains,

> All zoning is exclusionary, and is expected to be exclusionary; that is its purpose and intent. The provisions governing almost every zoning district operate to exclude certain uses of property from certain portions of the land, and thereby in the case of housing, the people who would occupy the housing excluded.[8]

When jurisdiction after jurisdiction implements exclusionary zoning, entire regions become unaffordable to low- and even middle-income households. Residents in search of affordable housing may move to exurbs that are far from many jobs and require long commutes, but at a certain point driving farther in search of affordability becomes untenable in terms of time and transportation costs.

Some early zoning proponents said that reducing population density would improve public health. During the COVID-19 pandemic, New York Governor Andrew Cuomo made a similar argument, tweeting of New York City, "Density is still too high and is still too dangerous." However, in both instances, overcrowding was the threat to public health rather than density. Crowding refers to the number of people sharing a room, whereas density refers to the number of people living on a fixed amount of land. Overcrowding can occur in high- or low-density locations and has contributed to the spread of Covid-19 from urban to rural low-income areas. Researchers at Johns Hopkins University have identified no correlation between either population density or crowding and Covid-19 infection rates at the county level.[9] However, other analyses have found a relationship between crowding and Covid-19 spread.[10] To the extent that reduced crowding improves public health, permitting more housing to be built at lower costs in the locations where people want to live supports not only economic opportunity, but better health outcomes as well.

Filtering: How the Market Can Deliver Housing Affordability

Through the mid-20th century, housing markets provided housing to residents at a wide range of income levels, even in the face of rapid population growth. In his book *Living Downtown*, Paul Groth explains that boarding houses and single-room-occupancy buildings provided a key source of market-rate housing that was affordable even to very low-wage workers in cities like San Francisco and New York.[11] By sharing a bathroom and relying on urban neighborhoods to provide affordable food options and space for socializing, these residents were able to keep their living costs affordable even in cities with high land prices. Today, land-use restrictions that require each new housing unit to be a minimum size and include prescribed amenities rule out lower-cost housing options.

Before zoning was implemented in Manhattan, neighborhoods that had been built as single-family homes were often repurposed as boarding houses to put real estate to its most profitable use in a rapidly growing city. While historically land use regulations allowed builders to provide housing that was designed for low-income tenants, housing that had been initially built for high- or middle-income residents also tended to become more affordable to less-well-off residents over time. Because lower-income residents were willing to share space in subdivided houses or purpose-built apartments, they were able to outbid higher-income residents for the most desirable locations.[12] Those who wanted to live in a single-family home surrounded by other single-family homes had to keep moving northward as land in the heart of the city was put to more valuable use over time as denser housing and commercial space.[13]

In liberal markets, housing becomes affordable to lower-income people over time in two ways. First, a household may sell a house to a landlord, who then rents it out as rooms or converts it into an apartment building. This process turns one large home into smaller, more affordable homes. But second, even housing that isn't subdivided becomes more affordable over time through a process called *filtering*. The majority of people moving into new-construction housing are moving out of older, somewhat less desirable housing. Today, land use regulations that limit new housing construction and set minimum standards for housing unit sizes have restricted both the rate of filtering and the price point it can start from. Nonetheless, filtering provides an important source of housing affordable to low- and middle-income Americans today. According to one estimate, filtering leads real home prices to fall by 1.9 percent per year.[14]

Economist Evan Mast looks at the moves that new construction causes in a study of 686 multifamily developments.[15] Mast finds that 100 new units open up 70 units in below-median income neighborhoods and 40 units in bottom-quintiles income neighborhoods.

The filtering process can start from a lower price point if localities allow for relatively low-cost new construction typologies, including multifamily construction. Additionally, the process accelerates when existing homes are allowed to be subdivided into smaller homes. Today, single-family zoning prevents such subdivision in the majority of the country's residential neighborhoods. Neighborhoods and cities that have set up severe obstacles to new housing construction may experience the reverse of filtering, in which a stagnant supply of housing becomes more expensive over time as demand increases and existing homes go to higher-income residents over time.[16]

Increasingly Binding Housing Supply Constraints

Not all land use regulations change development outcomes. In some cases when land at the outskirts of urban regions is developed for the first time, localities zone the land to match what homebuilders want to provide. In this case, regulations may be *non-binding.* Rules that do have an effect on development outcomes are called *binding* regulations.

Land use regulations in US cities have become more binding over time, and as a result they're having larger effects on housing supply and house prices.[17] Localities have been using zoning to limit development for more than 100 years, but it wasn't until the 1970s that entire regions began experiencing high and rising house prices in response to these supply constraints.[18] Before that time period, center cities typically courted growth while built-out suburbs sought to limit it in order to maintain low density.[19] Nonetheless, farther-flung suburbs generally still had plenty of undeveloped land that they were willing to make available for relatively low-cost development.

Economist William Fischel argues that the rise of the environmental movement led to a sympathetic argument that homeowners could use in support of limiting development.[20] Neighbors who oppose growth in their proximity may argue that development would harm local habitats. On a larger scale, however, infill growth—redeveloping existing neighborhoods at denser levels—is much less environmentally harmful than new growth at the urban fringe.[21] Nonetheless, homeowners, whom Fischel labels "homevoters" for their outsize influence on local policy decisions, have used environmental concerns to successfully block development in many jurisdictions.[22] By blocking change in their neighborhoods, homevoters may limit the risk that new construction could lower the value of their home, which is often their largest financial asset. They also create the potential for large windfall gains, should demand for housing increase in an area where building new supply is politically difficult.[23]

The problem of inelastic housing supply—a housing market in which increases in demand for housing result in relatively little construction and relatively large prices increases—in a policy environment shaped by homevoters is most severe in high-cost coastal cities. But it's not limited to these jurisdictions. During the housing boom from 2012 through 2017, house prices rose significantly faster than household incomes. Relative to the boom from 1996 to 2006, however, the housing supply response has been substantially smaller during the more recent boom.[24] Since the financial crisis, no metro area in the country has reached the rate of residential building permits per capita that it experienced from 1990 to 2007.[25]

The Land Use Regulations Preventing New Housing Construction

The most important land use regulation standing in the way of new housing is single-family zoning. In California, the state with the largest affordability problem, 80 percent of the land zoned for residential development is designated exclusively for single-family housing, and denser housing typologies are banned in these areas.[26]

On top of single-family zoning that restricts lower-cost multifamily housing construction, all US cities and suburbs enforce rules including minimum lot size requirements and setback requirements that require each home to sit on a certain amount of land. Using data from 2000, urban economists Edward Glaeser, Joseph Gyourko, and Raven Saks estimate the cost of regulations that limit residential construction. They find that New York; Boston; Los Angeles; Newport News, Virginia; Oakland, California; Salt Lake City; San Francisco; San Jose, California; and Washington, DC, all have "zoning taxes" that accounted for at least 10 percent of housing costs at the time of their study.[27] Housing affordability and the effects of land use regulations on new housing supply have certainly become worse since 2000.

Gyourko and coauthors Jonathan Hartley and Jacob Krimmel recently released an index of land use regulations and building permit approval processes across metropolitan areas. To develop their Wharton Residential Land Use Regulatory Index (WRLURI), they survey policymakers in jurisdictions across the country.[28] Of course, many market and policy factors beyond zoning affect house prices, such as regional demand for housing and geographic constraints on building new housing, among others. Nonetheless, local rules and institutions that determine what can be built in a locality and how long developers typically have to spend to get approvals are an important factor in determining house prices. Figure 1 shows the relationship between WRLURI and median house prices. WRLURI explains 40 percent of price variation across metropolitan areas.

In high-cost cities, limits on density clearly prevent the subdivision and redevelopment that market actors would otherwise make to increase housing supply and bring down prices. But new research shows that these regulations shape market outcomes even in places with relatively elastic housing supply. Researchers Nolan Gray and Salim Furth show that in three fast-growing Texas suburbs, new homes are concentrated close to the minimum zoned lot size, indicating the presence of binding regulations.[29] Additionally, many developers in these jurisdictions seek variances in order to build new homes on lots that are smaller than the minimum allowable lot size on the books.[30] Seeking regulatory exemptions adds to the costs of development, and the additional cost is passed on to consumers in the form of higher house prices.

In addition to density restrictions, in jurisdictions where land is expensive, parking requirements play an important role in driving up housing construction costs. When land is scarce, developers build mandated parking in aboveground or underground garages where each spot costs tens of thousands of dollars to build. In one typical Los Angeles multifamily project, parking was only feasible to build in an underground garage. For each one-bedroom unit in Los Angeles, developers are required to build two parking spots, at a cost of more than $100,000 per unit.[31] In the absence of parking requirements, residential builders would still provide parking to people willing to pay for it, but households willing to forgo a car (or to have one car instead of two) would have the freedom to economize on parking costs.

On top of restrictions that limit density and housing supply within cities, in some cases additional land use restrictions limit new building at the urban fringe. Urban growth boundaries (UGBs) are a key component of smart growth planning, a planning school that emerged in the 1970s as a response to traditional zoning practices that restrict traditional development patterns.

However, smart growth principles have never been fully implemented. Rather than repealing rules like parking requirements and single-family zoning that stand in the way of dense, walkable development, local policymakers who have implemented smart growth policies have generally layered UGBs on top of these traditional zoning

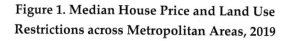

Figure 1. Median House Price and Land Use Restrictions across Metropolitan Areas, 2019

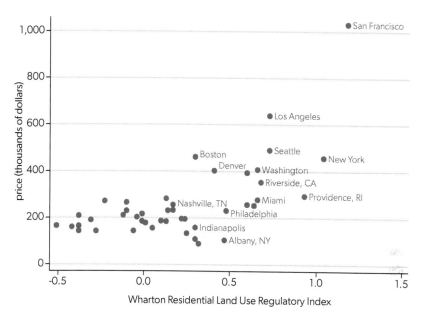

Sources: Index values are from Joseph Gyourko, Jonathan Hartley, and Jacob Krimmel, "The Local Residential Land Use Regulatory Environment across U.S. Housing Markets: Evidence from a New Wharton Index" (NBER Working Paper No. 26573, National Bureau of Economic Research, Cambridge, MA, December 2019); median house price data are from "Housing Data," Zillow Research, ZHVI All Homes Time Series ($) (data set), accessed February 24, 2020, https://www.zillow.com/research/data/.

restrictions. In turn, UGBs have further constrained new housing supply and contributed to house price increases.

Research is mixed on the effect of UGBs on house prices. Portland, Oregon, has perhaps the most binding UGB in the country. One study found that Portland's UGB did not cause house prices around Portland to rise between 1990 and 2000.[32] Since then, however, Portland house prices have more than doubled after accounting for inflation. Other studies have found that UGBs raise land prices for land inside the boundary,[33] and a study from the 1980s found the same effect for house prices.[34]

Historic neighborhoods often have the characteristics that smart growth advocates promote, including dense, walkable development.

But traditional zoning and historic preservation rules prevent new development in these neighborhoods that would allow more people to live in them. Historic preservation is particularly prevalent in Manhattan, where nearly one-third of buildings are landmarked.[35] One study of the effects of preservation on house prices finds that outside Manhattan in New York City, historic preservation increases property prices of homes that have redevelopment potential and those that are landmarked. However, within Manhattan, where the option to redevelop is most valuable, historic designation raises the prices of homes that are not preserved but has a smaller positive price effect for those that are.[36]

On the whole, there is a strong consensus among economists that in expensive coastal regions land use regulations are standing in the way of new housing construction and are causing high and rising house prices.[37]

Consequences of Supply Constraints and High Prices for Housing

Land use regulations that constrain building supply and lead to an inelastic supply of housing harm society's most vulnerable members the most. These regulations have devastating effects for low-income renters in high-cost cities. On average, households in the lowest income quintile spend more than 60 percent of their income on housing, whether they're renters or homeowners.[38] This means typical low-income households are severely cost-burdened: they may have insufficient funds to meet their other needs beyond housing, they may live in crowded conditions, or they may endure long and unpleasant commutes. A study from Zillow finds that as median rents exceed 32 percent of the median household's income, homelessness rates begin to rise.[39]

The consequences of land use regulations that constrain housing supply are not limited to residents who are directly burdened by high rents. Land use regulations also have macroeconomic consequences because they cause "spatial misallocation," meaning workers don't live in the locations with the best opportunities because of housing supply constraints.[40] While the highest-earning individuals can afford housing in the location of their choice, land use regulations may force those earning less to choose between living in the location where their best job opportunities are located and living in a location where they can afford decent housing and a reasonable commute.

Land use regulations reduce income mobility by shutting out relatively low-income residents from locations with high-paying jobs. Economists Peter Ganong and Daniel Shoag show that income convergence across states between 1990 and 2010 was less than half of the rate it was from 1880 to 1980, as people stopped moving from lower-income states to higher-income states.[41]

In addition to reducing income mobility, spatial misallocation reduces economic growth when people can't live in the locations where they could be most productive. Cities provide opportunities for a high density of people and firms to collocate and learn from each other. By locking out population growth, land use regulations stand in the way of growth and innovation. Macroeconomists have estimated that land use regulations reduce US GDP substantially, by between hundreds of billions[42] and trillions of dollars.[43]

Failed Solutions

In the face of high and rising housing costs in expensive cities, state and local policymakers are under pressure to pursue policies to increase affordability for their residents. In 2019, Oregon and California passed statewide rent control laws in an attempt to reduce rent burdens and rent hikes for current tenants, and New York reformed its rent control policy to allow stricter rent control across the state.

Rent control gives tenants some of the benefits of homeownership by offering relatively predictable housing costs. However, it comes with serious consequences for the supply of rental housing. A recent study of rent control in San Francisco found that buildings affected by the city's rent control law were 8 percentage points more likely to be converted to condos than buildings that were exempt from the law.[44] While rent control benefits those who live in rent-controlled units, the authors find that it reduced the supply of relatively low-cost rental housing, at the expense of renters who weren't lucky enough to secure a protected apartment.

While rent control is primarily limited to some of the highest-cost coastal cities, inclusionary zoning is a similar policy becoming increasingly common across the country.[45] Under inclusionary zoning, homebuilders are required or incentivized to build below-market-rate housing units as part of new market-rate projects. The subsidized units are required to be affordable to households making a certain percentage of the median income over time. Localities often offer density bonuses that allow homebuilders to build more market-rate housing than they would be permitted to construct under the underlying zoning.

A requirement that developers provide subsidized housing as a component of new housing developments is a tax on new construction that can be expected to reduce housing supply and drive up prices. However, the density bonuses that inclusionary zoning often incorporates allow more housing supply than would otherwise be permitted. This makes its overall effect on new housing construction and market-rate house prices ambiguous.

Five studies have estimated the effect of inclusionary zoning on house prices, and three find that it increases prices relative to the counterfactual. One finds mixed effects, and one finds that inclusionary zoning reduced median market-rate prices.[46] Further, the density bonuses that inclusionary programs typically include derive their value from the fact that traditional zoning regulations prevent homebuilders from providing as much housing as would be profitable given demand. Without exclusionary zoning that gives value to density bonuses, inclusionary zoning would be a clear tax on new housing construction.

Like rent control, inclusionary zoning can provide large benefits for the residents who receive price-controlled homes. Like rent control, it fails to address the core cause of housing unaffordability in growing regions—exclusionary zoning and limitations on relatively low-cost housing typologies. These policies give state and local politicians the tools to appear to address the problem of unaffordability without threatening the exclusionary zoning order that homevoters support.

Successful Reform at the Local Level

The homevoter dynamics at the local level create serious obstacles to reform at the local level. Relative to renters, homeowners are more likely to stay in the same jurisdiction over time[47], and they're more likely to vote.[48] Local politicians are therefore incentivized to appease these homevoters with exclusionary zoning policy rather than liberalizing housing policy to allow in new residents who might be less inclined to reelect them than the current electorate is.

Nonetheless, several US cities provide models for accommodating growth and maintaining affordability. Houston is famous for not having a zoning code and for allowing rapid suburban development on its urban fringe. But it also allows dense redevelopment. In 1999, Houston reduced the minimum lot size within its Interstate 610 loop to 1,400 square feet, making it possible for a single house to be redeveloped with three townhouses.[49] More recently, it eliminated parking requirements in some downtown neighborhoods. Localities across the country, from Portland to Atlanta have legalized accessory dwelling units (ADUs). And Minneapolis implemented a zoning reform to permit triplexes across the parts of the city where previously only single-family houses were allowed. Rather than permitting a bit more density across the city, Seattle has taken the approach of permitting high-rise residential development in its "urban villages."

These examples show that in some cases local reform is politically possible. However, local reform ends at the municipal limits, and metro areas comprise many jurisdictions, each of which sets its own land use regulations and is responsive to its own voters. In general, the incentives at the local level are biased in favor of the heavily regulated status quo.

Arguments in Support of Local Control in Land Use

In spite of the serious costs of allowing homevoters to have strong influence over land use regulations, local control over land use decisions remains popular among many groups. Historically, early progressive supporters of zoning and other land use regulations argued that these regulations were necessary for improving the living conditions of low-income people living in urban tenements. Conditions for low-wage workers in urban centers were indeed poor—homes were overcrowded, and crowding and poor sanitation contributed to public health problems.

As an alternative to urban apartments, progressives promoted moving the residents of tenements to suburbs, from which downtown jobs were newly accessible by streetcar. They argued that owner-occupied, single-family homes promoted healthy and virtuous lifestyles.[50] They promoted local land use regulations as a tool to maintain exclusively single-family development in the suburbs and to implement slum clearance policies to eliminate tenements in the cities.

Local control over land use regulations also has support among conservatives, who tend to prefer subsidiarity—the principle of devolving policy decisions to the lowest level of government possible. Political philosopher Loren King explains two justifications for this subsidiarity:

> One rationale appeals to personal autonomy and liberal-democratic legitimacy: leave political decisions at the institutional scale closest to those affected by those judgments, just because legitimate authority rests—in the first and most critical instance—with the free and informed consent of those moral agents most obviously affected by political decisions. Political decisions are always ultimately backed by coercion, and such coercion can only be legitimately authorized by reasons that are responsive to each citizen's equal moral standing as at once both the subject and the final author of that coercion. Decisions made closest to those most affected are more likely to satisfy this criterion of legitimacy, treating us as properly autonomous citizens. Another rationale is (moderately) communitarian in spirit. Our most cherished relationships tend to be in our families and communities, churches and neighborhoods—a variety of associations we are either born and raised into or sometimes choose to enter on the basis of our considered values and aspirations. It is typically within such communities that our broader conceptions of justice and the good life are formulated and affirmed. This associative richness is to be applauded, and if government must interfere with civic or nonpublic associations, best that it do so in ways that are least intrusive and most carefully tailored to

achieve whatever public purposes necessitated interference in the first place.[51]

In addition to both progressives and conservatives who offer ideological justifications for giving local governments control over land use, others support zoning from an efficiency perspective. They argue that bargaining over allowable land use is inefficient: A group of residents may be willing to pay a commercial landowner enough to entice the landowner to locate away from their neighborhood, but the residents face a coordination problem that keeps them from facilitating this transaction.[52] From this perspective, local governments stepping in to separate land uses is welfare-enhancing.

Edward Glaeser and Joseph Gyourko write, "Empirical investigations of the local costs and benefits of restricting building generally conclude that the negative externalities are not nearly large enough to justify the costs of regulation."[53] Land use regulations do prevent externalities, for instance when they block tall buildings that would cast shadows on neighboring properties. However, they also prevent the positive externalities that emerge when more people are able to afford housing in their preferred location. In the abstract, most people agree that more housing should be permitted in the regions where people want to live. This is reflected in the plethora of proposals from federal policymakers for encouraging local zoning reform.[54] But when it comes to specific proposals for new housing, particularly multifamily housing, local residents very often find a reason to oppose construction in their backyard.

The Role for State Preemption

While a few localities have implemented pro-housing reforms, in general states have clear legal and economic bases for setting limits on local land use regulations. Local jurisdictions are "creatures of their states," so even "home rule" states can limit local regulatory authority. The effects of local restrictions on new housing spill across local political boundaries, limiting population growth, economic growth, and income mobility at the state and national levels. Because reversing these trends are valid objectives for state policymakers, they have a role to play in limiting exclusionary zoning and protecting property owners' rights to build more housing.

From its beginning, zoning has been used to block multifamily housing and uphold the authority of local governments to create exclusively single-family neighborhoods.[55] This has arguably been more consequential than zoning's role in separating incompatible land uses, particularly as industrial uses have become cleaner over time and as changes in transportation networks have naturally led industrial users to want to move away from dense urban areas.

In the Supreme Court, local governments' police power to protect "general welfare" has been interpreted such that local policymakers may restrict property rights in land use to meet the preferences and financial interests of the jurisdiction's current residents, with no consideration for the costs of these policies to property owners or to prospective residents who are shut out of the jurisdiction by supply constraints.[56] But not all state courts share this jurisprudence. For example, New Jersey courts have held that municipalities must consider the effects of their zoning laws on residents who live outside their borders.[57]

Recent reforms at the state level show how states may set limits on local exclusionary zoning. In 2019, Oregon passed a state law that eliminated single-family zoning in much of the state. It requires all localities with at least 25,000 residents to allow up to fourplexes or "cottage clusters" of small single-family homes on lots currently zoned for single-family units exclusively.[58] For cities with between 10,000 and 25,000 residents, the law upzones single-family lots to allow duplex construction.

In 2016, California policymakers passed a law that requires all the state's localities to allow ADUs on all lots that have single-family homes. In Los Angeles particularly, the law has led to a surge in ADU permitting. Following the law's passage, at least 2,500 new ADUs have been built in the city, representing a 1,000 percent increase in permitting.[59] In 2019, California policymakers took an additional step, allowing all homeowners to build second "junior" ADUs—effectively setting the lower bound of density restrictions in the state to triplex zoning.[60]

Following the principle of subsidiarity provides advantages in some areas of local policymaking, increasing voters' options to live in a jurisdiction that matches their policy preferences. But land use regulations that prevent housing construction, thus reducing the potential for population growth, reduce residents' opportunities to choose between jurisdictions. When land use decisions are made at the neighborhood or municipal level, the costs of construction tend to be emphasized rather than the long-term benefits of allowing more people to live in their location of choice. Therefore, states have an important role to play in protecting individual rights from local restrictions by limiting the extent to which localities may restrict housing construction.

Conclusion

In particularly exclusionary jurisdictions, local land use regulations stand in the way of new housing supply being built in response to new demand. This situation leads to the price for a fixed supply of housing being bid up. This, in turn, creates painful trade-offs for all kinds of households, but it particularly burdens low-income renters.

While some cities have successfully liberalized land use regulations, incentives are stacked against liberalization at the local level. Local policymakers are incentivized to please homevoters in order to stay in office, and homevoters are incentivized to oppose development in order to increase their property's value through scarcity.

States have a role to play in limiting the extent to which localities constrain new housing construction, because the costs of housing supply constraints spill over across local borders. Municipalities derive from their states their authority to use their police power to protect their residents' interests through land use regulations, so states should require that localities consider the interests of all the state's residents when determining housing policy.

CHAPTER 10

Building Energy Codes: A Case Study in Regulation and Cost-Benefit Analysis

Matthew J. Holian

Including energy codes in building codes is a policy option for reducing energy consumption that has received increased attention since the 1970s, driven by concerns about energy security and climate change. How much have such building energy codes helped reduce energy consumption, and are they wise policies from the standpoint of society broadly conceived? This chapter introduces the major questions in the area of energy efficiency regulations in the residential sector, and then illustrates an economic technique known as cost-benefit analysis (CBA) by examining a recently published economic analysis of Florida's energy codes.[1]

My intention in presenting the case study from Florida is to illustrate the main steps in CBA, which is widely used throughout regulatory analysis. This chapter thus can be used by students, teachers, policy analysts, and others who wish to know more about how CBA could be applied to any of the regulations discussed in this volume. The practice of CBA integrates skills from across the theoretical and empirical subfields of economics, and consequently the study of CBA presents an excellent opportunity for meaningful student research projects. In the conclusion, I provide guidance that should be useful to students and professionals beginning an original CBA, and to teachers who are guiding students in this exercise.

Economists generally agree that CBA is an essential tool for selecting efficient regulations. CBA is often a part of regulatory impact analysis. It has been required for major regulations at the federal level for decades, and—at the subnational level—more and more states and cities have started to apply CBA to their public decision-making processes. For example, CBA is used at the California Department of Transportation to allocate funds among competing roadway improvement proposals.[2]

Building energy codes are a specific example of a more general category of public policies: technical and performance standards. Similar types of regulations exist for automobiles, appliances, buildings, construction equipment, and a host of other energy-consuming products. For example, the Corporate Average Fuel Economy (CAFE) program requires automobile manufacturers to achieve specified levels of fuel efficiency, as measured by miles per gallon.

Though performance standards like the CAFE standards are intended to be fuel-saving policies, they can have unintended consequences. As cars use less gasoline per mile, the effective price of driving falls and people drive more—this is the so-called rebound effect.[3] The increased driving causes congestion, pollution, and traffic accidents, which were not goals of the energy efficiency policy. It is even conceivable that more fuel-efficient vehicles could encourage suburban sprawl, as households find it easier to sustain car-based lifestyles.

Manufacturers of appliances from refrigerators to air conditioners have been required to meet increasingly tight standards since the 1970s. The average annual energy consumption of a refrigerator has fallen from 1,800 kilowatt hours in 1976 to 450 in 2001, a dramatic increase in efficiency.[4] What is responsible for the rise in efficiency of cars and refrigerators? Regulation may have played a role, but—as Arthur Rosenfeld and Deborah Poskanzer note—"the other factor contributing to the sudden drop in refrigerator energy use in the mid-1970s was the advent of a new manufacturing technology, blown-in foam insulation."[5] This example illustrates the empirical challenge of determining the independent impact of energy codes on energy demand by just examining trends in average fuel use. In the next section, I highlight two empirical techniques, randomized controlled experiments and multiple regression, that analysts can use to reach more accurate estimates of the causal effect of a policy on an outcome of interest.

State and local governments use energy codes to apply energy efficiency standards in the residential sector. We can distinguish between building codes in general and building energy codes in particular. Building codes cover many aspects of housing structures, including plumbing, accessibility, and safety. Energy codes are but one part of the overall set of regulations with which home builders have to comply.

California and Florida were among the first states to adopt building energy codes. Economists Kevin Novan, Aaron Smith, and Tianxia Zhou discuss how builders in California complied with the initial energy codes.[6] They calculate that building a 1,620-square-foot, fully compliant house in Sacramento would have cost $1,565 more than a noncompliant house (in 1980 dollars), owing to additional ceiling and wall insulation and to infiltration control (e.g., caulking and weather-stripping sources of air leakage). Its builders would have also been required to install a smaller air conditioner. Every few years, states with energy codes tend to strengthen them. Grant Jacobsen and Matthew Kotchen discuss how in Florida, a builder had multiple options for adjusting a home design feature to bring it into compliance when that state's energy codes were strengthened in 2002.[7] One option was installing low-emissivity windows, which would have increased costs of a standard Florida home by between $675 and $1,012.

The problem of asymmetric information, where a builder knows more about the home's design than the home buyer or tenants do, provides a market failure rationale for building codes. It is not easy for a home buyer or renter to see how much insulation is behind the walls, for example, and so if buildings are less energy efficient than they would be in a world without these types of informational challenges, both building codes in general and energy codes in particular could be justified on efficiency grounds.

Another motivation for building codes is energy cost myopia, a form of behavioral bias. This refers to situations where home buyers do not account for the long-term energy costs when they buy a home—they consider only the up-front costs. These are situations where consumers

are unable to rationally consider future costs. This chapter will introduce a concept called *discounting*, and we will see that energy cost
myopia could be modeled as homeowners behaving as if they have an
irrationally high discount rate. Of course, to the extent that discount
rates reflect personal preferences, an analyst imposing the "correct" discount rate on a homeowner is an example of paternalism—and there is
no consensus about what discount rate a homeowner "should" have.
In chapter 13 of this volume, James Broughel discusses the topic of
energy cost myopia in more detail.

While asymmetric information and energy cost myopia are two of
the most prominent justifications for energy codes, there are also some
ways codes could be counterproductive in terms of their intended purpose. The rebound effect, discussed above in the context of cars, also
pertains to homes. If homes are more energy efficient, the occupants
may use the air conditioner more than they otherwise would. They
may decide to bake a cake on a hot day, whereas otherwise they would
have postponed baking until the sun went down. It can be time consuming to open and close all the windows in a large home. If the home
is energy efficient, a household may decide to just keep the windows
closed and use the air conditioner all the time, whereas otherwise they
would have opened and closed the windows on the basis of the outside air temperature.

Energy efficiency regulations could also be harmful if they lull voters
into a sense of complacency regarding energy consumption. This is
a political economy point, related to one made by economist Arik
Levinson on a *Freakonomics Radio* podcast episode with Stephen Dubner.[8] Voters seem unwilling to enact a carbon tax, perhaps because
they assume the government is doing enough through energy efficiency regulations.

The subfield of economics known as public choice emphasizes the
possibility of so-called regulatory capture. Perhaps the home builders
that can most easily comply with energy codes (likely the larger builders with more ability to navigate regulations) lobby for making the
codes stricter because they know this will make smaller builders less
competitive. If the regulatory process is "captured" by private interests,

this would obviously reduce the efficiency of the new construction segment of housing markets.

A final issue that has received increased attention recently is the issue of distributional effects. Are energy codes and CAFE standards more equitable than energy or carbon taxes? In the context of homes, economists Chris Bruegge, Tatyana Deryugina, and Erica Myers find that "building energy codes result in more undesirable distortions for lower-income households."[9] In the context of automobiles, Lucas Davis and Christopher Knittel find that "fuel economy standards are more regressive than a gasoline tax with revenues returned lump sum." They conclude that "it is difficult to argue for fuel economy standards on the basis of distributional concerns."[10]

A typical view among economists is that there are often ways of reducing energy consumption that are less costly than energy efficiency regulations. In the case of CAFE standards, most of the top economists would prefer a gasoline tax over fuel economy performance standards.[11] Nobel laureate William Nordhaus writes about energy codes and related approaches that they "can supplement and buttress more comprehensive greenhouse-gas emissions limits or carbon taxes. However, they are inefficient because they require spending substantial sums for minimal impacts."[12] There may be rationales for some energy codes, especially in a world where we do not have carbon taxes, but regulators should be sensitive to the costs energy codes impose on builders. The costs and benefits of energy codes are the topics of the next section.

Evaluating Building Energy Codes: A Case Study

This section describes a recent economic analysis of building energy codes in Florida, which was carried out by Grant Jacobsen and Matthew Kotchen.[13] Jacobsen and Kotchen's analysis (hereinafter referred to as the JK analysis) has a lot in common with cost-benefit analysis, one specific type of economic analysis. Other methods of economic analysis include economic impact analysis and fiscal impact analysis, which are often mistakenly described as CBA. One of the goals is to section is to describe what CBA is, so a reader will be able to recognize when an analysis that is described as a CBA is in fact something else.[14]

CBAs are typically carried out in one of two settings. First, government agencies may commission CBAs or carry them out themselves. These studies typically strive to be comprehensive and adhere closely to the principles of CBA, but the quality of government CBAs varies widely. Second, academic journals sometimes publish CBAs, and while these may be comprehensive, they are usually shorter than the government-sponsored analyses. One reason for this is that academic studies often focus on one specific aspect of the policy in question. For example, the focus of the JK study was empirically estimating the impact of policy on energy demand. Jacobsen and Kotchen carry out an economic analysis as a secondary part of their study—six paragraphs out of the 16-page article. The fact that the JK analysis has relatively few moving parts is a virtue for my purposes, because it makes it an ideal candidate for an introduction to CBA.

Most CBAs share a common set of general features. Leading textbook authors Anthony Boardman, David Greenberg, Aidan Vining, and David Weimer describe them in a widely cited list containing nine steps:[15]

1. "Specify the set of alternative projects."
2. "Decide whose benefits and costs count (standing)."
3. "Catalogue the impacts and select measurement indicators."
4. "Predict the impacts quantitatively over the life of the project."
5. "Monetize (attach dollar values to) all impacts."
6. "Discount benefits and costs to obtain present values."
7. "Compute the net present value of each alternative."
8. "Perform a sensitivity analysis."
9. "Make a recommendation."

This list, or minor variations on it, is widely used in the literature. For example, in the context of CBA of crime, the authors of one 2016 book describe an essentially identical list that has ten steps.[16] My own opinion is that steps 6 and 7 could be combined, making this a list of eight steps. I use this list to organize the discussion that follows.

Jacobsen and Kotchen examine a change to Florida's energy codes. Florida initially adopted energy codes in 1978 and strengthened them in 2002. The details of Florida's 2002 energy code change are complicated, but—as a simplification—JK frame the policy as requiring new homes to use more expensive windows with a low-emissivity (low-E) coating, which should in turn reduce electricity and natural gas demand. This requirement was expected to lower household energy bills.

In terms of CBA step 1, one set of alternatives facing policymakers in 2002 was to change the code (require low-E windows) or not to change it. This set has only two options, and Jacobsen and Kotchen do not discuss whether policymakers at the time considered stronger or weaker versions of the code or other completely different policy instruments to promote energy efficiency, such as taxes or cap and trade. If these alternatives were included in an analysis, the set of alternatives would be larger than two. Many government-sponsored CBAs specify multiple alternatives, while academic CBAs are often less comprehensive in terms of alternatives.

In CBA step 2, *standing* refers to whose preferences count. This is a deeply philosophical question, but it is usually decided in CBAs on the basis of practical considerations. For example, a CBA conducted by a government agency may count costs and benefits to US citizens only. However, some economists hold that all impacted parties should have standing.[17] As we see next, the JK analysis incorporates negative externalities to third parties from the emissions produced by the burning of fossil fuels. Thus their implicit delineation of standing is a global one, although they do also consider a case where only the homeowner has standing, and a case that could be described as one where only citizens have standing.

CBA step 3 has to do with cataloging impacts. The JK analysis includes (1) the additional resources builders use in complying with the code, (2) the reduction in energy used by households, and (3) the reduction in negative externalities associated with producing the energy. Examples of these externalities include the suffering of third parties who breathe in sulfur dioxide produced during electricity generation and smaller catches for fishers because of ocean acidification caused by climate change. Other potential impacts that Jacobsen and Kotchen do not catalog include the impact of more or less comfortable indoor temperatures.[18]

CBA step 4 has to do with predicting impacts. Empirical training in causal inference is critical to doing this step well. Correlation is not causation, and the researcher needs to determine what impact was actually caused by the policy. It is not enough to discover that energy use was lower in homes built after energy codes were strengthened, because it is possible that other things changed along with regulations. For example, if for some reason homes were smaller on average after the codes were strengthened, it might appear that the codes were responsible for an observed lower energy use, but in fact the reason was that the smaller homes required less energy to heat and cool.[19]

One technique analysts use to estimate impacts is to get data and estimate impacts themselves. Another technique is to use "the literature." By the literature, I mean all the studies that have been written on a particular topic. An analyst who searches these studies will find estimates of impacts that have been produced by others. Because impact estimation is such a crucial step in any CBA, I discuss methods for this step in more detail in the appendix.

Jacobsen and Kotchen used residential billing data to estimate a multiple regression model that found that the change in Florida's energy code caused electricity consumption to fall by 48 kilowatt-hours (kWh) per month and natural gas consumption to fall by 1.5 therms. They then use the literature to find so-called plug-in values to estimate the size of reduced emissions. The four categories of emissions they include are carbon dioxide, sulfur dioxide, nitrous oxide, and particulates. Emissions factors are numbers drawn from the literature that are used to estimate the reduction in emissions from each energy source. For example, the JK analysis cites a study that found burning 1 therm of natural gas generates 0.006 tons of carbon dioxide. If households reduce natural gas use by 1.5 therms per month, carbon dioxide emissions will fall by 1.5 × 0.006, or 0.009 tons of carbon dioxide monthly.

CBA step 5 involves *monetization*—assigning a dollar amount to an impact to represent its social value. The stricter energy codes require builders to use low-E windows, and monetization involves valuing the additional resources that go into producing these windows. The JK analysis finds an estimate in the literature indicating the low-E windows

are 10 percent more expensive than non-low-E windows, and calculates that the change to the code has added between $675 and $1,012
to overall construction costs for a standard home.

Note that the increase in construction costs might not exactly corre-
spond to the social costs of the resources. For example, imagine that
the window manufacturing company is a monopoly and there is only
a trivial increase in its cost from producing the low-E windows. In that
case the higher price paid by builders to the window manufacturer
would be a transfer from the builder to the window manufacturer, not
a social cost. Now, it is unlikely that the window producer is a monopoly, and the technique Jacobsen and Kotchen adopt for monetizing the
impact seems very reasonable to me—but I construct this example to
illustrate that there are cases where a researcher cannot just use market
prices in the monetization step.

To monetize the energy use reduction impact, Jacobsen and Kotchen
multiply the energy savings (48 kWh of electricity and 1.5 therms of
natural gas per month) by the marginal price an average household
pays (14.6 cents per kWh for electricity and $1.22 per therm for natural
gas) to arrive at annual energy savings of $106.[20] As with the construc-
tion impact discussed in the preceding paragraph, this seems to be a
reasonable way of monetizing the social value of the saved resources,
but it may not be perfect. For example, if the energy price consumers
pay incorporates government taxes, then the price consumers pay will
overstate the social value of the resource savings, because part of the
price is a transfer rather than a resource cost.[21]

The third set of impacts that must be monetized are the four types of
emissions. Carbon dioxide causes climate change and the other three are
associated with public health problems. (Particulates—essentially soot—
can cause asthma, for example.) Earlier I discussed how Jacobsen and
Kotchen estimate that carbon dioxide emissions fall by 0.009 tons each
month, or 0.108 tons annually, because of reductions in natural gas use.
The social cost of carbon has been calculated by William Nordhaus as
$31 per ton of carbon dioxide (in 2010 dollars);[22] thus one way of mon-
etizing the reduction in natural gas use is by multiplying 0.108 by $31,
yielding an annual climate change mitigation benefit of $3.35. Jacobsen

and Kotchen do not report the marginal damage figures they used for carbon, but it is possible to calculate these values from the information they do present.[23] It turns out that they used a low estimate of $7.68 and high estimate of $93.70, in 2009 dollars; thus the $31 figure from Nordhaus lies on the lower end of the range they considered.[24] Hence the high-end estimate of the social value of reduced carbon emissions from natural gas is 0.108 tons times $93.70, or $10.12 annually. The JK analysis applies different marginal damage estimates to each pollutant and each fuel source, and finds that all together, reductions in the four types of emissions, owing to a household's lower electricity and natural gas demand, are valued at between $14.15 and $84.84 annually.

CBA steps 6 and 7 can be combined. Discounting refers to accounting for the fact that a dollar saved next year is not as valuable as a dollar saved now. Net present value (NPV) is the most widely used of several decision criteria in CBA. In fact, because the JK analysis was, strictly speaking, not a CBA, Jacobsen and Kotchen do not present NPV calculations. Instead they discuss three different types of payback periods. Besides NPV and the payback period, other decision criteria one sometimes encounters include the internal rate of return and the benefit-cost ratio. However, there are several advantages to NPV that make it the most widely used and accepted decision criterion.[25] If NPV is positive, this indicates that the investment, policy, project, or program produces more benefits than costs over its lifetime.

Using all the numbers presented in the JK analysis and discussed up until now, it is possible to calculate the NPV of the change in Florida's energy codes for a household in Gainesville:

$$NPV = -675 + \sum_{t}^{T} \frac{106 + 84}{(1 + r)^t}.$$

We can write this another way by specifying a time horizon. Say $t = 1$ and $T = 10$. Then we can express NPV using the equation below, which is less compact but avoids the use of the summation operator:

$$NPV = -675 + \frac{106 + 84}{1 + r} + \frac{106 + 84}{(1 + r)^2} + \cdots + \frac{106 + 84}{(1 + r)^{10}}.$$

In both equations, $675 is the low-end estimate of the social cost of the low-E windows, $106 is the estimate of the social benefit of energy resource savings, and $84 is the high-end estimate of the social benefit of the avoided emissions. Because the NPV uses both the low-end cost estimate and high-end benefit estimate, it can be said to be a best-case scenario NPV. There are two variables in this equation: the time horizon (t and T) and the discount rate (r), which affects how valuable future benefits are in the present. Like other decisions in CBA, the choice of a discount rate can be highly philosophical, but in practice analysts usually adopt a market interest rate.

The analyst selects the time horizon by choosing t and T. We could base the end of the time horizon, T, on the effective life of the low-E windows. Windows are long-lived durables, and arguably T should be substantially higher than 10—perhaps 50 or more. The JK analysis cites a 2007 study that reports the average ownership tenure in Florida as 11.5 years.[26] I selected a time horizon of 10 for the equation because it is close to this figure of 11.5 years, and because as a whole number it is convenient for purposes of demonstration. A longer time horizon will lead to a higher NPV, and I consider the effect of selecting different end periods below as part of the sensitivity analysis. Regarding the beginning of the time horizon, benefits will be realized once the house is built and occupied, but by starting with $t = 1$, the NPV calculation assumes that benefits are realized at the end of every year; we assume benefits are realized at the beginning of each year by setting it at $t = 0$.

Assuming a discount rate of 5 percent (so $r = 0.05$), the best-case NPV estimate is $792.[27] The fact that this is positive indicates that energy codes that require low-E windows are a good social investment.

How does this NPV estimate compare with the decision criteria presented in the JK analysis? Jacobsen and Kotchen presented three criteria, the first of which is a private payback period, which is calculated as the up-front costs of $675 divided by the annual savings of $106, and comes to 6.37 years. This is the amount of time it would take a homeowner to recover the investment in the thicker windows. This criterion assumes a discount rate of zero and does not account for impacts on third parties.[28] The second criterion could be called a global social payback period, which is the up-front costs of $675 divided by $190, the sum of private and social benefits, and comes out to 3.5 years. Third, Jacobsen and Kotchen recognize that "one might argue that the benefits associated with a lower CO_2 emissions should not be considered . . . as they are likely to occur for the most part outside the policy jurisdiction."[29] Excluding carbon dioxide reduction benefits reduces the value of emissions reductions from $84 to $22, and what could be called a national social payback period rises to 5.3 years ($675 divided by $128, where $128 is the sum of $106 and $22).

CBA step 8 involves sensitivity analysis, which refers to determining how the NPV estimate changes when one of the assumptions or estimates that went into the equation is changed. By considering payback periods that include more or fewer categories of benefits, Jacobsen and Kotchen do present some sensitivity analysis. They do not discuss how sensitive their findings are to changes in other assumptions.

In this and the next two paragraphs, I present some examples of further sensitivity analysis. The payback periods considered in the JK analysis were based on best-case assumptions, and so I first recalculate my NPV figure using the worst-case figures. Recall that the calculations above used the low-end cost estimate of the low-E windows: $675. The high-end estimate was $1,012.[30] In addition, they used the high-end estimate of the value of emissions reductions—$84—but the low-end estimate was $14. A worst-case NPV calculation would simply replace $675 with $1,012 and $84 with $14 in the equations above. With a discount rate of 5 percent, the worst-case NPV estimate is −$85. This negative value indicates that the discounted value of social benefits is not enough to justify the up-front costs of low-E windows.

Another assumption is the impact of the energy code changes on energy demand. Jacobsen and Kotchen find it to be 48 kWh per month for electricity and 1.5 therms for natural gas. However, in follow-up work using more recent data from the same study area, Kotchen finds that there are no electricity savings, but natural gas savings are about double.[31] From this it follows that, "following the same approach outlined by Jacobsen and Kotchen, the revised estimates imply social and private payback rates of about 10 and 16 years (up from 4 to 6), respectively."[32] In terms of the NPV calculation, in the original analysis above, natural gas savings were $22 and electricity savings $84, for combined energy savings of $106. If we double natural gas savings and ignore electricity savings, energy savings under the revised impact estimates are only $44. In addition, social benefits of avoided emissions under these revised impact estimates range from $1.84 to $20.74. Recalculating NPV under these assumptions, I find best- and worst-case NPV estimates of −$175 and −$658, respectively. Both best- and worst-case NPV figures are negative under Kotchen's revised impact estimate.[33]

Of course, the −$175 to −$658 NPV figures presented above use the 10-year time horizon, which—as mentioned above—might be too short. As a final check on the sensitivity of these estimates, I note that with a 50-year time horizon and using the revised impact estimates from Kotchen, the best- and worst-case NPV figures are $507 and −$175, respectively.[34]

What can we conclude from examining the effect of alternate sets of assumptions on the NPV estimate? The NPV estimates are quite sensitive to the assumptions. CBA does not give us a clear answer in this case. While it may seem as if CBA provides a nonanswer, the results do suggest that Florida's changes to its energy codes were not obviously good or bad. Then again, the sensitivity analysis does draw our attention to the fact that the marginal damage figure we use for carbon dioxide reductions is a key driver of whether the NPV is positive or negative. Assumptions about how carbon reductions impact climate change to a large extent determine whether the policy is efficient or not.

CBA step 9 entails making a recommendation. Jacobsen and Kotchen do not make a formal policy recommendation, but their initial study might offer an implicit suggestion that Florida policymakers were correct to strengthen the energy code in 2001. The authors never actually say this, but it is not hard to imagine a reader interpreting their results as encouragement to further strengthen energy codes in Florida, or to replicate Florida's changes in other states in similar climate zones. However, as we have just seen, the revised empirical estimates of the policy's impact show that the case for energy codes is weaker than Jacobsen and Kotchen initially found.

My examination of the JK analysis suggests that Florida's stricter building codes do not clearly pass a cost-benefit test. Of course, there is room for strengthening the analysis. Strictly speaking, Jacobsen and Kotchen set out to calculate payback periods for a representative household, not to carry out a social CBA. We have seen that it is possible to recast their analysis as a simple CBA just by specifying a time horizon and calculating NPV with the figures they provide. Thus, on one hand, the analysis they carry out is very close to a CBA. On the other hand, had their goal been a comprehensive CBA, they likely would have (among other things) factored in other impacts, such as the administrative costs of creating and enforcing energy codes.[35] Recent work by Kevin Novan, Aaron Smith, and Tianxia Zhou adopts a different approach to valuing the cost of complying with energy codes, and in their CBA of California's energy codes, these authors find evidence suggesting that the initial codes likely do pass a cost-benefit test (that is, NPV is likely positive).[36] The question of the efficiency of building energy codes remains an active area of scholarship that may evolve substantially in the years to come.

Conclusion

This chapter first described state-level building energy code regulations and surveyed the important concepts and controversies surrounding them. It then presented a case study which described a CBA of a change made to Florida's building energy codein 2002. In reconsidering the JK analysis as a CBA,[37] I calculated NPV—which is the most conventional decision criterion in CBA—under best- and worst-case scenarios, and I also updated the analysis to account for new policy impacts estimated in Kotchen's 2017 study.[38] I find that while NPV is positive in the best-case scenario, it is negative in the worst-case scenario. When the updated impact estimates are used, both best- and worst-case NPV figures are negative. With a longer time horizon and updated impact estimates, the best-case assumptions result in positive NPV while the worst-case assumptions result in negative NPV.

This case study shows how CBA can be applied in the specific setting analyzed in this chapter. In addition, because all CBAs follow the same steps, the case study can also be used to understand CBA in general so it can be applied to any of the areas discussed in other chapters of this book.

I emphasize that an analyst with empirical training in causal inference and econometrics will do a better job at the crucial step of impact estimation. To do CBA well, and to understand what it is and—maybe more importantly—what it is not, requires an analyst to have a mix of skills (including empirical skills), a grasp of neoclassical economic theory, and a familiarity with financial calculations such as NPV and inflation adjustments. It also requires a healthy dose of critical thinking skills, both in terms of cataloging impacts and selecting studies for the literature review that contain the most appropriate estimates to plug in at various points in the analysis.

Because doing CBA provides opportunities for using and developing all these different skills, I have started requiring that students write term papers when I teach the course in CBA to undergraduates at San Jose State University. There are many different types of term papers a student could write in a CBA course, from ones that lean econometric to literature reviews, but I've found that the method that works the best for most students is the benefits transfer method, exemplified in the second half of Alan Krueger's 2003 study.[39] The goal of a paper employing this method would be to replicate a previously published NPV (or related) calculation, exactly as I have done here, and then critically evaluate it and modify it in some ways. This may seem unoriginal, but in fact replicating CBAs can help lend badly needed transparency to the policy analysis literature. Moreover, the "replicate and extend" approach provides a student with a more obvious guide to writing a term paper than the "redesign the wheel" approach—an approach that I often observed (and unwittingly encouraged) in my earlier years teaching the CBA course.

In fact, the idea of replicate and extend can be used in courses beyond CBA. It can also be used successfully in courses in econometrics.[40] My suggestion for instructors in both introductory CBA and econometrics courses is the same: require students to write original term papers, but guide them in doing this by providing references to papers they should replicate and extend. More advanced students can then move beyond this approach in more advanced courses, after cutting their teeth on a replication assignment.

Finally, this chapter was also written for the professional policy analyst who needs to do an original CBA. While I have to recommend formal training in CBA, the best way to learn independently is to read published CBAs, replicate, and extend. Going through the calculations carefully enough to replicate them will provide a deeper understanding of all the moving pieces. Keep in mind that the perfect CBA has yet to be written, and there is always room for improvement. Our job is to do the best we can to inform decision makers. Ultimately decision makers have multiple criteria beyond NPV to consider, but the consequentialist underpinning of CBA and the neoclassical approach deserve a place at the table in any major decision involving public or shared resources.

Appendix on Impact Estimation: Do It Yourself, or Plug In Values?

Analysts can estimate the impacts of regulations themselves, or they can use estimates from the literature in a so-called plug-in approach. There are several ways analysts could estimate impacts themselves, but these ways all require getting data. The ideal data collection method is to conduct a randomized, controlled experiment. For example, researchers Meredith Fowlie, Michael Greenstone, and Catherine Wolfram do this as part of a large-scale weatherization project. A randomized, controlled experiment is the gold standard for isolating and estimating causal effects, because the researcher can assign treatment in a way that is uncorrelated with participant characteristics.[41]

Most of the time, however, experiments are infeasible because of their cost. Therefore, economists often have to rely on observational (as opposed to experimental) data. Jacobsen and Kotchen base their analysis on utility billing data, as well as house characteristics such as square footage and number of bathrooms.[42] They find that homes built just after the date that energy codes were strengthened use less energy compared to observationally identical homes built just before. Is this a compelling way to estimate the causal effect that building energy codes have on energy demand?

Arik Levinson argues not necessarily. Newer homes use less energy for reasons apart from their design, and Levinson argues Jacobsen and Kotchen conflate home vintage with home age.[43] In his 2017 follow-up to the JK analysis, Kotchen finds evidence suggesting that Levinson was correct, with regard to electricity at least: Kotchen finds that energy codes were not responsible for reducing electricity demand.[44] However, he does find that the savings from natural gas persisted and were twice as large as he and Jacobsen had found in their 2013 analysis.[45]

The econometric literature that estimates the impact of energy codes on energy demand is rich and evolving, and reviewing it all is beyond the scope of this chapter. Table A1 lists nine recent studies that are all at least somewhat comparable. Care must be taken in comparing the results summarized in the table, however, because the studies use different approaches and cover different study areas. Sometimes, a single study will provide the best estimate of an impact to use in a CBA. In other situations, averaging impacts may be appropriate. An analyst's ability to distinguish between correlation and causation is just as important when using the plug-in method as when estimating impacts from the raw data.[46]

Table A1. Estimating Impacts through Literature Review

Study	Finding	Area
Anin Aroonruengsawat, Maximilian Auffhammer, and Alan H. Sanstad, "The Impact of State Level Building Codes on Residential Electricity Consumption," *Energy Journal* 33, no. 1 (2012): 31-52.	Energy codes reduced electricity consumption by 0.3%–5.0%, depending on the state.	US
Bishwa S. Koirala, Alok K. Bohara, and Hui Li, "Effects of Energy-Efficiency Building Codes in the Energy Savings and Emissions of Carbon Dioxide," *Environmental Economics and Policy Studies* 15, no. 3 (2013): 271–90.	Energy codes reduced electricity expenditures by 1.8% and natural gas expenditures by 1.3%, on average.	US
Grant D. Jacobsen and Matthew J. Kotchen, "Are Building Codes Effective at Saving Energy? Evidence from Residential Billing Data in Florida," *Review of Economics and Statistics* 95, no. 1 (March 2013): 34–49.	A revision to Florida's energy codes in 2002 lowered electricity consumption by 4.3% and natural gas consumption by 6.7%.	FL

Study	Finding	Area
Matthew J. Kotchen, "Longer-Run Evidence on Whether Building Energy Codes Reduce Residential Energy Consumption," *Journal of the Association of Environmental and Resource Economists* 4, no. 1 (2017): 135–53.	A revision to Florida's energy codes in 2002 lowered electricity consumption by 0.0% and natural gas consumption by 13.5%.	FL
Dora L. Costa and Matthew E. Kahn, "Electricity Consumption and Durable Housing: Understanding Cohort Effects," *American Economic Review* 101, no. 3 (May 2011): 88–92.	Homes built in California in the 1980s do not use significantly less electricity than homes built in the 1970s, ceteris paribus.	CA
Holian, Matthew J. "The Impact of Building Energy Codes on Household Electricity Consumption," *Economics Letters* 186, no. 108841 (January 2020): 1-4.	Homes built in California in the 1980s use between 0% and 2% less electricity than homes built in the 1970s, ceteris paribus.	CA
Kevin Novan, Aaron Smith, and Tianxia Zhou, "Residential Building Codes Do Save Energy: Evidence from Hourly Smart-Meter Data" (E2e Working Paper 031, E2e Project, June 2017).	Homes built in Sacramento just after California adopted energy codes in 1978 use 1.6%–2.6% less electricity than those built just before.	CA
Arik Levinson, "How Much Energy Do Building Energy Codes Save? Evidence from California Houses," *American Economic Review* 106, no. 10 (2016): 286794.	Homes built in California just after the adoption of energy codes use 0% less electricity and 5% less natural gas than homes built before, but the difference is insignificant.	CA
Meredith Fowlie, Michael Greenstone, and Catherine Wolfram, "Do Energy Efficiency Investments Deliver? Evidence from the Weatherization Assistance Program," *Quarterly Journal of Economics* 133, no. 3 (2018): 1597–644. (experimental investigation)	The Weatherization Assistance Program reduced energy consumption by 10%–20%, but up-front costs were twice energy savings.	MI

Note: These nine studies use various methods to estimate the impact of energy codes on energy use.

CHAPTER *11*

The Tradeoffs between Energy Efficiency, Consumer Preferences, and Economic Growth

James Broughel

The traditional economic rationale for government intervention in the economy is market failure.[1] Underlying the market failure concept is the idea that, because of certain market frictions known as transaction costs, beneficial gains from trade are prevented from occurring that would otherwise increase social welfare. The usual cases where these kinds of transaction costs are present are situations involving externalities, asymmetric information, monopoly power, or the provision of public goods. In such situations, the government can potentially be a corrective force to improve welfare.

While these sources of market failure have led to no shortage of regulatory and other policy interventions, in recent years government agencies and academics have begun justifying policy interventions on the grounds that an additional form of market failure exists, known as a "behavioral market failure."[2] They extend the standard list of "neoclassical market failures" mentioned above to include instances of suboptimal individual decision-making. Behavioral market failures occur because of various cognitive biases afflicting individuals, which result in people making poor decisions that reduce their own welfare.

The concept of behavioral market failure is an outgrowth of research in the field of behavioral economics, a subset of economic theory that focuses on the intersection of economics and psychology and tends to emphasize the cognitive limitations of human beings. Behavioral economics can be contrasted with neoclassical economics, which assumes a high degree of rationality on the part of economic agents. According to the neoclassical view, consumers can generally be expected to act in a self-interested manner that accords with their own welfare, given the constraints they face in terms of resources and information. Neoclassical economists therefore assume that consumers' preferences can be inferred simply by observing their behavior. If a consumer engages in a particular transaction, that consumer is assumed to be made better off by the transaction. Otherwise, the consumer would have held on to his or her money and the transaction would not have taken place. In this way, consumers "reveal" their preferences through their actions, giving rise to the term *revealed preference*.

Behavioral economists hold a different view. They routinely drop this revealed preference assumption, instead arguing that cognitive bias prevents consumers from advancing their own welfare in many cases. The "true" preferences of individuals and their behavior in the marketplace are often not aligned, even in cases where consumers possess all the relevant information needed to make an informed choice. Consumers may buy unhealthy food, for example, because they act hastily and without regard for long-run consequences. They might come to regret their decision later, and would act differently with hindsight. It is for this reason that behavioral economists claim to be able to bestow a benefit on consumers—making them better off "as judged by themselves"[3]—by preventing certain market transactions from occurring. In other words, by overriding consumer choices that are influenced by biased decision-making, policymakers can potentially improve consumer welfare, as gauged by the consumers' own preferences.

Some neoclassical economists acknowledge that behavioral biases are a real phenomenon, but they downplay their importance. For example, biased behavior could be present in markets, but behavior may not be *systematically* biased in one direction or another. Just as there are people who consume more unhealthy food than is optimal, so too there are other people who take a healthy lifestyle too far. In the aggregate, perhaps these biases cancel each other out. Or perhaps over time biases are systematically weeded out of the marketplace, because biased behavior is punished by market forces while rational behavior is rewarded.[4]

Some examples of situations in which overriding consumer choice could have potentially welfare-improving results include banning or taxing certain unhealthy foods, banning addictive products such as cigarettes or alcohol, and capping interest rates on or banning certain kinds of payday lending. However, not all behavioral interventions are intended to override consumer choice—that is, to take the rather extreme step of banning the activity in question. Some interventions, such as so-called nudges, are choice-preserving.[5] The idea behind nudges is that choices are presented to consumers in a different arrangement (known as the *choice architecture*), or with a different default rule, such that a consumer is more likely to make the welfare-improving choice. For example, rather than banning sugary soda, government regulators could simply require supermarkets to place soda in a less visible part of the store. In that case consumers could still search for the soda if they truly want it, but the soda wouldn't be as salient to them as it might be if it were placed near the checkout aisle.

Similarly, employees could be opted into an employer-administered retirement plan by default, while still being left the option of refusing the plan if they prefer to make alternative arrangements for their retirement. However, even these seemingly benign nudges aren't entirely free of coercion. In the soda example, a supermarket is still told by the government where it must place soda, and in the retirement account example, an employer is told how it must enroll its employees in retirement plans.

According to the neoclassical view, the choice architecture that nudges focus on changing should matter only slightly in most cases. So long as information relevant to a consumer's choice is available relatively costlessly (e.g., is presented in a not-overly-complex manner), the consumer should be able to process the information and make the decision that best fits his or her circumstances. Empirically, however, the choice architecture presented to consumers does seem to matter: consumer choices often change if information is presented in a slightly different manner or if default options change. For example, when employees are defaulted into a retirement plan, more of them tend to sign up. Similarly, if signing up to be an organ donor becomes the default option at the DMV, more people tend to do so. In this manner, a nudge can potentially exploit biases and help guide consumers toward a better choice.

As may be evident from table 1, the line between a neoclassical market failure owing to asymmetric information and a behavioral market failure owing to cognitive bias can be a fuzzy one. One could easily argue that the choice architecture creates cognitive costs for consumers, and therefore that improving the choice architecture is just a sophisticated way of reducing transaction costs associated with collecting information. That would suggest that the real issue facing policymakers is how to present information in the best possible way to consumers, such that problems of asymmetric information can be overcome.

In fact, regulators sometimes assert both information problems and behavioral bias when they justify regulatory interventions. For example, the Department of Energy (DOE), the Environmental Protection Agency, and the Department of Transportation have done so when setting energy and fuel efficiency standards.[6] Energy efficiency regulations, which are the focus of this chapter, are not nudges because they do not rearrange the choice architecture presented to consumers. Rather, they are product bans, which simply remove certain classes of devices from the marketplace. Products that fail to meet the minimum standards set by the DOE are not legally permitted in the marketplace, and are therefore removed as an option for consumers.

Neoclassical economists generally view product bans as imposing costs on consumers, since they result in fewer options for consumers in the marketplace. In fact, these energy interventions raise up-front costs for consumers; equipment is made more expensive because it has to be remodeled to use less energy. However, at the same time a more energy-efficient device will generate a stream of financial benefits in the future through lower utility bills or (with an automobile) fewer stops at the gas station. A neoclassical economist would typically argue that consumers are in the best position to weigh these trade-offs between

Table 1. The Neoclassical View vs. the Behavioral View

	Neoclassical view	Behavioral view
Human beings . . .	. . . are assumed to be rational for modeling purposes.	. . . are viewed as sometimes systematically irrational.
Consumer and business decisions	. . . are individually optimal from the perspective of the agent, given budget and information constraints.	. . . can be systematically biased.
Market transactions	. . . reveal consumer preferences, absent information constraints.	. . . may or may not reveal consumer preferences.
Market failures	. . . result from transaction costs preventing mutually beneficial exchanges.	. . . result from biased decision-making—i.e., cognitive transaction costs—in addition to neoclassical market failures.
Individual behavior	. . . is individually optimal, assuming full information, but may not be socially optimal.	. . . may or may not be optimal from the perspective of the individual or society.
Choice architecture	. . . is not important so long as information is relatively inexpensive to obtain and process.	. . . can influence choices, owing to behavioral bias, even with freely available information.
Product bans	. . . reduce consumer choice. (Absent asymmetric information between buyer and seller, the consumer is made worse off: an unambiguous cost.)	. . . can improve consumer welfare: a potential benefit.
Behavioral market failures	. . . are impossible, because rational, self-interested behavior is assumed.	. . . are possible owing to any one of countless cognitive biases identified by researchers.

up-front costs and future savings. After all, consumers know their own preferences and their relevant financial constraints better than anyone else. If a consumer chooses to purchase a relatively less energy-efficient appliance, according to the neoclassical economist, it must be because that's the option best suited for his or her needs.

Behavioral economists don't see it this way. They believe consumers are often incapable of making the choice that corresponds with their own preferences—for example, because they are myopic, or because they are too present-oriented to fully appreciate benefits that will come to them in the future. Regulatory agencies therefore sometimes claim that eliminating energy-inefficient products from the marketplace (i.e., banning products that some consumers would otherwise purchase) confers a benefit on consumers. Neoclassical economists, on the other hand, view the removal of a product from the marketplace—except in cases where consumers lack critical information about the product— as an unambiguous cost to the consumers who would have opted to purchase the banned product in the absence of a regulation.

This chapter walks though the theory underlying behavioral market failures and provides a brief overview of the "energy efficiency gap," which is a potential behavioral market failure often asserted to exist in markets for energy-consuming devices. It turns out that the behavioral market failure concept fits squarely within the mainstream market failure theory in economics, suggesting that behavioral market failures need to be taken seriously. However, as we will see, traditional market failure theory is not fully satisfying. Moreover, there are significant knowledge problems facing policymakers when they try to correct behavioral market failures, which make these problems considerably more challenging to address than neoclassical market failures. For example, how should an analyst attempt to identify instances when consumers' actions deviate from their "true" preferences? Neoclassical market failures can be identified through revealed preferences, but if consumers' actions are not a credible reflection of their preferences, then what is? If an analyst can never be certain about what a consumer wants, neither can the analyst ever be certain that a behavioral market failure is present. Furthermore, so many behavioral biases have been identified in the academic literature that one could argue that almost any decision a consumer makes is biased by cherry-picking a bias that suits the situation, which suggests there is a danger that this kind of rationale for regulating will be abused.

This chapter also provides an example of a regulation where behavioral market failure forms an implicit rationale for the regulation. The example comes from the Department of Energy and involves energy efficiency standards recently set for ceiling fans. It turns out that 80 percent of the benefits the DOE claimed for the ceiling fan regulation, which amounts to $16.5 billion (2015 dollars), stem from overriding consumer choices. This estimate is highly dependent on an array of assumptions, including assumptions about a product's usage over its lifetime, quality remaining the same between more- and less-efficient devices, and the relevant consumer or business discount rate. Without these benefits, the regulation fails a cost-benefit test, according to the DOE's own analysis.

The chapter concludes with discussion of an underexplored rationale for these energy efficiency regulations: externalities imposed on future generations as a result of slower economic growth. Although evidence is at best ambiguous about whether an actual behavioral market failure exists to justify these regulations, there may be a basis for them that does not aim to correct consumer irrationality but instead aims to boost growth. Whether energy efficiency regulations are the best means to promote economic growth is far from clear. However, exploring this issue could prove useful in other contexts, since there are some significant gaps in the theory of market failure as it now stands. Walking through the logic of how present-day consumers impose externalities on future citizens will make the limitations of current market failure theory more clear.

Behavioral Market Failures

Behavioral market failures are similar in many respects to traditional market failures in that a behavioral market failure can be illustrated using the same static supply-and-demand framework commonly used to illustrate neoclassical market failures. Figure 1 shows a case where at every unit of production, total willingness to pay for a good is less than the private internal marginal benefit that consumers derive from consuming it. Under laissez-faire conditions, consumers demand quantity F of the good and pay a price of D, but consumers are demanding too little relative to what is internally optimal, thereby generating a deadweight loss represented by the triangle BCE. At each unit of production between quantities F and G, the internal marginal benefit to the consumer is greater than what the consumer is willing to pay for the resource. An optimal allocation of resources would therefore have production occur at the quantity G, with consumers paying a price of A. However, some behavioral bias is preventing the consumers' marginal willingness to pay from aligning with their internal marginal benefit.

This kind of situation has been referred to as an *internality* because of the divergence between willingness to pay and the internal benefit consumers enjoy.[7] In the case of an internality, there is a deviation between unbiased and biased, or rational and irrational, willingness to pay. The scenario presented in figure 1 is similar to the neoclassical case of a public good or a positive externality. Too little of a good is produced relative to what is socially optimal, so the social benefits of more production exceed private benefits at the margin under laissez-faire.

In the neoclassical case, a similar diagram might be used to describe the market for lawn improvements. Well-maintained lawns and gardens increase the desirability and value of property in a neighborhood, but most people do not fully take external benefits to their neighbors into account when deciding how much time and effort to spend on lawn care. Hence, people may invest too little in lawn maintenance from a social point of view. Similarly, in the behavioral case, people might demand too little healthy food or spend too few resources on exercise equipment or on a gym membership because they are myopic or put too little weight on the long-run benefits of a healthier lifestyle.[8] In either case, the market fails because socially or internally beneficial transactions should be taking place but are prevented from occurring, either because of transaction cost frictions such as externalities or as a result of behavioral bias, which can be thought of as a kind of cognitive transaction cost.

Figure 1. A Behavioral Market Failure

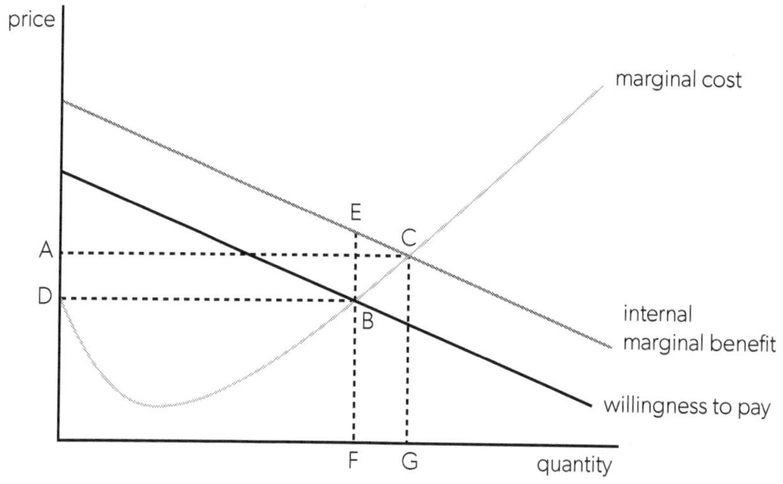

The Energy Efficiency Gap

Figure 1 might also describe a potential behavioral market failure in markets for energy-consuming appliances. If the x axis represents the quantity of investment in energy-efficient devices, investing quantity F would represent underinvestment relative to what is internally optimal for the consumer.[9] Such underinvestment could be explained by a lack of foresight or by some other behavioral problem that has led the consumer to undervalue future financial savings owing from using a less-energy-intensive device. Underinvestment of this kind provides a potential rationale for government intervention in this market to force people to conserve energy.

A large empirical literature explores the existence of an *energy efficiency gap*,[10] which is sometimes also referred to as the *energy paradox*[11]—phrases that reflect the idea that consumers may underinvest in energy efficiency. This literature traces its origins to a 1979 study that found very high implied consumer discount rates in markets for air conditioners.[12] Some individual discount rates ran as high as 90 percent annually, with an average rate of about 25 percent found in the study, leading the author to posit that consumers might be putting too little weight on future energy savings.

The evolution of the literature on a potential undervaluation problem in markets for energy-consuming products coincided with the explosion of research on behavioral economics, which identified countless biases that afflict individual decision-making. Many of the identified biases relate to situations that involve trade-offs that occur across time, suggesting that decisions could be problematic if they involve up-front costs that produce streams of benefits in the future.

For example, hyperbolic discounting is an anomaly involving discount rates that decline over time.[13] This phenomenon and others could explain why consumers might have difficulty optimizing consumption across their lifetimes,[14] and it is closely connected to the idea that consumers sometimes display "time inconsistent" behavior, in that the optimal choice today might not look optimal when reflecting at some point in the future. Not surprisingly, these issues are often associated with self-indulgent behavior or self-control problems. Examples of biases that could contribute to time inconsistent preferences include inertia, inattention, and procrastination. These biases explain why consumers might come to regret decisions that seem optimal in the moment.

Although the idea that consumers are not the perfectly rational automatons found in economic models is hardly controversial, the empirical evidence on the existence of an energy efficiency gap is somewhat mixed. New York University professor Hunt Allcott and University of Chicago economist Michael Greenstone reviewed the large literature on the energy efficiency gap,[15] concluding that there is only limited empirical support for it. Similarly, Yale economist Kenneth Gillingham and Resources for the Future economist Karen Palmer find evidence that the extent of the energy efficiency gap may be overestimated, although they acknowledge the true size of the energy efficiency gap is unknown.[16] More recently, a study by economists Todd Gerarden, Richard Newell, and Robert Stavins expresses more confidence that behavioral explanations play a significant role in explaining the energy efficiency gap, but these authors also suggest other factors, such as measurement and modelling errors in the studies evaluating these markets, are important.[17]

One challenge facing researchers studying the energy efficiency gap is that in order to measure the extent to which a bias is present, an analyst must make certain modeling assumptions and then calibrate the model with data to determine the extent to which real-world behavior deviates from some theoretical optimum. It is always possible—and indeed likely—that relevant variables are left out of the model and that the data used are imperfect. In other words, there is almost always something a neoclassical economist could point at to justify why the behavior of consumers is rational and the model being used to measure bias is imperfect.[18]

For instance, Hunt Allcott and economist Nathan Wozny estimate the extent to which automobile prices adjust in response to changes in gasoline prices,[19] since full adjustment would suggest a high degree of rationality on the part of car consumers. This kind of study inevitably makes certain assumptions about consumers' expectations about the path of future energy prices, as well as about the discount rate appropriate for a consumer to use to discount savings on future gasoline purchases. Allcott and Wozny conclude that automobile prices adjust in response to energy price increases, but probably not fully. They acknowledge the considerable uncertainty in their estimates, but it's also worth acknowledging that any effort to set policy on the basis of this study or similar studies would be highly premature.

Further complicating matters is the fact that many purchasers of automobiles are profit-oriented businesses. With their armies of lawyers and accountants, do corporations suffer from behavioral bias as well? At the very least, behavioral bias seems less likely on the part of managers in corporations than with individual consumers. While it's not surprising that businesses, through advertising or other means, might seek to exploit the behavioral biases of their customers, it also seems likely that businesses themselves would be savvy enough to identify such manipulations when the businesses are on the consumer side of transactions.

Despite the uncertainty surrounding the extent or even the existence of an energy efficiency gap, federal regulatory agencies have justified policies that cost billions of dollars on the grounds that an energy efficiency gap is present. Not surprisingly, many critics have emerged to condemn these regulations. Some worry about a cascade of potential dangers that could result if the traditional assumption of rationality that underpins standard economic analysis is discarded.[20] Others argue that even if behavioral bias is present in some markets, the same biases that afflict individual decision-making are also likely to be present in government.[21] This does not imply that regulators can never produce beneficial solutions if behavioral market failures occur. However, information problems, the poor incentives regulators often face, and the possibility that regulators will create traditional market failures or government failures in the process of correcting behavioral market failures are legitimate reasons to be wary of behavioral interventions, as they are of other kinds of regulatory interventions.[22] Furthermore, the evidence supporting many behavioral biases is often weaker than is commonly acknowledged, due to problems with the underlying psychological experiments used in academic research. Many of these studies fail attempts at replication, for example.[23]

At the end of the day, regulators do not know what consumers' true preferences are, which means regulators face a possibly insurmountable knowledge problem. Additionally, the list of behavioral biases identified by researchers is so long that almost any decision could be asserted to be either rational or irrational. Any claim that consumers are made "better off as judged by themselves" by overriding their choices is uncertain at best, because consumer preferences are always going to remain to some extent unobservable.[24]

An Example

While the theory that underlies behavioral market failure appears to follow a reasonable line of logic, demonstrating biased behavior empirically is an altogether different task. How can an outside observer ever know what other people's "true" preferences are? One could simply ask them, perhaps, but a whole host of problems emerge from "stated preference" studies that rely on questionnaires or surveys.[25] Such analyses may be even more unreliable than revealed-preference studies—for example, because there are fewer consequences to being wrong on a survey compared to being wrong in the real world. Survey respondents also often respond in a way that they think will please those conducting the survey, a phenomenon known as social desirability bias.[26]

Yet, despite these knowledge problems, government agencies have finalized dozens of energy efficiency standards based on explicit or implicit behavioral economics reasoning. In fact, some of the largest, most impactful regulations, known as economically significant regulations, fall into this category. Economically significant regulations are those expected to impose an impact of at least $100 million in a single year, and according to the Office of Information and Regulatory Affairs in Washington, DC, nine such regulations cleared its review process in 2016, three in 2015, and eight in 2014.[27] One regulation, which set energy conservation standard for ceiling fans, was published in the *Federal Register* on January 19, 2017—the day before Donald Trump took office.[28] This regulation is notable because in four years the Trump administration did not allow any new economically significant energy efficiency standards to clear the regulatory review process (although several leftover Obama-era rules were finalized in the last days of the Trump administration).

Consequently, this economically significant regulation, issued at the tail end of the Obama administration, is one of the most recent major-impact energy efficiency rules. In the technical support document associated with the rulemaking, the DOE estimated that consumers will see incremental installed cost increases of $2.5–$4.4 billion because of this rule. Meanwhile, consumer operating cost savings were estimated to be $7.0–$16.5 billion for the years 2020–2049. The combined net present value of all estimated costs and benefits, including environmental benefits, for the standard ranged from $8.5 billion to $16.3 billion (in 2015 dollars), depending on the discount rate used, according to the agency.[29]

The operating-cost savings reflect a prediction by the DOE that it will save consumers and businesses billions on lower utility bills. But it is worth asking why consumers are not taking into account of these savings on their own or if there are factors aside from energy efficiency that are more important to consumers when they make their final purchase decision.

Without the energy efficiency regulation, less-efficient products would almost certainly be available in the marketplace. Ceiling fan purchasers would have a wider array of choices among more efficient and less efficient fans. Perhaps they would also have a wider array of choices across other product attributes. The efficiency standard limits their range of choice, and in essence forces them to choose between a more efficient fan and an alternative product (for example, an air conditioner), or to purchase no product it all.

From a neoclassical perspective, when the option of a less efficient ceiling fan is removed from a consumer's choice set, an unambiguous cost to the consumer occurs, unless the consumer is acting with less than full information. There may well be other benefits associated with a product ban aside from energy savings (for example, benefits to the environment), but banning products that consumers would otherwise purchase is not a benefit *to them* in regulatory impact analysis.[30]

This is not the perspective of the DOE, however. The DOE estimates that the combined benefits of reducing carbon dioxide and nitrous oxide emissions are valued at $4.2 billion (at a 3 percent discount rate), which means that 80 percent of the claimed benefits of the regulation are related to "operating cost savings" to consumers—the value of reduced energy costs to consumers. If the regulation is evaluated solely on the basis of the environmental benefits,[31] it fails a cost-benefit test according to the DOE's own numbers (see table 2 and figure 2).

Implicit in the DOE's decision to include these operating cost savings as benefits is the assumption that a market failure must be present, which the agency is correcting with the regulation. If no market failure were present, then it would not be possible for the agency to improve the allocation of resources and produce corresponding benefits for the public. Two possible examples of market failures that could be present are the possibility that consumers are acting with less than perfect information when purchasing ceiling fans or that there is a behavioral market failure present. The DOE offers a few justifications for the regulation, including:

> The economics literature provides a wide-ranging discussion of how consumers trade off upfront costs and energy savings in the absence of government intervention. Much of this literature attempts to explain why consumers appear to un-

dervalue energy efficiency improvements. There is evidence
that consumers undervalue future energy savings (or appear
to do so) as a result of (1) a lack of information; (2) a lack of
sufficient salience of the long-term or aggregate benefits; (3) a
lack of sufficient savings to warrant delaying or altering purchases; (4) excessive focus on the short term, in the form of
inconsistent weighting of future energy cost savings relative
to available returns on other investments; (5) computational
or other difficulties associated with the evaluation of relevant
tradeoffs; and (6) a divergence in incentives (for example, between renters and owners, or builders and purchasers).[32]

Notably, the DOE offers no citations to support these assertions. There
is a kitchen-sink-like quality to the list, as if the DOE was searching for
any justification it could find for the regulation. Even if the DOE had
provided more direct evidence, the relevant literature—as discussed
earlier—is somewhat ambivalent about the extent of a market failure
in markets for energy-consuming goods. Furthermore, it's not clear
that the academic literature has much, if anything, to say about the ceiling fan market in particular. Many consumers of ceiling fans are also
businesses, which one would generally expect to be quite sophisticated
in their purchasing decisions.

Table 2. Benefits of Ceiling Fan Regulation

Benefit	Billions of 2015 dollars
Consumer operating cost savings	16.5
Carbon dioxide reduction	3.8
Nitrous oxide reduction	0.4

Note: CO_2 reduction is calculated using the estimated mean social cost of carbon. All
estimates calculated using a 3% discount rate.

Source: US Department of Energy, "Technical Support Document: Energy Efficiency
Program for Consumer Products and Commercial and Industrial Equipment: Ceiling
Fans," 2016, 1-2.

Figure 2. Benefits of Ceiling Fan Regulation

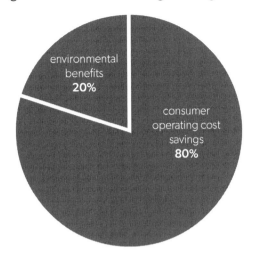

Source: US Department of Energy, "Technical Support Document: Energy Efficiency Program for Consumer Products and Commercial and Industrial Equipment: Ceiling Fans," 2016, 1-2.

Leaving aside the question of whether a market failure is present in the ceiling fan market, the operating cost savings calculations are based on a host of assumptions, some or all of which could turn out to be incorrect. For example, the DOE estimated the average lifetime of ceiling fans to be 13.8 years,[33] and assumed that a representative high-speed, small-diameter fan would operate 12 hours per day in active mode (with a range of about 6–18 hours), and that a large-diameter fan would also operate 12 hours per day.[34] The DOE also relied on predictions of the path of future energy prices, something that is notoriously difficult.

While it could be argued that the DOE made a good-faith effort to estimate these factors, and backed up its estimates with data that were available, it nonetheless seems likely one could find alternative assumptions and alternative data to justify a shorter lifespan for these products and less intensive use.[35] This could easily change the cost-benefit calculus.

Even assuming the DOE's assumptions in these areas are correct, the agency still estimated that almost 30 percent of consumers of standard ceiling fans would experience net costs,[36] and that the rule would result in an average installed cost of standard fans of $124.95,[37] which is no small sum. The DOE's assumptions about operating cost savings are also highly dependent on the several discount rates used in analysis. The agency estimates national benefits and costs using social discount rates, assumed to be 3 or 7 percent, while individual or household-specific discount rates are used to calculate payback periods—that is, the amount of time it takes consumers to recoup the up-front costs of more-energy-efficient devices.

The DOE is right that for social, or aggregate, purposes, the relevant discount rate is the social discount rate, not an individual's personal discount rate. Here, DOE analysts are being careful to distinguish impacts from an individual perspective, such as payback periods, from impacts from a social perspective, such as cumulative benefits and costs to society. It remains an open question whether the social discount rates used in the analysis are correct (an issue that is beyond the scope of this chapter). However, there are reasons to believe that the DOE's assessment of individual-level discount rates may be off the mark. The DOE calculated household-specific discount rates in the ceiling fan analysis by calculating a weighted average of various debt and equity instruments available to households across different income groups. These weighted average rates vary from 3.49 percent (for the highest-income earners) to 5.08 percent (for the second-lowest-income group), with an average rate of 4.43 percent.[38] The DOE also calculated the weighted average cost of capital discount rates for businesses in the office, retail, lodging, and food-service industries. These rates ranged from 4.9 percent to 6.0 percent, with a mean rate of 5.0 percent.[39] Tables 3 and 4 display the various discount rates used by the DOE in its payback period analysis, broken down across income and business sectors.

The DOE's approach, which is to calculate weighted averages of various debt and equity interest rates available to households and businesses, where weights are based on the share of each source of financing for each group, is defensible in that, according to standard economic theory, a rational agent's own personal discount rate—that is, the rate at which the agent trades present for future consumption—should equal the market interest rate the agent faces, in equilibrium.[40]

Table 3. Department of Energy Average Real Effective Discount Rate, by Income Group

Percentile of income	Discount rate (%)
1st to 20th	4.88
21st to 40th	5.08
41st to 60th	4.67
61st to 80th	3.95
81st to 90th	3.68
91st to 100th	3.49
Overall average	4.43

Source: US Department of Energy, "Technical Support Document: Energy Efficiency Program for Consumer Products and Commercial and Industrial Equipment: Ceiling Fans," 2016, 8–23, 8–27.

Table 4. Department of Energy Real Weighted Average Cost of Capital for Various Sectors

Sector	Mean Discount rate (%)
Office	5.1%
Retail	5.0%
Lodging	6.0%
Food service	4.9%
Other	5.0%
Average discount rate	5.0%

Source: US Department of Energy, "Technical Support Document: Energy Efficiency Program for Consumer Products and Commercial and Industrial Equipment: Ceiling Fans," 2016, 8-29.

In this sense, the DOE's basic approach—of identifying market rates consumers and businesses face and using these as a proxy for the consumer's or business's personal discount rate—is not unreasonable.[41] A key question is whether the particular rates and their corresponding weights that are used are actually representative of the market conditions consumers and businesses face.

Many consumers face interest rates far higher than those calculated by the DOE, especially those who are credit constrained. For instance, the real interest rates on credit cards the DOE uses range from 9.87 to 11.95 percent,[42] which seem low given that consumers routinely face nominal rates closer to 20 percent in the marketplace. Low-income earners are also likely to have higher discount rates than high-income earners,[43] which is evident in table 3 and suggests that these rules may have important distributional effects. Many consumers don't even have credit. For example, the Consumer Financial Protection Bureau reported in 2015 that 26 million Americans, or roughly 1 in 10 adults, have no credit history.[44] The DOE acknowledges that credit constraints are a potential problem, but the agency doesn't seem to recognize that for some individuals the relevant interest rate is infinity—they can't borrow at any rate.

While the DOE's broad approach to calculating consumer and business discount rates follows a certain logic that is (at least on the face of it) reasonable, from a neoclassical perspective, all this analysis of payback periods may turn out to be unnecessary. If one accepts revealed preference as a principle of economic analysis, then whatever discount rate the consumer uses must be the correct discount rate. Only he or she knows the market conditions and interest rates relevant to his or her personal situation. The DOE's approach would make sense if it can be demonstrated that consumers and businesses have some informational problem or constraint that prevents them from calculating these rates effectively for themselves, such that the DOE can calculate their cost of capital better than they can. Absent such evidence, DOE's payback period analysis rests on shaky foundations.

More concretely, if revealed preference holds, then those consumers who opt to buy a particular device, and subsequently cannot buy it because the device is banned by the DOE, suffer an unambiguous cost from the regulation. No payback period analysis need even be done, since such consumers are never paid back on net for their loss: the payback period is infinite. This is not to say that a regulation isn't worth promulgating. All policies create winners and losers, and the consumers that would have opted to purchase a product that is banned by regulators are simply some of the losers from the policy in question. This is not how the DOE markets its regulations, however. Instead, the agency routinely claims that consumers benefit from its appliance and equipment standards.[45]

There is also the possibility that consumers lose because product quality is impaired by energy-efficiency standards. One retrospective study identified a number of areas where appliance efficiency regulations tend to impose greater costs and lower cost savings on consumers than is typically estimated in the DOE's ex ante analyses. These areas include reduced product life and reliability, greater energy usage than anticipated, and additional operation and maintenance costs.[46]

One reason energy savings can be less than expected is that consumers sometimes respond to energy efficiency improvements by using a device more intensively, a phenomenon known as the *rebound effect*.[47] For example, drivers tend to drive more miles when the miles-per-gallon increases on their vehicle. The same general principle holds for appliances. While the DOE does acknowledge rebound effects and calculates some scenarios where a rebound effect occurs, it does not adjust operating-cost savings calculations due to a rebound effect in its core calculations for its ceiling fan rule.[48] In extreme cases, however, these unintended consequences have been known to fully offset the aim of reducing energy consumption.

Making a device more energy efficient can also complicate its mechanics, making it more prone to breaking—and shortening a product's life span adds to the likelihood that energy savings will not materialize. The DOE is supposed to account for the possibility of quality changes as a result of its regulations, according to various statutory mandates.[49] However, it is a change in relative quality, not just absolute quality, that should ideally be considered—that is, how quality has changed or stayed the same relative to how quality would have improved in absence of a regulation. Such changes can be exceedingly hard to measure. All told, the uncertainty facing regulators is considerable when it comes to energy efficiency standards.

Is There an Economic Growth Rationale for These Regulations?

Underlying revealed preference methods is the idea that consumers are generally most capable of deciding for themselves what is in their own interests. But what is in the individual's interest and what is in society-at-large's broader interest are not always the same thing. Market failures mean that individual and social interests often deviate, even under neoclassical assumptions.

However, standard portrayals of market failure, as illustrated in figure 1, often lack a temporal component. In other words, analysts tend to think of and explain market failures in a static context, without expressly considering a time element. They also fail to distinguish between social benefits and costs that come in the form of consumption from those that come in the form of investment. This is odd because the consumption choices of consumers today, even seemingly unimportant choices, can impact people in the future, not just those alive today. If I decide to purchase something as simple as an ice-cream cone for $5, that decision can have a future impact if, had I not bought the ice cream, I would have invested some of the $5 instead.[50]

Consider the hypothetical example of an energy efficiency regulation for an appliance that would result in savings of $1 million by reducing energy use. Perhaps these savings come at the expense of a loss of consumer utility valued by present consumers at $2 million— maybe because appliance functionality is impaired in some way. From the standpoint of the appliance's purchasers, this is clearly a bad deal. They value the lost product quality more than the financial savings from lower utility bills. They would be made worse off by this regulation, were it enacted.

But consider the same example from the standpoint of future consumers. If some fraction of the million dollars in financial savings were invested and reinvested continually, it would grow into far more than $1 million or even $2 million in the future. The short-run reduction in consumer utility as a result of lower-performing appliances seems trivial from this perspective, because it is a temporary loss. Utility, after all, can't be invested in an account as money can. Meanwhile, the compounding gains stemming from increased investment could potentially have far-reaching longer-run consequences.

In theory, it seems that it could be worthwhile to override consumer choices in the present in order to increase investment that can benefit individuals in the future. This is not to say that present consumers are made better off by having had their choices overridden. Unlike the behavioral approach, this rationale for energy efficiency regulations does not claim that overriding consumer choices is a benefit—it is clearly a cost—but all regulations override choice to some extent, so the fact that consumer choices are overridden is not a sufficient reason to preclude regulation.

In fact, if future consumers could participate in present-day markets, one might expect they would be willing to pay consumers in the present to accept a lower-functioning appliance. They would likely be willing to pay up to the future value of whatever the investment benefit will be worth to them in the future. In our example, they might be willing to pay consumers $2.1 million to accept some functionality impairment in their appliance. This is a small price for future consumers to pay if it leads to more investment in the economy, which could grow into huge sums owing to the power of compound interest.

If such compensation took place, then everyone would be made better off by the change without making anyone else worse off, a situation known as a Pareto improvement. Consumers today would be better off because, though they would have a worse device, they would also have some extra money that more than compensates them for it. Consumers in the future would be better off because of the increased investment that will have boosted economic growth and raised their incomes. Even without compensation, the winners would gain by more than the losers would lose, a situation which is known in economics as a Kaldor-Hicks improvement (or a potential Pareto improvement), and is a principle that underlies cost-benefit analysis.

In this example, time acts as a transaction cost, similar to how traditional externalities, asymmetric information, and poor decision-making result from physical and mental transaction costs. Time creates a market failure because time prevents mutually beneficial exchanges from occurring. The market failure associated with time is unique in that usually with traditional neoclassical market failures, harmed third parties are alive to lobby on behalf of their own interests. This is not the case with future generations.

One potential problem with this logic is that almost any consumption expenditure would seem to impose an externality on people in the future. After all, some of the resources consumed might have been invested instead. So there needs to be some limiting principle that would prevent the present generation from having to save all its income for the sake of the future. In fact, there *is* such a limiting principle. Future generations would be unlikely to want to pay current consumers to invest any more of present income than corresponds with the consumption-maximizing "Golden Rule" rate of economic growth. This is the rate of economic growth that maximizes consumption across generations. Beyond this point, any additional returns to investment would be eaten up by the maintenance of depreciating capital, and so, on net, the rate of return on investment is negative for society.

An interesting aspect of these kinds of intertemporal externalities is that they can override traditional market failures. For example, let's say that a polluting power plant reduces air quality in a particular city. The residents of the city, if they could organize, might be willing to pay the plant to reduce its emissions such that it would be profitable for the firm to do so. However, it is costly for residents to organize, owing to transaction costs, and so the exchange doesn't take place. Such an exchange, if it took place, would increase social welfare within the current time period, because both the residents and the power plant would be better off. However, there is still the future to consider. If the exchange simply increased consumer utility—say health—but at the expense of capital accumulation and economic growth, people in the future might well be willing to compensate present citizens to accept more pollution. On balance, social welfare might be improved if present citizens accepted more risk, in exchange for faster economic growth.

This example highlights how the efficient solution can change depending on whether time is considered in the analysis. If one focuses only on the present moment, it might appear that the efficient solution is for the power plant to pollute far less. But if one takes a perspective that accounts for the future as well, it may well be that the efficient outcome is for the power plant to produce more energy, and by extension, to increase present pollution somewhat. The irony, of course, is that regulators and academics seem to suffer from their own version of present bias, at least when it comes to the theory of market failure that is the basis for many regulatory interventions.

With energy efficiency regulations, the growth rationale for regulations is a moot point if financial savings never materialize. But if the energy savings are indeed real, any policy that on balance increases investment may actually increase social welfare, at least so long as the economy is operating below the consumption-maximizing Golden Rule rate of economic growth. This logic also extends to other behavioral interventions—such as default opt-in retirement accounts—that potentially increase savings and investment.

Conclusion and Policy Reform

The theory underlying behavioral market failures is not so different from the theory that explains market failures of other kinds; however, the knowledge problem facing regulators is likely to be harder to overcome with behavioral market failures. Moreover, the traditional theory of market failure is itself incomplete, because it doesn't fully consider how benefits and costs accrue to individuals over the course of time.

Even the growth rationale for energy efficiency regulations should have caveats attached to it. Almost any regulation that increases capital formation on balance could be justified on these grounds. And while there are sound economic reasons to believe that the market underperforms in this regard (most economic growth models predict that society will not achieve the consumption-maximizing rate of growth), it is far from obvious whether the best way to promote capital formation is through energy efficiency regulations, or through regulations at all. After all, if subpar growth is really such a big problem, why not encourage more investment in the marketplace, either by private firms or perhaps by the government itself—for example, through tax policy or the creation of a sovereign wealth fund? Energy efficiency regulations are unlikely to be the best method available to boost growth, or even to be a particularly good method.

All told, a dose of humility is likely in order. It may well be that the best option—even when behavioral market failures are present—is for policymakers to defer to the decisions of consumers. Identifying bias in the real world is likely to be extremely difficult, and the knowledge problem associated with proving the existence of behavioral market failures is severe. Even choice-preserving interventions, such as nudges, could well backfire. If a regulator switches a default option for retirement plans, how does the regulator know which default corresponds with employees' "true" preferences? Most likely some will be made better off and some worse off. On balance, the change could well be welfare-reducing, but how can the analyst ever know for sure?

Behavioral economists often argue that their interventions make consumers "better off as judged by themselves." At the end of the day, however, the knowledge constraints facing regulators make the behavioral rationale for promoting energy efficiency less than fully convincing. Fashionable new ideas and theories in academia are being used to justify regulatory interventions that have been around for decades.[51] Upon closer inspection, however, these new rationales end up looking a lot like the old ones: the same old paternalism that has existed throughout the ages.

Energy Markets and Environmental Regulations

CHAPTER 12

Cooperation or Conflict: Two Approaches to Conservation

Jordan K. Lofthouse and Megan E. Jenkins

In 2012, the mayor of a southern Utah town found herself working to protect the local cemetery from an invasion of small rodents. The Utah prairie dog had made itself at home in the cemetery, digging burrows that sank headstones and created hazards for those visiting their loved ones. Paragonah Mayor Constance Robinson explained that some of the animals had even made their way inside coffins buried in the cemetery. She noted, "When we found that out, we were devastated."[1]

Utah prairie dogs are a unique species that create complex underground "towns." In addition to damaging the local cemetery, the prairie dogs burrowed under the runway at the nearby Parowan Airport. The damage was so bad that the runway no longer met Federal Aviation Administration safety standards. Underground fencing had to be installed to keep the prairie dogs out so the airport could continue operating.[2]

Town residents such as Mayor Robinson hoped to remove the prairie dogs to stop the damage being done in their community. But the Utah prairie dog was listed as a threatened species under the Endangered Species Act. That meant that federal regulations made it illegal for anyone to harm or remove the animals without a permit, even if that harm occurred by accident in the course of otherwise legal activities such as maintaining the town's cemetery or airport runways.

While many were frustrated by these restrictions, others agreed with the need to protect the animal to prevent extinction. Lindsey Sterling Krank of the Prairie Dog Coalition expressed this sentiment: "Love 'em or hate 'em, we gotta have 'em. . . . If you were to remove a prairie dog from the prairie ecosystem, the prairie ecosystem could fall apart."[3]

This conflict over the Utah prairie dog eventually culminated in a lawsuit in which a group of local property owners and local governments, calling themselves "People for the Ethical Treatment of Property Owners," sued the federal government, alleging that federal restrictions on their ability to remove prairie dogs from their land were unlawful. In 2014 a US district court judge sided with the property owners, putting a halt on federal restrictions.[4]

But when federal restrictions were removed, the prairie dog was not left to fend for itself. Instead, the state stepped up and created its own plan to protect the species. That plan involved $400,000 in funding for habitat protection on state lands. State biologists were tasked with moving prairie dogs from residential areas to the state-owned conservation lands that were being improved for the specific purpose of providing quality habitat for the species. Soon after, prairie dog numbers rose to their highest counts in recorded history.[5]

What made these state-led efforts so successful? First, they aligned incentives so that landowners were encouraged to work toward conservation goals rather than against them. Prairie dogs, like most endangered species, rely on private land for their habitat. That makes it essential for governments to treat landowners as valued conservation partners through policies that encourage them to share their land with endangered species. Utah's plan did this by allowing landowners and conservationists to work together to achieve the desired environmental goal of recovering an imperiled species.

Second, the Utah plan relied on local knowledge by consulting state biologists and people with on-the-ground expertise in what it takes to help the species thrive. Conservation efforts are more likely to be successful if they have buy-in from local people. The state's plan achieved this by treating local stakeholders as partners in conservation rather than as obstacles.

Unfortunately for the prairie dog, in 2017 the 10th Circuit Court of Appeals overturned the district court's decision and made Utah's successful plan to move prairie dogs to more hospitable habitat unlawful.[6] The Supreme Court was then asked to review the case, but declined to do so in 2018.[7]

But the story of the Utah prairie dog didn't end with the 10th Circuit's decision. In 2018, the US Fish and Wildlife Service allowed Utah to resume its successful management of the species. The agency worked with the Utah Division of Wildlife Resources to create a 10-year conservation plan for the Utah prairie dog. The plan creates permits that allow limited removal or harm to the species as long as steps are taken to mitigate impacts to the species elsewhere. The new plan also involves relocating prairie dogs from private land to areas that are better suited to their survival, and it uses incentive-based approaches through conservation easements and conservation banks.

The fight over this rodent in southern Utah helps illustrate how environmental policy today often pits stakeholders against one another rather than allowing for cooperation. Protecting wildlife and preventing extinction are worthy goals, but environmental policies must be evaluated on the basis of their outcomes rather than their intentions. The approach we choose matters in determining whether we will get the desired outcome, as well as how much conflict, litigation, and controversy will happen along the way.

In the case of the Utah prairie dog, the initial implementation of the Endangered Species Act created a punitive regulatory approach that punished local actors for taking any action that harmed the species, even on their private property. This approach reduced the incentives for local landowners and environmental groups to work together to find a win-win solution. Because this approach did not provide a path for cooperative solutions to emerge, conflict and litigation were the result.

But the removal of federal restrictions created the opportunity for local stakeholders to formulate their own plan. Utah's innovative plan to help the prairie dog recover was successful because it relied on incentives and allowed bottom-up solutions to emerge. Even though the courts gave power back to federal officials, those officials allowed Utah's successful, cooperative conservation plan to continue.

Every sphere of social life is characterized by varying levels of cooperation and conflict. Cooperation occurs when people work together peacefully, and conflict entails people fighting against each other. Cooperation occurs on a massive scale every day when people voluntarily exchange their money and property in markets. Even if people don't have the same goals, they can bargain and exchange with one another to find mutually beneficial outcomes. This process of voluntary, mutually beneficial exchange allows people to coexist in a cooperative way.[8]

Government regulation can play an important and helpful role in getting good environmental outcomes. Some laws and regulations, however, are better at creating opportunities for cooperative solutions to emerge than others. Top-down policies tend to result in conflict rather than cooperation because they give people with different goals limited opportunities to compromise with each other. But policies that are flexible and allow people to compromise and exchange with one another tend to result in much more cooperative outcomes.

The story of the Utah prairie dog demonstrates how a conflict-ridden situation can become more cooperative through policy change. When state and federal policies were changed to allow people to find bottom-up solutions, more cooperation resulted, benefiting both the prairie dog and local people.

Many current environmental policies create incentives for opposing sides to engage in conflict by lobbying for policies that benefit their side at the expense of others. For example, environmental organizations are often pitted against energy and manufacturing companies, and they battle by spending billions of dollars lobbying for policies that benefit them. From 2000 to 2016, special interest groups spent more than $2 billion lobbying Congress for policies related to climate change. This activity made up almost 4 percent of total lobbying expenditures during those years.[9] Reforms to environmental policies could change the incentives so that resources are put to socially productive uses rather than wasted through lobbying.

The rest of this chapter will examine why some types of environmental policy lead to conflict and controversy and why other arrangements can result in more cooperation. First, we look at the types of institutions that facilitate cooperation and limit conflict. To do this, we explore some basic economic principles that show why cooperation through exchange is likely to be more successful in achieving positive environmental outcomes than top-down policies. Second, we examine how a nonprofit called American Prairie Reserve has relied on property rights and incentives rather than punishment to engage in large-scale conservation. We also discuss the shortcomings of American Prairie Reserve's approach. Finally, we explore key implications for public policy going forward that would likely help the US achieve better environmental stewardship. We use the Endangered Species Act as an example to explore potential reforms to improve environmental outcomes and decrease conflict.

Conflict or Cooperation? Finding Institutions That Work

From prairie dogs in southern Utah to wolves in Yellowstone, attempts at conservation often result in conflict. This conflict comes about for many different reasons. Sometimes conflict happens when different environmental goals clash—for example, advocates of large-scale solar power plants have butted heads with wildlife conservationists because the solar power plants can take up critical habitat for endangered species such as the desert tortoise.[10] Other conflicts arise when people disagree about which goals are most important, how different goals should be pursued, and who should bear the cost of reaching those goals.

Effective environmental policy must provide ways to resolve conflict and facilitate cooperation between people with interests that may be at odds. In this section, we compare a positive-sum system of property rights and voluntary exchange with the zero-sum system of political decision-making that is often used in environmental policy today.

Scarcity—the Root of Environmental Problems

To understand conflict in environmental policy from an economic point of view, it is helpful to first understand scarcity. Scarcity occurs because human desires often exceed the means to satisfy those desires. Given the right circumstances, every resource in the world can become scarce because no resource exists in unlimited amounts. People also value resources differently, and will inevitably disagree about how a particular resource should be used. Environmental problems arise when people place conflicting demands on scarce natural resources or disagree about how to achieve a particular environmental goal.

For example, the vast "sagebrush sea" of Wyoming is a prime location for oil and gas extraction, but it is also an important habitat for the greater sage-grouse—a bird that is native to much of the American West and has been considered for listing as an endangered species. Although the sagebrush sea of Wyoming is indeed vast, it is not unlimited. There are only so many areas where oil and gas production can take place, and likewise, there are only so many acres where sage-grouse can live. Without some sort of mechanism to decide the "who, what, how, and when," conflict will arise between the many parties who have competing visions for how Wyoming's sagebrush sea should be used.

While some level of conflict is inevitable, what matters is how institutions channel human behavior. Some institutions are more likely to encourage people to look for mutually beneficial outcomes, while others are more likely to spark conflict that results in more costs than benefits.

Property Rights, Exchange, and Cooperation

The positive-sum, cooperative system of property rights and voluntary exchange is important for dealing with competing visions for how any resource should be used. Property rights make it clear who has the ability to make decisions about a particular resource. Private property rights allow those who hold them to benefit from decisions that create value, and force the owner to bear the costs of choices that go poorly. Property rights also assign liability to people who damage another person's property, making it clear who has to pay whom when something goes wrong. Thus, property rights give owners a strong incentive to use their property wisely and give non-owners an incentive to be careful with another person's property.[11]

Property rights work best when they can be traded, exchanged, and contracted over. Markets allow property owners to trade, rent, or make contracts with one another on the basis of how much they value a particular property right. Markets thus facilitate cooperation on a massive scale. Humans can peacefully coexist because property rights clarify the rules about who can use what, and if one person does not like how another person's property is being used, the two people can bargain with one another to come to a mutually beneficial arrangement.[12] In markets, property rights incentivize owners to weigh the costs and benefits of their actions. When markets allow people to trade with one another, resources can flow to those who value them most. Thus, voluntary exchange is mutually beneficial because both parties see an exchange as making them better off (or they wouldn't choose to trade in the first place).

The concept of private property rights is not always easy to define because property rights are really a "bundle" of sub-rights that function together. For example, if a person owns a house, she has several sub-rights associated with her ownership. Her property rights mean that she has the right to do many different things: paint the house yellow, build a fence around it, sell it, transfer it to a family member, stop others from trespassing, run a business from it, use it as collateral for a loan, rent out a room, lease out the house entirely, and sue people who cause damage.

Property rights are not absolute, however. Property owners can choose to give up some of their sub-rights in the bundle. For example, in conservation easements, landowners can choose to give up the sub-right to develop the land that they own. Essentially, a conservation easement means that a landowner gives the sub-right of development to the government or another organization for the purpose of conservation. If the landowner sells the property in the future, the new owner likewise cannot build anything on the land because it is set aside for conservation.[13]

Property rights are complex. For example, sometimes property rights are not easily exchangeable. If property rights cannot be exchanged, it may be difficult to use them to solve problems. In other cases, there may be spillover effects, called externalities, when property rights are not defined. For example, it is difficult to assign property rights to air and therefore difficult to address air pollution through property rights. Another example where defining property rights is difficult is in the case of wildlife. For example, private landowners generally get to decide what to do with their land. These rights are not absolute, however, as government agencies may decide to regulate private landowners when endangered species live on or migrate across private land. In such cases, policymakers have to balance the private property rights of landowners and the public interest in protecting endangered species.

Government policies and property rights are interconnected. Governments help to clearly define the limits of property rights, keep records of property ownership, and enforce property rights through policing and the court system. Governments rely on private property and mutually beneficial exchange to function because government revenue comes largely through property taxes, sales taxes, and income taxes.[14]

Many renowned scholars, including Nobel Prize winners, have studied the role of property rights in solving social problems—these scholars have included Ronald Coase, Elinor Ostrom, Douglass North, Yoram Barzel, and Daron Acemoglu. They have spent decades researching how property rights contribute both to economic growth and to environmental solutions. But when private property rights are not clearly defined or enforced, people cannot engage in mutually beneficial, positive-sum exchanges. The lack of clear property rights can thus lead to conflict when opposing parties fight over who is being harmed and who should have to pay damages.

When resources are owned collectively, rules must be created to clarify who gets to use what resources. If rules are not established, individual users may face an incentive to overuse a resource to the point of depletion.[15] The ecologist Garrett Hardin coined the term "tragedy of the commons" to describe this situation, where a resource held in common is exhausted by overuse. When dealing with such a shared resource, Hardin argued that individuals will act in their own self-interest and deplete the resource, creating an outcome that no one desired.

In her Nobel Prize–winning work, Elinor Ostrom outlined how the tragedy of the commons could be avoided. One potential way is to divide the resource into private property. If privatization is not possible or desirable, there are other alternatives. For example, the resource could be managed collectively by the local community, which could create and enforce its own rules for governing the resource. Elinor Ostrom documented many successful cases of community management of communal resources all over the world.[16] Additionally, government officials could create regulations to determine who gets to use commonly owned resources and how they may use them. Although regulations can help overcome the tragedy of the commons, they can also pose other problems, such as favoritism and corruption. Each of these three ways to avoid the tragedy of the commons has trade-offs, so the appropriate course of action will depend on the unique circumstances and the preferences of local communities. In the real world, most solutions to environmental problems involve a combination of privatization, community management, and government regulation. Based on her observations, Elinor Ostrom rejected the idea that solutions to complex environmental problems must rely solely on either a private or a government approach.

Another key insight of Elinor Ostrom's research shows that one way to overcome complex environmental problems is through polycentric decision-making. Polycentric governance systems have multiple, overlapping decision-making centers, which allow societies to effectively solve environmental problems. A polycentric approach allows federal, state, and local governments, as well as private associations and markets, to come together to find solutions that are better tailored to local conditions, take better advantage of local knowledge, and have more direct involvement by local populations. Polycentric systems allow more freedom for people on the ground to develop their own rules and strategies that work with unique circumstances and preferences.[17]

Policymakers who impose centralized, one-size-fits-all laws may not have the necessary knowledge to solve the problems they want to solve, and such top-down policies often spawn conflict. In polycentric systems of governance, many day-to-day decisions are delegated to lower levels so that people with the on-the-ground experience and knowledge can use their experience and knowledge to solve the problem. Additionally, when local governments and local associations make decisions instead of far-removed "outsiders," their actions may receive more buy-in from the people on the ground.

The combination of private property rights and polycentric systems can and does help to solve real-world problems such as wildlife conservation. When wildlife can be owned as private property, people have a stronger incentive to engage in conservation. For example, American bison were nearly wiped out of existence in the 1800s, but a combination of government-led conservation efforts and the establishment of private property to bison brought the species back from the brink.

In the 1500s, an estimated 30–60 million bison roamed across North America. As white American settlers moved westward, their farming practices disrupted bison habitat, and their cattle passed diseases to bison. These bison were largely unowned, and people slaughtered them in huge numbers for food and leather, as well as for their bones, which were used for refining sugar, making fertilizer, and producing fine bone china. The bison slaughter was a tragedy of the commons on a massive scale. State legislatures and Congress made a few legal attempts in the 1800s to protect the dwindling number of bison, but most of these laws were either not passed or not enforced. By 1884, there were only around 325 wild bison left in the United States.[18]

It was not until the late 1800s, after most of the wild herds had vanished, that people found it worthwhile to capture and breed bison. Because wild herds had been eliminated and private individuals raised live bison, nearly all states changed their laws to treat bison as domestic livestock rather than wildlife. Bison became property just like ordinary cattle. In 1889, 256 bison were in captivity, and by 1901, private bison numbered over 600. In 1902, there were about 700 bison in private herds, and the wild Yellowstone herd consisted of 23 animals.

Once property rights to bison were established, the market for bison emerged. People realized that they could raise bison for meat or tourism. Ranchers bought and sold bison to each other, and they also sold bison to zoos, parks, and refuges.[19] Thanks largely to private efforts, the population of bison grew to 12,521 by 1919. In the 1990s, there were at least 250,000 bison in private herds. Over this time, the federal government also implemented its own conservation regulations for bison, particularly in Yellowstone. By the 1990s, there were an estimated 20,000–25,000 bison in government-managed public herds in North America.[20]

The combination of both private and public efforts helped bring bison back from the brink of extinction. In 2017, there were 183,780 privately owned bison in the United States and 119,314 privately owned bison in Canada. Today, the US federal government manages roughly 10,000 public bison, state and other public herds have about 9,000 bison, and Native American tribes manage about 20,000.[21] American bison are just one of many success stories in which private property rights have aided conservation.[22]

Winners and Losers in the Political Arena

When property rights are not or cannot be clearly defined, government regulation can play a role in helping to solve environmental problems. Although regulation has the potential to help improve environmental quality, the command-and-control approach assumes that centralized policymakers have the knowledge necessary to do so. In many cases, however, policymakers may not have the required knowledge to anticipate what the effects of their policies will be, leading to conflict and unintended consequences that may actually be harmful to the environment or cause other problems.[23]

To understand why policymakers do what they do, public choice economics uses economic principles to analyze both market and government activity. People in the market are assumed to be rational and self-interested, and so are those in the government. All people, whether they are in the public or the private sphere, respond to their incentives and constraints. With this perspective, public choice economics examines how real-world governments actually make policies, not how an ideal government should or could make policies.[24]

Public policies are a result of the collective choices of voters, special interest groups, and government officials. Governments have the power to require citizens to pay taxes and obey regulations. Special interest groups then hire lobbyists to persuade elected officials to enact certain public policies that benefit members of the groups, while the costs are dispersed among other groups.[25] Solving environmental difficulties through political means can be problematic because politicians and bureaucrats can be persuaded to choose policies that benefit one side at the other's expense.[26]

The conflict that arises from the rent-seeking process is a negative-sum game for society because special interest groups use resources to persuade government officials to adopt specific positions, but these resources don't produce new goods or services. In other words, rent-seeking isn't harmless. In some cases, rent-seeking can be negative-sum when competing rent-seekers collectively spend more than the government distributes. Rent-seeking has social costs because real resources are spent trying to capture part of a fixed pie rather than to make the pie bigger.[27]

Private property rights and voluntary exchange create the potential for both sides to be better off than they otherwise would have been. Politics, however, doesn't have the same potential for trade among opposing groups because both sides attempt to get their preferred policy enacted at the expense of the other side. In other words, private property rights and markets reward those who seek compromise through mutually beneficial exchange, whereas politics incentivizes conflict because some people bear more of the costs than others. Private property rights and markets allow cooperation to emerge and local knowledge to be accessed, which can improve outcomes and provide benefits to both sides. To avoid the problems associated with political rent-seeking, people can achieve desirable environmental outcomes through the cooperative process of market exchange.

Markets and Market-Like Regulations

Up to this point, we have focused on the strengths of markets and the downsides of government policies, but that does not imply that markets always produce the best result or that government policies always lead to bad outcomes. Although there are general patterns that occur in markets and government, the real world is messy, and solving real-world environmental problems is difficult. Dozens of examples show how markets have worked remarkably well to solve environmental problems when property rights are clearly defined and enforced. Unfortunately, some of the most dire environmental dilemmas concern issues where property rights are not clear. These include issues related to wildlife, water, and air.[28]

When it is too difficult or costly to assign property rights, government policies may be the best option available to solve environmental problems. That doesn't mean, however, that top-down, government-led conservation approaches will be perfect. Government approaches can also experience failures, impose high costs, and produce unintended consequences. Further, not all government policies are created equal.

The real question is how to merge the best aspects of markets with public policies, while also accounting for the limitations of politics. Many government policies, such as the Clean Air Act, the Clean Water Act, and the Endangered Species Act, have led to improved environmental outcomes. Each of those policies also has its shortcomings, unintended consequences, and costs. In the future, policymakers and citizens can think of new ways to reform environmental policies to limit conflict, facilitate cooperation, and produce desirable environmental outcomes.

Reforms to conservation policies could make the policies more market-like in the sense that they could allow for exchange between different people who have different preferences. The opposite of a market-like regulation would be a command-and-control regulation, one in which policymakers set clear rules and punish people who don't abide by the rules. The critical difference between a market-like policy and a command-and-control policy is who determines the means of reducing pollution. In market-like policies, people voluntarily exchange with one another to decide who reduces pollution, by how much, and by which means. Under command-and-control policies, the government makes these decisions. A government approach can be problematic because government officials may not have the knowledge to identify the most efficient or effective way to reduce pollution. That kind of knowledge can only be generated through market discoveries.

A common problem with command-and-control regulations is that special interest groups have a strong incentive to persuade policy-makers to craft the rules in a way that benefits them at the expense of other groups. Those who bear the costs of command-and-control regulations will try to find creative ways to get around them, which can lead to negative unintended consequences and limit the effectiveness of the regulations. Market-like regulations can be a workable alternative because they allow for mutually beneficial exchange.

One of the most successful market-like regulations enacted in the US was a cap-and-trade system for sulfur emissions, which were the chief cause of acid rain. The amendments to the Clean Air Act in 1990 created the cap-and-trade system, which consisted of two parts. First, total sulfur emissions were "capped" for the entire nation at 8.95 millions tons—a 50 percent reduction from 1980 levels. Second, the federal government issued tradable permits that allowed companies to legally emit sulfur in certain amounts. The combined amount of allowable emissions from all permits equaled the total "cap" on national emissions.

The federal government gave the permits, called allowances, to existing coal-fired power plants on the basis of their historical fuel use and an emissions performance standard.[29] These permits functioned as a form of government-assigned property rights that could then be traded.

Due largely to the market-like system of tradable permits, sulfur emissions significantly decreased after the cap-and-trade system was enacted. Emissions in 2000 were nearly 40 percent below those of 1980. Much of the sulfur pollution in the US comes from energy producers, and an important lesson from the cap-and-trade system was that firms generating electricity from clean sources made money by selling their permits to firms that produce electricity from dirty sources. The result was that clean energy was essentially subsidized voluntarily by other polluters.

The cap-and-trade system reduced sulfur emissions by millions of tons annually at a fraction of the expected costs. Some of the most important innovations that came from this system were improvements in the accuracy of emissions data, lower costs for every ton of sulfur eliminated, more efficient means of electricity production, shifts to less-polluting fuel, and more efficient pollutant-removing technology.[30] Figure 1 shows how sulfur dioxide decreased over time after the implementation of the cap-and-trade system, and it also shows the success of a similar cap-and-trade program for nitrogen oxides that was implemented in 2003.[31]

Compared to the traditional command-and-control approach, in a cap-and-trade system polluters have a stronger incentive to discover lower-cost ways of reducing pollution. Under a cap-and-trade system, the companies that can reduce pollution for a low cost have an opportunity to sell their permits to other companies that will have a more difficult time reducing their pollution cheaply. This means that all companies have a strong incentive to look for cheaper, more effective, and more efficient ways of reducing pollution because they can make money by doing so. Over time, an increasing number of companies will find it in their interest to implement the cheaper, more effective, and more efficient ways of reducing pollution.

Figure 1. Levels of Sulfur Dioxide and Nitrogen Oxides in the US, by Year

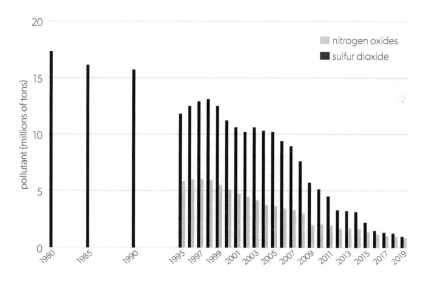

Source: "Air Markets Program Data," US Environmental Protection Agency, Clean Air Markets Division, accessed April 18, 2020, https://ampd.epa.gov/ampd/.

Anyone can participate in the cap-and-trade system, which means that environmentalists who care about decreasing emissions can buy the permits, tear them up, and choose not to pollute at all.[32] For example, the Clean Air Conservancy was a national nonprofit organization that would collect donations from environmentalists and then purchase sulfur permits from energy producers. The Conservancy would then retire the permits so that no one could use them to emit sulfur. The Conservancy used to mail donors certificates announcing the amount of sulfur that had been purchased and retired with the money they sent in.[33]

Cap-and-trade and other market-like regulations don't completely eliminate conflict. Deciding what the cap will be is a political decision that can bring about conflict. Different organizations may lobby for a higher or lower cap on emissions, which is a form of rent-seeking. Once a decision is made about what the cap should be, policymakers must then assign the permits. The initial assignment of permits can be contentious because the assignment determines who gains the benefits and who bears the costs, at least at first. Policymakers can assign permits in various ways. The Environmental Protection Agency has often used a sealed-bid auction, in which permits are sold to the highest bidders. Policymakers could also award permits to firms based on the amount of pollution they have historically emitted, or they could award permits in a blind lottery to any applicant. Each system of awarding permits will have trade-offs, and any decision is likely to spark some conflict.

Despite the inherent conflict in deciding how to assign permits initially, a cap-and-trade system is likely to be less conflict-ridden than command-and-control regulations. Once the permits have been assigned, anyone who is unhappy with the initial assignment can seek to buy more permits from those who have a surplus. Under command-and-control regulations, there is no possibility of exchange in a market, so people who are unhappy often resort to lobbying to change the regulations. If they are successful, the formerly favored side will become upset, and its members are likely to lobby to reinstate the old regulations. The back-and-forth of the rent-seeking process is socially wasteful when the total amount of money spent on lobbying by both sides is greater than the total social benefits.[34] Both systems can yield the same pollution outcomes, but cap-and-trade systems encourage a wider range of win-win situations.

Policymakers can look for creative, innovative ways of leveraging markets and market-like mechanisms, as they have for bison conservation and limiting sulfur pollution. These examples illustrate that conservation can and does happen without top-down, command-and-control regulations that spur conflict. The next section explores an innovative real-world approach to species conservation that takes advantage of both markets and market-like mechanisms to limit conflict and facilitate cooperation.

An Innovative Approach to Market-Based Conservation

The Great Plains of northeastern Montana might not seem like much to visitors passing through, but to one local nonprofit, these grasslands offer the potential for achieving key conservation goals. The American Prairie Reserve (APR) is currently working to patch together these seemingly endless grasslands to create one of the world's largest nature reserves. This group aims to restore the landscape and wildlife of the Great Plains to the conditions members of the Lewis and Clark Expedition saw in the early 19th century.

APR's ultimate goal is to create the largest wildlife reserve in the lower 48 states by piecing together approximately 3.2 million acres of both private and public lands. Once completed, the Reserve will contain roughly 500,000 acres of private land, accompanied by grazing leases on adjacent public lands.[35]

Cooperative Conservation on the Great Plains

APR operates primarily as a willing-buyer-willing-seller organization. It raises money from private donors to buy private land in northern Montana. The sellers are generally ranchers who own large tracts of private land that are accompanied by long-term grazing leases on federal land managed by the Bureau of Land Management (BLM) and state lands managed by the Montana Department of Natural Resources and Conservation. When APR buys private property, it can also acquire the accompanying leases on federal and state grazing lands if it follows the applicable rules and regulations.[36]

From 2004 to September 2020, APR had completed 31 transactions to build a habitat base of nearly 420,000 acres. Of the total land in the Reserve, nearly 105,000 acres are made up of private land owned directly by the Reserve. On APR's privately owned lands, the organization is relatively free to engage in its private goals of ecological restoration—for instance, it may reintroduce bison and remove fences to allow wildlife to roam freely, subject to existing laws and regulations. Just over 315,00 acres are leased public lands, mostly owned by the federal government with the remainder owned by the state of Montana.[37]

Many people are familiar with government-led conservation efforts, such as national parks and national monuments. APR's voluntary approach to large-scale conservation, however, follows a long but often overlooked history of voluntary conservation in the United States. One of the earliest examples was Thomas Jefferson's purchase of land to protect Virginia's Natural Bridge. After Jefferson died, his estate sold the land that contained Natural Bridge, but the land was privately protected until 2014, when the owner sold the property so that it could become a Virginia state park.[38]

By following this tradition of voluntary conservation, APR is strategically using private property rights to avoid much of the conflict that is associated with conservation through political means. Since property rights can be traded, exchanged, and contracted over, ranchers and conservationists can come to cooperative, mutually beneficial agreements through voluntary exchanges of land. APR supporters would like to see Montana's Great Plains be used for conservation, and traditional ranchers would like that same land to be available for agriculture. For private lands, property rights allow people with opposing views to bargain with one another to find an arrangement that works for both parties. If a rancher values his property at $1 million and APR offers the rancher anything over $1 million, both sides are made better off from an exchange.

In addition to buying land, one of APR's main goals is to create an environment where wildlife, including predators, can thrive. Many ranchers and farmers in the area, however, see wildlife as a threat to their livelihoods. As a result, APR's efforts at wildlife restoration could be undermined in surrounding areas if ranchers and farmers scare away or kill the returning wildlife. APR has started a program called Wild Sky to create incentives for ranchers and farmers that live near the reserve to view wildlife as an asset rather than a liability.

Wild Sky Beef is a for-profit subsidiary company of APR that funds an incentive program for ranchers who share their land with wild-life.[39] It contracts with ranchers across the United States, mainly in the Upper Midwest, to raise grass-fed cattle to sell at a premium price.[40] The profits from selling this beef are used to provide ranchers around the Reserve with financial rewards as incentives for making their land more conducive to wildlife. Ranchers in the program agree to certain conditions, such as not tilling the land, not killing predators or prairie dogs, and installing wildlife-friendly fencing.

The Wild Sky program provides participating ranchers with financial incentives to view wildlife as a benefit rather than a detriment.[41] Participating ranchers receive payments from the Wild Sky program that help offset the costs of protecting wildlife and promoting ecological health. For example, ranchers are paid for installing webcams on their property to show evidence that they are making their land welcome to predators and other wildlife. Each year, APR staff and a third-party evaluator determine to what extent participating ranchers are improving or maintaining ecological conditions. Participating ranchers that demonstrate ecological improvements to their land receive an annual premium through the Wild Sky program.[42]

By reducing conflict between ranchers and wildlife, the Wild Sky program provides another example of an arena of conflict transformed into an opportunity for mutually beneficial outcomes.

Political Conflict on the Great Plains

Despite the willing-buyer-willing-seller approach and compensation through the Wild Sky program, APR has led to political tension in Montana. APR operates in the public sphere because it relies on public grazing lands. Federal and state grazing land is a critical component of

APR's strategy because there is not enough contiguous private land in the region to create a self-sustaining prairie ecosystem.

APR functions under the same legal rules as traditional ranchers to acquire federal and state grazing leases. The leases stipulate specific types of animals that count as livestock, as well as where and when grazing can occur. Grazing permits are allocated to individuals with a privately owned "base property" adjacent to a leased plot. On BLM lands, when a lease is about to expire, the current lessee receives priority to renew the lease. If a lessee's base property is acquired by a new owner, the BLM grants this new owner priority to acquire the grazing lease.⁴³

Although APR operates within the same legal rules that apply to all public land lessees, many local cattle ranchers are skeptical, and sometimes hostile, to APR.⁴⁴ Several special interest groups have formed to oppose APR. Understanding the root cause of this tension is helpful in understanding how to make both market- and government-driven conservation more successful.

One of APR's main goals is to reintroduce bison to the landscape on its private and public lands. Bison serve a dual purpose on the reserve. First, bison are native to the region, which helps APR achieve its goal of restoring the land's historical ecology. Second, bison are institutionally important because according to BLM rules, leased lands must be used to graze livestock. To retain its leases to public lands, APR must graze approved livestock; otherwise it will lose its grazing permits. APR has been granted bison grazing permits on two BLM allotments and two state leases, totaling 19,314 leased public acres.⁴⁵

Since not all APR's grazing permits allow bison, APR has requested that the BLM and the Montana Department of Natural Resources and Conservation change the permits to allow bison on all APR's allotments.⁴⁶ In 2018, APR requested permission to graze bison on an additional 17 BLM grazing allotments and 18 state grazing leases.⁴⁷

While it waits for the federal and state agencies to make their decisions, APR grazes a minimal number of cattle on its leased public land so that it can retain those grazing permits.⁴⁸

The BLM has little oversight or control over what APR does with its private land, but access to federal grazing land is under the purview of

BLM decision makers. Federal grazing lands are subject to the National Environmental Policy Act (NEPA), which means that the BLM must complete the environmental assessment process required under NEPA. Depending on the BLM's environmental assessment, it could choose to disallow any bison grazing on APR's grazing leases, forbid season-long grazing, or forbid the removal of internal fencing. If the BLM takes any of these actions, it will be more difficult for APR to accomplish its overall goal.

Between 2018 and 2019, the BLM held several scoping meetings in local communities to facilitate its environmental assessment process. At the scoping meetings, farmers, ranchers, and local government representatives expressed concerns about APR's proposal. BLM spokesman Jonathan Moor said that environmental assessments do not usually involve public scoping meetings, but agency decision makers felt the contention over APR's request warranted such meetings.[49]

After the meetings, the BLM received 2,497 submissions about APR's proposal and the upcoming NEPA analysis. In February 2019, the BLM released 24 topics from the public comment process that will guide the environmental analysis. The BLM has stated that "the public will be notified once the environmental assessment is complete."[50]

Due to the political pushback, APR revised its application for permission to graze bison on its leased BLM lands in September 2019. After significant pushback, in September 2019, APR reduced its request by 80 percent, to just five BLM grazing allotments and five state leases.[51] Now APR is requesting permits for year-long continuous grazing on 48,000 acres of BLM land instead of on the previously requested 290,000 acres. APR's stated reason for this change is "the growing need to resolve concerns and provide more opportunity to publicly demonstrate the sustainability of year-long bison grazing with our neighbors, land managers, and other interested members of the public."[52]

The BLM's environmental assessment will move forward regarding APR's revised permit requests. After the BLM prepares the environmental assessment and notifies the public about it, there will be another public review and comment period, which will likely involve more meetings in towns near APR. After that period, the BLM will publish a revised environmental assessment. This assessment will determine whether the BLM allows APR to move forward toward its goals on the public land.[53]

But the conflict over public land management is not likely to end there. BLM decision makers must choose whether to support APR's goals or the goals of the opposing groups. The side that the BLM does not support is likely to look for alternative ways to change the outcome. That side might try persuade BLM decision makers to reconsider their decision, it might lobby members of Congress to change the laws, it might go to the courts to nullify the BLM's decision, or it might appeal to the president for an executive order that would change the outcome. In markets, opposing sides can bargain with one another to come to a mutual agreement. The political arena is different, however, because people in authority make decisions that they impose on other people. Special interest groups have a perpetual incentive to persuade decision makers to benefit their members at the expense of the members of other groups.

Learning from American Prairie Reserve

The story of APR is still unfolding, but it is a fascinating case study because it offers two distinct lessons. First, the willing-buyer-willing-seller approach and Wild Sky's financial incentives show how private property and markets can lead to a cooperative, mutually beneficial outcome for people who may have opposing ideas about wildlife conservation. Second, the political control of resources, such as public land, can lead to conflict over power and resources. Because APR is working with both private and public lands, the situation is complex, but it provides scholars and policymakers with a new way to look at species conservation.

Managing public lands for conservation or agriculture is difficult because one group may attempt to use the political structure to entrench its interests at the expense of others. When a new actor enters the political arena, the people who have traditionally been favored by political decision makers may see the new actor as challenging the status quo. Nobody wants to see political power shift away from their interests.

Although APR and traditional ranchers both operate under the same institutional rules that allow them to obtain leases to public lands, many ranchers seem to fear that APR could take away their influence on the decision-making process for public land management. For example, one group opposing APR is the Montana Community Preservation Alliance. This group's stated purpose is to preserve the agricultural lifestyle of Montana, fight national monument designations, and prevent the introduction of free-roaming bison.[54] United Property Owners of Montana is another group composed of local ranchers who want to preserve Montana's "unique agricultural heritage" from the perceived threat of APR's mission.[55] Several prominent residents who live near APR lands have publicly opposed the nature reserve project. Marko Manoukian, the secretary-treasurer for the Phillips County Livestock Association, and Vicki Olson, the chair of the Montana Public Lands Council, have spoken out against the project.[56]

Despite the conflict over government-owned land, APR's innovative approach on private land takes advantage of both markets and market-like mechanisms. No system, whether relying on markets or governments, will ever completely eliminate conflict. Some institutional arrangements, however, can help resolve conflict more effectively than others can. Markets can resolve conflict because groups that don't see eye to eye can bargain to come to mutually beneficial arrangements. The willing-buyer-willing-seller approach and the Wild Sky program's financial incentives are two important ideas that conservationists and policymakers should learn from.

Reforming Policy to Allow for Cooperation

Reforms to federal policies, such as the Endangered Species Act (ESA), can provide solutions that limit conflict and facilitate effective conservation. The environmental movement of the 1960s sparked legislation meant to help preserve species, reduce pollution, and preserve undeveloped lands. However, these environmental policies have undeniably created conflict over the decades. A prime example is the ESA, which has employed a top-down regulatory approach for roughly 50 years. Despite the good intentions behind the law, the ESA has been a source of contention and unintended consequences that can make life harder for the very species it is meant to protect.

One unintended consequence has been "shoot, shovel, and shut up." The ESA takes a punitive approach that punishes people who "take" a listed species. The ESA defines the term *take* to include harassing, harming, pursuing, hunting, shooting, wounding, killing, trapping, capturing, or collecting a listed species, or even attempting to engage in any of those actions. These restrictions under the ESA apply anywhere protected species are found—even on private land. Because these restrictions mean landowners risk losing autonomy over how their land can be used (and risk the possibility of real reductions in property values), landowners may choose to ignore the ESA and quietly eliminate endangered species that live on their land before government officials find out about the species' location. Rational and self-interested landowners who discover a listed species on their property may face a strong incentive to shoot, shovel, and shut up.[57]

Another unintended consequence of the punitive approach of the ESA has been preemptive habitat destruction. If a land-use restriction under the ESA is likely, landowners may find it in their interest to destroy the habitat of endangered species to make sure that the species is not attracted there. Landowners may try to beat the restrictions by developing their land more rapidly than they would have otherwise. In 2003, economists Dean Lueck and Jeffrey Michael found evidence that some forest landowners in North Carolina preemptively harvested timber to avoid land-use restrictions related to the endangered red-cockaded woodpecker.[58]

Private property rights give people an incentive to use property responsibly and to avoid harming other people's property. However, assigning property rights to wildlife is not always feasible. For example, how would we go about assigning property rights to red-cockaded woodpeckers in North Carolina? It would be extremely difficult, especially since the birds can easily travel across different landowners' property. When private property rights can't be clearly defined, there may be a justification for government regulation of some form. Private landowners usually control access to wildlife because wildlife often lives on private land, but government agencies regulate hunting and protect wildlife regardless of where the animals live.[59] Despite the complexities of wildlife ownership and management, policy reforms could improve species conservation.

Aligning Incentives with Regulatory Flexibility

First, policymakers could focus on incentive-based regulations rather than adopting a punitive approach. Instead of simply punishing people who harm an endangered species, policymakers could make the ESA more flexible so that private landowners are more likely to cooperate. For example, there could be a wider use of permits or agreements that allow for limited removal or harm to a species as long as steps are taken to mitigate impacts to the species elsewhere.

One such reform from the mid-1990s has successfully mitigated conflict and facilitated cooperation: Safe Harbor Agreements. A Safe Harbor Agreement (SHA) is a voluntary agreement between property owners whose land is affected by the ESA and the US Fish and Wildlife Service. If participating landowners contribute to the recovery of listed species on their land, the Fish and Wildlife Service agrees not to impose additional restrictions on their land.[60]

Policies like SHAs are important because they shift the incentives for private landowners. Without SHAs, private landowners have little incentive to go out of their way to improve the well-being of endangered species on their land. If landowners want to improve the environmental quality of their land, they might create an environment where listed species will want to live. But if no SHA is in place, landowners that manage their land to benefit listed species may be "rewarded" with legal restrictions on the way they use their land. SHAs allow good deeds to go unpunished because landowners can commit to do something beneficial for a listed species, even if there is no legal obligation to do it. The federal government then gives an assurance that the voluntary actions won't cause additional legal restrictions on the use of private land under the ESA.[61]

If the goal is conservation that is more cooperative and thus more effective, then policymakers should look for ways to expand the use of

SHAs and consider reforms in the same vein as SHAs that allow land-owners to find creative ways to offset their impacts to listed species without bearing the burden of strict regulatory compliance. Since SHAs make the ESA less punitive, landowners are more likely to comply and even cooperate in working toward conservation goals.

Policymakers could also expand the use of incentive-based conservation efforts such as the Conservation Reserve Program (CRP). Under this program, the US Department of Agriculture's Farm Service Agency pays farmers a yearly rent if they remove environmentally sensitive land from agricultural production and plant species that will improve environmental quality. These contracts typically last 10–15 years and are intended to help improve water quality, prevent soil erosion, and reduce loss of wildlife habitat. Since the CRP was enacted in 1985, it has been the largest private-lands conservation program in the United States.[62]

Research has found that due to the CRP, soil quality improved in several places across the country as highly erodible cropland was replaced with perennial grass.[63] The CRP has also helped increase the population of several species, including waterfowl, songbirds, fish, and macroinvertebrates.[64] The Congressional Research Service found that the CRP prevents 325 million tons of soil erosion annually, protects 2 million acres of wetlands, sequesters 52 million metric tons of carbon dioxide annually, and provides habitat for 13.5 million pheasants and 2.2 million ducks each year.[65]

Like all policies, however, the CRP has trade-offs and unintended consequences. For instance, some noncropland has been converted into crop production in part because of the incentives created under the CRP. Because the CRP reduces production, it drives up output prices for crops. As prices increase, farmers have an incentive to convert non-cropland into cropland to take advantage of the higher prices. Research indicates that for each 100 acres of cropland retired under the CRP in the central United States, 20 acres of noncropland were converted to cropland, offsetting 9 percent and 14 percent of CRP water and wind erosion reduction benefits, respectively.[66]

Despite the trade-offs, policymakers can still look for incentive-based conservation efforts like the CRP while learning from experience to mitigate unintended consequences. New conservation policy innovations that are yet undiscovered could also improve species conservation further while benefiting landowners in a win-win scenario.

Species Conservation through Polycentricity

Another effective way to enable cooperative approaches to conservation is through polycentricity, in which many overlapping decision-making centers are allowed to work together. A polycentric approach to conservation from 2010 to 2015 kept the greater sage-grouse off the endangered species list. Federal, state, and local policymakers, as well as private associations, cooperated to conserve the greater sage-grouse populations in the western United States. The example of the greater sage-grouse is helpful because it shows how various governments, businesses, and nonprofit organizations can effectively conserve species in a polycentric system.

After several years of legal battles, the US Fish and Wildlife Service announced in 2010 that the listing of the greater sage-grouse was "warranted but precluded," temporarily deferring listing the bird under the ESA.[67] The threat of a full listing, however, was a real possibility. The greater sage-grouse became a "candidate species" for full listing under the ESA. Candidate species don't receive statutory protection under the ESA, but the Fish and Wildlife Service encourages various levels of government and private organizations to form partnerships for candidate species' conservation. If conservation measures aren't taken, the Fish and Wildlife Service can choose to formally list a candidate species and give it the full statutory protection of the ESA, which can be punitive and lead to the unintended consequences mentioned previously. Through a candidate species designation, the Fish and Wildlife Service tries to address the needs of species so that the full regulatory restrictions of the ESA don't become necessary. A candidate species designation gives federal, state, and local policymakers, as well as private citizens, a wider range of options to experiment with conservation efforts because the full statutory requirements of the ESA do not apply.[68] The candidate species designation for the greater sage-grouse gave federal agencies, state governments, and private associations a chance to work on conservation efforts to avoid a full listing in the future.

Federal agencies, such as the BLM and the US Forest Service, drafted new management plans after the candidate species designation, which were adopted in 2015. The new plans amended the previous plans to increase the protection for sage-grouse across million acres of federal land across much of the western United States.[69] The new plans also expanded coordination between the BLM and the Forest Service. Finally, the plans also provided technical assistance and financial support for conservation on private lands.

A wide range of stakeholders, including farmers, ranchers, energy developers, state fish and wildlife agencies, and many others, helped the BLM and the Forest Service develop their new plans.[70] These new plans sparked some controversy, however, because the Obama administration did not adopt the state plans as it originally said it would.[71] Despite that, the federal government's approach still allowed polycentric decision-making in many regards.

One effective polycentric approach from the BLM and the Forest Service was the Sage Grouse Initiative. More than 1,100 private individuals across the West participated in the Sage Grouse Initiative, which had the dual goal of restoring about 4.4 million acres of sage-grouse habitat while also allowing economic development on federal lands. The Sage Grouse Initiative works through voluntary cooperation, incentives, and community support to protect sage-grouse habitat and increase sage-grouse populations. The initiative accomplishes these goals by helping ranchers on private rangeland secure conservation easements, promote deep-rooted perennial grasses to keep the range weed-free, remove conifers that threaten sage-grouse habitat, perform wetland restoration projects, and make fences more visible to sage-grouse to reduce deadly collisions.[72]

Utah developed its sage-grouse conservation plans in a highly polycentric structure because roughly half of Utah's greater sage-grouse live on private lands, making local communities and private landowners necessary participants for successful conservation. Utah policymakers created the Community-Based Conservation Program and Local

Working Groups. The Community-Based Conservation Program is run by a Utah State University extension program staffed predominantly by university-affiliated researchers. It provides incentives for private landowners and local communities to engage in conservation as an alternative to direct regulations. The program facilitates sage-grouse local working groups throughout Utah.[73]

Local Working Groups were first implemented in 1996 and were later expanded to accommodate the candidate species designation. These groups bring together state and federal agents, local landowners, and other interested parties to conserve sage-grouse. Each group has its own conservation plan and works to reverse the decline of sage-grouse in its area. Utah currently has 11 Local Working Groups, and several other states have adopted similar groups. Now there are more than 60 across the West.[74]

The sage-grouse example shows how a polycentric approach to public policy can effectively solve conservation problems. Policymakers should look for ways to take advantage of the benefits of polycentric systems to improve environmental policy.

Conclusion

Overhauling entire public policies, such as the ESA, may not be possible, but making small adjustments on the margin may be a politically palatable move toward more cooperative, effective conservation. People who care about saving endangered species should also care about finding the most effective ways of saving those species. The histories of many public policies, like the ESA, have been rife with controversy, conflict, and unintended consequences. Despite this conflict, policymakers and environmental groups alike have found innovative, creative ways to facilitate cooperation so that conservation is more effective.

The real-world examples presented here suggest that conservation is not achieved by good intentions alone, but by the actual rules that societies make. Creating or reforming policies that allow people to find cooperative, win-win situations is likely to lead to better conservation outcomes. Conservation and environmental stewardship in general could be improved by leveraging the power of private property and reforming public policies to better align incentives with desired outcomes. By recognizing and working to reform current policies that create conflict and unintended consequences, policymakers can help move toward a more cooperative and more effective model of conservation.

CHAPTER 13

Retail Electric Competition and Natural Monopoly: The Shocking Truth

Jerry Ellig[1]

During the past four decades, competition has come to several industries previously thought to be natural monopolies, including previously unlikely candidates such as telephone service and cable TV. Economic studies generally show that, contrary to what natural monopoly theory would predict, competition has produced cost reductions, price reductions, and other consumer benefits.[2] Indeed, competition in these industries has become explicit national policy.

In contrast, regulated monopoly remains the dominant paradigm for electricity retailing in the United States. Only in 13 states and the District of Columbia can most consumers choose their electricity supplier. These jurisdictions account for about one-third of the nation's power production and consumption.[3] Even in these states, electric distribution wires remain regulated monopolies. Direct competition between electric utilities that each own overlapping networks of distribution wires is quite rare. Retail competition—whether or not accompanied by competition in distribution—remains a controversial concept.

This chapter seeks to advance the policy discussion on electric competition by comparing the results of monopoly and competition in retail electricity sales. It reviews empirical research on two different models for achieving retail competition: competition between electricity retailers to serve customers who have access to a wires network that is a regulated monopoly, and duopolistic competition between electric utilities with overlapping wires networks. Under both models, competition is associated with substantial price reductions, substantial cost reductions, and some degree of innovative product differentiation.

Policymakers' interest in retail electric competition tends to increase when new technologies push the cost of power from new plants below the average cost of power from old plants.[4] In recent years the US has seen significant reductions in the cost of gas-fired generation (largely because of fracking) and the cost of renewable sources.[5] If history repeats itself, the availability of new, lower-cost power sources will lead to renewed interest in retail competition. Indeed, retail electric competition was the subject of a ballot initiative in Nevada in 2018; Virginia legislators introduced a bipartisan retail competition bill in January 2020; and retail competition has been proposed in South Carolina's ongoing debate over privatization of Santee Cooper, the state-owned electric utility.[6] A review of the economic evidence on retail electric competition is thus clearly timely.

The Theory

The electric industry consists of four conceptually distinct functions that operated as monopolies in most of the United States for most of the 20th century: (1) power generation, (2) high-voltage transmission wires, (3) lower-voltage distribution wires, and (4) retail sales to customers.[7] Power generation was believed to be a natural monopoly because of economies of scale: it was less expensive for one firm to operate a few large power plants than for many firms to operate smaller power plants. Similarly, the wires businesses are still usually assumed to be natural monopolies on the grounds that having one set of wires is less expensive than having duplicate sets of wires. The retail sales function was typically bundled with the monopoly local distribution function, as there seemed to be little reason to have competing retailers when power generation and wires were both monopolies. In addition, all four functions were frequently operated together by vertically integrated monopolies because of economies of scope—primarily efficiencies stemming from the need for minute-by-minute coordination of power generation with power use.

Technological changes altered these relationships beginning in the 1980s. Economies of scale became a questionable argument for monopoly in generation as smaller cogenerators and gas-fired power plants became competitive with larger, utility-owned power plants. Economies of scope became a questionable argument for vertical integration as computers and communication technology reduced coordination costs, enabling competition first in bulk (wholesale) power markets and then in retail sales. Wires are still almost always regulated by federal and state governments as monopolies, although there are some examples of competing local distribution companies with competing wires (discussed below).

The mere existence of retail competition does not necessarily refute the claim that retail competition sacrifices economies of scale or scope. As a matter of economic theory, an industry can be a natural monopoly and nevertheless be vulnerable to inefficient competition. Protection from competition is required to ensure economic efficiency if the natural monopoly is "unsustainable," which means a peculiar set of cost and demand conditions leads to the presence of competitors in the market even though one firm can serve the entire market at the lowest cost.[8] Thus, it is possible in theory that competition in electricity retailing could lead to higher prices or other less-favorable contract terms than customers would receive from a regulated monopoly.

On the other hand, if retail electricity sales do not involve large economies of scale or scope, then retail competition (as opposed to regulated monopoly) could potentially improve economic welfare in at least three ways: (1) by providing more efficient pricing, (2) by bringing price reductions driven by cost reductions, and (3) by product differentiation. Efficient pricing of a homogeneous commodity promotes the allocative efficiency described in textbook models of competition. But since real-world competition is a rivalrous process of experimentation and discovery, competition can also generate productive efficiency—reductions in cost, improvements in productivity, and increased innovation that lead to price reductions and product differentiation.[9]

More Efficient Pricing

Traditional public utility regulation tends to set prices equal to average costs, and it may also permit the utility to earn some monopoly profits. Prices that reflect marginal costs promote economic efficiency and enhance overall welfare.[10] Competition should be expected to eliminate monopoly profits and generate electricity prices that more closely reflect marginal costs—primarily the price of natural gas—instead of the utility's average costs.[11] True marginal cost retail prices would vary minute by minute as wholesale prices change, and few customers currently see such prices, even where retail competition exists.[12] However, one would expect prices in a competitive retail market to reflect marginal costs at least somewhat more closely than do prices set under rate-of-return regulation.

Of course, price increases due to spikes in marginal costs rarely seem like a benefit from the customer's perspective. When marginal costs in competitive markets jump, average-cost pricing under monopoly regulation can look like a better deal for the consumer, even if it does misallocate resources. Nevertheless, competition could improve overall welfare by driving prices closer to marginal costs, even if competitive retail prices (based on marginal cost) sometimes exceed regulated monopoly prices (based on average cost).

Price Reductions

Inefficiencies created by public utility regulation are well known in the economics literature. On the one hand, rate-of-return regulation can increase the regulated firm's costs by promoting an inefficient substitution of capital for labor.[13] On the other hand, utility regulation may diminish the firm's incentive to invest if the regulator cannot credibly commit that it will not expropriate the value of the firm's investments after these investments are made.[14] Utility regulation can reduce a firm's incentive to cut costs or innovate more generally, because the firm's rates are periodically adjusted to eliminate the profits from innovation.[15] In addition, protection from competition can also diminish a utility's incentive to control costs or innovate because it does not have to fear losing business to competitors; economists call this type of efficiency

"X-efficiency."[16] If these inefficiencies are sufficiently large, the introduction of competition can reduce costs, improve productivity, and increase service innovation.

Product Differentiation

If customers value differentiated electricity products, then competition creates the opportunity for diverse electricity providers to provide additional features, services, or quality attributes. Competition is the process that allows different retailers to offer additional features or services in order to discover which ones have enough value to customers to justify their costs.

MIT economics professor Paul Joskow notes several ways retailers might add value, such as by providing less expensive metering, billing, or customer service; by procuring power at lower cost; by installing more sophisticated metering and control technology; by offering products that let customers hedge risks; by supplying green power; and by offering products, applications, and services "behind the meter." He also argues that many value-added functions retailers fulfill in other industries—such as providing more convenient locations, offering more convenient delivery options, maintaining inventories, offering complementary products, providing point-of-sale service, providing post-sale service or returns, providing information about the product, and negotiating quantity discounts with manufacturers—are not very relevant in electricity. He recommends that retailers be allowed to compete but doubts that differentiated services will be attractive to many smaller customers.[17]

Stephen Littlechild, a University of Cambrdge professor who headed the United Kingdom's electricity regulatory agency from 1989-98, expresses a more sanguine view of the potential for product differentiation, noting that experiences in the Untied Kingdom and elsewhere suggest that consumers value fixed-price contracts, smoothed payment plans, and the bundling of electricity and gas.[18] Choice experiments provide additional insight about the potential for product differentiation in electricity retailing. A study published in *The Energy Journal* in 2019 finds that noticeable percentages of small and medium-sized commercial and industrial customers express a positive willingness to pay more for service from a company they are familiar with, service from a company with a local office, electricity generated from renewable sources, a choice of payment options, customized billing, a website that provides usage information, a real person answering customer service calls instead of a voice response system, a package that bundles electricity with other products such as other fuels or warranties, or service from a company that earmarks funds for local economic development or local charities. Signup bonuses are generally viewed negatively. The majority of customers regard variable rates and one-, two-, or three-year contracts negatively, but a sizeable minority value these kinds of arrangements.[19]

Whether competition in retail electricity supply enhances or diminishes economic welfare is ultimately an empirical question. Studies of formerly monopolized or cartelized network industries that were restructured to introduce competition typically find that competition leads to more efficient pricing, and that it also generates innovative cost reductions, productivity gains, and nonprice competition.[20] Thus, there is ample reason to consider whether retail electric competition has produced some of the same kinds of benefits.

Retail Competition with Monopoly Distribution: General Trends

Retail electric competition became a subject of significant debate in Washington, DC, and in state capitals during the 1990s. All states that implemented some form of retail competition continued to treat the wires used for long-distance transmission and local distribution as regulated monopolies. Power generation and marketing to retail customers were opened to competition.

There are, however, significant differences across state electricity restructuring plans. California enacted a sweeping restructuring law in 1996, then reversed course after wholesale prices spiked in 2000 and 2001. Michigan restructured but then capped the size of competitive sales at 10 percent of the market in 2009.[21] Texas enacted the most extensive plan in 1999, allowing approximately 8 million customers in the region covered by the Electric Reliability Council of Texas to choose their electricity suppliers. Unlike the other states with retail competition, Texas utilities do not offer a regulated default service for customers who decline to switch providers; such service has served as a barrier to entry in other states that have sought to implement retail competition.[22]

States can be divided roughly into three groups according to the extent of retail electric competition. Figure 1 shows weighted average electricity price trends for each group of states (in inflation-adjusted 2018 dollars). These data show the delivered price of electricity to customers (in other words, the total cost including wires charges). Therefore, the comparisons capture any effects of retail competition on economies of scale or scope that might ultimately affect the price paid by the customer. The cost of producing the electric power is generally less than half of the total cost of the delivered price.

Figure 1. Electricity Price Trends (Delivered Price of Electricity)

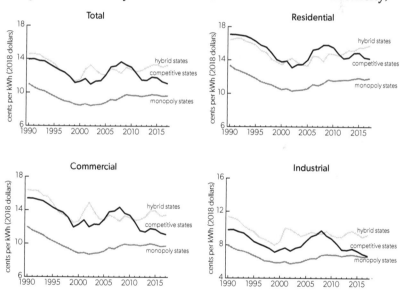

Note: "Competitive" states are Connecticut, Delaware, Illinois, Massachusetts, Maine, Maryland, New Hampshire, New Jersey, New York, Ohio, Pennsylvania, Rhode Island, and Texas; this category also includes Washington, DC. "Hybrid" states are Arizona, California, Michigan, Montana, Nevada, and Oregon. The rest of the states are "monopoly" states. (Alaska and Hawaii are excluded.)

Source: Author's calculations using data from the US Energy Information Administration, "Electricity" (database), accessed November 13, 2019, https://www.eia.gov/electricity/data.php.

Thirteen states and the District of Columbia currently allow most customers to choose their power suppliers;[23] these states are labeled "competitive" in figure 1. Arizona, California, Michigan, Montana, Nevada, and Oregon allow competition for a limited portion of the total load; these are the "hybrid" sates. The remaining states are the "monopoly" states. (Alaska and Hawaii are excluded because they have very high electricity prices owing to their unique geographic circumstances.) In a study conducted for the Retail Energy Supply Association, former Illinois Commerce Commission Chairman Philip O'Connor contended that the electric utilities' costs in the hybrid states are largely driven by regulation, since a minority of the market is open to competition.[24] His price comparisons include the hybrid states with the monopoly states. But, as figure 1 reveals, price levels and the pattern of price changes differ visibly in the hybrid and the competitive states, so in this chapter prices for these two groups are shown separately.

Figure 1 shows that electricity prices were falling in all three kinds of states during the 1990s. This occurred largely because of the lower marginal cost of new generation, primarily fueled by natural gas. The pattern was similar across all states, since the regulated monopoly model prevailed everywhere during that time. However, the states that eventually became the competitive and the hybrid states had substantially higher electricity prices than the states where retail sales remained a monopoly; indeed, the relatively high prices may have motivated the interest in competition and may be part of the reason the competitive states experienced price reductions.

During the transitional period to competition (roughly 1998–2008 for most states), the competitive and hybrid states implemented restructuring plans that opened retail markets to competition. Figure 1 shows that prices in these states became more volatile than prices in the monopoly states. Most of the empirical evidence suggests that retail competition aligned retail prices more closely with fluctuating marginal costs— usually the price of natural gas.[25] The primary exception comes from a study of Connecticut, which found that retail prices tracked the utilities' regulated rate for "standard offer service" more closely than they tracked wholesale electricity prices.[26]

In California, prices spiked owing to supply shortages and manipulation of the wholesale power market in 2001 and 2002. These California price spikes largely account for figure 1's spikes in the weighted average price of electricity in the hybrid states for those years. The competitive states experienced price increases later, between 2002 and 2008. These increases largely reflect the fact that the price of natural gas more than doubled during this period, from $3.32 per million British thermal units (mmBtu) in 2002 to $8.50 per mmBtu in 2008.[27]

In a survey of published academic literature on electricity restructuring, Northeastern University economist John Kwoka concluded that academic studies of the early years of electricity restructuring could not adequately separate the effects of fuel price changes, excess generation capacity, mandatory rate reductions, price caps, stranded cost recovery mechanisms, and other transitional issues to determine what, if any, price effects could be attributed to restructuring.[28] Most competitive states retained rate caps until at least 2007, which tended to blunt customers' incentive to shop for better electricity prices.[29]

By 2008, however, nonutilities owned a substantial amount of generation and served a substantial number of customers in the competitive states, and transitional issues had largely been resolved. Eight years later, nonutility competitors served almost three-quarters of the load that was eligible to switch in the 13 competitive states and DC, including 49 percent of residential customers.[30] As figure 1 shows, after 2008 the price trend in competitive states diverges significantly from the trend in the hybrid and the monopoly states. Prices in competitive states declined steeply after 2008, whereas prices in hybrid and monopoly states generally increased. Residential, commercial, and industrial customers all received price reductions in the competitive states. Table 1 shows the percent change in prices between 2008 and 2017 in all three types of states.

This comparison suggests that retail competition, when fully implemented, may have generated significant price reductions. But raw price data are only suggestive. Prices in many competitive electricity markets are lower than prior regulated prices, but that information alone does not tell us how much of the price difference is due to competition. Prices in competitive markets tend to be higher than prices in monopoly markets, but it would be erroneous to conclude that competition increases prices. Prices in the competitive states were higher than prices in the monopoly states before the former introduced competition. Numerous other factors that could affect prices in the two sets of markets may not be the same.

Table 1. Weighted Average Electricity Percent Changes in Price, 2008–2017

	Competitive states (%)	Hybrid states (%)	Monopoly states (%)
Overall	−19	+8	+2
Residential	−10	+14	+5
Commercial	−22	+6	0
Industrial	−31	−1	−2

Source: Author's calculations using data from the US Energy Information Administration, "Electricity" (database), accessed May 12, 2020, https://www.eia.gov/electricity/data.php.

An accurate assessment of the effects of competition requires a comparison of prices paid in competitive markets to a relevant counterfactual estimate of what the prices would have been in the absence of competition.[31] Two types of scholarly studies attempt to identify a relevant counterfactual by controlling for other factors that could increase electricity prices. Some compare price trends in competitive and monopoly states after controlling for other factors that influence prices. Others focus on the pattern of prices over time in a single state.

The studies comparing monopoly and competitive states generally find that competition is associated with at least small price reductions for residential customers. Some of these studies find no change in commercial or industrial rates, but one study finds that commercial and industrial rates fell too.[32]

Single-state studies have been conducted on Illinois, Ohio, and Texas. The Illinois study found that Illinois avoided price increases that affected neighboring states between 1997 and 2007, and the authors argue that this result can be attributed to competition in Illinois. A study of Ohio found that restructuring is associated with increased prices in parts of the state where utilities did not divest their generation assets to independent companies, but competition is associated with price reductions in the service territory of Duke Energy, which did divest its generation assets.[33] (Multiple studies of Texas will be discussed in the following section.)

One study assesses the extent of product differentiation in competitive versus noncompetitive states. Competitive states have more customers selecting green power and dynamic pricing.[34]

The available scholarly evidence suggests that well-designed and fully implemented retail competition programs more closely align prices with marginal costs, can reduce prices below the level where they would be in the absence of competition, and might promote some product differentiation. But attaining these results depends crucially on whether the competition program is well designed and fully implemented. For this reason, it is instructive to take a closer look at the two states commonly regarded as retail competition's most significant success and most spectacular failure. The most notable success occurred in the state of Texas, where approximately 8 million residential, commercial, and industrial customers have the right to choose their power supplier.[35] The most spectacular failure occurred in California, where skyrocketing electricity prices bankrupted one of the largest utilities in the state and led to the recall of Governor Gray Davis and the election of Governor Arnold Schwarzenegger in 2003.

The Texas Success

Texas is widely recognized for achieving the most extensive retail electric competition in the United States.[36] Texas introduced electric competition in the portion of the state covered by the Electric Reliability Council of Texas (ERCOT). The transmission grid in the ERCOT region is completely under the jurisdiction of the state; hence, the state of Texas has jurisdiction to regulate wholesale transactions as well as retail transactions within ERCOT.[37]

The Texas Restructuring Plan

Texas enacted its electricity restructuring bill in 1999. Senate Bill 7 allowed the approximately 60 electric co-ops and 50 municipal utilities within ERCOT to opt in to competition;[38] most of them declined to do so. Indeed, in 2018 Lubbock Power & Light became the first municipal utility to opt in to competition. The switch will occur once the construction of transmission interconnections with ERCOT is completed in 2021.[39]

Vertically integrated utilities were separated into a transmission and distribution utility, a power generation company, and a retail electricity provider. No generator was allowed to own generation capacity exceeding 20 percent of the load in its service territory.[40]

Retail competition began in 2002. For five years, each utility's marketing affiliate was required to offer residential and small commercial customers in its service territory a regulated "price to beat" that was set 6 percent below 1999 rates. After three years or after the utility lost 40 percent of its customers to competitors, the utility's marketing affiliate was permitted to offer service at rates below the price to beat.[41]

The price to beat could be adjusted twice yearly for changes in fuel costs.[42] This provision was critical because natural gas accounts for approximately half of the electric power consumed in Texas,[43] and gas-fired plants are the marginal source of power about 85 percent of the time.[44] If the regulated default price were not flexible, competitors would be reluctant to enter the market, because they would have to compete against an artificially low regulated price when the cost of gas is high. An inflexible regulated retail price also could have led to financial stress or even bankruptcy for the incumbent utilities as wholesale prices fluctuated.[45]

Substantial new generation entered the market in the years before competition. Between 1995 and 2000, 5,700 megawatts of new power plant capacity were built. Most of these plants were built by nonutility generators. The Texas wholesale power market is based largely on confidential, bilateral contracts rather than on a centralized spot market. ERCOT does operate an auction market for balancing energy and for ancillary services such as reserves.[46]

Price Trends

Figure 2 compares inflation-adjusted electricity price trends in Texas and in the monopoly states between 1990 and 2017. Texas residential

Figure 2. Price Trends in Texas vs. Monopoly States (Delivered Price of Electricity)

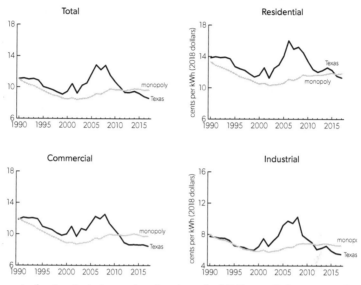

Source: Author's calculations using data from the US Energy Information Administration, "Electricity" (database), accessed November 13, 2019https://www.eia.gov/electricity/data.php.

Figure 3. Texas Electricity Rates in 2018 vs. Last Regulated Rate

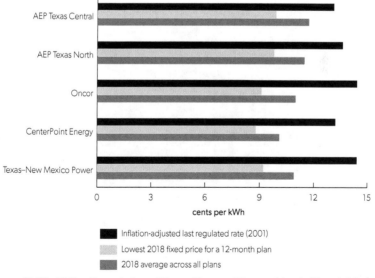

Source: Public Utility Commission of Texas, "Scope of Competition in Electric Markets in Texas" (Report to the 86th Legislature, Austin, TX, January 2019), 3.

and commercial customers paid higher prices than their counterparts
in monopoly states during the decade when competition was being
debated (1990–1999). Prices became more volatile during the transition years, 2000–2007. Texas prices peaked in 2008, then declined so
sharply that the average price in Texas was below the price in monopoly states after 2012.

Every two years, the Public Utility Commission of Texas produces
a report for the Texas legislature on competition in the electric industry. Figure 3 shows that in 2018, the average price for residential power
plans in all five ERCOT distribution regions was between 10 and 24
percent below the last regulated price. The least expensive 12-month
fixed price plan offered even larger savings.

Efficient Pricing

The available evidence suggests that under competition, the price of electricity is more closely linked to the price of natural gas. Figure 4 shows
that wholesale electricity prices in ERCOT's real-time balancing market
have tracked natural gas prices in most years since 2001. Gas prices
dropped substantially after 2008, largely because of fracking technology.[47]

**Figure 4. Average Real-Time Energy Prices and Natural Gas
Prices in the Electric Reliability Council of Texas Region**

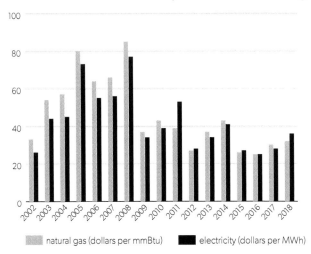

Source: *2018 State of the Market Report for the ERCOT Electricity Markets* (Fairfax, VA: Potomac Economics, June 2019), 5.

Competition and the fuel cost adjustments in the regulated price to beat conveyed these changes in the marginal cost of power to customers. Raw data show that Texas retail electricity prices have generally tracked wholesale prices since 2002.[48] The advent of retail electric competition in 2002 was followed by a run-up in the price of natural gas in 2003 and 2004, which led to increases in wholesale prices, the regulated price to beat, and the offers from competitive retail electricity providers.[49] As a result, a study published in *Energy Policy* in 2006 concluded that residential consumers in Texas markets open to competition paid more for electricity than consumers in Texas's monopoly markets in 2002–2004.[50] Because the price to beat was more directly linked to natural gas prices than were traditional regulated prices, the price to beat increased faster than prices in regulated monopoly markets between January 2002 and December 2004. Residential consumers who switched providers paid lower rates than the price to beat, but only 18 percent had done so by September 2004.[51]

In some cases, the price to beat allowed the utility to over-recover its costs; for example, one utility was permitted a 23.4 percent increase in the price to beat because gas prices increased 23.4 percent, even though gas-fired plants accounted for only 42 percent of the company's power supply.[52] This occurred because the Public Utility Commission of Texas recognized that the marginal cost of gas-fired generation sets the price in a competitive market.[53]

An econometric study using more recent data finds that retail prices more closely reflect marginal costs in the state's competitive markets than in the monopoly markets. The econometric analysis covers the years 2002–2016 and examines pricing trends for customers using 1,000 kilowatt-hours (kWh) of power per month. The authors analyzed factors that affect prices in the five competitive regions of ERCOT and eight noncompetitive markets: the territories served by two investor-owned utilities, three co-ops, and three municipal utilities. In all five competitive regions, retail residential prices are positively correlated with the wholesale price of power and utility wages. In other words, retail prices vary with marginal costs, as one would expect in a competitive market. Retail prices are positively correlated with wholesale electricity prices in only three of the noncompetitive markets and positively correlated with wages in only one of the noncompetitive markets.[54]

The study also examines the efficiency of pricing for commercial customers. Analysis using a sample of commercial rates gathered directly from customers shows that between 2005 and late 2009, commercial rates in competitive markets were above commercial rates in noncompetitive markets. Between late 2009 and 2016, commercial rates in competitive markets fell below commercial rates in noncompetitive markets by an ever-widening amount. The authors conclude that commercial rates more closely track wholesale prices in the competitive markets, and commercial customers in noncompetitive markets are likely cross-subsidizing other customers.[55]

Price Reductions

Several empirical studies have attempted to identify the price effect of retail competition in Texas after controlling for other factors that could influence prices. One early study found that competition likely reduced prices for larger customers but not for residential customers.[56]

Competition appears to have placed a significant constraint on prices only after the regulated price to beat was eliminated in 2007. A 2009 study found that the disappearance of the price to beat is associated with a drop in residential electricity prices of about 2.3–2.4 cents per kWh, or roughly 19–20 percent. There are several reasons why elimination of a price cap could be associated with lower prices. Natural gas prices peaked above 11 cents per mmBtu in 2005 and dropped below 6 cents per mmBtu in 2006, but the price to beat did not drop as quickly as the price of natural gas and was likely above the competitive level. Once it was eliminated, retail electricity providers competed against each other instead of competing against the artificially high price to beat. Alternatively, the existence of the cap may have reduced the profitability of entry and increased uncertainty for competitive providers, thus discouraging entry and constraining competition until the price to beat was eliminated.[57]

A 2019 study found evidence that competition has spurred retail cost reductions. A time trend variable in the econometric analysis reveals that the spread between retail and wholesale prices in competitive regions declined after the regulated price to beat expired in January 2007. The regression results indicate that the spread between retail and wholesale prices in competitive regions fell by between 0.6 cents and 2.0 cents per kWh between 2007 and 2016. By comparison, this spread increased over time in three of the noncompetitive regions and was unchanged in four others.[58] Thus, the existence of competition is associated with a noticeable reduction in retailers' nonenergy costs over time.

The raw data in figure 5 provide a visualization of the econometric results. At the advent of competition in 2002, retail prices in the five competitive markets were higher than retail prices in the eight noncompetitive markets. By 2016, inflation-adjusted retail prices had fallen in the competitive markets by between 1.04 cents and 1.82 cents per kWh. During that same time period, retail prices rose in the noncompetitive markets by between 0.23 cents and 2.07 cents per kWh. Between 2002 and 2016, wholesale prices fell by between 0.55 cents and 1.10 cents per kWh, depending on the wholesale region. Thus, retail prices in competitive markets fell by more than the wholesale price, at the same time that retail prices were rising in the noncompetitive markets.

Product Differentiation

The ability to choose among differentiated products can be a source of value to customers in addition to competition's effect on prices. Although retail electricity providers in Texas did not initially offer a lot of differentiated products,[59] product differentiation has expanded as the market has matured. As table 2 shows, in the competitive regions, residential customers could choose from between 24 and 51 different suppliers offering hundreds of different products in 2018. Product offerings include 100 percent renewable energy, time-of-use pricing, free electricity on weekends, prepaid plans, and price guarantees lasting from 1 to 60 months.[60] By 2018, 94 percent of residential customers, 94 percent of small nonresidential customers, and 98 percent of large nonresidential customers had affirmatively chosen an electricity supplier at least once.[61]

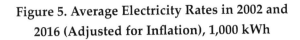

Figure 5. Average Electricity Rates in 2002 and 2016 (Adjusted for Inflation), 1,000 kWh

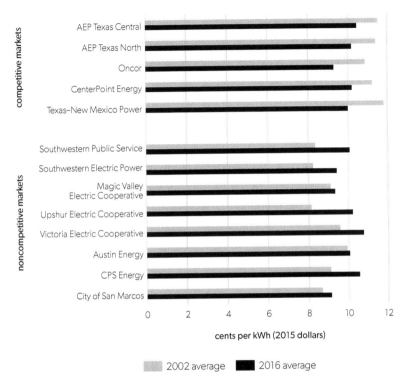

Source: Table 1 in Peter R. Hartley, Kenneth B. Medlock III, and Olivera Jankovska, "Electricity Reform and Retail Pricing in Texas," _Energy Economics_ 80 (2019): 7

Table 2. Number of Retail Suppliers and Products in Texas, 2018

Service territory	Number of residential suppliers	Number of products
AEP Texas Central	48	282
AEP Texas North	24	237
Oncor	50	311
CenterPoint Energy	52	305
Texas–New Mexico Power	42	247

Source: Public Utility Commission of Texas, "Scope of Competition in Electric Markets in Texas" (Report to the 86th Legislature, Austin, TX, January 2019), 2.

The California Debacle

California enacted its restructuring law in 1996. California did not fare nearly as well as Texas during its brief experiment with retail electric competition.

Figure 6 shows that California's electricity prices have always been substantially higher than the prices in the states where retail competition currently exists. Prices fell steadily until 1998 or 1999, then rose modestly for a year or two. Prices spiked in 2001 and 2002, especially for commercial and industrial customers. California prices began to rise after 2008 for residential customers and after 2010 for commercial and industrial customers. Prices in states with retail competition began a steady decline after 2008.

The atypical behavior of prices in California stems directly from unique features of the California market design. Customers were

Figure 6. Price Trends in California vs. Competitive States (Delivered Price of Electricity)

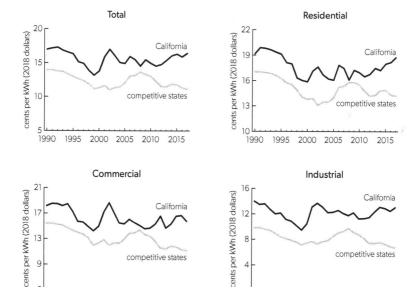

Source: Author's calculations using data from the US Energy Information Administration, "Electricity" (database), accessed November 13, 2019, https://www.eia.gov/electricity/data.php.

guaranteed price reductions, even if they did not shop around. They received the option to purchase power at a rate equal to 90 percent of the regulated rate in 1996.[62] Unlike Texas, with its adjustable price-to-beat mechanism, California provided for little retail price flexibility to accommodate fluctuations in the marginal cost of producing electricity. The retail price of electricity (not including transmission and distribution charges) was capped at about 6 cents per kWh.[63] These provisions discouraged new competitors from serving the residential market, so most residential customers continued to buy electricity from the incumbent utilities at a fixed price.

The three investor-owned California utilities—Pacific Gas and Electric, Southern California Edison, and San Diego Gas & Electric—were required to purchase all power in a state-mandated, day-ahead wholesale spot market. They retained no right to buy power under long-term contracts from generation facilities that they divested. The combination of inflexible retail prices and fluctuating wholesale prices left the utilities exposed to substantial financial risk, which they did not hedge.[64] The wholesale market commenced operation on April 1, 1998.[65]

Generators selling in the wholesale market learned that higher bids would not lead to a significant reduction in the quantity sold. The capped retail prices did not signal to consumers when power became more scarce. Since utilities were obligated to satisfy consumer demand at the fixed retail price, they had to procure sufficient power regardless of the wholesale price. The absence of demand response allowed generators to exercise market power by withholding supply and bidding high prices.

Unique features of California's electricity supply situation also made it easier for generators to exercise market power in 2000 and 2001. Just 672 megawatts of new power plants were built during 1995–2000 in the run-up to competition. California is heavily dependent on power imports from neighboring states, and hydroelectric power accounted for 20–25 percent of California's total supply. Owing to a dryer-than-normal year, hydroelectric imports in 2000 were 47 percent below their level in 1999.[66] Because there was less supply available on the market, individual generators had greater ability to influence prices by withholding supply.

Price spikes and shortages were the inevitable result. California experienced rolling blackouts in January, March, and May 2001.[67] One major utility, Pacific Gas and Electric, declared bankruptcy in March 2001. Other California utilities were allowed to increase their rates to prevent additional bankruptcies.

The state sought to prevent further wholesale price spikes by signing $45 billion worth of long-term contracts to purchase electricity in 2001:[68] "By mid-summer 2001, spot electricity prices were back to pre-crisis levels, and the state was committed to over $40 billion worth of long-term electricity contracts at prices that are likely more than 50 percent above the expected future spot prices."[69] Retail competition was also repealed.

Clearly, the failure of retail competition in California has nothing to do with any inherent tendency in electricity markets toward natural monopoly. Rather, California chose an inherently unstable combination of mandatory retail rate reductions, inflexible retail prices, and a requirement that utilities buy most of their power in a volatile day-ahead spot market that was highly vulnerable to manipulation.

Retail Competition with Competing Wires: The Electric Avenue Less Traveled

Not all network industries use shared access to monopoly infrastructure. Railroad transportation, cable television, wireless, broadband, satellite communications, and even wireline telephone involve significant competition between firms that build their own infrastructure.[70] Even in electricity, some duopolistic competition has existed in the United States between local distribution companies that own their own wires. These duopolies engage in both retailing and distribution, and sometimes also in transmission and generation. Empirical research finds that costs and prices are both substantially lower where competition exists; this result suggests that the salutary effects of competition outweigh any lost economies of scale.

In 1966, 49 US cities had direct competition between an investor-owned electric utility and a municipal electric utility; by 1981, that number had declined to 27.[71] Not surprisingly, economists have studied these duopoly electric markets to see how competition affects prices and service. Empirical research focuses on the municipal utilities because the data for these utilities are available for the individual cities where competition exists. The municipal utilities' prices are set by local officials, and they are not subject to rate-of-return regulation.[72]

The first extensive econometric studies were conducted by University of Illinois economist Walter Primeaux and summarized in his 1986 book, *Direct Electric Utility Competition*. There are two reasons that competition could lead to lower prices: competition could force firms to set prices closer to costs, and competitive firms may have lower costs owing to X-efficiency. Primeaux employed a sample that matched municipal utilities that faced competition with municipal utilities in similar cities with similar sources of electricity supply that did not face competition. He found that the marginal price of moving from the 750 kWh rate block to the 1,000 kWh rate block was 19 percent lower in cities with competition. Average revenue per KWh, a proxy for the average electricity rate, is 33 percent lower where competition exists.[73]

Primeaux also found that competition is associated with a reduction in average costs of 11 percent at the mean value of average cost.[74] The overall effect of competition on costs varies with the size of the firm, because competition sacrifices some economies of scale. The increased costs due to lost economies of scale exceed the decreased costs due to X-efficiency at annual sales above 222 million kWh. At the time of Primeaux's study, 92 percent of publicly owned systems and 60 percent of investor-owned systems had annual sales below 100 million kWh.[75] There was no difference in capacity utilization in monopoly and duopoly markets.[76]

The size of the cost reduction suggests that lower costs account for a significant portion, but not all, of the price reduction associated with competition. It appears that competitive rivalry also pushes prices closer to costs. Duopoly firms changed their prices more frequently than monopoly firms, which implies a greater degree of rivalry.[77]

If natural monopoly exists anywhere in electricity, it is likely in transmission and distribution.[78] Using data from 1961–1976, Primeaux and a coauthor estimated a cost function for transmission and distribution that controls for whether a utility faces direct competition. They find that the average cost curve for transmission and distribution is likely U-shaped, which suggests that larger, monopolized transmission and distribution utilities have exhausted the economies of scale.[79] Their analysis focused on the combined cost of transmission and distribution; it did not test whether there are economies of scope from combining transmission and distribution.

Case studies have revealed several examples of product differentiation in duopoly markets. Utilities serving multiple cities addressed customer complaints more quickly in cities where they faced competition. Competing utilities installed standby facilities so they could offer more reliable service, cut down trees for customers, provided free poles for television antennae, and furnished contractors with outside wiring for free.[80] Other inducements offered by competitors in some cities included free temporary service for new construction, free labor for inside wiring, appliance sales, and appliance service.[81] Companies rarely charged for connection or disconnection, and the deposits they required from new customers were low.[82]

In a 1996 study, John Kwoka identified 22 cities with multiple electric utilities where at least some customers were permitted to switch providers as of 1989. In 12 of these cities, current customers could switch; in the others, only new residents or new industrial customers could choose their electric company. Kwoka's regression results suggest that companies that face competition may have higher fixed costs (although the correlation is not statistically significant). Companies facing competition have lower variable costs, and this relationship is statistically significant. The net effect is that electric utilities that face competition have costs that are 16 percent lower than those of utilities that do not face competition.[83] Direct wire-on-wire competition is also associated with an 8.1 percent reduction in price, in addition to the effect on costs. Thus, direct competition is associated with a 24 percent reduction in electricity prices.[84]

It is interesting to compare the size of the price reductions associated with direct infrastructure competition with that of the price reductions associated with retail choice and open access to the wires. Direct infrastructure competition preserves economies of scope and subjects a larger portion of the industry to competition, but it also involves duplicative facilities. Retail choice with open access to the wires could sacrifice economies of scope, and it leaves the wires monopolized, but it avoids the cost of duplicating the wires.

Kwoka's and Primeaux's results suggest that direct infrastructure competition is associated with price reductions of 24–33 percent. The raw data in table 1 show that after 2008, when competition was fully implemented, average prices in competitive states declined by 19 percent while prices in monopoly states were rising. In Texas, residential electricity prices fell by about 19–20 percent after the price to beat was phased out.[85] The Public Utility Commission of Texas reports that average electricity prices in competitive regions of the state in 2018 were 10–23 percent below both the last regulated price and the national average.[86] These results suggest that retail competition between companies with their own distribution wires delivers price reductions at least as large as those produced by customer choice with monopoly wires. Indeed, the price reductions from infrastructure competition may be even larger. Such comparisons are, of course, only suggestive, since they involve studies conducted with different data sets at different times that control for different factors that influence prices.

Policy Reform

Scholarly research on retail competition suggests that competition can produce a more efficient retail price structure, reduce retail price levels, and promote the introduction of value-added services. The research also shows, however, that retail reform can be a quite complex undertaking. Results have varied greatly depending on how the rules and institutions governing the retail market are established.

The most common type of reform leaves transmission and distribution wires as regulated monopolies and implements competition in the retailing function. In general, policymakers who seek to introduce or expand this type of retail electric competition would do well to follow the Texas model, as described above and in chapter 15 of this volume. A key feature that allowed retail competition to flourish in Texas, even for residential customers, was the elimination of a standby regulated service offering from the incumbent electric utilities. The "price to beat" mechanism was temporary and adjusted to reflect changes in the marginal cost of generation. Competition intensified greatly, and consumers reaped greater benefits, after the price to beat expired.

California also offers two important lessons for electricity market reform. First, it is clear that requiring a utility to offer a regulated standby rate creates a substantial barrier to entry on the retail level—especially if the regulated rate gives customers who do not shop a guaranteed price cut. Second, requiring utilities to buy all their power in a spot market prone to manipulation is a recipe for disaster. Policymakers seem to have heeded the second lesson, because no state has tried to replicate California's mandatory spot market requirement. However, it is not clear whether the first lesson has been learned; other than Texas, even the states with retail competition still require the incumbent utility to offer consumers standby service at a regulated rate. This may explain why none of the other competitive states has seen as much competition for retail customers as Texas has.

Studies of duopolistic retail competition between vertically integrated utilities suggest that this form of competition can also be viable. However, the number of jurisdictions with duopolistic utility competition has fallen over time, and it is not clear why. Nevertheless, the empirical research suggests that there is no economic justification for granting exclusive monopoly territories to electric distribution companies. States should abolish monopoly electric franchises and allow competition to emerge if and where it is practicable.

Conclusions

The available scholarly evidence clearly refutes the idea that monopoly is the most efficient market structure for retail electricity sales. Many of the studies summarized in this chapter find that electricity prices in states that allow widespread retail choice tend to be lower than they would have been under monopoly, once the lengthy transition period concludes. Under competition, prices more closely reflect marginal costs, and costs themselves appear to have fallen. Moreover, at least in the state with the most developed retail market—Texas—there is evidence of product differentiation that may create additional value for consumers. Contrary to natural monopoly theory, no studies find that retail competition, per se, increased prices, although several studies find that flaws in market design have led to higher prices. Aside from California, whose experience was covered in depth above, the most common design flaw involves failure to sufficiently "quarantine" the remaining utility monopoly so it cannot distort the retail market.[87]

Studies of duopolistic competition between utilities that engage in both retailing and distribution produce results qualitatively similar to those of the studies of states that implemented retail competition while treating the wires as regulated monopolies. Econometric studies find that under duopoly, electric utilities have lower costs and charge lower prices than under monopoly—prices that seem to reflect both the cost difference and the effects of competitive rivalry. Case studies reveal numerous ways in which duopoly firms compete through product differentiation.

Regardless of which form retail competition takes, there is no economic justification for monopolizing electricity retailing.

Governance for Networks: Regulation by Networks in Electric Power Markets in Texas

Michael Giberson and L. Lynne Kiesling

Most electricity consumers, whether households or small businesses, have few (if any) choices when it comes to their electricity supplier. The electric power business works a little differently in Texas, where most consumers can choose from among dozens of suppliers and face as many as two hundred different plans.

Reforms in Texas and several other states over the past 30 years were intended to promote the growth of competition in the electric power industry. The political debate was framed as a choice between regulation and deregulation. Should government regulators oversee the industry or should oversight somehow be "left to the market"?

Astute industry observers, noting the voluminous regulations required to support the emergence of competition, see the *deregulation* label as misplaced. *Restructuring* is the preferred term of art. How and why is the reformed structure to work? The question draws attention to what in economics are called *governance institutions*.

Market exchange requires a background of social practices to define and enforce property rights. For a marketplace to emerge and endure, it further requires methods for resolving disputes. Governance institutions for market exchange are the collection of social practices concerning property rights and dispute resolution that enable durable market exchanges. Governance institutions have been studied in circumstances ranging from medieval trading coalitions to piracy to prison yards to diamond trading to the provision of municipal services. We add to this literature with a case study examining governance institutions arising in wholesale electric power markets.

Governance is often considered to come in two types: public or private. According to this classification, within a particular sphere either government authority dominates or voluntary private interaction dominates. Work on common-pool resource institutions has added a third category of analysis, in which governance is provided primarily by social custom. Most, perhaps all, market settings are hybrids, in which some governance issues are resolved within one institutional setting and others are addressed elsewhere.

In electric power markets government authority has long been the dominant governance institution, but reforms undertaken over the past 30 years have shifted governance purposefully in the direction of market institutions. Much industry analysis remains framed as regulation versus deregulation, which is to say it assumes that governance is either public or it is private. In addition, the development of governance institutions for wholesale power markets remains an ongoing process as rules are introduced or revised to adapt to changing conditions. The goals for this case study are two: First, we will illustrate the value of the governance literature for understanding the organization of wholesale power markets. Second, we will use the case of electric power markets to examine and develop the understanding of governance institutions in the explicitly hybrid circumstances of wholesale power markets integrated with power system operations. Wholesale power trading is both enabled and constrained by the networked physical infrastructure connecting producers and consumers. We therefore draw on and mix three kinds of materials for our study: the literature on governance institutions, the literature on networks, and the recent history and economics of electric power markets.

The term *governance* has broad application in social analysis, with similarly broad variation in the scope of the term and the use to which it is applied. University of California, Berkeley political scientist Mark

Bevir explores this variation in an essay in the *Encyclopedia of Governance*.[1] Within Bevir's typology, our approach fits most clearly within "rational choice theory," albeit without commitments to perfectly consistent preferences or completeness of information (commitments typical in formal modeling). In other words, we take our focus on governance to be about goal-oriented behavior by agents working within an environment of formal and informal rules, which they rely on to plan activity and coordinate with other agents.

Often it becomes easier to see how governance institutions work in everyday cases if one first considers the institutions that arise in relatively unusual environments.[2] In the 11th century, a time when few people traveled far from home, the overseas trading networks employed by Maghribi traders provides one example of an unusual case.[3] George Mason University economist Peter Leeson's work on pirate governance studies cooperation (among pirates, if not their victims) in a seafaring environment.[4] Brown University political scientist David Skarbek's work on prison gangs presents another environment quite unlike the everyday world most buyers and sellers inhabit.[5] We offer the electric power industry as another relatively extreme environment within which to explore governance. Our exploration draws on the analysis of common-pool resources produced by Indiana University political scientist and Nobel prizewinner Elinor Ostrom and her colleagues,[6] the analysis of network governance offered by University of Illinois law professor Amitai Aviram,[7] and historical and institutional detail about the development of electric power markets.

The electric power trading environment is relatively extreme owing to the somewhat unforgiving nature of service delivery over an electric power grid. At the moment of the power transaction, the range of potential buyers and sellers is fixed by the network of physical electrical infrastructure connecting consumers and producers. The service must be produced the moment it is consumed. Successful delivery of electric power service involves meeting demanding technical requirements. Within the electric grid, individual power transactions may be complementary to some other uses of the grid while they create or shift patterns of congestion and thus compete against others. Overall maintaining grid stability can require electric generation to sacrifice the sale of electricity to provide grid support services, often without direct payment.[8] The physical demands of managing the production, delivery, and consumption of electric power create a distinctive, and in this respect extreme, economic environment. These physical constraints also affect the institutional framework or governance structure in which exchange occurs.[9]

We investigate the topic of governance in networks with a focus on electric power markets in Texas. Texas is the only US state with a market design fully integrating competitive wholesale and competitive retail transactions.[10] In the United States, electricity has traditionally been sold predominantly by privately owned companies granted monopoly territory protection by the state and constrained by state regulation of rates and other terms of service. These privately-owned electric utilities tend to be vertically integrated across a range of activities including electric power generation, long-distance transmission service, local distribution service, and retailing power to captive consumers. The fundamental governance systems within the traditional system are state and federal utility regulations, constrained somewhat by capital markets and manager-shareholder relations, as well as the broader environment of property and contract law.

The Texas approach retains significant portions of the traditional governance framework but limits the monopoly portions of the regulated electric utility to the transmission and distribution systems and shifts electric generation and retailing functions to predominantly market governance. Much of the governance of the wholesale power market occurs through the Electric Reliability Council of Texas (ERCOT), an independent system operator (ISO) that runs the wholesale power market and oversees operations of the transmission grid.

Briefly, in Texas electric power retailers buy power from electric generation and offer to sell it to end-use customers in competitive retail markets.[11] The rest of this chapter will explore key features of governance institutions in general and how those governance institutions are shaped by a networked environments. This survey of the governance literature is employed to show how market-based governance institutions replace traditional rate-based regulation of vertically-integrated electric utilities and identify some advantages of making such replacement.

Governance and Networks

Effective governance institutions reflect the opportunities for gains from exchange and the related risks of opportunistic behavior.[12] A one-off trade for an inexpensive, immediately consumed product differs from the purchase of a durable consumer appliance. It also differs from an employment contract. Whether trade is within a social circle or between groups, whether potential failures are easy or difficult to recover from, whether parties have high-quality alternatives to the trade—all these features of transactions and the trading environment affect which rules are well-suited to govern behavior and to help people accomplish their various goals.[13]

Economic analysis, including analysis of the electric power system, has commonly focused on only two governance systems—government regulation and market competition—as if they represented the full range of options. Discussions of reforms to the electric power industry over the past three decades exemplify this simple analysis when the discussions are framed as being about deregulation, as if all regulation of potential opportunism is government-imposed regulation and the only alternative is the "free market."[14] Yale law professor Robert Ellickson, in *Order without Law*, identifies five types of governance systems: first-party controllers (self-regulation), second-party controllers (counterparty regulation), and three kinds of third-party controllers—social forces, organizations, and governments.[15] Aviram draws on this categorization, explaining networks as one particularly significant form of third-party organizational regulator.[16] The work of Elinor Ostrom and others on common-pool resource governance offers a complementary and more extensive examination of these issues.

On the basis of her own fieldwork and surveys of many other studies, Ostrom identified eight general principles that characterize durable governance institutions for common-pool resources:[17]

1. *"Clearly defined boundaries.* The identity of the group and the boundaries of the shared resource are clearly delineated."

2. *"Proportional equivalence between benefits and costs.* Members of the group must negotiate a system that rewards members for their contributions. High status or other disproportionate benefits must be earned. Unfair inequality poisons collective efforts."

3. *"Collective-choice arrangements.* Group members must be able to create at least some of their own rules and make their own decisions by consensus. People hate being told what to do but will work hard for group goals that they have agreed upon."

4. *"Monitoring.* Managing a commons is inherently vulnerable to free-riding and active exploitation. Unless these undermining strategies can be detected at relatively low cost by norm-abiding members of the group, the tragedy of the commons will occur."

5. *"Graduated sanctions.* Transgressions need not require heavy-handed punishment, at least initially. Often gossip or a gentle reminder is sufficient, but more severe forms of punishment must also be waiting in the wings for use when necessary."

6. *"Conflict resolution mechanisms.* It must be possible to resolve conflicts quickly and in ways that are perceived as fair by members of the group."

7. *"Minimal recognition of rights to organize.* Groups must have the authority to conduct their own affairs. Externally imposed rules are unlikely to be adapted to local circumstances and violate principle 3."

8. "For *groups that are part of larger social systems*, there must be *appropriate coordination among relevant groups.* Every sphere of activity has an optimal scale. Large scale governance requires finding the optimal scale for each sphere of activity and appropriately coordinating the activities, a concept called polycentric governance."

Together, the eight principles characterize a system of rules useful in sustaining mutually beneficial cooperation in an environment that might otherwise encourage opportunistic behavior.

Further analysis of the eight principles by environmental scientists Michael Cox, Gwen Arnold, and Sergio Villamayor-Tomás suggested useful refinements to three of the eight principles (1, 2, and 4). For principle 1, "clearly defined boundaries," Cox, Arnold, and Villamayor-Tomás suggest separating attention to community boundaries from attention to resource boundaries. For principle 2, "proportional equivalence between benefits and costs," they note that concern for proportional equivalence should be considered both with respect to local conditions and with respect to the individual benefit-cost position of individual community members. Similarly, for principle 4, "monitoring," they suggest separating the monitoring of resource status from the monitoring of the behavior of group members and nonmembers.[18]

In "Regulation by Networks," Aviram describes network exchange and explains how the network influences the efficacy of governance institutions available to the network. His analysis is not limited to physical networks such as power grids or natural gas pipelines, but extends to trade associations, commodity exchanges, and other social networks. So long as the network offers significantly positive network effects to its members and has privileged access to the information flow created by transactions, his analysis of network regulation should apply.

All networked environments shape the opportunities for gains from exchange and the potential for opportunism. "Network effects" are benefits that increase as more people are connected. The value of a telecommunication system to a member party increases with the number of other parties the member can communicate with. The larger a trading community becomes, the greater the likelihood that there will be a good fit between the goals of buyers and the goals of sellers. In two-sided markets such as credit card payment systems, the value to consumers increases with the number of sellers accepting the card and the value to sellers increases with the number of consumers using the card.

The presence of strong network effects turns the threat of effective exclusion from the network into a powerful disciplining device. In private, non-networked exchange, the possibility of future gains from trade provides disciplining effects on opportunistic behavior. Opportunistic behavior extracts additional benefits now while sacrificing gains from trade with the same counterparty in the future. However, if the opportunistic agent has sufficiently attractive alternative counterparties, the loss of one will be of small consequence. Information-sharing within a network, however, can result in the loss of all member counterparties, substantially raising the cost of and thereby deterring opportunistic behavior.

Networks can also improve the agents' ability to secure gains from trade because they reduce the risks arising from counterparties' failures, whether due to opportunism or accident. Some gains from trade can only be secured through sustained cooperation over time. When one counterparty fails to deliver, networks may be able to replace the nonperforming party and readily mitigate harms that would otherwise result. Reduction of risks enhances the ability to trade.

At the same time, networked systems are exposed to a unique kind of opportunistic behavior for which they cannot be the best regulator: degradation of quality. Aviram offers the example of two interconnected networks, one larger than the other.[19] The interconnection benefits members of each networks by expanding the number of potential counterparties, but the networks' owners profit most from—and therefore prefer—trades between their own members. In this situation, the larger network faces an incentive to degrade the quality of the interconnection, perhaps by reducing the number of simultaneous transactions that can be supported. The reduction in capacity of the interconnection imposes higher costs on members of the smaller network and thereby increases the relative benefit of switching membership from the smaller to the larger network. The benefits of switching (as opposed to remaining members of the smaller network) increase with each agent that switches, threatening a cascading effect. In the absence of governance structures outside the networks themselves, either the small network will collapse or it will be forced to bear a disproportionate share of the costs of maintaining the interconnection.

The potential case of degradation shows one application of this approach to analysis. Even as a network should be expected to effectively promote certain kinds of transactions, namely those among its members, at the same time it is unlikely to be the most effective regulator of transactions among members of separate networks. If transactions across networks appear to leave potential gains from trade unexploited, this situation suggests that competition among institutions has not yet fully adapted to the environment. Reform consumes resources, so one possibility is that the costs of reform outweigh potential gains. However, improving trade between networks may create winners and losers within separate networks, and losers will have an incentive to frustrate potential reforms.

Markets are networks in both a general and a specific sense. Exchange and transactions are inherently social, requiring parties to be connected. A network of buyers and sellers benefits both sides of the market by increasing the number of potential trading partners, which is a more general phenomenon than demand-side complementarity. More specifically, modern markets are often digital platforms, which means that the market provider is decreasing transaction costs and enabling parties to find each other for mutual benefit.[20] In such market platforms, the market rules defined by the platform provider and the formal legal context combine to provide an institutional framework that is neither government regulation nor purely private ordering. Digital market platforms that establish rules to mitigate opportunistic behavior are networks capable of regulation in Aviram's sense.

We can apply Ostrom's eight principles specifically to the case of ISOs by mixing in Aviram's work and industry knowledge (see table 1). ISOs offer strong two-sided market effects: the more electric generators connected to the system, the more valuable the system becomes to consumers; the more consumers connected to the system, the more valuable it becomes to electric generators. The ISO can control membership and participation on its network (principle 1), making exclusion a simple and powerful deterrent to opportunistic behavior. Monitoring power flows on the transmission network is central to the ISOs' function (principle 4), making detection and deterrence of opportunistic behavior an inexpensive feature for an ISO to provide. The ISO market offers easy access to substitute transactions in the case of nonperformance by a counterparty (for example, intentional or accidental failure to supply power as contracted), reducing counterparty risk. The nonperforming party typically settles with the ISO at the market price for deviation from schedules, a type of graduated sanction (principle 5).

Table 1. Principles for Stable Governance Applied to Independent System Operators (ISOs)

1) Clearly defined boundaries

The ISO maintains a list of transmission system components and a list of ISO members by industry segment. The capabilities of individual members differ by industry segment and are described in ISO rules.

ISO rules determine the basis for membership and grounds for terminating that membership, making expulsion from the network a powerful disciplinary option.

2) Proportional equivalence between benefits and costs

Many transactions conducted with the ISO are priced in accordance with ISO rules. Additional member obligations are also established in the rules. Disagreements about proportionality arise among members on the basis of differences in industry segment, business strategies, or technologies employed. Such differences are often discussed in stakeholder proceedings and disagreements are sometimes raised in regulatory proceedings.

3) Collective-choice arrangements

ISO members participate in the development of new rules and the reform of existing rules through stakeholder processes. Typical ISO rules provide for industry-segment representation in approval processes.

4) Monitoring

The ISO engages in constant monitoring of conditions on the transmission grid, including metering of injections, losses, and withdrawals of electric power as well as monitoring for other conditions relevant to the stability of the physical transmission grid. At the same time, the ISO engages in monitoring of the financial capabilities of members commensurate with credit risks raised by their participation in the market.

The ISO's ability to monitor the physical system and member interactions in real time enables rapid detection of (some) rule violations and provides for mitigation of potential harms to the system or to other members.

5) Graduated sanctions

Violations of ISO rules are met with a variety of sanctions, ranging from warnings to fines to expulsion from the system. The detailed monitoring of the electric power grid allows finely graded sanctions to be applied.

6) Conflict resolution mechanisms

The ISO offers little in the way of direct dispute resolution service for disputes between members. Such disputes may be addressed before regulatory commissions or through the judicial system.

7) Minimal recognition of rights to organize

ISOs have been collaboratively developed by transmission owners and wholesale power market stakeholders under the oversight and approval of federal and state authorities.

8) Appropriate coordination among relevant groups

ISOs are embedded within a system of federal and state laws and regulations. External authorities often defer to ISO rules and actions within ISO rules when those rules appear to reflect the consensus of ISO members.

Source: The list of principles for stable governance comes from David Sloan Wilson, Elinor Ostrom, and Michael E. Cox, "Generalizing the Core Design Principles for the Efficacy of Groups," *Journal of Economic Behavior and Organization* 90 (2013): S21–S32.

However, ISOs have persistently faced difficulty in overcoming barriers to efficient trades with resources or consumers in neighboring ISOs.[21] This version of a degradation strategy is, as Aviram suggested, difficult for the network itself to overcome.

In the next section we explore a particular market platform—wholesale power markets operated by ERCOT, the ISO in Texas—as a form of governance institution. Our study is limited to the ERCOT ISO in Texas. While other ISOs in the United States share similar governance structures, we made no effort to examine or compare governance across the seven US ISOs.

Electric Power Markets: The Texas Model and Regulation by Network

The Texas electric power industry works differently enough from what is typical that it is worth explaining what makes it different, why Texas policymakers switched (most of) the state from monopoly to competitive supply, and how the changes affect consumers. Here we introduce the Texas model, give some background, and then discuss how well the Texas system has been working. The Texas approach is recognized among industry specialists as being distinctive—some experts say it is one of the best such markets.[22]

Industry History and Structure

Electric power was long seen as an exception to the stereotypical American enthusiasm for free enterprise and rivalry among companies seeking to win loyal customers through low prices and good service. But a wave of deregulation in other industries that had earlier been tightly regulated, with apparent benefits to consumers, led some in the electric power industry to ask "why not here?"

In fact, the electric power industry was once a hotbed of competition. At the beginning of the 20th century, a large city like Chicago would have had 20 or 30 small power companies competing for business. Electric power was slower to come to smaller towns, but by 1920 even a small West Texas town like Lubbock, which had only a few thousand residents at the time, featured two competing electricity suppliers.[23] But the view was spreading that one company could serve an area more cheaply than two or more, and state-protected monopolies soon dominated the industry.

Monopolies did have several advantages. There were economies of scale and scope that allowed bigger companies to capture technical efficiencies. In addition, the electric power system is composed of several parts that had to be carefully coordinated to maintain service. Before the age of computers and advanced communication technologies, it would have been difficult to maintain the coordination necessary to operate a competitive system. In today's interconnected world, that old justification for monopoly has fallen away.

The electric power industry can be divided into three basic parts: the electric power generators, the transmission and distribution "wires," and the retailing end of the business—see Figure 1. The difficulties involved in carefully coordinating electricity generation with the carrying capacity of the wires to constantly meet the varying demands of end consumers made monopoly seem necessary. Allowing too much power to flow over particular transmission wires can lead to costly failures. A failure to keep production closely matched to consumption could be costly as well. The economies of scale and scope that also supported the monopoly model apply differently to the generation and transmission parts of the industry, and have almost no bearing on the retail side of things.

Early electric companies had just two or three generators, and at the time larger generators could be much more efficient than smaller ones. These economies of scale at the power plant meant that a single company with a few large power plants could operate more cheaply than several smaller companies with smaller power plants. The logic of efficiency drove the industry to larger and larger power plants. The five-megawatt steam turbine installed in Chicago in 1903 was the largest

Figure 1. The Traditional Vertically Integrated Utility

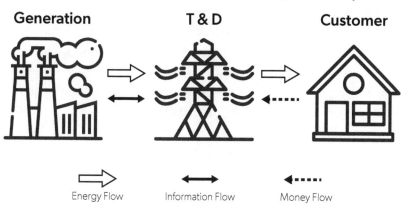

Source: U.S. Department of Energy, Office of Electricity Delivery and Energy Reliability, United States Electricity Industry Primer, (Washington, DC. June 2015). Retrieved from www.energy.gov.

of its time and produced power at half the cost of smaller power plants. But by the 1970s, new power plants were being built that were 100 times larger, and sometimes bigger than that.[24]

Of course, the technology of small power plants improved over the century as well, and by the 1970s a small power plant—when fit to the right situation and the right location—could sometimes be just as cost-effective as a large power plant. The economies-of-scale justification for bigger power plants owned by one large monopoly, once a major force in the industry, faded in importance.

The wires connecting generators and end consumers continue to show significant economies of scale. (Here we use *wires* as a catch-all term for a range of equipment, including poles, transformers, relays, some very high-tech components, meters, and a lot of actual wires.) High-voltage transmission systems connect distant power supplies to big cities, while lower-voltage distribution systems in cities and towns deliver power to end users. The electric meter, almost always owned by the distribution company, is the "end of the line," so to speak.

While the generation business upstream of the wires and the retailing business downstream quickly became settings for potential competition in Texas, the wires business itself has remained a monopoly regulated by state and federal regulators. The wires business has been changing, meanwhile: digital meters may be the most obvious change to end consumers, but high-tech digital components are growing in importance as well for the efficient and reliable operation of transmission systems. The increase in customer-owned generation, such as rooftop solar, has also created new challenges for distribution systems. Still, economies of scope remain important to the wires network, so monopoly with regulatory oversight remains the dominant business model.

At the retail end of the industry, where electric power is sold to the end user, simplicity rather than economies of scale drove monopolization. Since a single company owned the power generators and the wires linking that supply to consumers, it seemed natural that a single company would sell the power to consumers. Retail consumers range from large industrial consumers to individual households, with a wide array of businesses in between. As regulated monopoly became the dominant system for selling power, regulated rates tended to come in three basic categories: industrial, commercial, and residential. Sometimes customers within a category would have two or three options, but increased variety made regulation more difficult, so the number of offerings were limited.

The first state regulators of investor-owned electric utilities emerged in 1907, and by the early 1920s a majority of states had adopted state grants of monopoly power to private electric utilities in exchange for oversight over utility rates. Texas was relatively slow to adopt such regulation. Texas left rate regulation of private electric utilities to local governments until the state established the Public Utility Commission in 1975.[25]

Regulatory Reforms and Wholesale Power Markets

Technological changes in generation in the 1980s contributed to a move toward liberalizing the wholesale (bulk) power portion of the electric industry. New generation technologies such as the combined-cycle gas turbine made generation more economical at smaller scales and reduced the time and cost of turning generators on and off, and these changes made competitive wholesale power markets feasible. Wholesale power markets grew on the foundations of power pools that had been established (in the mid-Atlantic states, as early as the 1930s) to enable vertically integrated monopoly utilities to make bulk power sales to each other in emergency circumstances.

The emergence of non-utility generating resources in the 1980s led to increasing interest on the part of large industrial customers in bypassing utility service and purchasing power directly from independent producers. Congress responded to this interest with the Energy Policy Act of 1992, which required regulated transmission owners to provide third parties with nondiscriminatory access to the transmission grid. Transmission owners were often reluctant to accommodate third-party transactions because typically such deals resulted in the loss of power sales by affiliated local electric power companies. In effect, transmission owners could profit from employing what Aviram describes as a "degradation strategy,"[26] and they were often accused of doing so when third-party requests were denied.

The complexity of handling third-party requests and frequent costly regulatory appeals when requests were denied led many to support the development of ISOs, regional power systems integrating transmission system management with a competitive wholesale markets. The new approach enabled both utility and nonutility generators to compete to serve customers at the wholesale level, while managing power flows over the wires in a safe manner. Wholesale competition among power generators provides a part of the foundation needed to offer a choice of suppliers to retail consumers.

In Texas the Electric Reliability Council of Texas expanded to take on these oversight functions in the 1990s.[27] ERCOT has its origins in a 1941 organizational effort, the Texas Interconnected System (TIS), to help Texas utilities better coordinate their production for the war. In 1970 TIS reorganized as ERCOT and became the regional electric reliability council covering most of the state.. ERCOT opened its competitive wholesale power market in 1995. In the same year the first commercial wind farm began operation in Texas. ERCOT became an official ISO in 1996—its organizational mission called for it to be an independent third party to operate and coordinate flows in the transmission grid, ensuring open access to the grid and to wholesale power markets for all market participants. ERCOT describes itself as follows:

The Electric Reliability Council of Texas (ERCOT) manages the flow of electric power to more than 25 million Texas customers—representing about 90 percent of the state's electric load. As the independent system operator for the region, ERCOT schedules power on an electric grid that connects more than 46,500 miles of transmission lines and 650+ generation units. It also performs financial settlement for the competitive wholesale bulk-power market and administers retail switching for 8 million premises in competitive choice areas. ERCOT is a membership-based 501(c)(4) nonprofit corporation, governed by a board of directors and subject to oversight by the Public Utility Commission of Texas and the Texas Legislature. Its members include consumers, cooperatives, generators, power marketers, retail electric providers, investor-owned electric utilities, transmission and distribution providers and municipally owned electric utilities.[28]

Figure 2 shows ERCOT's governance structure. ERCOT is overseen by a board of directors composed of market-segment directors, consumer directors, and unaffiliated directors, with market-segment directors allocated across six areas: generators, investor-owned utilities, power marketers, retail energy providers, municipal utilities, and cooperatives.[29] The board is advised by a Technical Advisory Committee (TAC) composed of industry stakeholders, with similar market-sector and consumer membership. The TAC is further supported by four subcommittees and various working groups and task forces. Directors affiliated with market participants are elected by members within the market segment. Unaffiliated directors are selected by affiliated directors. The state's Office of Public Utility Counsel is assigned to represent residential and small commercial customers on the board and the TAC. The chair of the Public Utility Commission of Texas serves as a nonvoting member of the board.

ERCOT's members represent the various participants (buyers and sellers) in its markets, and they work with ERCOT staff to develop and implement market rules, use data to analyze the performance of those

Figure 2. Governance Structure of the Electric Reliability Council of Texas (ERCOT)

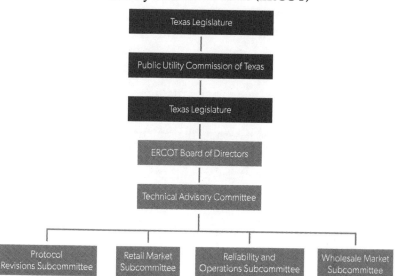

rules, assess penalties for the violation of those rules, and revise those rules through well-communicated procedures if they perceive a potential for improvement.[30] Any member can propose changes to ERCOT rules. Proposed rule changes are subject to a review-and-comment period, and this process is overseen by the Protocol Revisions Subcommittee of the TAC. The TAC makes recommendations to the board for protocol and other changes, and the board is empowered to adopt or reject proposed changes.

In many respects, therefore, ERCOT is an important central entity for enabling regulation by networks to occur in Texas. The ERCOT market platform is a network of digitally and physically connected parties and interconnected resources. ERCOT participants gain informational advantages by participating in this market network, advantages to which they would not otherwise have access. As an organization, ERCOT focuses on developing market rules that serve this regulatory function:

> Balanced market rules are a basic element in Texas competition. Clear, predictable and well-designed rules help foster a

stable electricity market. Electric Reliability Council of Texas (ERCOT) market rules are developed by participants from all aspects of the electricity industry. The rules and amendments are reviewed by the Public Utility Commission of Texas to ensure that they satisfy the public interest.[31]

In his discussion of network regulation, Aviram lists organized exchanges as a third party that can reduce the likelihood of opportunistic behavior and thus have a regulatory function.[32] Exchanges such as ERCOT also possess the informational advantages that can make network membership and participation valuable, and the ability to assess penalties or restrict access to the market network makes the threat of punishment credible. As Aviram also notes, networks cannot be the best guard against opportunistic behavior for all such potential threats. For that reason, oversight from the Public Utility Commission of Texas offers some protection for consumers and for others outside the ERCOT system. This external oversight can either support or overwhelm the internal governance at the ISO, so care is needed, but such external authorities are common in sustainable governance systems, as suggested by Ostrom's principle 8 ("appropriate coordination among relevant groups").

Trends in Power Generation, Consumption, and Prices

One way to evaluate how well the ERCOT market network is performing this regulatory role is by examining generation, consumption, and prices in ERCOT's main wholesale power market.[33]

Figure 3 presents the annual power generation by fuel source since 1990. Natural gas generation has shown a consistent upward trajectory, growing from roughly 136 terawatt-hours (TWh) in 1990 to almost 240 TWh in 2010. In contrast, generation from nuclear and nonwind renewables has been relatively flat. Generation from wind increased from 4 TWh in 2005 to more than 75 TWh in 2018—a nearly 1,700 percent increase over this time frame. The production costs of both natural gas and wind generation have fallen, and the ERCOT market has facilitated investment in those increasingly economical resources.

Figure 3. Texas Annual Electricity Generation by Fuel Type

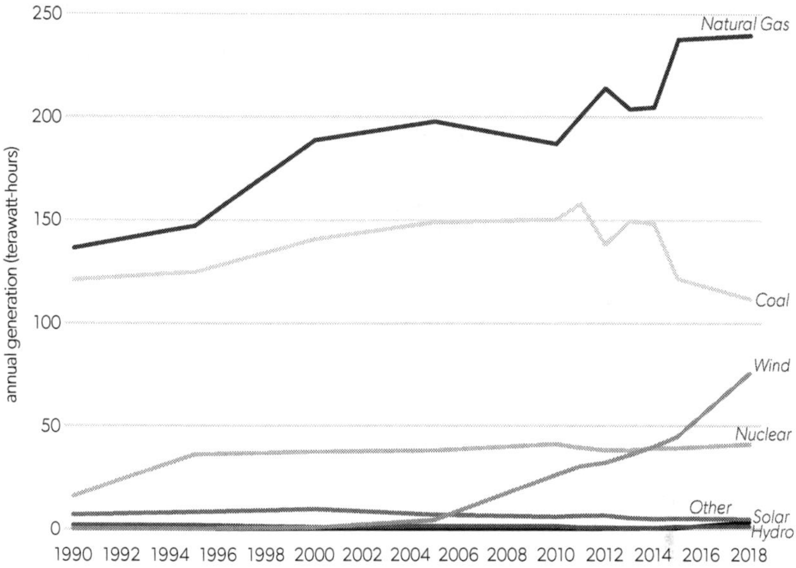

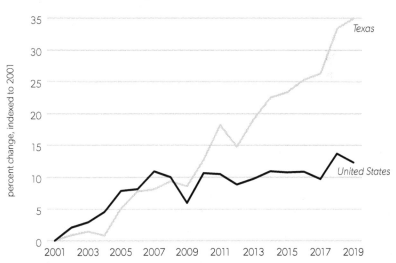

Source: US Energy Information Administration, *Electric Power Annual 2018* (Washington, DC: October, 2019).

Figure 4. Retail Sales of Electricity, All Sectors, United States and Texas

Source: US Energy Information Administration, *Electric Power Annual 2018* (Washington, DC: October, 2019).

Figure 4 indicates that total electricity consumption in Texas has been increasing, a phenomenon that is generally associated with economic growth. In the comparison with national consumption, the divergence after the 2008 recession is striking—consumption in the country as a whole has remained relatively constant while consumption in Texas has grown (and an increasing share of that power is from wind and natural gas, while a decreasing share is from coal).

At the same time that electricity consumption in Texas has been increasing, prices in Texas have risen much slower than in the nation as a whole, reflecting competition in both wholesale and retail markets.[34] After the Texas retail market opened up to competition in 2002, prices in Texas rose faster than the US average for a few years, but then they dropped below the average for the country in 2009 and have remained lower. Meanwhile, the national average electricity price has slowly crept higher, as figure 5 shows. Since 2009 the average retail price in Texas has been lower than the national average. Figure 6 reinforces this conclusion by comparing wholesale and retail prices over time. While average wholesale prices have been more volatile than average retail prices, both have declined since 2009.

While these production, consumption, and pricing trends don't provide enough data for causal inferences, they do suggest that the market-based governance structure that prioritizes regulation by networks in ERCOT is associated with welfare-enhancing exchange.

More careful econometric analysis supports this conclusion. A paper by Rice University economists Peter Hartley, Kenneth Medlock, and Olivera Jankovska reports the results of an in-depth analysis of retail and wholesale power prices in Texas since the 2002 opening of retail competition.[35] Hartley and his colleagues take advantage of the fact that not all electricity consumers in Texas gained access to competitive retail offers. This allows the researchers to, in effect, do a side-by-side comparison of price trends for competitive and noncompetitive areas.

The analysis produced "strong evidence that residential price movements . . . more accurately reflected corresponding movements in wholesale power markets"—suggesting again that fuel and other wholesale cost changes were more rapidly passed through to end

Figure 5. Average Retail Price of Electricity, All Sectors, United States and Texas

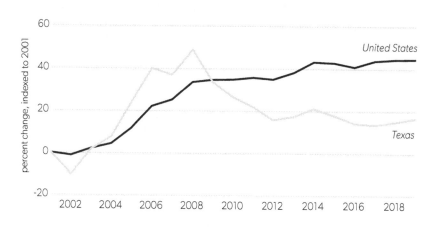

Source: US Energy Information Administration *Electric Power Annual 2018* (Washington, DC: October, 2019).

Figure 6. Texas Wholesale and Retail Electricity Prices

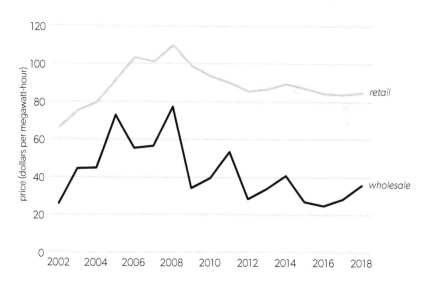

Sources: Potomac Economics, *2018 State of the Market Report for the ERCOT Electricity Markets*, June 2019; US Energy Information Administration, *Electric Power Annual 2018* (Washington, DC: October, 2019).

consumers with competition. In addition, "the difference between residential and wholesale prices declined on average over the period in the competitive market areas"—meaning that competitive suppliers appear to have lower operating costs than monopoly suppliers. Figure 7 shows Hartley, Medlock, and Jankovska's comparison of commercial and residential retail prices in competitive and monopoly areas. Comparison to the average wholesale prices (the lowest line) suggests that competitive retail prices better reflected underlying trends in wholesale power prices than did monopoly prices.[36] It is also noteworthy that prices for both residential and commercial customers began much higher than rates in monopoly areas, but ended at or below monopoly rates by 2016 (the end of the data set).

Investment in Renewable Energy and Infrastructure

Texas policy has relied primarily on competition within markets to induce investment in wind and solar resources, while investment in the transmission infrastructure to deliver remote wind power to urban consumers required legislative and regulatory action. New investment in electric generation is within the normal range of activities for the ERCOT market, and generally does not produce challenges to the ERCOT governance system. Transmission, on the other hand, was reserved for continued regulation as a monopoly service. In addition, the substantial size of the transmission infrastructure needed to access remote potential wind and solar resource sites could produce significant shifts of costs and benefits for existing ERCOT members. Policy decisions involving significant shifts in costs and benefits are difficult to address within the stakeholder-driven ERCOT governance system.

While wind and solar resources have attractive economic and environmental features, they are intermittent and require some form of backup energy—either a substitute generation source or storage—if they are to be considered resources for reliability or resilience purposes.

Texas's history of small-scale distributed generation for industrial activity goes back to the early 20th century, with an emphasis on energy-efficient cogeneration, also known as combined heat and power.[37] Little of this distributed generation was renewable—through the 1990s

Figure 7. Retail Electricity Prices in Competitive and Monopoly Areas of Texas

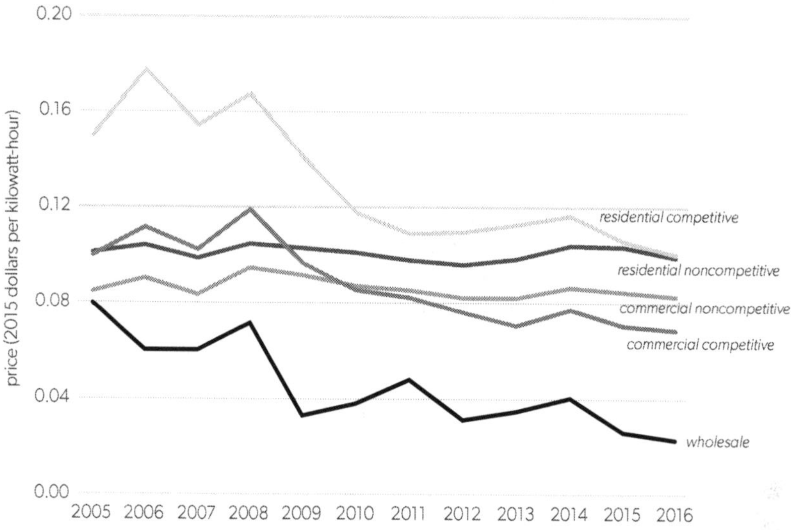

Source: Peter Hartley, Kenneth B. Medlock III, and Olivera Jankovska, "Electricity Reform and Retail Pricing in Texas," *Energy Economics* 80 (2019): 10.

Texas had modest amounts of wind and solar capacity, and what renewable capacity existed in the state was small hydroelectric generation. By the late 1990s, though, wind generation technologies had improved enough that investment in wind capacity increased, particularly in wind-intensive areas in West Texas.

The original deregulation legislation in Texas, S.B. 7 in 1999, incorporated several provisions to encourage renewable energy development as a way to address air pollution issues in the state's urban areas while also enabling economic development of the best wind resources of all 50 states.[38] S.B. 7 included a renewable portfolio standard that was modest by comparison with those of other states, but served as a policy platform for signaling the combined economic and environmental value of investing in wind generation.[39] S.B. 20 in 2005 augmented the original renewable target,[40] as energy economist Jay Zarnikau noted in 2011:

> SB 7 set an initial goal for renewable energy capacity of
> 2000MW by 2009. SB 20 in the 2005 legislative session in-

creased Texas' goal for renewable energy to 5880MW in 2015
and set a "voluntary" target of 10,000MW of wind power for
2025. Texas has already met the 2015 goal and is on track to
meet the 2025 goal well ahead of schedule.[41]

Texas also learned from the beneficial economic and environmental
effects of federal sulfur dioxide emission permit trading and implemented tradable renewable energy credits as a tool for meeting
renewable generation targets. Load-serving entities, which are the
retail energy providers in Texas, are required to have a market-share-
weighted number of renewable energy credits as their contribution to
the state's renewable energy goals, and they can meet that requirement
either by purchasing renewable energy to sell to their customers or by
purchasing renewable energy credits in the market.[42]

While West Texas is rich in wind energy potential, the ability to cap-
italize on wind investments there was constrained by the lack of a
transmission network. Increases in wind capacity would create congestion on the existing network, which would lead to price differences in
a balkanized wholesale power market. To facilitate wind investments,
S.B. 20 in 2005 also included provisions to reduce the regulatory siting
and permitting costs for transmission in key areas of wind development.
These Competitive Renewable Energy Zones (CREZ) connected wind-
rich areas of West and South Texas to the transmission grid, enabling
increased sales of wind power to meet demand in urban areas elsewhere in the state. By the time the transmission projects in the five CREZ
were completed in 2013, investments in installed wind capacity had
increased while transmission congestion fell, and wholesale market
prices converged across ERCOT, creating an integrated market capable
of capitalizing on Texas's wind resources.[43] Developers find that development costs are generally lower in Texas than in other states owing to
faster permitting and a regulatory environment conducive to investment and innovation.[44]

As a consequence of state policies that harness competition and markets to facilitate energy innovation by reducing transaction costs in
adoption and deployment, wind and solar investments have grown

in Texas since 1990. Figure 8 shows the amount of power generated annually from wind and solar photovoltaic systems from 1990 to 2018. Note the dramatic increase in wind generation as capacity increased and more wind resources were integrated into ERCOT's markets after the CREZ-enabled investments of 2006–2013. Solar power took a different growth trajectory because of its less attractive cost profile and lower energy efficiency compared to wind through the mid-2010s. Both wind and solar photovoltaic projects have seen larger-than-expected cost reductions as energy efficiency improves, production grows, and a competitive solar installation market drives down installation costs.[45]

Figure 9 shows that while total electricity generation in Texas has increased slowly, particularly over the past decade, solar and wind's share of that generation has increased dramatically since 2007 because market policies have been conducive to innovation and investment while the underlying technology costs are falling. The falling cost of both wind and solar technologies make them increasingly economical and better able to help cut pollution and greenhouse gas emissions.

Federal tax policies have also stimulated investment in wind and solar energy, although as the technologies become more economical those subsidies are being phased out. The federal wind production tax credit (PTC) was implemented in 1992 and has been modified and extended several times. The PTC allows a wind developer to claim a tax credit of 2.5 cents (inflation-adjusted) per kilowatt-hour generated. The PTC remains available for projects that began construction before January 1, 2020, and will be discontinued for subsequent wind projects.[46] Solar projects are eligible for a federal investment tax credit of 30 percent of the project's invested basis. This credit was implemented in 2006; it is currently scheduled to phase out by 2022. Phasing out the wind PTC and solar investment tax credit as wind and solar technologies become commercially attractive will reduce the distortions that the subsidies have introduced into ERCOT markets—particularly their suppression of prices and amplification of periods of negative prices.

Although markets typically have positive prices, sometimes power markets have negative market-clearing prices. Negative prices mean a power supplier will pay someone to take power. They arise in ERCOT for three main reasons: transmission constraints, the construction of new wind capacity in regions with less transmission capacity (leading to a mismatch in time and place between supply and demand), and the production tax credit paid to wind-resource owners.

In markets with large-scale central generation and demand that is stable (but that fluctuates over the day), negative prices may occur because of the cost of ramping down the generator's production. Turning down a nuclear power plant is expensive, so paying someone to take the power can be cheaper than ramping down generation. Markets enable buyers to benefit from this situation: for example, electricity consumers might be paid for precooling a commercial building, thereby reducing their electricity demand for air conditioning later in the day.

The increasing share of renewables in the generation portfolio introduces a new context for negative prices. In the first decade of the 21st century, as more wind generation came online in West Texas (and storage meanwhile was costly and uneconomical), the West Texas zone of ERCOT saw more periods with negative prices. Wind's intermittent nature contributed to these negative prices, which occurred because of a combination of insufficient transmission capacity to move the wind power to areas with more demand and insufficient local demand for the power. Thus high-wind periods can also be periods with negative prices.

In a transmission network with no congestion, inexpensive wind in West Texas could power consumption on the Gulf Coast. But when network capacity to deliver that power does not exist, markets balkanize, prices diverge, and plentiful West Texas wind power sells locally at a negative price. (In rare cases, negative prices for electricity briefly covered the entire ERCOT system, which reflects a limited ability to transmit electric power into power grids bordering the ERCOT system.)

Wind is challenging because it tends to be most available in sparsely populated locations and when demand is relatively low, such as overnight in winter months. Figure 10 shows the percentage of time that ERCOT experienced negative prices overall and in the West Texas zone.

Figure 8. Wind and Solar Photovoltaic Generation in Texas

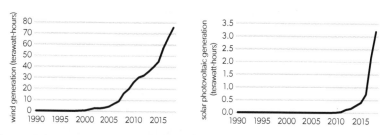

Source: US Energy Information Administration, *Electric Power Annual 2018* (Washington, DC: October 2019).

Figure 9. Total Electricity Generation in Texas vs. Solar and Wind Share

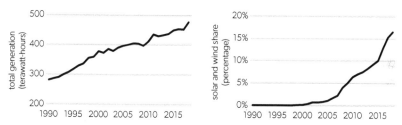

Source: US Energy Information Administration, *Electric Power Annual 2018* (Washington, DC: October 2019).

Figure 10. Negative Prices in Texas Compared to Wind Share of Total Generation

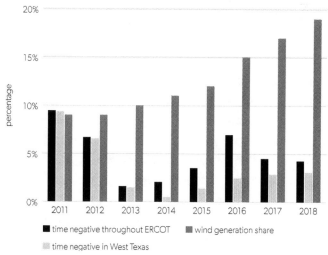

Note: ERCOT = Electric Reliability Council of Texas.
Source: Electric Reliability Council of Texas annual reports for 2011–2018.

The increasing incidence of negative prices gave extra impetus to the CREZ transmission investments that went live in 2012 and 2013.[47] ERCOT and the Public Utility Commission of Texas used negative price data as signals indicating congestion and market balkanization that could be reduced through transmission capacity investment.[48] As figure 10 shows, negative price incidence fell sharply in 2013, indicating the effects of CREZ investments. More recently, ERCOT has experienced more negative prices in West Texas, as wind's share of generation has grown from 15 to 19 percent.

A third factor contributing to negative prices in ERCOT has been the production tax credit. Wind companies receive the PTC on the basis of actual generation, so they are willing to pay up to the amount of the PTC (roughly $34 per megawatt-hour) to continue generating and not curtail production. The PTC subsidy has introduced a distortion into ERCOT markets by amplifying the phenomenon of negative prices. The elimination of the wind PTC in 2020 should reduce this distortion.

When transmission capacity is insufficient to transport wind energy as it is generated, then the generator may be curtailed, which means that the dispatch controllers in ERCOT tell these generators that they cannot send out their energy. Figure 11 shows the curtailment rate in ERCOT in comparison to the share of generated energy coming from wind resources. Curtailment was particularly high in 2008–2011 (and especially in 2009), and was alleviated starting in 2012 as the CREZ program's transmission investments increased network capacity. Low curtailment rates along with increasing wind shares since 2013 show the effects of the CREZ program, although curtailment has increased again recently. Reducing transmission constraints and congestion reduced the incidence of negative prices and curtailment and integrated the regional zones in ERCOT into a well-connected market.

ERCOT and the Public Utility Commission of Texas view the informative role of the price system as an important aspect of how the competitive market adapts to innovation. Everything has trade-offs, and wind power is no exception. Wind provides clean and increasingly affordable power, but exploiting this requires investments in transmission and backup. Negative prices send both an investment signal and

Figure 11. Wind Curtailment and Share of Generation in Texas

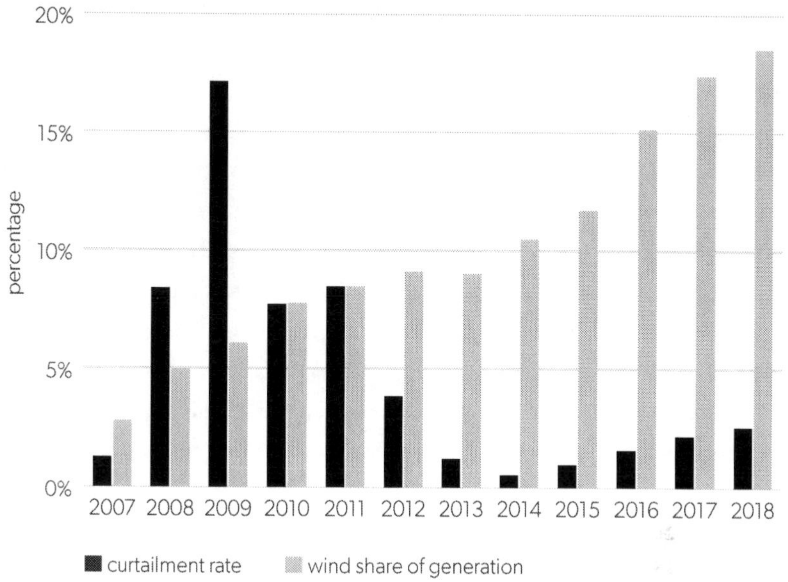

Source: Figure 42 in US Department of Energy, *2018 Wind Technologies Market Report*, August 2019, available at https://www.osti.gov/servlets/purl/1559881.

a purchase signal. The CREZ program explicitly used such price signals to coordinate transmission investment, bringing investment to the places where it was likely to be most valuable. The ability of electric generators to participate in markets, often using automation, means that generators that can respond with flexibility can profit from that capability. ERCOT's market rules and the economic value of having access to ERCOT markets create incentives to invest in such flexible and adaptable resources.

The Role of Network Governance in Texas Electricity

Aviram's "regulation by network" analysis holds as long as the network offers positive network effects and the network has privileged access to the information flow created by transactions. As described in more detail earlier, positive network effects arise when the addition of members to the network increases the value of the network to other members. Privileged access to information flows results when transactions between members of the network are necessarily observable by the network operator. The electric grid exhibits these characteristics to a high degree, and wholesale power markets are a network institution. While a consumer can self-supply power isolated from connections to others with a sufficient investment in the capability, connection to a grid often offers improved service quality and lower overall system cost. The grid operator closely monitors the supply and consumption of power across the high-voltage grid in order to manage the safe operation of transmission facilities, a process that produces vast quantities of transactional information. The result is that electric power grids are naturally set up to take advantage of "regulation by network" as elaborated in Aviram's work.

Aviram's work does not provide a complete discussion of governance institutions, and for that reason we nest it within the broader framework provided by Ostrom's eight principles. Aviram's work overlaps with principles 1 and 4. A successful network governance system will also attend to each of the other six principles.

For electric power grids operated as ISOs, the issues raised by principles 7 ("minimal recognition of rights to organize") and 8 ("appropriate coordination among relevant groups") are key. For ERCOT, the Public Utility Commission of Texas remains an important overseer. While the commission often defers to stakeholders about the details of ERCOT rules and procedures, the commission's position provides an independent venue for resolving differences, particularly when differences over proposed rules arise. Disputes can sometimes spill over into the courts or lead to legislative inquiries and other action. For this reason, the relations between ERCOT, the Public Utility Commission, and other outside entities are worthy of further attention in future research. It is in this area, too, that ERCOT is most distinctive from other ISOs, each of which is formally overseen by the Federal Energy Regulatory Commission rather than (primarily) by state legislative and regulatory authorities.

Conclusion: How to Promote Customer Choice and Retail Competition

Like other parts of the economy, the electric industry is a realm of cooperation, competition, and conflict. Securing opportunities in the electric industry usually requires decades-long commitments in uncertain environments. Long-run forecasts of expected costs and revenues must turn out to be approximately right often enough to give investors confidence to make investments. These opportunities for value creation often depend on governance institutions that are conducive to investment and innovation. In the case of Texas, those institutions are primarily governance by market networks, yielding more investment in increasingly economical and cleaner resources, for the benefit of producers and consumers.

Sometimes uncertainties are simply inherent in the world, from the point of view of potential cooperators—future climate outcomes, for example, are largely unknowable because of complexity and the impossibility of foresight. Other sources of uncertainty are social, such as public policy changes or the creditworthiness of potential counterparties in a proposed venture. Potential opportunistic behavior by counterparties is another source of uncertainty. Governance systems, the social and political rules of the game, can help reduce uncertainty and thereby enable parties to choose longer-run or otherwise riskier ventures when such ventures promise better overall results.

The essential physical network for delivery of electric power enables the industry itself to self-regulate efficiently for a wide range of possible transactions. Aviram's analysis highlights the specific characteristics of networks for aiding institutional governance, and Ostrom's much broader governance framework allows us to identify other aspects of the ERCOT system that allow it to be an effective, sustainable governance system. The economic environment within which the ERCOT grid operates and the electric power system itself are constantly changing, and such changes introduce new challenges to be addressed within the governance system. Understanding what aspects of the current ERCOT arrangements help them be effective can ensure that responses to those changes work to sustain rather than undermine ERCOT's successes.

Our analysis examines governance institutions within competitive electric power markets, a topic too often addressed in terms that assume the black-and-white dichotomy of regulated versus unregulated markets. Elsewhere we have advocated policy reforms to enable retail competition in electric power.[49] Our two key points for effective implementation are as follows:

1. Quarantine the monopoly to the wires and lines that form the platform where retail electric companies compete.
2. Bring the wholesale and retail electricity markets closer together.

First, unbundle vertically integrated monopolies. Power generation and retailing operations should be completely separated from transmission and distribution operations. Transmission and retailing should be competitive businesses with low barriers to entry and exit. The transmission and delivery business will remain a regulated monopoly utility. The rallying cry here is "quarantine the monopoly!" States that have permitted the monopoly to consume larger parts of the transmission and distribution processes have seen competition and prices suffer because of it.

Second, a competitive retail market also requires access to competitive wholesale power markets. The Texas model of competition in both retail and wholesale electric power is one of the best. We discussed the Texas model in a recent research report titled "Electric Competition in Texas: A Successful Model to Guide the Future."[50] There are many more details to establishing consumer choice and competitive markets in electric power, of course, but these recommendations provide a foundation.

We can also learn from the states where market performance has been disappointing.[51] As a guide for states seeking to transition from regulation to competition, other reform advocates have suggested five steps for improving competition:

- Unbundle distribution and retailing.
- Phase out default service.
- Allow efficient price signals to emerge.
- Promote access to information.
- Enforce consumer protection.

Each of these steps is important. Unbundling distribution and retailing creates a platform for electric retail companies to compete on. Phasing out the default service provider forces consumers to come into the market and choose a provider. It removes an barrier to competition, because the existing monopoly's position as the default service provider significantly reduces consumers' willingness to investigate alternatives.

If policymakers fail to do away with default service providers, then the opportunity for competition to emerge dwindles significantly. It's important here to promote awareness of the changing regulatory regime as a matter of both consumer protection and market efficiency.

The best recipe for consumer protection is providing clear and trusted information to consumers while aggressively pursuing bad actors who violate consumer-protection laws. Texas's "Power to Choose" website is an excellent example of an effective consumer education effort as part of the transition to competition.[52] And we should expect third-party rating and education services to arise as well, just as many such services have arisen for comparing credit card offers and other financial services.

Throughout all these steps, policymakers should keep in mind that efficient price signals emerge from well-functioning markets. A key here is preparing for dramatic swings in prices and the rise and fall of many electric retail companies. This is the normal process of market competition that reveals efficient prices. It is often compared to the biological process of evolution. The messy lives and deaths of companies represent the same idea as "survival of the fittest."

In market systems, the survival test indicates how well companies care for consumers. Attempts by regulators to soften the blows of competition by aiding companies can distort the incentives that companies have to serve consumers. The emergence of negative prices because of the federal production tax credit for wind energy serves as one example. In lieu of giving companies support, if there is an intense demand for such aid because of the turbulence in the electricity market, a better system would provide direct aid to consumers. Consumers can then choose among companies, picking what suits them best.

Texas's electricity market is an example of the potential for a greater reliance on network governance in place of monopoly regulation. It exemplifies the insights of institutionalists and network thinkers such as Elinor Ostrom. Fundamentally, it reveals that many states rely on a monopoly system despite promising opportunities for a reliance on institutions and networks that emphasize individual choice in a market. As in Texas, there is an opportunity for policymakers to move from a world where there is one choice into a world where consumers can choose from as many as 200 different plans.

Divisive Cases of Regulating Products and Services

CHAPTER 15

Net Neutrality: Internet Regulation and the Plans to Bring It Back

Ted Bolema

Net neutrality is a term like *pro-choice* or *right to work* that sounds uncontroversial but is used by its proponents to refer to a specific and highly contentious policy. This chapter defines *net neutrality* as the policy adopted by the Federal Communications Commission (FCC) majority in its 2015 rule titled "Protecting and Promoting the Open Internet" (hereinafter referred to as the 2015 Open Internet order) to describe the regulatory policy followed by the FCC in the Open Internet Order before it was repealed in 2017.[1] For the brief time the FCC's net neutrality regulation was in effect, it was applied unevenly, it prohibited conduct that could be beneficial to internet users, and it suppressed capital investment needed to support growth in a dynamic industry. Since the repeal of net neutrality regulation in 2017, we have seen increases in internet speeds, capital investment, and access to wireless cell sites.

Banning conduct and increasing regulatory oversight of conduct in the telecommunications sector is the wrong approach. The better regulatory response to the concerns that net neutrality was supposed to address is to promote faster and easier access to the internet through clear rules that embrace vigorous competition on the internet. If Congress will take the lead and clarify how internet access is to be regulated, or not regulated, then infrastructure investments can be planned knowing the layout of the playing field, and competition among providers can continue to drive new technological advances and growth of the U.S. economy.

A Brief History of Internet Regulation

The FCC is an independent federal agency that regulates interstate and international communications by radio, television, wire, satellite, and cable delivery. The FCC is led by five commissioners who are appointed by the president and approved by the Senate. Typically (and at all times that are relevant for this chapter), three of the commissioners are from the president's party and two are chosen by the leader of the other party in the Senate.

The FCC was created by the Communications Act of 1934, which Congress enacted to impose regulatory control over perceived monopolies in communications services. The original regulatory structure is still largely intact, even though competition concerns raised by today's broadband, digital, and wireless technologies are far different from the regulatory issues of nearly a century ago. The Communications Act of 1934 draws a distinction between Title I "information services" and Title II "telecommunications services." Title I information services are regulated lightly, if at all, while Title II telecommunications services may be subject to the same public utility–style regulation that the FCC used to regulate landline telephone service for much of the past century.

The internet was first launched in 1969, but until the 1990s traffic was fairly limited and relatively few people were using it. When regulators started to pay attention to the internet, internet service providers were classified as Title I information services, which allowed the internet to develop and thrive with relatively little regulatory oversight. That did not mean, however, that the internet was the unregulated Wild West. Instead, until 2015 the Federal Trade Commission, state attorneys general, and other state and federal consumer protection agencies had the same authority over internet service providers that they have over most other businesses.

During President Obama's administration, the FCC commissioners appointed as Democrats began to question whether more regulatory oversight was needed, while the commissioners appointed as Republicans generally resisted increased regulation of the internet. In 2010, the FCC, by a 3–2 party-line vote, promulgated the first version of the net neutrality regulation.[2] Internet service providers challenged this regulation, which was struck down by the DC Circuit Court of Appeals in its 2014 *Verizon v. FCC* decision.[3]

In *Verizon v. FCC*, the court held that the FCC did not have the authority to impose its 2010 version of net neutrality regulation under Title I, but would have that authority if the FCC reclassified internet service providers as Title II telecommunications services. The FCC majority at the time got the message, and by a 3–2 party-line vote promulgated a revised rule—the 2015 Open Internet order—to reclassify internet service providers as telecommunications services under Title II and impose its concept of "net neutrality."[4]

In 2017, soon after taking office, President Trump appointed a Republican replacement for an outgoing Democratic FCC commissioner. In December 2017, the FCC, with four holdover commissioners and the one new commissioner, voted again along party lines to promulgate the "Restoring Internet Freedom" order,[5] which largely undid the net neutrality regulations of the Open Internet order and restored internet service providers to their previous status as Tile I information services. The majority in favor of deregulation may only last, however, until the first commissioner vacancy following the 2020 election. Net neutrality regulation was imposed by a 3–2 vote in 2015, and it could be imposed again in 2021 with the change of a single commissioner.

Net Neutrality Regulation under the FCC's 2015 Open Internet Order

The term *net neutrality* is not well defined, and the lack of clarity about what is meant by net neutrality causes a great deal of confusion in policy debates. For the purposes of this chapter, *net neutrality* will be defined as the regulatory policy toward internet service providers found in the 2015 Open Internet order.

The 2015 Open Internet order divides the internet marketplace into internet service providers (ISPs), to be regulated under Title II, and "edge providers," which remain under Title I. The terminology used by the FCC majority indicates these commissioners' view that ISPs are looking to extort punitive rents from edge providers that can't fight back without the protection of the FCC. But edge providers are hardly fringe players on the internet—they are anyone that provides content on the internet, including Google and Amazon, the two largest companies in the world by market capitalization.[6] ISPs include wireless carriers such as AT&T and Verizon and cable companies such as Comcast, Cox, and Spectrum. These ISPs are substantial companies, but nowhere near the size of some of the edge providers.

The Open Internet order's analysis of why its net neutrality regulation was needed was based on what the FCC called the "virtuous cycle" theory. The FCC majority did not offer very much explanation in the Open Internet order for its conclusion that the virtuous cycle theory would lead to ISPs choking off demand for the very service they offer:

> The key insight of the virtuous cycle is that broadband providers have both the incentive and the ability to act as gatekeepers standing between edge providers and consumers. As gatekeepers, they can block access altogether; they can target competitors, including competitors to their own video services; and they can extract unfair tolls. Such conduct would, as the [Federal Communications] Commission concluded in 2010, "reduce the rate of innovation at the edge and, in turn, the likely rate of improvements to network infrastructure." In other words, when a broadband provider acts as a gatekeeper, it actually chokes consumer demand for the very broadband product it can supply.[7]

The FCC majority then justified banning certain conduct by internet service providers using a "bright-line" approach:

> The record in this proceeding reveals that three practices in particular demonstrably harm the open Internet: blocking, throttling, and paid prioritization. . . . [W]e find each of these

practices is inherently unjust and unreasonable, in violation of section 201(b) of the [Communications] Act [of 1934], and that these practices threaten the virtuous cycle of innovation and investment that the Commission intends to protect under its obligation and authority to take steps to promote broadband deployment under section 706 of the 1996 [Telecommunications] Act. We accordingly adopt bright-line rules banning blocking, throttling, and paid prioritization by providers of both fixed and mobile broadband Internet access service.[8]

The Open Internet order further described its three specific regulatory prohibitions:

No Blocking. Consumers who subscribe to a retail broadband Internet access service must get what they have paid for—access to all (lawful) destinations on the Internet. This essential and well-accepted principle has long been a tenet of Commission policy, stretching back to its landmark decision in Carterfone, which protected a customer's right to connect a telephone to the monopoly telephone network. . . .

No Throttling. The 2010 open Internet rule against blocking contained an ancillary prohibition against the degradation of lawful content, applications, services, and devices, on the ground that such degradation would be tantamount to blocking. . . . A person engaged in the provision of broadband Internet access service, insofar as such person is so engaged, shall not impair or degrade lawful Internet traffic on the basis of Internet content, application, or service, or use of a non-harmful device, subject to reasonable network management. . . .

No Paid Prioritization. Paid prioritization occurs when a broadband provider accepts payment (monetary or otherwise) to manage its network in a way that benefits particular content, applications, services, or devices. To protect against "fast lanes," this Order adopts a rule that establishes that: A person engaged in the provision of broadband Internet access service, insofar as such person is so engaged, shall not engage in paid prioritization.[9]

The Open Internet order had several other effects that are also important, but will not be analyzed in detail here. First, by classifying broadband providers as Title II telecommunications services, the Open Internet order effectively stripped the Federal Trade Commission of jurisdiction over broadband ISP practices that are potentially harmful to consumers, including practices affecting online privacy.[10] Second, the Open Internet order created an uneven playing field between ISPs and edge providers by treating their relationship as predominantly that of suppliers and users of internet access, when in fact regulated ISPs and unregulated edge providers are direct competitors in many markets.[11] Third, the Open Internet order contained a "general conduct standard," which was a catch-all provision that allowed the FCC to sanction almost any conduct that three commissioners deem undesirable.[12]

Problems with the Economic Analysis in the 2015 Open Internet Order

The 2015 FCC majority, applying its virtuous cycle theory, conjectured three ways in which ISPs might benefit from throttling, blocking, and paid prioritization: (1) ISPs could avoid the cost of making new investments, (2) they could charge more for access with capacity restricted by the lack of new investments, and (3) they could further enhance their revenues by making "slow lane" traffic less attractive, forcing content providers to move their content to "fast lanes" where the ISPs would charge extra for better service. The FCC majority argued that the 2015 Open Internet order's three bright-line prohibitions, when combined with the general conduct standard in the order, would take away broadband providers' incentives to game the system and encourage them to invest more in broadband infrastructure.

One obvious concern with the Open Internet order's analysis is that there is very little evidence that any of the allegedly harmful conduct by ISPs was actually occurring under Title I regulatory oversight. Then Commissioner Ajit Pai (he is now FCC chairman) pointed this out in his dissent to the Open Internet order:

> The Order ominously claims that "threats to Internet openness remain today," that broadband providers "hold all the tools necessary to deceive consumers, degrade content or disfavor the content that they don't like," and that the FCC continues "to hear concerns about other broadband provider practices involving blocking or degrading third-party applications." The evidence of these continuing threats? There is none; it's all anecdote, hypothesis, and hysteria. A small ISP in North Carolina allegedly blocked VoIP calls a decade ago. Comcast capped BitTorrent traffic to ease upload congestion eight years ago. Apple introduced FaceTime over Wi-Fi first, cellular networks later. Examples this picayune and stale aren't enough to tell a coherent story about net neutrality. The bogeyman never had it so easy. . . . One would think that a broken Internet marketplace would be rife with anticompetitive examples. But the agency doesn't list them. And it's not for a lack of effort.[13]

Apart from the lack of evidence of actual harm from any existing internet practices, the FCC's theory is not based on any conventional analysis of market power. Instead, the FCC based the Open Internet order's rules on the specious "gatekeeper" concept, which in essence is an assertion by the FCC majority that customers have a unique relationship with ISPs that gives ISPs monopoly power over them. Thus, the FCC extended Title II to ISPs with only a few subscribers and zero market power:

> This Order need not conclude that any specific market power exists in the hands of one or more broadband providers in order to create and enforce these rules. Thus, these rules do not address, and are not designed to deal with, the acquisition or maintenance of market power or its abuse, real or potential.[14]

The 2015 FCC majority was arguing that all ISPs are "terminating access monopolists" because they are the gatekeepers to the internet and because the cost of switching providers is so high for users. Even if those claims were true, a better response than imposing a sweeping regulatory structure that would discourage future competition, would rather be to address the specific anticompetitive harm the FCC claimed to have identified.[15] Instead, the FCC created the very problem that it was supposed to fix—except that it effectively made the FCC the internet access gatekeeper, injecting itself into ISPs' decisions to innovate, interconnect, and invest.[16]

Profits based on taking advantage of leverage from high market shares in a dynamic market are not sustainable because they attract new entry and investment by competitors. Such increases in competition should be encouraged, because competition defeats the incentive to restrict capacity described by the virtuous cycle theory, and also brings new firms into the market that can be the source of new innovation. But that is not what the Open Internet order did, as Commissioner Ajit Pai pointed out in his dissent:

> And yet, literally nothing in this Order will promote competition among Internet service providers. To the contrary, reclassifying broadband, applying the bulk of Title II rules, and half-heartedly forbearing from the rest "for now" will drive smaller competitors out of business and leave the rest in regulatory vassalage. Monopoly rules designed for the monopoly era will inevitably move us in the direction of a monopoly.[17]

One of the bright-line bans imposed by the Open Internet order is particularly problematic. The two relatively uncontroversial bright-line bans concern the blocking of traffic based on content and the "throttling," or slowing, of traffic based on content. While it might be argued that these bans were mostly harmless and contain qualifying language that should prevent the worst misapplications by regulators, they are unnecessary if the ISP market is reasonably competitive. But the rubber meets the road with the ban on paid prioritization arrangements, by which the FCC tried to prevent ISPs from charging for priority access.

Consumers Benefit from Paid Prioritization in Many Markets

Paid prioritization is used in many markets, regulated and unregulated. It is striking how common the practice is, and how widely accepted different forms of paid prioritization have become in diverse markets. Directly contradicting what the FCC's virtuous cycle theory predicts, existing paid prioritization arrangements do not lead to firms trying to choke off demand for their products. Instead, they consistently lead to more investment and more choices that benefit customers.

Another federal agency, the US Postal Service, makes extensive use of its own fast lanes and slow lanes for customers. Customers can pay for various forms of expedited delivery for packages and mail, or they can pay regular postage or bulk rates for mail that will be delivered on a slower schedule. FedEx and other private delivery services offer similar expedited "fast lane" schedules, but—contrary to the virtuous cycle theory—that has not given them the incentive to slow down deliveries of packages for customers who do not pay extra for higher-priority deliveries.[18]

Many states now offer actual "fast lanes" on highways, for a toll, as a way of attracting investment for highway projects. For example, Virginia has used the optional toll system to attract private investment for highway construction, and is currently relying on new private investment to expand the toll network to a stretch of highway on Interstate 395 going into the District of Columbia. Terry McAuliffe, Virginia's former Democratic governor, touted this expansion as "the latest step in our ongoing effort to move more people and provide more travel choices in one of the most congested corridors in the country."[19] Commuters willing to pay for a faster trip now have the option to do so. Even drivers who do not pay the toll stand to benefit from the private investment in and expansion of the highway, which reduces congestion in the nontoll lanes while giving them the option to use the faster toll lanes when they wish to use them.[20]

One paid prioritization practice that has been extensively analyzed over many years by the US antitrust agencies is the usage of slotting allowances at grocery stores, bookstores, and other retailers.[21] A supplier seeking to sell its merchandise at a retailer may agree to pay a slotting allowance in order to have its products placed on the most favorable shelf space, while other suppliers may be willing to accept less favorable shelf space. The practice of paying for favorable slotting may be an effective strategy for introducing new products that would otherwise require more spending on advertising and other forms of marketing. Former Commissioner Joshua D. Wright of the Federal Trade Commission, in his review of the economic effects of slotting allowances, finds that the practice generally benefits consumers:

> My results show that slotting contracts are primarily associated with brand-shifting of sales within a product category, but not increases in category level prices or a reduction in category output or variety. To the extent that slotting contract revenue is passed on to consumers in competitive retail markets, an assumption generally warranted in the grocery retail industry, the results here imply that slotting contract competition is likely to benefit consumers. In sum, my findings are inconsistent with anticompetitive theories and, in practice, demonstrate that such agreements are likely procompetitive and consistent with the promotional services theory.[22]

In a wide range of markets, customers have shown they are willing to voluntarily enter into paid prioritization arrangements, and usually are better off for it. For example, airlines charge passengers extra for a variety of enhanced services, including first-class seats, priority boarding, seats with extra leg room, and seats near the front of the airplane. The airlines' goal is not to exclude passengers who do not pay for these services or force them to pay higher fares. In fact, the opposite effect is much more likely. Regular air travelers can see that airlines try to fill as many seats as they can, and even offer "economy" fares that may not include any choice of seat, for example.

The customers who do not pay extra for better airline service are unlikely to be made worse off by the presence of other passengers on the plane who choose to pay extra for better service. Instead, it is more likely that passengers who pay less are better off if the airline chooses to offer more flights over more routes to attract customers willing to pay extra, and then offers lower fares to fill the remaining seats on those flights. Put another way, even though many customers today may feel as if they are being nickeled-and-dimed by airlines because of the fees associated with nearly every aspect of flying, forcing airlines to charge the same fares to everyone will almost certainly lead to fewer flights and routes, as well as to less investment for increasing capacity, which will raise fares and reduce choices for the most cost-conscious customers, leaving those customers worse off as a result.

Similarly, sports stadiums provide luxury boxes and favorable seating for higher prices, but that does not mean that the stadium operators want to exclude other customers who are unwilling to pay for premium seating or amenities, nor that they want to build smaller stadiums to restrict the supply of seats in order to drive up prices. Having some customers pay extra for better seats generates revenue that may be used to upgrade the stadium, to offer extra amenities to all customers, or to attract free agent professional players to make the home team more competitive—all of which may make games more enjoyable for all fans, even the ones paying the least.

These and other variations on paid prioritization have developed over time as suppliers, distributors, and customers have experimented in the market to find the arrangements that provide the greatest benefits. So long as markets are reasonably competitive, paid prioritization arrangements that try to take advantage of other parties will not survive for long, because the parties at a disadvantage can find alternative arrangements.

When Paid Prioritization May Be Necessary for Attracting Investment

Some specialized services for dedicated users require a high level of internet speed and reliability. The benefits of video phone calls and video streams from Netflix, for example, are reduced when they are delayed by slow buffering. Other internet uses do not necessarily require a prioritized internet connection. Email traffic, most file downloading, and many other uses lose little of their value if their transmission is delayed somewhat in a slow lane, although too long of a delay could diminish their value.

Paid prioritization offers benefits both to services that are sensitive to delays and to services that are not. Those that pay more are better off because they receive better quality service, in the same way that some people shipping packages are willing to pay extra for priority mail services that arrive faster, while others will not see enough benefit from avoiding delays to justify paying more.

Many future web applications are unlikely to develop if their developers cannot be assured that they will have access to fast and stable internet connections. One real-world example is Aira, a company that is providing smart glasses for people with vision impairments. Aira helps the visually impaired "see" by employing the capabilities of emerging 5G networks. Its customers receive instant wireless access to visual information through smart glasses, augmented reality, machine learning, geolocation, sensors, and trained human agents. Aira's customers can use their glasses to navigate city streets and airports, review printed material, catch public transportation, and get real-time assistance for job applications, shopping, and travel. But Aira glasses won't work without a robust network with dependable connectivity.[23]

Autonomous vehicles, interactive e-learning, and telemedicine are other examples of applications in the early stages of development. Investors may be unwilling to take the risk of investing in these applications if they cannot be assured of reliable prioritized broadband connections. For example, telemedicine is an emerging private application that may require prioritization in order to become widely available and accepted. Telesurgery is already allowing specialized surgeons in one location to operate on patients in completely different locations. The emerging market for telesurgery can give patients in small hospitals or remote areas access to highly skilled specialists who otherwise would not serve those areas. According to a medical journal article,

The ultimate goal of telerobotic surgery is to replicate the normal process of surgery from a distance. The success of telesurgery (or any aspect of telemedicine for that matter) depends largely on how faithfully and without incident remote activities duplicate their on-site equivalents. Because of its direct impact on surgeon performance, a frequent metric in real-time telesurgery research is that of system delay.[24]

The FCC's prohibition of paid prioritization may well prevent these services from developing, as well as other new applications that no one is yet anticipating. Their loss is difficult to measure because we cannot easily anticipate what will never happen.

Banning Paid Prioritization Doesn't Advance the FCC's Stated Objectives

Even if it were established that ISPs try to use paid prioritization in ways that do not benefit users, a sweeping regulatory ban on paid prioritization creates two problems that are likely to be worse than the problem the regulation is intended to address. First, such a ban prevents the paid prioritization arrangements that benefit final customers, who may want to pay extra for the reliability needed for their applications. Second, the ban on paid prioritization limits the return on investment by ISPs, so that they will invest less in situations where they do not have market power and protection from new entry.

The claim by the 2015 FCC majority that ISPs' status as "terminating access monopolists" requires the FCC to ban paid prioritization arrangements is inconsistent with the usual economic analysis of how firms with monopoly power behave. Basic economic analysis tells us that if ISPs are seeking to abuse whatever monopoly power they might have, they would be better off raising prices for internet access for all their customers until they reach the monopoly price rather than creating a new pricing arrangement that would only collect extra revenues from the minority of customers that need the priority access.

While the 2015 Open Internet order's ban on paid prioritization was framed as protecting consumers, it is worth asking whether consumers really want this protection. As the examples in the previous section show, a ban on paying for faster internet service is aimed at preventing internet users from paying for higher-quality or faster service. People choose to pay for better service all the time in many different markets, and rarely is that considered controversial or exploitative of the customers who want better service.

To the extent that there are any remaining concerns about broadband providers having market power and abusing it, these concerns should be addressed in a more closely tailored way to resolve the specific harm that arises from clearly anticompetitive instances of paid priority. Tailored responses used to address anticompetitive harms and inefficiencies in other industries, including antitrust laws, consumer protection laws, and minimum quality standards, may be sufficient to prevent the harms that could plausibly result from paid prioritization by broadband providers. More targeted approaches are less likely to destroy the real benefits and efficiencies that can be achieved using voluntary contracting arrangements, and less likely to discourage investment for the applications and new entrants that may require fast and reliable broadband connections.

Importance of Telecommunications Investment to the US Economy

The broadcast and telecommunications sector of the US economy is an important part of the US economy in and of itself, accounting for 2.1 percent of the US GDP in 2018.[25] The impact of telecommunications investment spreads far beyond the telecommunications sector, affecting many other sectors of the economy. Telecommunications are used by firms in other sectors as a crucial part of their production process, for marketing their products, for placing orders, and for credit validation to facilitate business transactions. Innovative new telecommunications products are emerging, building on the facilities created from past investment. As Chairman Pai points out, "Broadband has also made many sectors of the economy more productive, from shipping to energy. And it has given birth to entirely new industries, like the mobile apps economy, telemedicine, online education, and the nascent Internet of Things."[26]

Figure 1. Increase in Telecommunications Regulatory Restrictions

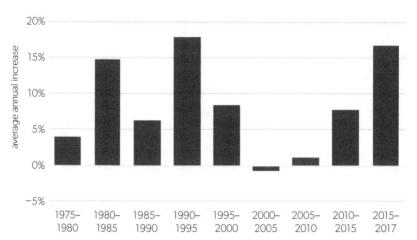

Source: RegData for three-digit North American Industry Classification System code 517: Telecommunications. Patrick A. McLaughlin and Oliver Sherouse, RegData US 3.0 Daily (data set), QuantGov, Mercatus Center at George Mason University, 2017.

The US telecommunications sector has experienced ongoing and consistent increases in regulation over time, except for about a decade where the regulatory accumulation leveled off from approximately 2000 to 2010. Figure 1 shows the accumulation of federal telecommunications regulations, using the RegData database at the three-digit level of the North American Industry Classification System (NAICS).[27] NAICS category 517 is for the telecommunications industry, and it includes wired and wireless telephone and internet carriers, including voice over internet protocols, cable and satellite distribution services, and telecommunications reselling services.

Federal regulatory restrictions have increased steadily in the US telecommunications sector, other than a decrease in 2000-2005, with an acceleration of new regulation additions after 2010. These increases represent net changes in the number of federal restrictions in place in the different time periods—that is, they consider both regulations that are added and regulations that are removed. Only changes in federal regulation are noted, however; regulatory burdens created at the state or local level are not included. As regulations are added, the amount of interaction between regulations increases, so the negative effect of regulatory accumulation results in a compounding effect as new regulations continue to accumulate.[28]

Regulatory controls that have outlived their intended purposes may be misapplied in ways that deprive the US economy of the benefits of new competition, greater innovation, and new investment that would otherwise lead to greater benefits for American customers. Even regulations that were promoted as ways to encourage investment by new firms can have the opposite effect. Michał Grajek and Lars-Hendrik Röller, economics professors at the European School of Management and Technology in Berlin, find that the European Union's open-access approach discourages entrants' individual investment even as new entry increases. They conclude, "Because facilities-based entry is likely to require substantial firm-level investment, our results are consistent with the view that the regulatory framework in Europe fails to deliver effective incentives to move toward facilities-based competition."[29]

Weak growth in the telecommunications sector is a problem not only for telecommunications firms, but also for firms and entrepreneurs throughout the economy that depend on telecommunications in their businesses and for their own innovation. As Chairman Pai explained,

> Today, with a powerful plan and a broadband connection, you can raise capital, start a business, immediately reach customers worldwide, and disrupt entire industries. Never before in history has there been such opportunity for entrepreneurs with drive and determination to transcend their individual circumstances and transform their world.
>
> And achieving this success does not require you to move to Silicon Valley or Stockholm or Seoul any other tech hub around the world. There are opportunities in every city in every corner of the world, *if*—and this is a big if—you have high-speed access to the Internet.[30]

Chairman Pai further explained how his concern about the 2015 Open Internet order's impact on investment was an important consideration when he sought to have the order repealed:

The FCC decided to apply last-century, utility-style regulation to today's broadband networks. Rules developed to tame a 1930s monopoly were imported into the 21st century to regulate the Internet. This reversal wasn't necessary to solve any problem; we were not living in a digital dystopia. The policies of the Clinton Administration, the Bush Administration, and the first term of the Obama Administration had produced both a free and open Internet *and* strong incentives for private investment in broadband infrastructure.

Two years later, it has become evident that the FCC made a mistake. Our new approach injected tremendous uncertainty into the broadband market. And uncertainty is the enemy of growth. After the FCC embraced utility-style regulation, the United States experienced the first-ever decline in broadband investment outside of a recession. In fact, broadband investment remains lower today [in early 2017] than it was when the FCC changed course in 2015.[31]

Pai was referring to the estimate by Hal Singer, a senior fellow at the Progressive Policy Institute, of a decline in domestic broadband capital expenditures of $3.6 billion in 2016, or 5.6 percent, relative to 2014 levels.[32] As shown in figure 2, the only two years in which US broadband investment has declined were 2015 and 2016, which were while the Open Internet order was in effect. When it became clear in 2017 that the FCC intended to undo the net neutrality regulations of the Open Internet order, capital investment in broadband internet capacity began to recover, and reached a record level in 2018 compared to recent years.

These trends are continuing, as Chairman Pai pointed out in October of 2020 when he described the increase in internet speeds, investment, and access to wireless cell sites since 2017:

And what's been the result [following the *Restoring Internet Freedom* order]? The Internet has remained free and open. And it's stronger than ever. Millions more Americans have access to the Internet today than in 2017. In 2018 and then again in 2019, the United States set records for annual fiber deployment, and we've seem network investment hit levels that our nation hadn't seen in over a decade. In fact, since we adopted the *Restoring Internet Freedom Order*, average download speeds for fixed broadband in the United States have doubled, increasing by over 99% (so much for getting the Internet one word as a time). And in 2018 and 2019, we added over 72,000 wireless cell sites in the United States, after adding fewer than 20,000 in the prior four years.

The potential for net neutrality regulation being readopted and then retracted has a cost, however, and one that is difficult to measure. Uncertainty about what the future regulatory environment will be like creates business uncertainty. Singer explained the effects of this uncertainty in 2013, as the FCC was beginning to consider how to replace the 2010 version of net neutrality regulation that was about to be struck down in court:

> ISPs will likely hedge against this new regulatory risk by conserving cash or paying out dividends rather than investing in continued network improvements. This reduction is not academic: In the few months since the [draft] Open Internet order was released, several small ISPs announced their intention to abandon investment plans due to heightened uncertainty injected by the reclassification.[33]

The emergence of cross-platform competition for data, video, and voice services presents a particular problem for accumulated telecommunications regulations. The old regulatory structures did not anticipate this competitive development enabled by technological advances and the digital revolution. The result is an uneven application of regulation, which discourages investment by the platforms most restricted by regulation. This situation also potentially weakens the incentive for the less-regulated platforms to invest, because they may be insulated from cross-platform competition.

Figure 2. US Broadband Investment by Year

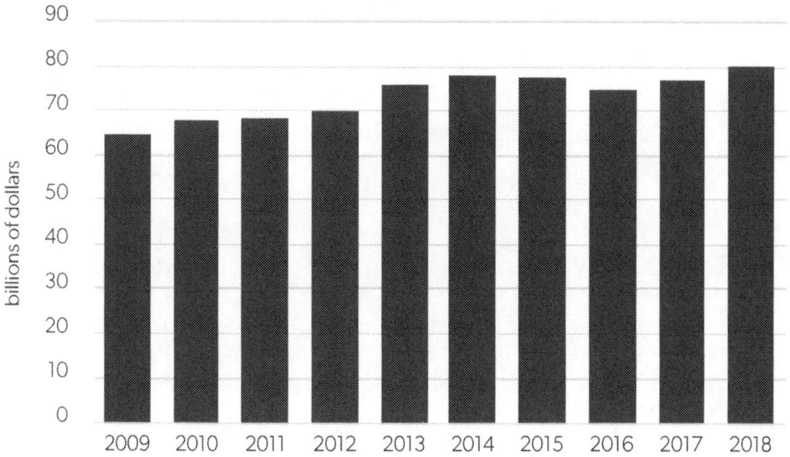

Source: USTelecom, "USTelecom Industry Metrics and Trends 2020," February 2020, https://www.ustelecom.org/wp-content/uploads/2020/02/USTelecom-State-of-Industry-2020.pdf.

Even when regulatory compliance compels more investment spending, complying will alter the mix of regulations, which introduces distortions that may not produce new or improved goods and services that consumers value more than those they had to give up.[34] These types of investments crowd out beneficial investment activity in favor of investments offering fewer benefits.[35]

Professor Richard A. Epstein of the New York University School of Law summarizes the importance of investment in telecommunications:

> The adjudication with respect to our telecommunications systems in the next generation will determine, for better or for worse, whether or not this nation, or other nations, will maintain its energetic drive. Every time tough regulations apply to networks, content providers will benefit to some extent in the short run but at the cost of retarding additional investment in the network itself. Voluntary arrangements are still the best way to determine the optimal way to structure interactions between content providers and carriers outside the control of the regulatory state. In the short term,

the battle over the Internet may well look like some form of second-best monopolistic competition. Nonetheless, in the long run, allowing technology to be free from regulation will make the system both more competitive and more efficient. The weight of the evidence supports light-handed regulation.[36]

The Repeal of Net Neutrality and How It Might Return

The FCC in December 2017 repealed the net neutrality regulations of the 2015 Open Internet order when it issued its Restoring Internet Freedom order.[37] This reversal was made possible by the change of one FCC commissioner, giving the FCC a 3–2 majority for the party-line vote to repeal.

The Restoring Internet Freedom order, like nearly every other major order by the FCC, was followed by legal challenges. In 2019, the DC Circuit's decision in *Mozilla v. FCC* held that the FCC had acted within its legal authority to reclassify ISP services from Title II telecommunications services to Title I information services.[38] But the *Mozilla* decision was not a complete win for the FCC. The DC Circuit pushed back on several specific provisions in the Restoring Internet Freedom order that were not specific to a repeal of the Open Internet order. In particular, the DC Circuit forced the FCC to make changes that related to internet access for public safety purposes, pole attachments for broadband deployment, and benefit eligibility for low-income households.

Most significantly, the *Mozilla* majority, over the dissent of one judge, struck down a provision in the Restoring Internet Freedom order that would have imposed a blanket preemption on states, preventing them from passing their own net neutrality laws that contravene the FCC's deregulatory policy. The court's majority did acknowledge that the FCC has the power to review state laws individually and preempt those that are inconsistent with clearly articulated FCC policies. Even so, the *Mozilla* decision is likely to lead to years of litigation, and regulatory uncertainty, as states such as California try to impose their own versions of net neutrality.[39]

The repeal of the Open Internet order has also been used as a justification for cities to build and operate their own broadband networks in hopes of achieving certain "net neutrality" outcomes at the local level that supposedly will comply with net neutrality regulations. For example, Mark Howell, the chief information officer for Concord, Massachusetts, claimed in a *Washington Post* op-ed that the Concord municipal broadband utility is providing a road map for "saving net neutrality."[40] A report by the American Civil Liberties Union (ACLU) claims that "states, cities, towns, and counties should take matters into their own hands by creating publicly owned services that do honor those [net neutrality] values and can help ensure an open internet."[41]

The ACLU report claims that government-run broadband networks will give more people access to the internet and will promote the "net neutrality" policies the ACLU favors. But then the ACLU goes even further, suggesting that First Amendment rights may be violated unless municipal governments operate their own communications networks.[42]

Thus, the ACLU, despite its long and distinguished history of protecting First Amendment free speech rights against government infringement, is now advocating for government ownership and operation of communications networks as a means of protecting free speech, under the beguiling guise of net neutrality. The ACLU report implicitly assumes that local governments can be trusted with this new power to be arbiters of what speech is permissible on the internet. But even leaving aside the issue of giving governments more control over communications networks, government-run broadband providers in the United States have a troubling history of blocking or otherwise restricting online content and failing to respect their users' privacy concerns.[43]

Policy Reform for Preserving and Promoting a Fast and Open Internet

Ultimately, the uncertainty about the status of internet freedom versus regulation in the name of net neutrality reflects a failure on Congress's part to give clear guidance to the regulatory agency. Congress should end the FCC's back-and-forth policy regarding net neutrality with legislation clarifying the issues the FCC has been addressing.

First, rather than leaving the FCC to decide whether to fit ISPs into the Title I or Title II regulatory boxes, Congress should declare what the regulatory policy toward ISPs should be. Ideally, Congress should declare that ISPs should be regulated as they have been—as Title I information services. Then Representative (now Senator) Marsha Blackburn of Tennessee introduced such a bill in 2017. As a compromise, Congress might consider a bill that would retain the ban on the blocking and throttling of internet traffic from the Open Internet order. These bans, while unnecessary in a reasonably competitive market where internet users can switch providers, might allow for a bipartisan agreement by acknowledging some of the concerns raised by net neutrality proponents but also permitting new technologies and applications that can only develop if paid prioritization is tolerated.

Second, Congress should declare under the Commerce Clause of the US Constitution a single national regulatory policy toward ISPs and preclude states from passing their own patchwork of different regulatory regimes. The internet allows people anywhere in the country to interact, with little regard for state borders. Requiring ISPs, edge providers, or anyone else doing business on the internet to keep track of different and potentially conflicting state regulatory requirements can only hold back the growth of exciting new markets and technologies that rely on internet access.[44]

Alternatively, if Congress does not act either to clarify its intended regulatory policy toward ISPs or to preempt state regulation in the name of net neutrality, the FCC might seek a bipartisan consensus among FCC commissioners to issue a net neutrality–type regulation that bans throttling and blocking but not paid prioritization. Such a regulation might do little harm and could help ward off the patchwork of state and local regulations that could replace federal regulations.

Third, Congress, as well as the FCC acting according to its power delegated from Congress, should resist the temptation to impose new regulation on the internet and in closely related telecommunications markets. While some eras (as shown in figure 1) are characterized by great regulatory accumulation and others by little or no accumulation, the overall direction has been toward a greater regulatory burden. Some of these regulations are now outdated owing to changes in markets and technologies. Other regulations, like the net neutrality regulations of the 2015 Open Internet order, are overly broad and prescriptive, or are not designed to address anticompetitive harms. It is no coincidence that the era with the least accumulation of new regulation—from 1995 to 2010—was also the era in which the internet and e-commerce emerged and new commerce thrived in the new markets created by rapid growth in internet access in the United States.

Conclusion

Internet service is better than ever since the repeal of the FCC's net neutrality policy at the end of 2017. Investment in internet infrastructure, which had slowed while net neutrality was in effect, grew in the first year of the order's repeal. In any event, the outcomes the FCC claimed to be pursuing with the Open Internet order can be better achieved by promoting competition among internet service providers than by regulation that discourages competition and deprives internet users of choices among providers and of applications that can only work with reliable access.

The partisan politics surrounding net neutrality regulations are hard to escape. The FCC's position on net neutrality will likely continue to seesaw each time the balance of power changes at the agency—which happens each time the presidency switches parties. But solutions are available if Congress acts to adopt a national policy toward internet regulation, one that will embrace vigorous competition among providers and guide both the FCC and state regulatory policies.

Unintended Consequences of Regulating Private School Choice Programs: A Review of the Evidence

Corey A. DeAngelis and Lindsey M. Burke[1]

The number of private school choice options has continued to grow ever since 1990, when the first modern-day school choice program in the United States was established in Milwaukee. Today, 65 private school choice programs are in operation in 29 states, the District of Columbia, and Puerto Rico. These include vouchers, tax credit scholarships, and education savings accounts.[2] During the Trump administration, officials put a renewed spotlight on school choice using the bully pulpit to make the case for its efficacy, signing into law a reauthorization of the DC Opportunity Scholarship Program, and in its push for a federal tax credit scholarship program. Increased interest in, and availability of, private school choice programs raises questions about the extent to which these programs will generate a genuine variety of education options for families. Growth in school choice programs has also generated a debate about the extent to which these programs should be regulated, the form regulations should take, and whether regulations increase or impede the quantity and quality of education options available to families.

Private school choice programs enable families to move from public schools to private schools and to access other education products and services. Many families do so because they are looking for something not offered in the public-school sector, and believe that the private-education sector offers something different that will better suit the needs of their child. Government regulations, in the form of oversight provided through mechanisms such as state standardized testing, are appropriate for providing accountability in the *public* sector, since public schools are accountable to government officials and are less-directly accountable to parents.[3] But government regulations designed to hold the public system accountable are inappropriate for a system of private education, which is supposed to offer something different to families than the public system, and which is held to an arguably higher form of accountability: the market.[4] Families that are unhappy with any element of their child's private school can vote with their feet and leave—an exit option that is more difficult for most families to execute in the residentially assigned public school system. Nevertheless, some scholars have made the moral case for government regulation of the *private* sector.

Former Hoover Institution research fellow Tibor Machan argued that there is a fundamental difference between government management and government regulation, contrasting national forests and parks and highways, which are government managed, with food and drug production, car sales, toy production, and so on, which are government regulated, but not managed.[5] Private schooling falls into the latter category: private schools are privately managed and operated, but exist within a patchwork quilt of regulatory environments in the states. Moral cases for government regulation of the private sector have generally taken four forms: (1) Private corporations are chartered by the states in which they reside, and thus the government has a foothold to regulate the behavior of private entities. (2) Market failures—that is, instances when the market "fails to achieve maximum efficiency"—can produce waste.[6] (3) Government regulations are needed to protect individual rights. And (4) there is sometimes judicial inefficiency—as seen, for example, in the adjudication of disputes involving pollution.[7]

Proponents of the regulation (sometimes referred to as accountability) of private school choice programs tend broadly to appeal to these moral arguments for government regulation of private entities. They argue that government "open admissions" regulations are necessary to ensure that private schools participating in school choice programs accept all students who apply, that the government should cap how much tuition a private school can charge so that it will not exceed the voucher amount and families on a scholarship can be guaranteed to afford it; that the government should require accreditation and standardized testing to ensure quality among participating schools. Moreover, proponents of private school choice regulations argue that such regulations are more likely to deter lower-performing schools from participating and therefore to increase the average quality of the private schools that participate.[8]

This chapter examines these arguments, with a particular emphasis on the Louisiana Scholarship Program—the most heavily regulated private school choice program in the country, and the only private school choice program that has produced negative academic outcomes for participants. We begin by looking at the experimental research on the impact of school choice broadly on academic achievement and attainment. Next, we review the literature on the impact of regulations on the quantity and quality of private schools in school choice programs. We conclude with a discussion of implications for federal and state policy.

Background to the Research Literature

We review the literature on the impact of regulations on private school choice programs. Our review strategy was twofold: First we gathered the universe of randomized controlled trial evaluations examining the impact of private school choice on student educational outcomes, including academic achievement and attainment. These randomized controlled trials include 16 studies on student academic achievement, published between 1998 (the first such evaluation ever conducted) and 2019 (the most recent evaluation published). Next we surveyed the correlational and descriptive literature on the impact of regulations on the supply of private schools and their quality, within the context of private school choice programs. We have included quantitative studies (seven studies), which use data to assess the types of schools that do or do not participate in voucher programs, and qualitative studies (eight studies), to understand the types of private schools that elect to participate in choice programs.

As shown in table 1, most evaluations of private school choice programs suggest that school choice indeed leads to higher test scores for students overall or for student subgroups.[9] However, the first experimental evaluation of a voucher program that found that the program had statistically significant negative effects on student test scores came out in 2015.[10] While students using vouchers to attend private schools caught up to their peers academically by the third year,[11] by the fourth (and final) year of the evaluation, large negative effects on math test scores had returned.[12] Specifically, the Louisiana Scholarship Program (LSP) substantially reduced students' math test scores, but did not have a statistically significant negative effect on reading test scores overall, or for any student subgroups, after four years.[13] The effects of the LSP on math scores were less negative for black students than for nonblack students.[14]

Table 1. Effect of Private School Choice on Math and Reading Test Scores

Study	Location	Method	Outcome	Result
Wolf et al., "School Vouchers"	Washington, DC	RCT	reading	positive
Cowen, "School Choice"	Charlotte, NC	RCT	math and reading	positive
Greene, "Effect of School Choice"	Charlotte, NC	RCT	math and reading	positive
Greene, Peterson, and Du, "Effectiveness of School Choice"	Milwaukee	RCT	math and reading	positive
Rouse, "Private School Vouchers"	Milwaukee	RCT	math	positive
Howell et al., "School Vouchers"	Washington, DC	RCT	math and reading	positive
	New York City	RCT	math and reading	null to positive
	Dayton, OH	RCT	math and reading	null to positive
Barnard et al., "Principal Stratification Approach"	New York City	RCT	math	null to positive

Study	Location	Method	Outcome	Result
Jin, Barnard, and Rubin, "Modified General Location Model"	New York City	RCT	math	null to positive
Krueger and Zhu, "Another Look"	New York City	RCT	math and reading	null
Bitler et al., "Distributional Analysis"	New York City	RCT	math and reading	null
Bettinger and Slonim, "Using Experimental Economics"	Toledo, OH	RCT	math	null
Webber et al., *Evaluation*	Washington, DC	RCT	math and reading	null
Mills and Wolf, "Louisiana Scholarship Program"	Louisiana	RCT	math	negative
Abdulkadiroğlu, Pathak, and Walters, "Free to Choose"	Louisiana	RCT	math and reading	negative

* Statistically significant positive effects are detected for subgroups.

Note: RCT = randomized controlled trial. "Positive" means that the study indicates a statistically significant test score benefit of private school choice overall. "Negative" means that the study finds a statistically significant negative effect of private school choice on test scores overall. "Null" indicates that the overall result reported for the outcome is not statistically significant. "Null to positive" means that statistically significant positive effects are detected for subgroups. Research on existing school voucher programs in Indiana and Ohio also found null to negative impacts on the academic achievement outcomes of participating students. These two studies, however, are not included because they are observational and cannot demonstrate that the negative outcomes were caused by voucher program participation.

Sources: Patrick J. Wolf et al., "School Vouchers and Student Outcomes: Experimental Evidence from Washington, DC," *Journal of Policy Analysis and Management* 32, no. 2 (2013): 246–70; Joshua M. Cowen, "School Choice as a Latent Variable: Estimating the 'Complier Average Causal Effect' of Vouchers in Charlotte," *Policy Studies Journal* 36, no. 2 (2008): 301–15; Jay P. Greene, "The Effect of School Choice: An Evaluation of the Charlotte Children's Scholarship Fund Program," *Civic Report* 12 (2000): 1–15; Jay P. Greene, Paul E. Peterson, and Jiangtao Du, "Effectiveness of School Choice: The Milwaukee Experiment," *Education and Urban Society* 31, no. 2 (1999): 190–213; Cecilia Elena Rouse, "Private School Vouchers and Student Achievement: An Evaluation of the Milwaukee Parental Choice Program," *Quarterly Journal of Economics* 113, no. 2 (1998): 553–602; William G. Howell et al., "School Vouchers and Academic Performance: Results from Three Randomized Field Trials," *Journal of Policy Analysis and Management* 21, no. 2 (2002): 191–217; John Barnard et al., "Principal Stratification Approach to Broken Randomized Experiments: A Case Study of School Choice Vouchers in New York City," *Journal of the American Statistical Association* 98, no. 462 (2003): 299–323; Hui Jin, John Barnard, and Donald B. Rubin, "A Modified General Location Model for Noncompliance with Missing Data: Revisiting the New York City School Choice Scholarship Program Using Principal Stratification," *Journal of Educational and Behavioral Statistics* 35, no. 2 (2010): 154–73; Alan B. Krueger and Pei Zhu, "Another Look at the New York City School Voucher Experiment," *American Behavioral Scientist* 47, no. 5 (2004): 658–98; Marianne Bitler et al., "Distributional Analysis in

Educational Evaluation: A Case Study from the New York City Voucher Program," *Journal of Research on Educational Effectiveness* 8, no. 3 (2015): 419–50; Eric Bettinger and Robert Slonim, "Using Experimental Economics to Measure the Effects of a Natural Educational Experiment on Altruism," *Journal of Public Economics* 90, no. 8–9 (2006): 1625–48; Ann Webber et al., *Evaluation of the DC Opportunity Scholarship Program: Impacts Three Years after Students Applied*, NCEE 2019-4006 (National Center for Education Evaluation and Regional Assistance, US Department of Education, 2019); Jonathan N. Mills and Patrick J. Wolf, "The Effects of the Louisiana Scholarship Program on Student Achievement after Four Years" (EDRE Working Paper No. 2019-10, University of Arkansas, Department of Education Reform, 2019); Atila Abdulkadiroğlu, Parag A. Pathak, and Christopher R. Walters, "Free to Choose: Can School Choice Reduce Student Achievement?," *American Economic Journal: Applied Economics* 10, no. 1 (2018): 175–206.

Explanations for the Negative Results

What might explain the LSP's negative effects on student test scores? Although the LSP is not the sole private school choice program to produce negative impacts on student academic achievement, it is the only program for which an experimental evaluation has demonstrated a causal effect. However, it is important to first provide some broader context for the overall evidence (including nonexperimental evaluations) on the impact of private school choice programs on student academic achievement.

Research on existing school voucher programs in Indiana and Ohio also found negative impacts on the academic achievement outcomes of participating students. A matching study (comparing students in Indiana's voucher program to a closely matched sample of their public school peers) found that Indiana's private school voucher program, currently serving some 34,000 students, led to a reduction in math achievement of 15 percent of a standard deviation after the students initially entered the voucher program, but that the students' math performance improved in later years. The researchers found no significant effect on English language arts performance.[15] Notably, the 2017 working paper version of this same evaluation found no effects on math and marginally significant positive effects on reading after four years.[16] This change in results after the peer-review process reinforces our decision to focus on randomized controlled trials rather than matching evaluations. Matching studies are less rigorous and possibly prone to bias introduced by the model specification decisions made by researchers.

A similarly structured matching study examining the impact of the Ohio EdChoice scholarship program on student academic achievement found that students who used a scholarship to attend a private school of choice performed worse in math and English than their matched peers who attended public schools.[17] Although this study found negative achievement effects on student academic achievement, it found positive competitive effects on test scores for students in nearby public schools.

Understanding the research in Indiana and Ohio provides important, but limited, context. Both of these states regulate their private school choice programs, though not to the extent that Louisiana regulates its program. Perhaps not consequently, the percentage of private schools that participate is higher in Ohio and Indiana than in Louisiana.[18] But readers should be cautious in interpreting the findings from Indiana and Ohio, because the existing studies on the impact of these school voucher programs are arguably correlational, and regulations are just one possible explanation for negative effects.

The strongest theories explaining the causal studies showing negative effects—the research concerning Louisiana—have to do with curriculum misalignment and the burdensome regulations on private schools participating in the program. First, there could be a curriculum alignment problem. Private schools have weaker incentives to teach to the test and less experience with the state's preferred curriculum than public schools. That being so, using vouchers to enable students to attend a private school could decrease their standardized test scores without actually reducing their cognitive skills. At the same time, recent empirical evidence suggests that the theory of curricular misalignment has merit. Researchers have found that private schools are more concerned about state standardized testing mandates than requirements to take nationally norm-referenced exams.[19] In addition, a survey experiment has found that state testing mandates largely reduce anticipated participation in voucher programs, while nationally norm-referenced testing mandates have no statistically significant effect.[20] Furthermore, every experimental voucher program evaluation following students for at least three years has found neutral to positive effects on test scores; the only exception is the LSP, which requires private schools to administer the state test.

Second, regulations might be responsible for the negative effects. Private schools participating in the LSP must administer the state standardized test, admit students on a random basis (open-admissions), and accept the voucher funding amount as payment in full (see table 2). The large negative effects of the LSP on math test scores persisted after four years of participation—a period that should have given private schools adequate time to adjust to new students and tests. Some education scholars have argued that the negative effects would have been even worse in Louisiana if not for the program's quality-enhancing regulations—after all, they argued, the highest-quality private schools should be the most likely to not participate in the program regardless of the regulatory burden, because they want to remain exclusive.[21] In these scholars' view, program regulations are more likely to deter lower-quality schools from participating in the program, and therefore increase the average quality of private schools that participate.

On the other hand, lower-quality private schools might be more likely to participate in the program regardless of the regulatory burden, because they are the most desperate for additional enrollment and funding.[22] Higher-quality private schools might be more likely to be deterred by regulations if they can afford to turn down the voucher funding and wish to remain autonomous and specialized. If so, voucher program regulations can be expected to decrease the average quality of private schools that participate. Some scholars have found, for example, that random-admissions mandates and state testing mandates are negatively associated with program participation. A 2020 study leveraged data from the 2015/16 Private School Universe Survey and found that both state testing requirements and open-admissions mandates depressed private school program participation across seven locations.[23]

Both sides of the debate tend to agree that program regulations reduce the quantity of schools that accept voucher students, since regulations are costs associated with participation.[24] Moreover, regulations such as state standardized testing requirements and random-admissions mandates might be particularly costly for the most specialized schools. If matching the unique needs of students to schools affects program success, regulations might reduce the effectiveness of voucher

Table 2. Private School Choice Program Characteristics

Variable	MPCP (Milwaukee)	OSP (Washington, DC)	Ed-Choice (Ohio)	LSP (Louisiana)	CSP (Indiana)	WPCP (Wisconsin)	North Carolina
Date enacted	1990	2004	2005	2008	2011	2013	2013
Average funding relative to public school	67%	46%	41%	54%	47%	67%	46%
Eligibility rate	69%	34%	10%	30%	50%	26%	45%
Private school participation rate (in sample)	92%	63%	39%	28%	44%	15%	50%
Standardized testing requirement	yes	yes	yes	yes	yes	yes	yes
State testing requirement	yes	yes	yes	yes	yes	yes	—
Government accreditation requirement	yes[a]	yes	—	—	yes	yes[a]	yes
Financial reporting requirement	yes	yes	—	yes	—	yes	yes
Copay prohibited	yes[b]	—	yes[c]	yes	—	yes[b]	—
Open-admissions process	yes	—	—	yes	—	yes	—
Teacher requirements	yes	yes	—	—	—	yes	—
Must allow students to opt out of religious programs	yes	—	—	—	—	yes	—

[a] School must be accredited within three years of initial program participation.

[b] Parents of students in grades 9–12 with an income greater than 220 percent of the federal poverty level may be charged additional tuition above the voucher amount.

[c] Copay is prohibited for students from families that are at or below 200 percent of the federal poverty level.

Note: MPCP = Milwaukee Parental Choice Program, WPCP = Wisconsin Parental Choice Program, CSP = Choice Scholarship Program, LSP = Louisiana Scholarship Program, OSP = Opportunity Scholarship Program. Eligibility rate means the percent of families living in the area that have students who are eligible for the program. Private school participation rate means the percentage of private schools participating in the programs. Copay prohibited refers to the practice that a voucher must be accepted as payment-in-full.
Source: Corey A. DeAngelis, "Which Schools Participate? An Analysis of Private School Voucher Program Participation Decisions across Seven Locations" (working paper, 2019), https://ssrn.com/abstract=3309754.

programs simply by reducing the number of specialized options available to families.

Finally, although it doesn't explain the negative effects, the program might improve character skills that are simply not captured by standardized math and reading tests. If so, standardized test scores might not be strong proxies for long-term outcomes such as college enrollment and degree attainment. In fact, two recent reviews of the evidence find that schools' effects on students' test scores often do not predict schools' effects on students' long-term outcomes. The authors of the first study compile all the evidence linking choice schools' effects on test scores and attainment and find that "a school choice program's impact on test scores is a weak predictor of its impact on longer-term outcomes."[25] For example, the study finds that 61 percent of schools' effects on math test scores—and 50 percent of their effects on reading test scores—did not successfully predict their effects on high school graduation. The second study similarly reviewed 11 studies indicating disconnects between private schools' effects on standardized test scores and their effects on long-term outcomes such as crime and college enrollment.[26]

But what does the evidence say? For the first time, we review the empirical evidence on the effects of school choice program regulations. Specifically, the preponderance of the evidence suggests that regulations are associated with reductions in the quantity, quality, and specialization of private schools participating in such programs. These unintended consequences could partially explain the recent negative effects of certain school choice programs on student achievement. Decreasing certain program regulations could improve the effectiveness of private school choice programs by increasing the number of meaningful options available to the families that need them the most.

Review Findings

We use the following inclusion criteria for reviewing the evidence linking private school choice program regulations to the quantity, quality, and specialization of participating private schools:

- quantitative studies (which use data to assess the types of schools that do or do not participate in voucher programs)

- studies that examine at least one of three outcomes: the quantity, quality, or specialization of private schools participating in choice programs

Quantity

Regulations could have negative effects on the supply of private schools available to families.[27] Private school leaders weigh costs and benefits when deciding whether to participate in private school choice programs each year. Because regulations are additional costs associated with participation, regulations should decrease the number of private schools that participate in choice programs.

The limited evidence on the subject supports this theory. Most of the literature linking regulations to the quantity of private schools participating in school choice programs is either correlational or merely descriptive (see table 3). Three descriptive studies examining private school choice programs in Indiana, North Carolina, Florida, and Louisiana find that private school leaders are concerned with current or future program regulations.

Megan Austin, senior researcher at American Institutes for Research, finds that the private schools electing to participate in Indiana's Choice Scholarship Program (CSP) are most concerned about how regulations would affect their academic and religious identities. Indeed, Austin finds that schools participating in the CSP experience changes to the religious and academic composition of their students, as anticipated.[28] Austin also finds that private schools not participating in the CSP are most concerned about the program's procedural requirements.[29]

The authors of a report evaluating North Carolina's Opportunity Scholarship find that the top concern for private schools participating in the program is future regulations. (Eighty-two percent of the participating schools list future regulations as a concern). Regulations are also the top reason private school leaders list for declining to participate in the program. (Fifty-seven percent of nonparticipating schools list future regulations as a concern.)[30]

Table 3. Effect of School Choice Regulations on Private School Participation Decisions

Study	Location	Method	Outcome	Effect
DeAngelis, Burke, and Wolf, "Effects of Regulations: California and New York"	CA, NY	RCT	expected participation	negative
DeAngelis, Burke, and Wolf, "Effects of Regulations: Florida"	FL	RCT	expected participation	negative
Stuit and Doan, *School Choice Regulations*	DC, FL, GA, IA, IN, LA, OH, PA, RI, WI	logistic regression	participation	negative
Sude, DeAngelis, and Wolf, "Supplying Choice"	DC, IN, LA	OLS	participation	negative
Austin, "Schools' Responses"	IN	descriptive	reasons for nonparticipation	negative
Egalite et al., *School Leaders' Voices*	NC	descriptive	reasons for nonparticipation	negative
			concerns about participation	negative
Kisida, Wolf, and Rhinesmith, *Views from Private Schools*	FL, IN, LA	descriptive	reasons for nonparticipation	negative

Note: RCT = randomized controlled trial, OLS = ordinary least squares regression. "Negative" indicates that the study found a statistically significant negative relationship between program regulations and private school participation.

Sources: Corey A. DeAngelis, Lindsey M. Burke, and Patrick J. Wolf, "The Effects of Regulations on Private School Choice Program Participation: Experimental Evidence from California and New York" (EDRE Working Paper No. 2019-07, University of Arkansas, Department of Education Reform, 2019); Corey A. DeAngelis, Lindsey M. Burke, and Patrick J. Wolf, "The Effects of Regulations on Private School Choice Program Participation: Experimental Evidence from Florida," *Social Science Quarterly* 100, no. 6 (2019), 2316–36; David Stuit and Sy Doan, *School Choice Regulations: Red Tape or Red Herring?* (Washington, DC: Thomas B. Fordham Institute, 2013); Yujie Sude, Corey A. DeAngelis, and Patrick J. Wolf, "Supplying Choice: An Analysis of School Participation Decisions in Voucher Programs in Washington, DC, Indiana, and Louisiana," *Journal of School Choice* 12, no. 1 (2018): 8–33; Megan J. Austin, "Schools' Responses to Voucher Policy: Participation Decisions and Early Implementation Experiences in the Indiana Choice Scholarship Program," *Journal of School Choice* 9, no. 3 (2015): 354–79; Anna J. Egalite et al., *School Leaders' Voices: Private School Leaders' Perspectives on the North Carolina Opportunity Scholarship Program, 2018 Update*, OS Evaluation Report #6 (NC State College of Education, October 2018); Brian Kisida, Patrick J. Wolf, and Evan Rhinesmith, *Views from Private Schools: Attitudes about School Choice Programs in Three States* (American Enterprise Institute, January 2015).

The authors of a 2015 study surveyed the leaders of nonparticipating private schools in Florida, Indiana, and Louisiana.[31] The researchers found that 64 percent of leaders of nonparticipating private schools in Louisiana, 62 percent in Indiana, and 26 percent in Florida listed "future regulation that might come with participation" as a major reason for nonparticipation. In addition, they found that leaders participating in the LSP—the most heavily regulated of the three locations—are the most concerned about future regulations.[32] In fact, 100 percent of the leaders of private schools participating in the LSP reported that future regulations are a general concern and 64 percent reported that future regulations are a major concern. Fifty-four percent of private school leaders participating in the CSP reported that future regulations are a major concern, while 44 percent of private school leaders participating in the Florida Tax Credit Scholarship Program—the least-regulated program of the three—reported future regulations as a major concern.

A 2018 study shows that only a third of the private schools in Louisiana participate in the heavily regulated LSP, whereas over twice that proportion of private schools participate in less-regulated programs in Washington, DC, and Indiana.[33] Co-founder of Basis Policy Research, David Stuit, and Associate Policy Researcher at RAND Corporation, Sy Doan, use school-level data from the 2009/10 round of the Private School Universe Survey to examine the relationship between school choice program regulatory burden and private school participation in school choice programs.[34] After controlling for other factors that might influence a school's decision to participate—such as school size, urbanicity, religiosity, and enrollment trends—Stuit and Doan find that increases in regulatory burdens are associated with decreases in private school participation rates. Specifically, the authors find that an increase in the regulatory burden score from 10 to 75 is associated with a 9 percentage point decrease in the likelihood of private school participation.[35]

Most studies examining the effects of school choice regulations are descriptive because regulations are not randomly assigned to private schools. Furthermore, the correlational literature is limited because regulatory packages are relatively similar across programs and tend not to change much over time. Two survey experiments attempt to establish causal relationships between specific voucher program regulations and private school participation. They use surveys to randomly assign different regulations—or a control condition—to private school leaders in three different states and ask them whether they would participate in new private school choice programs during the following school year.[36] The first experiment surveys private school leaders in Florida and finds that the open-admissions mandate reduces the likelihood that private school leaders say they are "certain to participate" by about 17.4 percentage points, while state standardized testing requirements reduce the likelihood that private school leaders say they are "certain to participate" by about 11.6 percentage points.[37] Similarly, the second surveys private school leaders in California and New York and find that the open-admissions mandate reduces certain participation by about 19 percentage points, while state standardized testing requirements reduce certain participation by about 9 percentage points.[38] However, neither experimental study finds evidence that nationally norm-referenced testing requirements or the prohibition of parental copayment reduce private school participation overall.[39]

Quality

In theory, regulations might be less likely to deter lower-quality private schools from participating in school choice programs than higher-quality private schools, since lower-quality schools are more in need of additional funding and enrollment—and, thus, more open to adhering to a regulatory regime in order to secure additional revenue. For their part, higher-quality private schools might be more selective when it comes to the types of voucher programs they opt into, since they are less likely to need the additional revenues to stay afloat.

The research on this question is limited since school quality is difficult to define, particularly because it is multidimensional. Families choose schools for their children on the basis of numerous priorities, including safety, culture, civic skills, religiosity, peer groups, location, and standardized test scores, among other factors. That said, eight empirical evaluations have examined the types of private schools that elect to participate in choice programs using six different measures of quality: tuition, enrollment, Google review scores, GreatSchools review scores, school safety, and standardized test scores. The preponderance of the evidence suggests that schools judged to be lower quality—on the basis of these six metrics—tend to be more likely to participate in choice programs (see table 4).

A 2018 study finds that schools with higher tuitions, enrollments, and GreatSchools review scores are less likely to participate in the Louisiana voucher program; however, the result for GreatSchools review scores is not statistically significant.[40] Two random assignment evaluations of the LSP find that the overall negative effects of the program are largely driven by private schools with lower tuition levels and enrollment trends,[41] suggesting that these two measures are also valid proxies for test score value-added. Furthermore, tuition levels represent the price customers are willing to pay for a school's bundle of education services, while enrollment represents the quantity of a school's education services demanded by families. Three other correlational studies indicate that schools with higher levels of tuition, larger enrollment, higher customer reviews, greater safety, and greater test score value-added tend to be less likely to participate in voucher programs in Milwaukee, Wisconsin; Ohio; Indiana; Colombia; and Chile.[42]

Although most of the correlational evidence indicates that lower-quality private schools tend to be more likely to participate in school choice programs, these studies cannot establish that program regulations are actually responsible. However, regulations are the largest cost associated with participation, in theory, and private school leaders report that program regulations are major deterrents.[43] Only two studies have randomly assigned regulations—or a control condition—to private school leaders using a survey.[44] One of these experiments finds limited evidence to suggest that higher-quality private schools in Florida are more likely to be deterred by various regulations.[45]

The clearest result of this experiment is that more expensive schools are more likely to be deterred by the regulation mandating that all schools accept the voucher amount as full payment. This result is intuitive: it is much more costly for a school with tuition of $20,000 to accept a $6,000 voucher as payment in full than for a school with tuition of $10,000 to do so. In addition, the researchers' model, with all controls, finds that a $1,000 increase in tuition is associated with a 1.4 percentage point increase in the magnitude of the negative effect of a state standardized testing mandate on intended program participation. The researchers also find that a 10 percentage point increase in enrollment growth from 2014 to 2016 is associated with a 2 percentage point increase in the magnitude of the negative effect of the open-admissions regulation on intended program participation.

The survey experiment examining the relationship between regulations and private school participation in voucher programs in California and New York mostly does not find heterogeneous effects by school quality. However, one marginally significant result suggests that a one-point increase in Google review scores (on a five-point rating scale) is associated with a 14.5 percentage point increase in the magnitude of the negative effect of the state testing mandate on anticipated program participation.

Table 4. Effect of School Choice Regulations on Quality of Participating Private Schools

Study	Location	Method	Quality measure	Effect
DeAngelis, Burke, and Wolf, "Effects of Regulations: California and New York"	California, New York	RCT	tuition	null
			enrollment trends	null
			GreatSchools reviews	null
			Google reviews	null to negative
DeAngelis, Burke, and Wolf, "Effects of Regulations: Florida"	Florida	RCT	tuition	negative
			enrollment trends	null to negative
Abdulkadiroğlu, Pathak, and Walters, "Free to Choose"	Louisiana	RCT	tuition	negative
			enrollment trends	negative
Lee, Mills, and Wolf, "Heterogeneous Impacts"	Louisiana	RCT	tuition	negative
			enrollment	negative
DeAngelis and Hoarty, "Who Particpates?"	Milwaukee; Ohio	Probit regression	tuition	negative
			enrollment	null
			GreatSchools reviews	negative
			Google reviews	null

Study	Location	Method	Quality measure	Effect
DeAngelis and Lueken, "Are Choice Schools Safe Schools?"	Indiana	Probit regression	school safety	negative
Bettinger et al., "School Vouchers"	Colombia	OLS	tuition	negative
Sánchez, "Understanding School Competition"	Chile	OLS	tuition	negative
			math test scores	negative
			test score value-added	negative
Sude, DeAngelis, and Wolf, "Supplying Choice"	DC, Indiana, Louisiana	OLS	tuition	negative
			enrollment	negative
			GreatSchools reviews	null

Note: RCT = randomized controlled trial, OLS = ordinary least squares regression. "Negative" indicates that the study found a statistically significant negative relationship between program regulations and the quality of the participating private schools. "Null" indicates that the study found no relationship between program regulations and the quality of the participating private schools. "Null to negative" indicates that the study found null to negative relationships between program regulations and the quality of the participating private schools.

Sources: Corey A. DeAngelis, Lindsey M. Burke, and Patrick J. Wolf, "The Effects of Regulations on Private School Choice Program Participation: Experimental Evidence from California and New York" (EDRE Working Paper No. 2019-07, University of Arkansas, Department of Education Reform, 2019); Corey A. DeAngelis, Lindsey M. Burke, and Patrick J. Wolf, "The Effects of Regulations on Private School Choice Program Participation: Experimental Evidence from Florida," *Social Science Quarterly* 100, no. 6 (2019), 2316–36; Atila Abdulkadiroğlu, Parag A. Pathak, and Christopher R. Walters, "Free to Choose: Can School Choice Reduce Student Achievement?," *American Economic Journal: Applied Economics* 10, no. 1 (2018): 175–206; Matthew H. Lee, Jonathan N. Mills, and Patrick J. Wolf, "Heterogeneous Impacts across Schools in the First Four Years of the Louisiana Scholarship Program" (EDRE Working Paper 2019-11, University of Arkansas, Department of Education Reform, Fayetteville, AR, April 23, 2019); Corey A. DeAngelis and Blake Hoarty, "Who Participates? An Analysis of School Participation Decisions in Two Voucher Programs in the United States" (Policy Analysis No. 848, Cato Institute, 2018); Corey A. DeAngelis and Martin F. Lueken, "Are Choice Schools Safe Schools? A Cross-Sector Analysis of K–12 Safety Policies and School Climates in Indiana" (Working Paper 2019-2, EdChoice, April 3, 2019); Eric Bettinger et al., "School Vouchers, Labor Markets and Vocational Education" (Borradores de Economía No. 1087, Banco de la República, Colombia, 2019); Cristián Sánchez, "Understanding School Competition under Voucher Regimes" (working paper, September 17, 2018), http://econweb.umd.edu/~sanchez/files/csanchez_jmp.pdf; Yujie Sude, Corey A. DeAngelis, and Patrick J. Wolf, "Supplying Choice: An Analysis of School Participation Decisions in Voucher Programs in Washington, DC, Indiana, and Louisiana," *Journal of School Choice* 12, no. 1 (2018): 8–33.

Specialization

As Michael McShane, director of national research at EdChoice, the-orized, "overregulation can have a chilling effect on diversity and innovation."[46] Regulations might lead to homogenization in the pri-vate school market for a couple of reasons.[47] First, because program regulations largely mirror regulations in traditional public schools, the switching costs associated with program participation will be higher for the most specialized private schools. Private schools that already oper-ate similarly to traditional public schools, on the other hand, will tend to face lower switching costs associated with program requirements. Second, some of the regulations associated with program participation make it particularly difficult for private schools to remain specialized. For example, the Louisiana voucher program requires that participat-ing private schools use random admissions processes, which could make it challenging for schools to maintain high academic standards or specialized missions.[48] Private schools participating in the LSP must also administer the state's standardized tests, which could increase the costs associated with deviating from the government's uniform curric-ulum. Private schools participating in the Milwaukee Parental Choice Program must use random admissions processes and must allow stu-dents to opt out of religious programs.[49]

Again, most of the evidence on the subject of specialization is merely correlational. However, just about all the correlational evi-dence indicates that more-specialized schools tend to be less likely to participate in voucher programs (see table 5). Four descriptive studies find that a significant share of private school leaders report that they are concerned about school choice programs' effects on their schools' specialized identities.[50] One 2015 study finds that 55 percent of pri-vate school leaders in Louisiana, 63 percent in Indiana, and 39 percent in Florida were concerned about school choice programs having an effect on their "independence, character, or identity."[51] Megan Austin has found that "schools choosing to participate in the Indiana Choice Scholarship Program were most concerned with how their academic and religious identity would be affected."[52] She interviewed principals of 10 Catholic schools that had chosen to participate in the program and finds additional costs associated with adapting to the needs of new students while maintaining school identity.[53] The authors of a 2018 study find that 14 to 18 percent of private school leaders in North Carolina reported concerns about the voucher program's effects on their school's identity.[54]

A 2019 study finds that private schools identifying as "regular schools" are more likely than nonregular schools to participate in school choice programs in Indiana, Louisiana, North Carolina, Ohio, Wisconsin, and Washington, DC.[55] Overall, schools that identify as primarily serving students with special needs, schools that focus on early childhood education, and alternative schools are less likely to participate in voucher programs than schools that identify as regular. Private schools that focus on supporting homeschooled students are less likely to participate than those that do not, and non-coeducational schools are less likely to participate than coeducational schools. Two studies have found that individual private schools in Indiana, Florida, Louisiana, Ohio, and Washington, DC, tend to be less likely to identify as specialized or alternative—and more likely to identify as regular—when they switch into voucher program environments.[56] A 2019 study finds that individual private schools in Indiana, Louisiana, and Washington, DC, are around two percentage points less likely to report that they focus on supporting homeschooling after they switch into voucher program environments.[57]

Two survey experiments address this question. One finds that the random admissions mandate has around a 25 percentage point negative effect on expected participation for nonregular (specialized) private schools and around a 17 percentage point negative effect on expected participation for regular (nonspecialized) private schools.[58] However, while the difference of around 8 percentage points suggests that the random admissions regulation is more costly for specialized private schools, it is not statistically significant. The second study similarly finds that the negative effects of school choice regulations on expected program participation do not differ by private school specialization.[59]

Table 5. Effect of School Choice Regulations on Specialization of Participating Private Schools

Study	Location	Method	Specialization measure	Effect
DeAngelis, Burke, and Wolf, "Effects of Regulations: California and New York"	CA, NY	RCT	nonregular	null
DeAngelis, Burke, and Wolf, "Effects of Regulations: Florida"	FL	RCT	nonregular	null
DeAngelis and Burke, "Does Regulation Reduce Specialization?"	DC, IN, FL, LA, OH	OLS	specialized	negative
			alternative	negative
DeAngelis and Burke, "Does Regulation Induce Homogenisation?"	DC, IN, LA	OLS	specialized	negative
			alternative	negative
DeAngelis and Dills, "Is School Choice a Trojan Horse?"	DC, IN, LA	OLS	homeschool focus	negative
DeAngelis, "Which Schools Participate?"	DC, IN, LA, NC, OH, WI	OLS	specialized	null
			focus on students with special needs	negative
			alternative	negative
			early childhood	negative
			homeschool focus	negative
			non-coeducational	negative
Austin, "Organizational and Social Costs"	IN	descriptive	reported concerns of effects on specialized identities	negative
Austin, "Schools' Responses"	IN	descriptive	reported concerns of effects on specialized identities	negative
Egalite et al, *School Leaders' Voices*	NC	descriptive	reported concerns of effects on specialized identities	null to negativea
Kisida, Wolf, and Rhinesmith, *Views from Private Schools*	FL, IN, LA	descriptive	reported concerns of effects on specialized identities	negative

a While Egalite et al. find that 14 to 18 percent of private school leaders in North Carolina report that the voucher program's effects on their school's identity is a concern, 82 to 86 percent indicate that this is not a concern.

Note: RCT = randomized controlled trial, OLS = ordinary least squares regression. "Negative" indicates that the study found a statistically significant negative relationship between program regulations and the specialization of the participating private schools. "Null" indicates that the study found no relationship between program regulations and the specialization of the participating private schools. Null to negative indicates that the study found null to negative relationships between program regulations and the specialization of the participating private schools.

Sources: Corey A. DeAngelis, Lindsey M. Burke, and Patrick J. Wolf, "The Effects of Regulations on Private School Choice Program Participation: Experimental Evidence from California and New York" (EDRE Working Paper No. 2019-07, University of Arkansas, Department of Education Reform, 2019); Corey A. DeAngelis, Lindsey M. Burke, and Patrick J. Wolf, "The Effects of Regulations on Private School Choice Program Participation: Experimental Evidence from Florida," *Social Science Quarterly* 100, no. 6 (2019): 2316–36; Corey A. DeAngelis and Lindsey M. Burke, "Does Regulation Reduce Specialization? Examining the Impact of Regulations on Private Schools of Choice in Five Locations" (Working Paper 2019-1, EdChoice, March 14, 2019); Corey A. DeAngelis and Lindsey M. Burke, "Does Regulation Induce Homogenisation? An Analysis of Three Voucher Programmes in the United States," *Educational Research and Evaluation* 23, no. 7–8 (2017): 311–27; Corey A. DeAngelis and Angela K. Dills, "Is School Choice a Trojan Horse? The Effects of School Choice Laws on Homeschool Prevalence," *Peabody Journal of Education* 94, no. 3 (2019): 342–54; Corey A. DeAngelis, "Which Schools Participate? An Analysis of Private School Voucher Program Participation Decisions across Seven Locations" (working paper, 2019), https://ssrn.com/abstract=3309754; Megan J. Austin, "Organizational and Social Costs of Schools' Participation in a Voucher Program," in *School Choice at the Crossroads: Research Perspectives*, ed. Mark Berends, R. Joseph Waddington, and John Schoenig (New York: Routledge, 2019); Megan J. Austin, "Schools' Responses to Voucher Policy: Participation Decisions and Early Implementation Experiences in the Indiana Choice Scholarship Program," *Journal of School Choice* 9, no. 3 (2015): 354–79; Anna J. Egalite et al., *School Leaders' Voices: Private School Leaders' Perspectives on the North Carolina Opportunity Scholarship Program, 2018 Update*, OS Evaluation Report #6 (NC State College of Education, October 2018); Brian Kisida, Patrick J. Wolf, and Evan Rhinesmith, *Views from Private Schools: Attitudes about School Choice Programs in Three States* (American Enterprise Institute, January 2015).

Conclusion and Policy Implications

If a family is unhappy with the education services provided by their residentially assigned public school, they generally only have four options: (1) pay for a private school out of pocket while still paying for the public school through property taxes, (2) incur the costs associated with homeschooling while still paying for the public school through property taxes, (3) move to a different residence that is assigned to a better public school, or (4) tell the residentially assigned public school to change and hope that things get better soon. Because each of these options is highly costly for families—especially for low-income households—either in terms of actual financial costs or of time lost while waiting for the public school to change, economists would argue that residentially assigned public schools hold significant monopoly power in the education market.[60] In fact, the costs of these options are so high that parents have even gone to jail for trying to get their children into better *public* schools by lying about their residencies.[61]

Private school choice programs decrease the costs associated with the first option by allowing families to use a fraction of their public education dollars to send their children to private schools. In theory, private school choice is expected to improve student outcomes by introducing competitive pressures into the market for education and putting power into the hands of consumers.[62] Families want their children to receive great educations, and parents are better positioned to understand their children's education needs than distant bureaucrats. Public and private schools must cater to the needs of families if they wish to keep their doors open when families can vote with their feet. Private school choice programs might also lead to better education outcomes by improving matches between schools and students.[63]

This review of the academic literature examines the impact of regulations on the quantity, quality, and specialization of private schools that decide to participate in school choice programs. On balance, the literature suggests that regulations are a net negative for school choice program design. Seven studies consider the relationship between regulations and private school participation in a school choice program, and all seven find negative effects, suggesting that onerous regulations reduce the likelihood of school participation. Eight studies look at the relationship between regulations and school quality; seven find that regulations could reduce the quality of the private schools that participate in school choice programs, and one finds null effects. Finally, ten studies examine the relationship between regulations and school specialization; seven studies suggest negative effects and three find null effects.

These findings also offer some possible explanations for the LSP's persistent and large negative effects on math test scores. First, private schools might have a comparative advantage at shaping character skills that are not easily captured by standardized test scores. In other words, standardized math and reading test scores may not be strong proxies for students' long-term success.[64] Public schools have stronger incentives to teach to the test—and more experience with test taking—than private schools, meaning private school choice programs could decrease performance on standardized tests without actually negatively affecting learning in the short run.

However, it is also possible that students participating in the LSP are learning less than children in public schools. Because this is possible, we should be especially concerned about how the design of school choice programs could influence their effectiveness. The empirical evidence on the topic tends to suggest that regulations unintentionally decrease the quantity, quality, and specialization of private schools that elect to participate in choice programs. Of course, this doesn't mean that policymakers should get rid of all school choice program regulations; instead, they need to more carefully weigh the intended benefits of regulations against the unintended—but realized—costs of regulations.

The most rigorous evidence suggests that while the open-admissions mandate aims to achieve equality, it has the largest negative effects on private school participation. The unintended result of the open-admissions mandate is the exact opposite of its intended effect. The regulation actually leads to less equality because fewer private schools participate, meaning that the least advantaged groups of students will have virtually no chance of attending those schools, while children from high-income families are still able to attend without financial assistance. Two survey experiments find that the state testing mandate significantly reduces the number of private schools available to students, whereas the nationally norm-referenced testing mandate is not associated with any significant reduction in options. In other words, if a testing regulation is necessary for the appearance of accountability to the public, policymakers should choose nationally norm-referenced tests to avoid the demonstrated unintended consequences of mandating the state test. The negative effects of state testing mandates are especially important to consider since research consistently finds that families do not strongly value standardized testing when they choose schools.[65]

The evaluation of the LSP was the first experiment in the world to find statistically significant negative effects of a private school voucher program on student test scores. The negative effects were large. The LSP also has the two most intrusive program regulations—the random-admissions mandate and the requirement that private schools administer the state standardized tests. The LSP also mandates that private schools accept the voucher amount as full payment, which keeps the most expensive private schools from participating in the program. Only a third of the private schools in Louisiana elect to participate in the LSP, whereas over twice that proportion tend to participate in less-regulated programs. In addition, schools with declining enrollment and lower tuitions—proxies for school quality—are more likely to participate in in the LSP, perhaps because they most need additional voucher funding.

Policymakers should consider the real costs associated with well-meaning regulations. The empirical evidence tends to suggest that regulations reduce the quantity, quality, and specialization of the private schools that participate in school choice programs. Policymakers could increase the number of meaningful options available to families by reducing top-down regulations of private school choice programs. Giving families real options—by avoiding onerous regulations—could increase the chances of success for the children that are most in need of better education options. If regulations reduce the variety and quality of private schools that choose to participate in school choice programs, they cut against the primary purpose of education choice: to provide more families with more options when it comes to their children's education.

Much more research is needed on the impact of regulations on the supply and quality of private schools choosing to participate or not participate in a private school choice program. And policymakers and government officials will need to pay particular attention to the design of school choice programs and the regulations that govern them as education becomes more piecemeal and customized in the years to come. New modes of K–12 education delivery are unfolding every year, from new approaches to education financing with education savings accounts to changes in delivery through micro-schooling, online learning, private tutoring, and homeschooling co-ops, among other options. How the public and governments conceive of accountability, and how they understand the impact of specific regulations on these options, will shape the education landscape for decades.

CHAPTER 17

"Blue Laws" and Other Cases of Bootlegger/Baptist Influence in Beer Regulation

Stephan F. Gohmann and Adam C. Smith

Alcohol is perhaps the most peculiarly regulated commodity in the US economy today.[1] The locus of regulatory control lies mainly at the state level, owing to the Twenty-First Amendment and other legacies of the Prohibition era. This has created a wilderness of different distribution laws that have contributed to the limited variety of American beer for most of the 20th century. An uprising occurred in the late 1970s when the craft beer industry disrupted many of the old ways of bringing beer to the masses. Craft alcohol expert Alistair Williams comments on this shift from the perspective of the demand side of the market, noting that "American tastes in beer are changing. Consumers want increased choice in beer styles, moving away from American light lager which has dominated the market for generations."[2] The shift was further propelled by changes in self-distribution laws in the first decade of the 21st century that allowed small craft brewers to meet burgeoning demand from younger drinkers.[3] While this movement has dramatically changed the market for alcohol, the three-tier system, that is the impetus for much of the regulation of alcohol, is still very much in place, and is widely endorsed at multiple points along the supply chain.[4]

This chapter focuses on state laws that pertain to alcohol regulation, with particular emphasis on the relationship between economic and moral interests that motivate much of the policy discussion. We use Bruce Yandle's "Bootleggers and Baptists" metaphor[5] to frame these interests and their subsequent influence on the political process. We examine several of the more common types of alcohol regulation, including limits on self-distribution, franchise agreements, and, of course, the blue laws that motivated the metaphor. We also provide a brief case study of two states, Indiana and Kentucky, examining how local interests attempted to use regulations for their own advantage.

Blue Laws and the Origin of Bootleggers and Baptists

Economist Bruce Yandle originally used so-called blue laws, found especially in the southern region of the United States, as the inspiration for his popular Bootleggers-and-Baptists metaphor.[6] As Yandle explains, "Bootleggers, you will remember, support Sunday closing laws (Blue Laws) that shut down all the local bars and liquor stores. Baptists support the same laws and lobby vigorously for them. Both parties gain, while the regulators are content because the law is easy to administer."[7] While blue laws do indeed spring from religious origins, as shown by their association with the Sabbath, their use in modern times correlates with bootlegger influence as much as Baptist influence. As Michael Lovenheim and Daniel Steefel explain, "A common justification for these laws put forth by policymakers is that they provide a secular benefit to society by curtailing drinking and thereby reducing alcohol-related crimes."[8] Yet the authors found that states that have repealed these laws saw little change in the rate of fatal accidents. Yandle's theory exposes the "Bootlegger" influence behind what would otherwise seem to be ineffective and outdated legislation.

The Bootleggers and Baptists in Yandle's theory need not literally be illegal alcohol sellers and churchgoers—though the theory readily lends itself to the alcohol market.[9] Instead, Yandle borrows these terms to make sense of political outcomes that would otherwise seem curious. As we explain below, the Prohibition era was especially rife with abuse of the legal system as actual bootleggers found aggressive means of quenching public thirst. Similarly, the Bootleggers in Yandle's theory are the economic interests that seek to gain from public spoils. They are an inevitable part of the political process, as demonstrated through the ever-expanding literature on rent-seeking.[10]

On the other hand, the Baptist and Methodist clergymen who seek to curb alcohol use represent an overarching appeal to the public interest. Similarly, the Baptists in Yandle's theory seek to bring benefits to the public in a way that is recognizable by others. Going back to *The Theory of Moral Sentiments* by the original Adam Smith (and namesake to one of the authors of this chapter), there is an alertness to sympathy from and for others that motivates our actions and beliefs. In a sense, our propensity to reciprocate trust is as deeply embedded as our propensity to truck and barter. When we find ourselves in sympathy with others, it becomes difficult to disentangle this public-spiritedness from underlying economic interests.[11]

Triumph of the Baptists

Prohibition speaks marvelously to this theory in that the intentions of the "drys" who instigated the legislation were intricately linked with other economic and moral interests. Historian Richard Gamble writes,

> Not every prohibitionist was motivated by the brand of Christian activism represented by the Christian Century, the Federal Council of Churches, the leaders of mainline or other denominations, or the countless reform associations. The more technocratic prohibitionists emphasized industrial efficiency, safety, and medical science rather than moralism or the Bible. But an appeal to religion pervaded the campaign as a whole. In the case of some Christians, war and Prohibition united them as never before—with such success that Protestant ecumenists considered it yet another sign of the approaching Kingdom of God (whatever that might mean). War and Prohibition divided other Christians; but for the moment, fundamentalists and modernists fought on the same side when it came to Prohibition.[12]

This alliance created a veneer of moral support for what became an unwieldy enforcement process. Daniel Okrent offers,

> Consider, for instance, the two constituencies that had the greatest stake in the Eighteenth Amendment and were thus implicit allies. No one had a stronger moral interest in Prohibition than the Baptist and Methodist clergymen who were its tribunes, but no one had a greater financial stake than the criminals who daily sought to undermine it. It's not easy to prove that the big-time mobsters, on-the-take cops, corrupt judges, speak-easy operators, and all the other economic beneficiaries of the Eighteenth Amendment and the Volstead Act gave their financial support to dry politicians. Researchers are unlikely to discover a canceled check made out to a political campaign and signed "Alphonse Capone."[13]

However, the incentives are evident. As Mark Thornton explains, "Not only did spending on alcohol increase, so did spending on substitutes for alcohol. In addition to patent medicines, consumers switched to narcotics, hashish, tobacco, and marijuana."[14] We'll discuss these substitution effects further below in reference to modern-day alcohol regulation.

Anti-Saloon League members and bootlegging mobsters were just the actors of that particular era. The more general point of the Bootleggers-and-Baptists framework is that economic interests will appeal to public-interest arguments to use the political process to their advantage.[15] Unlike distillers who were the main focus of prohibitionists, breweries had a chance to possibly keep beer legal during Prohibition, but they faced considerable obstacles in gaining public sympathy. First, World War I (1914–1918) made German brewers a prime target for prohibitionists. Anti-German sentiment during the war was used to the advantage of the prohibitionists. For example, the Woman's Christian Temperance Union used postcards claiming "the Saloon Backer is a Traitor to his Country."[16] Okrent relates the story of a dry politician saying to a local paper, "We have German enemies across the water.

We have German enemies in this country too. And the worst of all our German enemies, the most treacherous, the most menacing, are Pabst, Schlitz, Blatz, and Miller."[17]

Second, treated potable drinking water was becoming the norm. Throughout history, people have boiled water to remove contaminants. In the east, tea was the drink of choice. In the west, beer was the drink of choice. Frederick the Great complained when imported coffee began to replace beer as the drink of choice.[18] Bert Vallee argues that "western civilization has wine and beer to thank for nourishment and hydration during the past 10,000 years."[19] Before the very recent availability of clean, pure water, alcoholic beverages may have been the only safe liquids to drink. Although many large US cities had water piped into homes in the late 1800s, much of the water was pumped from the same river that was receiving untreated sewage. It wasn't until 1908 that Jersey City became the first city to continuously chlorinate and filter the city's drinking water.[20] As more cities started chlorinating and filtering their water, the need for beer declined.

Finally, brewers were not well organized. This is partly because the larger breweries were not ready to help out smaller breweries, which generally operated "tied houses" in the city in which they brewed. A *tied house* is a saloon that only serves a particular brewery's beer. According to Martin Stack and Myles Gartland, "From 1877 to 1895, the large national shipping breweries such as Anheuser-Busch and Pabst grew much faster than the industry. Yet, from 1895 to 1915, the largest breweries began to see their sales stagnate, and the industry grew at a faster rate, propelled by local and regional firms."[21] Since most bars only served the beer of one brewery, the larger breweries that shipped their beers had few alternatives and mostly sold their products in hotels and restaurants. Stack and Gartland argue that, after Prohibition, new rules were developed that favored larger shippers over local brewers. The larger shippers had a seat at the table when the legislation was being developed, and the local brewers were on the menu. The consequence was the three-tier system of regulation that is prevalent in most states today. In effect, the large national brewers (or "macro-breweries") became the Bootleggers, albeit legal ones.[22]

Impact of the Twenty-First Amendment

Prohibition, the failed "noble experiment," ended with the Twenty-First Amendment in 1933, which gave over authority to regulate alcohol to the individual states. From then on, each state was able to determine whether alcohol could be sold and to regulate its manufacture and distribution, tax it, and stipulate when and where people could consume it. As agricultural economist Bradley Rickard and co-authors observe, "the heterogeneity of alcohol availability laws in the United States is striking."[23] Underpinning all of this regulatory apparatus is the three-tier distribution system. Seventeen states directly control the sale of alcohol while the remaining states use a three-tier system.[24] But even in control states, the rules differ as to what types of alcohol are controlled. The three-tier system requires alcohol producers (tier 1) to sell to distributors (tier 2), who then sell and deliver the product to retailers such as liquor stores, bars, and restaurants (tier 3). Only at this point is the consumer able to purchase the product. Before the three-tier system, alcohol producers often sold directly to retailers or consumers, and led to the tied houses for breweries discussed above. It's unclear whether breweries would have consolidated as aggressively as they did had Prohibition not severely disrupted the American alcohol market. Nevertheless, under the three-tier system, the sales of small brewers immediately fell (see figure 1).

Okrent writes, "Of the 1,345 American brewers who had been operating in 1915, a bare 31 were able to turn on their taps within three months of the return of legal beer." Under the three-tier system, local breweries were no longer able to sell beer in their own saloons: they had to rely on other bars and restaurants to sell their beer. This made it easier for the out-of-town, larger brewers to sell their beer, since they were now in the same market position as the local brewers, though with greater ability to advertise their products. Moreover, economies of scale reduced the costs of mass-produced beer and the larger brewers bought up many of the regional brewers. As a consequence, the number of breweries fell from 756 in 1934 to 89 in 1978.

The Volstead Act was the legislation that detailed the enforcement of the Eighteenth Amendment. The legislation allowed individuals to make wine at home but not beer.[25] The Twenty-First Amendment repealed Prohibition and gave states the right to regulate alcohol sales and production, but was silent on home-brewing beer. In 1978, President Carter signed a bill which came to be known as the Cranston Act since it has an amendment by senators Alan Cranston, Harrison Schmitt, Dale Bumpers, and Mike Gravel that allowed home-brewing of 100 gallons of beer per adult and up to 200 gallons per household. Soon after, the craft brewing industry started to grow.[26]

Figure 1 shows the number of breweries in the United States from 1887 until 2018. Prohibition reduced the number of breweries dramatically, and the decline started well before the Eighteenth Amendment took effect, because many states had their own prohibition laws. When the Twenty-First Amendment passed, the few breweries that had survived during Prohibition by producing other products such as malt, ice cream, and other drinks started to scale up and buy out smaller breweries. This led to a decline in the number of breweries. After the Cranston Act in 1978, many homebrewers wanted to open breweries. Since states had the power to determine the production and distribution of alcohol, some states, such as California and Oregon, became early adopters of legal craft breweries, while others, such as Mississippi and Alabama, were late adopters, waiting until 2013 to legalize craft breweries.

A consequence of the Cranston Act was dramatic growth in the number of breweries, from 89 in 1978 to 8,386 in 2019. However, the number of breweries per capita varies dramatically by state and is partly dependent on when a state legalized small breweries, and particularly on whether self-distribution is possible, as we explain below. Some may question the relationship between the Cranston Act of 1978 and the more recent growth in breweries, which generally accelerated in the past 15 years. However, home brewing was the first step. The next step was that states had to pass laws allowing brewpubs to open. Research shows that Washington was the first state to legalize brewpubs, in 1982, followed by California and Oregon in 1983. Half of the states had legalized brewpubs by 1988.[27] Once brewpubs have been legalized, entrepreneurs hoping to open one must find funding and acquire all the appropriate licenses and government certifications.

Figure 1. Number of US Breweries, 1887–2018

Source: "National Beer Sales & Production Data," Brewers Association, accessed October 7, 2020, https://www.brewersassociation.org/statistics-and-data/national-beer-stats/.

Laws that allow for self-distribution, be it on-site (as in the case of brewpubs) or in local retail outlets, are particularly beneficial to craft brewery growth and are responsible for much of the postmillennial growth in number of breweries.[28] Recall that the three-tier system requires alcohol producers to sell to distributors, which then sell to liquor stores, bars, and other sellers of alcohol. Some states, however, have carved out an exception for smaller breweries that allows them to self-distribute their beer. For example, North Carolina recently raised its distribution cap from 25,000 to 50,000 after a contentious political battle between distributors and craft brewers.[29] Table 1 shows the number of breweries and breweries per 100,000 population over age 21 as well as self-distribution status in 2019. Notice that the average number of breweries per 100,000 is 3.2 in states that do not allow self-distribution but 4.8 in states that do allow self-distribution. Having 50 percent more breweries per capita results in a greater variety of beer, more competition, and lower prices.[30]

Self-distribution laws ultimately determine the capacity for growth, because they establish when the brewer must work with an outside distributor. Agricultural economist Daniel Toro-Gonzalez and co-authors

Table 1. Breweries per Capita and Self-Distribution Laws, 2019

Jurisdiction	Breweries per 100,000 population*	Allows self-distribution?
Mississippi	0.7	no
Louisiana	1.2	no
Alabama	1.4	no
Georgia	1.5	no
Texas	1.7	yes
New Jersey	1.9	yes
Arkansas	1.9	yes
Oklahoma	1.9	yes
Nevada	2.0	no
Utah	2.0	yes
Florida	2.0	no
West Virginia	2.0	yes
Kentucky	2.1	no
Tennessee	2.1	yes
Washington, DC	2.2	yes
South Carolina	2.3	no
Hawaii	2.3	yes
Arizona	2.4	yes
Maryland	2.5	yes
Kansas	2.9	no
New York	2.9	yes
Illinois	3.0	yes
Missouri	3.1	no
California	3.1	yes
Massachusetts	3.3	yes
Ohio	3.6	yes
Delaware	3.7	no
Connecticut	3.9	yes
Indiana	3.9	yes
Nebraska	4.0	no
North Dakota	4.0	yes
Rhode Island	4.1	no
Pennsylvania	4.1	yes
North Carolina	4.3	yes
Iowa	4.6	yes
Virginia	4.6	yes
Wisconsin	4.7	yes
Minnesota	4.7	yes
South Dakota	5.2	yes
Michigan	5.4	yes
Idaho	5.8	yes
New Mexico	6.2	yes
Washington	7.5	yes
New Hampshire	8.7	yes
Alaska	8.8	yes
Oregon	9.7	yes
Wyoming	9.8	yes
Colorado	10.0	yes
Montana	11.5	yes
Maine	12.7	yes
Vermont	14.2	no
Avg. where self-distribution allowed	4.8	
Avg. where self-distribution prohibited	3.2	

* The number of breweries per 100,000 population over age 21.

Source: "State Craft Beer Sales & Production Statistics, 2019," Brewers Association, accessed October 7, 2020, https://www.brewersassociation.org/statistics/by-state/.

note that "the variety of products available in the market at a given point in time is not an outcome of the market, but a result of distributors' decisions."[31] In addition, distributors for the macro-brewers would rather avoid competition for shelf space and taps at restaurants from craft breweries, since such competition will cut into the profits of their high-value clients. As a consequence, these interests have historically pushed for state alcohol laws that make it difficult for craft breweries to self-distribute. But as younger millennials, who favor product differentiation and customization, have reached legal drinking age, they have propelled the growth in the craft sector , putting pressure on distributors to include craft brands in their overall beer portfolio. Toro-Gonzalez and his co-authors explain that while "consumers who purchase [mass-produced] American lagers are highly loyal to this type of beer,"[32] craft beer drinkers are equally consistent in avoiding these types of brands.

Moreover, beer sales have been falling in the past 10 years. In 2008 beer captured 50.3 percent of alcohol revenues. Spirits accounted for 33.1 percent of sales, and wine for 16.6 percent. By 2019, these numbers were 45.2 percent for beer, 37.8 percent for spirits, and 17.0 percent for wine.[33] At the same time, the share of beer produced by craft brewers increased from 4.0 percent to 13.2 percent.[34] The reduction in sales has fallen hardest on the larger macro-brewers with mass-consumed products. Most macro-breweries have simply acquired craft breweries in order to maintain their market presence.[35] Nevertheless, the macro-brewers continue to resist competition from the craft sector through their relationships with distributors as enforced by the three-tier regulatory process.

In short, the "Bootleggers" in today's alcohol market are both distributors and macro-brewers. However, these economic interests need "Baptists," or a genuine moral argument, to keep the current legal structure in place. Fortunately for the Bootleggers, there are groups willing to oblige. Recent research has examined how the number of craft breweries per capita is related to the percentage of the population that is Baptist, to the number of distributors per capita, and to the percentage of state legislators' campaign contributions coming from macro-breweries.[36]

The influence of the percentage of the population that is Baptist on the number of breweries is pretty straightforward. In 2006, the Southern Baptist Convention passed the following resolution:

> WHEREAS, Years of research confirm biblical warnings that alcohol use leads to physical, mental, and emotional damage (e.g., Proverbs 23:29–35); . . .

> RESOLVED, That we urge Southern Baptists to take an active role in supporting legislation that is intended to curb alcohol use in our communities and nation.[37]

So, we should expect states with larger percentages of Southern Baptists to have legislators who will keep laws on the books that make it difficult for a brewery to open.

One of us (Gohmann) examined brewery growth from 2004 to 2012. He found that in the South, where literal Baptists make up a large portion of the population, laws that made it easier for breweries to open were indeed slow to change.[38] In southern states where the percentage of Baptists was larger, the number of breweries per capita was lower. Likewise, in southern states the number of breweries per capita was negatively associated with more beer distributors per capita and a larger percentage of state officers' campaign contributions coming from big breweries. This relationship did not hold in any other region of the country—likely because other regions lack a sufficient number of Baptists to elect legislators who would keep such distribution control laws in place.[39]

This relationship seems to be waning, however. In the past five years, the number of craft breweries has almost doubled—from 4,847 in 2015 to 8,386 in 2019.[40] Much of this growth took place in the South.

All Bootleggers-and-Baptists Politics Is Local
In many cases, states have complicated the Bootleggers-and-Baptists

situation further by ceding governing authority to local government. Section 2 of the Twenty-First Amendment allows states to determine the rules for alcohol distribution, including whether to be wet or dry. A dry state or county does not allow any alcohol sales. Several states decided to let counties determine their wet/dry status through local-option votes. Currently, 12 states have jurisdictions where alcohol sales are prohibited—that is, dry counties. For example, as in many other southeastern states, North Carolina "set into place the Alcohol Boards of Control (ABC) structure, giving local jurisdictions control over the production, distribution and sale of alcohol across N.C. County ABC Boards are local independent political subdivisions of the State Boards, operating as separate entities, establishing their own policies and procedures."[41]

There are several Bootleggers-and-Baptists implications of having wet and dry counties. First, in wet counties that border dry counties, many liquor stores locate right on the county border. These liquor stores are often keen to fight any move in the dry county to become wet. So in this case, the out-of-county liquor stores are the Bootleggers and the local residents in the dry county who wish to remain dry are the Baptists. For example, an article on a statewide vote in Arkansas to legalize the sale of alcohol throughout the state reported that the initiative was strongly opposed by the Arkansas Beverage Retailers Association. "The association says the initiative's passage would be 'catastrophic for county line liquor stores' and would allow large-scale retailers like Walmart and Kroger to dominate the market."[42] There was no mention in the article of the greater variety of beer and lower prices such competition would bring.

Laws prohibiting alcohol sales in a county might benefit the Bootleggers and assuage the consciences of the Baptists, but these laws have consequences. The three-tier system allows extensive political interference in alcohol markets in a way that significantly increases the cost of regulatory compliance for local brewers. For example, in today's alcohol market, economists Trey Malone and Dustin Chambers "show that each step of the beer value chain is subject to more than 20,000 regulations, with the majority of the total regulations affecting the brewery level," which corresponds to tier 3 where consumers buy alcohol. They continue, "In total our estimates suggest that more than 94,000 federal regulations influenced the production and sale of a single bottle of beer in 2012."[43] As a consequence, consolidating into larger brands often makes the most sense for brewers wanting to distribute in multiple states.

An additional constraint involves franchising law and pertains to how distributors bargain with brewers. As economist Douglas Whitman explains, "Alcohol wholesalers have regularly sought legislative protection to limit the power of suppliers to terminate their contracts."[44] While franchise agreements routinely contain certain stipulations, their enforcement is typically left to the market process; that is to say, agreements that result in mutual benefit will gain traction over time.[45] When franchising agreements are enforced not by market process but by government coercion, then their propensity to benefit all parties becomes less credible. Indeed, Francine Lafontaine and Margaret Slade claim that they "have found clear evidence that restrictions on vertical integration that are imposed, often by local authorities, on owners of retail networks are usually detrimental to consumers. Given the weight of the evidence, it behooves government agencies to reconsider the validity of such restrictions."[46]

Furthermore, many states require alcohol distributors to operate in exclusive territories. This ensures that distributors gain market power because they need not directly compete with one another for local contracts. The use of exclusive territories to properly incentivize contracts is credible when these contracts are entered into voluntarily. For example, Armen Alchian and William Allen explain how Coors used exclusive territories to motivate distributors to properly refrigerate their beer in transit.[47] As with franchising laws, however, this contracting solution is less credible when it is enacted by legislative decree. Together, these laws create significant entry barriers for new breweries at the local level. Distributors have enormous bargaining power since they are able to (1) control distribution of the product, (2) help structure contracts so that the contracts specifically favor their own interests, and (3) influence state governments directly through their role as part of the larger fiscal apparatus.

The trouble with all this regulatory interference is that it fails to even accomplish its stated goal: namely, to influence the consumption of alcohol by limiting production. Malone and Lusk find that, "at least for the US beer market, consumption habits are not directly correlated with the number of producers. By extension," they continue, "our results suggest that constructing policies with the intention of influencing consumer behavior by limiting decisions made by the seller is unlikely to accomplish the law's intended goals."[48]

For example, regulation can influence alcohol-related traffic fatalities in a way unintended by lawmakers. Economic theory suggests that the implicit price of alcohol will be higher in dry counties. A consumer in a dry county who wishes to purchase alcohol has two options. The first is to purchase it illegally from a literal bootlegger. In this case, the price will be higher than the price in a wet county, since the bootlegger—acting as a middleman—will charge for procuring the alcohol and also for the risk of getting caught. The second option is to drive to a wet county to purchase alcohol. In this case, the consumer has to add the costs of the trip, including time costs, to the purchase price of the alcohol. If the consumer plans on drinking in the wet county, the drinker may have to have a designated driver, find a place to stay to sober up, or take the risk of driving while intoxicated. If the consumer decides to drink in a wet county and then drive home, the potential for a motor vehicle fatality might be higher than it would have been if the consumer had been drinking locally.

Research into fatalities caused by driving under the influence of alcohol has shown mixed results. A study published in 1996 found no association between wet or dry counties and fatalities for 15-to-24-year-olds.[49] But data from the National Highway Traffic Safety Administration show that the number of alcohol-related deaths in 2006 was 6.8 per 10,000 people in dry Texas counties, compared to 1.9 per 10,000 in wet Texas counties.[50]

Moreover, the same set of substitution effects that encouraged illegal consumption activities during Prohibition is still present today. The availability of alcohol in wet counties also lowers its cost relative to the cost of other illegal substances such as marijuana, heroin, and methamphetamines. Michael Conlin, Stacy Dickert-Conlin, and John Pepper examine the influence of alcohol access in Texas on drug-related crimes and mortality. During the time period of their study, 1978 to 1996, Texas raised the legal drinking age from 18 to 19 and then from 19 to 21. Also, 26 counties changed from dry to wet. This change allowed the researchers to examine the unintended consequences of alcohol prohibition on illicit drug use arrests and deaths. They find that illegal drugs are substitutes for alcohol access. They also find that a jurisdiction changing from dry to wet status in Texas is related to a 14 percent reduction in drug-related mortality.[51] In a study comparing wet and dry counties in Kentucky, another set of researchers find that the number of meth lab seizures is twice as high in dry counties as in wet ones. If all counties in Kentucky became wet, the number of meth lab seizures would decrease by 35 percent.[52]

Comparing the prices of alcohol and marijuana gives similar results. John DiNardo and Thomas Lemieux examine marijuana use by high school seniors when the minimum drinking age is increased. When the drinking age increases, the relative price of now-illegal alcohol rises compared to that of marijuana. The researchers find that alcohol consumption decreases with this increase in the minimum drinking age, but that marijuana use increases.[53] Raising the minimum legal drinking age makes alcohol a forbidden fruit. Barış Yörük and Ceren Yörük find that, in the United States, the probability of drinking alcohol over the past month increases by 13 percent when people turn 21.[54] However, other studies find that a higher minimum drinking age reduces alcohol-related traffic fatalities.[55]

These public health issues could be amplified by an increase in craft breweries. For example, if the surge in craft breweries results in more alcohol-related deaths, then this would justify regulations that discourage the development of microbreweries. However, as stated earlier, Malone and Lusk find that consumption is not related to the number of producers—and, furthermore, beer consumption has been declining since 1981.[56] A 2018 study examined the propositions distributors appeal to in favor of limiting self-distribution, including the fact that some jobs are created by the three-tier system itself and various public health concerns.[57] These arguments are intended to appeal to public interest, but—as the researchers explain—each also has questionable empirical bearing on the way alcohol is consumed today. In other words, an alternative take is that distributors are using Baptist arguments to bolster their Bootlegging position.

A recent paper goes even further, documenting spending by interest groups tied to the respective Bootlegger and Baptist positions in the state of Arkansas. Specifically, the author—economist Jeremy Horpedahl—finds that "legalization of alcohol sales at the county level is opposed by religious organizations and by liquor sellers in adjacent counties."[58] In this case, Bootleggers typically supply funding in the form of advertising and legal fees, while Baptists organize opposition groups and provide local outreach. Also, Walmart is a notable proponent of legalization in Arkansas, since it has stores across the state that would be able to distribute beer and wine in newly wet counties. Nevertheless, Horpedahl notes, "even the largest corporation in the world, operating in its own state with a clear economic interest, apparently often is not able to defeat the concentrated interests of county-line liquor stores and passionate preachers."[59]

A Tale of Two States

As we have discussed so far, in most cases the rules are made at the state or the local level. Two recent cases expose the influence of distribution laws on different groups of competitors. Until recently, Kentucky had a state law that prohibited breweries within the state from distributing their beer. However, no law existed that prohibited a brewery outside the state from owning a distributorship in Kentucky. In the 1970s, Anheuser-Busch bought a distributorship in Louisville. Since craft brewing had not yet started in the state, this purchase was not an issue. However, in 2014 Anheuser-Busch wanted to purchase a distributor in Owensboro, in the western part of the state. The local craft brewers feared that such an acquisition would limit their ability to have their beers distributed in that area. They claimed that the current law favored out-of-state breweries over in-state breweries. The market solution would have been to allow any brewery to distribute within the state, and—as noted above—this would likely have led to increases in the number of breweries and the variety of beer in Kentucky. Instead, by passing H.B. 168 in 2015, the legislature decided that no brewery could own a distributor or distribute its own beer.[60]

Anheuser-Busch fought this bill, since the company would have to sell one of its distributorships and would lose the opportunity to own a second one. Owning the distributorship would have given Anheuser-Busch much more control over how its beer is marketed in Kentucky. One indicator of the importance of this to Anheuser-Busch is the company's lobbying expenditures. Many large companies pay lobbyists in each state to represent their interests. In 2014, Anheuser-Busch's lobbying expenses were $94,064. During the legislative session when H.B. 168 was passed, Anheuser-Busch's lobbying expenditures increased to $447,342[61] The following year, expenditures dropped to $69,998. During the same period, Miller Brewing Company, which was not involved in the distribution debate, had lobbying expenditures each year of $18,812. Another lobbying group, Kentuckians for Entrepreneurship and Growth, appeared in late 2014. It is a coalition of wholesalers, craft brewers, and other groups that pushed for H.B. 168. The group's lobbying expenditures were $16,058 in 2014, increased to $133,297 during the legislative session, and then fell to zero the following year. These expenditures paid off with the passage of H.B. 168.

Another legal debate happened in Indiana in 2018. The laws in Indiana that regulate selling beer are complicated. If you want cold beer, you can only buy it at a liquor store. Grocery stores (plus pharmacies) and convenience stores (which often accompany gas stations) can sell warm beer. In addition, until 2018 Indiana did not allow any alcohol sales on Sundays. These two rules—the one about cold beer and the one about Sunday sales—led to some perverse incentives for liquor stores, grocery stores, and convenience stores.

Liquor stores had the best deal, since they have the exclusive right to carry cold beer and also did not have to be open on Sunday, unlike most grocery stores and convenience stores. New legislation introduced in 2018 threatened to disrupt these privileges, and led to strange coalitions. The liquor stores did not want either Sunday sales or anybody else selling cold beer. This is an example of the transitional gains trap.[62] The liquor stores feared that allowing others to sell cold beer would hurt liquor store revenues, since the liquor stores were currently the only option. So the benefit of owning a liquor store, which an entrepreneur may have bought from its previous owner at a price that reflected the additional profits derived from the ability to sell cold beer, would disappear. Thus the liquor store owners wanted to maintain their monopoly. They opposed Sunday sales because this would require them to be open one more day a week with little additional expected weekly sales. They reasoned that consumers would buy all their alcohol on Saturdays for any Sunday consumption, and that any time open on Sunday would require the cost of employing workers.

Grocery stores wanted to be able to sell cold beer and also to sell alcohol on Sundays, since their stores were open for grocery business on Sundays. (Before 2018, the state had made an exception to the Sunday-sales rule for Super Bowl XLVI in 2012, which was hosted in Indianapolis.) Sunday sales might have been the most beneficial rule change for grocery stores, since they are able to stock a large amount of alcohol and would capture sales from many Sunday shoppers.

Convenience stores and gas stations are only allowed to sell warm beer. They wanted to be able to sell cold beer also, since many drivers might pick up a cold six-pack after filling up their gas tank on their way home from work. Sunday sales would also be beneficial, but cold-beer sales would be most beneficial rule change for this group.

The three competitors (liquor stores, grocery stores, and convenience stores) all wanted different rules. Liquor stores wanted the status quo, but grocery chains had the most clout and the most influence on how the legislation would change. If the grocery stores pushed for cold-beer sales, then convenience stores would benefit and be in the grocery stores' camp, and liquor stores would lose out on their cold-beer monopoly. If the grocery stores pushed for Sunday sales, then liquor stores would lose out, but even though it would cost them and additional day of being open, they could maintain the cold-beer monopoly. Seeing the writing on the wall, the liquor stores teamed up with the grocery stores, and in 2018 Governor Eric Holcomb signed a bill that legalized alcohol sales on Sundays from noon to 8 p.m. Indiana became the 41st state to allow Sunday alcohol sales.

Indiana's law pitted liquor stores against big-box retailers—grocery stores and pharmacies. Liquor store lobbying expenditures were over $150,000, and they donated more than $750,000 to lawmakers.[63] One has to wonder who will be in coalition with the big-box stores the next time legislation comes up about cold-beer sales.

Conclusion

It is hard to gaze on the regulatory landscape of the three-tier system and not see room for improvement. While marginal improvements continue to occur, deeper reform of the three-tier system remains elusive. The coalitions of Bootlegger and Baptist interests manifested in macro-breweries, distributors, and state governments work diligently to keep the existing regulatory apparatus in place. With that said, the 2020 pandemic has brought into intense focus the arcane distribution laws that interfere with brewers' ability to sell alcohol directly to consumers.[64] The pandemic has led to distribution laws across the United States being rescinded temporarily,[65] and some have even been eliminated altogether.[66] Perhaps now is the perfect time to provide blueprints for reforms that would bring needed change to this hopelessly entangled industry.[67]

The most crucial change would be increasing limits on self-distribution.[68] Small brewers in control states, states where the government controls the sales of distilled spirits at the wholesale level, are dependent on distributors to grow and scale their businesses. Preventing craft brewers from distributing their own product stymies the kind of marketing and brand recognition that would otherwise allow each brewer to scale its business as the market allows. The status quo instead sees distributors favoring macro-brewers in a way that makes it difficult for smaller brands to compete. The infamous "100 percent share of mind" campaign in the mid-1990s, in which Budweiser required its distributors to jettison any competing brands, is an excellent example of this.[69] These anticompetitive measures are predictable under the three-tier system, in which distributors wield powerful influence over underlying market share.

Even if distribution is controlled by the state, there should be ample room for competition among distributors by territory. Evidence suggests that when territorial arrangements between wholesalers and retailers are mutually beneficial, these arrangements will come into being naturally without government coercion.[70] Enforcing territorial monopolies by government decree, on the other hand, leverages bargaining ability in favor of distributors, which can in turn be used to prevent small brewers from gaining market share in their local area.[71] In addition to these monopoly provisions, there are numerous laws that favor distributors under existing franchise agreements. These include laws that make it tremendously difficult to terminate a relationship with a distributor, even when the brewer is able to demonstrate "good cause" that the contract has not been fulfilled. Typically, beer franchise laws allow the wholesaler a grace period to correct the underlying issues.[72]

Finally, taxes have been historically tied to alcohol in a way that seeks to accomplish public policy goals that are at times conflicting.[73] If state governments want to raise as much revenue as possible through alcohol consumption, then this should be a stated policy goal, giving rise to a strategy of removing all unnecessary barriers to the alcohol market. On the other hand, if the purpose of taxation is to limit consumption, then policymakers need to find a tax rate that would overwhelm even the most inelastic of beer drinkers. Regardless, greater research in this area is critical to further unpacking these cases of Bootlegger and Baptist influence in alcohol regulation.[74]

Smoke or Vapor? Regulation of Tobacco and Vaping

James E. Prieger

Given the well-known health harms of smoking, tobacco is regulated and taxed nearly everywhere in the world. With the introduction of electronic nicotine delivery systems (ENDS), commonly known as e-cigarettes, new questions have arisen about the risks to health from their use and whether they should be regulated as strictly as tobacco. In some quarters, the possibility that e-cigarettes and vaping could deliver an attractive, smoking-like sensory experience while avoiding the health harms that accompany combusting and inhaling tobacco has been greeted with enthusiasm, since the new products could help some smokers transition to a less risky product. In other quarters, and in much of the American public health community, e-cigarettes were greeted with skepticism and hostility, since they could potentially renormalize smoking, set back the great gains in tobacco control of the past several decades, and hook a new generation of young people on nicotine and smoking. This chapter covers the regulatory history of tobacco and e-cigarettes, summarizes upcoming regulatory actions and challenges, discusses the key issues involved in the regulation of these activities, and includes suggestions for better regulation.

Readers will benefit from an understanding of some vaping technology and terminology. All e-cigarettes work by means of a battery-operated heater that vaporizes a solution containing nicotine and flavoring (known as an eliquid), which is then inhaled by the user. Sometimes grouped with e-cigarettes are heat-not-burn products that heat ground tobacco without combustion. There are many types of e-cigarettes and vaping systems, from cartridge-based "closed" systems, in which the consumer buys a disposable, unmodifiable eliquid cartridge, to tank-based "open" systems, in which the vaper buys vials of eliquid for refill and can customize what is vaped. All of these will be referred to as "e-cigarettes" in this chapter, and their consumption will be called "vaping," unless a distinction among products is required. The exception is that discussions of the scientific literature on the health effects of e-cigarettes exclude heat-not-burn products, which are typically not included in the studies. Finally, note that using e-cigarettes is not "smoking"—nothing is combusted and there is no smoke.

History of Tobacco Regulation in the United States

From 1900 to 1963, per capita consumption of cigarettes grew rapidly, from a low figure in 1900 until in the latter year the daily average was more than half a pack per adult.[1] The watershed moment in the history of smoking in the United States was the publication of the Surgeon General's report in 1964, which stated that "cigarette smoking is a health hazard of sufficient importance in the United States to warrant appropriate remedial action."[2] After that year, consumption began its long decline, falling to 0.13 packs sold a day per adult in 2018.[3]

Of course, the average smoker consumes more than that. In 2018, adult smokers reported smoking a bit more than half a pack a day, while retail sales of cigarettes averaged a bit less than one pack per day per adult smoker.[4] That same year, there were about 34 million adult cigarette smokers in the US and 49 million adult users of any tobacco product, including e-cigarettes.[5] These figures imply that the prevalence of cigarette smoking has fallen to 13.7 percent among US adults, while the prevalence of any form of tobacco consumption is 19.7 percent. Adult cigarette smoking prevalence has declined about two-thirds from its peak in the 1960s.

The sale and use of tobacco in the US has been regulated in various ways for decades, although much of the regulatory action has come relatively recently compared to the long history of smoking. The first federal action regarding the tobacco industry and the health effects of its products was the requirement that cigarette manufacturers add the notice that smoking "may be hazardous to your health" on packs. The health warning, which came into effect in 1966, was the first of its kind in the world.[6]

Despite the landmark surgeon general's report in 1964, until the 1980s tobacco was specifically exempted from legislation (e.g., the Toxic Substances Control Act) and regulation (e.g., by the Consumer Product Safety Commission) that otherwise would have curtailed the industry or the freedom to smoke.[7] Starting in 1985, a set of four rotating health warnings with stronger wording were required on cigarette packaging.[8] The FDA sought to add graphical health warnings in 2011, but legal action by the tobacco industry has delayed the requirement for almost a decade.[9]

The first federally mandated restrictions on where one could smoke came in the late 1980s, with bans on smoking on certain domestic airline flights.[10] The so-called Synar Amendment of 1992 required all states to adopt and enforce restrictions on the sales and distribution of tobacco to minors; federal enforcement of the restrictions (through the withholding of certain federal payments to the states) went into effect in 1996.[11] While as recently as the 1980s some states had no restrictions on sales to minors, however defined, by 1995 all states and the District of Columbia prohibited the sale and distribution of tobacco products to those under 18 years of age.[12]

In 1998, the three major tobacco manufacturers signed the Master Settlement Agreement (MSA) with 46 states. In exchange for immunity from legal claims by these states for costs incurred for smoking-related illnesses and deaths, the three major tobacco manufacturers agreed to pay the states an estimated $206 billion, finance a $1.5 billion anti-smoking campaign, and cease various forms of advertising, product placement, and event sponsorship, as well as any form of marketing aimed at youth. While the settling states say that "the central purpose of the MSA is to reduce smoking, especially in American youth,"[13] it appears that the states spend little of the money collected from the MSA and tobacco taxes on tobacco prevention and cessation programs—well under 3 percent of it in 2020.[14]

The entering wedge for direct federal regulation of tobacco as a consumer product came in the form of Family Smoking Prevention and Tobacco Control Act of 2009, which granted the FDA authority to regulate tobacco products. The FDA's first action under the act was to issue a rule in 2010 prohibiting the sale of cigarettes and smokeless tobacco to any person under age 18. (Such sales were already illegal in all states.)[15] Since that time, there has been a steady flow of proposed and final rules and "guidance" from the FDA regarding tobacco regulation. Figure 1 shows the growth of federal regulation regarding tobacco over time, as measured by the cumulative number of pages of rules in the *Federal Register*. By 2015, there were over 200 pages of binding regulations, and by the beginning of 2020 there were 224 pages of rules, more than 150 pages of guidance regarding those rules, and well over 400 accumulated pages of proposed rules. The pages of proposed rules nearly doubled in 2019 with recent actions by the FDA (about which more will be said below).

In the first of two recent federal regulatory actions, the age threshold for retail sales of tobacco products after December 2019 was raised from 18 to 21 years.[16] Before that time, well fewer than half the states had an age restriction that high. In its most recent action, the FDA issued rules requiring graphical warnings on cigarette packages.[17] These new color graphics depicting the negative health consequences of smoking will occupy the entire top half of the area of the front and rear faces of cigarette packages.[18] Some research indicates that such large graphical warnings are more likely to be noticed by smokers or more likely to lead them to consider cessation or smoking less.[19]

In addition to tobacco regulations, the federal government has levied excise taxes on cigarettes continuously since the time of the Civil War.[20] The tax remained at 8 cents a pack from 1951 until 1983, when it was doubled. In the early 1990s the tax was raised to 24 cents, and in the early 2000s it was raised by stages to 39 cents. In 2009, the largest increase yet resulted in a per-pack federal tax of $1.01, where it remains in 2020.

Figure 1. Growth of Federal Regulation from the FDA Regarding Tobacco and E-cigarettes

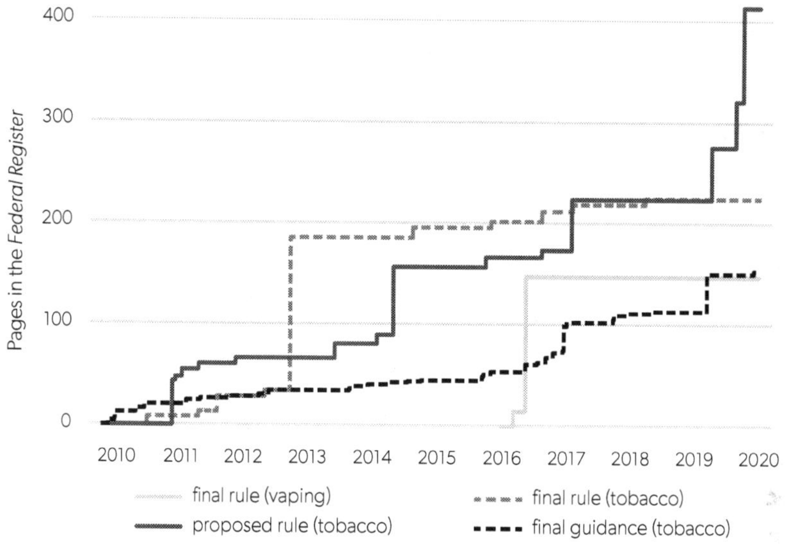

Source: Author's calculations from FDA data, https://www.fda.gov/media/88873/download.

State taxes on tobacco vary widely, although most states have increased their cigarette taxes in the past two decades. From 1970 to 2018, the average state excise tax (not weighted for population or consumption) increased from 9.6 cents per pack to $1.74—an annualized nominal growth rate of 7.5 percent and an inflation-adjusted growth rate of 3.6 percent (see figure 2). State taxes grew exceptionally quickly after 2000, with an inflation-adjusted growth rate of the average tax of 5.5 percent per year. Adding the federal tax on top of the state taxes shows that the combined nominal rates rose by an average of 5.7 percent per year between 1970 and 2018 and have risen by 6.9 percent per year since 2000. These large increases in the taxes over time resulted in almost 40 percent of the retail sales prices of cigarettes going to excise taxes in 2018—or, to put it another way, an effective 65 percent tax rate on a pack.

Figure 2 also shows the population-weighted averages of the taxes; these reflect the excise taxes facing the average person in the nation. For the most part these are similar to the simple averages, with the exception of a divergence in 2017 owing to California enacting a large tax increase. Overall, these levels of taxation make cigarettes one of the most highly taxed products in the nation. By comparison, state alcohol taxes averaged only three to five cents per drink in 2015.[21]

History of E-cigarette Regulation in the United States

The market for e-cigarette products in the United States began to take off around 2006. In 2008, the e-cigarette market had only $28 million in revenue from an estimated 190,000 vapers, but by 2017 it was a $4.6 billion market with an estimated 8.4 million vapers.[22] Those figures represent a revenue growth rate of over 50 percent per year. Given the recent emergence of e-cigarettes as a significant product, it is unsurprising that the regulatory history of vaping is short. In 2016, the FDA "deemed" e-cigarettes (or, more properly speaking, ENDS) to be tobacco products.[23]

While the FDA has the legal authority to deem new or existing products to be tobacco products, and thus subject to its regulatory authority, it is worth noting that ENDS do not contain tobacco. While nicotine is

Figure 2. Growth of State and Federal Excise Taxation on Cigarettes

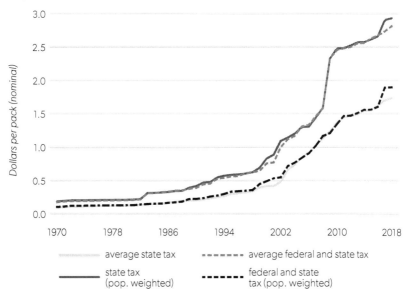

Source: Data from the Centers for Disease Control and Prevention, *"Tax Burden on Tobacco, 1970-2018,"* August 13, 2020, https://chronicdata.cdc.gov/Policy/The-Tax-Burden-on-Tobacco-1970-2018/7nwe-3aj9.

the addictive substance found in tobacco, it is the other constituents in tobacco that, when combusted and inhaled, cause the main health problems associated with smoking. In particular, to quote a report from the National Academies of Sciences, Engineering, and Medicine, "There is no evidence to indicate that nicotine is a carcinogen."[24] Thinking of e-cigarettes as tobacco products thus greatly confuses the issue, a point to which I will return below.

After deeming e-cigarettes to be tobacco products, the FDA aimed its entire set of tobacco-related regulations at vaping products as well. Manufacturers of existing products had to register with the FDA and submit lists of products, their ingredients, and evidence about their health effects.[25] Manufacturers are now required to place on product packaging a warning that they contain nicotine and that nicotine is an addictive chemical. Products introduced between 2007 and August 2016 could continue to be sold while their applications for regulatory approval were considered by the FDA.[26] New e-cigarette products are not allowed to be introduced after August 2016 without premarket approval. Since the FDA has not ruled on any e-cigarette application yet, in part because continuing legal action made uncertain the deadline for submission of applications, anti-vaping advocates can still truthfully claim that there are no FDA-approved e-cigarettes on the market.[27] In January 2020, the FDA also effectively prohibited sales of flavored cartridge-based e-cigarettes (other than tobacco-, mint-, and menthol-flavored e-cigarettes).[28] However, flavored eliquids for open-system tank vaping (typically available at vape shops) remain allowed.[29]

With e-cigarettes added to the regulatory purview of the FDA, age restrictions on sales to youth under age 18 and the prohibition of sales from vending machines came into force in 2016.[30] Most states had already banned sales to youth before the federal action (see figure 3), and over time many states raised their age restrictions on sales to 19 or 21 years. Near the end of 2019, as mentioned above, the federal age limit was raised to 21 for all tobacco products, including e-cigarettes.

States have also been free to impose other regulation on the sales and usage of e-cigarettes. The increasing number of other regulations among the states is depicted in figure 4. Some states require retailers to obtain special licenses to sell e-cigarettes, typically with the goal of limiting youth access to vaping products; some place the same restrictions on vapers regarding using the devices in public as on smokers (thus applying "smoke-free" rules to a smoke-free product). Finally, a minority of states levy excise taxes on e-cigarettes (in contrast to ubiquitous state taxes on cigarettes).

Upcoming Potential Regulatory Changes

The FDA is currently undertaking several rulemaking processes on tobacco regulation. One regulatory proceeding is considering whether menthol flavoring in cigarettes will be banned (other flavors are already illegal).[31] Perhaps the most ambitious regulatory action contemplated by the FDA is to lower the nicotine content in cigarettes to minimally addictive or nonaddictive levels.[32] While the FDA does not have the authority to ban cigarettes outright, such action would effectively kill the legal market for the product as it exists today. Public comments on the latter two proceedings were due in the summer of 2018, but the FDA has not issued final rules for either (or announced that it is abandoning the effort) as of the start of 2020.

As discussed earlier, apart from a single heat-not-burn product, the FDA has not issued rulings on any of the submissions for regulatory product approval for e-cigarette products. Thus, the industry faces a large degree of uncertainty going forward regarding the amount of effort required for successful submissions. The fact that the one approved product, IQOS by Philip Morris International, purportedly required billions of dollars for regulatory compliance on the part of the manufacturer and experienced two years of regulatory delay until approval does not bode well for any maker of e-cigarettes, apart from the largest tobacco manufacturers.[33]

The main upcoming regulatory action by the FDA—eagerly awaited by industry and the public health community—is not new regulation per se, but rather a definitive ruling on any of the regulatory approvals sought for e-cigarette products (discussed above). It remains to be seen whether any such products will be allowed to claim that they are safer than cigarettes or that they aid in cessation of smoking. It is also

Figure 3. Growth of State Regulation
regarding E-cigarette Sales to Youth

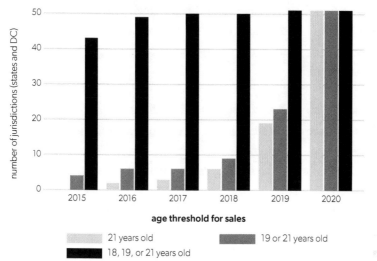

Sources: Tobacco Control Legal Consortium, *U.S. E-cigarette regulation: a 50-state review*, 2020. Available from https://publichealthlawcenter.org/resources/us-e-cigarette-regulations-50-state-review.

Figure 4. Growth of State Regulations
Regarding E-cigarette Sales and Usage

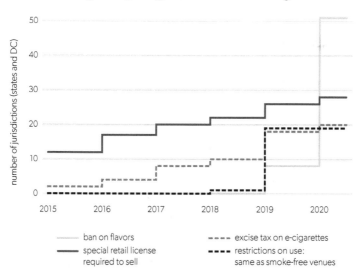

Sources:Public Health Law Center, "E-Cigarette Tax : States with Laws Taxing E-Cigarettes," 2020; Public Health Law Center, Retail Licensure on E-Cigarettes: States with Laws Requiring Licenses for Retail Sales of E-Cigarettes, 2020; Public Health Law Center, "U.S. E-Cigarette Regulation: A 50-State Review."

unclear whether any cartridge-based ENDS flavored with something other than mint or menthol will be approved; despite the current sales ban, the FDA has not ruled out granting regulatory approval for such products. As mentioned above, the only ruling to date has been on a heat-not-burn product, which differs in many ways from traditional vaping products.

Issues Involved with Taxing and Regulating Tobacco

This section covers the various rationales offered for regulating tobacco and some of the unintended consequences of doing so. The three main rationales for excise taxes and regulations on tobacco fall into two categories. The main *economic* rationale has traditionally been to tax tobacco to align the private and social costs of smoking. The main *actual* rationale appears to be paternalism. In recent years, a hybrid rationale has emerged in which theories from behavioral economics are used to justify paternalistic taxation and regulation. These rationales are all discussed here.

The economic rationale for regulation: externalities.

The traditional economic rationale for tobacco taxation is that it serves to correct consumers' faulty incentives (i.e., it is taxation to correct for externalities, à la economist Arthur C. Pigou). In other words, the main economic rationale for tobacco taxation depends on the presence of negative externalities.

An externality in this context is an effect of consumption that creates adverse consequences for persons other than the decision maker. So-called Pigovian taxes are set to correct for the externalities, so that consumers consider the costs and benefits of their actions from the social rather than merely the personal perspective. The two externalities discussed for consumption of tobacco are the burdens imposed on taxpayers (fiscal externalities) and the burdens imposed on nonsmokers (health externalities).[34] When smokers degrade their likely future health by their consumption of tobacco, they create future expected costs for publicly funded health programs such as Medicare. However, whether it is proper to treat such "fiscal externalities" identically to other externalities in the social calculus is debated.[35] Externalities require attention and possibly correction because they create inefficiencies, not because they transfer benefits from one party to another in the economy. The inefficiencies associated with fiscal externalities, however, are due to the inefficiencies inherent in subsidized healthcare, not to smoking per se. That is, the inefficiency (if any) arises because of the policy (Medicare), not the individual's action (smoking).

The remaining difficulties with an argument based on fiscal externalities, for those wishing to justify high tax rates on cigarettes, are twofold. First, the cost of a pack is borne today (by the buyer), but any external costs for society to fund healthcare are far in the future. The present expected discounted value of those future healthcare costs is small, and thus so would be the corrective taxes. (Note, however, that if healthcare cost increases continue to outpace general inflation, this first rebuttal loses some force.) Second, since smokers on average die younger than nonsmokers, they *reduce* the drain on the public purse for social security payments and have fewer years of eligibility for (costly) Medicare.[36]

Thus it is unsurprising that studies taking these considerations into account while computing the optimal tax to account for fiscal externalities alone generally find that current excise tax levels are too high compared to the net externalities.[37] Even using an astronomically high figure for the health cost to society of smoking a single pack ($35), the optimal tax to correct for negative externalities would be only 40 cents per pack (compared to the actual excise tax, which averaged around $2.80 in 2018).[38] The weight of the literature instead finds similarly small externalities, but some notable exceptions actually find social savings from smoking (although these tend to be in countries with higher public expenditures on health than the United States).[39]

However, fiscal externalities are not the only costs imposed on society by smokers. The other negative externality created by smoking is the burden imposed on nonsmokers, primarily through second-hand smoke. Such burdens include the annoyance of being exposed to others' smoke and any adverse health effects. Health-related externalities based on second-hand smoke gained prominence in arguments for taxation and tobacco control in the US in the 1990s, after the earlier studies concluding that tobacco taxes were too high. Given that "everyone knows" how harmful secondhand smoke is, many people would be surprised to learn how weak the scientific evidence used to justify the indoor smoke-free laws of the 1990s actually was.[40] A landmark study in 1993 from the Environmental Protection Agency purported to show the adverse health effects of secondhand smoke and was influential in the passage of many local and state smoke-free ordinances. However, the report was savaged by a federal court.[41] The study, which stated that it reviewed the best available scientific evidence at the time, was thrown out by the court in part because it "did not demonstrate a statistically significant association between [secondhand tobacco smoke] and lung cancer," which was its main claim. The point of rehearsing the story behind the first smoke-free ordinances is not to suggest that secondhand smoke does not have adverse health effects; that link is better established today. Rather, it is to note that, as is likely the case with the debate about e-cigarettes today (as will be covered below), the call to regulate smoking was sustained by political and social factors beyond those supported directly by the scientific knowledge at the time.[42]

Today, it is estimated that there are about 41,000 deaths per year in the United States attributable to secondhand smoke.[43] That figure represents about 1.5 percent of all deaths.[44] The negative effects of maternal and passive smoking on infant and child health are considered some of the most important negative externalities.[45] Various studies have associated smoking during pregnancy with reduced fetal growth, low birth weight, and, later in life, obesity, cardiovascular disease, and respiratory ailments. However, it remains the case that some of the links are weaker than people often assume. For example, one meta-analysis covering 76 studies on environmental tobacco smoke exposure found that there was no statistically significant association between environmental tobacco smoke in the home and premature births, low birthweight, spontaneous abortions, or lower Apgar scores at birth.[46] On the other hand, the same meta-analysis found a positive association of secondhand smoke with congenital malformations.[47] Furthermore, many studies find that anti-smoking regulations are associated with better infant and child health.[48]

Before leaving the subject of negative externalities, it is important to note that a tax is a blunt instrument for reducing environmental tobacco smoke exposure. The price elasticity of market demand for cigarettes is estimated to be around 0.4, implying that a 10 percent increase in the price of cigarettes reduces total consumption in the market by only 4 percent. Other, more direct interventions can have much larger impacts. For example, consider concerns about the health of unborn children in a smoking household. One behavioral intervention that involved advising about health risks, introducing strategies within the home to eliminate exposure to smoke, and cognitive behavioral therapy for depression or intimate partner violence when necessary reduced the odds of secondhand smoke exposure by one-half.[49] From the viewpoint of political economy, it is important to recognize that policymakers may prefer tobacco taxes to behavioral intervention programs because the former raise revenue for the state while the latter require public expenditure.

The behavioral rationale for regulation: "internalities."
Since taxes on tobacco may already be adequate or too high from the usual point of view of taxing to correct for externalities, tobacco control advocates in recent years have turned to justifications based on behavioral economics. The nontechnical version of these arguments proceeds along the following lines: "Youth are not rationally forward-thinking consumers, and most smokers begin smoking in their youth." The former assertion, coupled with the latter empirical observation, and supplemented with survey evidence showing that most smokers say that they wish they had not started smoking,[50] have led many advocates to call for higher tobacco taxes despite the absence of the usual economic rationales.

Arguments against this rationale include the observation that (as discussed earlier) taxes are blunt instruments to prevent smoking, especially since many youth do not pay for their cigarettes and, in particular, for their *first* cigarettes.[51] The greatest weight of a cigarette tax falls on adults, not youth. Furthermore, sales of tobacco to youth are already illegal; if the "infinite tax" tacitly imposed by a ban does not prevent youth from starting to smoke, then why would a finite tax do so—especially since both forms of tax can be evaded, as discussed below? The evidence is inconclusive regarding the impact of cigarette prices on youth smoking. At least some studies find that higher prices lower the propensity of youth to smoke,[52] although other research indicates that the actual primary driver affecting youth's smoking behavior is anti-smoking sentiment or regulations in the state rather than prices per se.[53]

Extending the behavioral economic rationale for tobacco taxes to adults requires a theory involving so-called internalities—irrational behavior due to limited self-control or foresight. Such theories, when applied to tobacco consumption, assume that there is a "behavioral wedge" between the price of the good and the value to the consumer of the last unit consumed.[54] Whereas a rational consumer (roughly speaking) spends money on a commodity to the point where it is just worth it, in terms of satisfaction gained for the price paid, the behavioral wedge implies that the individual "overconsumes" the good, even as evaluated by the person's own (eventual) preferences. Such individuals will look back on past decisions and wish that they had not consumed so much of the good. This may happen, for example, if youth, when they first try smoking, underestimate the likelihood that they will get addicted and become lifelong smokers (with all the resulting pecuniary and health costs). The implication is that, theoretically, increasing the price of a good by increasing an excise tax may actually increase some people's welfare. Thus, a tax may help "nudge" a consumer toward an outcome that is better for that person, in the estimation of that person. One study adopting this approach arrived at the conclusion that an "optimal" tax to correct for internalities might be as high as $15 per pack—far higher than any tax in the nation.[55] Such conclusions regarding optimal taxes make the behavioral approach a convenient rationale for parties advocating for higher tobacco taxes.

The paternalistic rationale for regulation.
As is clear from the discussion of the behavioral rationale for tobacco regulation, many policy analysts and policymakers approach the subject

of tobacco regulation with a heavy dose of paternalism. They view smokers as faulty decision makers who need to be saved from their own poor choices. Some authors are quite explicit about this. For example, in one behavioral economic study performed for a lung cancer group, the authors explain, "we will focus on failures of individual self-control which lead to excessive smoking relative to desired levels. In such a case, tobacco taxation can provide a corrective force to combat failures of self-control."[56] In this approach, the power of the state to tax provides a corrective force to nudge (or shove) irrational, tricked, or self-deluded smokers toward cessation.

Paternalism is a comfortable position for many policymakers to adopt, since—given smoking's negative correlation with income and education—relatively few of them smoke today. As Kip Viscusi, a University Distinguished Professor at Vanderbilt University, has pointed out, since policymakers have chosen not to smoke, it is therefore easy for them to assume that smokers are mistaken, irrational, or in need of policy nudges toward cessation.[57] Of course, the fact that a behavior is hard to quit does not necessarily prove that the choice to begin was irrational (as most coffee drinkers would attest).[58] Furthermore, assumed faulty choices based on mistaken perceptions of the health effects of smoking appear to be unlikely, since, if anything, the American public *over*estimates the risks of smoking today.[59] (The evidence about whether youth in particular hold correct perceptions of the risks involved in smoking is inconclusive, however.)[60]

Evidence for intertemporal irrationality and time inconsistency in decision-making (by which economists mean that the future self will regret decisions made by the present self) comes mainly from lab experiments. These are typically performed on college students at elite universities—hardly a representative demographic. There is also a small empirical literature that claims to find time inconsistency in real-world economic decisions (other than decisions about smoking).[61] Such apparent irrationality follows from individuals in the data not making the choices that the economic theorists think that they should after estimating impressively technical yet still restrictive models of consumers' choices. It remains to be seen whether these findings will hold up when more realistic models of economic behavior based on less restrictive assumptions are investigated.

While the arguments for paternalistic action by the state thus assume that smokers "need help helping themselves," arguments for less paternalism can be based on normative and positive grounds.[62] Normative ideas include the idea that the proper role of government is to protect the liberty of the citizens regarding—among other concerns—economic decisions, and the idea that (absent compelling reasons to the contrary) individuals should be free to make choices without government interference. Conversely, even granting the premise of limited cognition and the desire to optimize the behavior of individuals who cannot do so themselves, bounded rationality can raise the costs of government decision-making relative to private decision-making.[63] Positive arguments against paternalistic tobacco taxes are based on the unintended consequences that such taxes can have. For example, evidence from the 1990s indicates that higher prices caused smokers to switch to cigarettes that were higher in tar and nicotine, and therefore more harmful and addictive.[64] Other unintended consequences are covered in the next subsection.[65]

Unintended consequences of taxes and regulations.
An effective approach to policy must focus less on what policymakers hope will happen and more on what is likely to happen. This takes us into the realm of unintended consequences.

A standard desideratum for taxation is equity, based on the ability-to-pay principle. This principle leads to the system of progressive income taxation in the United States, for example. Excise taxes on cigarettes are regressive, however: poorer individuals spend a greater share of their income on consumption, and therefore an excise tax takes a greater share of a poor person's income than it does of a wealthy person's income. Furthermore, cigarette smoking is more prevalent among lower-income groups in the United States. These facts compound to make tobacco taxes doubly regressive.[66] While tobacco taxes may constitute only a small part of the total financial burden facing most smokers, in some cases the tax burden could be onerous. Consider, as an extreme example, a full-time minimum-wage worker in Chicago, where combined federal, state, county, and local tobacco taxes during the second half of 2019 were $8.17 per pack.[67] During that period, the taxes alone on a pack-a-day smoking habit would have taken up 12 percent of the individual's gross wages.[68]

If higher taxes encouraged many low-income individuals to quit smoking, then one could argue that the regressive impact of tobacco taxes would be blunted or removed entirely. The evidence for the predicate is weak, however. There is evidence that higher prices are associated with a lower number of smokers, even among the low-income population, but evidence for a link between prices and cessation is less clear (in part because cessation is harder to study than smoking prevalence). One study found that there is no correlation between successful cessation among smokers below the poverty line and cigarette prices in their state of residence, either in bivariate analysis or after controlling for other factors.[69] Low-income individuals who still smoke tend to be hard-core smokers whose behavior is difficult to change; taxing them simply raises their financial burdens if they do not quit.[70]

The indirect evidence for higher taxes leading to cessation is stronger: several studies show that tax increases lead to a lower smoking prevalence among older adults.[71] Given that few people begin smoking once out of their twenties, a lower prevalence of smoking among older smokers than younger smokers is indicative of cessation.[72] Regardless, another study found that, cigarette tax increases remain regressive even accounting for the different sensitivity among income groups of smoking to prices.[73]

Proponents of higher tobacco taxes often respond to the regressivity argument by contending that revenue from the taxes should be directed toward cessation programs intended to help low-income smokers quit or toward relieving these smokers' financial burdens.[74] Funding cessation programs may be an admirable intention, but—as mentioned earlier—less than 3 percent of current tobacco tax and MSA payments are spent on cessation.[75] Taxing to relieve a household's financial burden is an odd argument, since no scheme taxing a subset of the poor could result in net financial gains for those taxed. A final open question regarding the equity of taxes is whether the health benefits of reduced smoking accrue disproportionately to lower-income individuals and families. If so, the direct regressivity of the taxes would be attenuated (or even reversed) by the offsetting health benefits.

Illicit trade in response to tobacco taxes is also a concern. As stated in a leading economics textbook on public finance, "markets do not take taxes lying down."[76] Furthermore, to borrow a statement attributed to John Maynard Keynes, "the avoidance of taxes is the only pursuit that still carries any reward." A large body of research indicates that increasing tobacco taxes can have the unintended consequence of stimulating illicit trade in tobacco products (ITTP).[77] In the United States, most ITTP takes the form of legitimately manufactured cigarettes that are transported between states to be sold illicitly, avoiding state and local excise taxes at the point of retail sale. ITTP also involves counterfeit cigarettes, untaxed sales from Native American reservations, illicit whites (cigarettes legal in the country of manufacture but intended for illegal sales in other markets), and gray market reimported goods.[78] ITTP is big business. The National Academy of Sciences found in 2017 that illicit sales compose between 8.5 percent and 21 percent of the total market for cigarettes in the United States. This range represents between 1.24 and 2.91 "billion packs of cigarettes annually and between $2.95 billion and $6.92 billion in lost gross state and local tax revenues."[79] Worldwide, the avoided taxes from ITTP are estimated to be in the tens of billions of dollars per year, putting ITTP in the same financial class as the global traffic in illicit drugs.[80]

The economic explanation for ITTP is simple: licit and illicit cigarettes are substitutes, and when the tax-inclusive price of the licit good rises, some users will switch to the illicit substitute. The degree to which tax increases and tax differentials among states and localities cause substitution toward ITTP depends on many factors, including the rule of law, enforcement at customs borders and at points of sale, the ease of access to illicit sources, the price differential between licit and illicit cigarettes, and the moral sentiments of the smoker.[81]

While the basic fact that an increase in taxes leads to more ITTP, holding other factors constant, is generally accepted by most economists, there is much disagreement over the policy implications. If tax rates across states were unified, then presumably raising a unified rate would not stimulate as much ITTP as raising an already high local tax (such as in Chicago or New York City), given the large role that interstate tax arbitrage currently plays in ITTP.[82] Some in the public health community downplay any suggestion that taxes are linked to ITTP, dismissing the argument through guilt by association, since the tobacco industry makes this claim.[83] Others argue either that the effects are small or that other measures can be taken to combat illicit trade.[84] Careful empirical investigation has shown, however, that raising taxes can lead to sizeable increases in ITTP.[85] Notwithstanding, the evidence is clear that in most cases ITTP may erode but does not reverse revenue gains from increased taxes. Similarly, taxes do decrease consumption of tobacco products, even though ITTP may attenuate the amount by which they do so.[86]

Before leaving the subject of ITTP, it is important to note that it creates harms to health additional to those of smoking genuine, fully taxed cigarettes. Counterfeit cigarettes have been shown to contain pesticides, human and animal waste, heavy metals, and other harmful substances.[87] Furthermore, law enforcement directed at ITTP can create other harms, including those from incarceration and violence, given the well-known link between enforcement action against illicit drug markets and violence.[88]

Issues Involved with Taxing and Regulating E-cigarettes

This section reviews the most prominent issues regarding the regulation of ENDS and potential unintended consequences.

The main issues surrounding vaping concern its safety, its relationship to smoking (including whether it is a promising avenue for harm reduction), and unintended consequences of regulation and taxation. Harm reduction refers to policies and approaches aimed at reducing the harms from an addictive substance, but not the use of the substance per se.[89] The viewpoint of harm reduction is widely accepted in the public health community for alcohol and illicit drugs, but it is controversial in the tobacco control community, mainly because of guilt by association with Big Tobacco, which "has been seen by some to lead the harm reduction push (through the development of new nicotine delivery devices)."[90] Thus, in traditional tobacco control abstinence is taken as the goal, rather than finding safer ways to consume nicotine. The rejection of harm reduction as a guiding philosophy is sometimes justified with reference to the precautionary principle, which posits that lack of scientific certainty should not delay action to regulate or ban new products such as e-cigarettes.[91] Notwithstanding, the discussion to follow examines the issue through the lens of harm reduction and whether e-cigarettes could be part of such an approach.

Is vaping safer than smoking?

What many consider to be the most important question is the easiest to answer: Is vaping safer than smoking? Because e-cigarettes do not involve combustion, and because the combustion of the organic material in a cigarette creates nearly all the health hazards, it would be surprising indeed if e-cigarettes were found to be as risky for health as smoking. This simple expectation has been greatly muddied in the public mind by certain public health advocates who hold a priori goals of abstinence for both smoking and vaping. Thus, a review of the state of current knowledge on this topic may be useful.

To begin with, from the standpoint of harm reduction, the question is not whether e-cigarettes pose *no* health risks at all (except perhaps for the subject of initiation by youth, a subject to which I will return below). In the context of the public health disaster caused by smoking, the proper first question must be whether e-cigarettes are *safer* than cigarettes, and to what degree. After considering the state of the evidence, the official health ministry of England declared that vaping is at least 95 percent less harmful to health than smoking.[92] The purpose of Public Health England's statement in 2015 was not to present a precise risk multiple, but instead to effectively encourage smokers who have been unable to quit by other methods to switch to vaping instead of smoking.[93]

Eliquids and vapor contain substances known to be harmful to human health when inhaled, including irritants, carcinogens, and particulates.[94] Then again, much of modern life exposes individuals to harmful substances. Thus the question is what the short- and long-term health effects from such exposure are, and how they compare with those from smoking.

One difficulty in discussing the health effects of vaping is the great multiplicity of products: there is no "standard" vapor, concentration of chemicals in eliquids, or intensity of inhalation. Notwithstanding, one study found that along the spectrum of products tested, the preponderance of products produced vapor with cancer potencies of less than 1 percent of those of tobacco smoke.[95] Fewer harmful substances in the vapor means that fewer end up in the body. Another study concluded that switching completely from cigarettes to e-cigarettes "substantially reduced levels of measured carcinogens and toxins" in the body.[96] Overall, the National Academy of Sciences report on e-cigarettes found that "there is conclusive evidence that completely substituting e-cigarettes for combustible tobacco cigarettes reduces users' exposure to numerous toxicants and carcinogens present in combustible tobacco cigarettes."[97]

Perhaps the strongest case against vaping on the grounds of deleterious health effects would be based on respiratory disease, since exposure to particulates and flavorings in e-cigarette vapor could potentially impair the function of the lungs. Several studies find that vaping can cause acute respiratory symptoms such as coughing and wheezing, particularly among adolescents. Some of these studies do not control for concurrent or past smoking; controlling for these confounding factors removes the positive associations between vaping and respiratory symptoms in some studies.[98] Even here, however, the recent National Academy of Sciences report concluded that "there is no available evidence whether or not e-cigarettes cause respiratory diseases in humans."[99] Conversely, the same report found "limited evidence" for improvement in symptoms from asthma and chronic obstructive pulmonary disease when smokers who suffered from those ailments switched completely to vaping. Summarizing evidence concerning a variety of potential ill health effects, the report found that there is "substantial evidence that completely switching from regular use of combustible tobacco cigarettes to e-cigarettes results in reduced short-term adverse health outcomes in several organ systems," including the respiratory system.

To conclude, while there is great uncertainty about the long-term effects of vaping, the answer to whether using e-cigarettes is better for health than smoking is almost surely yes. Viewed as part of a continuum of nicotine delivery methods arranged in terms of health risk, e-cigarettes appear to be much closer to nicotine replacement therapies than to smoking. However, the strongest arguments for the potential for e-cigarettes to reduce health harms to users can be made for users who switch completely away from smoking. There is no available evidence about whether long-term e-cigarette use among users who continue to smoke, called dual users, changes morbidity or mortality compared to smokers who do not vape.[100]

Do e-cigarettes aid in cessation?

Is vaping a useful aid to help smokers quit smoking, or does it just prolong the habit by allowing smokers another way to consume nicotine when they are temporarily unable to smoke? It appears likely that e-cigarettes would be a more appealing cessation aid than nicotine replacement therapies (NRTs) such as patches, gum, or lozenges, given the sensory and behavioral similarity of vaping to smoking. The scientific literature on e-cigarettes and cessation is still in its early stages; given the novelty of vaping, no long-term studies on e-cigarettes and cessation have been performed. However, the initial literature is mainly encouraging.

A review of existing studies conducted in 2015 found that, overall, use of e-cigarettes was positively associated with both cessation of smoking and reduction in the intensity of smoking (for those who did not quit).[101] A more recent review of studies on cessation came to a similar conclusion, but only after excluding numerous published studies that did not meet standard levels of quality for scientific research in medicine or public health.[102] The latter meta-analysis found that rates of smoking cessation with e-cigarettes were generally similar to rates of cessation with NRT, while the former found e-cigarettes to be twice as effective as NRT.[103] Some research conducted after these reviews also suggests that e-cigarettes can play a role in cessation.[104]

Are kids getting addicted to e-cigarettes?

There have been many dire, headline-grabbing reports issued in recent years referring to the "vaping epidemic" among youth. For example, in 2019 many variations on the headline "Teen Vaping Surges to More Than One in Four Students" appeared.[105] However, the much-publicized "27 percent" statistic pertains to the proportion of high school students who have used an e-cigarette once or more during the past 30 days. There is clearly a lot of casual use among high schoolers, since the prevalence of *substantial* use of e-cigarettes among high school students (defined as use on 20 or more days out of the past 30) is less than 10 percent.[106]

Furthermore, substantial use of e-cigarettes is mostly confined to youth who already smoke. Among students who had never tried any actual tobacco product in 2018, the prevalence of substantial use of e-cigarettes was found to be only 1.0 percent.[107] For such never-smokers, only 3.8 percent reported craving nicotine and only 3.1 percent reported wanting to use an e-cigarette within 30 minutes of waking. Combined with evidence that most dual-using high schoolers began with smoking, not vaping (see the next subsection), the researchers computing these statistics conclude that the data "do not support claims of a new epidemic of nicotine addiction stemming from use of e-cigarettes."[108] Nevertheless, the prevalence of vaping—however it is measured—continues to rise among youth, and consequently it will require continued monitoring.

Finally, it is worth noting that not all youth vaping represents net health harms to the individual and society, given that in a counterfactual "no e-cigarettes" world, some young vapers would be smokers instead (or, in the case of dual use, potentially heavier smokers). The relationship between vaping and smoking is discussed in the next subsection.

Does vaping lead to smoking among youth?

The findings discussed in the previous subsection that most e-cigarette use by youth is by smokers, coupled with other evidence that the same is true for adults,[109] lead to the question of which came first. Does vaping lead to smoking (the "gateway hypothesis"), or do underage smokers just find vaping a more convenient (and likely cheaper)[110] way to consume nicotine while at school or elsewhere? First, it should be noted that many of the claims that e-cigarette use "causes" smoking are based on nothing more than the observation in population studies that many youth are dual users. However, it is likely that part of the association between vaping and smoking among youth is due to smoking leading to vaping. Another large part of the association is likely due to underlying (confounding) factors (such as a desire for risk-taking or exposure to smoking family members or peers) that make a youth more likely to vape *and* smoke.[111]

Given that it is unethical to perform randomized controlled trials involving exposure to vaping on youth, evidence can only come from observational studies of the population. Such studies, however, are inescapably beset by potential confounding factors. Population studies can control for certain observable demographic and behavioral confounders. Studies doing so that follow youth over time who do not initially smoke find that there is, in the estimation of the National Academy of Sciences report, "substantial evidence" that e-cigarette use increases the risk of trying cigarettes among youth and young adults.[112] However, it is impossible to control for all of the many genetic, behavioral, psychological, and environmental factors that surely must influence the propensities to smoke and vape, and none of the studies use econometric techniques designed to give some assurance that causal effects were identified. Some researchers, therefore, conclude that the association between vaping and smoking is more likely to be spurious than to be evidence for the gateway hypothesis.[113] As better data and more sophisticated statistical techniques are brought to bear on this question, it may be hoped that researchers, policy-makers, and the public can place greater confidence on one conclusion or the other.

If the conclusion in the National Academy of Sciences report is statistically meaningful, one would expect that as vaping among youth has risen, so will have youth smoking rates. This is not the case, however. Simply put, youth smoking initiation has been falling while the prevalence of vaping has been rising. A recent trend analysis of the relationship between vaping and youth smoking found that "while trying electronic cigarettes may causally increase smoking among some youth, the aggregate effect at the population level appears to be negligible."[114] Furthermore, the criterion of temporal precedence for causality states that if vaping causes smoking, then vaping must come before smoking. However, for the great majority of high school smokers, cigarettes were tried before e-cigarettes.[115] In 2014, only 2 percent of current high school age e-cigarette users who had smoked at least 25 cigarettes in their lifetimes said that they began with e-cigarettes. In 2015, that proportion had risen, but was still only between 8 percent and 15 percent.[116]

Another way to pose the question is whether restrictions on youth access to e-cigarettes will decrease smoking. The scant evidence on this subject appears to point to the opposite conclusion. Imposing minimum age laws for sales of e-cigarettes is estimated to have increased youth smoking participation by about one percentage point, which suggests that some youth who otherwise would have purchased e-cigarettes either began smoking or failed to quit.[117] Evidence in a similar vein comes from another study of underage rural girls: laws restricting sales of e-cigarettes to youth increased the prevalence of smoking during pregnancy by 0.6 percentage points, and evidence indicates that the cause was reduced cessation of smoking.[118] Given that the goal of minimum age laws is not just to discourage vaping but ultimately to improve health, these iatrogenic effects partially dilute the benefits of such laws.

Will the new federal minimum age law reduce youth vaping?

People between 18 and 21 years of age could legally purchase e-cigarettes in the majority of states at the beginning of 2019 (see figure 3), whereas none of them could a year later. How much the new age restrictions will reduce vaping among youth is as yet unknown. On the basis of previous experience with tobacco minimum age laws, we should expect that without enforcement the new law will have little to no effect on underage use.[119] With enforcement, it is natural to expect that youth vaping would decline at least to some extent, if experience with earlier tobacco laws and youth smoking is any guide.[120]

However, several factors suggest that the minimum age laws will not eliminate use by underage vapers. First, most youth do not buy their own e-cigarettes at retail stores, since in most places those under 18 have already been disallowed from purchasing them since 2016; acquiring e-cigarettes from social sources (e.g., friends and family) is much more common.[121] However, the hope of those raising the legal purchasing age is that younger teens will have fewer members of their social sourcing networks who are over 21. Furthermore, many youth who vape have already demonstrated willingness to break the law. Over two-fifths of youth who use e-cigarettes report vaping THC (tetrahydrocannabinol), which is illegal for youth even in states that have legalized cannabis.[122] Finally, even in relatively high-enforcement states such as California, approximately 7 percent of stores in 2018 were willing to sell e-cigarettes illegally to underage vapers.[123] This latter finding is in accord with research showing that the majority (75%) of underage smokers who attempt to purchase tobacco in the US are not refused because of age.[124]

Does vaping create externalities?

As discussed earlier, a classic argument for taxing tobacco rests on health harms created by secondhand smoke. What about secondhand exposure to vapor from e-cigarettes, or even thirdhand exposure to chemical residue that settles from vapor onto surfaces? If secondhand and thirdhand exposure create large health harms, then taxes on e-cigarettes and restrictions on where they can be used may be justified.

Given that the health harms of vaping are not yet known with precision, it is unsurprising that the secondary and tertiary health impacts are also largely unknown, at least in the sense that no "optimal tax" can be calculated yet to align private and social incentives. One systematic review of the scientific literature led to no stronger a statement than that second- and thirdhand exposure to vapor from e-cigarettes has "the *potential* to lead to adverse health effects."[125] The influential National Academy of Sciences report concluded that using an e-cigarette indoors "may involuntarily expose non-users to nicotine and particulates" but also that the effects of such exposure remain unknown.[126] Even if exposure to others' vapor proves eventually to be harmful, it is highly likely to be less harmful than exposure to secondhand smoke. The two studies just cited state that the "risk from being passively exposed to . . . vapor is likely to be less than the risk from passive exposure to conventional cigarette smoke"[127] and that there is "moderate evidence that second-hand exposure to nicotine and particulates is lower from e-cigarettes compared with combustible tobacco cigarettes."[128]

Do restrictions on advertising tobacco apply to e-cigarettes? Should they?

Many of the restrictions on advertising tobacco do not apply to e-cigarettes, since the most important restrictions—most notably, the ban on advertising cigarettes on television and radio—are not FDA regulations. When the FDA deemed e-cigarettes to be tobacco products, any regulations promulgated by that agency thenceforth applied to e-cigarettes. Thus, since 2018, by federal law all advertisements for e-cigarettes must display the warning that "This product contains nicotine derived from tobacco. Nicotine is an addictive chemical." The notice must occupy at least 20 percent of the area of the advertisement.[129] However, there is no federal law against advertising e-cigarettes on television, radio, websites, billboards, public transportation, and other outdoor venues, whereas these advertisements are prohibited in most of the US for cigarettes.[130] Some states, however, ban advertising e-cigarettes on billboards.

Whether advertising e-cigarettes helps or hinders public health depends on how youth and adults respond to advertising, the health effects of vaping, and whether smokers use e-cigarettes to aid cessation. One recent study found that viewing television (but not magazine) advertising of e-cigarettes encouraged smokers to quit, with most of the effect due to greater success per quit attempt rather than to an increase in attempts.[131] The authors estimate that 3 percent of the decrease in the prevalence of adult smoking is due to television advertising. This evidence, which the authors call "tentative" since it was gathered from a relatively short period (two years of data), should give policymakers pause if they are considering indiscriminate bans on advertising e-cigarettes. Whether and how ads targeting or particularly attractive to youth can be prevented without banning all advertising remains an open question, both for vaping and for other goods, such as alcohol.[132]

What about the recent health scares involving vaping and lung illness?

In mid-2019, a spate of visits to emergency rooms around the country linked vaping to acute lung injuries, and the government responded promptly—by creating an acronym for the phenomenon: e-cigarette- or vaping-associated lung injury (EVALI). While by the end of the year the tide of cases of illness and death from EVALI appeared to be reced- ing, the highly publicized events raised the issue of the health effects of e-cigarettes to prominence in the public's eye. As I write this chapter, officials are still investigating the causes of EVALI, and given that prod- ucts of questionable legality appear to be involved in many cases, the true causes may never be nailed down. However, the following para- graphs summarize what seems to be known at the present.

As of February 18, 2020, there were 2,739 hospitalizations and 68 deaths connected with EVALI.[133] The emergency room visits rose sharply in August 2019 and peaked in September. Note that since e-cig- arette usage had been growing smoothly and steadily since at least 2006, a suddenly appearing (and declining) epidemic such as EVALI cannot logically be caused by vaping in general. The most plausible current guess about the cause of EVALI centers on vitamin E acetate, a chemi- cal added to e-cigarettes containing THC (loosely speaking, "marijuana vapes") that the Centers for Disease Control and Prevention says is "strongly linked to the EVALI outbreak." In government tests, 48 of 51 EVALI patients examined had vitamin E acetate in their lung fluid, compared to *none* found in a comparison group of 99 healthy people.[134] Of the roughly 2,000 EVALI patients for whom data were available, 82 percent reported using THC-containing products; given that such products are illegal in some places under state law and illegal every- where under federal law, this percentage is undoubtedly lower than the actual proportion of THC vapers. Of those using THC-containing products, 84 percent reported acquiring products from informal sources other than physical commercial sources such as dispensaries and vape shops: friends, dealers, off the street, or online sellers.[135] Furthermore, the most commonly used brand in a sample of 86 EVALI patients was a generic THC cartridge made by multiple unregulated manufacturers and sold on the black market.[136] On the basis of the evidence, the Centers for Disease Control and Prevention concludes that vitamin E acetate has been identified "as a primary cause of EVALI."[137]

While some public health officials seized upon the epidemic as evidence that vaping in general is deleterious to health, the official recommendations from the Centers for Disease Control and Prevention (as I write this chapter) are to avoid vaping THC, to avoid the additive vitamin E acetate, to be aware of "the wide range of health effects" associated with THC use, and to seek help for abuse of cannabis from a healthcare professional. In particular, the CDC specifically warns against returning to smoking instead of vaping for those who quit smoking or are trying to quit.

If we heavily regulate, tax, or ban e-cigarettes, what might be the unintended consequences?

Some of the potential unintended consequences of over-regulating e-cigarettes are similar to those discussed earlier for tobacco, while others differ. The tax equity issue because of the regressivity of excise taxation remains, although not to the same extent as for cigarette taxes, since it is not the case that lower-income individuals are more likely to vape than higher-income individuals.[138] The more important consideration concerns the health consequences of discouraging the use of a nicotine product at the lower end of the continuum of risk and the potential for black-market substitution.

The harm reduction (as opposed to the abstinence) approach to tobacco control views tobacco and nicotine-containing products as lying along a continuum of risk.[139] Combustible products, most notably cigarettes, pose the greatest hazards, while nicotine replacement therapies are the least hazardous products. Some public health authorities embracing the harm reduction approach, perhaps most notably Public Health England, place e-cigarettes close to the low-risk end of the continuum. The key question for harm reduction is what will happen if e-cigarettes are banned, heavily taxed, or saddled with overly burdensome regulation? If more people continue to smoke instead of switching to vaping or quitting, then the evidence reviewed above indicates that it is highly likely that public health would suffer. Per-unit or ad valorem taxation of e-cigarettes may also encourage substitution toward products with higher concentrations of nicotine, which may increase health harms for youth.[140] On the other hand, if vaping renormalizes smoking and increases initiation among youth, public health could suffer in the future. (Discussion of these consequences continues in the next section.)

Given the relative novelty of vaping, illicit trade in e-cigarette products is much less studied than illicit trade in tobacco products.[141] Apparently a thriving black market in counterfeit e-cigarettes already exists, although the prevalence is unknown and claims by manufacturers may be overstated. A worrisome feature of counterfeit eliquids is the uncertainty about what they contain; one study found that many of them contain nicotine even when they are labeled as zero-nicotine products.[142] Black-market THC vaping products have been found to contain pesticides, heavy metals, and lead, and counterfeit nicotine eliquids have been traced to illicit, unsanitary facilities in China.[143] Packaging and supplies to assemble counterfeit vaping products are readily available online.[144] The barriers to entry into the market for counterfeit products therefore seem to be low. As in any other market, as taxes or sales restrictions on licit products rise, substitution of illicit sources by some users should be expected, although the sensitivity to taxation of illicit trade in e-cigarette products has not been explored yet.

There is another important factor linking regulation of e-cigarettes to illicit trade, however. When e-cigarettes are readily available to smokers at reasonable prices, they offer smokers an attractive alternative to buying illicit tobacco products to reduce the costs of consuming nicotine. E-cigarettes could thus attenuate the link between higher cigarette taxes and stricter regulation of traditional tobacco products and ITTP. An econometric study found empirical support for this hypothesis.[145] Using data from Europe, econometric analysis showed that in places lacking availability of e-cigarettes, there was a sizeable, statistically significant positive relationship between tax increases for cigarettes and ITTP. However, the availability of e-cigarettes attenuated the size of that link: "the more available e-cigarettes become, the less the ITTP market share rises in response to tax-driven price increases for conventional cigarettes."[146] In places where e-cigarette markets are large enough, cigarette prices no longer have any significant effect on illicit trade.

Steps toward Better Regulation

If more were understood about the actual health effects of vaping and exactly what the relationships are among the prices of tobacco and e-cigarettes, vaping, and youth initiation of smoking, and furthermore if society agreed that vapers and smokers need to be "saved from themselves" because of irrational choices, then in principal one could compute optimal prices for tobacco and e-cigarettes and levy taxes to achieve them. Complicating the analysis are the additional factors discussed above regarding the relationships among the price of tobacco, the price and attractiveness of vaping, and illicit trade. Furthermore, policymakers would also have to decide whether and how to weigh the equity considerations raised by tobacco taxation. Given the great uncertainty about the precise degree to which vaping is safer than smoking, no such tax rates can be computed at present. However, although a "first best" regulatory policy toward tobacco and vapor cannot be determined, there are sensible steps that can be taken that are likely to be in the right direction.

For tobacco, difficult and honest discussion needs to take place about the role of high rates of excise taxation. Given the evidence discussed above that current tax rates are higher than those required to correct for externalities and that the burden falls heavily on low-income individuals, the remaining rationales for taxation rest on paternalism, whether it is dressed in the clothing of behavioral economics or not.[147] How much of states' and localities' desire to tax tobacco stems from the ease of raising revenue from a socially disfavored minority?

Regarding e-cigarettes, the following seven recommendations can guide policymakers toward better regulation. First, the overriding principle that shapes thinking about regulating tobacco and e-cigarettes should be risk-proportionate regulation.[148] Products that are not as harmful to health as cigarettes should be regulated less stringently, taxed at lower levels, or even encouraged if they aid in cessation of tobacco use. By deeming e-cigarettes to be "tobacco products," the

FDA created a setting that prompted all the anti-tobacco crusading zeal to be indiscriminately directed at vaping as well. But since vaping is almost surely less harmful to health than smoking, the regulatory touch should also be lighter.

Second, the public health community in the United States needs to curb its tendency to understate the likely health benefits of switching from cigarettes to e-cigarettes. Sometimes this understatement happens because people confuse the absolute risk from vaping with the relative risk of vaping versus smoking, since the absolute risk is often characterized in more certain or inflated terms than the current body of scientific evidence warrants. Since e-cigarettes may cause some health harms (this argument runs), therefore vaping is no better than smoking. When anti-vaping advocates in the public health community take the uncertainty in the scientific literature as license to make statements implying that e-cigarettes could be comparably risky to cigarettes—or even more dangerous—their statements are technically true, since the long-term health effects of vaping are unknown. But they are also highly misleading.[149]

Such statements have helped convince many members of the public to hold potentially dangerous attitudes about the relative health harms of smoking and vaping. Surveys indicate that today the majority of Americans believe e-cigarettes are just as harmful as cigarettes, and about 10 percent think that vaping is more dangerous than smoking.[150] Fewer than 3 percent of adults think that e-cigarettes are much less harmful than cigarettes.[151] These negative perceptions of e-cigarettes have grown rapidly in recent years. This is concerning, given that the perceived risk of smoking relative to vaping is known to affect the decision to use e-cigarettes.[152]

Third, the uncertainty regarding the health effects of e-cigarettes should not be used to discourage smokers from switching to vaping. The personal negative health impacts from smoking are large and well studied. Switching completely away from such a harmful activity to an activity that is very likely to be less harmful—even if the degree of relative risk is uncertain—is likely to improve the health prospects of the individual switching. The potential costs to public health of discouraging smokers from switching to e-cigarettes are high. One study found that, compared to the status quo, replacement of cigarette use by e-cigarette use over a 10-year period would result in 1.6–6.6 million fewer premature deaths and 20.8–86.7 million fewer years of life lost.[153]

Fourth, given the potential benefits to adult smokers from switching to e-cigarettes and the potential harms to youth from taking up vaping or, in consequence, smoking, targeting regulation narrowly at youth may be better than blunt, broadly applied rules. Thus the current age limits on purchases of e-cigarettes are mainly uncontroversial, as is the FDA's enforcement against eliquids designed to resemble child-friendly food products. So would be, presumably, future restrictions on advertising aimed at youth. Of course, youth-oriented restrictions may prevent some young people who already smoke from switching to a less harmful product, since most current smokers began their habit before age 18. (As noted earlier, the age restriction for e-cigarette sales is now 21.)

Expending tobacco control funds on campaigns and information to alert youth to the potential dangers of vaping, in principle, is also relatively uncontroversial, since nicotine may have adverse health effects for adolescents that it does not have for adults.[154] However, as with any abstinence campaign, it is likely that some youth will reject such messages, particularly if they sense that the claims are overblown or manipulative. Given the absence of solid knowledge about adverse health effects, some youth-oriented anti-vaping messages instead rely on false syllogisms along these lines: "Big Tobacco wants you to vape, and tobacco kills—therefore vaping will kill you." Others attempt to parlay the recent epidemic of EVALI into messages not to use licit products such as JUUL and other commercially available, non-THC e-cigarettes, which does not appear to be a supportable conclusion (given the current but evolving knowledge reviewed earlier in this chapter).[155] It is an open question why the same public health community that rejects fear-based anti-drug messages as ineffective or, worse, causing a boomerang effect[156] embraces them for the anti-vaping crusade.

Fifth, given the benefits of using regulation to target vaping by youth, heavily taxing e-cigarettes is not likely to be in the best interests of public health. As discussed previously, a tax (or any general regulation affecting all ages of users) is a very blunt instrument. While higher prices may deter some youth from using e-cigarettes, given the apparently large current appetite for black-market vapes that the EVALI epidemic revealed, coupled with the evidence from tobacco taxes and ITTP, it seems very likely that high taxes on e-cigarettes will drive more youth demand toward less reputable and potentially much more dangerous sources. In any event, sales to those under 21 years of age are already banned, which is equivalent to an infinitely high tax that applies only to youth. Furthermore, burdening adult smokers with high taxes will discourage some of them from switching to vaping, to the likely detriment of their health.

Indeed, if e-cigarettes are viewed as a form of nicotine-replacement therapy, there might even be a case for subsidizing them for smokers attempting cessation (as NRTs are subsidized through private health insurance and various public programs) rather than taxing them. Thus, proposed legislation such as the E-cigarette Tax Parity Act, which seeks to tax nicotine equally regardless of the mode of delivery, not only almost certainly violate the principle of risk-proportionate regulation but also may be harmful to public health.[157]

Sixth, careful consideration is warranted about whether banning the use of e-cigarettes in public spaces is appropriate. As reviewed above, it is far more certain that switching from smoking to vaping is beneficial for the health of the user than it is that e-cigarettes create substantial health harms from secondary exposure. But the ability to use e-cigarettes to consume nicotine, even if only in designated areas, while at work or in public spaces could be a powerful incentive for a smoker to switch. On the flip side, the ability to consume nicotine more easily may also prevent or delay some smokers from cessation (the "dual use" case). More study will be required to resolve these uncertainties, but it is not at all clear that excessive caution is better than cautious optimism regarding the social costs and benefits of vaping bans in public and work spaces. Banning vaping where smoking is banned also sends the message that the two activities are equally harmful, when they most likely are not—see again the second and third points discussed above.

Seventh, efforts to resolve the regulatory uncertainty at the federal level should be regarded as highly important. The FDA currently states that "no ENDS products have been authorized by the FDA—meaning that all ENDS products currently on the market are considered illegally marketed and are subject to enforcement, at any time, in the FDA's discretion."[158] Yet the agency has so far allowed sales of commercial nicotine e-cigarette products, as long as there are no sales or marketing to youth. The current regulatory environment is thus one in which the industry and the specific manufacturers and retailers in the industry are subject to a higher degree of regulatory dependence and uncertainty than affects most other industries. The negative effects of regulatory uncertainty and regulatory delay on investment and product innovation are well studied in other industries.[159] If e-cigarettes aid cessation or otherwise reduce harms from smoking, then innovation in that product space should be encouraged rather than discouraged.

Finally, in regard to both tobacco and e-cigarettes, policymakers must pay serious attention to the interplay among taxation, regulation, and illicit markets. If e-cigarettes are inexpensive, attractive to users, easy to obtain, and able to be used in places where smoking is forbidden, then current smokers will be less likely turn to the black market when they are faced with higher taxes on cigarettes or increased restrictions on smoking.[160] Because the argument that higher taxes stimulate ITTP is convenient for tobacco manufacturers lobbying for lower tax rates, the public health community has a long history of discounting the possibility out of hand. This is despite the well-established links economists have found between cigarette taxation and smuggling.[161] The already-present black market in tobacco, e-cigarettes, and eliquids should not be viewed as a theoretical possibility of limited practical import. Instead, illicit trade in all these product markets—and the likelihood that stricter regulation and higher taxation will exacerbate it—must be part of the policy calculus from the beginning.

Policymakers should plan for enforcement against illicit markets, and this enforcement must include action stronger than the tool currently preferred by the FDA—warning letters sent to noncompliant retailers and manufacturers.[162] Policymakers must also recognize that harsher, more effective enforcement can create its own harms—a notion familiar to the harm reduction community regarding illicit drugs, but curiously absent among anti-tobacco advocates.[163]

Moving Forward: A Guide for Regulatory Policy

Adam Hoffer and Todd Nesbit

The causes of our social and financial problems are myriad; to suggest that regulation is the primary cause of all such societal problems would be irresponsible. Yet our regulatory policies do impose real costs. Those costs should cause us to pause to reconsider the proper role of government. Such an undertaking is likely to lead to the conclusion that regulatory policy be held to a higher standard than the whims of appointed bureaucrats. While many regulations undoubtedly improve public well-being and pass a cost-benefit test, many others neither expand liberties nor come close to achieving the lofty goals set forth by their proponents.

Millions of Americans, particularly those from lower-income households, regularly are prohibited from entering more financially promising careers, are prevented from receiving proper medical care, pay higher prices than necessary, and generally have their daily lives complicated as a result of unjustified or ineffective regulation. A significant share of such unnecessary costs is the outcome of a political process that caters to special interests and is plagued by imperfect information and the unchecked personal ambitions of policymakers.

The chapters compiled in this book apply fundamental economics to evaluate regulatory policy. We incorporate lessons from public choice theory, law and economics, and constitutional economics, among other fields, to examine the expected behavior of self-interested individuals involved in the enactment and enforcement of regulatory policy. In this final chapter of the book, we summarize some common themes observed across the contributed chapters. We then present some policy recommendations that promise to make regulatory policy less burdensome and more effective at enhancing individual liberties and well-being.

Broad Research Findings

Government intervention, according to standard economic theory, may be justified to correct so-called market failures. In the case of regulation, such failures generally involve information problems and circumstances in which the costs of defining and enforcing private property rights exceed the benefits of doing so. Consequently, the theoretical justification for regulation is much more limited than the practice of regulating has generally been. Consider, for instance, occupational licensing and alcohol sales regulation.

As discussed by Alicia Plemmons and Edward Timmons in chapter 6, the public call for occupational licensing generally centers on a concern for consumer safety based on a presumption that private firms lack proper incentives for adequate training. If this argument is true and providers' inadequate training puts consumers at risk, one would reasonably expect regulators to require more extensive training programs for professions in which inadequately trained providers place consumers at greater risk. We suggest it is fair to assert that the risks of an improperly or inadequately trained emergency medical technician exceed those of, say, an interior designer. Yet occupational licensing requirements often do not match well with the potential for consumer risk:

For example, Michigan requires 1,460 days of education and training to become an athletic trainer, but just 26 to be an emergency medical technician (EMT). In fact, across all states, interior designers, barbers, cosmetologists, and manicurists all face greater average licensing requirements than do EMTs.[1]

The data clearly show a disconnect between the true motivation for occupational licensing and its theoretical justification.

Equally questionable is the regulation of alcohol sales, which is discussed in chapter 17. Again, such rules are generally motivated by a publicly stated concern for consumer safety. Their proponents often explicitly argue that consumers just do not understand or properly account for the risks. But the regulations often fail to match intentions with outcomes. Alcohol regulation better reflects a situation in which well-intended concerns are exploited to intentionally enrich a select few—a classic bootleggers-and-Baptists example. For instance, Pennsylvania still monopolizes the sale of liquor to state liquor stores, and sales to consumers are limited to no more than a six-pack at retail outlets other than licensed beer distributors.

The personal incentives of elected and appointed public officials at all levels of government rarely square with the goal of promoting the public's interest, should such a single goal inclusive of all individuals even be feasible. Instead, the incentives of politicians and bureaucrats often are more aligned with catering to special interests. For the elected legislator, such behavior is consistent with reelection motives. For the appointed bureaucrat, such behavior is consistent with job security, promotion in rank, and more generous perquisites of office, all of which are influenced heavily or controlled by elected legislators and chief executives. The result is more restrictive, complex, and burdensome regulatory rules that protect the interests of the politically connected (and often wealthy) few at the expense of their smaller, less politically connected rivals and the broader public.

Such overregulation—regulatory powers extending beyond the economically justified limits—comes at a steep cost. The costs of regulatory failures and the lessons to be learned from these failures have been detailed throughout this book and are summarized below.

Section I: Regulation, Entrepreneurship, and Opportunity

Entrepreneurship and market exchange are the primary drivers of wealth accumulation and prosperity. Indeed, poverty is the default status in nature, and the pursuit of profit through innovation and market exchange has lifted a large majority of the world's population far from those dire circumstances. Unfortunately, these benefits have not reached all individuals. The ability of market exchange to create wealth relies on formal and informal institutions, including private property rights and social trust. Regulation can play an important role in enhancing wealth creation in cases where private property rights cannot be defined or properly protected and when social trust is difficult to establish.

Unfortunately, the political marketplace in which regulation is enacted is rife with rent-seeking and suffers from substantial information asymmetries. These characteristics often lead to excessive regulation that hinders entrepreneurship, particularly small business start-ups. Rent-seeking exacerbates the social environment by pitting individuals and groups with stakes in the outcomes of regulatory processes against one another, creating winners and losers in zero- or negative-sum games, further eroding social trust, and undermining markets' ability to function properly.

Consumers don't trust producers because firms lobby government regularly to enact policies that restrict competition, allowing incumbents to increase their prices and profits. Newcomers attempting to enter a trade often are excluded by regulations supported by those already practicing the trade who seek to restrict competition. As a result, the poor often are trapped on the lower rungs of the income ladder. Given the obstacles erected by the political marketplace to contributing legally to wealth creation, many individuals turn their efforts to the shadow economy, where trust is more difficult to establish, the returns on investment are smaller, and the incentives for destructive entrepreneurship are stronger.

In summary, while the rule of law plays an important role in supporting market exchange and enhancing wealth creation, the incentives inherent in the political marketplace often lead to excessive regulation. Overregulation slows economic growth by degrading social trust and redirecting entrepreneurs away from productive activities and toward unproductive and sometimes destructive ones. Individuals who are marginalized politically, most often the poor, are those who suffer the most.

Section II: Regulation and Labor Market Outcomes

Virtually all economic and social regulations tend to reduce employment, on average, in the regulated industry. Their effect on wages is more varied and depends on the specific type of regulation imposed. For example, occupational licensing, minimum wages, and "make-work" rules all tend to increase average wages. At the same time, most other labor market regulations are expected to reduce them.

We draw particular attention to occupational licensing laws. As discussed earlier in this chapter, while some theoretical support can be found for the limited use of licensing, it is reasonably clear that the current extent of occupational licensing far exceeds the level that is beneficial. Workers in states with more expansive occupational licensing have fewer occupational choices and less job mobility, effects that are particularly harmful for minorities who are more likely to experience unemployment. Some of the costs of higher wages are passed on to consumers in the form of higher product prices or are borne by workers in the form of fewer hours of work and less-valuable fringe benefits. However, product or service quality is improved marginally in some cases.

Certificate-of-need (CON) laws are particularly common in the healthcare industry and are found to fail in delivering on the lofty promises of their proponents. CON laws were justified on the basis of improving access to healthcare, particularly in rural areas, while also driving down healthcare costs. Certificate-of-need regulations have, in most cases, done exactly the opposite: reduced access and increased costs. Relaxing or eliminating CON laws would do much to expand access to healthcare, particularly in rural areas.

Section III: Land Use and Energy Standards

Affordable housing is a major policy goal in many large U.S. cities such as San Francisco and New York City. Counterproductive land use regulations have contributed to the shortages of affordable housing. Restrictive zoning laws, minimum unit size requirements, rent controls, and "green space" rules guide urban redevelopment and limit new housing construction. Such regulations indulge the preferences of constituent homeowner-voters, who seek through regulatory intervention to raise the value of what likely is their single most valuable asset. The direct result is, as intended, elevated real estate prices. The indirect results include pricing the less wealthy out of the market, job immobility for people who occupy rent-controlled housing, and longer commuting times (and more tailpipe emissions), particularly for the less wealthy who must look farther away from the central business district to find affordable housing.

In addition to following zoning and minimum unit size requirements, developers must comply with building codes and energy efficiency codes, which raise construction costs. Likewise, homeowners' appliance choices are limited by energy efficiency standards. Such regulations are well intended and are justified by their proponents as necessary to correct home buyers' and homeowners' biases toward underestimating the long-run benefits of more-energy-efficient systems that increase up-front purchase prices. However, to the extent that consumers do not value energy conservation as highly as environmental activists do (perhaps because time-of-day electricity pricing is not yet widespread) and thus do not face incentives to reduce power consumption, the codes and standards can be counterproductive. Assessing energy efficiency regulations thus raises empirical questions that should be answered by well-informed cost-benefit analyses.

Section IV: Energy Markets and Environmental Regulations

While it is common for regulatory policy to pit against one another individuals and groups with different stakes in the regulatory process, this is particularly true of environmental and energy regulation. Regulations in these areas have consistently favored the goals of one politically-popular group over those of other less-politically-popular groups, regardless of the relative costs and benefits for those affected by the regulation. For example, environmental activists often battle for influence over a proposed regulation with the owners of business enterprises who would incur substantial compliance costs should the regulation be imposed. In other cases, large public utility providers seek protection from competition to take advantage of monopoly pricing while consumers want to prevent such protections and the resulting higher prices.

"Market-like regulation" is but one approach that has been shown to increase the effectiveness of regulatory outcomes, particularly in the realm of environmental and energy rules, and to foster wealth creation—or, at worst, to impair prosperity to lesser extents. Market-like regulations harness the best aspects of markets and public policy interventions while limiting the worst aspects of political influence on regulatory outcomes. Consider the regulation of electricity markets. The traditional approach for the electricity distribution and retail industries has been to impose and maintain regulation largely on the basis of claims that electricity markets are natural monopolies. However, when competition is introduced at the retail or distribution levels, lower prices, cost reductions, and more robust innovation are observed. Texas's regulatory model for electricity introduces competitive market design at both the wholesale and retail levels and serves as an excellent example of market-like regulation.

Section V: Divisive Cases of Regulating Products and Services

Regulation of the internet, school choice, alcohol, and tobacco and vaping products exemplifies the dangers of overregulation. The pursuit of "net neutrality" was a heavy-handed, top-down approach to regulation. It failed miserably and was repealed just two years after its promulgation. Because opposition to overregulating the internet is far from over, bureaucrats would be wise to employ market-like regulatory strategies to avoid the pitfalls of their first regulatory attempt.

Student performance has benefited from school choice precisely because school choice places competitive pressures on traditional public schools to improve their performances in educating children, many of whom are currently limited to only one option in their geographically defined public school district. Special interests, mainly in the form of teachers' unions, likely have led some states to enact regulations that limit the ability of private or charter schools to compete directly with the public school monopoly. Mandates requiring that students be admitted randomly to alternative schools and that these schools administer state-approved tests appear to be the most intrusive, leading to substantial reductions in the numbers, qualities, and instructional methods of the private schools participating in school choice programs. To the extent that the regulation of school choice programs is intended to foster better student performance, it is counterproductive and serves little purpose other than to protect public school teachers and administrators from competition.

The political marketplace can make for some strange bedfellows. Religious groups that oppose the consumption of alcohol can find themselves aligned with large breweries or beer distributors that seek to reduce their competition. Similarly, health advocates may have found themselves on the same side politically as big tobacco in support of regulations that simultaneously reduce competition for tobacco companies and increase product prices or restrict the number of tobacco flavors available to consumers. On the one hand, such regulations that benefit politically connected firms are representative of public-and-private-sector cronyism. On the other hand, to the extent that reducing the consumption of such "sin goods" is welfare-enhancing, more efficient and effective alternatives to selective taxes and paternalistic "nudges" are available.

Prescribing Better Regulatory Policy

The broader takeaway from this book is that the regulatory process could be vastly improved by decreasing the influence of special interests and increasing the dedication to a set of general guiding principles. We conclude the book with a discussion of those guiding principles of regulation.

An obvious potential solution to at least some of the regulatory issues discussed in this book is to repeal or substantially limit the extent of the regulations in question. However, such a generic suggestion does very little to advance the discussion of improving regulatory policy, in part because policy decisions are made in the political marketplace. We want the present volume to offer politically feasible yet truly helpful policy prescriptions and guiding principles. These are what we attempt to offer in the remainder of this chapter.

First-Best Solutions

The first three policy prescriptions would provide the greatest benefits, but implementing them may prove politically challenging.

1) Mandate sunset provisions. All regulations should include automatic sunset provisions; such provisions cannot be routinely extended or renewed. Policymakers should view attempts to solve societal problems by public policy interventions—regulatory or otherwise—as experiments, best undertaken at the state or local levels of government. Any policy's outcomes and implications cannot be known or anticipated fully before it is put in place. Individuals may respond in unexpected ways. Innovators may create new technologies. Pandemics may happen.

A multitude of scenarios could play out that render the regulation ineffective or perverse. The regulation could be too restrictive or inflexible. It might not be restrictive enough. One size does not fit all. Or maybe the regulation will become no longer desirable or needed. A sunset provision prevents us from being locked into a bad policy or one that has become obsolete given unpredictable changes in society over time. Such a requirement should not only be imposed on new regulations, but also be phased in retroactively for existing regulations.

We propose that every regulation be automatically repealed after X years. The sponsoring agency should be allowed to resubmit the regulation for another X years through the normal approval process, but the proposal will then need to include evidence that the regulation has mitigated the targeted "market failure" and generated positive net benefits.

The length of time for sunsetting may need to be tailored to the problem addressed. Whereas five years may be enough time to determine whether a regulation has effectively reduced informational barriers and improved efficiency in a particular industry, such a time frame may be too short for many environmental, pharmaceutical, and medical device issues. Measuring the effects of a policy on climate change, population changes for slow-reproducing species, and other issues will likely require at least ten years of observation. It may take a generation for any adverse effects of approved prescription drugs and healthcare procedures to materialize.

2) Require cost-benefit analysis. As has been true since Ronald Reagan issued Executive Order 12291, all new significant regulatory action at the federal level should be subject to sound cost-benefit analyses to provide evidence that the proposed regulation will produce greater benefits than costs. At a minimum, only regulations that produce positive net benefits should be implemented. A more restrictive alternative would mandate not only that all regulations produce positive net benefits but also that their net benefits be larger than those expected from other reasonable alternatives. This proposed policy is not all that different from Executive Order 12866, which has been signed by every president since Clinton. (Presidents Carter and Reagan also signed similarly motivated orders during their terms.)[2] Executive Order 12866 applies to significant regulations (i.e., those with potential impacts of $100 million or more on the economy in any given year), but we suggest that its application be broadened to all regulations. Conducting the necessary regulatory impact study is costly; should such a cost not be warranted given the extent of the problem, the issue is inframarginal and should be left unaddressed by regulatory policy.

Requiring cost-benefit analyses is certainly not a panacea. The accuracy and reliability of the estimates could vary substantially across agencies and over time. Regulatory economist Jerry Ellig used the Regulatory Report Card, published by the Mercatus Center at George Mason University, to quantify the quality of the analysis in regulatory impact analyses of regulations falling under the provisions of Executive

Order 12866. He finds that of federal agencies conducting more than five regulatory impact analyses, the Department of Energy produced the best analyses while the Department of Health and Human Services produced the worst.[3] Despite the varying quality of the regulatory impact analyses, the requirement is a step in the right direction and, at a minimum, it should help agencies avoid implementing the most damaging regulations and meanwhile increase the transparency of the regulatory process.

3) Create a federal regulatory approval agency. Some readers may be perplexed by the suggestion of more bureaucracy as a solution to bureaucratic problems. Bear with us. Again, our goal is to promote institutions and rules that improve regulatory policy. While a regulatory approval agency would not be foolproof, it should lead to improved regulatory policy. Reaching this goal need not require the creation of a new agency. Rather, implementing this recommendation could take the form of expanding the existing Office of Information and Regulatory Affairs (OIRA). We suggest that it may be time to establish an independent agency, likely OIRA, to review all federal regulation concerning fiscal policy. At minimum, it is time to expand the definition of which regulations meet the significant regulatory action criteria such that more regulations are reviewed.

We provide here a broad idea of how such an approval agency might work. All existing bureaus and agencies would remain in place with their same duties, but without authority to implement the regulations they craft. Any agency would be able to draft and recommend a new regulation; however, that regulation would have to be submitted to the federal regulatory approval agency for review and approval.

All regulatory proposals would need to include a cost-benefit analysis, as we suggested in solution number 2. Any individual or organization that opposes a proposed regulation would be able to object to the proposed regulation and present arguments against it to the federal regulatory approval agency. All hearings and documents would be open to the public for full review and comment before any final ruling. The federal regulatory approval agency itself could not create any new regulations; it would be authorized only to approve or not approve those submitted to it. The review process likewise would apply to proposals to renew sunsetting regulations.

The federal regulatory approval agency's structure could be similar to that of the Federal Reserve, with independent member-experts located in regional offices across the country (and perhaps with specialties in different industries). The agency would review regulatory impact analyses to confirm that the sponsoring agency has adequately justified the provisions contained within proposed regulations—in this way it would be similar to OIRA. Indeed, expanding and restructuring OIRA, rather than creating a new agency, is likely the most efficient means of establishing the prescribed federal regulatory approval agency.

As Ellig notes, it is reasonable to expect the regulatory approval agency to return regulations to the sponsoring agencies and demand higher-quality analysis when it is operating under a presidential appointee rather than a career civil service administrator.[4] Ellig finds empirical support for the hypothesis that the quality of regulatory analysis improves when OIRA is headed by a political appointee. He finds, further, that the primary benefit of OIRA is to ensure "that agencies base their estimates of benefits on more careful analysis, develop alternatives, and explain how their analysis affected decisions."[5] We expect that a broader federal regulatory approval agency likewise might improve the quality of regulatory impact analyses, which also should lead to sounder final regulations.

Second-Best Solutions

Even if the first three policy prescriptions prove too difficult politically to implement right away, substantial gains in regulatory quality can still be achieved by pursuing the following policies in the meantime.

4) Reduce the volume of the current regulatory code. Multiple politicians have suggested eliminating one or more existing regulations for every new one promulgated. In our opinion, that approach is an inefficient way of lightening the regulatory burden because it does not necessarily get rid of the most problematic regulations. However, mandating the elimination of old regulations before a new one is implemented would send the correct message to regulatory agencies: namely, that the regulatory drag on the economy needs to be taken seriously and reduced where and when possible.

5) Institute broad reciprocity for licenses at the state and local levels. Household mobility is restricted greatly by current occupational licensing rules. Instituting broad reciprocity for licenses and professional certifications will open employment opportunities for people who move or travel across state or city borders, especially to locations where their skills are in short supply; businesses will have an easier time operating in new locations. As highlighted by the reciprocity offered to most doctors and nurses during the COVID-19 pandemic, removing barriers to employment can offer significant benefits with low or zero costs.

Rules of Thumb

Each of the above five policy prescriptions involve action by the legislative branch and, thus, may take substantial time to gain enough political support to enact. However, the sponsoring regulatory agencies can improve regulatory outcomes by following the following rules of thumb.

A) Base rulemaking on reliable, scientific evidence. Relying on scientific evidence as the basis for evaluating rulemaking will help minimize the influence of vested interest groups' efforts to nudge the process by misinforming regulators. This principle comes with two caveats. First, this is not to suggest that all lobbying is without value; indeed, lobbying can provide useful information and can permit large numbers of less wealthy individuals to have their voices heard. However, given the existing political climate, the voices that dominate the policy process tend to be the individuals and businesses that are already successful and that seek to block the entry of new competitors or to drive existing rivals from the market. Such influence has led to inefficient and exclusionary regulatory policy.

Second, we by no means argue that science is uninfluenced by the political process. While scientists are often viewed as benevolent truth seekers, scientists are bound by the shortcomings common to all humans, including the limitations often referenced in the public choice literature. In a recent article published in the academic journal *Public Choice*, Diana Thomas and Michael Thomas argue that scientists can be best characterized as self-interested individuals who participate in coordination processes similar to those that participate in markets and politics.[6] Indeed, the institutions of scientific disciplines sometimes create incentives for researchers to participate in rent-seeking activities. Consequently, science itself can be complicit in the lobbying process, either as special interest group itself or selectively justifying the intentions of other interest groups. That scientists are not the ideal truth seekers we want them to be is no reason to throw scientific evidence out the window; however, it does suggest that rule makers should bear in mind that scientific researchers may be influenced by political biases and should therefore seek out more evidence rather than relying on the popular study of the day.

B) Avoid blunt or broad regulation. Regulatory policy is most effective when it targets a very specific problem precisely; it is less effective when its language is broad. This is not to argue for command-and-control rules that dictate the exact measures a firm must take. Rather, we suggest that regulation be written such that it cannot be later interpreted to apply to other industries not originally under consideration. For example, if youth smoking and vaping is the concern, tailor policy to youth rather than to all smokers and vapers. Precise, targeted regulation will lessen the frequency and extent of unintended consequences and improve the overall efficiency of the policy.

C) Incentivize state and local coordination. Given the existing political marketplace, homeowner-voters have strong incentives to support local policies that raise their own home values without regard to the spatial spillovers imposed on neighboring jurisdictions or on the less wealthy. Consequently, state governments can contribute in major ways to limiting the inefficiencies stemming from local regulations. For example, states may provide guidelines regarding economic development and land use policies.

D) Establish market-like regulation. Market-like regulations in energy and education, to name just two areas, facilitate competition and innovation while limiting the costs of the political marketplace. Competitive pressures encourage firms to control costs and limit price increases while still innovating and improving product quality. Furthermore, choices about which technologies to invest in and what risks to take are left in the hands of the people who stand to gain or lose rather than subjected to political whim. Market-like institutions will improve the efficiency of the means used to achieve the intended goals of regulatory policies.

E) Incorporate more analysis of economic risk. Rulemaking should incorporate an analysis of risk to determine the extent of regulation needed. When the risk of negative outcomes is economically small, regulation should be minimal or nonexistent. When the risk of negative outcomes is economically large, regulation might be more involved. The fact that the risk of negative outcomes is large does not guarantee that regulation is wise, because the costs of the regulation can have the unintended effect of lowering income and increasing the risk of harm and death in other ways. In a recent Independent Institute Briefing, economists Kevin Gomez, Diana Thomas, and Ryan Yonk use the example of chemical regulations to detail how regulations have the potential to cause far more harm than the estimated risks that the regulations are crafted to mitigate.[7]

F) Avoid uncertainty. Our final rule of thumb is twofold. First, regulations should be clear about what is permitted and what is not. Second, regulators should not erect burdensome regulation to protect individuals from the uncertain; doing so often prevents people from developing private solutions to deal with unwanted uncertainty. If a private solution shows a good deal of promise for abating or minimizing a problem, there is little need for regulation to begin with. Further, market innovations may address the problem in the near future, making restrictive regulation not only unnecessary but also inefficient.

Endnotes

FOREWORD

1   George J. Stigler, "Supplementary Note on Economic Theories of Regulation (1975)," in *The Citizen and the State: Essays on Regulation*, by George J. Stigler (Chicago: University of Chicago Press, 1975), 140.

2   George J. Stigler, "The Theory of Economic Regulation," *Bell Journal of Economics and Management Science* 2, no. 1 (1971): 3–21.

3   Stigler, "Supplementary Note on Economic Theories," 140 (emphasis in original).

4   Harold Demsetz, "Information and Efficiency: Another Viewpoint," *Journal of Law and Economics* 12 (1969): 1–22.

5   Frédéric Bastiat, "What Is Seen and What Is Not Seen," in *Selected Essays on Political Economy*, ed. George B. de Huszar (1850; repr., Irvington-on-Hudson, NY: Foundation for Economic Education, 1964).

6   Adam Smith, *The Theory of Moral Sentiments*, ed. D. D. Raphael and A. L. Macfie (1759 repr., Indianapolis: Liberty Fund, 1982), 233–34.

7   Smith, *Theory of Moral Sentiments*, 234.

8   F. A. Hayek, "The Use of Knowledge in Society," *American Economic Review* 35 (1945): 519–30.

9   Stigler, "Theory of Economic Regulation," 3.

10 Robert Higgs, *Crisis and Leviathan: Critical Episodes in the Growth of American Government*, 25th anniv. ed. (Oakland, CA: Independent Institute, 2013).

11 Mancur Olson, *The Logic of Collective Action: Public Goods and the Theory of Groups* (Cambridge, MA: Harvard University Press, 1965).

12 Gordon Tullock, "The Welfare Costs of Tariffs, Monopolies and Theft," *Western Economic Journal* 5 (1967): 224–32; Anne O. Krueger, "The Political Economy of the Rent-Seeking Society," *American Economic Review* 64 (1974): 291–303.

13 Gordon Tullock, "The Transitional Gains Trap," *Bell Journal of Economics and Management Science* 6 (1975): 671–78.

14 Robert E. McCormick, William F. Shughart II, and Robert D. Tollison, "The Disinterest in Deregulation," *American Economic Review* 74 (1984): 1075–79; Fred S. McChesney, "Of Stranded Costs and Stranded Hopes: The Difficulties of Deregulation," *Independent Review* 3 (1999): 485–509.

15 Louis De Alessi, "Property Rights: Private and Political Institutions," in *The Elgar Companion to Public Choice*, ed. William F. Shughart II and Laura Razzolini (Cheltenham, UK: Edward Elgar, 2001).

16 Gary M. Anderson, William F. Shughart II, and Robert D. Tollison, "On the Incentives of Judges to Enforce Legislative Wealth Transfers," *Journal of Law and Economics* 32 (1989): 215–28.

INTRODUCTION

1 "Total Pages Published in the *Code of Federal Regulations* (1950–2017)," Regulatory Studies Center, George Washington University, last updated January 30, 2019, https://regulatorystudies.columbian.gwu.edu/sites/g/files/zaxdzs1866/f/downloads/Total%20Pages%20Published%20in%20the%20CFR.pdf.

2 Lee Rainie, Scott Keeter, and Andrew Perrin, "Trust and Distrust in America," Pew Research Center, July 22, 2019.

3 "Congress and the Public," Gallup, accessed February 11, 2021, https://news.gallup.com/poll/1600/congress-public.aspx.

4 Data in this paragraph come from "Special Report: The State of Consumer Trust," Morning Consult, Most Trusted Brands 2020, accessed February 11, 2021, https://morningconsult.com/wp-content/uploads/2020/01/Morning-Consult-The-State-of-Consumer-Trust.pdf.

5 Omar Al-Ubaydli and Patrick A. McLaughlin, "RegData: A Numerical Database on Industry-Specific Regulations for All United States Industries and Federal Regulations, 1997–2012," *Regulation & Governance* 11 (2015): 109–23.

6 William Baumol, "Entrepreneurship: Productive, Unproductive and Destructive," *Journal of Political Economy* 98 (1990): 893–921.

CHAPTER 1: REGULATION AND ENTREPRENEURSHIP: THEORY, IMPACTS, AND IMPLICATIONS

1 Paul D. Reynolds, Michael Hay, and S. Michael Camp, *Global Entrepreneurship Monitor: 1999 Executive Report* (Kansas City, MO: Kauffman Center for Entrepreneurial Leadership, 1999); Andrew L. Zacharakis, William D. Bygrave, and Dean A. Shepherd, *Global Entrepreneurship Monitor: National Entrepreneurship Assessment; United States of America* (Kansas City, MO: Kauffman Center for Entrepreneurial Leadership, 2000).

2 Joseph A. Schumpeter, *Capitalism, Socialism, and Democracy* (New York: Harper, 1942).

3 Israel M. Kirzner, "Entrepreneurial Discovery and the Competitive Market Process: An Austrian Approach," *Journal of Economic Literature* 35, no. 1 (1997): 60–85.

4 See Russell S. Sobel, "Testing Baumol: Institutional Quality and the Productivity of Entrepreneurship," *Journal of Business Venturing* 23, no. 6 (November 2008): 641–55; Russell S. Sobel, "Economic Freedom and Entrepreneurship," in *What America's Decline in Economic Freedom Means for Entrepreneurship and Prosperity*, ed. Donald J. Boudreaux (Vancouver, BC: Fraser Institute, 2015).

5 Lecture in 1755, quoted in Dugald Stewart, *Account of the Life and Writings of Adam Smith LLD*, section IV, p. 25, which is included in Adam Smith, *Essays on Philosophical Subjects*, ed. W. P. D. Wightman and J. C. Bryce (Indianapolis, IN: Liberty Fund, 1982).

6 For more information about the public interest view, see Richard A. Posner, "The Social Costs of Monopoly and Regulation," *Journal of Political Economy* 83, no. 4 (1975): 807–27.

7 See James M. Buchanan and Gordon Tullock, *The Calculus of Consent: Logical Foundations of Constitutional Democracy* (Ann Arbor: University of Michigan Press, 1962); "Public Finance and Public Choice," chapter 10 in James M. Buchanan, *What Should Economists Do?* (Indianapolis, IN: Liberty Press, 1979).

8 See Posner, "Social Costs of Monopoly and Regulation"; George J. Stigler, "The Theory of Economic Regulation," *Bell Journal of Economics and Management Science* 2, no. 1 (1971): 3–21.

9 The best discussion of this can be found in Frédéric Bastiat, *The Law* (1850; repr., Indianapolis, IN: Liberty Fund, 2013).

10 Bruce Yandle, "Bootleggers and Baptists—the Education of a Regulatory Economist," *Regulation* 7, no. 3 (1983): 12–16.

11 See the wonderful essay by Frédéric Bastiat, "What Is Seen and What Is Not Seen," in *Selected Essays on Political Economy*, ed. George B. de Huszar (1850; repr., Irvington-on-Hudson, NY: Foundation for Economic Education, 1964).

12 Gordon Tullock, "The Transitional Gains Trap," *Bell Journal of Economics* 6 (Autumn 1975): 671–78.

13 See Russell S. Sobel and John A. Dove, "Analyzing the Effectiveness of State Regulatory Review," *Public Finance Review* 44, no. 4 (July 2016): 446–77.

14 Thomas DeLeire, "The Unintended Consequences of the Americans with Disabilities Act," *Regulation* 23, no. 1 (2000): 21–24.

15 Associated Press, "Rare Woodpecker Sends a Town Running for Its Chain Saws," *New York Times*, September 24, 2006.

16 Jonathan Klick and Joshua D. Wright, "Grocery Bag Bans and Foodborne Illness" (Research Paper No. 13-2, University of Pennsylvania Institute for Law and Economics, November 2, 2012), https://ssrn.com/abstract=2196481.

17 See Gordon Tullock, "The Welfare Cost of Tariffs, Monopolies, and Theft," *Western Economic Journal* 5, no. 3 (June 1967): 224–32.

18 OpenSecrets.org, Center for Responsive Politics, accessed April 21, 2020, https://www.opensecrets.org/.

19 Sobel, "Testing Baumol."

20 Sobel, "Testing Baumol."

21 Not all these reductions in business activity are unintentional, however. Sometimes regulations are enacted to intentionally lower the consumption or production of goods such as cigarettes, marijuana, alcohol, gambling, and assisted suicide. More troubling economically, however, are the seemingly well-intended health and safety regulations that create reductions in prosperity that are unintentional.

22 Michael Greenstone, "The Impacts of Environmental Regulations on Industrial Activity," *Journal of Political Economy* 110, no. 6 (December 2002): 1175–217.

23 See Alberto Alesina et al., "Regulation and Investment," *Journal of the European Economic Association* 3, no. 4 (June 2005): 791–825.

24 Patrick A. McLaughlin and Oliver Sherouse, "RegData 2.2: A Panel Dataset on U.S. Federal Regulations," *Public Choice* 180, no. 1–2 (2019): 43–55.

25 James Bailey and Diana Thomas, "Regulating Away Competition: The Effect of Regulation on Entrepreneurship and Employment," *Journal of Regulatory Economics* 52 (2017): 237–54. Nathan Goldschlag and Alex Tabarrok use these data to examine measures of industry dynamism such as the job destruction rate and the start-up rate; however, they do not find that regulation was a major factor driving the overall decline in industry dynamism that has occurred in the United States in the past few decades. Nathan Goldschlag and Alex Tabarrok, "Is Regulation to Blame for the Decline in American Entrepreneurship?," *Economic Policy* 33 (2018): 5–44.

26 Peter T. Calcagno and Russell S. Sobel, "Regulatory Costs on Entrepreneurship and Establishment Employment Size," *Small Business Economics* 42, no. 3 (March 2014): 541–59.

27 Joseph A. Schumpeter, *The Theory of Economic Development* (Cambridge, MA: Harvard University Press, 1934); William J. Baumol, "Education for Innovation: Entrepreneurial Breakthroughs vs. Corporate Incremental Improvements" (NBER Working Paper No. 10578, National Bureau of Economic Research, Cambridge, MA, June 2004); Clayton M. Christensen, *The Innovator's Dilemma: When New Technologies Cause Great Firms to Fail* (Boston: Harvard Business School Press, 1997).

28 See Milton Friedman and Rose Friedman, *Free to Choose: A Personal Statement* (New York: Harcourt Brace Jovanovich, 1979); William J. Baumol, "Contestable Markets: An Uprising in the Theory of Industry Structure," *American Economic Review* 72, no. 1 (1982): 1–15.

29 See Annie Karni, "This Gas Station Is a Landmark?!," *New York Post*, April 8, 2012, https://nypost.com/2012/04/08/this-gas-station-is-a-landmark/.

30 See Toke S. Aidt, "Rent Seeking and the Economics of Corruption," *Constitutional Political Economy* 27 (2016): 142–57; Arye L. Hillman and John G. Riley, "Politically Contestable Rents and Transfers," *Economics and Politics* 1 (1989): 17–39.

31 See Nabamita Dutta and Russell S. Sobel, "Does Corruption Ever Help Entrepreneurship?," *Small Business Economics: An Entrepreneurship Journal* 47, no. 1 (June 2016): 179–99.

32 See, for example, Richard Rose, "Getting Things Done in an Anti-modern Society: Social Capital Networks in Russia," in *Social Capital: A Multifaceted Perspective*, ed. Partha Dasgupta and Ismail Serageldin (Washington, DC: World Bank, 2000), and Vartuhí Tonoyan et al., "Corruption and Entrepreneurship: How Formal and Informal Institutions Shape Small Firm Behavior in Transition and Mature Market Economies," *Entrepreneurship Theory and Practice* 34 (2010): 803–31.

33 Michael Schwirtz, "In Filing, Casino Operator Admits Likely Violation of an Anti-bribery Law," *New York Times*, March 2, 2013.

34 See, for example, Andrei Shleifer and Robert Vishny, "Corruption," *Quarterly Journal of Economics* 108, no. 3 (1993): 599–617; Edward Glaeser and Raven Saks, "Corruption in America," *Journal of Public Economics* 90, no. 6–7 (2006): 1053–72, and Sergey Anokhin and William S. Schulze, "Entrepreneurship, Innovation, and Corruption," *Journal of Business Venturing* 24 (2009): 465–76.

CHAPTER 2: REGULATION AND THE PERPETUATION OF POVERTY IN THE US AND SENEGAL

1 Deirdre N. McCloskey, *The Bourgeois Virtues* (Chicago: University of Chicago Press, 2006).

2   We have chosen Senegal because one of the authors (Wade) is Senegalese and spends considerable time in Senegal, where she operates a business.

3   Laura Silver and Courtney Johnson, "Internet Connectivity Seen as Having Positive Impact on Life in Sub-Saharan Africa," Pew Research Center, October 9, 2018, https://www.pewresearch.org/global/2018/10/09/internet-connectivity-seen-as-having-positive-impact-on-life-in-sub-saharan-africa/.

4   McCloskey, *The Bourgeois Virtues*20. (We have updated the world population number from 6 billion to 7 billion.)

5   Note that this is a *factor* of 119, not 119 percent. In percentage terms, we are 11,900 percent better off in terms of total quality of adult years.

6   All the statistics in this paragraph are from Steven Horwitz, "Inequality, Mobility, and Being Poor in America," *Social Philosophy and Policy* 31, no. 2 (Spring 2015): 70–91 and the references therein.

7   W. Michael Cox and Richard Alm, *Myths of Rich and Poor: Why We're Better Off Than We Think* (New York: Basic Books, 1999).

8   World Bank, "Decline of Global Extreme Poverty Continues but Has Slowed: World Bank," press release, September 19, 2018, https://www.worldbank.org/en/news/press-release/2018/09/19/decline-of-global-extreme-poverty-continues-but-has-slowed-world-bank.

9   For documentation of the historical importance of the Industrial Revolution and the liberal institutions that made it possible see McCloskey, *Bourgeois Virtues*; Joel Mokyr, *The Lever of Riches* (New York: Oxford University Press, 1990); Douglass C. North, *Structure and Change in Economic History* (New York: W.W. Norton, 1981).

10 On "permissionless innovation," see Adam Thierer, *Permissionless Innovation: The Continuing Case for Comprehensive Technological Freedom*, rev. and exp. ed. (Arlington, VA: Mercatus Center at George Mason University, 2016), https://www.mercatus.org/system/files/Thierer-Permissionless-revised.pdf. On "trade-tested betterment," see Deirdre N. McCloskey, *Bourgeois Equality: How Ideas, not Capital or Institutions, Enriched the World* (Chicago: University of Chicago Press, 2016).

11 McCloskey, *Bourgeois Equality*.

12 For a more complete development of this idea, see Mancur Olson, *The Rise and Decline of Nations* (New Haven, CT: Yale University Press, 1982).

13 Bruce Yandle, "Bootleggers and Baptists—the Education of a Regulatory Economist," *Regulation* 7, no. 3 (1983): 12–16.

14 Diana Thomas, "Regressive Effects of Regulation," *Public Choice* 180 (2019): 1–10.

15 Thomas, "Regressive Effects of Regulation," 5.

16 See the review of the literature by David Neumark and William Wascher, "Minimum Wages and Employment," *Foundations and Trends in Microeconomics* 3, no. 1+2 (2007): 1–182.

17 See the discussion in Thomas C. Leonard, *Illiberal Reformers: Race, Eugenics and American Economics in the Progressive Era* (Princeton, NJ: Princeton University Press, 2016).

18 James B. Bailey, Diana W. Thomas, and Joseph R. Anderson, "Regressive Effects of Regulation on Wages," *Public Choice* 180 (2019): 91–103.

19 Bailey, Thomas, and Anderson, "Regressive Effects of Regulation," 101.

20 Steven Horwitz, "The Costs of Inflation Revisited," *Review of Austrian Economics* 16 (2003): 77–95.

21 The following discussion is adapted from Steven Horwitz, "Breaking Down the Barriers: Three Ways State and Local Governments Can Get Out of the Way and Improve the Lives of the Poor" (Mercatus Research, Mercatus Center at George Mason University, July 2015), http://mercatus.org/publication/breaking-down-barriers-three-ways-state-and-local-governments-can-improve-lives-poor.

22 Morris Kleiner and Alan Krueger estimate that licensing increases wages by about 15 percent, and that when licensing is combined with union membership, the wage premium averages 24 percent. See Morris M. Kleiner and Alan B. Krueger, "The Prevalence and Effects of Occupational Licensing," *British Journal of Industrial Relations* 48 (December 2010): 685.

23 Dick M. Carpenter II et al., *License to Work: A National Study of Burdens from Occupational Licensing*, 1st ed. (Arlington, VA: Institute for Justice, May 2012), https://ij.org/report/license-to-work/.

24 The fact that some states require licenses for certain occupations but other states do not require licenses for the same occupations suggests that the goal of licensing is not to protect public safety, but instead to serve as an opportunity for "bootleggers" to benefit by foreclosing competition. After all, if an occupation is safe in one state, why would it be unsafe in another?

25 Carpenter et al., *License to Work*.

26 Chapter Two, pages 19–44 in this volume, by Alicia Plemmons and Edward Timmons, provides additional depth to many of the issues about occupational licensing raised in the last few paragraphs.

27 Carpenter et al., *License to Work*.

28 This is the consensus view among economists, as found in Jeremy Horpedahl, "Ideology Über Alles? Economics Bloggers on Uber, Lyft, and Other Transportation Network Companies," *Econ Journal Watch* 12, no. 3 (2015).

29 Ryan Bourne, "The Regressive Effects of Child-Care Regulations," *Regulation* 41, no. 3 (2018): 8–11.

30 Elizabeth Milnikel and Emily Satterthwaite, *Regulatory Field: Home of Chicago Laws*, special updated ed. (Arlington, VA: Institute for Justice, November 2010), http://ij.org/images/pdf_folder/city_studies/ij-chicago_citystudy.pdf.

31 Milnikel and Satterthwaite, *Regulatory Field*.

32 Milnikel and Satterthwaite, *Regulatory Field*.

33 Elan Shpigel, "Chicago's Over-Burdensome Regulation of Mobile Food Vending," *Northwestern Journal of Law and Social Policy* 10 (2015): 354–88.

34 Michael Lucci and Hilary Gowins, *Chicago's Food-Cart Ban Costs Revenue, Jobs* (Special Report, Illinois Policy Institute, Chicago, IL, August 2015), https://www.illinoispolicy.org/reports/chicagos-food-cart-ban-costs-revenue-jobs/.

35 Lucci and Gowins, *Chicago's Food-Cart Ban*.

36 Robert McNamara, "No Brotherly Love for Entrepreneurs," Institute for Justice, Arlington, VA, November 2010, http://ij.org/images/pdf_folder/city_studies/ij-philly_citystudy.pdf.

37 Entrepreneurs seeking to open a food cart also need a separate permit for their cart, and the number of those permits is capped.

38 Miriam Berger, "Your Favorite Food Vendor Could Get Arrested," *Salon*, November 24, 2013, http://www.salon.com/2013/11/24/your_favorite_food_vendor_could_get_arrested/.

39 US Chamber of Commerce Foundation, "Enterprising Cities: Regulatory Climate Index 2014—Section 1," accessed August 27, 2020, http://www.uschamberfoundation.org/regulatory-climate-index-2014-section-i.

40 Dustin Chambers, Patrick A. McLaughlin, and Laura Stanley, "Regulation and Poverty: An Empirical Examination of the Relationship between the Incidence of Federal Regulation and the Occurrence of Poverty across the US States," *Public Choice* 180 (2018): 134.

41 World Bank, *Doing Business 2019: Training for Reform*, 2019, https://www.doingbusiness.org/content/dam/doingBusiness/media/Annual-Reports/English/DB2019-report_print-version.pdf and James Gwartney et al., *Economic Freedom of the World: 2019 Annual Report* (Vancouver, BC: Fraser Institute, 2019).

42 See the data on Senegal at the Fraser Institute's Economic Freedom database, https://www.fraserinstitute.org/economic-freedom/map?geozone=world&page=map&year=2017&countries=SEN#country-info (accessed August 27, 2020), which uses data from James Gwartney et al., *Economic Freedom of the World: 2019 Annual Report* (Vancouver, BC: Fraser Institute, 2019).

43 https://data.worldbank.org/indicator/NY.GDP.PCAP.PP.CD?most_recent_value_desc=true

44 World Bank, *Doing Business 2019: Training for Reform; Economy Profile of Senegal*, n.d., http://documents.worldbank.org/curated/en/529461541164094928/pdf/131734-WP-DB2019-PUBLIC-Senegal.pdf.

45 World Bank, *Doing Business 2019: Training for Reform*, 2019.

46 This demonstrates both the interconnections among various businesses and the insight dating back to Adam Smith that the division of labor is limited by the extent of the market. There is a chicken-and-egg problem here in that there would be more small entrepreneurs if there were more other small entrepreneurs selling supplies for that market.

47 Ekta Jhaveri, "Closing the Gap: Identifying Key Challenges for the Missing Middle SMEs in Francophone West Africa," *Next Billion*, February 20, 2018, https://nextbillion.net/closing-the-gap-identifying-key-challenges-for-the-missing-middle-smes-in-francophone-west-africa/.

48 In 2010, Senegal was ranked 172nd out of 183 nations in the Ease of Doing Business index, which indicates that it is one of the most difficult nations in the world in which to employ workers. Subsequent *Doing Business* reports quit reporting rankings on employing workers because of labor organization pressure. World Bank, "Ease of Doing Business Rankings," *Doing Business 2019*, accessed September 17, 2020, https://www.doingbusiness.org/en/rankings.

49 See the data from the World Bank at "Senegal Imports, Tariff by Country and Region 2018," World Integrated Trade Solution database, accessed August 27, 2020, https://wits.worldbank.org/CountryProfile/en/Country/SEN/Year/LTST/TradeFlow/Import/Partner/all/.

50 John Page, "For Africa's Youth, Jobs Are Job One," in *Foresight Africa: Top Priorities for the Continent in 2013* (Washington, DC: Brookings Institution, 2013), https://www.brookings.edu/wp-content/uploads/2016/06/Foresight_Page_2013.pdf.

51 The work of Hernando de Soto is instructive along these lines about the relationship between in the informal and formal sectors in poorer countries. See, for example, Hernando de Soto, *The Mystery of Capital: Why Capitalism Triumphs in the West and Fails Everywhere Else* (New York: Basic Books, 2000).

CHAPTER 3: SOCIAL TRUST AND REGULATION: A TIME-SERIES ANALYSIS OF THE UNITED STATES

1   Lee Rainie, Scott Keeter, and Andrew Perrin, "Trust and Distrust in America," Pew Research Center, July 22, 2019, 29, https://www.pewresearch.org/politics/2019/07/22/trust-and-distrust-in-america/.

2   Pew Research Center, "Public Trust in Government: 1958-2019." Pew Research Center, April 171 2019, https://www.pewresearch.org/politics/2019/04/11/public-trust-in-government-1958-2019/

3   Rainie, Keeter, and Perrin, "Trust and Distrust in America."

4   Gallup, "Trust in Government," *In Depth: Topics A to Z*, accessed May 9, 2020, https://news.gallup.com/poll/5392/trust-government.aspx.

5   Gallup, "Confidence in Institutions," *In Depth: Topics A to Z*, accessed May 9, 2020, https://news.gallup.com/poll/1597/confidence-institutions.aspx.

6   Simeon Djankov et al., "The Regulation of Entry," *Quarterly Journal of Economics* 117, no. 1 (2002): 1–37; William A. Niskanen, "The Peculiar Economics of Bureaucracy," *American Economic Review* 58, no. 2 (1968): 293–305.

7   Simeon Djankov, Caralee McLiesh, and Rita Maria Ramalho, "Regulation and Growth," *Economics Letters* 92, no. 3 (2006): 395–401.

8   Silvia Ardagna and Annamaria Lusardi, "Explaining International Differences in Entrepreneurship: The Role of Individual Characteristics and Regulatory Constraints" (NBER Working Paper No. 14012, National Bureau of Economic Research, Cambridge, MA, 2008); Peter T. Calcagno and Russell S. Sobel, "Regulatory Costs on Entrepreneurship and Establishment Employment Size," *Small Business Economics* 42, no. 3 (2014): 541–59; Nathan Goldschlag and Alex Tabarrok, "Is Regulation to Blame for the Decline in American Entrepreneurship?," *Economic Policy* 33, no. 93 (2018): 5–44; Leora Klapper, Luc Laeven, and Raghuram Rajan, "Entry Regulation as a Barrier to Entrepreneurship," *Journal of Financial Economics* 82, no. 3 (2006): 591–629; André van Stel, David J. Storey, and A. Roy Thurik, "The Effect of Business Regulations on Nascent and Young Business Entrepreneurship," *Small Business Economics* 28, no. 2–3 (2007): 171–86.

9   Daron Acemoglu and Joshua D. Angrist, "Consequences of Employment Protection? The Case of the Americans with Disabilities Act," *Journal of Political Economy* 109, no. 5 (2001): 915–57.

10 Bruce Yandle, "Bootleggers and Baptists—the Education of a Regulatory Economist," *Regulation* 7, no. 3 (1983): 12–16.

11 Dustin Chambers, Courtney A. Collins, and Alan Krause, "How Do Federal Regulations Affect Consumer Prices? An Analysis of the Regressive Effects of Regulation," *Public Choice* 180, no. 1–2 (2019): 57–90; Morris M. Kleiner, "Occupational Licensing," *Journal of Economic Perspectives* 14, no. 4 (2000): 189–202.

12 George J. Stigler, "The Theory of Economic Regulation," *Bell Journal of Economics and Management Science* 2, no. 1 (1971): 3–21.

13 Gordon Tullock, "Efficient Rent Seeking," in *Efficient Rent-Seeking*, ed. Alan A. Lockard and Gordon Tullock (Boston: Springer, 2001).

14 Hans Pitlik and Ludek Kouba, "Does Social Distrust Always Lead to a Stronger Support for Government Intervention?," *Public Choice* 163, no. 3–4 (2015): 355–77.

15 Vernon L. Smith and Bart J. Wilson, *Humanomics: Moral Sentiments and the Wealth of Nations for the Twenty-First Century* (Cambridge: Cambridge University Press, 2019).

16   Thomas A. Rietz et al., "Trust, Reciprocity, and Rules," *Economic Inquiry* 56, no. 3 (2018): 1526–42.

17   Philippe Aghion et al., "Regulation and Distrust," *Quarterly Journal of Economics* 125, no. 3 (2010): 1015–49.

18   Paolo Pinotti, "Trust, Honesty and Regulations" (MPRA Paper 7740, Munich Personal RePEc Archive, 2008).

19   See Ardagna and Lusardi, "Explaining International Differences in Entrepreneurship"; Klapper, Laeven, and Rajan, "Entry Regulation as a Barrier to Entrepreneurship"; van Stel, Storey, and Thurik, "Effect of Business Regulations."

20   Niskanen, "Peculiar Economics of Bureaucracy"; Barry Weingast, Kenneth Shepsle, and Christopher Johnsen, "The political economy of benefits and costs: A neoclassical approach to distributive politics," *Journal of Political Economy*, 89, no. 4, (1981): 642–664; Robert B. Ekelund and Robert D. Tollison, "The Interest-Group Theory of Government," in *The Elgar Companion to Public Choice*, ed. William F. Shughart II and Laura Razzolini (Cheltenham, UK: Edward Elgar, 2001).

21   Yandle, "Bootleggers and Baptists."

22   Djankov et al., "Regulation of Entry." The quality of private goods is measured by a country's compliance with international quality standards. The quality of public goods in a country is measured by the level of water pollution, the number of deaths from accidental poisoning, and the number of deaths from intestinal infection.

23   Christian Bjørnskov and Nicolai J. Foss, "Do Economic Freedom and Entrepreneurship Impact Total Factor Productivity?" (SMG Working Paper No. 8/2010, Center for Strategic Management and Globalization, Copenhagen Business School, September 2010); Kristina Nyström, "The Institutions of Economic Freedom and Entrepreneurship: Evidence from Panel Data," *Public Choice* 136, no. 3–4 (2008): 269–82.

24   Andrew Hale, David Borys, and Mark Adams, "Regulatory Overload: A Behavioral Analysis of Regulatory Compliance" (Working Paper No. 11-74, Mercatus Center at George Mason University, Arlington, VA, 2011). The authors support their argument with a review of relevant literature on safety regulation.

25   Russ Sobel, "Testing Baumol: Institutional quality and the productivity of entrepreneurship," *Journal of Business Venturing*, 23, (2008): 641–655; van Stel, Storey, and Thurik, "Effect of Business Regulations." For Baumol's theory, see William Baumol, "Entrepreneurship: Productive, unproductive and destructive." *Journal of Political Economy*, 98(5), (1990) 893–921.

26   Goldschlag and Tabarrok, "Is Regulation to Blame?"

27   Noel D. Campbell, Tammy M. Rogers, and Kirk C. Heriot, "The Economic Freedom Index as a Determinant of Firm Births and Firm Deaths," *Southwest Business and Economics Journal* 16 (2007): 37–50.

28   Calcagno and Sobel, "Regulatory Costs on Entrepreneurship."

29   Feng Gao, Joanna Shuang Wu, and Jerold Zimmerman, "Unintended Consequences of Granting Small Firms Exemptions from Securities Regulation: Evidence from the Sarbanes-Oxley Act," *Journal of Accounting Research* 47, no. 2 (2009): 459–506; Daron Acemoglu and Joshua D. Angrist. "Consequences of Employment Protection? The Case of The Americans With Disabilities Act," *Journal of Political Economy*, 109 (2001): 915-957.

30   Gao, Wu, and Zimmerman, "Unintended Consequences of Granting Small Firms Exemptions."

31 Acemoglu and Angrist, "Consequences of Employment Protection?"

32 Joseph E. Stiglitz, "Government Failure vs. Market Failure: Principles of Regulation," in *Government and Markets: Toward a New Theory of Regulation*, ed. Edward J. Balleisen and David A. Moss (Cambridge: Cambridge University Press, 2009).

33 Stiglitz, "Government Failure vs. Market Failure."

34 Lynn A. Stout, "Are Stock Markets Costly Casinos? Disagreement, Market Failure, and Securities Regulation," *Virginia Law Review* 81, no. 3 (April 1995): 611–712.

35 Stiglitz, "Government Failure vs. Market Failure," 13.

36 Cass R. Sunstein, "Nudges.gov: Behavioral Economics and Regulation," in *The Oxford Handbook of Behavioral Economics and the Law*, ed. Eyal Zamir and Doron Teichman (Oxford: Oxford University Press, 2014).

37 Richard H. Thaler and Cass R. Sunstein, *Nudge: Improving Decisions about Health, Wealth, and Happiness* (New Haven: Penguin, 2009).

38 Patrick A. McLaughlin, Nita Ghei, and Michael Wilt, "Regulatory Accumulation and Its Costs: An Overview" (Policy Brief, Mercatus Center at George Mason University, Arlington, VA, November 2018), https://www.mercatus.org/publications/regulation/regulatory-accumulation-and-its-costs-0.

39 Robert D. Putnam, *Making Democracy Work: Civic Traditions in Modern Italy*, with Robert Leonardi and Raffaella Y. Nanetti (Princeton, NJ: Princeton University Press, 1993), 167.

40 Stephen Knack and Philip Keefer, "Does Social Capital Have an Economic Pay-Off? A Cross-Country Investigation," *Quarterly Journal of Economics* 112, no. 4 (1997): 1251–88.

41 Christian Bjørnskov, "How Does Social Trust Affect Economic Growth?," *Southern Economic Journal* 78, no. 4 (2012): 1346–68.

42 Bjørnskov, "How Does Social Trust Affect Economic Growth?"

43 Peter Nannestad, "What Have We Learned about Generalized Trust, If Anything?," *Annual Review of Political Science* 11 (June 2008): 413–36.

44 Ryan Murphy, Meg Tuszynski, and Jeremy Jackson, "Some Dynamics of Socioeconomic Relationships: Well-Being, Social Capital, Economic Freedom, Economic Growth, and Entrepreneurship," *American Journal of Entrepreneurship* 13, (June 2020):4-44.

45 Jeremy Jackson, Art Carden, and Ryan A. Compton, "Economic Freedom and Social Capital," *Applied Economics* 47, no. 54 (2015): 5853–67; Jeremy J. Jackson, "Economic Freedom and Social Capital: Pooled Mean Group Evidence," *Applied Economics Letters* 24, no. 6 (2017): 370–73.

46 Niclas Berggren and Henrik Jordahl, "Free to Trust: Economic Freedom and Social Capital," *Kyklos* 59, no. 2 (2006): 141–69.

47 Christian Bjørnskov, "The Multiple Facets of Social Capital," *European Journal of Political Economy* 22, no. 1 (2006): 22–40.

48 Wendy M. Rahn and Thomas J. Rudolph, "A Tale of Political Trust in American Cities," *Public Opinion Quarterly* 69, no. 4 (2005): 530–60.

49 Aaron C. Weinschenk and David J. Helpap, "Political Trust in the American States," *State and Local Government Review* 47, no. 1 (2015): 26–34.

50 Nannestad, "What Have We Learned?"

51 Andreas Bergh and Christian Bjørnskov, "Historical Trust Levels Predict the Current Size of the Welfare State," *Kyklos* 64, no. 1 (2011): 1–19; Christian Bjørnskov

and Gert Tinggaard Svendsen, "Does Social Trust Determine the Size of the Welfare State? Evidence Using Historical Identification," *Public Choice* 157, no. 1–2 (2013): 269–86.

52 Bo Rothstein, Marcus Samanni, and Jan Teorell, "Explaining the Welfare State: Power Resources vs. the Quality of Government," *European Political Science Review* 4, no. 1 (2012): 1–28.

53 Art Carden, Steven Castello, and Benjamin Priday, "Religious Freedom and Private Enterprise," *Journal of Private Enterprise 35*, (2020): 47-59 .

54 Knack and Keefer, "Does Social Capital Have an Economic Pay-Off?"; Rafael La Porta, Florencio Lopez-de-Silanes, Andrei Shleifer, and Robert Vishny. "Trust in Large Organizations," *American Economic Review*, 87(2) (1997): 333–38.

55 Knack and Keefer, "Does Social Capital Have an Economic Pay-Off?"

56 Christian Bjørnskov and Stefan Voigt, "Constitutional Verbosity and Social Trust," *Public Choice* 161, no. 1–2 (2014): 91–112.

57 David Ahnen and Peter T. Calcagno, "Constitutions and Social Trust: An Analysis of the US States," *Journal of Private Enterprise* 34, no. 3 (2019): 11–33.

58 Aghion et al., "Regulation and Distrust."

59 Aghion et al., "Regulation and Distrust."

60 Pinotti, "Trust, Honesty and Regulations."

61 Paolo Pinotti, "Trust, Regulation and Market Failures," *Review of Economics and Statistics* 94, no. 3 (2012): 650–58.

62 Pitlik and Kouba, "Does Social Distrust Always Lead to a Stronger Support for Government Intervention?" *Public Choice 163*, (2015): 355-377.

63 Smith and Wilson, *Humanomics*.

64 Rietz et al., "Trust, Reciprocity, and Rules."

65 Robert D. Putnam, *Bowling Alone: The Collapse and Revival of American Community* (New York: Simon & Schuster, 2000); Eric M. Uslaner and Mitchell Brown, "Inequality, Trust, and Civic Engagement," *American Politics Research* 33, no. 6 (2005): 868–94.

66 In total, 19 values for trust are imputed.

67 Pitlik and Kouba, "Does Social Distrust Always Lead to a Stronger Support?"

68 Knack and Keefer, "Does Social Capital Have an Economic Pay-Off?"

69 Guglielmo Barone and Sauro Mocetti, "Inequality and Trust: New Evidence from Panel Data," *Economic Inquiry* 54, no. 2 (2016): 794–809; Eric M. Uslaner, "Trust, Democracy and Governance: Can Government Policies Influence Generalized Trust?," in *Generating Social Capital: Civil Society and Institutions in Comparative Perspective*, ed. Marc Hooghe and Dietlind Stolle (New York: Palgrave Macmillan, 2003).

70 Francesco Daveri and Guido Tabellini, "Unemployment, Growth and Taxation in Industrial Countries," *Economic Policy* 15, no. 30 (2000): 48–104; Horst Feldmann, "The Unemployment Effects of Labor Regulation around the World," *Journal of Comparative Economics* 37, no. 1 (2009): 76–90.

71 Vector autoregression is well known, as a methodology, to suffer from parameter overproliferation. Too many estimated parameters relative to the number of observations weakens the statistical power available. Also, many potential control variables end up moving together over time, causing further statistical problems of collinearity.

72   This first differencing a technical requirement need to apply the VAR methodology to our data.

73   It is important to note that Granger causality is a very specific type of causality. It should not be confused with a more general concept of causality that might be gleaned from an experimental research design.

74   Aghion et al., "Regulation and Distrust."

75   All the variables in the model are first differenced. The summary statistics for the difference variables are presented in table A1 in the appendix.

76   Knack and Keefer, "Does Social Capital Have an Economic Pay-Off?"

77   Eric M. Uslaner, *The Moral Foundations of Trust* (Cambridge: Cambridge University Press, 2002); John F. Helliwell, "How's Life? Combining Individual and National Variables to Explain Subjective Well-Being," *Economic Modelling* 20, no. 2 (2003): 331–60; John F. Helliwell, "Well-Being, Social Capital and Public Policy: What's New?," *Economic Journal* 116, no. 510 (2006): C34–C45.

78   Aghion et al., "Regulation and Distrust"; Pinotti, "Trust, Regulation and Market Failures."

79   Each variable in the regression equations represents a log difference. These differences are calculated following a similar pattern. For example, is the log level of trust at time t minus the log level of trust at time $t - 1$.

CHAPTER 4: REGULATION AND THE SHADOW ECONOMY

1   Douglas North, "Institutions," *Journal of Economic Perspectives* 5, no. 1 (1991): 97–112.

2   William Baumol, "Entrepreneurship: Productive, Unproductive and Destructive," *Journal of Political Economy* 98 (1990): 893–921.

3   Several studies investigate this hypothesis. See, for example, Russell S. Sobel, "Testing Baumol: Institutional Quality and the Productivity of Entrepreneurship," *Journal of Business Venturing* 23, no. 6 (2008): 641–55; Travis Wiseman and Andrew Young, "Economic Freedom, Entrepreneurship & Income Levels: Some US State-level Empirics," *American Journal of Entrepreneurship* 6, no. 1 (2013): 100–119. Additionally, Young and I examine productive and unproductive outcomes in the context of informal, religious institutions. Travis Wiseman and Andrew Young, "Religion: Productive or Unproductive," *Journal of Institutional Economics* 10, no. 1 (2014): 21–45. Rent-seeking involves using the political process to transfer wealth, typically from one group to another.

4   The shadow economy has many synonyms—the underground economy, the second economy, black markets, the informal sector, the extra-legal sector, off-the-books economic activity, under-the-table economic activity, hidden economy, parallel economy, cash economies, etc.

5   See Friedrich Schneider, "The Shadow Economy and Work in the Shadow: What Do We (Not) Know?" (IZA Discussion Paper No. 6423, Institute for the Study of Labor, Bonn, Germany, 2012).

6   This is the common claim made in the literature, though one that is highly debatable. Consider, for example, the electricity consumption variable often used as a shadow economy indicator in estimating shadow economic activity: electricity consumption statistics will measure electricity used for legal market activity and for illegal market activity, such as manufacturing marijuana. Similarly, unemployment statistics used to estimate shadow economy size tell us very little about what unemployed persons are actually doing in the shadow economy.

7   Andreas Buehn and Friedrich Schneider, "Shadow Economies around the World: Novel Insights, Accepted Knowledge, and New Estimates," *International Tax and Public Finance* 19 (2012): 139–71.

8   Table 3 in Buehn and Schneider, "Shadow Economies around the World."

9   Robert Neuwirth, *Stealth of Nations: The Global Rise of the Informal Economy* (New York: Random House, 2011), 117.

10 Hans F. Sennholz, *The Underground Economy*, online ed. (Ludwig von Mises Institute, 1984), 10, https://cdn.mises.org/The%20Underground%20Economy_3.pdf.

11 Table 3 in Buehn and Schneider, "Shadow Economies around the World."

12 Friedrich Schneider and Dominik Enste, "Shadow Economies: Sizes, Causes, and Consequences," *Journal of Economic Literature* 38 (2000): 77–114.

13 Hernando de Soto, *The Other Path: Economic Answers to Terrorism* (New York: Basic Books, 1989); Hernando de Soto, *The Mystery of Capital: Why Capitalism Triumphs in the West and Fails Everywhere Else* (New York: Basis Books, 2000); Neuwirth, *Stealth of Nations.*

14 Schneider and Enste, "Shadow Economies."

15 See, for example, Maria Lacko, "The Hidden Economies of Visegrad Countries in International Comparison: A Household Electricity Approach," in *Hungary: Towards a Market Economy* (Cambridge, UK: Cambridge University Press, 1998); Maria Lacko, "Electricity Intensity and the Unrecorded Economy in Post-socialist Countries," in *Underground Economies in Transition* (Farnham, UK: Ashgate, 1999); Maria Lacko, "Do Power Consumption Data Tell the Story? Electricity Intensity and Hidden Economy in Post-socialist Countries," in *Planning, Shortage, and Transformation: Essays in Honor of Janos Kornai* (Cambridge, MA: MIT Press, 2000); Maria Lacko, "Hidden Economy: An Unknown Quantity? Comparative Analysis of Hidden Economies in Transition Countries, 1989–1995," *Economies in Transition* 8, no. 1 (2000): 117–49; Simon Johnson, Daniel Kaufmann, and Andrei Shleifer, "The Unofficial Economy in Transition," *Brookings Papers on Economic Activity*, no. 2 (1997): 159–239.

16 For more detail, see Travis Wiseman, "US Shadow Economies: A State-Level Study," *Constitutional Political Economy* 24, no. 4 (2013): 310–35. See also other recent studies of the shadow economy.

17 Sidney L. Carroll and Robert J. Gaston, "Occupational Restrictions and the Quality of Service Received: Some Evidence," *Southern Economic Journal* 47, no. 4 (1981): 959–76.

18 Wiseman, "US Shadow Economies"; Richard J. Cebula and Edgar L. Feige, "America's Unreported Economy: Measuring the Size, Growth and Determinants of Income Tax Evasion in the U.S.," *Crime, Law and Social Change* 57, no. 3 (2011): 265–58.

19 Lynda Richardson, "Nannygate for the Poor: The Underground Economy in Day Care for Children," *New York Times*, May 2, 1993.

20 Wiseman, "US Shadow Economies."

21 Shadow economy value estimates are based on the author's own calculations. Real GDP and real GDP per capita estimates come from the Bureau of Economic Analysis, and shadow economy size (9.54%) comes from Wiseman, "US Shadow Economies." The value of shadow economic activity is derived as *real GDP*$_{2016}$ × 9.54%, or \$95.3 billion × 0.0954 = \$9.1 billion. Similarly, shadow economy value per capita is measured as *real GDP per capita*$_{2016}$ × 9.54% = \$31,881 × 0.0954 = \$3,044.

22 Dean Stansel, José Torra, and Fred McMahon, *Economic Freedom of North America 2016* (Vancouver, BC: Fraser Institute, 2016).

23 Dick M. Carpenter II et al., *License to Work: A National Study of Burdens from Occupational Licensing*, 2nd ed. (Arlington, VA: Institute for Justice, 2017).

24 Productive entrepreneurship scores come from my index of Productive and Unproductive Entrepreneurship Scores and are based on state-level per capita venture capital investments, patents per capita, self-proprietorship (self-employment) growth rates, establishment birth rates, and large establishment (500 employees or more) birth rates. The index offers a 48-point productive entrepreneurship scale, increasing in greater percentages of productive activity. Travis Wiseman and Andrew Young, "Religion: Productive or Unproductive," *Journal of Institutional Economics* 10, no. 1 (2014): 421-33..

25 Schneider and Enste, "Shadow Economies."

26 For measures of both taxes and charges as a percentage of GDP, see Wiseman, "US Shadow Economies."

27 Recent examples of such innovations include the dark web—a peer-to-peer web platform that houses many services designed to maintain user anonymity in exchanges. Silk Road is one dark web exchange forum where anonymous buyers and sellers exchange illicit goods and services, typically using a cryptocurrency (such as Bitcoin) as a store of monetary value.

28 Luis Buñuel, *My Last Sigh: The Autobiography of Luis Buñuel* (New York: Random House, 1982), 45.

29 Jeffrey Miron and Jeffrey Zweibel, "Alcohol Consumption during Prohibition," *AEA Papers and Proceedings* 81, no. 2 (1991): 242–47.

30 Ken Burns and Lynn Novick recently directed a three-part documentary series that outlines many of the unintended consequences of Prohibition—including mafia wars and increased fatalities owing to poisoning from poor-quality underground alcohol. *Prohibition*, directed by Ken Burns and Lynn Novick, written by Geoffrey C. Ward (Prohibition Film Project, 2011).

31 Mark Thornton, "Alcohol Prohibition Was a Failure" (Policy Analysis No. 157, Cato Institute, 1991).

32 For more details about the impact of marijuana legalization on crime, public health, traffic fatalities, etc., see Jeffrey Miron, Angela Dills, and Sietse Goffard, "Common Myths about Marijuana Legalization," *Cato at Liberty*, November 4, 2016, https://www.cato.org/blog/common-myths-about-marijuana-legalization. Also, policy analyst Ashley Bradford and economist David Bradford demonstrate that prescription drug dependency and Medicare program spending are reduced in states that permit medical marijuana use. Ashley Bradford and David Bradford, "Medical Marijuana Laws Reduce Prescription Medication Use in Medicare Part D," *Health Affairs* 35, no. 7 (2016): 1230–36.

CHAPTER 5: AN INTRODUCTION TO THE EFFECT OF REGULATION ON EMPLOYMENT AND WAGES

1 See, for example, Ban of Hazardous Lawn Darts, 16 C.F.R. pt. 1306 (2016).

2 That is, it is negative unless the effect on consumer safety is so profound as to itself constitute a major boon to employment. That is unlikely for the ban on lawn darts, but plausible for its near neighbor in the *Code of Federal Regulations*, Ban of Lead-Containing Paint and Certain Consumer Products Bearing Lead-Containing Paint, 16 C.F.R. pt. 1303 (2016). See, for example, Rick Nevin, "The Answer Is Lead Poisoning" (working paper, December 19, 2012), https://9zc.d79.myftpupload.

com/wp-content/uploads/2020/09/Nevin-2012-The-Answer-is-Lead-Poisoning.
pdf.

3   Steven C. Salop, David T. Scheffman, and Warren Schwartz, "A Bidding Analysis
of Special Interest Regulation: Raising Rivals' Costs in a Rent Seeking Society"
(Working Paper No. 114, Federal Trade Commission, Washington, DC, September
1984).

4   "Agency Regulatory Restrictions over Time", QuantGov, accessed September 24
2020 https://www.quantgov.org/agency-restrictions

5   The Department of Labor is the sixth largest agency as measured by total regulatory restrictions in the *Code of Federal Regulations*. The five agencies with the most
restrictions are, in order, the Environmental Protection Agency, the Department of
the Treasury, the Department of Agriculture, the Department of Transportation,
and the Department of Homeland Security.

6   Lawrence Summers, "Some Simple Economics of Mandated Benefits," in "Papers
and Proceedings of the Hundred and First Annual Meeting of the American
Economic Association," special issue, *American Economic Review* 79, no. 2 (1989):
177–83.

7   For example, in the United States the Worker Adjustment and Retraining Notification Act requires firms with 100 or more employees to give at least 60 days notice
before mass layoffs (affecting 50 or more employees), and some states have stricter
laws of their own; see "Plant Closings and Layoffs," US Department of Labor,
accessed April 28, 2020, https://www.dol.gov/general/topic/termination/plant-
closings.

8   Some effects may also change over time. Using a more complex theoretical model
with monopolistic competition and bargaining, Olivier Blanchard (former Chief
Economist of the International Monetary Fund) and economist Francesco Giavazzi
argue that a typical regulation leads to higher wages and employment in the short
run by protecting incumbents before lowering employment and wages in the long
run by discouraging new firms from entering. Olivier Blanchard and Francesco
Giavazzi, "Macroeconomic Effects of Regulation and Deregulation in Goods and
Labor Markets," *Quarterly Journal of Economics* 118, no. 3 (2003): 879–907.

9   Nevin, "Answer Is Lead Poisoning."

10 Think, perhaps, of selling flowers, which requires a license in Louisiana: Shoshana
Weissmann and C. Jarrett Dieterle, "Louisiana Is the Only State That Requires
Occupational Licenses for Florists. It's Absurd," *USA Today*, March 28, 2018.

11 A similar logic holds to a lesser degree for "make-work" jobs (in the purest form,
think of digging a hole and filling it in again). While these jobs do not actually
harm others, they are simply an unnecessarily costly way of transferring money. If
the goal is to make workers better off, forget about the make-work and write them
a check. See also Travis Wiseman's chapter on unproductive entrepreneurship
(chapter 4 in this volume).

12 "Doing Business: Measuring Business Regulations," World Bank, accessed April
28, 2020, https://www.doingbusiness.org/en/doingbusiness.

13 *Doing Business 2019: Training for Reform*, 16th ed. (Washington, DC: World Bank,
2019).

14 Simeon Djankov et al., "The Regulation of Entry," *Quarterly Journal of Economics*
117, no. 1 (2002): 1–37.

15 Ryan Decker et al., "The Role of Entrepreneurship in US Job Creation and Economic Dynamism," *Journal of Economic Perspectives* 28, no. 3 (2014): 3–24.

16 Milton Friedman and Simon Kuznets, *Income from Independent Professional Practice* (New York: National Bureau of Economic Research, 1954); Morris Kleiner and Alan Krueger, "Analyzing the Extent and Influence of Occupational Licensing on the Labor Market," *Journal of Labor Economics* 31, no. 2 (2013): S173–S202.

17 Jonathan Meer and Jeremy West, "Effects of the Minimum Wage on Employment Dynamics," *Journal of Human Resources* 51.2 (2016): 500–22. For an excellent summary of the state of minimum wage research, see Jeffrey Clemens and Michael Strain, "Estimating the Employment Effects of Recent Minimum Wage Changes: Early Evidence, an Interpretative Framework, and a Pre-commitment to Future Analysis" (NBER Working Paper No. 23084, National Bureau of Economic Research, Cambridge, MA, 2017). For a meta-analysis of recent work, see Paul Wolfson and Dale Belman, "15 Years of Research on US Employment and the Minimum Wage," *Labour* 33 (2019): 488–506.

18 Jonathan T. Kolstad and Amanda E. Kowalski, "Mandate-Based Health Reform and the Labor Market: Evidence from the Massachusetts Reform," *Journal of Health Economics* 47 (2016): 81–106; Conor Lennon, "Are the Costs of Employer-Provided Health Insurance Passed On to Workers at the Individual Level?" (working paper, August 5, 2019), http://www.conorjlennon.com/uploads/3/9/6/0/39604893/lennon_ehb_revision_sept_2020.pdf.

19 Jonathan Gruber, "The Incidence of Mandated Maternity Benefits," *American Economic Review* 84, no. 3 (1994): 622–41; Joanna N. Lahey, "The Efficiency of a Group-Specific Mandated Benefit Revisited: The Effect of Infertility Mandates," *Journal of Policy Analysis and Management* 31, no. 1 (2012): 63–92; James Bailey, "Who Pays the High Health Costs of Older Workers? Evidence from Prostate Cancer Screening Mandates," *Applied Economics* 46, no. 32 (2014): 3931–41.

20 Summers, "Some Simple Economics."

21 Gruber, "Incidence of Mandated Maternity Benefits."

22 For one example where health insurance benefit mandates had little effect on employment because firms were able to use a self-insurance loophole (though self-insuring added its own costs), see James Bailey and Douglas Webber, "Health Insurance Benefit Mandates and Firm Size Distribution," *Journal Risk and Insurance* 85 (2018): 577–95.

23 Bailey, "Who Pays the High Health Costs of Older Workers?"

24 Thomas DeLeire, "The Wage and Employment Effects of the Americans with Disabilities Act," *Journal of Human Resources* 35 (Fall 2000): 693–715; Daron Acemoglu and Joshua D. Angrist, "Consequences of Employment Protection? The Case of the Americans with Disabilities Act," *Journal of Political Economy* 109, no. 5 (2001): 915–57.

25 J. R. Shackleton, "The Economics of Employment Regulation," *Economic Affairs* 25.3 (2005).

26 "Employment Rate: Aged 25–54: Males for the United States," FRED, Federal Reserve Bank of St. Louis, accessed September 24, 2020, https://fred.stlouisfed.org/series/LREM25MAUSA156S.

27 Didem Tuzemen, "Why Are Prime-Age Men Vanishing from the Labor Force?," *KC Fed Economic Review* (Federal Reserve Bank of Kansas City), February 21, 2018.

28 McLaughlin and Sherouse, RegData US 3.1 Annual (data set).

29 Kleiner and Krueger, "Analyzing the Extent and Influence of Occupational Licensing."

30 Susan Laudicina, Joan Gardner, and Kim Holland, "State Legislative Healthcare and Insurance Issues" (Technical Report, Blue Cross Blue Shield Association, 2011).

31 Tuzemen, "Why Are Prime-Age Men Vanishing from the Labor Force?"

32 Diana Thomas, "Regressive Effects of Regulation" Mercatus Center Working Paper No. 12-35, November 2012; James Bailey, Diana Thomas, and Joseph Anderson, "Regressive Effects of Regulation on Wages," *Public Choice* 180 (2019): 91–103; Dustin Chambers, Patrick A. McLaughlin, and Laura Stanley, "Barriers to Prosperity: The Harmful Impact of Entry Regulations on Income Inequality," *Public Choice* 180 (2019): 165–90.

33 W. Mark Crain and Nicole V. Crain, "The Cost of Federal Regulation to the U.S. Economy, Manufacturing and Small Business" (report, National Association of Manufacturers, September 10, 2014).

34 John W. Dawson and John J. Seater, "Federal Regulation and Aggregate Economic Growth," *Journal of Economic Growth* 12, no. 2 (2013): 137–77.

35 McLaughlin and Sherouse, RegData US 3.1 Annual (data set).

36 James Bailey and Diana Thomas, "Regulating Away Competition: The Effect of Regulation on Entrepreneurship and Employment," *Journal of Regulatory Economics* 52 (2017): 237–54.

37 Dustin Chambers, Patrick A. McLaughlin, and Tyler Richards, "Regulation, Entrepreneurship, and Firm Size" (Mercatus Working Paper, Mercatus Center at George Mason University, Arlington, VA, 2018).

38 David S. Lucas and Christopher Boudreaux, "Federal Regulation, Job Creation, and the Moderating Effect of State Economic Freedom: Evidence from the United States" (working paper, July 19, 2018), http://home.fau.edu/cboudreaux/web/Regional%20Studies%20Article%207.20.18%20.pdf. Indices that measure economic freedom generally include some measures of regulation and researchers have evaluated their effects on a variety of outcomes, including labor market outcomes. See, for example, Stephan F. Gohmann, Bradley K. Hobbs, and Myra McCrickard, "Economic Freedom and Service Industry Growth in the United States," *Entrepreneurship Theory and Practice* 32, no. 5 (2008): 855–74. I generally do not discuss such work in this chapter because these indices include many nonregulatory measures along with the regulatory measures.

39 Bentley Coffey, Patrick A. McLaughlin, and Pietro Peretto, "The Cumulative Cost of Regulations" (Mercatus Working Paper, Mercatus Center at George Mason University, Arlington, VA, 2016). This figure was also endorsed by an October 2, 2017, report of the Council of Economic Advisers, "The Growth Potential of Deregulation."

40 McLaughlin and Sherouse, RegData US 3.1 Annual (data set).

41 Mark Febrizio, "Analyzing the Economic Effects of State-Level Regulation" (working paper, July 18, 2018), https://papers.ssrn.com/sol3/papers.cfm?abstract_id=3220171.

42 Crain and Crain, "Cost of Federal Regulation."

43 Clyde Wayne Crews Jr., "Ten Thousand Commandments: An Annual Snapshot of the Federal Regulatory State," 2019 ed. (report, Competitive Enterprise Institute, Washington, DC, 2019).

44 Crews, "Ten Thousand Commandments."

45 "The Economic Effects of Federal Deregulation since January 2017: An Interim Report" (report, Council of Economic Advisers, June 2019).

46 Idaho did sunset its entire regulatory code in 2019, but plans to reinstate much of it in 2020. See James Broughel, "Idaho Repeals Its Regulatory Code," *The Bridge* (Mercatus Center at George Mason University), May 9, 2019; J. Kennerly Davis, "Man Bites Dog—Idaho Repeals Its Regulatory Code," Federalist Society blog, July 18, 2019.

47 British Columbia did reduce regulation by 43 percent in the years after 2000, as measured in Laura Jones, "Cutting Red Tape in Canada: A Regulatory Reform Model for the United States?" (Mercatus Research, Mercatus Center at George Mason University, Arlington, VA, 2015).

48 "The Economic Effects of Federal Deregulation since January 2017: An Interim Report."

CHAPTER 6: OCCUPATIONAL LICENSING: A BARRIER TO OPPORTUNITY AND PROSPERITY

1 Morris Kleiner, "Occupational Licensing," *Journal of Economic Perspectives* 14, no. 4 (2000): 189–202.

2 Bureau of Labor Statistics, "Labor Force Statistics from the Current Population Survey: Data on Certifications and Licenses," last modified January 22, 2020, https://www.bls.gov/cps/certifications-and-licenses.htm.

3 Bureau of Labor Statistics, "Characteristics of Minimum Wage Workers, 2017," BLS Reports, Report 1072, March 2018, https://www.bls.gov/opub/reports/minimum-wage/2017/home.htm.

4 Bureau of Labor Statistics, "Union Members Summary," news release, January 22, 2020, https://www.bls.gov/news.release/union2.nr0.htm.

5 Dick M. Carpenter III, Lisa Knepper, Kyle Sweetland, and Jennifer McDonald, "The Continuing Burden of Occupational Licensing in the United States," *Economic Affairs* 38, no. 3 (2018): 380-405. ; Edward Timmons and Robert Thornton, "The Licensing of Barbers in the USA," *British Journal of Industrial Relations* 48, no. 4 (2010): 740–57.

6 The Knee Center for the Study of Occupational Regulation. *Barber Licensing Data.* https://csorsfu.com/

7 Barbering/Barber Career Program Tuition & Fees Comparison, College Tuition Compare, https://www.collegetuitioncompare.com/compare/tables/vocational-program/barbering-barber/

8 Bureau of Labor Statistics, "Barbers, Hairstylists, and Cosmetologists," *Occupational Outlook Handbook*, last modified September 1, 2020, https://www.bls.gov/ooh/personal-care-and-service/barbers-hairstylists-and-cosmetologists.htm.

9 Quoted in Casey Frizzell, "Barbers Upset with Cuts Proposed Bill Would Make in Arkansas," *5 News*, March 7, 2019.

10 Gordon Tullock, "The Transitional Gains Trap," *Bell Journal of Economics* 6, no. 2 (1975): 671–78.

11 Quoted in Zack Briggs, "Bill Would Abolish Arkansas Barber Board, No License or Education Required to Cut Hair," *KATV*, March 6, 2019.

12 Quoted in Camille Connor, "Barbers, Cosmetologists against Texas Bill That Would Do Away with Licenses," *News Channel 6*, March 13, 2019.

13 For a study that utilizes a similar approach of defining the relevant theories on the effects of licensing, see A. Frank Adams, John Jackson, and Robert Ekelund, "Occupational Licensing in a 'Competitive' Labor Market: The Case of Cosmetology," *Journal of Labor Research* 23, no. 2 (2002): 261–78.

14 Milton Friedman, *Capitalism and Freedom* (Chicago: University of Chicago Press, 1962); Mancur Olson, *The Logic of Collective Action: Public Goods and the Theory of Groups* (Cambridge, MA: Harvard University Press, 1965).

15 George J. Stigler, "The Theory of Economic Regulation," *Bell Journal of Economics and Management Science* 2, no. 1 (1971): 3–21.

16 George Akerlof, "The Market for 'Lemons': Quality Uncertainty and the Market Mechanism," *Quarterly Journal of Economics* 84, no. 3 (1970): 488–500; Hayne Leland, "Quacks, Lemons, and Licensing: A Theory of Minimum Quality Standards," *Journal of Political Economy* 87, no. 6 (1979): 1328–46.

17 Carl Shapiro, "Investment, Moral Hazard, and Occupational Licensing," *Review of Economic Studies* 53, no. 5 (1986): 843–62.

18 Morris Kleiner and Evan Soltas, "A Welfare Analysis of Occupational Licensing in U.S. States" (NBER Working Paper No. 26383, National Bureau of Economic Research, Cambridge, MA, 2019).

19 Ryan Nunn and Gabriel Scheffler, "Occupational Licensing and the Limits of Public Choice Theory," *Administrative Law Review Accord* 4, no. 2 (2019): 25–41.

20 Adam Thierer et al., "How the Internet, the Sharing Economy, and Reputational Feedback Mechanisms Solve the 'Lemons Problem'" (Mercatus Working Paper, Mercatus Center at George Mason University, Arlington, VA, May 2015).

21 Chiara Farronato et al., "Consumer Protection in an Online World: An Analysis of Occupational Licensing" (NBER Working Paper No. 26601, National Bureau of Economic Research, Cambridge, MA, 2020).

22 Morris Kleiner, *Licensing Occupations: Ensuring Quality or Restricting Competition?* (Kalamazoo, MI: W.E. Upjohn Institute for Employment Research, 2006).

23 Bureau of Labor Statistics, "Labor Force Statistics from the Current Population Survey."

24 Robert Thornton and Edward Timmons, "The De-licensing of Occupations in the United States," *Monthly Labor Review*, May 2015.

25 John K. Ross, "The Inverted Pyramid: 10 Less Restrictive Alternatives to Occupational Licensing" (report, Institute for Justice, November 2017).

26 Benjamin Elman, *Civil Examinations and Meritocracy in Late Imperial China* (Cambridge, MA: Harvard University Press, 2013).

27 Yüan-ling Chao, *Late Imperial China: A Study of Physicians in Suzhou, 1600–1850* (New York: Peter Lang, 2009).

28 *Occupational Licensing Legislation in the States* (Chicago: Council of State Governments, 1952).

29 Smith. Chapter X: On Wages and Profit in the different Employments of Labor and Stock. *An Inquiry into the Nature and Causes of the Wealth of Nations*. (1776)

30 Paul Larkin Jr., "Public Choice Theory and Occupational Licensing," *Harvard Journal of Law and Public Policy* 39, no. 1 (2016): 209–331.

31 Dent v. West Virginia, 129 U.S. 114 (1889).

32 Before 1870, a minority of states had early occupational licensing for attorneys, dentists, insurance brokers, physicians, and teachers. Between 1870 and the beginning of the Progressive Era, in 1890, some states also added additional licensing requirements for pharmacists and veterinarians. Marc Law and Sukkoo Kim, "Specialization and Regulation: The Rise of Professionals and the Emergence of Occupational Licensing Regulation," *Journal of Economic History* 65, no. 3 (2005): 723–56.

33 Friedman. Chapter IX: Occupational Licensing. *Capitalism and Freedom*. (1962)

34 Thomas Duffy, "The Flexner Report—100 Years Later," *Yale Journal of Biology and Medicine* 84, no. 3 (2011): 269–76.

35 Law and Kim, "Specialization and Regulation."

36 Law and Kim, "Specialization and Regulation"; Bureau of Labor Statistics, "Labor Force Statistics from the Current Population Survey."

37 Kenneth Arrow, *Essays in the Theory of Risk-Bearing* (United States: Markham, 1971); Morris Kleiner and Alan Krueger, "The Prevalence and Effects of Occupational Licensing," *British Journal of Industrial Relations* 48, no. 4 (2010): 1–12.

38 Alicia Plemmons, "Occupational Licensing Effects on Firm Entry and Employment" (Working Paper no. 2019.008, Center for Growth and Opportunity at Utah State University, 2019); Peter Blair and Bobby Chung, "Job Market Signaling through Occupational Licensing" (NBER Working Paper No. 24791, National Bureau of Economic Research, Cambridge, MA, 2018); Brian Meehan et al., "The Effects of Growth in Occupational Licensing on Intergenerational Mobility," *Economics Bulletin* 39, no. 2 (2019): 1516–28.

39 *Occupational Licensing Legislation in the States.*

40 Bureau of Labor Statistics, "Labor Force Statistics from the Current Population Survey."

41 Council on Licensure, Enforcement & Regulation, "Sunrise, Sunset and Agency Audits," accessed February 22, 2020, https://www.clearhq.org/page-486181.

42 Arlene Holen, "The Economics of Dental Licensing" Arlington, VA: Public Research Institute of the Center for Naval Analysis, 1978 .

43 Sidney Carroll and Robert Gaston, "Occupational Licensing and the Quality of Service: An Overview," *Law and Human Behavior* 7, no. 2–3 (1983): 139–46; Morris Kleiner and Robert Kudrle, "Does Regulation Affect Economics Outcomes? The Case of Dentistry," *Journal of Law and Economics* 43, no. 2 (2000): 547–82.

44 Carroll and Gaston, "Occupational Restrictions and the Quality of Service Received: Some Evidence" *Southern Economics Journal*, 47, no. 4, (1981): 959-976.

45 Shapiro, "Investment, Moral Hazard, and Occupational Licensing."

46 Edward Timmons and Robert Thornton, "Licensing One of the World's Oldest Professions: Massage," *Journal of Law and Economics*, 56, no. 2, (2013): 371-88.

47 Edward Timmons and Robert Thornton, "The Licensing of Barbers in the USA," *British Journal of Industrial Relations*, 48, no. 4 (2010):740-57, December 2010; Edward Timmons and Robert Thornton, "The Effects of Licensing on the Wages of Radiologic Technologists," *Journal of Labor Research* 29, no. 4 (2008): 333–46; Morris Kleiner and Kyoung Park, "Battles among Licensed Occupations: Analyzing Government Regulations on Labor Market Outcomes for Dentists and Hygienists" (NBER Working Paper No. 16560, National Bureau of Economic Research, Cambridge, MA, 2010); Jeffrey Perloff, "The Impact of Licensing Laws on Wage Changes in the Construction Industry," *Journal of Law and Economics* 23, no. 2 (1980): 409–28; Mark Gius, "The Effects of Occupational Licensing on Wages: A State-Level Analysis," *International Journal of Applied Economics* 12, no. 20 (2016): 30–45; Edward Timmons and Anna Mills, "Bringing the Effects of Occupational Licensing into Focus: Optician Licensing in the United States," *Eastern Economic Journal*, 44, no. 1 (2018): 69-83

48 Morris Kleiner and Evgeny Vorotnikov, "Analyzing Occupational Licensing among the States," *Journal of Regulatory Economics* 52, no. 2 (2017): 132–58.

49 Peter Blair and Bobby Chung, "How Much of a Barrier to Entry Is Occupational Licensing," *British Journal of Industrial Relations* (forthcoming).

50 Benjamin McMichael, "The Demand for Healthcare Regulation: The Effect of Political Spending on Occupational Licensing Laws," *Southern Economic Journal* 84, no. 1 (2017): 297–316.

51 Adam Summers, "Occupational Licensing: Ranking the States and Exploring Alternatives" *Policy Study #361*, Reason Foundation, 2007.

52 Jessica Silver-Greenberg, Stacy Cowley, and Natalie Kitroeff, "When Unpaid Student Loan Bills Mean You Can No Longer Work," *New York Times*, November 18, 2017.

53 Blair and Chung, "Job Market Signaling."

54 Blair and Chung, "How Much of a Barrier to Entry Is Occupational Licensing." See also Kleiner and Soltas, "Welfare Analysis of Occupational Licensing."

55 Federal Aviation Administration, "Basic Requirements to Become an Aircraft Mechanic" https://www.faa.gov/mechanics/become/basic/

56 NYC Business, "Sightseeing Guide License" https://www1.nyc.gov/nycbusiness/description/sightseeing-guide-license

57 The section summarizes the findings of Edward Timmons et al., "Assessing Growth in Occupational Licensing of Low-Income Occupations: 1993–2012," *Journal of Entrepreneurship and Public Policy* 7, no. 2 (2018): 178–218.

58 Dick M. Carpenter II et al., *License to Work: A National Study of Burdens from Occupational Licensing*, 1st ed. (Arlington, VA: Institute for Justice, May 2012).

59 Timmons et al., "Assessing Growth in Occupational Licensing."

60 David P. Bianco, ed., *Professional and Occupational Licensing Directory: A Descriptive Guide to State and Federal Licensing, Registration, and Certification Requirements* (Detroit: Gale Research, 1993).

61 Dick M. Carpenter II et al., *License to Work: A National Study of Burdens from Occupational Licensing*, 2nd ed. (Arlington, VA: Institute for Justice, November 2017).

62 Alex Bryson and Morris Kleiner. "Re-Examining Advances in Occupational Licensing Research: Issues and Policy Implications" *British Journal of Industrial Relations* 57, no. 4 (2019): 721-731

63 Alex Bryson and Morris Kleiner, "Re-examining Advances in Occupational Licensing Research: Issues and Policy Implications," *British Journal of Industrial Relations* 57, no. 4 (2019): 721–31.

64 Benjamin Shimberg, Barbara Esser, and Daniel Kruger, *Occupational Licensing: Practices and Policies* (Washington, DC: Public Affairs Press, 1972).

65 Simon Rottenberg, ed., *Occupational Licensure and Regulation* (Washington, DC: American Enterprise Institute, 1980).

66 White House, *Occupational Licensing: A Framework for Policymakers*, July 2015, https://obamawhitehouse.archives.gov/sites/default/files/docs/licensing_report_final_nonembargo.pdf.

67 Thornton and Timmons, "The De-licensing of Occupations."

68 Robert Thornton, Edward Timmons, and Dante DeAntonio, "Licensure or License? Prospects for Occupational Deregulation," *Labor Law Journal* 68, no. 1 (2017): 46–57.

69 Updates on home page of "Braiding Freedom: A Project of the Institute for Justice," accessed February 22, 2020, http://braidingfreedom.com/ and Institute for Justice, accessed September 15, 2020, http://ij.org.

70 S.B. 2469, 109th Gen. Assemb., Reg. Sess. (Tennessee 2016); S.B. 1437, 53rd Leg., 1st Sess. (Arizona 2017). See also "Tennessee HB2201," TrackBill, accessed February 22, 2020, https://trackbill.com/bill/tennessee-house-bill-2201-professions-and-occupations-as-enacted-enacts-the-right-to-earn-a-living-act-amends-tca-title-4-title-7-title-38-title-62-title-63-and-title-67/1238736/.

71 Angela Gonzales, "Goldwater Institute Helps Behavioral Health Counselors Continue Practicing in Arizona," *Phoenix Business Journal*, November 7, 2017.

72 Arizona also enacted a reform in 2019 that conditionally recognizes many licenses for new residents of the state. This reform did not change occupational licensing requirements for current residents, however.

73 S.B. 2489, 2017 Leg., Reg. Sess. (Mississippi 2017).

74 The governor did veto legislation that would have tripled the experience requirement for real estate brokers in March 2018, but this was a more traditional veto of a pending bill rather than a rule change occurring outside the legislative process.

75 One issue with the sunset process is that it is subject to executive review. A great example of a sunset recommendation being overturned occurred with plumbers in Texas in June 2019. See Elizabeth Byrne, "Abbott Extends State Plumbing Board until 2021 after Legislature Abolished It," *Texas Tribune*, June 13, 2019.

76 Office of the New Mexico Governor, "Martinez Issues Executive Order Implementing Comprehensive Occupational Licensing Reform," *KRWG*, October 3, 2018.

77 Ellen Marks, "Licensing Reforms Require Legislative Approval," *Albuquerque Journal*, October 23, 2018.

78 H.B. 2697, 2019 Leg., Reg. Sess. (West Virginia 2019).

CHAPTER 7: GENDER, RACE, AND EARNINGS: THE DIVERGENT EFFECT OF OCCUPATIONAL LICENSING ON THE DISTRIBUTION OF EARNINGS AND ON ACCESS TO THE ECONOMY

1 Djankov et. Al (2002), Klapper, Laeven, Rajan (2006) Simeon Djankov, Raphael La Porta, Florenzio Lopez-de-Silanes, and Andrei Shleifer, (2002). "The Regulation of Entry," *The Quarterly Journal of Economics* 117 (2002), No. 1: 1-37; Simeon Djankov, Caralee McLiesh, and Rita Ramalho, "Regulation and Growth," *Economics Letters*, 92 (2006): 395-401; Leora Klapper, Luc Laeven, and Raghuram Rajan, "Entry regulation as a barrier to Entrepreneurship," *Journal of Financial Economics* , 82 (2006), No:3: 591-629; James Bailey and Diana Thomas, "Regulating Away Competition: the effect of regulation on entrepreneurship and employment," *Journal of Regulatory Economics,* 52 (2017): 237-254.

2 Diana W. Thomas, "Regressive Effects of Regulation," *Public Choice* 180, no. 1/2 (2019): 1–10.

3 Dustin Chambers, Courtney A. Collins, and Allan Krause, "How Do Federal Regulations Affect Consumer Prices? An Analysis of the Regressive Effects of Regulation," *Public Choice* 180, no. 1/2 (2019): 57–90.

4 James Bailey, Diana W. Thomas, and Joseph Anderson, "Regressive Effects of Regulation on Wages," *Public Choice* 180, no. 1/2 (2019): 91–103.

5   Dustin Chambers, Patrick A. McLaughlin, and Laura Stanley, "Barrier to Prosperity: The Harmful Impact of Entry Regulations on Income Inequality," *Public Choice* 180, no. 1/2 (2019): 165–90.

6   Bureau of Labor Statistics, "Labor Force Statistics from the Current Population Survey," last modified January 22, 2020, https://www.bls.gov/cps/cpsaat49.htm.

7   Ryan Nunn, *Occupational Licensing and American Workers* (Washington, DC: Brookings Institution, 2016).

8   For more information on this point, see chapter 7 in this volume by Alicia Plemmons and Edward Timmons.

9   Milton Friedman, *Capitalism and Freedom* (Chicago: University of Chicago Press, 1962).

10 Robert B. Ekelund and Robert D. Tollison, "The Interest-Group Theory of Government," in *The Elgar Companion to Public Choice*, ed. William F. Shughart II and Laura Razzolini (Northampton, MA: Edward Elgar, 2001).

11 Maury Gittleman, Mark A. Klee, and Moriss M. Kleiner, "Analyzing the Labor Market Outcomes of Occupational Licensing," *Industrial Relations* 57, no. 1 (2018): 57–100.

12 Dustin Chambers, Patrick A. McLaughlin, and Laura Stanley, "Barrier to Prosperity: The Harmful Impact of Entry Regulations on Income Inequality," *Public Choice* 180, no. 1/2 (2019): 165–90.

13 Morris M. Kleiner and Evan J. Soltas, "A Welfare Analysis of Occupational Licensing in U.S. States" (NBER Working Paper No. 26383, National Bureau of Economic Research, Cambridge, MA, October 2019).

14 Bureau of Labor Statistics, "Highlights of Women's Earnings in 2018," BLS Report 1083. https://www.bls.gov/opub/reports/womens-earnings/2018/pdf/home.pdf

15 Francis D. Blau and Lawrence M. Kahn, "Gender Differences in Pay," *Journal of Economic Perspectives* 14, no. 4 (2000): 70.

16 Francis D. Blau and Lawrence M. Kahn, "The Gender Wage Gap: Extent, Trends, and Explanations," *Journal of Economic Literature* 55, no. 3 (2017): 789–865.

17 Blau and Kahn, "Gender Wage Gap," 797.

18 Gary S. Becker, *The Economics of Discrimination* (Chicago: University of Chicago Press, 1957).

19 Claudia Goldin, "A Grand Gender Convergence: Its Last Chapter," *American Economic Review* 104, no. 4 (2014): 1091–119.

20 Claudia Goldin and Lawrence F. Katz, "A Most Egalitarian Profession: Pharmacy and the Evolution of a Family-Friendly Occupation," *Journal of Labor Economics* 34, no. 3 (July 2016): 705–46.

21 Goldin and Katz, "Most Egalitarian Profession."

22 Morten Bennedsen et al., "Do Firms Respond to Gender Pay Gap Transparency?" (NBER Working Paper No. 25435, National Bureau of Economic Research, Cambridge, MA, January 2019).

23 Marlene Kim, "Pay Secrecy and the Gender Wage Gap in the United States," *Industrial Relations* 54, no. 4: 648–67.

24 Janna E. Johnson and Morris M. Kleiner, "Is Occupational Licensing a Barrier to Interstate Migration?," *American Economic Journal: Economic Policy*, 12(3):347-73.

25 Summarizing the existing literature on the topic of tied migration and labor force participation and employment, a 2009 study suggests that women are more likely than men to be tied migrants. Thomas J. Cooke et al., "A Longitudinal Analysis of Family Migration and the Gender Gap in Earnings in the United States and Great Britain," *Demography* 46, no. 1 (2009): 147–67.

26 William T. Bielby and Denise D. Bielby, "I Will Follow Him: Family Ties, Gender-Role Beliefs, and Reluctance to Relocate for a Better Job," *American Journal of Sociology* 97, no. 5 (1992): 1241–67.

27 Cooke et al., "Longitudinal Analysis of Family Migration." Additional contributions, which corroborate the findings of Cooke and his coauthors, include the following: Thomas J. Cooke, "Family Migration and the Relative Earnings of Husbands and Wives," *Annals of the Association of American Geographers* 93 (2003): 338–49; Joyce P. Jacobsen and Laurence M. Levin, "Marriage and Migration: Comparing Gains and Losses from Migration for Couples and Singles," *Social Science Quarterly* 78, no. 3 (1997): 688–709; Felicia B. LeClere and Diana K. McLaughlin, "Family Migration and Changes in Women's Earnings: A Decomposition Analysis," *Population Research and Policy Review* 16 (1997): 315–35; Kimberlee A. Shauman and Mary C. Noonan, "Family Migration and Labor Force Outcomes: Sex Differences in Occupational Context," *Social Forces* 85, no. 4 (2007): 1735–64.

28 Jeremy Burke and Amalia R. Miller, "The Effects of Job Relocation on Spousal Careers: Evidence from Military Change of Station Moves," *Economic Inquiry* 56, no. 2 (2018): 1261–77.

29 A 2013 Pew Research Center study reports that 42% of mothers and 28% of fathers said they had to reduce work hours in order to care for a child or a family member. In the same study, 39% of mothers and 24% of fathers said they had taken a significant amount of time off in order to care for a child or a family member, and 27% of mothers and 10% of fathers said they had quit a job in order to care for a child or family member. Pew Research Center, *On Pay Gap, Millennial Women Near Parity—for Now* (Washington, DC: Pew Research Center, 2013). In 2011, mothers spent, on average, 14 hours per week caring for children, while fathers spent only 7 hours. For more information regarding the differences between mothers and fathers in terms of the amount of time spent on childcare and housework, see Pew Research Center, *Modern Parenthood* (Washington, DC: Pew Research Center, 2013).

30 Benjamin Powell and Evgeny Vorotnikov, "Real Estate Continuing Education: Rent Seeking or Improvement in Service Quality?," *Eastern Economic Journal* 38, no. 1 (2012): 57–73.

31 David Neumark, "Wage Differentials by Race and Sex: The Roles of Tastes Discrimination and Labor Market Information," *Industrial Relations 38*, no. 3 (1999): 414-445.

32 Amanda Agan and Sonja Starr, "Ban the Box, Criminal Records, and Racial Discrimination: A Field Experiment," *Quarterly Journal of Economics* 133, no. 1 (2018): 191–235.

33 A 2017 study by the National Student Clearinghouse Research Center examined educational outcomes by race and ethnicity and found, approximately, that Hispanic students completed a degree or certificate program within six years at a rate of 46 percent and black students completed such a program within six years at a rate of 38 percent, while white students completed it within six years at a rate of 62 percent. Doug Shapiro et al., "Completing College: A National View of Student Attainment Rates by Race and Ethnicity—Fall 2010 Cohort" (Signature Report No. 12b, National Student Clearinghouse Research Center, Herndon, VA, April 2017).

34 Sarah K. S. Shannon et al., "The Growth, Scope, and Spatial Distribution of People with Felony Records in the United States, 1948–2010," *Demography* 54 (2017): 1795–818.

35 For example, a report issued by the Federal Reserve Bank of Atlanta and the Federal Reserve Bank of Cleveland based on the 2016 Small Business Credit Survey suggests that black-owned firms have difficulty obtaining credit for business expansions. For more information on these challenges, see Federal Reserve Bank of Cleveland and Federal Reserve Bank of Atlanta, *2016 Small Business Credit Survey Report on Minority-Owned Firms*, November 2017.

36 Alison Cathles, David E. Harrington, and Kathy Krynski, "The Gender Gap in Funeral Directors: Burying Women with Ready-to-Embalm Laws?," *British Journal of Industrial Relations* 48, no. 4 (2010): 688–705.

37 Peter Q. Blair and Brian W. Chung, "Job Market Signaling through Occupational Licensing" (NBER Working Paper No. 24791, National Bureau of Economic Research, Cambridge, MA, 2019).

38 Beth Redbird, "The New Closed Shop? The Economic and Structural Effects of Occupational Licensure," *American Sociological Review* 82, no. 3 (2017): 600–624. Note that Deyo, Kleiner, and Timmons question the validity of Redbird's findings. They specifically criticize Redbird's lack of a theoretical framework, the data she uses, and her empirical methodology. Darwin Deyo, Edward Timmons, and Morris Kleiner, "A Response to 'New Closed Shop: The Economic and Structural Effects of Occupational Licensure'," *Mercatus Policy Brief*, November 2018.

39 Blair and Chung, "Job Market Signaling."

40 Agan and Starr, "Ban the Box."

41 Kleiner and Soltas, "Welfare Analysis of Occupational Licensing."

42 Ryan Nunn, "How Occupational Licensing Matters for Wages and Careers," Brookings Institution, March 2018 and Ryan Nunn, "Occupational Licensing and American Workers," *Economic Analysis – The Hamilton Project*, Brookings Institution, June 2016.

43 Peter Q. Blair and Brian W. Chung, "How Much of a Barrier to Entry Is Occupational Licensing?," *British Journal of Industrial Relations* 57, no. 4 (2019): 919–43.

44 Morris M. Kleiner, "A License for Protection," *Regulation* 29, no. 3 (Fall 2006): 17–21.

45 John S. Heywood and James H. Peoples, "Deregulation and the Prevalence of Black Truck Drivers," *Journal of Law and Economics* 37, no. 1 (1994): 133–55.

46 Sandra E. Black and Philip E. Strahan, "The Division of Spoils: Rent-Sharing and Discrimination in a Regulated Industry," *American Economic Review* 91, no. 4 (2001): 814–31.

47 Bailey, Thomas, and Anderson, "Regressive Effects of Regulation on Wages."

48 Gordon Tullock, "The Transitional Gains Trap," *Bell Journal of Economics* 6, no. 2 (1975): 671–78.

49 See several contributions to a special issue of *Public Choice* on the topic, most importantly Michael D. Thomas, "Reapplying Behavioral Symmetry: Public Choice and Choice Architecture," *Public Choice* 180, no. 1/2 (2019): 11–25; Chambers, Collins, and Krause, "How Do Federal Regulations Affect Consumer Prices?"; Bailey, Thomas, and Anderson, "Regressive Effects of Regulation on Wages"; G. P. Manish and Colin O'Reilly, "Banking Regulation, Regulatory Capture, and Inequality," *Public Choice* 180, no. 1/2 (2019): 145–64. For a discussion of regulation more generally, see

Bentley Coffey, Patrick A. McLaughlin, and Pietro Peretto, "The Cumulative Cost of Regulations," *Review of Economic Dynamics*, forthcoming.

50 David Skarbek, "Occupational Licensing and Asymmetric Information: Post-hurricane Evidence from Florida," *Cato Journal* 28, no. 1 (2008): 71–80.

CHAPTER 8: HOW CAN CERTIFICATE-OF-NEED LAWS BE REFORMED TO IMPROVE ACCESS TO HEALTHCARE?

1 Pamela C. Smith and Kelly Noe, "Is the Community Health Needs Assessment Replacing the Certificate of Need?," *Journal of Health Care Finance* 42, no. 2 (Fall 2015).

2 Katelin Davis, "Modernizing Certificate of Need Laws to Match the Post–Affordable Care Act Landscape: Using Mississippi as a Case Study for Reform in Healthcare Costs and Access to Rural Care," *Mississippi Law Journal* 89, no. 3 (2020): 479–523.

3 James F. Blumstein and Frank A. Sloan, "Health Planning and Regulation through Certificate of Need: An Overview," Utah Law Review 3 (1978): 37.

4 James F. Blumstein and Frank A. Sloan, "Health Planning and Regulation through Certificate of Need: An Overview."

5 "National Health Planning and Resources Development Act of 1974, Pub. L. No. 93-641, 88 Stat. 2225 (1975).

6 James B. Simpson, "State Certificate-of-Need Programs: The Current Status," *American Journal of Public Health* 75, no. 10 (October 1985): 1225–29.

7 Simpson, "State Certificate-of-Need Programs: The Current Status."

8 "CON – Certificate of Need State Laws," National Conference of State Legislatures, December 2019, accessed October 10, 2020, https://www.ncsl.org/research/health/con-certificate-of-need-state-laws.aspx#:~:text=a%20community%20need.,Interactive%20Map%20of%20State%20CON%20Laws,each%20state%20as%20December%202019

9 James F. Blumstein and Frank A. Sloan, "Health Planning and Regulation through Certificate of Need: An Overview," *Utah Law Review* 3 (1978): 37.

10 James F. Blumstein and Frank A. Sloan, "Health Planning and Regulation through Certificate of Need: An Overview."

11 "Total Knee Replacement," OrthoInfo (American Academy of Orthopaedic Surgeons), accessed July 27, 2020, https://orthoinfo.aaos.org/en/treatment/total-knee-replacement/

12 Susan L. Averett, Sabrina Terrizzi, and Yang Wang, "Taking the CON Out of Pennsylvania: Did Hip/Knee Replacement Patients Benefit? A Retrospective Analysis," *Health Policy and Technology* 8, no. 4 (December 2019): 349–55.

13 David M. Cutler, Robert S. Huckman, and Jonathan T. Kolstad, "Input Constraints and the Efficiency of Entry: Lessons from Cardiac Surgery," *American Economic Journal: Economic Policy* 2, no. 1 (February 2010): 51–76.

14 Vivian Ho, Meei-Hsiang Ku-Goto, and James G. Jollis, "Certificate of Need (CON) for Cardiac Care: Controversy over the Contributions of CON," *Health Services Research* 44, no. 2p1 (2009): 483–500.

15 Thomas Stratmann et al., "Certificate-of-Need Laws: How CON Laws Affect Spending, Access, and Quality across the States," Mercatus Center at George Mason University, August 29, 2017, accessed February 15, 2020, https://www.mercatus.org/publications/corporate-welfare/certificate-need-laws-how-con-laws-affect-spending-access-and-quality.

16 Mercatus Center at George Mason University, "Certificate-of-Need Laws: Virginia State Profile," accessed February 10, 2020, https://www.mercatus.org/system/files/virginia_state_profile.pdf; Thomas Stratmann and David Wille, "Certificate-of-Need Laws and Hospital Quality" (Mercatus Working Paper, Mercatus Center at George Mason University, Arlington, VA, September 2016).

17 Stratmann and Wille, "Certificate-of-Need Laws and Hospital Quality."

18 Stratmann and Wille, "Certificate-of-Need Laws and Hospital Quality."

19 Stratmann and Wille, "Certificate-of-Need Laws and Hospital Quality."

20 Stratmann and Wille, "Certificate-of-Need Laws and Hospital Quality."

21 Thomas Stratmann and Matthew C. Baker, "Are Certificate-of-Need Laws Barriers to Entry? How They Affect Access to MRI, CT, and Pet Scans" (Mercatus Working Paper, Mercatus Center at George Mason University, Arlington, VA, January 2016).

22 Stratmann and Baker, "Are Certificate-of-Need Laws Barriers to Entry? How They Affect Access to MRI, CT, and Pet Scans."

23 Stratmann and Baker, "Are Certificate-of-Need Laws Barriers to Entry? How They Affect Access to MRI, CT, and Pet Scans. "

24 Thomas Stratmann et al., "Certificate-of-Need Laws: How CON Laws Affect Spending, Access, and Quality across the States.", Mercatus Center at George Mason University, August 29, 2017, accessed February 15, 2020, https://www.mercatus.org/publications/corporate-welfare/certificate-need-laws-how-con-laws-affect-spending-access-and-quality.

25 Aaron J. Casp et al., "Certificate-of-Need State Laws and Total Hip Arthroplasty," *Journal of Arthroplasty* 34, no. 3 (March 2019): 401–7.

26 "CON Process and How to Apply," Tennessee Health Services and Development Agency, accessed January 30, 2020, https://www.tn.gov/hsda/certificate-of-need-information/how-to-apply-for-con.html.

27 Applications can take 110 days if they are initially rejected and the applicant chooses to appeal.

28 Daniel Sherman, "The Effect of State Certificate-of-Need Laws On Hospital Costs: An Economic Policy Analysis," *Federal Trade Commission* (1988): 97.

29 Sherman, "The Effect of State Certificate-of-Need Laws On Hospital Costs: An Economic Policy Analysis."

30 Carolina Ophthalmology,P.A., "Petition for a change in the basic policies and methodologies for the 2009 state medical facilities plan," *North Carolina Division of Health Service Regulation* (2008) : 18

31 Carolina Ophthalmology,P.A., "Petition for a change in the basic policies and methodologies for the 2009 state medical facilities plan."

32 Brian C. Stagg et al., "Trends in Use of Ambulatory Surgery Centers for Cataract Surgery in the United States, 2001–2014," *JAMA Ophthalmology* 136, no. 1 (January 2018): 53–60.

33 Stagg et al., "Trends in Use of Ambulatory Surgery Centers for Cataract Surgery in the United States, 2001–2014."; Muayad Kadhim et al., "Do Surgical Times and Efficiency Differ between Inpatient and Ambulatory Surgery Centers That Are Both Hospital Owned?," *Journal of Pediatric Orthopaedics* 36, no. 4 (2016): 423–28; David Shactman, "Specialty Hospitals, Ambulatory Surgery Centers, and General Hospitals: Charting a Wise Public Policy Course," *Health Affairs* 24, no. 3 (2005): 868–73; Aparna Higgins, German Veselovskiy, and Jill Schinkel, "National Estimates of

Price Variation by Site of Care," *American Journal of Managed Care* 22, no. 3 (2016): e116–e121.

34 Geetha Davis, "The Evolution of Cataract Surgery," *Missouri Medicine* 113, no. 1 (2016): 58–62.

35 "Increased Use of Ambulatory Surgery Centers for Cataract Surgery," *Michigan Medicine*, November 22, 2017.

36 "History of LASIK: Invention, Iteration & Current Status," NVISION Eye Centers, accessed January 14, 2020, https://www.nvisioncenters.com/lasik/history-and-invention/.

37 Sarah Gantz, "How Lasik and Botox Could Point the Way to Health Care Price Transparency," *Philadelphia Inquirer*, February 28, 2018.

38 Forrest Saunders, "Cedar Rapids Doctor Fights State over Certificate of Need Requirements," *KCRG.com*, June 14, 2017.

39 Thomas Stratmann and Christopher Koopman, "Entry Regulation and Rural Health Care: Certificate-of-Need Laws, Ambulatory Surgical Centers, and Community Hospitals" (Mercatus Working Paper, Mercatus Center at George Mason University, Arlington, VA, February 2016).

40 Matthew D. Mitchell, "Do Certificate-of-Need Laws Limit Spending?" (Mercatus Working Paper, Mercatus Center at George Mason University, Arlington, VA, September 2016).

41 Stratmann et al., "Certificate-of-Need Laws: How CON Laws Affect Spending, Access, and Quality across the States," Mercatus Center at George Mason University, August 29, 2017, accessed February 15, 2020, https://www.mercatus.org/publications/corporate-welfare/certificate-need-laws-how-con-laws-affect-spending-access-and-quality.

42 Stratmann et al., "Certificate-of-Need Laws: How CON Laws Affect Spending, Access, and Quality across the States."

43 James Bailey and Tom Hamami, "Competition and Health-Care Spending: Theory and Application to Certificate of Need Laws" (Working Paper 19-38, Federal Reserve Bank of Philadelphia, October 2019).

44 Stratmann et al., "Certificate-of-Need Laws: How CON Laws Affect Spending, Access, and Quality across the States."

45 Christopher J. Conover and Frank A. Sloan, "Does Removing Certificate-of-Need Regulations Lead to a Surge in Health Care Spending?," *Journal of Health Politics, Policy, and Law,* Vol 23, no.3 (June 1998).

46 Gary Scott Davis, Adam J. Rogers, and Carole M. Becker, "Florida Repeals Significant Portions of Certificate of Need Law," *National Law Review* 9, no. 182 (July 2019).

47 Andrew Whitney, "Georgia Pares Back CON Laws," Heartland Institute, May 31, 2019.

48 Jack Pitsor, "States Modernizing Certificate of Need Laws," *LegisBrief* (National Conference of State Legislatures) 27, no. 41 (December 2019).

49 Gary Scott Davis, Adam J. Rogers, and Carole M. Becker, "Florida Repeals Significant Portions of Certificate of Need Law," *National Law Review* 9, no. 182 (July 2019).

50 Andrew Whitney, "Georgia Pares Back CON Laws," Heartland Institute, May 31, 2019.

51 Lacie Glover, "Why Does an MRI Cost So Darn Much?," *Money*, July 16, 2014.

52 Maryland Health Care Commission, "Modernization of the Maryland Certificate of Need Program: Final Report," draft, December 11, 2018.

53 Maryland Health Care Commission, "Modernization of the Maryland Certificate of Need Program: Final Report."

54 Pamela C. Smith and Kelly Noe, "Is the Community Health Needs Assessment Replacing the Certificate of Need?," *Journal of Health Care Finance* 42, no. 2 (Fall 2015).

55 Smith and Noe, "Is the Community Health Needs Assessment Replacing the Certificate of Need?"

56 Matthew D. Mitchell, Elise Amez Droz, and Anna K. Parsons, "Phasing Out Certificate-of-Need Laws: A Menu of Options" (Policy Brief, Mercatus Center at George Mason University, Arlington, VA, February 2020).

57 Mitchell, Droz, and Parsons, "Phasing Out Certificate-of-Need Laws."

58 Daylight Saving Time Amendments, S.B. 59, 2020 Gen. Sess. (Utah 2020).

59 Daylight Saving Time Amendments, S.B. 59.

60 Mitchell, Droz, and Parsons, "Phasing Out Certificate-of-Need Laws."

61 Mitchell, Droz, and Parsons, "Phasing Out Certificate-of-Need Laws."

62 "Coronavirus Disease (COVID-19)—Events as They Happen," World Health Organization, accessed May 31, 2020, https://www.who.int/emergencies/diseases/novel-coronavirus-2019/events-as-they-happen; "Coronavirus Global Health Emergency: Coverage from UN News," *UN News*, accessed May 31, 2020, https://news.un.org/en/events/coronavirus-global-health-emergency-coverage-un-news?page=45.

63 "States Are Suspending Certificate of Need Laws in the Wake of COVID-19 but the Damage Might Already Be Done," *Pacific Legal Foundation* (blog), March 31, 2020.

64 Angela C. Erickson, "States Are Suspending Certificate of Need Laws in the Wake of COVID-19 but the Damage Might Already Be Done," *Pacific Legal Foundation* (blog), March 31, 2020.

65 Justin Haskins, "America's Hospitals Are Unprepared for Coronavirus—Here's Why You Should Blame Government," *The Hill*, March 21, 2020.

66 Haskins, "America's Hospitals Are Unprepared."

CHAPTER 9: LAND USE REGULATION AND HOUSING AFFORDABILITY

1 Robert Caro, *The Power Broker: Robert Moses and the Fall of New York* (New York: Knopf, 1974), 1024.

2 Raphael Fischler, "Health, Safety, and the General Welfare: Markets, Politics, and Social Science in Early Land-Use Regulation and Community Design," *Journal of Urban History* 24, no. 6 (September 1998): 675–719.

3 Ryan Holeywell, "Forget What You've Heard, Houston Really Does Have Zoning (Sort Of)," Kinder Institute for Urban Research, September 8, 2015. While Houston does have some land use regulations that would be found in a typical zoning ordinance, it does not have use restrictions that prevent housing from being built on land zoned for commercial or industrial use.

4 Euclid v. Ambler, 272 U.S. 365 (1926).

5 Seymour Toll, *Zoned American* (New York: Grossman, 1969), 158-9.

6 Buchanan v. Warley, 245 U.S. 60 (1917). See also "Buchanan v. Warley," Oyez, accessed May 5, 2020, https://www.oyez.org/cases/1900-1940/245us60.

7   Though the Supreme Court overturned explicitly race-based zoning in 1916, local, state, and federal policy continued segregation in real estate for decades after. In 1934, in response to a housing shortage, the Federal Housing Authority was established to subsidize homebuying by insuring mortgages. However, the agency refused to insure homes in neighborhoods where black Americans lived. For a history of government-imposed segregation in housing, see Richard Rothstein, *The Color of Law: A Forgotten History of How Our Government Segregated America* (New York: Liveright, 2017).

8   Bernard Siegan, *Land Use without Zoning* (Lexington, MA: D.C. Heath, 1972), 88. See also Fischler, "Health, Safety, and the General Welfare."

9   Shima Hamidi, Sadegh Sabouri, and Reid Ewing, "Does Density Aggravate the COVID-19 Pandemic?" *Journal of the American Planning Association* 86, no. 4 (June 2020), 495-509.

10   Ian Lovett, Dan Frosch, and Paul Overberg, "Covid-19 Stalks Large Families in Rural America," *The Wall Street Journal,* June 7, 2020.

11   "Appendix: Hotel and Employment Statistics" in Paul Groth, *Living Downtown: The History of Residential Hotels in the United States* (Berkeley: University of California Press, 1994).

12   Charles Lockwood, *Manhattan Moves Uptown: An Illustrated History* (Boston: Houghton Mifflin, 1976; repr., Dover, 2014), 293.

13   Lockwood, *Manhattan Moves Uptown.*

14   Stuart Rosenthal, "Are Private Markets and Filtering a Viable Source of Low-Income Housing? Estimates from a 'Repeat Income' Model," *American Economic Review* 104, no. 2 (February 2014): 687–706.

15   Evan Mast. "The Effect of New Market-Rate Housing Construction on the Low-Income Housing Market," (Upjohn Institute Working Paper 19-307, 2019).

16   Rosenthal, "Are Private Markets and Filtering a Viable Source of Low-Income Housing?" Rosenthal points out that house price inflation, which occurs when demand for housing increases in places with severe zoning constraints, can cause housing to "filter up."

17   Joseph Gyourko and Raven Molloy, "Regulation and Housing Supply," in Gilles Duranton, J. Vernon Henderson, William C. Strange, eds., *Handbook of Regional and Urban Economics* Volume 5, (2015): 1291-2.

18   William A. Fischel, "The Rise of the Homevoters: How OPEC and Earth Day Created Growth-Control Zoning That Derailed the Growth Machine" (working paper, Marron Institute, February 2016).

19   Harvey Molotch, "The City as a Growth Machine: Toward a Political Economy of Place," *American Journal of Sociology* 82, no. 2 (1976): 309–32.

20   William A. Fischel, "An Economic History of Zoning and a Cure for Its Exclusionary Effects," *Urban Studies* 41, no. 2 (February 2004).

21   For a review of the evidence on the environmental effects of infill development versus new suburban development, see David Owen, *Green Metropolis: Why Living Smaller, Living Closer, and Driving Less Are the Keys to Sustainability* (New York: Penguin, 2009).

22   Fischel, "Economic History of Zoning."

23   Fischel, "Economic History of Zoning."

24   Knut Are Aastveit, Bruno Albuquerque, and André Anundsen, "Time-Varying Housing Supply Elasticities and US Housing Cycles" (working paper, January

31, 2018), https://editorialexpress.com/cgi-bin/conference/download.cgi?db_name=IAAE2018&paper_id=397.

25 Sarah Holder, "The Cities Where Job Growth Is Outpacing New Homes," *CityLab*, September 9, 2019.

26 Kerry Cavanaugh, "Holy Cow! California May Get Rid of Single-Family Zoning," *Los Angeles Times*, April 24, 2019.

27 Edward L. Glaeser, Joseph Gyourko, and Raven Saks, "Why Is Manhattan So Expensive? Regulation and the Rise in House Prices" (NBER Working Paper No. 10124, National Bureau of Economic Research, Cambridge, MA, November 2003).

28 Joseph Gyourko, Jonathan Hartley, and Jacob Krimmel, "The Local Residential Land Use Regulatory Environment across U.S. Housing Markets: Evidence from a New Wharton Index" (NBER Working Paper No. 26573, National Bureau of Economic Research, Cambridge, MA, December 2019). This paper updates the WRLURI, which was first published in Joseph Gyourko, Albert Saiz, and Anita Summers, "A New Measure of the Local Regulatory Environment for Housing Markets: The Wharton Residential Land Use Regulatory Index," *Urban Studies* 45, no. 3 (March 2008): 693–729.

29 Nolan Gray and Salim Furth, "Do Minimum-Lot-Size Regulations Limit Housing Supply in Texas?" (Mercatus Working Paper, Mercatus Center at George Mason University, Arlington, VA, November 2015).

30 Gray and Furth, "Do Minimum-Lot-Size Regulations Limit Housing Supply?"

31 Donald C. Shoup, *The High Cost of Free Parking* (Chicago: American Planning Association, 2011), 90.

32 Myung-Jin Jun, "The Effects of Portland's Urban Growth Boundary on Housing Prices," *Journal of the American Planning Association* 72, no. 2 (2006): 239–43.

33 Gerrit J. Knaap, "The Price Effects of Urban Growth Boundaries in Metropolitan Portland, Oregon," *Land Economics* 61, no. 1 (1985): 26.

34 Keith R. Ihlanfeldt, "The Effect of Land Use Regulation on Housing and Land Prices," *Journal of Urban Economics* 61, no. 3 (2007): 420–35.

35 Ingrid Gould Ellen, Brian J. McCabe, and Eric Edward Stern, "Fifty Years of Historic Preservation in New York City" (Fact Brief, Furman Center at New York University, March 2016).

36 Vicki Been et al., "Preserving History or Hindering Growth? The Heterogeneous Effects of Historic Districts on Local Housing Markets in New York City" (NBER Working Paper 20446, National Bureau of Economic Research, September 2014).

37 Joseph Gyourko and Raven Molloy, "Regulation and Housing Supply" (NBER Working Paper No. 20536, National Bureau of Economic Research, Cambridge, MA, October 2014).

38 Jenny Schuetz, "Cost, Crowding, or Commuting? Housing Stress on the Middle Class," Brookings Institution, May 7, 2019.

39 Chris Glynn and Alexander Casey, "Homelessness Rises Faster Where Rent Exceeds a Third of Income," Zillow Research, December 11, 2018.

40 Chang-Tai Hsieh and Enrico Moretti, "Housing Constraints and Spatial Misallocation," *American Economic Journal: Macroeconomics* 11, no. 2 (2019): 1-39.

41 Peter Ganong and Daniel Shoag, "Why Has Regional Income Convergence in the U.S. Declined?" *Journal of Urban Economics* 102 (2017).

42 Kyle F. Herkenhoff, Lee E. Ohanian, and Edward C. Prescott, "Tarnishing the Golden and Empire States: Land-Use Restrictions and the U.S. Economic Slow-down," *Journal of Monetary Economics* 93 (2018): 89–109;

43 Hsieh and Moretti, "Housing Constraints and Spatial Misallocation."

44 Rebecca Diamond, Tim McQuade, and Franklin Qian, "The Effects of Rent Control Expansion on Tenants, Landlords, and Inequality: Evidence from San Francisco" (NBER Working Paper No. 24181, National Bureau of Economic Research, Cambridge, MA, January 2018).

45 Brian Stromberg and Lisa Sturtevant, "What Makes Inclusionary Zoning Happen?" (Inclusionary Housing policy brief, National Housing Conference, May 2016).

46 For a review of the studies that estimate the effects of inclusionary zoning on new housing construction and market-rate house prices, see Emily Hamilton, "Inclusionary Zoning and Housing Market Outcomes" (Mercatus Working Paper, Mercatus Center at George Mason University, Arlington VA, September 2019).

47 Derrick Moore, "Overall Mover Rate Remains at an All-time Low," U.S. Census Bureau, December 21, 2017.

48 In 2016, 49% of renters voted, compared to 60% of homeowners. See Chris Salviati, "Renters vs. Homeowners at the Ballot Box—Will America's Politicians Represent the Voice of Renters?," Apartment List, October 30, 2018.

49 M. Nolan Gray and Adam A. Millsap, "Subdividing the Unzoned City: An Analysis of the Causes and Effects of Houston's 1998 Subdivision Reform," *Journal of Planning and Education Research* (2020).

50 Kenneth Jackson, *Crabgrass Frontier: The Suburbanization of the United States* (Oxford: Oxford University Press, 1985), 192.

51 Loren King, "Cities, Subsidiarity, and Federalism," *Nomos* 55 (2014): 291–331.

52 William A. Fischel, *Zoning Rules! The Economics of Land Use Regulation* (Cambridge, MA: Lincoln Institute of Land Policy, 2015), 229–30.

53 Edward L. Glaeser and Joseph Gyourko, "The Economic Implications of Housing Supply," *Journal of Economic Perspectives* 32, no. 1 (Winter 2018): 3–30.

54 Michael Andersen, "It's Official: DC Politicians Have Woken Up to Housing Abundance," Sightline Institute, October 14, 2019.

55 See, for example, Lionshead Lake, Inc. v. Township of Wayne, 10 N.J. 165, 89 A.2d 693 (1952). "People who move into the country rightly expect more land, more living room, indoors and out, and more freedom in their scale of living than is generally possible in the city. City standards of housing are not adaptable to suburban areas and especially to the upbringing of children. But quite apart from these considerations of public health which cannot be overlooked, minimum floor-area standards are justified on the ground that they promote the general welfare of the community."

56 Euclid v. Ambler, 272 U.S. 365 (1926).

57 Southern Burlington County NAACP v. Township of Mount Laurel, 67 N.J. 151, 336 A.2d 713 (1975). For a history of the Mount Laurel decision, see David L. Kirp, John P. Dwyer, and Larry A. Rosenthal, *Our Town: Race, Housing, and the History of Suburbia* (Rutgers, NJ: Rutgers University Press, 1997).

58 H.B. 2001, 80th Leg. Assemb., Reg. Sess. (Oregon 2019). See also "2019 Session: House Bill 2001," Your Government website (OregonLive.com), accessed May 5, 2020, https://gov.oregonlive.com/bill/2019/hb2001/.

59 Luis Arias, "Is the Answer to LA's Housing Crisis in Your Backyard?," *LAist*, August 8, 2019.

60 A.B. 68, 2019–20 Leg., Reg. Sess. (California 2019). See also "AB-68 Land Use: Accessory Dwelling Units," California Legislative Information, accessed May 5, 2020, https://leginfo.legislature.ca.gov/faces/billNavClient.xhtml?bill_id=201920200AB68.

CHAPTER 10: BUILDING ENERGY CODES: A CASE STUDY IN REGULATION AND COST-BENEFIT ANALYSIS

1 Grant D. Jacobsen and Matthew J. Kotchen, "Are Building Codes Effective at Saving Energy? Evidence from Residential Billing Data in Florida," *Review of Economics and Statistics* 95, no. 1 (March 2013): 34–49.

2 Matthew J. Holian and Ralph McLaughlin, "Benefit-Cost Analysis for Transportation Planning and Public Policy: Towards Multimodal Demand Modeling" (MTI Report 12-42, Mineta Transportation Institute, San Jose, CA, August 2016).

3 Kenneth Gillingham, "Rebound Effects," in *The New Palgrave Dictionary of Economics*, edited by Palgrave Macmillan (London: Palgrave Macmillan, 2014). https://doi.org/10.1057/978-1-349-95121-5_2875-1

4 Arthur H. Rosenfeld and Deborah Poskanzer, "A Graph Is Worth a Thousand Gigawatthours: How California Came to Lead the United States in Energy Efficiency (Innovations Case Narrative: The California Effect)," *Innovations: Technology, Governance, Globalization* 4, no. 4 (2009): 57–79.

5 Rosenfeld and Poskanzer, "A Graph Is Worth a Thousand Gigawatthours," 70.

6 Kevin Novan, Aaron Smith, and Tianxia Zhou, "Residential Building Codes Do Save Energy: Evidence from Hourly Smart-Meter Data" (E2e Working Paper 031, E2e Project, June 2017).

7 Jacobsen and Kotchen, "Are Building Codes Effective at Saving Energy?"

8 Stephen J. Dubner, "How Efficient Is Energy Efficiency?," February 5, 2015, in *Freakonomics Radio*, podcast, https://freakonomics.com/podcast/how-efficient-is-energy-efficiency-a-new-freakonomics-radio-podcast/.

9 Chris Bruegge, Tatyana Deryugina, and Erica Myers, "The Distributional Effects of Building Energy Codes," *Journal of the Association of Environmental and Resource Economists* 6, no. S1 (2019): S95.

10 Lucas W. Davis and Christopher R. Knittel, "Are Fuel Economy Standards Regressive?," *Journal of the Association of Environmental and Resource Economists* 6, no. S1 (2019): S61.

11 Davis and Knittel, "Are Fuel Economy Standards Regressive?"

12 William D. Nordhaus, *The Climate Casino: Risk, Uncertainty, and Economics for a Warming World* New Haven: Yale University Press, 2013), 261.

13 Jacobsen and Kotchen, "Are Building Codes Effective at Saving Energy?"

14 The focus in CBA is on human welfare broadly conceived, while economic impact analysis and fiscal impact analysis are narrower and focus on specific impacts. For example, fiscal impact analysis may focus on the impact of some policy or program on the state government's budget, while economic impact analysis may focus on the policy or program's impact on GDP. CBA, on the other hand, recognizes that social welfare can go up even as state budgets and GDP go down. For an example of economic impact analysis, see Anoshua Chaudhuri and Susan G. Zieff, "Do Open Streets Initiatives Impact Local Businesses? The Case of Sunday Streets in San Francisco, California," *Journal of Transport Health* 2, no. 4 (2015):

529–39. For an example of fiscal impact analysis, see Dennis P. Culhane, Stephen Metraux, and Trevor Hadley, "Public Service Reductions Associated with Placement of Homeless Persons with Severe Mental Illness in Supportive Housing," *Housing Policy Debate* 13, no. 1 (2002): 107–63.

15 Quoted from Anthony E. Boardman et al., *Cost-Benefit Analysis: Concepts and Practice* (Cambridge: Cambridge University Press, 2017), 6.

16 Matthew Manning et al., *Economic Analysis and Efficiency in Policing, Criminal Justice and Crime Reduction: What Works?* London: Palgrave Macmillan, 2016), 36.

17 Diana Fuguitt and Shanton J. Wilcox, *Cost-Benefit Analysis for Public Sector Decision Makers* (Westport, CT: Greenwood, 1999), 53.

18 This impact was included in the analysis in Meredith Fowlie, Michael Greenstone, and Catherine Wolfram, "Do Energy Efficiency Investments Deliver? Evidence from the Weatherization Assistance Program," *Quarterly Journal of Economics* 133, no. 3 (2018): 1597–644.

19 For further discussion, see Matthew J. Holian, "The Impact of Building Energy Codes on Household Electricity Consumption," *Economics Letters* 186, no. 108841 (January 2020): 1-4. In this piece I discuss the exact case mentioned here, where home size changes over time along with energy efficiency, and show how multiple regression techniques can be used to estimate causal effects in this setting.

20 The details behind this calculation are 48 kWh × 12 months × 14.6 cents = $84 annual electricity cost savings. For natural gas, the calculation is 1.5 therms × 12 months × $1.22 = $21.96. Adding these together, $22 + $84 = $106, which is the value of the annual energy savings.

21 It is a subtle point, but the reason monetizing with market prices is appealing is because neoclassical perfect competition theory teaches us that price equals marginal cost. Perfect competition is a theoretical condition not always met in the real world, however, and there are times when the use of market prices is not appropriate. In these cases, analysts have to be creative in calculating a so-called shadow price, which is simply the true social value of an impact.

22 Nordhaus, William D. "Revisiting the Social Cost of Carbon," *Proceedings of the National Academy of Sciences of the United States of America* 114, no. 7 (February 2017): 1518–23.

23 Table 5 in Jacobsen and Kotchen, "Are Building Codes Effective at Saving Energy?"

24 Jacobsen and Kotchen's table 5 indicated the low- and high-end figures for carbon dioxide reduction owing to a fall in natural gas use as $0.83 and $10.12, respectively. Thus the marginal damage figures are calculated as follows: $0.83 ÷ 0.108 = $7.68, and $10.12 ÷ 0.108 = $93.70. I have verified with the authors that these were the marginal damage figures they used, and I thank Matthew Kotchen for sharing his analysis file with me.

25 Fuguitt and Wilcox, *Cost-Benefit Analysis*.

26 Dean Stansel, Gary Jackson, and Howard Finch, "Housing Tenure and Mobility with an Acquisition-Based Property Tax: The Case of Florida," *Journal of Housing Research* 16, no. 2 (2007): 117–29.

27 NPV can be calculated in a spreadsheet, or with the following handy formula:

$$-675 + 190 \times \left(\frac{1}{0.05} - \frac{\frac{1}{0.05}}{1.05^{10}} \right).$$

There is actually an intuition behind this equation. The term $1/r$ is the present value of a dollar received every year forever (an annuity that pays out forever is called a perpetuity), which is $20 when $r = 0.05$. The second term in parentheses is the present value of $20 ten years from now, which is $12.28. So the term in parentheses can be thought of as the present value of a $1 perpetuity that is taken away in ten years. This is $20 minus $12.28, or $7.72. Given that there are $190 in benefits every year for ten years, we can multiply $190 by $7.72 to find $1,467, the present value of benefits. From this we subtract $675, which is the initial up-front costs, to find a present value of $1,467 minus $675, or $792.

28 Assuming a zero discount rate is a simplifying assumption, but it is not realistic. Households that have investment options value current money more than future money. The issue of myopic behavior discussed in the introduction can be modeled through the NPV equation. If households have an irrational level of impatience when it comes to home energy efficiency, they will not make investments with positive NPV. How to account for possible consumer myopia is an ongoing debate in policy analysis, but keep in mind that it is not easy to discern when people are behaving irrationally and when they have preferences concerning future values that differ from the preferences a policy analyst or decision maker thinks they should have.

29 Jacobsen and Kotchen, "Are Building Codes Effective at Saving Energy?," 47.

30 Florida's energy code gives the builder flexibility about how to meet the energy use requirements specified in the home. If there is a design change that enables a builder to comply with the code more cheaply than by using low-E windows, the builder could select that design feature instead. This means that the $675 figure might overstate the actual cost of compliance—though I still refer to $675 as the low-end estimate.

31 Matthew J. Kotchen, "Longer-Run Evidence on Whether Building Energy Codes Reduce Residential Energy Consumption," *Journal of the Association of Environmental and Resource Economists* 4, no. 1 (2017): 135–53.

32 Kotchen, "Longer-Run Evidence," 152.

33 Kotchen, "Longer-Run Evidence."

34 Kotchen, "Longer-Run Evidence."

35 A final consideration is well worth mentioning. The analysis described above was for a representative home. If all homes in the study area are the same, we could simply multiply the NPV for a single home by the number of homes. But because homes differ, a more careful analysis would have to account for this. Many homes in Florida do not use natural gas at all, for example, and natural gas savings were the only benefit of the stricter codes found in Kotchen, "Longer-Run Evidence."

36 Novan, Smith, and Zhou, "Residential Building Codes Do Save Energy."

37 Jacobsen and Kotchen, "Are Building Codes Effective at Saving Energy?"

38 Kotchen, "Longer-Run Evidence."

39 Alan B. Krueger, "Economic Considerations and Class Size," *Economic Journal* 113, no. 485 (2003): F34–F63.

40 My forthcoming book, *Data and the American Dream: Contemporary Social Controversies and the American Community Survey* (London: Palgrave Macmillan, 2021) elaborates on how the replicate and extend method can be used in learning introductory econometrics and R programming.

41 Fowlie, Greenstone, and Wolfram, "Do Energy Efficiency Investments Deliver?"

42 Jacobsen and Kotchen, "Are Building Codes Effective at Saving Energy?"

43 Arik Levinson, "How Much Energy Do Building Energy Codes Save? Evidence from California Houses," *American Economic Review* 106, no. 10 (2016): 286794.

44 Kotchen, "Longer-Run Evidence."

45 Kotchen, "Longer-Run Evidence."

46 The debate between Hanushek and Krueger highlights this important issue, in the context of education. Eric A. Hanushek, "The Failure of Input-Based Schooling Policies," *Economic Journal* 113, no. 485 (2003): F64–F98, and Krueger, "Economic Considerations and Class Size."

CHAPTER 11: THE TRADEOFFS BETWEEN ENERGY EFFICIENCY, CONSUMER PREFERENCES, AND ECONOMIC GROWTH

1 Susan Dudley and Jerry Brito, *Regulation: A Primer*, 2nd ed. (Arlington, VA: Mercatus Center at George Mason University, 2012).

2 Cass R. Sunstein, *Why Nudge? The Politics of Libertarian Paternalism* (New Haven, CT: Yale University Press, 2014).

3 This is a phrase routinely used in the behavioral economics literature. See Richard H. Thaler and Cass R. Sunstein, *Nudge: Improving Decisions about Health, Wealth, and Happiness*, rev. and exp. ed. (New York: Penguin Books, 2009); Richard H. Thaler, *Misbehaving: The Making of Behavioral Economics* (New York: W.W. Norton, 2016); Alexander C. Cartwright and Marc A. Hight, "'Better Off as Judged by Themselves': A Critical Analysis of the Conceptual Foundations of Nudging," *Cambridge Journal of Economics* 44, no. 1 (January 2020): 33–54.

4 The rationality assumption in economics is sometimes thought of as an assumption desirable for its predictive properties rather than its realism. Milton Friedman, for example, argued that billiards players act as if they know complex mathematical formulas. Thus, an analyst might be able to predict their behavior with mathematics, even though billiards players do not think in terms of math, generally. See "The Methodology of Positive Economics," in Milton Friedman, *Essays in Positive Economics* (Chicago: University of Chicago Press, 1953).

5 Thaler and Sunstein, *Nudge*.

6 Ted Gayer and W. Kip Viscusi, "Overriding Consumer Preferences with Energy Regulations," *Journal of Regulatory Economics* 43, no. 3 (June 2013): 248–64.

7 Hunt Allcott and Dmitry Taubinsky, "The Lightbulb Paradox: Evidence from Two Randomized Experiments" (NBER Working Paper No. 19713, National Bureau of Economic Research, Cambridge, MA, December 2013); Hunt Allcott and Cass R. Sunstein, "Regulating Internalities," *Journal of Policy Analysis and Management* 34, no. 3 (June 2015): 698–705; David Weimer, *Behavioral Economics for Cost-Benefit Analysis: Benefit Validity When Sovereign Consumers Seem to Make Mistakes* (Cambridge: Cambridge University Press, 2017).

8 Interestingly, gym memberships are sometimes used as an example of businesses *exploiting* the biases of their customers, who are overly optimistic about their future likelihood of working out. This example highlights how dueling biases—in this case, a present bias and an optimism bias—can influence behavior in opposite directions.

9 Figure 1 could also describe too little investment in energy efficiency from a neoclassical perspective, as there could be social benefits external to the consumer associated with energy efficiency, such as benefits from reduced pollution.

10 Hunt Allcott and Michael Greenstone, "Is There an Energy Efficiency Gap?," *Journal of Economic Perspectives* 26, no. 1 (February 2012): 3–28.

11 Adam B. Jaffe and Robert N. Stavins, "The Energy Paradox and the Diffusion of Conservation Technology," *Resource and Energy Economics* 16, no. 2 (May 1994): 91–122.

12 Jerry A. Hausman, "Individual Discount Rates and the Purchase and Utilization of Energy-Using Durables," *Bell Journal of Economics* 10, no. 1 (1979): 33–54.

13 Richard H. Thaler and H. M. Shefrin, "An Economic Theory of Self-Control," *Journal of Political Economy* 89, no. 2 (1981): 392–406.

14 Neoclassical economists generally assume rational consumers exhibit constant exponential discounting, although exceptions can arise as a result of uncertainty or risk.

15 Allcott and Greenstone, "Is There an Energy Efficiency Gap?"

16 Kenneth Gillingham and Karen Palmer, "Bridging the Energy Efficiency Gap: Policy Insights from Economic Theory and Empirical Evidence," *Review of Environmental Economics and Policy* 8, no. 1 (January 2014): 18–38.

17 Todd D. Gerarden, Richard G. Newell, and Robert N. Stavins, "Assessing the Energy-Efficiency Gap," *Journal of Economic Literature* 55, no. 4 (2017): 1486–525.

18 Behavioral economists sometimes hand-wave away such neoclassical explanations, calling them "explainawaytions." However, one could just as easily argue that cherry-picking biases to condemn behavior one doesn't like is also a form of explainawaytion. See Richard H. Thaler, "Behavioral Economics: Past, Present, and Future," *American Economic Review* 106, no. 7 (July 2016): 1577–600.

19 Hunt Allcott and Nathan Wozny, "Gasoline Prices, Fuel Economy, and the Energy Paradox," *Review of Economics and Statistics* 96, no. 5 (October 2013): 779–95.

20 Gayer and Viscusi, "Overriding Consumer Preferences."

21 W. Kip Viscusi and Ted Gayer, "Behavioral Public Choice: The Behavioral Paradox of Government Policy," *Harvard Journal of Law and Policy* 38, no. 3 (2015): 973–1007; Michael David Thomas, "Reapplying Behavioral Symmetry: Public Choice and Choice Architecture," *Public Choice* 180 (2019): 11–25.

22 Brian F. Mannix and Susan E. Dudley, "Please Don't Regulate My Internalities," *Journal of Policy Analysis and Management* 34, no. 3 (June 2015): 715–18.

23 Mario J. Rizzo and Glen Whitman. *Escaping Paternalism: Rationality, Behavioral Economics, and Public Policy.* Cambridge, UK: Cambridge University Press (2020).

24 Cartwright and Hight, "Better Off as Judged by Themselves."

25 Richard B. Belzer and Richard P. Theroux, "Criteria for Evaluating Results Obtained from Contingent Valuation Methods," in *Valuing Food Safety and Nutrition,* ed. Julie A. Caswell (Boulder, CO: Westview, 1995).

26 Pamela Grimm, "Social Desirability Bias," in *Wiley International Encyclopedia of Marketing* (American Cancer Society, 2010).

27 See Reginfo.gov (database), Office of Information and Regulatory Affairs, accessed September 29, 2020, https://www.reginfo.gov/public/.

28 Last-minute regulations like this one are not uncommon, as administrations often rush regulations out the door in their final weeks and months in office. See Veronique de Rugy and Antony Davies, "Midnight Regulations and the Cinderella Effect," *Journal of Socio-economics* 38, no. 6 (December 2009): 886–90.

29 US Department of Energy, "Technical Support Document: Energy Efficiency Program for Consumer Products and Commercial and Industrial Equipment: Ceiling Fans," 2016, 1-2.

30 As I will discuss below in the discussion about economic growth, the energy savings could still prove a benefit to future consumers even if, on balance, current consumers are made worse off.

31 It's also worth noting that the environmental benefits for these regulations are calculated from a global perspective while the costs to consumers and businesses are calculated from a domestic perspective only, implying an imbalance in the aggregate cost and benefit estimates. Government guidelines recommend that any significant benefits or costs accruing to individuals outside the borders of the United States be presented separately from domestic impacts. US Office of Management and Budget, *Circular A-4: Regulatory Analysis*, September 17, 2003.

32 US Department of Energy, Energy Conservation Program: Energy Conservation Standards for Ceiling Fans, 82 Fed. Reg. 6826, 6878 (January 19, 2017).

33 82 Fed. Reg. at 6850.

34 US Department of Energy, "Technical Support Document: Ceiling Fans," 7-5.

35 Scholars have questioned these kinds of assumptions in DOE's analyses. See, for example, Art Fraas and Sofie Miller, "Measuring Energy Efficiency: Accounting for the Hidden Costs of Product Failure" *Economics of Energy & Environmental Policy* 9, no. 2 (2020): 1-18. .

36 US Department of Energy, "Technical Support Document: Ceiling Fans," 8-31.

37 US Department of Energy, "Technical Support Document: Ceiling Fans," 8-31.

38 US Department of Energy, "Technical Support Document: Ceiling Fans," 8-27.

39 US Department of Energy, "Technical Support Document: Ceiling Fans," 8-29.

40 This is an implication of the Fisher model and the Ramsey growth model, for example (two popular economic models).

41 Of course, it is possible the market is not in equilibrium or that distortions of various kinds cause market interest rates not to reflect the subjective time preferences of members of society.

42 US Department of Energy, "Technical Support Document: Ceiling Fans," 8-25.

43 Sofie Miller, "One Discount Rate Fits All? The Regressive Effects of DOE's Energy Efficiency Rule," *Policy Perspectives* 22 (2015): 40–54.

44 Consumer Financial Protection Bureau, "CFPB Report Finds 26 Million Consumers Are Credit Invisible," press release, May 5, 2015, https://www.consumerfinance.gov/about-us/newsroom/cfpb-report-finds-26-million-consumers-are-credit-invisible/.

45 See, for example, US Department of Energy Fact Sheet, Saving Energy and Money with Appliance and Equipment Standards in the United States, October 2016.

46 Fraas and Miller, "Measuring Energy Efficiency."

47 Kenneth Gillingham, David Rapson, and Gernot Wagner, "The Rebound Effect and Energy Efficiency Policy," *Review of Environmental Economics and Policy* 10, no. 1 (January 2016): 68–88.

48 US Department of Energy, "Technical Support Document: Ceiling Fans," 10C-1.

49 See, for example, 42 U.S.C. § 6295(o)(2)(A) and 42 U.S.C. § 6295(o)(2)(B).

50 To put it another way, each additional spending decision affects our savings surplus or deficit for the year, which in turn affects the bequest amount we leave to our heirs.

51 It's easy to forget this, but energy security and independence were the chief concerns at the time energy efficiency standards were first implemented in the United States in the 1970s.

CHAPTER 12: COOPERATION OR CONFLICT: TWO APPROACHES TO CONSERVATION

1   Quoted in Aaron Vaughn, "Utah Towns Fight Federally Protected Prairie Dogs," *Fox 13*, May 21, 2012.

2   "Utah Residents in Battle to Rid Town of Prairie Dogs," *Fox News*, June 26, 2012.

3   Quoted in "Utah Residents in Battle," *Fox News*.

4   Lindsay Whitehurst, "Trump Administration Loosens Utah Prairie Dog Restrictions," *AP News*, April 13, 2018.

5   Jonathan Wood, "A Prairie Home Invasion: How Environmental Federalism Can Lead to Real Recovery of Endangered Species," *PERCReports* (Property and Environment Research Center) 36, no. 2 (Winter 2017).

6   Lacey Louwagie, "Utah Prairie Dogs Get Federal Protection, Circuit Rules," *Courthouse News Service*, March 30, 2017.

7   Associated Press, "Supreme Court Declines to Hear Prairie Dog Protections Lawsuit," *New York Post*, January 29, 2018.

8   F. A. Hayek, *Law, Legislation and Liberty*, vol. 2 (Chicago: University of Chicago Press, 1977).

9   Robert Brulle, "The Climate Lobby: A Sectoral Analysis of Lobbying Spending on Climate Change in the USA, 2000 to 2016," *Climatic Change* 149, no. 3–4 (August 2018): 289–303.

10 Julie Cart, "Saving Desert Tortoises Is a Costly Hurdle for Solar Projects," *Los Angeles Times*, March 4, 2012.

11 Terry L. Anderson and Donald Leal, *Free Market Environmentalism for the Next Generation* (New York: Palgrave Macmillan, 2015).

12 Ronald H. Coase, "The Problem of Social Cost," *Journal of Law and Economics* 56, no. 4 (November 2013): 837–77.

13 "Resources," specifically "What Is a Conservation Easement?," National Conservation Easement Database, accessed September 23, 2020, https://www.conservationeasement.us/resources/.

14 Terry L. Anderson and Fred S. McChesney, *Property Rights: Cooperation, Conflict, and Law* (Princeton, NJ: Princeton University Press, 2003).

15 Garrett Hardin, "The Tragedy of the Commons," *Science* 162, no. 3859 (December 1968): 1243–48.

16 Elinor Ostrom, *Governing the Commons* (New York: Cambridge University Press, 1990).

17 Elinor Ostrom, "Beyond Markets and States: Polycentric Governance of Complex Economic Systems," *American Economic Review* 100, no. 3 (June 2010): 641–72; Elinor Ostrom, "Polycentric Systems for Coping with Collective Action and Global Environmental Change," *Global Environmental Change* 20, no. 4 (2010): 552.

18 "Time Line of the American Bison," US Fish and Wildlife Service, accessed September 23, 2020, https://www.fws.gov/bisonrange/timeline.htm.

19 Dean Lueck, "The Extermination and Conservation of the American Bison," *Journal of Legal Studies* 31, no. S2 (2002): S609–S652.

20 "Time Line of the American Bison," US Fish and Wildlife Service.

21 "Bison by the Numbers: Data & Statistics," National Bison Association, accessed September 23, 2020, https://bisoncentral.com/bison-by-the-numbers/.

22 Michael 't Sas-Rolfes, "Saving African Rhinos: A Market Success Story," ed. Laura Huggins (PERC Case Studies, Property and Environment Research Center, Bozeman, MT, n.d.); Anderson and Leal, *Free Market Environmentalism*.

23 Sanford Ikeda, "The Dynamics of Interventionism," *Advances in Austrian Economics* 8 (2005): 21–58.

24 Gordon Tullock, *Virginia Political Economy*, ed. Charles Kershaw Rowley (Indianapolis, IN: Liberty Fund, 2004).

25 Gary S. Becker, "A Theory of Competition among Pressure Groups for Political Influence," *Quarterly Journal of Economics* 98, no. 3 (1983): 371–400; Mancur Olson, *The Logic of Collective Action: Public Goods and the Theory of Groups* (Cambridge, MA: Harvard University Press, 1995); George J. Stigler, "The Theory of Economic Regulation," *Bell Journal of Economics and Management Science* 2, no. 1 (1971): 3–21; Sam Peltzman, "Toward a More General Theory of Regulation" (NBER Working Paper No. 133, National Bureau of Economic Research, Stanford, CA, April 1976).

26 Randall G. Holcombe, *Political Capitalism: How Economic and Political Power Is Made and Maintained* (Cambridge: Cambridge University Press, 2018).

27 Gordon Tullock, "The Welfare Costs of Tariffs, Monopolies, and Theft," *Western Economic Journal* 5, no. 3 (1967): 224–32.

28 Anderson and Leal, *Free Market Environmentalism*.

29 Stephanie Benkovic and Joseph Kruger, "U.S. Sulfur Dioxide Emissions Trading Program: Results and Further Applications," *Water, Air, and Soil Pollution* 130, no. 1–4 (August 2001): 241–46.

30 Benkovic and Kruger, "U.S. Sulfur Dioxide Emissions Trading Program."

31 "NOx Budget Trading Program," US Environmental Protection Agency, accessed September 23, 2020, https://www.epa.gov/airmarkets/nox-budget-trading-program.

32 Anderson and Leal, *Free Market Environmentalism*; Tyler Cowen and Alexander Tabarrok, *Modern Principles: Microeconomics* (New York: Worth, 2013), 191–94.

33 Marguerite Lamb, "Keeping Coal-Burning Electric Power Plants in Check," *Mother Earth News*, December 1999/January 2000.

34 Tullock, "Welfare Costs of Tariffs, Monopolies, and Theft," 224–32.

35 "Building the Reserve," American Prairie Reserve, accessed September 23, 2020, https://www.americanprairie.org/building-the-reserve; "Building the Reserve FAQs," American Prairie Reserve, accessed September 23, 2020, https://www.americanprairie.org/building-the-reserve-faqs.

36 "The Federal Land Policy and Management Act of 1976, as amended," Bureau of Land Management, September 2016, https://www.blm.gov/sites/blm.gov/files/AboutUs_LawsandRegs_FLPMA.pdf.

37 "Building the Reserve," American Prairie Reserve; "Building the Reserve FAQs," American Prairie Reserve.

38 Annys Shin, "Natural Bridge, Once Owned by Jefferson, to Become Virginia State Park," *Washington Post*, February 6, 2014.

39 "FAQ," Wild Sky Beef, accessed September 23, 2020, http://wildskybeef.org/about-beef/faq; "How Wild Sky Works," Wild Sky Beef, accessed September 23, 2020, http://wildskybeef.org/wildlife-friendly-ranching/how-wild-sky-works;

"Pocket Guide to Wildlife-Friendly Ranching," Wild Sky Beef, accessed September 23, 2020, http://wildskybeef.org/sites/default/files/rancher-pocket-guide_sm.pdf.

40 "FAQ," Wild Sky Beef; "How Wild Sky Works," Wild Sky Beef; "Pocket Guide," Wild Sky Beef.

41 "FAQ," Wild Sky Beef; "How Wild Sky Works," Wild Sky Beef.

42 "FAQ," Wild Sky Beef; "Pocket Guide," Wild Sky Beef.

43 "Fact Sheet on the BLM's Management of Livestock Grazing," Bureau of Land Management, 2016; "Federal Land Policy and Management Act of 1976 as Amended," Bureau of Land Management.

44 Traci Eatherton, "Free-Range Bison Stir Up Dispute on Grazing," *Tri-state Livestock News*, May 11, 2018; David Murray, "'Not on My Property': Central Montana Ranchers Say No to Bison," *Great Falls Tribune*, March 24, 2017; Karl Puckett, "Prairie Reserve Still Attracting Fans, Foes," *Great Falls Tribune*, June 18, 2015.

45 "Updated Bison Proposal Submitted," American Prairie Reserve, accessed September 23, 2020, https://www.americanprairie.org/news-blog/updated-bison-proposal-submitted.

46 Bureau of Land Management, "Public Input Sought on Bison Grazing Proposal," news release, March 21, 2018, https://www.blm.gov/press-release/public-input-sought-bison-grazing-proposal.

47 "American Prairie Reserve NEPA Comments Regarding APR Bison Grazing Proposal," American Prairie Reserve, accessed September 23, 2020, https://www.americanprairie.org/sites/default/files/2018-06-11%20APR%20NEPA%20Comments.pdf.

48 "Updated Bison Proposal Submitted," American Prairie Reserve.

49 Eatherton, "Free-Range Bison Stir Up Dispute on Grazing."

50 Bureau of Land Management, "BLM Releases Report with Public Comments on Bison Grazing Proposal," news release, February 8, 2019, https://www.blm.gov/press-release/blm-releases-report-public-comments-bison-grazing-proposal.

51 "Updated Bison Proposal Submitted," American Prairie Reserve.

52 "Updated Bison Proposal Submitted," American Prairie Reserve.

53 "Environmental Assessment Process: An Overview," Bureau of Land Management, April 2018, https://eplanning.blm.gov/epl-front-office/projects/nepa/103543/139891/171995/EAHandout_final.pdf.

54 Puckett, "Prairie Reserve Still Attracting Fans, Foes."

55 "Our Organization," United Property Owners of Montana, accessed September 23, 2020, http://upom.org/.

56 Kevin Mooney, "Hunters and Tourists Beware: Free-Range Bison Could Destroy This Small Town," *Washington Examiner*, June 4, 2018.

57 Daniel Dierker, "Shoot, Shovel, and Shut Up: An Analysis of Several Potential Means of Endangered Species Protection in an Agricultural Landscape" (PhD diss., University of Saskatchewan, 2002).

58 Dean Lueck and Jeffrey Michael, "Preemptive Habitat Destruction under the Endangered Species Act," *Journal of Law and Economics* 46, no. 1 (April 2003): 27–60.

59 Dean Lueck, "Property Rights and the Economic Logic of Wildlife Institutions," *Natural Resources Journal* 35, no. 3 (June 1995).

60   US Fish and Wildlife Service, "Safe Harbor Agreements for Private Landowners," October 2017, https://www.fws.gov/endangered/esa-library/pdf/harborqa.pdf.

61   Michael J. Bean, "Overcoming Unintended Consequences of Endangered Species Regulation," *Idaho Law Review* 38, no. 2 (2002): 409–20.

62   Farm Service Agency, "Conservation Reserve Program," US Department of Agriculture, accessed September 23, 2020, https://www.fsa.usda.gov/programs-and-services/conservation-programs/conservation-reserve-program/.

63   D. L. Karlen et al., "Conservation Reserve Program Effects on Soil Quality Indicators," *Journal of Soil and Water Conservation* 54, no. 1 (1999): 439–44.

64   Susanne Szentandrasi et al., "Conserving Biological Diversity and the Conservation Reserve Program," *Growth and Change* 26, no. 3 (July 1995): 383–404.

65   Megan Stubbs, "Conservation Reserve Program (CRP): Status and Issues" (CRS Report No. R42783, Congressional Research Service, Washington, DC, 2014), 14.

66   JunJie Wu, "Slippage Effects of the Conservation Reserve Program," *American Journal of Agricultural Economics* 82, no. 4 (November 2000): 979–92.

67   Endangered and Threatened Wildlife and Plants; 12-Month Findings for Petitions to List the Greater Sage-Grouse (*Centrocercus urophasianus*) as Threatened or Endangered, 75 Fed. Reg. 13909–4014 (March 23, 2010).

68   US Fish and Wildlife Service Ecological Services Program, "Candidate Species: Section 4 of the Endangered Species Act," October 2017, https://www.fws.gov/endangered/esa-library/pdf/candidate_species.pdf.

69   National Sage-Grouse Habitat Conservation Strategy, US Department of the Interior, Bureau of Land Management, Oregon/Washington State Office, "Oregon Greater Sage-Grouse Approved Resource Management Plan Amendment," September 2015, https://www.blm.gov/sites/blm.gov/files/greater_sage-grouse_rmp_amendment.pdf; Bureau of Land Management, "Sage-Grouse Conservation Plan Amendments Supported by Affected States' Governors," press release, March 15, 2019, https://www.blm.gov/press-release/sage-grouse-conservation-plan-amendments-supported-affected-states-governors.

70   US Forest Service, "Fact Sheet: BLM, USFS Greater Sage-Grouse Conservation Effort," US Department of Agriculture, September 22, 2015, https://www.fs.usda.gov/sites/default/files/fact-sheet-greater-sage-grouse.pdf.

71   Devin Henry, "Feds Release Sage Grouse Conservation Plan," *The Hill*, May 28, 2015.

72   "Proactive Conservation," Sage Grouse Initiative, National Resources Conservation Service, accessed September 23, 2020, https://www.sagegrouseinitiative.com/our-work/proactive-conservation/; "Partner List," Sage Grouse Initiative, National Resources Conservation Service, accessed September 23, 2020, https://www.sagegrouseinitiative.com/about/partners/.

73   Terry A. Messmer et al., "Utah's Adaptive Resources Management Greater Sage-Grouse Local Working Groups 2018 Annual Report" (Utah Community-Based Conservation Program, Jack H. Berryman Institute, Department of Wildland Resources, and Utah State University Extension, Logan, UT, 2018).

74   "Working with Sage-Grouse Local Working Groups: A Practical Guide for NRCS Staff," US Department of Agriculture, Natural Resources Conservation Service, Agricultural Wildlife Conservation Center, Utah State University, April 2009, http://digitalcommons.usu.edu/cgi/viewcontent.cgi?article=1092&context=extension_curall; Lorien R. Belton, S. Nicole Frey, and David K. Dahlgren, "Partici-

patory Research in Sage-Grouse Local Working Groups: Case Studies from Utah," *Human–Wildlife Interactions* 11, no. 3 (January 2017): 287–301.

CHAPTER 13: RETAIL ELECTRIC COMPETITION AND NATURAL MONOPOLY: THE SHOCKING TRUTH

1   Acknowledgments: The author would like to thank Mark Febrizio, two anonymous referees, and the editors of this volume for helpful comments on an earlier draft of this chapter.

2   For a sample of the relevant literature, see Robert W. Crandall, *After the Breakup: U.S. Telecommunications in a More Competitive Era* (Washington, DC: Brookings Institution, 1991); Robert W. Crandall and Jerry Hausman, "Competition in U.S. Telecommunications Services: Effects of the 1996 Legislation," in *Deregulation of Network Industries: What's Next?*, ed. Sam Peltzman and Clifford Winston (Washington, DC: AEI-Brookings Joint Center for Regulatory Studies, 1991); Robert W. Crandall and Jerry Ellig, *Economic Deregulation and Customer Choice: Lessons for the Electric Industry* (Fairfax, VA: Center for Market Processes, 1997); Thomas W. Hazlett, "Cable Television," in *Handbook of Telecommunications Economics: Technology Evolution and the Internet*, ed. Sumit Majumdar et al. (Amsterdam: Elsevier Science, 2006); Thomas W. Hazlett, *The Political Spectrum* (New Haven, CT: Yale University Press, 2017).

3   Philip R. O'Connor, "Restructuring Recharged: The Superior Performance of Competitive Electricity Markets 2008–2016" (white paper, Retail Energy Supply Association, Hummelstown, PA, April 2017), 12.

4   Severin Borenstein and James Bushnell, "The U.S. Electric Industry after 20 Years of Restructuring" (NBER Working Paper No. 21113, National Bureau of Economic Research, Cambridge, MA, April 2015).

5   Regarding fracking, see Catherine Hausman and Ryan Kellogg, "Welfare and Distributional Implications of Shale Gas," *Brookings Papers on Economic Activity*, March 2015, 71–125. Regarding renewable energy, see Michael Giberson and L. Lynne Kiesling, "Governance for Networks: Regulation by Networks in Electric Power Markets in Texas," chapter 14 in this volume.

6   Kelsey Misbrener, "Energy Choice Coalition Supports New Virginia Energy Reform Act," *Solar Power World*, January 9, 2020; "Nevada Question 3, Changes to Energy Market and Prohibit State-Sanctioned Electric-Generation Monopolies Amendment (2018)," *Ballotpedia*, accessed May 12, 2020, https://ballotpedia.org/Nevada_Question_3,_Changes_to_Energy_Market_and_Prohibit_State-Sanctioned_Electric-Generation_Monopolies_Amendment_(2018); Oran P. Smith and Michael T. Maloney, "Energizing Enterprise: How Energy Market Reforms in the Wake of the V.C. Summer Debacle Can Transform South Carolina's Economy" (Report, Palmetto Promise Institute, November 2018); Jerry Ellig, "Selling Santee Cooper: Competition Should Be Part of the Plan," *Post and Courier* (Charleston, SC), April 14, 2019.

7   The first two paragraphs in this section are based largely on Giberson and Kiesling, "Markets as Network Governance." Readers are referred to that chapter for a more extensive discussion.

8   William J. Baumol, John C. Panzar, and Robert D. Willig, *Contestable Markets and the Theory of Industry Structure* (New York: Harcourt Brace Jovanovich, 1982), 192–208.

9   F. A. Hayek, *New Studies in Philosophy, Politics, Economics, and the History of Ideas* (London: Routledge & Kegan Paul, 1978), chapter 12, "Competition as a Discovery Procedure." On the distinction between allocative and productive efficiency, see

518

W. Kip Viscusi, Joseph E. Harrington Jr., and John M. Vernon, *Economics of Regulation and Antitrust*, 4th ed. (Cambridge, MA: MIT Press, 2005), 79–95.

10 Borenstein and Bushnell, "U.S. Electric Industry," 10.

11 Jay Zarnikau and Doug Whitworth, "Has Electricity Utility Restructuring Led to Lower Electricity Prices for Residential Consumers in Texas?," *Energy Policy* 34, no. 15 (2006): 2199–200.

12 L. Lynne Kiesling, "Incumbent Vertical Market Power, Experimentation, and Institutional Design in the Deregulating Electricity Industry," *Independent Review* 19, no. 2 (Fall 2014): 239–64. Kiesling describes experimental programs that show that consumers value and respond to real-time price signals when they have access to technology (smart meters) that enables them to preprogram their responses.

13 Harvey Averch and Leland L. Johnson, "Behavior of the Firm under Regulatory Constraint," *American Economic Review* 52 (December 1962): 1052–69.

14 Graeme Guthrie, "Regulating Infrastructure: The Impact on Risk and Investment," *Journal of Economic Literature* 44, no. 4 (December 2006): 925–72.

15 M. E. Beesley and Stephen C. Littlechild, "The Regulation of Privatized Monopolies in the United Kingdom," *Rand Journal of Economics* 20, no. 3 (1989): 454–72; Mark W. Frank, "An Empirical Analysis of Electricity Regulation on Technical Change in Texas," *Review of Industrial Organization* 22 (2003): 313–31; Israel Kirzner, *Discovery and the Capitalist Process* (Chicago: University of Chicago Press, 1985), chapter 6: "The Perils of Regulation: A Market Process Approach."

16 Harvey Leibenstein, "Allocative Efficiency versus 'X-efficiency,'" *American Economic Review* 56 (1966): 392–413; Rodney Stevenson, "X-inefficiency and Interfirm Rivalry: Evidence from the Electric Utility Industry," *Land Economics* 58, no. 1 (1982): 52–66.

17 Paul L. Joskow, "Why Do We Need Electricity Retailers? Or Can You Get It Cheaper Wholesale?" (working paper, Harvard Electricity Policy Group, 2000).

18 Stephen C. Littlechild, "Wholesale Spot Price Pass-Through," *Journal of Regulatory Economics* 23, no. 1 (2003): 71.

19 Andrew A. Goett, Kathleen Hudson, and Kenneth E. Train, "Customers' Choice among Retail Energy Suppliers: The Willingness-to-Pay for Service Attributes," *Energy Journal* 21, no. 4 (2000): 1–28.

20 Crandall, *After the Breakup*; Crandall and Ellig, *Economic Deregulation*; Crandall and Hausman, "Competition in U.S. Telecommunications"; Hazlett, *Political Spectrum*; Jerry Ellig, "Railroad Deregulation and Consumer Welfare," *Journal of Regulatory Economics* 21, no. 2 (2002): 143–67; Clifford Winston, "U.S. Industry Adjustment to Economic Deregulation," *Journal of Economic Perspectives* 12 (1998): 89–110; Clifford Winston, "Economic Deregulation: Days of Reckoning for Microeconomists," *Journal of Economic Literature* 31 (1993): 1263–89.

21 Michael Giberson and Arthur R. Wardle, "The Consequences of Retail Electric Choice in the United States: An Assessment of Empirical Studies" (working paper, Center for Growth and Opportunity, September 2019 draft), 6.

22 Kiesling, "Incumbent Vertical Market Power."

23 O'Connor, "Restructuring Recharged," 13.

24 O'Connor, "Restructuring Recharged," 12.

25 Giberson and Wardle, "Consequences of Retail Electric Choice," 12.

26 Giberson and Wardle, 20–21.

27 *2018 State of the Market Report for the ERCOT Electricity Markets* (Fairfax, VA: Potomac Economics, June 2019), 5.

28 John Kwoka, "Restructuring the US Electric Power Sector: A Review of Recent Studies," *Review of Industrial Organization* 32, no. 3–4 (2008): 165–96.

29 Giberson and Wardle, "Consequences of Retail Electric Choice," 13–14.

30 O'Connor, "Restructuring Recharged," 13–16.

31 L. Lynne Kiesling, "Retail Restructuring and Market Design in Texas," in *Electricity Restructuring: The Texas Story*, ed. L. Lynne Kiesling and Andrew N. Kleit (Washington, DC: AEI Press, 2009), 171–72.

32 Giberson and Wardle, "Consequences of Retail Electric Choice," 15–17.

33 Giberson and Wardle, "Consequences of Retail Electric Choice," 14–19.

34 Mathew J. Morey and Laurence D. Kirsch, "Retail Choice in Electricity: What Have We Learned in 20 Years?" (report, Christensen Associates Energy Consulting LLC for Electric Markets Research Foundation, February 11, 2016).

35 "About ERCOT," Electric Reliability Council of Texas website, accessed May 12, 2020, http://www.ercot.com/about.

36 Borenstein and Bushnell, "U.S. Electric Industry," 9.

37 For more detailed descriptions of ERCOT, see Giberson and Kiesling, "Markets as Network Governance"; David Spence and Darren Bush, "Why Does ERCOT Have Only One Regulator?," in *Electricity Restructuring: The Texas Story*, ed. L. Lynne Kiesling and Andrew N. Kleit (Washington, DC: AEI Press, 2009).

38 Jay Zarnikau, "A Review of Efforts to Restructure Texas' Electricity Market," *Energy Policy* 33 (2005): 15.

39 "The ERCOT Solution," Lubbock Power & Light, accessed May 12, 2020, http://lpandl.com/ercot/.

40 Kiesling, "Incumbent Vertical Market Power," 156–57.

41 Pat Wood III and Gürcan Gülen, "Laying the Groundwork for Power Competition in Texas," in *Electricity Restructuring: The Texas Story*, ed. L. Lynne Kiesling and Andrew N. Kleit (Washington, DC: AEI Press, 2009), 30.

42 Kiesling, "Retail Restructuring," 166.

43 Public Utility Commission of Texas, "Scope of Competition in Electric Markets in Texas" (Report to the 85th Legislature, Austin, TX, January 2017), 15.

44 Zarnikau and Whitworth, "Has Electric Utility Restructuring Led to Lower Electricity Prices?," 2193.

45 Wood and Gülen, "Laying the Groundwork," 30; Zarnikau, "Review of Efforts," 20.

46 Zarnikau, "Review of Efforts," 30.

47 Hausman and Kellogg, "Welfare and Distributional Implications."

48 Figure 4 in Giberson and Kiesling, "Markets as Network Governance."

49 Linhong Kang and Jay Zarnikau, "Did the Expiration of Retail Price Caps Affect Prices in the Restructured Texas Electricity Market?," *Energy Policy* 37, no. 5 (2009): 1713–14.

50 Zarnikau and Whitworth, "Has Electric Utility Restructuring Led to Lower Electricity Prices?," 2200.

51 Public Utility Commission of Texas, "Scope of Competition in Electric Markets in Texas" (Report to the 79th Legislature, Austin, TX, January 2005), 60.

52 Robert W. Michaels, "Competition in Texas Electric Markets: What Texas Did Right & What's Left to Do" (report, Texas Public Policy Foundation, Austin, TX, March 2007), 9.

53 Kiesling, "Retail Restructuring," 158–59.

54 Peter R. Hartley, Kenneth B. Medlock III, and Olivera Jankovska, "Electricity Reform and Retail Pricing in Texas," *Energy Economics* 80 (2019): 1–11.

55 Hartley, Medlock, and Jankovska, "Electricity Reform," 10.

56 Zarnikau and Whitworth, "Has Electric Utility Restructuring Led to Lower Electricity Prices?"

57 Kang and Zarnikau, "Did the Expiration Affect Prices?"

58 Hartley, Medlock, and Jankovska, "Electricity Reform," 9.

59 Kiesling, "Retail Restructuring," 163; Zarnikau, "Review of Efforts," 24.

60 Public Utility Commission of Texas, "Scope of Competition in Electric Markets in Texas" (Report to the 86th Legislature, Austin, TX, January 2019), 3.

61 Electric Reliability Council of Texas, "Supplemental Information: Retail Electric Market, September 2017–September 2018," PowerPoint file, accessed May 12, 2020, http://ercot.com/content/wcm/key_documents_lists/89277/Observed_Selection_of_Electric_Providers_September_2018.ppt.pptx.

62 Frank A. Wolak, "Diagnosing the California Electricity Crisis," *Electricity Journal* 16, no. 7 (2003): 16.

63 Severin Borenstein, "The Trouble with Electricity Markets: Understanding California's Restructuring Disaster," *Journal of Economic Perspectives* 16, no. 1 (2002): 193.

64 Wolak, "Diagnosing the California Electricity Crisis," 17–18.

65 Borenstein, "Trouble with Electricity Markets," 195.

66 Wolak, "Diagnosing the California Electricity Crisis," 20–21.

67 Wolak, 29.

68 Wolak, 30.

69 Borenstein, "Trouble with Electricity Markets," 209.

70 Crandall and Ellig, *Economic Deregulation*; Hazlett, *Political Spectrum*; Ellig, "Railroad Deregulation."

71 Walter J. Primeaux Jr., *Direct Electric Utility Competition* (New York: Praeger, 1986), 19, 188.

72 Walter J. Primeaux Jr., "Estimate of the Price Effect of Competition: The Case of Electricity," *Resources and Energy* 7 (1985): 327–30.

73 Primeaux, "Estimate of the Price Effect of Competition," 336-37. The marginal price result is statistically significant at the 5 percent level, and the average revenue result is significant at the 10 percent level.

74 Walter J. Primeaux Jr., "An Assessment of X-efficiency Gained through Competition," *Review of Economics and Statistics* 59, no. 1 (1977): 105–8; Walter J. Primeaux Jr., "A Re-examination of the Monopoly Market Structure for Electric Utilities," in *Promoting Competition in Regulated Markets*, ed. Almarin Phillips (Washington, DC: Brookings Institution, 1974), 175–200.

75 Primeaux, "Re-examination of the Monopoly Market Structure," 195–96.

76 Primeaux, *Direct Electric Utility Competition*, 66–68.

77 Walter J. Primeaux Jr. and Mark Bomball, "A Re-examination of the Kinky Oligopoly Demand Curve," *Journal of Political Economy* 82 (1974): 851–62.

78 Kiesling, "Incumbent Vertical Market Power."

79 Randy A. Nelson and Walter J. Primeaux Jr., "The Effects of Competition on Transmission and Distribution Costs in the Municipal Electric Industry," *Land Economics* 64, no. 4 (1988): 338–46.

80 Primeaux, *Direct Electric Utility Competition*, 123, 134–39.

81 Primeaux, *Direct Electric Utility Competition*, 208.

82 Nelson and Primeaux, "Effects of Competition on Transmission and Distribution Costs," 304.

83 John Kwoka, *Power Structure: Ownership, Integration, and Competition in the U.S. Electric Industry* (Boston: Kluwer Academic, 1996), 62–65.

84 Kwoka, *Power Structure*, 91–92.

85 Kang and Zarnikau, "Did the Expiration Affect Prices?"

86 Public Utility Commission of Texas, "Scope of Competition" (2019), 3.

87 Kiesling, "Incumbent Vertical Market Power."

CHAPTER 14: GOVERNANCE FOR NETWORKS: REGULATION BY NETWORKS IN ELECTRIC POWER MARKETS IN TEXAS

1 Mark Bevir, "Governance," in *Encyclopedia of Governance*, ed. Mark Bevir (Thousand Oaks, CA: Sage, 2007).

2 While not focused on governance issues per se, LSE Fellow and author Richard Davies's recent book suggests a similar perspective—that our understanding of the everyday present can be deepened by examining extreme cases. Richard Davies, *Extreme Economies: What Life at the World's Margins Can Teach Us about Our Own Future* (New York: Farrar, Straus, and Giroux, 2019).

3 Avner Greif, "Reputation and Coalitions in Medieval Trade: Evidence on the Maghribi Traders," *Journal of Economic History* 49, no. 4 (1989): 857–82.

4 Peter T. Leeson, "An-arrgh-chy: The Law and Economics of Pirate Organization," *Journal of Political Economy* 115, no. 6 (2007): 1049–94; Peter T. Leeson, *The Invisible Hook: The Hidden Economics of Pirates* (Princeton, NJ: Princeton University Press, 2009).

5 David Skarbek, "Governance and Prison Gangs," *American Political Science Review* 105, no. 4 (2011): 702–16; David Skarbek, *The Social Order of the Underworld: How Prison Gangs Govern the American Penal System* (Oxford: Oxford University Press, 2014).

6 Elinor Ostrom, *Governing the Commons: The Evolution of Institutions for Collective Action* (Cambridge: Cambridge University Press, 1990).

7 Amitai Aviram, "Regulation by Networks," *BYU Law Review*, 2003, 1179-1238.

8 Federal Energy Regulatory Commission, *Payment for Reactive Power*, Commission Staff Report AD14-7, April 22, 2014.

9 As an implication of these claims, we would predict that a rise of decentralized, relatively inexpensive battery storage capability would precipitate dramatic changes to governance systems surrounding electric power.

10 For background on the electric industry in Texas and its regulatory reforms over the past two decades, see L. Lynne Kiesling and Andrew N. Kleit, eds., *Electricity Restructuring: The Texas Story* (Washington, DC: AEI Press, 2009).

11 While several other states participate in ISO-style wholesale markets integrated with transmission-grid operations and some of these states also allow some de-

gree of retail electric competition, the Texas approach is frequently regarded as the most complete integration of competition in wholesale and retail markets.

12 Following Aviram, we rely on the definition of opportunism provided by Robert Cooter: "an act in which someone destroys part of the cooperative surplus to secure a larger share of it." Robert D. Cooter, "The Theory of Market Modernization of Law," *International Review of Law and Economics* 16, no. 2 (1996): 150; cited in Aviram, "Regulation by Networks," 1184.

13 Ostrom, *Governing the Commons*.

14 More sophisticated analysis employs the term *restructuring* instead, in part simply because government regulation is not removed—the number of regulations may actually increase—while responsibility for certain transactions is shifted away from government regulators and to agents in the market.

15 Robert C. Ellickson, *Order without Law: How Neighbors Settle Disputes* (Cambridge, MA: Harvard University Press, 1991), 126–32, 241–46; cited in Aviram, "Regulation by Networks," 1186.

16 Aviram, "Regulation by Networks."

17 The version of Ostrom's principles quoted here is from David Sloan Wilson, Elinor Ostrom, and Michael E. Cox, "Generalizing the Core Design Principles for the Efficacy of Groups," *Journal of Economic Behavior and Organization* 90 (2013): S21–S32. The eight design principles were originally set out in Ostrom, *Governing the Commons*.

18 Michael Cox, Gwen Arnold, and Sergio Villamayor-Tomás, "A Review of Design Principles for Community-Based Natural Resource Management," *Ecology and Society* 15, no. 4 (2010): 38.

19 Aviram, "Regulation by Networks," 1210.

20 For a seminal work on multisided platform economics, see Jean-Charles Rochet and Jean Tirole, "Platform Competition in Two-Sided Markets," *Journal of the European Economic Association* 1, no. 4 (2003): 990–1029. For a transaction cost economics analysis of digital platforms, see L. Lynne Kiesling, Michael C. Munger, and Alexander Theisen, "From Airbnb to Solar: Toward a Transaction Cost Model of a Retail Electricity Distribution Platform" (working paper, 2019), https://papers.ssrn.com/sol3/papers.cfm?abstract_id=3229960.

21 For an overview see Rishi Garg, *Electric Transmission Seams: A Primer*. National Regulatory Research Institute, NBRRI Report No. 15-03 (February 2015). Garg notes the potential for inefficient coordination between ISOs was raised as early as 2000 as the Federal Energy Regulatory Commission was developing rules to govern Regional Transmission Owners. The 2015 report assesses both progress made and continuing challenges in obtaining efficient coordination among neighboring. See also Michael A. Giberson, *Improving coordination between regional power markets*. Doctoral dissertation, George Mason University (2004).

22 Here are a few expert observations: "The ERCOT market is generally considered to be the most successful of the restructured electricity markets in North America." Jay Zarnikau, "The Evolution of a Competitive Electricity Market in Texas," paper presented at 28th USAEE/IAEE North American Conference, New Orleans, LA (December 2008). The ERCOT market is "the most robust restructured retail market in North America and one of the top three in the world." Young Kim, "Unfinished business: The evolution of US competitive retail electricity markets", Ch 12 (pp 331-361) in Fereidoon P Sioshansi, *Evolution of Global Electricity Markets*, Elsevier: Academic Press, 2013. "Texas is the competitive residential electricity market leader for the eighth consecutive year." Treadway, Nat. "Annual Baseline

Assessment of Choice in Canada and the United States (ABACCUS)." Distributed Energy Financial Group LLC (2015). "Texas is widely regarded as the most successful retail electricity market in the US." Stephen Littlechild, *The regulation of retail competition in US residential electricity markets*. Technical Report. University of Cambridge, 2018.

23 Walter J. Primeaux, *Direct electric utility competition: The natural monopoly myth.* (New York: Praeger Scientific, 1985).

24 Thomas R. Casten. *Turning off the Heat: Why America must double energy efficiency to save money and reduce global warming.* (New York: Prometheus Books, 1998).

25 William J. Hausman and John L. Neufeld, "How Politics, Economics, and Institutions Shaped Electric Utility Regulation in the United States: 1879–2009," *Business History* 53, no. 5 (2011): 723–46; Robert A. Webb, "The 1975 Texas Public Utility Regulatory Act: Revolution or Reaffirmation," *Houston Law Review* 13 (1975): 1.

26 Aviram, "Regulation by Networks."

27 "About ERCOT," Electric Reliability Council of Texas website, accessed October 7, 2020, http://www.ercot.com/about. See also David Spence and Darren Bush, "Why Does ERCOT have Only One Regulator?" in Kiesling and Kleit, *Electricity Restructuring*.

28 "About ERCOT," Electric Reliability Council of Texas website, accessed October 7, 2020, http://www.ercot.com/about.

29 *Amended and Restated Bylaws of Electric Reliability Council of Texas, Inc.*, July 31, 2020 See "Governance," Electric Reliability Council of Texas website, ,October 30, 2020 http://www.ercot.com/about/governance.

30 An example of the rule change process was the decision to change the price formation rules from a zonal design (with the ERCOT territory divided into zones and a single price representing the whole zone) to a nodal design (with a price reflecting congestion costs at each node in the network in the territory). For a thorough discussion of this process, see Eric S. Schubert and Parviz Adib, "Evolution of Wholesale Market Design in ERCOT," in Kiesling and Kleit, *Electricity Restructuring*.

31 "Market Rules," Electric Reliability Council of Texas website, accessed October 7, 2020, http://www.ercot.com/mktrules.

32 Aviram, "Regulation by Networks," 1189.

33 For an earlier evaluation of the competitive performance of ERCOT's markets, see Steven L. Puller, "Competitive Performance of the ERCOT Wholesale Market," in Kiesling and Kleit, *Electricity Restructuring*.

34 These price trends also reflect the high share of natural gas generation in Texas, as well as the growth in the natural gas supply after 2008 from fracking, which reduced prices in both wholesale and retail markets. For an outstanding analysis of the effects of fracking in the natural gas industry, see Catherine Hausman and Ryan Kellogg, "Welfare and Distributional Implications of Shale Gas," *Brookings Papers on Economic Activity*, 2015, 71–125.

35 Peter Hartley, Kenneth B. Medlock III, and Olivera Jankovska, "Electricity Reform and Retail Pricing in Texas," *Energy Economics* 80 (2019): 1–11.

36 Data are available from the Baker Institute for Public Policy's web page for Hartley, Medlock, and Jankovska, "Electricity Reform and Retail Pricing in Texas," June 7, 2017, https://www.bakerinstitute.org/research/electricity-reform-and-retail-pricing-texas/.

37 Nat Treadway, "Distributed Generation Drives Competitive Energy Services in Texas," in Kiesling and Kleit, *Electricity Restructuring*.

38 Dennis Elliott et al., "New Wind Energy Resource Potential Estimates for the United States," National Renewable Energy Laboratory and AWS Truepower, January 27, 2011, https://www.nrel.gov/docs/fy11osti/50439.pdf. Additionally, maps of potential wind capacity and generation are available at "U.S. Installed and Potential Wind Power Capacity and Generation," WINDExchange (US Department of Energy), accessed October 7, 2020, https://windexchange.energy.gov/maps-data/321.

39 S.B. 7, 76th Leg., Reg. Sess. (Texas 1999).

40 S.B. 20, 79th Leg., Reg. Sess. (Texas 2005).

41 Jay Zarnikau, "Successful Renewable Energy Development in a Competitive Electricity Market: A Texas Case Study," *Energy Policy* 39 (2011): 3909.

42 ERCOT's description of the renewable energy credit program is available at "Renewable Energy Credit Program," Electric Reliability Council of Texas website, accessed October 7, 2020, https://www.texasrenewables.com/recprogram.asp.

43 Xiaodong Du and Ofir Rubin, "Transition and Integration of the ERCOT Market with the Competitive Renewable Energy Zones Project," *Energy Journal* 39, no. 4 (October 2018): 235–59.

44 Zarnikau, "Successful Renewable Energy Development," 3910, citing Will Ferguson, "Texas Wind

Industry's Rapid Growth Creates New Challenges," *Texas Business Review* (February 2010): 1-5.

45 Adelina Jashari, Jana Lippelt, and Marie-Theres von Schickfus, "Unexpected Rapid Fall of Wind and Solar Energy Prices: Backgrounds, Effects and Perspectives," *CESifo Forum* 19, no. 2 (2018): 65–69. For an analysis of wind turbine cost reductions, see US Department of Energy, *2018 Wind Technologies Market Report*, August 2019, available at https://www.osti.gov/servlets/purl/1559881.

46 Congressional Research Service, *The Renewable Electricity Production Tax Credit: In Brief*, CRS Report R43453, November 27, 2018. Closed-loop biomass projects and geothermal projects are also eligible for the PTC. Other renewable technologies were also eligible for the PTC, but have been reduced to half credit. See table 1 in Congressional Research Service, *Renewable Electricity Production Tax Credit*, 2.

47 Jess Totten, "Texas Transmission Policy," in Kiesling and Kleit, *Electricity Restructuring*, 103.

48 Schubert and Adib, "Evolution of Wholesale Market Design in ERCOT."

49 Michael Giberson and Lynne Kiesling, "The Need for Electricity Retail Market Reforms," *Regulation*, Fall 2017.

50 Lynne Kiesling and Michael Giberson, *Electric Competition in Texas: A Successful Model to Guide the Future*, Conservative Texans for Energy Innovation, July 2020, https://www.conservativetexansforenergyinnovation.org/research--/.

51 Erik Desrosiers, "Competitive Electricity Retailing: Why Restructuring Must Go On," *Utility Dive*, July 11, 2017.

52 "Power to Choose" website, Public Utility Commission of Texas, accessed October 7, 2020, http://powertochoose.org.

CHAPTER 15: NET NEUTRALITY: INTERNET REGULATION AND THE PLANS TO BRING IT BACK

1   Protecting and Promoting the Open Internet, 80 Fed. Reg. 19737 (April 13, 2015).

2   Preserving the Open Internet, 76 Fed. Reg. 59192 (September 23, 2011).

3   Verizon v. Federal Communications Commission, 740 F.3d 623 (D.C. Cir. 2014).

4   For a brief history of internet regulation and the net neutrality debate, see the introduction in Randolph J. May and Seth L. Cooper, *A Reader on Net Neutrality and Restoring Internet Freedom* (Potomac, MD: Free State Foundation, 2018).

5   Restoring Internet Freedom, 83 Fed. Reg. 21927 (May 11, 2018).

6   These categorizations are somewhat inconsistently applied. For example, Google operates its own infrastructure that is not considered an "ISP" network. Tom Foremski, "Google Is Building a Private Internet That's Far Better, and Greener, than the Internet," *ZDNet*, March 18, 2010, Tom Evslin, "Internet Fast Lanes: You May Be Surprised by Who Actually Has Them," *Morning Consult*, August 4, 2017.

7   Protecting and Promoting the Open Internet, 80 Fed. Reg. 19737, 19740 (April 13, 2015), citing Preserving the Open Internet, 76 Fed. Reg. 59191, 59194 (September 23, 2011).

8   Protecting and Promoting the Open Internet, 80 Fed. Reg. at 19752.

9   Protecting and Promoting the Open Internet, 80 Fed. Reg. at 19740.

10 Theodore R. Bolema, "The FTC Has the Authority, Expertise, and Capability to Protect Broadband Consumers," *Perspectives from FSF Scholars* (Free State Foundation) 12, no. 35 (October 19, 2017).

11 Evslin, "Internet Fast Lanes."

12 Introduction in May and Cooper, *Reader on Net Neutrality*.

13 Protecting and Promoting the Open Internet, GN Docket N0. 14-28(dissenting statement of Ajit Pai, Commissioner, FCC) at 14.

14 Protecting and Promoting the Open Internet, 80 Fed. Reg. at 19739.

15 At the time of the 2015 Open Internet order, the ISP market was more competitive and dynamic than monopolistic: 99 percent of US consumers had a choice of providers. Chart III.A.2 in Federal Communications Commission, "Annual Report and Analysis of Competitive Market Conditions with Respect to Mobile Wireless, Including Commercial Mobile Services" (WT Docket No. 16-137, September 23, 2016), 31.

16 Introduction in May and Cooper, *Reader on Net Neutrality*.

17 Protecting and Promoting the Open Internet, GN Docket N0. 14-28(dissenting statement of Ajit Pai, Commissioner, FCC) at 10.

18 Kenneth Button and David Christiansen, "Unleashing Innovation: The Deregulation of Air Cargo Transportation" (Mercatus on Policy, Mercatus Center at George Mason University, Arlington, VA, November 2014).

19 Terry McAuliffe, "Governor McAuliffe Announces Acceptance of Private Sector Proposal to Deliver I-395 Express Lanes Extension," news release, February 25, 2017, http://www.vdot.virginia.gov/newsroom/statewide/2017/governor_mcauliffe_announces_acceptance111748.asp.

20 Robert Krol, "Tolling the Freeway: Congestion Pricing and the Economics of Managing Traffic" (Mercatus Working Paper, Mercatus Center at George Mason University, Arlington, VA, May 2016).

21 Federal Trade Commission, "Slotting Allowances in the Retail Grocery Industry, Selected Case Studies in Five Product Categories" (Federal Trade Commission Staff Study, November 2003).

22 Joshua D. Wright, "Slotting Contracts and Consumers Welfare," *Antitrust Law Journal* 74, no. 2 (2007): 440.

23 Roslyn Layton, "Prioritization: Moving Past Prejudice to Make Internet Policy Based on Fact," *AEIdeas*, April 17, 2018.

24 Eric J. Hanly and Timothy J. Broderick, "Telerobotic Surgery," *Operative Techniques in General Surgery* 11, no. 2 (2005): 173, citations omitted.

25 Bureau of Economic Analysis, US Department of Commerce, "Industry Economic Accounts Underlying Detail," news release, October 29, 2019.

26 Ajit Pai, "Infrastructure Month at the FCC," news release, Federal Communications Commission, March 30, 2017, https://www.fcc.gov/news-events/blog/2017/03/30/infrastructure-month-fcc.

27 RegData measures regulatory restrictions at the industry level according to the two-, three-, and four-digit levels of the NAICS. It is particularly useful because it is an industry-specific quantification of federal regulation that counts the number of actual regulatory restrictions using text analysis of the *Code of Federal Regulations* rather than relying on proxies such as the number of pages in the *Code of Federal Regulations* or in the *Federal Register*. Patrick A. McLaughlin and Oliver Sherouse, RegData US 3.2 Annual (data set), QuantGov, Mercatus Center at George Mason University, 2020; Omar Al-Ubaydli and Patrick A. McLaughlin, "RegData: A Numerical Database on Industry-Specific Regulations for all United States Industries and Federal Regulations, 1997–2012," *Regulation & Governance* 11 (2015): 109–23.

28 Michael Mandel and Diana G. Carew, "Regulatory Improvement Commission: A Politically-Viable Approach to U.S. Regulatory Reform" (Policy Memo, Progressive Policy Institute, Washington, DC, May 2013).

29 Michał Grajek and Lars-Hendrik Röller, "Regulation and Investment in Network Industries: Evidence from European Telecoms," *Journal of Law and Economics* 55, no. 1 (2012): 211.

30 Ajit Pai, "Remarks of the Federal Communications Commission Chairman Ajit Pai at the Mobile World Congress," Barcelona, Spain, February 28, 2017, speech.

31 Ajit Pai, "Remarks of the Federal Communications Commission Chairman Ajit Pai at the Mobile World Congress" (speech at the Mobile World Congress, Barcelona, Spain, February 28, 2017).

32 Hal Singer, "2016 Broadband Capex Survey: Tracking Investment in the Title II Era," *Hal Singer* (blog), March 1, 2017.

33 Hal Singer, "Three Ways the FCC's Open Internet Order Will Harm Innovation" (Policy Memo, Progressive Policy Institute, Washington, DC, May 2015).

34 Richard Williams, "The Impact of Regulation on Investment and the US. Economy" (Mercatus Research, Mercatus Center at George Mason University, Arlington, VA, January 2011).

35 John W. Mayo, "Regulation and Investment: Sk(r)ewing the Future for 21st Century Telecommunications?" (Economic Policy Vignette, Georgetown Center for Business and Public Policy, June 2016).

36 Richard A. Epstein, "Can Technological Innovation Survive Government Regulation?," *Harvard Journal of Law and Public Policy* 36 (2013): 97.

37 Restoring Internet Freedom, 83 Fed. Reg. 21927 (May 11, 2018).

38 Mozilla v. Federal Communications Commission, 940 F.3d 1 (D.C. Cir. 2019).

39 Professor Daniel Lyons of Boston College Law School provides an excellent analysis of the implications of the *Mozilla* decision striking down the provision in the Restoring Internet Freedom order that would have preempted states from passing their own net neutrality laws. Daniel A. Lyons, "Conflict Preemption of State Net Neutrality Efforts after Mozilla," *Perspectives from FSF Scholars* (Free State Foundation) 14, no. 29 (October 14, 2019).

40 Mark Howell, "Saving Net Neutrality, One House at a Time," *Washington Post*, April 22, 2018.

41 American Civil Liberties Union, *The Public Internet Option: How Local Governments Can Provide Network Neutrality, Privacy, and Access for All*, March 2018, 5.

42 American Civil Liberties Union, *Public Internet Option*, 12.

43 Enrique Armijo, "Municipal Broadband Networks Present Serious First Amendment Problems," *Perspectives from FSF Scholars* (Free State Foundation) 10, no. 11 (February 23, 2015); Enrique Armijo, "A Case of Hypocrisy: Government Network Censors Support Net Neutrality for Private ISPs," *Perspectives from FSF Scholars* (Free State Foundation) 13, no. 1 (January 3, 2018).

44 Lyons, "Conflict Preemption."

CHAPTER 16: UNINTENDED CONSEQUENCES OF REGULATING PRIVATE SCHOOL CHOICE PROGRAMS: A REVIEW OF THE EVIDENCE

1 The content of this chapter is solely the responsibility of the authors and does not necessarily represent the views of Reason Foundation, the Cato Institute, or the Heritage Foundation.

2 EdChoice, *The ABCs of School Choice: The Comprehensive Guide to Every Private School Choice Program in America*, 2020 ed.

3 Jason Bedrick, "Leave School Choice to the States," *TownHall.com*, April 16, 2015.

4 Bedrick, "Leave School Choice to the States."

5 Tibor R. Machan, "Government Regulation of Business: The Moral Arguments," Foundation for Economic Education, July 1, 1988.

6 Machan, "Government Regulation of Business."

7 Machan, "Government Regulation of Business."

8 Douglas Harris, "The Reform Debate, Part II: The Difference between Charter and Voucher Schools," *Education Week*, November 11, 2015.

9 John Barnard et al., "Principal Stratification Approach to Broken Randomized Experiments: A Case Study of School Choice Vouchers in New York City," *Journal of the American Statistical Association* 98, no. 462 (2003): 299–323; Joshua M. Cowen, "School Choice as a Latent Variable: Estimating the 'Complier Average Causal Effect' of Vouchers in Charlotte," *Policy Studies Journal* 36, no. 2 (2008): 301–15; Jay P. Greene, Paul E. Peterson, and Jiangtao Du, "Effectiveness of School Choice: The Milwaukee Experiment," *Education and Urban Society* 31, no. 2 (1999): 190–213; Jay P. Greene, "The Effect of School Choice: An Evaluation of the Charlotte Children's Scholarship Fund Program," *Civic Report* 12 (2000): 1–15; William G. Howell et al., "School Vouchers and Academic Performance: Results from Three Randomized Field Trials," *Journal of Policy Analysis and Management* 21, no. 2 (2002): 191–217; Hui Jin, John Barnard, and Donald B. Rubin, "A Modified General Location Model for Noncompliance with Missing Data: Revisiting the New York City School Choice Scholarship Program Using Principal Stratification," *Journal of Educational and Behavioral Statistics* 35, no. 2 (2010): 154–73; Cecilia Elena Rouse, "Private

School Vouchers and Student Achievement: An Evaluation of the Milwaukee Parental Choice Program," *Quarterly Journal of Economics* 113, no. 2 (1998): 553–602; Patrick J. Wolf et al., "School Vouchers and Student Outcomes: Experimental Evidence from Washington, DC," *Journal of Policy Analysis and Management* 32, no. 2 (2013): 246–70.

10 Jonathan N. Mills, "The Effectiveness of Cash Transfers as a Policy Instrument in K-16 Education" (University of Arkansas Theses and Dissertations, 2015); Jonathan N. Mills and Patrick J. Wolf, "Vouchers in the Bayou: The Effects of the Louisiana Scholarship Program on Student Achievement after 2 Years," *Educational Evaluation and Policy Analysis* 39, no. 3 (2017): 464–84; Abdulkadiroğlu, Pathak, and Walters, "Free to Choose."

11 Mills and Wolf, "Vouchers in the Bayou."

12 Jonathan N. Mills and Patrick J. Wolf, "The Effects of the Louisiana Scholarship Program on Student Achievement after Four Years" (EDRE Working Paper No. 2019-10, University of Arkansas, Department of Education Reform, 2019).

13 The fully specified and preferred model used in the study by Jonathan Mills and Patrick Wolf did not find statistically significant negative effects of the LSP on reading test scores; however, the model that did not control for students' baseline test scores did detect statistically significant negative effects on reading test scores overall and for subgroups. Mills and Wolf, "Louisiana Scholarship Program after Four Years."

14 Mills and Wolf, "Louisiana Scholarship Program after Four Years." In the interest of brevity, this review focuses on the effects of private school choice programs on test scores for participating students. The rigorous scientific evidence tends to suggest that private school choice programs lead to better civic outcomes, higher levels of college enrollment, more racial integration, more safety, and higher test scores for public school students. For civic outcomes, see Corey A. DeAngelis, "Do Self-Interested Schooling Selections Improve Society? A Review of the Evidence," *Journal of School Choice* 11, no. 4 (2017): 546–58; Patrick J. Wolf, "Civics Exam: Schools of Choice Boost Civic Values," *Education Next* 7, no. 3 (2007): 66–73. For college enrollment, see, for example, Matthew M. Chingos et al., "The Effects of Means-Tested Private School Choice Programs on College Enrollment and Graduation" (Research Report, Urban Institute, Washington, DC, July 2019); Leesa M. Foreman, "Educational Attainment Effects of Public and Private School Choice," *Journal of School Choice* 11, no. 4 (2017): 642–54. On racial integration, see Elise Swanson, "Can We Have It All? A Review of the Impacts of School Choice on Racial Integration," *Journal of School Choice* 11, no. 4 (2017): 507–26. On safety, see, for example, Ann Webber et al., *Evaluation of the DC Opportunity Scholarship Program: Impacts Three Years after Students Applied*, NCEE 2019-4006 (National Center for Education Evaluation and Regional Assistance, US Department of Education, 2019); Patrick J. Wolf et al., *Evaluation of the DC Opportunity Scholarship Program: Final Report*, NCEE 2010-4018 (National Center for Education Evaluation and Regional Assistance, US Department of Education, 2010). For higher test scores for public school students, see Anna J. Egalite, "Measuring Competitive Effects from School Voucher Programs: A Systematic Review," *Journal of School Choice* 7, no. 4 (2013): 443–64.

15 R. Joseph Waddington and Mark Berends, "Impact of the Indiana Choice Scholarship Program: Achievement Effects for Students in Upper Elementary and Middle School," *Journal of Policy Analysis and Management* 37, no. 4 (2018): 783–808.

16 R. Joseph Waddington and Mark Berends, "Impact of the Indiana Choice Scholarship Program: Achievement Effects for Students in Upper Elementary and Middle School" (working paper, 2017).

17 David Figlio and Krzysztof Karbownik, *Evaluation of Ohio's EdChoice Scholarship Program: Selection, Competition, and Performance Effects* (Columbus, OH: Thomas B. Fordham Institute, 2016).

18 Corey A. DeAngelis, "Regulatory Compliance Costs and Private School Participation in Voucher Programs," *Journal of School Choice* 14, no. 1 (2020): 95–121.

19 Brian Kisida, Patrick J. Wolf, and Evan Rhinesmith, *Views from Private Schools: Attitudes about School Choice Programs in Three States* (American Enterprise Institute, January 2015).

20 Corey A. DeAngelis, Lindsey M. Burke, and Patrick J. Wolf, "The Effects of Regulations on Private School Choice Program Participation: Experimental Evidence from California and New York" (EDRE Working Paper No. 2019-07, University of Arkansas, Department of Education Reform, 2019).

21 Harris, "Reform Debate, Part II."

22 Jason Bedrick, "The Folly of Overregulating School Choice," *Education Next*, January 5, 2016.

23 DeAngelis, "Regulatory Compliance Costs."

24 Harris, "Reform Debate, Part II."

25 Hitt, McShane, and Wolf, "Do impacts on test scores even matter? Lessons from long-run outcomes in school choice research" (American Enterprise Institute, 2018). .

26 Corey A. DeAngelis, "Divergences between Effects on Test Scores and Effects on Non-cognitive Skills," *Educational Review* 2019.

27 Frederick M. Hess, "Does School Choice 'Work'?," *National Affairs* 5, no. 1 (Fall 2010): 35–53; Michael Q. McShane, ed., *New and Better Schools: The Supply Side of School Choice* (Lanham, MD: Rowman & Littlefield, 2015).

28 Megan J. Austin, "Schools' Responses to Voucher Policy: Participation Decisions and Early Implementation Experiences in the Indiana Choice Scholarship Program," *Journal of School Choice* 9, no. 3 (2015): 354–79.

29 Austin, "Schools' Responses to Voucher Policy."

30 Anna J. Egalite et al., *School Leaders' Voices: Private School Leaders' Perspectives on the North Carolina Opportunity Scholarship Program, 2018 Update*, OS Evaluation Report #6 (NC State College of Education, October 2018).

31 Kisida, Wolf, and Rhinesmith, *Views from Private Schools*.

32 Kisida, Wolf, and Rhinesmith, *Views from Private Schools*.

33 Yujie Sude, Corey A. DeAngelis, and Patrick J. Wolf, "Supplying Choice: An Analysis of School Participation Decisions in Voucher Programs in Washington, DC, Indiana, and Louisiana," *Journal of School Choice* 12, no. 1 (2018): 8–33.

34 David Stuit and Sy Doan, *School Choice Regulations: Red Tape or Red Herring?* (Washington, DC: Thomas B. Fordham Institute, 2013).

35 Stuit and Doan, *School Choice Regulations*.

36 Corey A. DeAngelis, Lindsey M. Burke, and Patrick J. Wolf, "The Effects of Regulations on Private School Choice Program Participation: Experimental Evidence from Florida," *Social Science Quarterly* 100, no. 6 (2019), 2316–36; DeAngelis, Burke, and Wolf, "Effects of Regulations: California and New York."

37 DeAngelis, Burke, and Wolf, "Effects of Regulations: Florida."

38 DeAngelis, Burke, and Wolf, "Effects of Regulations: California and New York."

39 The literature on this topic has important limitations. The two survey experiments are limited because they draw conclusions on the basis of stated—rather than revealed—preferences. See Paul A. Samuelson, "Consumption Theory in Terms of Revealed Preference," *Economica* 15, no. 60 (1948): 243–53. The nonexperimental studies are limited because they are merely correlational.

40 Sude, DeAngelis, and Wolf, "Supplying Choice."

41 Abdulkadiroğlu, Pathak, and Walters, "Free to Choose"; Matthew H. Lee, Jonathan N. Mills, and Patrick J. Wolf, "Heterogeneous Impacts across Schools in the First Four Years of the Louisiana Scholarship Program" (EDRE Working Paper 2019-11, University of Arkansas, Department of Education Reform, Fayetteville, AR, April 23, 2019).

42 Eric Bettinger et al., "School Vouchers, Labor Markets and Vocational Education" (Borradores de Economía No. 1087, Banco de la República, Colombia, 2019); Corey A. DeAngelis and Blake Hoarty, "Who Participates? An Analysis of School Participation Decisions in Two Voucher Programs in the United States" (Policy Analysis No. 848, Cato Institute, 2018); Corey A. DeAngelis and Martin F. Lueken, "Are Choice Schools Safe Schools? A Cross-Sector Analysis of K–12 Safety Policies and School Climates in Indiana" (Working Paper 2019-2, EdChoice, April 3, 2019); Cristián Sánchez, "Understanding School Competition under Voucher Regimes" (working paper, September 17, 2018), http://econweb.umd.edu/~sanchez/files/csanchez_jmp.pdf.

43 Egalite et al., *School Leaders' Voices*; Kisida, Wolf, and Rhinesmith, *Views from Private Schools*.

44 DeAngelis, Burke, and Wolf, "Effects of Regulations: Florida"; DeAngelis, Burke, and Wolf, "Effects of Regulations: California and New York."

45 DeAngelis, Burke, and Wolf, "Effects of Regulations: Florida."

46 Michael Q. McShane, *Rethinking Regulation: Overseeing Performance in a Diversifying Educational Ecosystem* (Indianapolis: EdChoice, May 2018).

47 Lindsey M. Burke, "Avoiding the "Inexorable Push toward Homogenization' in School Choice: Education Savings Accounts as Hedges against Institutional Isomorphism," *Journal of School Choice* 10, no. 4 (2016): 560–78.

48 "Louisiana Scholarship Program," EdChoice, accessed May 19, 2020, https://www.edchoice.org/school-choice/programs/louisiana-scholarship-program/.

49 "Wisconsin—Milwaukee Parental Choice Program," EdChoice, accessed May 19, 2020, https://www.edchoice.org/school-choice/programs/wisconsin-milwaukee-parental-choice-program/.

50 Austin, "Schools' Responses to Voucher Policy"; Megan J. Austin, "Organizational and Social Costs of Schools' Participation in a Voucher Program," in *School Choice at the Crossroads: Research Perspectives*, ed. Mark Berends, R. Joseph Waddington, and John Schoenig (New York: Routledge, 2019); Egalite et al., *School Leaders' Voices*; Kisida, Wolf, and Rhinesmith, *Views from Private Schools*.

51 Kisida, Wolf, and Rhinesmith, *Views from Private Schools*.

52 Austin, "Schools' Responses to Voucher Policy."

53 Austin, "Organizational and Social Costs."

54 Egalite et al., *School Leaders' Voices*.

55 Corey A. DeAngelis, "Which Schools Participate? An Analysis of Private School Voucher Program Participation Decisions across Seven Locations" (working paper, 2019), https://ssrn.com/abstract=3309754.

56 Corey A. DeAngelis and Lindsey M. Burke, "Does Regulation Induce Homogenisation? An Analysis of Three Voucher Programmes in the United States," *Educational Research and Evaluation* 23, no. 7–8 (2017): 311–27; Corey A. DeAngelis and Lindsey M. Burke, "Does Regulation Reduce Specialization? Examining the Impact of Regulations on Private Schools of Choice in Five Locations" (Working Paper 2019-1, EdChoice, March 14, 2019).

57 Corey A. DeAngelis and Angela K. Dills, "Is School Choice a Trojan Horse? The Effects of School Choice Laws on Homeschool Prevalence," *Peabody Journal of Education* 94, no. 3 (2019): 342–54.

58 DeAngelis, Burke, and Wolf, "Effects of Regulations: California and New York."

59 DeAngelis, Burke, and Wolf, "Effects of Regulations: Florida."

60 Milton Friedman, "The Role of Government in Education," in *Economics and the Public Interest*, ed. Robert A. Solo (New Brunswick, NJ: Rutgers University Press, 1955).

61 Erika Sanzi, "While Rich People Bribe Their Kids' Way into College, Parents of Color Sit in Jail for Wanting Better Schools," *Education Post*, March 13, 2019.

62 John E. Chubb and Terry M. Moe, "Politics, Markets, and the Organization of Schools," *American Political Science Review* 82, no. 4 (1988): 1065–87; Corey A. DeAngelis, "Is Public Schooling a Public Good? An Analysis of Schooling Externalities" (Policy Analysis No. 842, Cato Institute, May 9, 2018); Caroline M. Hoxby, ed., *The Economics of School Choice* (Chicago: University of Chicago Press, 2007).

63 DeAngelis and Holmes Erickson, "What Leads to Successful School Choice Programs? A Review of the Theories and Evidence," *Cato Journal* 38, no. 1 (2018): 247–63.

64 DeAngelis, "Divergences"; Hitt, McShane, and Wolf, "Do impacts on test scores" .

65 Jason Bedrick and Lindsey M. Burke, *Surveying Florida Scholarship Families: Experiences and Satisfaction with Florida's Tax-Credit Scholarship Program* (Indianapolis: EdChoice, October 2018).

CHAPTER 17: "BLUE LAWS" AND OTHER CASES OF BOOTLEGGER/BAPTIST INFLUENCE IN BEER REGULATION

1 See Richard E. Wagner, *Politics as a Peculiar Business: Insights from a Theory of Entangled Political Economy* (Cheltenham, UK: Edward Elgar, 2016).

2 Alistair Williams, "Exploring the Impact of Legislation on the Development of Craft Beer," *Beverages* 3, no. 2 (2017): 2.

3 Derek Thompson, "Craft Beer Is the Strangest, Happiest Economic Story in America," *The Atlantic*, January 8, 2018.

4 For example, the Brewers Association argues in its list of position statements that "state laws should support an independent distribution tier that is unencumbered by undue influence, ownership or control by the largest brewers and ensures access to market for all brewers." See "Position Statements," Brewers Association, accessed March 3, 2020, https://www.brewersassociation.org/government-affairs/position-statements/. See also https://www.nbwa.org/news/what-three-tier-system.

5   See Bruce Yandle, "Bootleggers and Baptists—the Education of a Regulatory Econ-
    omist," *Regulation* 7, no. 3 (1983): 12–16; Bruce Yandle. "Bootleggers and Baptists
    in retrospect." Regulation 22 (1999): 5.

6   As other authors have before us, we use the "Bootlegger" and "Baptist" labels to
    refer to the parties concerned in a wide variety of regulatory activity—the term
    Bootlegger in this sense does not imply illegal action, but rather points to those
    engaged in political action in pursuit of narrow economic gains. See especially
    Adam C. Smith and Bruce Yandle, *Bootleggers and Baptists: How Economic Forces and
    Moral Persuasion Interact to Shape Regulatory Politics*, (Cato institute Press, 2014),
    189. Accordingly, we will denote this group of people as "Bootleggers" with a
    capital *B*. References to actual bootleggers engaged in selling illegal booze will be
    distinguished with a lowercase *b*.

7   Yandle, "Bootleggers and Baptists," 13.

8   Michael F. Lovenheim and Daniel P. Steefel, "Do Blue Laws Save Lives? The Effect
    of Sunday Alcohol Sales Bans on Fatal Vehicle Accidents," *Journal of Policy Analysis
    and Management* 30, no. 4 (2011): 798.

9   See Jeremy Horpedahl, "Bootleggers, Baptists and Ballots: Coalitions in Arkansas'
    Alcohol-Legalization Elections," *Public Choice*, 2020, 1–17.

10 See, e.g., Gordon Tullock, "The Welfare Costs of Tariffs, Monopolies, and Theft,"
    Economic Inquiry 5, no. 3 (1967): 224–32; Robert D. Tollison, "Rent Seeking: A
    Survey," *Kyklos* 35, no. 4 (1982): 575–602; Roger D. Congleton and Arye L. Hillman,
    eds., *Companion to the Political Economy of Rent Seeking* (Cheltenham, UK: Edward
    Elgar, 2015).

11 See Adam Smith, *The Theory of Moral Sentiments* ed. D. D. Raphael and A. L. Macfie
    (1759; repr., Indianapolis: Liberty Fund, 1982).

12 Richard Gamble, "'Two Kaisers in the Same Grave': Prohibition at 100," *Law &
    Liberty*, October 1, 2019.

13 Daniel Okrent, *Last Call: The Rise and Fall of Prohibition* (New York, NY: Simon and
    Schuster, 2010), 302.

14 Mark Thornton, "Alcohol Prohibition Was a Failure" (Policy Analysis No. 157,
    Cato Institute, 1991), 4.

15 See Jason F. Shogren, "The Optimal Subsidization of Baptists by Bootleggers,"
    Public Choice 67, no. 2 (1990): 181–89.

16 See for example https://themobmuseum.org/blog/world-war-played-key-role-
    passage-prohibition/ accessed 10/7/2020

17 Okrent, *Last Call*, 100.

18 Bert L. Vallee, "Alcohol in the Western World," *Scientific American* 278, no. 6 (1998):
    80–85.

19 Vallee, "Alcohol in the Western World."

20 Victor Kimm, Joseph Cotruvo, and Arden Calvert, *Drinking Water: A Half Century
    of Progress* (EPA Alumni Association, 2016).

21 Martin Stack and Myles Gartland, "The Repeal of Prohibition and the Resurgence
    of the National Breweries: Productive Efficiency or Path Creation?," *Management
    Decision* 43, no. 3 (2005): 422.

22 One indicator of the larger breweries' influence was that the day Prohibition end-
    ed, August Anheuser Busch Jr. decided to have Clydesdale horses pull a wagon of
    beer down Pennsylvania Avenue to deliver beer to FDR in the White House. This
    was the first appearance of these horses for Budweiser. Kat Eschner, "The Bud-

weiser Clydesdales' First Gig Was the End of Prohibition," *Smithsonian Magazine*, March 28, 2017.

23 Bradley J. Rickard, Marco Costanigro, and Teevrat Garg. "Economic and social implications of regulating alcohol availability in grocery stores." Applied Economic Perspectives and Policy 35, no. 4 (2013): 613-633.

24 "Control State Directory and Info," National Alcohol Beverage Control Association, https://www.nabca.org/control-state-directory-and-info, last accessed 7 October, 2020.

25 This was a political nod to the Catholic clergy. See Gamble, "Two Kaisers in the Same Grave."

26 The Brewers Association defines craft brewers as those that produce 6 million barrels or fewer, with no controlling interest from non-craft brewers. See "Craft Brewer Definition," Brewers Association, accessed March 3, 2020, https://www.brewersassociation.org/statistics-and-data/craft-brewer-definition/.

27 Kenneth G. Elzinga, Carol Horton Tremblay, and Victor J. Tremblay, "Craft Beer in the United States: History, Numbers, and Geography," *Journal of Wine Economics* 10, no. 3 (2015): 242–74.

28 See Jacob Burgdorf, "Trouble Brewing? Brewer and Wholesaler Laws Restrict Craft Breweries" (Mercatus on Policy, Mercatus Center at George Mason University, Arlington, VA, September 2016).

29 Jennifer Thomas, "Pending NC Legislation Could Signal End to Craft-Beer Battle over Self-Distribution Cap," *Charlotte Business Journal*, March 14, 2019.

30 See Stephan F. Gohmann, "Why Are There So Few Breweries in the South?," *Entrepreneurship Theory and Practice* 40, no. 5 (2016): 1071–92; Trey Malone and Jayson L. Lusk, "Brewing Up Entrepreneurship: Government Intervention in Beer," *Journal of Entrepreneurship and Public Policy* 5, no. 3 (2016): 325–42.

31 Toro-González, Daniel, Jill J. McCluskey, and Ron C. Mittelhammer. "Beer snobs do exist: Estimation of beer demand by type." Journal of agricultural and resource economics (2014): 174-187.

32 Ibid., p. 19.

33 "Supplier gross revenue of alcoholic beverages in the United States from 2008 to 2019, by beverage type," Statista, https://www.statista.com/statistics/237868/us-revenue-of-alcoholic-beverages-by-type/ last accessed October 7, 2020.

34 See "National Beer Sales & Production Data," Brewers Association, accessed March 3, 2020, https://www.brewersassociation.org/statistics/national-beer-sales-production-data/.

35 John Kell, "Anheuser-Busch InBev Buys 9th Craft Brewer," *Fortune*, November 3, 2016; James Brumley, "More Craft Beer Can't Help Big Brewers," *Motley Fool*, January 28, 2020.

36 Gohmann, "Why Are There So Few Breweries in the South?"

37 Southern Baptist Convention, "On Alcohol Use in America," accessed Oct. 7 2020, http://media2.sbhla.org.s3.amazonaws.com/annuals/SBC_Annual_2006.pdf

38 Gohmann, "Why Are There So Few Breweries in the South?"

39 Gohmann, "Why Are There So Few Breweries in the South?"

40 https://www.brewersassociation.org/statistics-and-data/national-beer-stats/, accessed October 7, 2020.

41 Alistair Williams, "Exploring the Impact of Legislation," 3.

42 Jack Holmes, "Will Arkansas' Prohibition Finally End?," *Daily Beast,* updated April 14, 2017.

43 Trey Malone and Dustin Chambers, "Quantifying Federal Regulatory Burdens in the Beer Value Chain," *Agribusiness* 33, no. 3 (2017): 2. By way of comparison, 11,000 regulations affect railroads, as of 2012. See Jerry Ellig and Patrick A. Mc-Laughlin, "The Regulatory Determinants of Railroad Safety," *Review of Industrial Organization* 49, no. 2 (2016): 371–98.

44 Douglas Glen Whitman, *Strange Brew: Alcohol and Government Monopoly* (Oakland, CA: Independent Institute, 2003), 7.

45 See James C. Cooper et al., "Vertical Antitrust Policy as a Problem of Inference," *International Journal of Industrial Organization* 23, no. 7–8 (2005): 639–64.

46 Francine Lafontaine and Margaret Slade, "Vertical Integration and Firm Boundaries: The Evidence," *Journal of Economic Literature* 45, no. 3 (2007): 680.

47 Armen A. Alchian and William R. Allen, *Universal Economics* (Indianapolis: Liberty Fund, 2018), 383–84.

48 Malone and Lusk, "Brewing Up Entrepreneurship," 337.

49 Kelly J. Kelleher et al., "Alcohol Availability and Motor Vehicle Fatalities," *Journal of Adolescent Health* 19, no. 5 (1996): 325–30.

50 "'Dry Towns' in the USA," American Addiction Centers, accessed March 3, 2020, https://www.alcohol.org/statistics-information/dry-towns/.

51 Michael Conlin, Stacy Dickert-Conlin, and John Pepper, "The Effect of Alcohol Prohibition on Illicit-Drug-Related Crimes," *Journal of Law and Economics* 48, no. 1 (2005): 215–34.

52 Jose Fernandez, Stephan F. Gohmann, and Joshua C. Pinkston, "Breaking Bad in Bourbon Country: Does Alcohol Prohibition Encourage Methamphetamine Production?," *Southern Economic Journal* 84, no. 4 (2018): 1001–23.

53 John DiNardo and Thomas Lemieux, "Alcohol, Marijuana, and American Youth: The Unintended Consequences of Government Regulation," *Journal of Health Economics* 20, no. 6 (2001): 991–1010.

54 Barış K. Yörük and Ceren Ertan Yörük, "The Impact of Minimum Legal Drinking Age Laws on Alcohol Consumption, Smoking, and Marijuana Use: Evidence from a Regression Discontinuity Design Using Exact Date of Birth," *Journal of Health Economics* 30, no. 4 (2011): 740–52.

55 Brent D. Mast, Bruce L. Benson, and David W. Rasmussen, "Beer Taxation and Alcohol-Related Traffic Fatalities," *Southern Economic Journal* 66, no. 2 (1999): 214–49; Thomas S. Dee, "State Alcohol Policies, Teen Drinking and Traffic Fatalities," *Journal of Public Economics* 72, no. 2 (1999): 289–315.

56 Malone and Lusk, "Brewing Up Entrepreneurship"; "Percentage Change in Per Capita Alcohol Consumption, United States, 1977–2016," National Institute on Alcohol Abuse and Alcoholism, accessed March 3, 2020, https://pubs.niaaa.nih.gov/publications/surveillance110/fig3.htm.

57 Christopher Koopman and Adam C. Smith. "The Political Economy of Craft Beer in North Carolina (and Beyond)." *Political Economy in the Carolinas* 1 (2018): 76-98. For evidence that opponents of reform used the argument that changing the system would cost jobs, see Steve Bittenbender, "Would Liquor Access Expansion in Pennsylvania Cost Jobs? Lawmakers, Interested Parties Debate Bills," *Center Square,* November 6, 2019.

58 Jeremy Horpedahl, "Bootleggers, Baptists and Ballots," 2.

59 Horpedahl, "Bootleggers, Baptists and Ballots," 15.

60 H.B. 168, 2015 Leg., Reg. Sess. (Kentucky 2015).

61 The lobbying data are from https://www.followthemoney.org/ last accessed October 7, 2020

62 See Gordon Tullock, "The Transitional Gains Trap," *Bell Journal of Economics* 6, no. 2 (1975): 671–78.

63 Brian Slodysko and Tom Davies, "Governor Signs Historic Indiana Sunday Alcohol Sales Bill," *South Bend Tribune*, February 28, 2018.

64 Trey Malone, "Craft Beer Revolution Is in Danger amid Coronavirus Crisis. Here's What Can Help Save It," *USA Today*, April 22, 2020.

65 Alex Gangitano, "Coronavirus Brings Quick Changes to State Alcohol Laws," *The Hill*, April 1, 2020.

66 See "Direct Shipment of Alcohol Bill Heading to Governor," *Richmond Register*, March 28, 2020.

67 https://www.usatoday.com/story/opinion/2020/05/18/coronavirus-forces-changes-outdated-alcohol-regulations-column/5194183002/

68 For example, North Carolina recently increased self-distribution to 100,000 barrels. See Brooklynn Cooper, "N.C. Breweries Can Produce Quadruple the Amount of Beer Now. Here's What They Plan to Do with It," *Charlotte Observer*, June 6, 2019.

69 See Tom Acitelli, *The Audacity of Hops: The History of America's Craft Beer Revolution* (Chicago: Chicago Review, 2017), 238.

70 See Whitman, *Strange Brew*, 27.

71 Jim Morrill, "Craft Brewers Say This Document Shows the Distribution System Is 'Rigged,'" *Charlotte Observer*, May 25, 2017.

72 See Williams, "Exploring the Impact of Legislation," 6.

73 C. Jarrett Dieterle and Kevin Kosar, "GOP Tax Reform Impact on Booze," January 2018, R Street Institute, https://www.rstreet.org/wp-content/uploads/2018/01/2018-R-Sheet-2-GOP-Tax-Reform-Impact-on-Booze.pdf.

74 For examples of research that explicitly examines and measures these Bootlegger-Baptist relationships, see Gohmann, "Why Are There So Few Breweries in the South?"; Jacob Burgdorf, "Impact of Mandated Exclusive Territories in the US Brewing Industry: Evidence from Scanner Level Data," *International Journal of Industrial Organization* 63 (2019): 376–416; and Horpedahl, "Bootleggers, Baptists and Ballots."

CHAPTER 18: SMOKE OR VAPOR? REGULATION OF TOBACCO AND VAPING

1 Institute of Medicine, *Ending the Tobacco Problem: A Blueprint for the Nation*, ed. Richard J. Bonnie, Kathleen Stratton, and Robert B. Wallace (Washington, DC: National Academies Press, 2007).

2 US Department of Health, Education, and Welfare, *Smoking and Health: Report of the Advisory Committee to the Surgeon General of the Public Health Service* (Washington, DC: US Government Printing Office, 1964), 32.

3 Euromonitor International, *Tobacco in the United States*, Country Report, January 2019, Passport.

4 The smoking intensity figure of 11.5 cigarettes per day (with a 95% confidence interval for the mean of [11.2, 11.8]) is calculated by the author from the 2018 Tobacco Use Supplement to the Current Population Survey. The retail sales figures are from Euromonitor International, *Tobacco in the United States*. The discrepancy

between self-reported smoking behavior and sales per adult smoker is due to the well-known fact that survey respondents tend to underreport smoking and to the fact that many underage smokers consume some of the sales.

5   MeLisa R. Creamer et al., "Tobacco Product Use and Cessation Indicators among Adults—United States, 2018," *Morbidity and Mortality Weekly Report* 68, no. 45 (2019): 1013–19.

6   Heikki Hiilamo, Eric Crosbie, and Stanton A. Glantz, "The Evolution of Health Warning Labels on Cigarette Packs: The Role of Precedents, and Tobacco Industry Strategies to Block Diffusion," *Tobacco Control* 23, no. 1 (2014): e2.

7   Institute of Medicine, *Ending the Tobacco Problem.*

8   Hiilamo, Crosbie, and Glantz, "Evolution of Health Warning Labels."

9   See Tobacco Products; Required Warnings for Cigarette Packages and Advertisements, 84 Fed. Reg. 42754 (August 16, 2019), and the discussion below.

10 Pub. L. No. 100-202 (1987) banned smoking on domestic airline flights scheduled for two hours or less, while Pub. L. No. 101-164 (1989) did the same for flights scheduled for six hours or less.

11 States were required to have (and enforce through random inspections) laws "prohibiting any manufacturer, retailer or distributor of tobacco products from selling or distributing such products to any individual under the age of 18." In the event of noncompliance, a state would lose eligibility for a Substance Abuse Prevention and Treatment Block Grant. See Tobacco Regulation for Substance

Abuse Prevention and Treatment Block Grants, 61 Fed. Reg. 1492 (January 19, 1996).

12 See Dorie E. Apollonio and Stanton A. Glantz, "Minimum Ages of Legal Access for Tobacco in the United States from 1863 to 2015," *American Journal of Public Health* 106, no. 7 (2016): 1200–207; and D. M. Shelton et al., "State Laws on Tobacco Control—United States, 1995," *Morbidity and Mortality Weekly Report Surveillance Summaries* 44, no. 6 (1995): 1–28.

13 The statement is from the National Association of Attorneys General Center for Tobacco and Public Health, the organization set up by the attorneys general of the settling states to handle matters pertaining to the MSA. See "NAAG Center for Tobacco and Public Health," National Association of Attorneys General, accessed July 2, 2020, https://www.naag.org/naag/about_naag/naag-center-for-tobacco-and-public-health.php.

14 "A State-by-State Look at the 1998 Tobacco Settlement 21 Years Later," Campaign for Tobacco-Free Kids, last modified January 16, 2020, https://www.tobaccofreekids.org/what-we-do/us/statereport.

15 See Regulations Restricting the Sale and Distribution of Cigarettes and Smokeless Tobacco to Protect Children and Adolescents, 75 Fed. Reg. 13225 (March 19, 2010). The rule was a revised version of a 1996 FDA rule that was ultimately voided by the Supreme Court, which ruled in 2000 that the FDA lacked the authority to regulate tobacco as a drug. FDA v. Brown & Williamson Tobacco Corp. (98-1152), 529 U.S. 120 (2000), 153 F.3d 155, affirmed.

16 The new regulation (which took effect immediately when President Trump signed the bill on December 20, 2019) amends the Federal Food, Drug, and Cosmetics Act at 21 U.S.C. 387f(d) to include the higher minimum age of retail sale for any tobacco product, including ecigarettes (because of the FDA deeming action described in the next section).

17 Tobacco Products; Required Warnings for Cigarette Packages and Advertisements, 84 Fed. Reg. 42754 (August 16, 2019).

18 For the final rule, see Tobacco Products; Required Warnings for Cigarette Packages and Advertisements, 85 Fed. Reg. 15638 (March 18, 2020).

19 See David Hammond et al., "Text and Graphic Warnings on Cigarette Packages: Findings from the International Tobacco Control Four Country Study," *American Journal of Preventive Medicine* 32, no. 3 (2007): 202–9; Seth M. Noar et al., "Pictorial Cigarette Pack Warnings: A Meta-analysis of Experimental Studies," *Tobacco Control* 25, no. 3 (2016): 341–54. However, apparently no study has shown that graphical warnings lead to an increase in actual cessation (versus stated intentions to quit).

20 *The Tax Burden on Tobacco: Historical Compilation* (Arlington, VA: Orzechowski and Walker, 2014).

21 See Timothy S. Naimi et al., "Erosion of State Alcohol Excise Taxes in the United States," *Journal of Studies on Alcohol and Drugs* 79, no. 1 (2018): 43–48.

22 Euromonitor International, *Tobacco in the United States.*

23 Ned Sharpless, "How FDA is Regulating E-Cigarettes," September 10, 2019, https://www.fda.gov/news-events/fda-voices/how-fda-regulating-e-cigarettes.

24 National Academies of Sciences, Engineering, and Medicine, *Public Health Consequences of Ecigarettes* (Washington, DC: National Academies Press, 2018).

25 See the review of the regulatory status of ecigarettes provided by the Ned Sharpless, the acting commissioner of the FDA. Ned Sharpless, "How FDA Is Regulating Ecigarettes," Food and Drug Administration, September 10, 2019, https://www.fda.gov/news-events/fda-voices-perspectives-fda-leadership-and-experts/how-fda-regulating-e-cigarettes.

26 After a court decision, the deadline for filing the applications with the FDA was initially set at May 12, 2020, but this was later extended by 120 days because of impacts from COVID-19 in April. The court ordered that products with timely applications could remain on the market for one year pending FDA review.

27 The one partial exception is Philip Morris International's heat-not-burn product IQOS, which heats tobacco (unlike conventional ENDS, which vaporize an eliquid) without combustion so that the vapor can be inhaled. Heat-not-burn products are often considered a different category from ecigarettes by users, researchers, and manufacturers.

28 See Food and Drug Administration, *Enforcement Priorities for Electronic Nicotine Delivery Systems (ENDS) and Other Deemed Products on the Market without Premarket Authorization: Guidance for Industry*, January 2020, https://www.fda.gov/media/133880/download.

29 More properly speaking, they are technically still illegal (as with all ENDS apart from IQOS), but are not candidates for FDA enforcement at the present time.

30 However, as discussed in note 11 above, rather than functioning as an outright restriction, the federal age limit is instead enforced through financial consequences for states that do not so restrict sales. As figure 3 shows, nearly all states followed the FDA's prompting. Michigan, however, did not restrict sales of ecigarettes to minors until April 2019. See Malachi Barrett, "Michigan Senate Approves Ban on Ecigarette Sales to Minors," *MLive*, April 23, 2019.

31 For the advance notice of proposed rulemaking, see 83 Fed. Reg. 12294 (March 21, 2018). The due date for comments from interested parties was extended to July; see 83 Fed. Reg. 26618 (June 8, 2018).

32 For the advance notice of proposed rulemaking, see 83 Fed. Reg. 11818 (March 16, 2018).

33 For the rough cost estimate, see Jennifer Maloney, "FDA Clears Philip Morris International Heat-Not-Burn IQOS Device for Sale in U.S.," *Wall Street Journal*, April 30, 2019.

34 The discussion here follows Kenneth Warner et al., "Criteria for Determining an Optimal Cigarette Tax: The Economist's Perspective," *Tobacco Control* 4, no. 4 (1995): 380–86.

35 The argument presented here is from Edgar K. Browning, "The Myth of Fiscal Externalities," *Public Finance Review* 27, no. 1 (January 1999): 3–18.

36 See Jane G. Gravell and Dennis Zimmerman, *Cigarette Taxes to Fund Health Care Reform: An Economic Analysis* (Washington, DC: Library of Congress, 1994); and Willard G. Manning et al., "The Taxes of Sin: Do Smokers and Drinkers Pay Their Way?" *JAMA* 261, no. 11 (1989): 1604–9.

37 It is also important to note that studies (such as those cited in note 35) were reaching such conclusions well *before* the recent rounds of increases in tobacco taxes. See figure 2.

38 For the average tax rate, see figure 2; for the study, see Jonathan Gruber and Botond Köszegi, *A Modern Economic View of Tobacco Taxation* (Paris: International Union against Tuberculosis and Lung Disease, 2008). This estimate of the net negative externality does not include any harmful effects of secondhand smoke.

39 Sijbren Cnossen, "Tobacco Taxation in the European Union," *FinanzArchiv/Public Finance Analysis* 62, no. 2 (2006): 305–22.

40 See W. Kip Viscusi, "The New Cigarette Paternalism," *Regulation* 25, no. 4 (2002): 58–64; and Gary L. Huber, Robert E. Brockie, and Vijay K. Majhajan, "Smoke and Mirrors: The EPA's Flawed Study of Environmental Tobacco Smoke and Lung Cancer," *Regulation* 16, no. 3 (1993): 44–54.

41 A US district court found that the "EPA's study selection is disturbing" and that the agency had cherry-picked the data, excluding almost half the available evidence—the half that did not support its preferred conclusion. See Flue-Cured Tobacco Co-op. v. U.S.E.P.A., 4 F. Supp. 2d 435 (M.D.N.C. 1998). While this court decision was later overturned for the reason that the EPA's study was not a reviewable action under the Administrative Procedure Act, the findings regarding the scientific weakness of the report were left unrebutted. See Flue-Cured Tobacco Cooperative Stabilization Co. et al. v. Environmental Protection Agency et al., 313 F.3d 852 (4th Cir. 2002).

42 For a fascinating sociological perspective on why the anti-smoking crusade began to succeed when it did after "centuries of failure," see Randall Collins, "Tobacco Ritual and Anti-ritual: Substance Ingestion as a History of Social Boundaries," in *Interaction Ritual Chains* (Princeton, NJ: Princeton University Press, 2004). Collins points out the importance of nonscientific factors such as the "enjoying the moral prestige of a popular progressive movement" [p. 344].

43 See *The Health Consequences of Smoking—50 Years of Progress: A Report of the Surgeon General* (Atlanta: US Department of Health and Human Services, 2014). Note that such estimates are typically reported without confidence intervals, but—given the uncertainty in the relative risks underlying the calculations—the confidence intervals would be wide.

44 See Melanie Heron, "Deaths: Leading Causes for 2014," *National Vital Statistics Reports* 65, no. 5 (2016): 1–95.

45 See G. Banderali et al., "Short and Long Term Health Effects of Parental Tobacco Smoking during Pregnancy and Lactation: A Descriptive Review," *Journal of Translational Medicine* 13 (2015); Kerry Anne McGeary et al., "Impact of Comprehensive

Smoking Bans on the Health of Infants and Children," *American Journal of Health Economics* 6, no. 1 (2020): 1–38.

46 See Giselle Salmasi et al., "Environmental Tobacco Smoke Exposure and Perinatal Outcomes: A Systematic Review and Meta-analyses," *Acta Obstetricia et Gynecologica Scandinavica* 89, no. 4 (2010): 423–41. Note that the results regarding low birthweight are equivocal: while there is no statistically significant association between environmental tobacco exposure and low birthweight, when the latter is defined as a binary variable for birthweight less than 2.5 kilograms, there is a statistically significant association with lower birthweight when defined as a continuous variable. Such equivocal results hint at (perhaps substantial) nonlinearity or threshold effects in the relationship between environmental tobacco exposure and birthweight. Regardless, comparison with the results of other studies shows that the negative impact on birthweight of drinking one additional cup of coffee a day is more certain than the impact of a father smoking preterm (where certainty is ascertained by statistical significance and the width of confidence intervals). For the impact of a father smoking, see Ting-Jung Ko et al., "Parental Smoking during Pregnancy and Its Association with Low Birth Weight, Small for Gestational Age, and Preterm Birth Offspring: A Birth Cohort Study," *Pediatrics and Neonatology* 55, no.1 (2014): 20–27. For the impact of drinking coffee, see Jongeun Rhee et al., "Maternal Caffeine Consumption during Pregnancy and Risk of Low Birth Weight: A Dose-Response Meta-analysis of Observational Studies," *PLOS ONE* 10, no. 7 (2015): 1–18.

47 The difficulty with measuring how detrimental maternal and passive smoking may be to neonatal and child health is exacerbated by the high likelihood that unobserved factors are correlated with these causes and the health outcomes. Most of the public health studies in the meta-analysis cited use cross-sectional data and cannot control for such confounding factors. A better-designed study demonstrates that the impact of maternal smoking on infant health and the infant healthcare cost savings associated with ceasing smoking during pregnancy are typically overestimated by an order of magnitude. See Douglas Almond, Kenneth Y. Chay, and David S. Lee, "The Costs of Low Birth Weight" *Quarterly Journal of Economics* 120, no. 3 (2005): 1031–83.

48 See, for example, the many studies cited in Timor Faber et al., "Effect of Tobacco Control Policies on Perinatal and Child Health: A Systematic Review and Meta-Analysis" *The Lancet Public Health* 2, no. 9 (2017): e420–37 and Timor Faber et al., "Smoke-Free Legislation and Child Health" *npj Primary Care Respiratory Medicine* 26, art. no. 16067 (2016): 1–8. As discussed in the previous note, most such studies suffer potential bias from confounding factors. One recent study using methodology to reduce the impact of omitted variable bias (and, interestingly, one cited by a referee as bolstering the link between smoking and the health of infants and children) showed that after controlling for unobserved confounding factors at the county level, there was no association (at the standard 5% significance level) between comprehensive smoking bans and birthweight or the prevalence of low birthweight (see the bottom of panel b of table 3 of McGeary et al., "Impact of Comprehensive Smoking Bans.") or the prevalence of hay fever, any respiratory allergies, asthma, ear infections, or being in "excellent or very good" general health. Out of nine child health outcomes studied, the only two displaying significant association with a ban were emergency room visits and being in "fair or poor" general health.

49 Ayman El-Mohandes et al., "An Intervention to Reduce Environmental Tobacco Smoke Exposure Improves Pregnancy Outcomes," *Pediatrics* 125, no. 4 (2010): 721–28.

50 For example, roughly 90% of US smokers agreed with the following statement: "If you had to do it over again, you would not have started smoking." Geoffrey T. Fong et al., "The Near-Universal Experience of Regret among Smokers in Four Countries: Findings from the International Tobacco Control Policy Evaluation Survey," *Nicotine & Tobacco Research* 6, no. 3 (2004): 341–51.

51 More than 60% of child smokers in one study said that they were given their first cigarettes. See Janet G. Baugh et al., "Development Trends of First Cigarette Smoking Experience of Children: The Bogalusa Heart Study," *American Journal of Public Health* 72, no. 10 (1982): 1161–64.

52 Hana Ross and Frank J. Chaloupka, "The Effect of Cigarette Prices on Youth Smoking," *Health Economics* 12, no. 3 (2003): 217–30; Dean R. Lillard, Eamon Molloy, and Andrew Sfekas, "Smoking Initiation and the Iron Law of Demand," *Journal of Health Economics* 32, no. 1 (2013): 114–27.

53 Philip DeCicca et al., "Youth Smoking, Cigarette Prices, and Anti-smoking Sentiment," *Health Economics* 17, no. 6 (2007): 733–49; Jeffrey Wasserman et al., "The Effects of Excise Taxes and Regulations on Cigarette Smoking," *Journal of Health Economics* 10, no. 1 (1991): 43–64.

54 In the theories discussed here, the value to the consumer of the last unit consumed is measured as the money-metric marginal utility from consumption. See Emmanuel Farhi and Xavier Gabaix, "Optimal Taxation with Behavioral Agents," *American Economic Review* 110, no. 1 (2020): 298–336.

55 Gruber and Köszegi, *Modern Economic View of Tobacco Taxation*.

56 Gruber and Köszegi, *Modern Economic View of Tobacco Taxation*, p. 2.

57 Viscusi, "New Cigarette Paternalism."

58 For a discussion of assumptions under which a rational individual would choose to become addicted, see Gary S. Becker and Kevin M. Murphy, "A Theory of Rational Addiction," *Journal of Political Economy* 96, no. 4 (1988): 675–700.

59 Viscusi shows that at a time when medical science indicated that the risk of lung cancer for an average smoker was 6%–13%, the public thought it was 47%. Similar overestimation of risk is also present for premature mortality and life-years lost. Viscusi, "New Cigarette Paternalism."

60 The evidence in one study shows that among 14-to-22-year-olds, 70% of smokers and 79% of nonsmokers overestimated the risks of lung cancer. The same researchers found that only 34% of smokers and 41% of nonsmokers overestimated the total mortality risk of smoking, which the researchers take to be around 50%. Daniel Romer and Patrick Jamieson, "Do Adolescents Appreciate the Risks of Smoking? Evidence from a National Survey," *Journal of Adolescent Health* 29, no. 1 (2001): 12–21. However, at the time of that study, the public was being told by the surgeon general's report on smoking and the National Cancer Institute that the mortality risk was 18 percent to 36 percent. See Viscusi, "New Cigarette Paternalism." It appears unlikely that any average smoker or nonsmoker would be looking at the technical academic or clinical literature indicating higher risk. Thus, the large majority of both smokers and nonsmokers were overestimating the risks compared to what they were being told by the most prominent sources of information. One would expect that as the higher estimates of mortality risk diffused into the public-facing messaging in the tobacco control community, people's perceptions of risk would rise in response, if the degree of overestimation were to remain similar. However, apparently no more recent studies on risk perception have been performed.

61 For example, one strand of literature finds time inconsistency in labor market and welfare program participation decisions. See Hanming Fang and Dan Silverman, "Time-Inconsistency and Welfare Program Participation: Evidence from the NLSY," *International Economic Review* 50, no. 4 (2009): 1043–77.

62 See Russell S. Sobel and Joshua C. Hall, "In Loco Parentis: A Paternalism Ranking of the States," in *For Your Own Good: Taxes, Paternalism, and Fiscal Discrimination in the Twenty-First Century*, ed. Adam J. Hoffer and Todd Nesbit (Arlington, VA: Mercatus Center at George Mason University, 2018).

63 The argument follows from the observations that consumers have stronger incentives to correct their behavior than do government decision makers and that consumers have stronger incentives to make good choices when choosing what to buy than when choosing how to vote. See Edward L. Glaeser, "Paternalism and Psychology," *Regulation* 29, no. 2 (2006).

64 See M. C. Farrelly et al., "The Effects of Higher Cigarette Prices on Tar and Nicotine Consumption in a Cohort of Adult Smokers," *Health Economics* 13, no. 1 (2004): 49–58. Despite the oft-heard slogan that "there is no such thing as a safer cigarette," the epidemiological evidence indicates that low-tar cigarettes reduce the risk of lung cancer and total mortality for smokers. See G. C. Kabat, "Fifty Years' Experience of Reduced-Tar Cigarettes: What Do We Know about Their Health Effects?," *Inhalation Toxicology* 15, no. 11 (2003): 1059–102.

65 For more complete critiques of paternalism and taxation, see Adam J. Hoffer and Todd Nesbit, eds., *For Your Own Good: Taxes, Paternalism, and Fiscal Discrimination in the Twenty-First Century* (Arlington, VA: Mercatus Center at George Mason University, 2018); Adam J. Hoffer, William F. Shughart II, and Michael D. Thomas, "Sin Taxes and Sindustry: Revenue, Paternalism, and Political Interest," *Independent Review* 19, no. 1 (2014): 47–64.

66 See Matthew C. Farrelly et al., "Response by Adults to Increases in Cigarette Prices by Sociodemographic Characteristics," *Southern Economic Journal* 68, no. 1 (2001): 156–65; Don Fullerton and Diane L. Rogers, *Who Bears the Lifetime Tax Burden?* (Washington, DC: Brookings Institution Press, 1993); Andrew B. Lyon and Robert M. Schwab, "Consumption Taxes in a Life-Cycle Framework: Are Sin Taxes Regressive?," *Review of Economics and Statistics* 77, no. 3 (1995): 389–406; and Dahlia K. Remler, "Poor Smokers, Poor Quitters, and Cigarette Tax Regressivity," *American Journal of Public Health* 94, no. 2 (2004): 225–29.

67 See "Increases and Changes to Consumer Taxes in Chicago for 2020," Civic Federation, January 10, 2020, https://www.civicfed.org/civic-federation/blog/increases-and-changes-consumer-taxes-chicago-2020. The minimum wage in Chicago at the time was $12 per hour.

68 See Matthew C. Farrelly, James M. Nonnemaker, and Kimberly A. Watson, "The Consequences of High Cigarette Excise Taxes for Low-Income Smokers," *PLOS ONE* 7, no. 9 (2012): e43838. The authors conclude after an empirical examination that high cigarette taxes "can impose a significant financial burden on low-income smokers." See also James E. Prieger et al., *The Impact of Ecigarette Regulation on the Illicit Trade in Tobacco Products in the European Union* (Geneva, Switzerland: BOTEC Analysis, 2019), which discusses at length the issue of "specific impoverishment" caused by tobacco taxes.

69 Maya Vijayaraghavan et al., "The Effectiveness of Cigarette Price and Smoke-Free Homes on Low-Income Smokers in the United States," *American Journal of Public Health* 103, no. 12 (2013): 2276–83. Furthermore, while some evidence shows that higher prices are associated with lower smoking prevalence among low-income individuals, this evidence does not by itself imply that taxes cause cessation, since

it could just as well mean that fewer low-income individuals ever started smoking.

70 See Michael L. Marlow and Sherzod Abdukadirov, "Taxation as Nudge: The Failure of Anti-obesity Paternalism," in Hoffer and Nesbit, *For Your Own Good*.

71 Philip DeCicca and Logan McLeod, "Cigarette Taxes and Older Adult Smoking: Evidence from Recent Large Tax Increases," *Journal of Health Economics* 27, no. 4 (2008): 918–29.

72 Even here, the evidence is mixed, because when the estimated smoking responses to tax increases are used to simulate trends in the prevalence of smoking in the US, the models greatly underpredict actual smoking rates. Philip DeCicca et al., "The Economics of Smoking Prevention," in *Oxford Research Encyclopedia of Economics and Finance* (Oxford: Oxford University Press, 2018). That is, if tax increases discouraged adult smoking so much, then there would not be so many actual smokers still. Thus, DeCicca et al. conclude that "the true [price] elasticity lies between zero and −0.1, which is considerably smaller than the corresponding consensus estimate."

73 Gregory J. Colman and Dahlia K. Remler, "Vertical Equity Consequences of Very High Cigarette Tax Increases: If the Poor Are the Ones Smoking, How Could Cigarette Tax Increases Be Progressive?," *Journal of Policy Analysis and Management* 27, no. 2 (2008): 376–400. This study also explains how under extreme behavioral models (as discussed earlier) cigarette taxes can be progressive, but nevertheless concludes that "taxes and other hindrances on smoking benefit higher-income more than lower-income smokers who are planning to quit." Colman and Remler, "Vertical Equity Consequences," 396.

74 See, for example, Vijayaraghavan et al., "Effectiveness of Cigarette Price and Smoke-Free Homes."

75 See "State-by-State Look," Campaign for Tobacco-Free Kids. While this fact may appear to be at odds with the common recent practice of earmarking tax increases for cessation programs or other public health initiatives, the fungibility of state tax revenue implies that earmarking a dollar does not mean that an *additional* dollar will be spent on the targeted cause. See George R. Crowley and Adam J. Hoffer, "Earmarking Tax Revenues: Leviathan's Secret Weapon?," in Hoffer and Nesbit, *For Your Own Good*.

76 See Jonathan Gruber, *Public Finance and Public Policy* (New York: Worth Publishers, 2005), 547.

77 See Roger Bate, Cody Kallen, and Aparna Mathur, "The Perverse Effect of Sin Taxes: The Rise of Illicit White Cigarettes," *Applied Economics* 52, no. 8 (2020): 789–805; James E. Prieger and Jonathan Kulick, "Cigarette Taxes and Illicit Trade in Europe," *Economic Inquiry* 56, no. 3 (2018): 1706–23; James E. Prieger and Jonathan Kulick, "Tax Evasion and Illicit Cigarettes in California: Part IV—Smokers' Behavioral and Market Responses to a Tax Increase," BOTEC Analysis, January 24, 2019, https://ssrn.com/abstract=3322095; Philip DeCicca, Donald Kenkel, and Feng Liu, "Excise Tax Avoidance: The Case of State Cigarette Taxes," *Journal of Health Economics* 32, no. 6 (2013): 1130–41; Michael LaFaive, "Prohibition by Price: Cigarette Taxes and Unintended Consequences," in Hoffer and Nesbit, *For Your Own Good*; and the numerous empirical studies cited in these studies.

78 See James E. Prieger, Jonathan Kulick, and Mark A. R. Kleiman, "Unintended Consequences of Cigarette Prohibition, Regulation, and Taxation," *International Journal of Law, Crime and Justice* 46 (2016): 69–85.

79 National Research Council and Institute of Medicine, *Understanding the U.S. Illicit Tobacco Market: Characteristics, Policy Context, and Lessons from International Experiences*, ed. Peter Reuter and Malay Majmundar (Washington, DC: National Academies Press, 2015), 4.

80 See discussion of this comparison in Prieger et al., *Impact of Ecigarette Regulation*.

81 For empirical evidence on the final point, see Prieger and Kulick, "Tax Evasion and Illicit Cigarettes in California: Part IV."

82 Rajiv Goel and James W. Saunoris, "Cigarette Smuggling: Using the Shadow Economy or Creating Its Own?," *Journal of Economics and Finance* 43 (2019): 582–93.

83 See Julia Smith, Sheryl Thompson, and Kelley Lee, "Death and Taxes: The Framing of the Causes and Policy Responses to the Illicit Tobacco Trade in Canadian Newspapers," *Cogent Social Sciences* 3, no. 1 (2017).

84 See Luk Joossens and Martin Raw, "From Cigarette Smuggling to Illicit Tobacco Trade," *Tobacco Control* 21, no. 2 (2012): 230–34.

85 See in particular Prieger and Kulick, "Cigarette Taxes and Illicit Trade in Europe."

86 A group of economists with diverse perspectives on tobacco taxation and ITTP state that "little disagreement exists that an increase in the tax rate would generate significant increases in revenue, or that it would decrease consumption." Warner et al., "Criteria for Determining an Optimal Cigarette Tax."

87 See Lee Moran, "Fake Cigarettes Containing Human Feces, Rat Droppings Flood British Market: Report," *New York Daily News*, November 11, 2014; W. Edryd Stephens, Angus Calder, and Jason Newton, "Source and Health Implications of High Toxic Metal Concentrations in Illicit Tobacco Products," *Environmental Science and Technology* 39, no. 2 (2005): 479–88; and Oliver Bennett, "How Counterfeit Cigarettes Containing Pesticides and Arsenic Make It to Our Streets," *Independent*, August 7, 2018.

88 See Prieger, Kulick, and Kleiman, "Unintended Consequences of Cigarette Prohibition"; James E. Prieger and Jonathan Kulick, "Violence in Illicit Markets: Unintended Consequences and the Search for Paradoxical Effects of Enforcement," *B.E. Journal of Economic Analysis and Policy* 15, no. 3 (2015): 1263–95; and James Prieger and Jonathan Kulick, "Unintended Consequences of Enforcement in Illicit Markets," *Economics Letters* 125, no. 2 (2014): 295–97.

89 See Alison Ritter and Jacqui Cameron, "A Review of the Efficacy and Effectiveness of Harm Reduction Strategies for Alcohol, Tobacco and Illicit Drugs," *Drug and Alcohol Review* 25, no. 6 (2006): 611–24.

90 Ritter and Cameron, "Review of the Efficacy and Effectiveness," 613.

91 See the discussion of harm reduction versus the precautionary principle in Lawrence W. Green, Jonathan E. Fielding, and Ross C. Brownson, "The Debate about Electronic Cigarettes: Harm Minimization or the Precautionary Principle," *Annual Review of Public Health* 39 (2018): 189–91.

92 See A. McNeill et al., *Ecigarettes: An Evidence Update* (London: Public Health England, 2015).

93 "Based on current knowledge, stating that vaping is at least 95% less harmful than smoking remains a good way to communicate the large difference in relative risk unambiguously so that more smokers are encouraged to make the switch from smoking to vaping." McNeill et al., *Ecigarettes: An Evidence Update*. Given the clarity of the statement, the obvious implication that switching should be encouraged, and the resistance of some in the American public health community to that message, it is unsurprising that Public Health England has been attacked for its

statement. See, for example, Thomas Eissenberg et al., "Invalidity of an Oft-Cited Estimate of the Relative Harms of Electronic Cigarettes," *American Journal of Public Health* 110, no. 2 (2020): 161–62. A good discussion of the issues involved and a rebuttal may be found in Clive Bates, "Vaping Is Still at Least 95% Lower Risk than Smoking—Debunking a Feeble and Empty Critique," *The Counterfactual* (blog), January 17, 2020.

94 Tianrong Cheng, "Chemical Evaluation of Electronic Cigarettes," *Tobacco Control* 23, no. S2 (2014): 11–17.

95 William E. Stephens, "Comparing the Cancer Potencies of Emissions from Vapourised Nicotine Products Including Ecigarettes with Those of Tobacco Smoke," *Tobacco Control* 27, no. 1 (2018): 10–17.

96 See Lion Shahab et al., "Nicotine, Carcinogen, and Toxin Exposure in Long-Term Ecigarette and Nicotine Replacement Therapy Users: A Cross-Sectional Study," *Annals of Internal Medicine* 166, no. 6 (2017): 390–400.

97 See National Academies of Science, Engineering, and Medicine, *Public Health Consequences of Ecigarettes.*

98 For example, one study found that the odds of wheezing in adolescents are affected by ecigarette use only when past cigarette use is not controlled for. See Rob McConnell et al., "Electronic Cigarette Use and Respiratory Symptoms in Adolescents," *American Journal of Respiratory and Critical Care Medicine* 195, no. 8 (2017): 1043–49. Conversely, the association between vaping and the odds of having symptoms of bronchitis was reduced in magnitude but not removed when past cigarette use was controlled for.

99 See National Academies of Science, Engineering, and Medicine, *Public Health Consequences of Ecigarettes.*

100 See National Academies of Science, Engineering, and Medicine, *Public Health Consequences of Ecigarettes.*

101 See Muhammad Aziz Rahman et al., "Ecigarettes and Smoking Cessation: Evidence from a Systematic Review and Meta-analysis," *PLOS ONE* 10, no. 3 (2015).

102 See Andrea C. Villanti et al., "How Do We Determine the Impact of E-cigarettes on Cigarette Smoking Cessation or Reduction? Review and Recommendations for Answering the Research Question with Scientific Rigor," *Addiction* 113, no. 3 (2018): 391–404. The observation that this review found that *most* studies on vaping and cessation (all but four out of 91) failed to constitute reliable scientific evidence is important, because public health researchers who oppose vaping sometimes claim that "the weight of the evidence" shows that ecigarette use does not aid cessation.

103 The cessation rate, defined as the 12-month quit rate, was found to be about 10% with NRTs and 20% with ecigarettes. See Rahman et al., "Ecigarettes and Smoking Cessation."

104 Some recent studies finding that ecigarettes may aid cessation use quasi-experimental designs. See Dhaval Dave et al., "Does Ecigarette Advertising Encourage Adult Smokers to Quit?," *Journal of Health Economics* 68 (2019): 102227; Henry Saffer et al., "Ecigarettes and Adult Smoking: Evidence from Minnesota" (NBER Working Paper No. 26589, National Bureau of Economic Research, Cambridge, MA, December 2019). Other studies employ randomized controlled trials. See Peter Hajek et al., "A Randomized Trial of Ecigarettes versus Nicotine-Replacement Therapy," *New England Journal of Medicine* 380 (2019): 629–37. The authors find that ecigarettes were more effective for smoking cessation than nicotine-replacement therapy.

105 See, for example, Angelica LaVito, "CDC Says Teen Vaping Surges to More than 1 in 4 High School Students," CNBC, September 12, 2019.

106 Karen A. Cullen et al., "Ecigarette Use among Youth in the United States, 2019," *JAMA* 322, no. 21 (2019): 2095–103. This figure is derived by multiplying the any-use prevalence of 27.5% by the proportion of current users using 20 days or more out of the past 30 (34.2%).

107 Robert West, Jamie Brown, and Martin Jarvis, "Epidemic of Youth Nicotine Addiction? What Does the National Youth Tobacco Survey Reveal about High School Ecigarette Use in the USA?," *Qeios* preprint, submitted October 7, 2019.

108 West, Brown, and Jarvis, "Epidemic of Youth Nicotine Addiction?"

109 See, for example, Scott R. Weaver et al., "Use of Electronic Nicotine Delivery Systems and Other Tobacco Products among USA Adults, 2014: Results from a National Survey," *International Journal of Public Health* 61, no. 2 (2016): 177–88.

110 Given that cigarette taxes are generally higher than taxes on ecigarettes (if there are any), among other reasons, vaping is generally seen as cheaper than smoking. Depending on the cigarettes and vaping device or method compared, the cost differences can be very large. See, for example, Ethan Wolff-Mann, "Vaping Is 95% Healthier and 40% Cheaper Than Smoking," *Money*, August 20, 2015; and Lindsay Fox, "Smoking vs. Vaping: The Ultimate Cost Comparison," *EcigaretteReviewed* (blog), February 25, 2016.

111 This is known as the *common liability hypothesis*. See Lynn T. Kozlowski and Kenneth E. Warner, "Adolescents and Ecigarettes: Objects of Concern May Appear Larger Than They Are," *Drug and Alcohol Dependence* 174 (2017): 209–14.

112 National Academies of Science, Engineering, and Medicine, *Public Health Consequences of Ecigarettes.*

113 See Jean-Francois Etter, "Gateway Effects and Electronic Cigarettes," *Addiction* 113, no. 10 (2018): 1776–83.

114 See D. T. Levy et al., "Examining the Relationship of Vaping to Smoking Initiation among US Youth and Young Adults: A Reality Check," *Tobacco Control* 28, no. 6 (2019): 629–35.

115 West, Brown, and Jarvis, "Epidemic of Youth Nicotine Addiction?"

116 West, Brown, and Jarvis, "Epidemic of Youth Nicotine Addiction?" The relevant survey question was not asked in more recent waves of the relevant survey.

117 Similarly sized effects were found by two studies. See Dhaval Dave, Bo Feng, and Michael F. Pesko, "The Effects of E-cigarette Minimum Legal Sale Age Laws on Youth Substance Use," *Health Economics* 28, no. 3 (2019): 419–36; A. S. Friedman, "How Does Electronic Cigarette Access Affect Adolescent Smoking?," *Journal of Health Economics* 44 (2015): 300–308.

118 Michael F. Pesko and Janet M. Currie, "Ecigarette Minimum Legal Sale Age Laws and Traditional Cigarette Use among Rural Pregnant Teenagers," *Journal of Health Economics* 66 (2019): 71–90.

119 Nancy A. Rigotti, "Youth Access to Tobacco," *Nicotine and Tobacco Research* 1, suppl. 2 (1999): S93–S97.

120 There is remarkably little evidence on this topic from the US context. Nancy Rigotti reports on two controlled studies from the US: In one, enforcement of minimum age laws to purchase tobacco had no effect on youth smoking, but in the other, enforcement was associated with lowering the growth rate of youth smoking. Rigotti, "Youth Access to Tobacco." The 2015 National Academies study on the issue found no studies at all on the topic in the US but cited evidence from

Europe that minimum age laws reduce youth smoking prevalence. Richard J. Bonnie, Kathleen Stratton, and Leslie Y. Kwan, eds., *Public Health Implications of Raising the Minimum Age of Legal Access to Tobacco Products* (Washington, DC: National Academies Press, 2015).

121 Only 10.5% of 15-to-17-year-old vapers bought their own ecigarettes; it is much more common that they asked someone to buy on their behalf (17.3%) or got them from someone else (57%). Susanne Tanski et al., "Youth Access to Tobacco Products in the United States: Findings from Wave 1 (2013–2014) of the Population Assessment of Tobacco and Health Study," *Nicotine and Tobacco Research* 21, no. 12 (December 2019): 1695–99. See similar evidence from Hannah M. Baker et al., "Youth Source of Acquisition for Ecigarettes," *Preventive Medicine Reports* 16 (2019); and Jessica K. Pepper et al., "How Do Adolescents Get Their Ecigarettes and Other Electronic Vaping Devices?," *American Journal of Health Promotion* 33, no. 3 (2019).

122 Amy Fairchild et al., "Evidence, Alarm, and the Debate over Ecigarettes," *Science* 366, no. 6471 (December 2019): 1318–20.

123 Lisa Henriksen et al., "Assurances of Voluntary Compliance: A Regulatory Mechanism to Reduce Youth Access to Ecigarettes and Limit Retail Tobacco Marketing," *American Journal of Public Health* 110, no. 2 (2020): 209–15.

124 Tanski et al., "Youth Access to Tobacco Products."

125 Isabel M. R. Hess, Kishen Lachireddy, and Adam Capon, "A Systematic Review of the Health Risks from Passive Exposure to Electronic Cigarette Vapour," *Public Health Research and Practice* 26, no. 2 (2016). Emphasis added.

126 National Academies of Science, Engineering, and Medicine, *Public Health Consequences of Ecigarettes*.

127 Hess, Lachireddy, and Capon, "Systematic Review of the Health Risks."

128 National Academies of Science, Engineering, and Medicine, *Public Health Consequences of Ecigarettes*. Note also that the careful (and carefully worded) conclusions of these scientific assessments stand in contrast to statements by the World Health Organization, which comes down strongly against vaping. The World Health Organization answered the question "are secondhand ENDS emissions dangerous?" unequivocally: "Yes. The aerosols in ENDS typically contain toxic substances, including glycol which is used to make antifreeze. ENDS pose risks to users and non-users." World Health Organization, "Q&A Detail: Ecigarettes," accessed January 23, 2020, https://www.who.int/news-room/q-a-detail/e-cigarettes-how-risky-are-they. (The "yes" in the answer was later removed.) For discussion of the merits of this statement, see Clive Bates, "World Health Organisation Fails at Science and Fails at Propaganda—the Sad Case of WHO's Anti-vaping Q&A," *The Counterfactual* (blog), January 30, 2020.

129 See Required Warning Statement Regarding Addictiveness of Nicotine, 21 C.F.R. 1143.3 (April 1, 2019).

130 The television and radio ad ban for cigarettes is nationwide (under a federal law—it is not an agency regulation), but the other use of the venues mentioned is prohibited under the Tobacco Master Settlement Agreement, which applies in 46 states. Andrew Glass, "Congress Bans Airing Cigarette Ads, April 1, 1970," *Politico*, April 1, 2018.

131 See Dhaval Dave et al., "Does E-Cigarette Advertising Encourage Adult Smokers to Quit?" *Journal of Health Economics* 68 art. no. 102227 (2019):1–13.

132 See, for example, Michele Simon, "Reducing Youth Exposure to Alcohol Ads: Targeting Public Transit," *Journal of Urban Health* 85, no. 4 (2008): 506–16.

133 The information here and the statistics to follow are from the Centers for Disease Control and Prevention's information page, "Outbreak of Lung Injury Associated with the Use of Ecigarette, or Vaping, Products," accessed October 9, 2020, https://www.cdc.gov/tobacco/basic_information/e-cigarettes/severe-lung-disease.html. The Centers for Disease Control and Prevention is a part of the US Department of Health and Human Services.

134 See Blount, et al., "Vitamin E Acetate in Bronchoalveolar-Lavage Fluid Associated with EVALI," *New England Journal of Medicine* 382, no. 8 (2020):697-705. If the test group with EVALI were typical of the general population of vapers with regard to the presence of vitamin E acetate in their lungs, as would be the case if vitamin E acetate (and hence THC) had nothing to do with the illnesses, then the probability of observing *no* vitamin E acetate in the control group is a vanishingly small number: $1.5 \times 10\text{--}122$—a zero followed by a decimal point and 121 more zeroes.

135 The total percentage cited includes 6 percent who reported acquiring products from both commercial and informal sources.

136 The brand is Dank Vapes. See Jennifer Maloney and Daniela Hernandez, "Vaping's Black Market Complicates Efforts to Combat Crises," *Wall Street Journal*, October 6, 2019.

137 See the CDC webpage cited in note 133.

138 A review of studies found that "no clear patterns emerged" in the relation between socioeconomic status and ecigarette usage, and that, if anything, income appears to be positively associated with use. See Greg Hartwell et al., "Ecigarettes and Equity: A Systematic Review of Differences in Awareness and Use between Sociodemographic Groups," *Tobacco Control* 26, no. e2 (2017): e85–e91.

139 See, for example, David B. Abrams, "Promise and Peril of Ecigarettes: Can Disruptive Technology Make Cigarettes Obsolete?," *JAMA* 311, no. 2 (2014): 135–36.

140 As of early 2020, every state tax on ecigarettes is ad valorem: a specific tax per milliliter of eliquid or per cartridge, or a combination of the two; in particular, no state taxes the concentration of nicotine. National Conference of State Legislatures, "Ecigarette & Vaping Product Taxes," April 6, 2020, https://www.ncsl.org/research/fiscal-policy/electronic-cigarette-taxation.aspx. On the potential for nicotine to harm the development of the adolescent brain, see note 147.

141 For one of the rare examples of research on illicit trade in ecigarette products, see Prieger et al., *Impact of Ecigarette Regulation.*

142 See Esther E. Omaiye et al., "Counterfeit Electronic Cigarette Products with Mislabeled Nicotine Concentrations," *Tobacco Regulatory Science* 3, no. 3 (2017): 347–57.

143 See Maloney and Hernandez, "Vaping's Black Market."

144 See Daniela Hernandez, "Sales of Illicit Vaping Products Find Home Online," *Wall Street Journal*, September 20, 2019.

145 See Prieger et al., *Impact of Ecigarette Regulation.* The study has not yet undergone peer review, however.

146 Prieger et al., *Impact of Ecigarette Regulation.*

147 "Government measures to reduce smoking through higher taxes would seem to be a form of paternalism about which economics has little to say." Cnossen, "Tobacco Taxation in the European Union, p. 315."

148 See Frank J. Chaloupka, David Sweanor, and Kenneth E. Warner, "Differential Taxes for Differential Risks—Toward Reduced Harm from Nicotine-Yielding Products," *New England Journal of Medicine* 373, no. 7 (2015): 594–97. For discussion

of proportionate regulation regarding ecigarettes, see also Prieger et al., *Impact of Ecigarette Regulation.*

149 See, for example, the statement that "we don't know whether ecigarette use is as lethal as combustible cigarette use, less lethal than combustible cigarette use, or more lethal than combustible cigarette use," by one public health researcher. Virginia Commonwealth University, "An Often-Made Claim that Ecigarettes are '95% Safer' Is Not Valid," news release, *EurekAlert*, January 8, 2020, https://www.eurekalert.org/pub_releases/2020-01/vcu-aoc010820.php.

150 Jidong Huang et al., "Changing Perceptions of Harm of Ecigarette vs Cigarette Use among Adults in 2 US National Surveys from 2012 to 2017," *JAMA* 2, no. 3 (2019).

151 See the data from the National Cancer Institute, HINTS: Health Information National Trends Survey, "Compared to Smoking Cigarettes, Would You Say That Electronic Cigarettes Are . . . ," accessed October 9, 2020, https://hints.cancer.gov/view-questions-topics/question-details.aspx?nq=1&qid=1282.

152 See, for example, Olivia A. Wackowski and Cristine D. Delnevo, "Young Adults' Risk Perceptions of Various Tobacco Products Relative to Cigarettes: Results from the National Young Adult Health Survey," *Health Education and Behavior* 43, no. 3 (2016): 328–36.

153 David T. Levy et al., "Potential Deaths Averted in USA by Replacing Cigarettes with Ecigarettes," *Tobacco Control* 27, no. 1 (2018): 18–25.

154 The scientific evidence "is suggestive" that exposure to nicotine during adolescence may have "lasting adverse consequences for brain development," resulting in adversely affected cognitive function and development. *Health Consequences of Smoking—50 Years of Progress*, 126.

155 For example, see the article for schoolchildren sponsored by the Centers for Disease Control and Prevention, part of its "The Real Cost" ecigarette prevention campaign: "The Health Impacts of Ecigarettes: Discover the Truth about How These Devices Can Harm You," *Scholastic*, 2019, http://www.scholastic.com/youthvapingrisks/healthrisksofcigarettes_studentarticle_A.pdf. The article uses the EVALI cases to lead into the anti-ecigarette message, clearly wanting the reader to link those health harms with uses of any ecigarette.

156 "We continue to be concerned that many of [the Office of National Drug Control Policy]'s advertisements are exaggerated fear appeals, which most experts in public health communications have concluded almost never work." William Dejong and Lawrence Wallack, "The Drug Czar's Anti-drug Media Campaign: Continuing Concerns," *Journal of Health Communication* 5, no. 1 (2000): 77–82. See also the article cited by Dejong and Wallack: R. F. Soames Job, "Effective and Ineffective Use of Fear in Health Promotion Campaigns," *American Journal of Public Health* 78, no. 2 (1988): 163–67.

157 Ecigarette Tax Parity Act, S. 2463, 116th Cong. (2019).

158 See Food and Drug Administration, "FDA Finalizes Enforcement Policy on Unauthorized Flavored Cartridge-Based Ecigarettes That Appeal to Children, Including Fruit and Mint," news release, January 2, 2020, https://www.fda.gov/news-events/press-announcements/fda-finalizes-enforcement-policy-unauthorized-flavored-cartridge-based-e-cigarettes-appeal-children.

159 See, e.g., George Bittlingmayer, "Regulatory Uncertainty and Investment: Evidence from Antitrust Enforcement," *Cato Journal* 20, no. 3 (2001): 295–326; James E. Prieger, "Regulation, Innovation, and the Introduction of New Telecommunications Services," *Review of Economics and Statistics* 84, no. 4 (2002): 704–15; and Kira

R. Fabrizio, "The Effect of Regulatory Uncertainty on Investment: Evidence from Renewable Energy Generation," *Journal of Law, Economics, and Organization* 29, no. 4 (2013): 765–98.

160 See Prieger et al., *Impact of Ecigarette Regulation*. See also the discussion in the previous section.

161 See the discussion in the previous section.

162 See Food and Drug Administration, *Enforcement Priorities for Electronic Nicotine Delivery Systems*, § IV.E.

163 For discussion with reference to drug markets, see Jonathan Caulkins and Peter Reuter, "Towards a Harm-Reduction Approach to Enforcement," *Safer Communities* 8, no. 1 (2009): 9–23. For discussion with reference to tobacco markets, see Prieger, Kulick, and Kleiman, "Unintended Consequences of Cigarette Prohibition."

CONCLUSION

1 Brad Hershbein, David Boddy, and Melissa S. Kearney, "Nearly 30 Percent of Workers in the U.S. Need a License to Perform Their Job: It Is Time to Examine Occupational Licensing Practices," Brookings Institution, January 27, 2015.

2 Executive Order No. 12866, 58 Fed. Reg. 190 (October 4, 1993).

3 Jerry Ellig, "Evaluating the Quality and Use of Regulatory Impact Analysis: The Mercatus Center's Regulatory Report Card, 2008–2013" (Mercatus Working Paper, Mercatus Center at George Mason University, Arlington, VA, July 2016), 29.

4 Ellig, "Quality and Use of Regulatory Impact Analysis," 52–53.

5 Ellig, 73–74.

6 Diana W. Thomas and Michael D. Thomas, "Behavioral Symmetry, Rent Seeking, and the Republic of Science," *Public Choice* 183, no. 3 (June 2020): 443–59.

7 Kevin Gomez, Diana Thomas, and Ryan Yonk. "Precaution Can Kill: Chemical Benefits and Regulatory Risks." Independent Institute Briefing, May 15, 2020.

Made in the USA
Middletown, DE
01 November 2023

41758982R00342